Mississippi Black History Makers

Mississippi Black History Makers

Revised and Enlarged Edition

by
GEORGE A. SEWELL
and
MARGARET L. DWIGHT

UNIVERSITY PRESS OF MISSISSIPPI
Jackson

Copyright 1984 by the
University Press of Mississippi
All rights reserved
First Edition published 1977

Print-on-Demand Edition

This volume sponsored by
ALCORN STATE UNIVERSITY

Library of Congress Cataloging in Publication Data

Sewell, George Alexander.
  Mississippi black history makers.

  Includes bibliographical references and index.
  1. Afro-Americans—Mississippi—Biography.
2. Mississippi—Biography. I. Dwight, Margaret L.
II. Title.
E185.93.M6S48   1984   920'.0092'960730762   84-3511

Contents

Preface   x
Politics   3
    Hiram Hodes Revels   7
    Blanche Kelso Bruce   16
    John Roy Lynch   26
    James D. Lynch   38
    James Hill   48
    Thomas W. Stringer   49
    Josiah T. Settle   52
    Roscoe Conklin Simmons   55
    Robert H. Wood   58
    James Charles Evers   59
    Unita Blackwell Wright   66
    Eddie James Carthan   67
    Marion Shepilov Barry   72
    Evan Doss   73
    W. E. Mollison   75
    Constance Slaughter-Harvey   76
    Henry Jay Kirksey   77
    Robert George Clark   80
    Aaron Henry   84
    Douglas Leavon Anderson   87
    Fred Lee Banks   87
    Horace Lawson Buckley   87
    Credell Calhoun   88
    Tyrone Ellis   88
    Hillman Jerome Frazier   89
    Isiah Fredericks   89
    David Leo Green   89
    Clayton P. Henderson   90
    Leslie Darnell King   90
    Barney J. Schoby   91
    Charles Bernard Sheppard   91
    Percy Willis Watson   91

    Charles Lemuel Young 92
    Deborah Jones Gambrell 92
    Melvin Redmond 93
    James Winfield 93
    Eddie Lucas 94
    Eddie L. McBride 94
    Clifford Jennings 95
    James C. Cooper 95
    Vernon C. Johnson 96
    Charles E. Pugh 96
    William K. Dease, Sr. 96
    Betty Jones 97
Civil Rights 99
    Ida B. Wells 103
    Margaret Murray Washington 111
    Jack Harvey Young, Sr. 112
    Medgar Evers 117
    Fannie Lou Hamer 122
    Clyde Kennard 131
    James Meredith 133
    James Chaney 143
    Willie Tatum 145
Business 147
    William T. Johnson 149
    The Montgomerys: Ben and Isaiah 154
    George Washington Lee 163
    Joseph Edison Walker 170
    Clarie Collins Harvey 176
    George Johnson 180
    Robert Earl Jones 181
    Jessie R. Chambliss 182
    Sam Baker 183
    Vernon Floyd 184
    Charlene Owens 185
    Rose Morgan 185
    Louise K. Quarles 186
    Randolph T. Myrick 187
    Emorrie Jenkins 187
    E. W. Green 187
    Thelma Sanders 187
    Naomi Sims 188

Education   189
   John Dewey Boyd   193
   Walter Washington   195
   B. Baldwin Dansby   198
   Jacob L. Reddix   199
   John A. Peoples, Jr.   204
   Ernest A. Boykins, Jr.   206
   Joe Louis Boyer   208
   George A. Owens   209
   Laurence C. Jones   211
   Jane Ellen McAllister   217
   Florence Octavia Alexander   222
   Cleopatra D. Thompson   223
   Hazael McFarland Thompson   226
   William H. Holtzaw   228
   Willa B. Player   229
   William Arthur Butts   230
   Edward Allen Jones   231
   Romeo Benjamin Garrett   233
   Melerson Guy Dunham   236
   Charlemae Hill Rollins   237
   Ruby Stutts Lyells   238
   Joffre T. Whisenton   239
   William Smith Demby   240
   The J. E. Johnsons   242
   Arenia C. Mallory   245
   McKinley Charles Martin   245
   Joyce Ladner   246
   Gladys Noel Bates   246
   Lou Emma Holloway   246
   Janice White Sikes   247
   Dorothy Gordon Gray   248
   Julius Eric Thompson   248
Literature and Journalism   249
   Richard Nathaniel Wright   252
   Margaret Walker Alexander   267
   Anne Moody   269
   Percy Green   270
   The William A. Scott Family   273
   Lerone Bennett, Jr.   277
   Wililam Dilday   280

    Jessie Mosley 281
    Sarah Harvey Stevens 281
    William Gordon 281
The Performing and Visual Arts 283
    Elizabeth Taylor Greenfield 285
    William Grant Still 285
    Leontyne Price 292
    B. B. King 302
    Ellas "Bo Diddley" McDaniel 312
    Charley Pride 315
    Arthur Crudup 320
    Frederick O'Neal 321
    James Earl Jones 322
    Richmond Barthé 325
    Sam Gilliam 325
    Lavern Hamberlin 326
    Joseph Overstreet 327
    Beah Richards 327
    William Fischer 327
    Frederick Douglass Hall 328
    Raeschelle Potter 328
    Lucia Hawkins 329
    Albert King 329
    Little Milton 330
    Levion Dillon 330
    Ike Turner 330
    Bukka White 331
    Bobby Bryant 331
Religion 333
    Alexander Preston Shaw 336
    Sherman Lawrence Greene, Sr. 337
    Lucy C. Jefferson 341
    H. Hartford Brookins 342
    Homer C. McEwen, Sr. 345
    Joseph Harrison Jackson 347
    L. Venchael Booth 349
    Mae Frances Spencer 351
Science, Medicine, and Social Work 353
    Sidney D. Redmond 355
    L. T. Miller 361
    George H. Lane 364

Deborah Hyde-Rowan 364
Eliza J. Pillars 365
Rhetaugh G. Dumas 367
Jessie O. Thomas 368
Lucille Price 373
Cleo Walter Blackburn 374
Walter Massey 376
Natalia Tanner Cain 376
Margaret Lawrence 377
Gwendolyn Nero Loper 377
Georgie Catchings Coleman 377
Jennifer O. Hicks 378

Sports 379
Walter Payton 381
Lusia Harris Stewart 387
Pete Brown 388
Spence Haywood 389
Eugene Short 389
George Scott 390
Mildrette Netter 390

Military 391
Thomas J. Money, Jr. 393
Jesse Leroy Brown 395
John Mitchell Brown 398
Modis A. Smiley 399
Glennie M. Rowland 400
Daniel L. Jennings 400

Notes 401
Appendix 443
Index 453

Preface

This edition of *Mississippi Black History Makers*, like the first edition published in 1977, presents a panorama of biographical profiles on Mississippi blacks who have made significant contributions in bringing about the uplift of the black race, from the mid-nineteenth century to the present. Its purpose is to reveal the most effective struggles of a people who dared to venture forth into white society and who succeeded in breaking down racial barriers. Within the biography of each individual mentioned is also the life and story of a people who resisted oppression and survived. Collectively, the biographies of those featured show the transformation of Mississippi from a closed society to a pluralistic one.

For the first edition, we are indebted to the late George Alexander Sewell, whose foresight and dedication made *Mississippi Black History Makers* possible. Dr. Sewell began the project in the early 1970s when he was a distinguished professor of sociology at Alcorn State University. This scholar, minister, and civic leader rendered decades of unselfish service to the university and surrounding communities and imprinted the pages of history as surely as those he honored.

In her introduction to the first edition, author-educator Margaret Walker Alexander wrote about the significance of black achievements in Mississippi:

> Slavery, Reconstruction, and segregation, all so difficult, have presented such overwhelming obstacles in the path of the Negro that, like the handicapped horse winning the race, the black Mississippian has been more than determined to succeed, to rise about every obstacle that has impeded him, and to achieve national greatness. Surely the hardships, the provincial atmosphere, the oppressive social system all have contributed to a climate for genius in Mississippi. This is an anomaly, a peculiar irony, but nevertheless true: Mississippi has truly become a climate for genius. If, then, such a great record of achievement has been accomplished under slavery and segregation what will such people do with freedom in an open society? Surely greater things are yet to come, for a great racial heritage always envisions a greater destiny!

Preface

Freedom came, and new leaders emerged. Because of these changes and because of the inadvertent omission of some well-known figures, it became necessary to revise *Mississippi Black History Makers*. Several changes characterize this edition. In an effort to chronicle the accomplishments of black Mississippians systematically, the book has been organized into ten thematic sections; each section is introduced with an historical overview. For this edition, seventy five black history makers have been added, and information about the contemporary figures has been updated with primary source material.

This work is not intended to be an exhaustive study of all Mississippi black heroines or heroes. It would be impossible to discover every individual whose life reflects the uplift and assimilation of the black race into the mainstream of society. Yet it is the task of the scholars of each generation to identify, record, and place in perspective the work of those figures who, they believe, have improved the quality of life for mankind. The selection process was by no means an easy one. Guided by responses from community leaders and organizations and by the availability of primary and secondary sources—particularly oral sources, I included representative figures from several professions.

For this book, a Mississippi black history maker is a person who was either born in Mississippi and spent a part of his life here or one who migrated into the state and remained. Some of those included achieved national, even international, prominence in their chosen fields. Others made lasting contributions within the state, as pioneers in fields where blacks had previously not been allowed, in so doing creating new avenues for others. A third group of lesser known history makers is included because these individuals have made outstanding contributions within their own community or profession and represent the many others not included who have similarly affected a select group of people.

It is impossible to acknowledge by name all the many individuals who gave invaluable assistance to this project. To all those who provided information and technical assistance, I extend a sincere "thank you." I want to express my gratitude specifically to Dr. Walter Washington, president of Alcorn State University; Dr. Rudolph Waters, vice-president; Dr. Malvin Williams, academic dean; and Ralph Payne, director of public relations. Each believed that the task could be accomplished and entrusted me to complete it. Furthermore, throughout this project. Dr. Washington was encouraging and gave unselfishly of his time to make this book a success.

Very few individuals realize the magnitude of help, patience, and understanding that a writer receives from the publishing staff. I must singly and collectively thank Barney McKee, JoAnne Prichard, and others on the staff of the University Press of Mississippi. I also sincerely appreciate the time Mattie Sanders and Alice Dwight spent in typing the manuscript.

The sources of my inspiration were my mother, Lula M. Dwight, and my father, Benton Dwight, Sr. They and Dr. Ray Davis gave me moral support when I needed it. I am most grateful to them.

Margaret L. Dwight
Alcorn State University

Mississippi Black History Makers

POLITICS

To appreciate the impact that black politicians have had upon Mississippi society, one must understand that southern politics has historically been based upon the racial doctrine of white supremacy, Jim Crowism, and conservatism. Southern politics was oppressive to blacks and fed upon the denial of civil liberties, executive, judicial, and legislative inequality, and reinforced violence.

In the 1960s black politicians in Mississippi assessed their political strength, unified, and organized and used their political power base to influence change and control electoral decisions. Their political *modus operandi* depended upon the reinforcement of group values and participation as well as the consolidation of their power base. The election of blacks as U.S. Congressmen, state legislators, and city officials further increased the political awareness and political consciousness of black Mississippians. From Reconstruction to the present blacks exercised the elective franchise when they were not hampered by legal and illegal methods.

When blacks were emancipated in Mississippi three issues were important to them: suffrage, education, and land. Many believed that by obtaining the right to vote, they would get education and land. Consequently, they devoted much time and effort to acquiring the elective franchise. Under the Radical Republicans' Reconstruction plan of 1867 seven hundred thousand blacks registered to vote. The temporary suffrage arrangement under the Fourteenth Amendment became permanent with the passage and ratification of the Fifteenth Amendment in 1870—the right to vote. Subsequently blacks were elected as lieutenant governor, secretary, superintendent of education, and Speaker of the House in Mississippi. Hiram R. Revels and Blanche K. Bruce were chosen as United States senators.

However, participation in the political processes by blacks was hindered by harassment and intimidation. Furthermore, the compromise of 1877 eroded blacks political strength in the state. When southern Democrats who advocated white supremacy took control of the state under the guise of establishing "Home Rule," a few blacks managed to retain the right to vote and hold office. They were able to retain some power through the fusion principle, which provided for reciprocity: white Democrats consulted with black leaders on the number of offices to be distributed to blacks in exchange for black support of their election.

The 1890 Mississippi Constitutional Convention sealed the disenfranchisement fate of blacks when it adopted a resolution that stipulated as a prerequisite for registration a "reasonable" interpretation of the constitution. Although this resolution violated blacks' civil rights, it was deemed legal. In addition, between 1890 and 1910, whites disrobed black voters with extralegal legislative requirements for voting such as good character test, literacy test, poll taxes, grandfather clause,[1] understanding clause,[2] white primary,[3] criminal offenses,[4] and property qualifications. Illegal reinforcement included terrorist tactics as well as wholesale violence. The result was the wholesale debasement of the black race and the containment of blacks within geographical perimeters.

Gradually, blacks regained the right to vote as the U.S. Supreme Court declared the grandfather clause (U.S. v. Guinn 1915) and white primary (Smith v. Allwright 1944) unconstitutional, constitutional amendment invalidated the poll tax in 1961, and the remaining restrictions were removed through the passage of the civil rights acts of 1957, 1960, 1964, and 1965. The 1965 Voting Rights Act called for direct federal action to enable blacks to register and vote without the protracted litigation required by previous legislation.

For fourteen years following the Voting Rights Act of 1965, litigation dealing with redistricting and reapportionment dominated Mississippi politics, unified the black electorate, and led to the election of black public officials. Numerous black Mississippians believed that redistricting was a political ploy to divide black voters, and that it was synonymous with gerrymandering. The issue was resolved when the U.S. Supreme Court ruled gerrymandering unconstitutional, thereby preventing the split or exclusion of black votes in local and state elections, particularly in predominantly black counties. The overall effects of the court ruling became evident in the 1979 legislative election.

The election of 1979, which sent seventeen blacks to the state legislature—the largest number since Reconstruction—marked a turning point in Mississippi politics. Mississippi ranked second to Georgia in legislative members. (Georgia had twenty-three.) Accordingly, the National Roster of Black Elected Officials reported that

Louisiana superceded Mississippi by a slim margin of 333 to 303 black public officials.

Within the black community, the election of black public officials in 1979 symbolized several meaningful occurrences in Mississippi history. First, the election represented a giant step in the political advancement of the black race. Second, the same identical site, the House chambers in the Old Capitol where black lawmakers were sworn into duty during Reconstruction, became the location for the special swearing-in ceremonies of the seventeen black elected legislators. Hinds County Judge Reuben Anderson ordered that the Old Capitol be used for the occasion instead of the Mississippi legislature's temporary dwelling, old Central High School in Jackson.

The swearing-in proceedings of the seventeen-member Mississippi Legislative black caucus attracted a few whites and more than 400 blacks. Because of the tardiness of some members of the legislature and a new and unusual lengthy seating process, the audience endured a ninety-minute delay to pay tribute to the largest contingent of Mississippi black legislators since Reconstruction. Representative Robert Clark of Lexington, the master of ceremonies, assured the audience that the seating process was a necessary procedure and not an attempt to stall the awaiting ceremony.

Many had traveled from as far away as Illinois, Michigan, and California to witness the ceremony only to be informed that there were no more passes and they could not gain admittance. "Nobody told us we needed passes before we spent our money to come all this way," one person commented, "This is history for some of us and I'm very disappointed that we aren't allowed inside." Inside the Old Capitol, Governor Cliff Finch stalked the halls, shaking hands and issuing his usual invitation to everyone to stop by the Governor's Mansion on their way out of town.[5]

Perhaps the prevailing sentiment of the waiting crowd was best expressed by Robert Spense of Water Valley. Nodding toward the inside of the second-floor house chamber, where his friend, Representative Aaron Henry of Clarksdale, had just been sworn in, Spense exclaimed, "I didn't think I'd ever live to see this day, I hope I live to see it again."[6]

By 4:45 p.m., the last of the seventeen black legislators arrived at the Old Capitol and Judge Reuben Anderson began the long awaited protocol. "These seventeen men," Anderson remarked, "reflect the aspirations and hopes of their various communities and the state in general." Quoting from John R. Lynch, Anderson continued, "The impartial historian will record the fact that the colored people of the South have contended for their rights with a bravery and gallantry that is worthy of the highest commendation. . . . Although the bondman's yoke of oppression was upon their necks, yet they were true and loyal to their government."[7]

The next speaker, E. C. Foster, professor of history at Jackson State University, reminded his listeners that the 1890 Constitutional Convention—attended by seventeen black delegates—produced a document that stripped political representation from blacks for over ninety years. But, predicting that history would not repeat itself, Foster declared, "Our challenge now is to go beyond Reconstruction."[8]

Hiram Rhodes Revels
First Black United States Senator

Black Mississippians perceived political Reconstruction as the "golden age" of high expectations. At no other time in Mississippi history, except during the civil rights movement, did blacks have the option of making freedom a reality through the political processes. Opportunities to vote, to hold office, to receive an education, and to share in the state's wealth were available. Because of blacks' participation in Mississippi politics during Reconstruction, numerous black leaders were nominated and elected. Among those selected was Hiram Rhodes Revels, who rose to prominence as the state and nation's first black United States Senator.

Revels, the first of three blacks seated in the exclusive chambers of the United States Senate, was born free in Fayetteville, North Carolina, on September 27, 1822. Frequently, Revels was referred to as a quadroon, one who is one-fourth black. His ethnic heritage consisted of African, Anglo-American, and Indian ancestry.[1]

During his youthful years, Revels had an insatiable desire for education; therefore, he enrolled in North Carolina segregated schools for blacks. He continued his educational pursuits, uninterrupted, until the Nat Turner slave insurrection in Virginia in 1831. Prior to this revolt, North Carolina, had allowed free blacks opportunities to obtain an education. Then the law changed, and the state denied blacks the right to an education and public officials implemented and stringently enforced an involuntary black migration policy, thus ridding North Carolina of its free black population.[2] Consequently, Revels moved to Ohio and then to Indiana, both free states, in order to obtain an education.

Driven by a desire to acquire professional religious training to prepare him for the ministry, Revels enrolled in 1844 at a Quaker coeducational school, probably Beach Grove Seminary, in Union County, Ohio. He was the only black among wealthy white students. Believing it would be economically and socially advantageous to matriculate at a black seminary in Drake County, Ohio, Revels transferred. At the black theological center, Revels studied more earnestly to keep a pace with the advanced students. Upon graduation in 1845, Revels was ordained a minister in the African Methodist Episcopal Church at Baltimore, Maryland.[3]

Revels's continuous quest for knowledge and spiritual well-being led him to Knox College in Galesburg, Illinois. While pursuing his academic career, Revels preached, taught, and lectured blacks in Indiana, Illinois, Ohio, Missouri, and Maryland. When Revels was twenty-five years old, the A.M.E. Church bishop assigned him a pastorate in Indiana.[4]

During his lecture and evangelistic tours, Revels revealed his conservative theology and duplicity. On one occasion, he recalled that he sedulously refrained from doing anything that would incite slaves to run away from their masters. "It being understood that my object was to preach the gospel to them" reminisced Revels, "and improve their moral and spiritual conditions; even slave holders were tolerant toward me. But when in free states, I always assisted the fugitive to make escape . . . ."[5]

With the advent of the Civil War in 1861, Revels temporarily abandoned his ministry in order to recruit blacks for the Union Army. He assisted in organizing the first black regiments in Baltimore, Maryland. In 1863, he moved to St. Louis, recruited a black regiment, and initiated educational programs for blacks.

Dedicated to the education and elevation of the black race, Revels devoted his time to the creation of black educational institutions. In 1863, he founded a large school for freedmen in St. Louis. Revels, however, "met with considerable opposition in Missouri, but was never subjected to violence. He was once arrested for illegally teaching slaves, but was soon released." In late 1864, Revels left St. Louis and went to Vicksburg, Mississippi, to assist the provost marshal of the Freedmen's Bureau in establishing schools for the freedmen. During that period, he also served as chaplain of a black regiment and minister of Bethel A.M.E. Church in Vicksburg, the mother church of that denomination in Mississippi. He settled at Natchez where he pastored the large, newly established congregation Zion Chapel A.M.E. Church.[6]

Because of his poor health, Revels spent two years in the North and Midwest before returning to Mississippi, where he reluctantly launched a political career that eventually led to national recognition. He settled in Natchez where he pastored the large, newly erected Zion Chapel A.M.E. Church. In 1868 Revels hastily accepted an appointment as city alderman from General Adelbert Ames, provisional military governor. John R. Lynch lived in Natchez and undoubtedly used his influence to persuade Revels to enter politics. Thus at the state Republican Convention held in Natchez, Revels's political career began with his nomination for United States Senator.

According to the 1869 Constitution, Adams County was entitled to one state senator. Minister Henry P. Jacobs, a stalwart, bolted the local Republican organization and announced his candidacy for that position, while the Lynch regulars supported J. M. P. Williams another black Baptist minister. That contest was interesting and exciting, though not bitter, and turned out very close.

The district convention was composed of thirty-three delegates, evenly divided between the regular and bolted Republicans. Several secret-ballot votes were taken, resulting in a sixteen to sixteen tie. One delegate did not vote. That delegate, a Negro Baptist minister, the Reverend Noah Buchanan, was approached by both sides, but would not submit to the efforts and pleadings of either. Consequently, the delegates adjourned and each faction began caucusing. The Jacobs delegates decided to stay with their man. At the Williams meeting, the Honorable H. C. Griffin, white Republican leader, suggested the name of Hiram R. Revels as a compromise candidate. Revels, a newcomer, seemed ideal: he had never voted or attended a political meeting in the county but was an educated black and presumed to be a Republican. These qualities might get the Reverend Noah Buchanan's support.

A committee from the Williams faction called on Buchanan who concurred with the decision of his friends. Then the committee approached an unsuspecting and surprised Hiram Revels, who at his request was given until seven o'clock the following morning to decide. Promptly at seven the next morning he notified the chairman of his acceptance. At the next balloting Revels, the compromise candidate, was elected the state senator by a margin of one vote, seventeen to sixteen.[7]

When the legislature convened on the first Monday in January 1870, someone suggested to Lieutenant Governor Powers, the presiding officer of the senate, that Revels be invited to give the opening prayer. "That prayer—one of the most impressive and eloquent . . . that had ever been delivered in the Senate Chamber—made Revels a United States Senator."[8]

By prior agreement among Republicans, the unexpired term in the U.S. Senate involuntarily vacated by Jefferson Davis, ex-president of the Confederacy, was reserved for a black man. Reverend James Lynch, who had just been elected secretary of state for a four-year term, was the first choice. To elect Lynch to the U.S. Senate, however, would have necessitated another state election, which they wanted to avoid. The next name suggested was Hiram R. Revels. The white Republicans assured blacks that if they united for Revels, the whites would support him. Governor Alcorn also endorsed Revels' candidacy. In the joint legislative session every Republican voted for Revels, except for Senator William M. Hancock, who stated, "that as a lawyer, he did not believe that a colored man was eligible to a seat in the United States Senate."[9] Again, Revels, the compromise candidate, was elected, this time by a vote of thirty-nine to eighteen.

The election of Revels as a replacement for Jefferson Davis took the country by surprise. As the time drew near for Revels to take his seat, the interest intensified. The nation was apprehensive and the world silently amazed at this sudden new phase of American Democracy. "The bottom rail is on top," wrote one author; "the newly emancipated unfranchised citizen enters upon the dignified position of U.S. Senator, to mingle his voice with the law-makers and to cast his vote in behalf of God and his country."[10]

Various press releases questioned Revels's eligibility. While the *New York Herald* predicted his exclusion, the *Chicago Times* declared him ineligible because he was not a citizen before 1866. The *Baltimore Gazette* charged that as a Kansas pastor Revels was guilty of immoral conduct, a charge which was untrue. The *Mobile Register* (of February 15, 1870), a southern press, very appropriately remarked, however, that "If immorality were made a test the senate would be swept clean of its members."[11]

On January 30, 1870, Revels, tall, portly and dignified, arrived in Washington to familiarize himself with the nation's social and political affairs. Immediately, he attracted attention. The senator-elect made as his second Capitol Hill home the restaurant of George T. Downing, a man whose political judgment many black leaders relied heavily upon because of his influence within the black community and on Capitol Hill.

Revels, however, relied upon his own political experiences and trusted his own judgment regarding political issues. He was opposed to political extremists, and radicals, whom he believed hampered the political success of the Republican party in Mississippi. Observers usually described Revels as a renowned orator, self-assured politician, and respected individual who knew what he wanted.

During the three week interval while the senate debated the reentry of Mississippi into the Union and the acceptance of Revels's credentials, he was entertained by Dr. Charles Purvis, a respected black Washingtonian who welcomed him into his interracial circle of associates. A fitting climax was a party hosted by John W. Forney, where President Grant and cabinet members were present. Grant received Revels "with great kindness and hoped he would be admitted without difficulty."[12]

On February 23, 1870, Senator Henry Wilson set the stage for a dramatic scene when he presented Revels's credentials. Charges and countercharges converted the senate chambers into a political forum. Some bitterly charged that the radicals did not want a Negro in the Senate but were using the issue as a means of getting the Negro vote and keeping them loyal to the Republican party. Moreover, they alleged that the radicals desired Revels's rejection. Others claimed the radicals were using Revels to humiliate the South. The fact that Revels's credentials were signed by Military Goveror General Ames raised the question of their validity. Senator Garrett Davis denied Revels's eligibility under the nine-year clause, and Senator J. P. Stockton insisted the credentials be referred to a committee. Senator James W. Nye, elated that a Negro was replacing Jefferson Davis, asserted: "I had hoped that prejudice was over; color never made a man; color never unmade a man . . . ."[13] The debate was so prolonged that no vote was taken. The following day Revels's credentials became the priority item on the senatorial agenda.

On the third day of the hearings, Wilson, rejoicing that a black man had come from Mississippi, argued in favor of seating Revels. This action justified Stockton's rejoinder that Revels was a legal representative. The opposition argued the legal and moral implications of a black man replacing the ex-president of the Confederacy in the same chamber where such men as Henry Clay, John C. Calhoun, and Daniel Webster had sat.

Throughout the deliberations Senator Charles Sumner of Massachusetts, the devout and dedicated abolitionist, remained silent. Yet, the issues were of paramount concern to him. Late in the day Sumner, who never regained his health after suffering a brutal beating from John C. Calhoun in the senate chambers in 1856, rose to deliver a powerful speech. Concluding, Sumner proclaimed "All men must be equal before the law, regardless of color."[14]

The senators voted forty-eight to eight against referring Revels's nomination to the judiciary committee, and a motion to seat Revels followed. The chamber bristled with excitement. Within a few minutes, the senate approved the seating of Revels by the same margin, forty-eight to eight. When Vice-President Schuyler Colfax asked Revels to come forward, the silence thickened. While the vast crowd stood silently, Senator Henry Wilson of Massachusetts escorted

Senator-elect Revels to the desk. Revels, dressed in a clerical black suit with a long coat and waistcoat and holding black gloves and a brown cane, walked forth self-possessed and dignified. Hiram Rhodes Revels was sworn in and seated as the nation's first black in the United States Senate at 4:40 p.m., on February 24, 1870.

Reflecting, Senator Simon Cameron, related an incident that occurred in 1861. Prior to Jefferson Davis's departure from Washington, Cameron had prophesied to Davis, "I believe in the justice of God, that a Negro some day will come to occupy your seat."[15] Cameron rejoiced that the prophecy had come true.

One year in the U. S. Senate is a very brief period to make a record; however, Revels lost no time plunging into the routine. He delivered his maiden speech on March 16, within three weeks after the swearing-in. This gala and momentous occasion for his race attracted an overflow crowd, including numerous politicians and congressmen. The best journalists in the nation reported this gala event, and even the southern press gave him due credit for making a good impression. The *Philadelphia Press* commented, "Never since the birth of the republic has such an audience been assembled under one single roof. It embraced the greatest and the least American citizens."[16]

When the novelty of having a black man in the United States Senate ceased, the senate resumed its legislative session. Since committee assignments were made earlier in the session, Revels was at a disadvantage. He was, however, assigned to the committee on education and labor. As a committee member, he suggested donating the old marine hospital at Natchez to the state of Mississippi for educational purposes.[17]

Politically, Revels was a conservative and conciliator. His voting record indicates that he usually aligned himself with Republicans but occasionally voted against party legislation or took unpopular stances on controversial issues that affected the South. Revels's conciliatory attitude toward southern whites alienated him from blacks and some Republicans. For instance, the readmission of Georgia to the union was a decisive and unpopular question, particularly among radical, moderate, and conservative Republicans. Disregarding the political fervor created by the Georgia controversy and ignoring the Republican stance, Hiram Revels, voted for readmission. He also tenaciously supported the removal of political disabilities of Southern whites. He claimed that the freedmen in Georgia "bear toward their former masters no revengeful thoughts, no hatreds, no animosities. "And now, sir, I protest in the name of truth and human rights against any and every attempt to fetter the hands of 100,000 white and colored citizens of the state of Georgia."[18] Revels's political stance alienated him from his cherished friend, Senator Sumner.

In a speech on May 17, Revels further jeopardized his political career when, claiming that harmony between the races prevailed in Mississippi, he advocated amnesty for all former Confederates who pledged their loyalty to the U. S. government. Indeed, this meant good news for Mississippians. In the state legislature, Senator A. T. Morgan, a cultured and formerly affluent planter who had moved to Yazoo City from Ohio and married to an octoroon, made a motion to create a new county to be named for Revels; although this was a worthy gesture, it received no serious support.[19]

Because of his controversial position, demands for Revels as a speaker increased, and he toured large cities, making resounding presentations. At Baltimore before an interracial audience, he stressed economic nationalism and education for Negroes. He persuasively advised Negroes to be true to themselves, to the country, and to the Republican party. On one occasion, the popular orator Wendell Phillips dramatically introduced Revels as "the Fifteenth Amendment in flesh and blood."[20]

When the new Congress convened in December, Revels, who arrived a week late, had been named to the District of Columbia Committee. But he seemed more interested in a good levee system for Mississippi than in the blacks of the District.

As his term in office drew to a close, Senator Revels delivered on February 8, 1871, his conciliatory speech advocating integrated schools in the District of Columbia. An interracial school system, he believed, would diminish racial prejudice in the nation's capitol. He stressed that common schools for blacks and whites would not lead to social relationships between the races. He pointed to New England as an example of harmonious race relations. According to Revels, black and white children learned together, but lived separate existence. "The white race has no better friend than I," he assured his listeners; "I am true to my own race. The Negro should be built up but not at the expense of the white man."[21] Revels further vowed to leave the Republican party before enacting legislation that was damaging to whites.

Whenever feasible, Revels tried to promote the economic and political advancement of blacks. Revels appointed a black to West Point and succeeded in getting blacks hired as mechanics in the U.S. Navy Yard. He filed claims with the federal government for compensations for Mississippians whose property was utilized for the union's purposes during the Civil War. He voted consistently for the controversial annexation of the Dominican Republic, an issue that divided the black community. Some blacks felt annexation would protect an otherwise weak, defenseless people; others predicted that such action would destroy a fledgling black republic.

Prior to the expiration of his term, several colleagues interceded, without Revels's consent, to find some position in government for him lest he fall into obscurity upon leaving the senate. Such plans might have materialized had not Revels declined in favor of returning to Mississippi. Governor Alcorn had written Revels that he had a "dignified service" for him.

Meanwhile, "A good deal of nervousness existed among the whites (of Mississippi) for fear that some colored student would demand admission to the university." The state constitution prohibited any distinctions and discriminations based upon race or color. The Supreme Court had upheld the Civil Rights Act in the case of a black who had refused to occupy a particular seat in a Jackson theater.[22]

The governor needed Revels's assistance in establishing a university for the "benefit of the colored people of the state of Mississippi." Relying heavily upon Revels's political influence in the state and in the Mississippi Legislature to guarantee the establishment of such a university, Governor Alcorn and Senator Revels prepared an educational bill that would pass in both houses of the legislature. As predicted, the act was approved May 17, 1871, with an annual budget of $50,000, the same as that for the University of Mississippi, a white institution. The legislature recommended that the university bear the name of Hiram Rhodes Revels; however, Revels declined the honor and suggested the Alcorn University as a tribute to the governor of Mississippi.[23]

Former senator Revels was named president of Mississippi's first state-supported, predominantly black institution of higher education, only four months after he had argued for integrated common schools for Washington, D.C. Alcorn University opened on the former campus of Oakland College, a Presbyterian school for white males built with black slave labor. Now the sons of slaves were attending school there.

In 1873 charges of mishandling school funds were lodged against the Revels's administration. A full scale investigation by the board of trustees revealed that the charges were completely groundless and that, to the contrary, the finances had been cautiously and prudently managed. The board praised the administration, "emphasizing that they were administering a great institution of learning and making it perfect in all its parts."[24]

Also in 1873 James L. Alcorn lost the Republican gubernatorial nomination to Adelbert Ames. As the newly elected governor, Ames dismissed Revels as president of Alcorn University because he had supported the candidacy of former governor Alcorn during the gubernatorial campaign. In spite of adamant protests voiced by Alcorn University's faculty and students, the governor's decision remained unchangeable. In addition, the state legislature reduced the university's annual appropriations from $50,000 to $15,000.[25]

In the bitter election of 1875, Revels supported the Democrats, who won control of the state with a conservative platform. After the premature death of Secretary of State James D. Lynch, Revels filled his unexpired term. Refusing to run for the post in the forthcoming election, Revels accepted in 1876 the reappointment as president of Alcorn University under a Democratic regime. Revels had lost political support from both black and white Republicans; therefore, he plunged into his work at Alcorn with renewed vigor and enthusiasm. In 1878 the school was reorganized and rechartered under the name of Alcorn Agricultural and Mechanical College. For reasons of health, Revels resigned as president of Alcorn in 1882.

Essentially, Revels seemed more adept at politics than educational administration. In assessing his tenure as college president, one writer observed, "the school was quiet, unobtrusive, and uninspired, which of course, was precisely what native Mississippi whites thought Negro schools should be."[26] Had Revels not joined the fight to establish Alcorn State University, however, educational growth and advantages for blacks might have been stifled.

Revels's character was impeccable. In Washington, as in Mississippi, he was respected as intelligent and conscientious. One editor characterized Revels as well educated and one of the most polite men in the country. Senior citizens recalled that Revels bowed and tipped his hat every time he passed anyone on the street.[27] As a minister, he never brought reproach upon his calling. Voluntarily, he withdrew from the independent A.M.E. Church and joined the white Methodist Episcopal Church.

In *Men of Mark* Revels's biographer, William J. Simmons, wrote, "As the first Negro senator he stands the solitary figure in history, too, for the black man who sat in the seat of Jefferson Davis, the president of the Southern Confederacy. The Negro was no longer chattels, beast of burden, but a Senator mingling with the exalted in exalted stations and attracting the attention of the world. The irrepressible Negro is hard to 'keep in his place.' He succeeds persistently in getting some white man's place, or his own held wrongly so long by another."[28]

"In spite of his extreme caution and timidity," Samuel Smith, southern historian surmised, "Revels throughout his career was a credit to his race. Had there been more like him, both white and black, some compromise would have brought peace to Mississippi."[29]

Revels died on January 16, 1901, after suffering an attack while attending the Upper Mississippi Annual Conference of the Methodist Episcopal Church, at Aberdeen. His remains lie in the cemetery at Holly Springs, Mississippi.

Revels was married to Phoeba Bass of Zanesville, Ohio; she bore him six daughters, three of whom died at an early age. Susie married Horace Cayton, Sr., a journalist of Seattle, Washington; Ida became the wife of Sidney Redmond of Jackson, Mississippi; and Maggie married attorney Perry W. Howard.

Blanche Kelso Bruce

First Black To Serve A Full Term In U.S. Senate

Blanche K. Bruce was the first black man to serve a full six-year term in the United States Senate, to preside over that body, and to sign his name on the nation's currency. Born a slave in Farmville, Virginia, on March 1, 1841, Bruce, broad shouldered and erect, typified the model American black male of average height. His countenance and manner provoked no antagonism, and his personality harmonized with the many political successes he achieved during the Reconstruction era in Mississippi.

Bruce rose to the status of United States Senator from humble beginnings. His mother, Polly, a house slave, gave birth to eleven children. As a mulatto, Bruce's plight was difficult. The mantle of slavery so engulfed him that frequently he could not see beyond its limits. Yet, he and his brother enjoyed more freedom and privileges than other slaves. Contrary to the legislative ban against educating slaves, Bruce received a rudimentary education from his young master's tutor. Tradition affirms that Bruce was more adept at learning than his young master. As a slave, Bruce traveled with his owner to Brunswick, Missouri, where he acquired skills in graphic communication as a printer.[2]

When his young master joined the Confederate forces, Bruce and his brother journeyed to Hannibal, Missouri, to enlist in the Union Army only to be informed that blacks were unacceptable as enlisted men. Thereafter, Bruce emancipated himself by discarding his slavery name, Branch, and changing it to Blanche Kelso Bruce.[3]

In 1864 within a few months after Bruce moved to Hannibal, a free town, he founded the first public school for black Missourians. Previously at Lawrence, Kansas, he had opened the first school for blacks in the United States. While teaching school Bruce became convinced that he needed more education; subsequently, he entered Oberlin College in 1866, a move that awakened his dormant thirst for knowledge and a desire for its practical application.[4]

After two years, financial reality forced Bruce to seek employment in St. Louis. For approximately a year he worked on the river steamer *Columbia*, which operated out of St. Louis, with a regular run up the Missouri River to Council Bluffs, Iowa. The colorful river life offered little permanent prospects for an ambitious young black. Bruce was intrigued by the stories of the Deep South as a place where energetic and educated black men could assume leadership positions. There, land was sold cheaply as a result of the impoverishment caused by the Civil War. He left the steamboat service and ventured forth, first to Arkansas and later to Tennessee.

In 1868, Bruce visited Mississippi at the invitation of Samuel Ireland, a prominent black leader whom he had met in St. Louis. In Mississippi, Ireland introduced Bruce to James L. Alcorn, the ex-Confederate general and Delta planter who identified with newly formed Republican leadership. Alcorn extended an invitation to Bruce to settle in Mississippi.[5]

Later that year, at the age of twenty-seven, Bruce moved to Floreyville, Bolivar County, Mississippi. Floreyville, a steamboat landing town had begun an economic revival, through newly developed farm lands and new modes of transportation. Although practically penniless, the personable, energetic, and shrewd Bruce had little difficulty in establishing himself as a successful planter. As such, every aspect of the state economy was of interest to him. His attraction to politics immediately led to his election as election commissioner of Tallahatchie County and eventually to the U.S. Senate. Bruce possessed those qualities which prepared him for positions of honor and trust that boosted his public career. Good judgment, tact, and executive ability became the hallmark of his vocation.

Bruce's affiliation and participation in local and state politics linked him with prominent politicians as he rose to power. In 1870 Bruce attended the inaugural festivities in Jackson for the new Republican governor and legislature and was elected sergeant-at-arms of the state senate. Bruce also attended local and state party conventions. Thus, he established political alliances with Adelbert Ames and James L. Alcorn, two powerful white Republican leaders. Affiliations with John R. Lynch and Jim Hill were mutually beneficial— Lynch became a U.S. Congressman for three terms; Hill became secretary of state in Mississippi and later federal Internal Revenue collector; and Bruce went to the U.S. Senate. That alliance gained control of the state party machinery. At nearly every state Republican convention, Bruce or Lynch served as chairman with Hill as floor manager. Bruce, a professional politician, mastered all the tricks of the trade.

At Floreyville, Bruce joined H. T. Florey, the principal landowner and local Radical Republican leader, and others in a political alliance that secured passage of a bill to make Floreyville the county seat of Bolivar County. Bruce built the first house in Floreyville after it became the county seat. (When Bruce later moved to Washington, D.C., his house, a fine structure for that day, was sold to a prominent white resident.) In 1876 the Democrats regained control of the state government and changed the name of the town from Floreyville to Rosedale.[6]

After 1871 Bruce's political career took an upward turn. In 1871, Bruce was appointed tax assessor of Bolivar County, one of the state's richest counties. The preceding year he easily raised, with the assistance of whites, the required $125,000 for sheriff's bond and was elected to the consolidated offices of sheriff and tax collector. He was also appointed to the Board of Commissioners for the Mississippi River levee. Unopposed in 1874, Bruce was re-elected to those same official trusts. Later he was chosen superintendent of the county schools. Earlier in the election of 1873, Bruce had positively refused the nomination of lieutenant governor on the ticket headed by Adelbert Ames. Had Bruce accepted that slot, Ames might have resigned the governorship and returned to the U.S. Senate, leaving the governor's office to Bruce. Bruce was assured of the senatorship.

He supported the regular Republican Ames–A. K. Davis ticket. Davis, a Negro, ran to attract the black vote and became Mississippi's first black lieutenant governor. Bruce was steadily gaining wealth as a planter and popularity as a politician.[7]

As one of twelve black sheriffs in Mississippi, Bruce's record was perhaps the most outstanding of any state sheriff—white or black—during a period marked with tensions and constant provocations to disorder. Even his most outspoken political opponents praised his conduct and cooperated with him to avoid racial strife which plagued the state and almost led to race war in 1875. Even though it was fashionable in later years to besmirch Reconstruction leaders of the state, "it was never customary to deride Senator Bruce in Bolivar County, where his record was too well known."[8]

In 1872 when Bruce was enroute to the Republican National Convention as a delegate, he stopped in Washington at the senate building with James Hill, Mississippi's secretary of state. Pointing to a desk occupied previously by Mississippi senators, Hill asked Bruce if he would like to occupy that seat. Bruce allegedly said that was "out of the question." Hill declared, "I can and will put you there; no one can defeat you."[9] That was the beginning of a determined, low key, but well-planned campaign that led Bruce to the U. S. Senate.

Prior to the adoption of the Seventeenth Amendment, senators were chosen by state legislatures. Subsequently, Bruce's campaign was limited to members of the Mississippi legislature in 1874. Unlike his predecessor, Hiram R. Revels, Bruce deliberately set out to get the position and worked hard to gain it. He carefully cultivated personal contacts; and his sponsor, Secretary of State Jim Hill, kept him informed of all developments. The *Floreyville Star*, a weekly published in Bolivar County, led an editorial campaign in behalf of the election of a Negro senator, with Bruce as the paper's pointed choice, indicating, incidentally that Bruce "was too valuable a man to be spared from the county at that time."[10] Bruce's record as sheriff and his ability to work with all people were cited among his qualifications. However, Bruce was reported to have been the proprietor and editor-in-chief of the *Star*.[11]

Initially Governor Ames supported Bruce's candidacy for the U.S. Senate, but on March 4, 1875, Ames also announced his candidacy for the position. The tactful yet determinant Jim Hill rose to the challenge and defied the governor. Convening in January 1874, the Mississippi legislature with a nominal Republican majority had to decide whether it would elect a black man as United States Senator or maintain its "lily white" tradition. Many whites opposed the idea, which resulted in the formation of separate white and black caucuses to consider the candidates. Some whites adopted the strategy of nominating several blacks in an attempt to split black votes in the legislature. Refusing to be divided by this stratagem, the black legislators guided by Secretary of State Hill remained committed to Bruce, assuring his nomination.[12]

As Bolivar County sheriff, Bruce associated with powerful white legislators who reciprocated favors. Thirty-six legislators held notes due from the state auditor of public accounts for warrants issued because the state lacked sufficient cash to meet its obligations. The current value of the notes was sixty-five cents on the dollar. Under the law, however, a county sheriff could turn in the warrants at face value in transmitting county taxes due in payments to the state. Sheriff Bruce redeemed state warrants of legislators at face value and made valuable friends. When he was elected to the senate in 1875, three white Democratic senators were among those who voted for Bruce.[13]

On his thirty-fourth birthday, March 5, 1875, Senator-elect Bruce appeared before a special session of Congress and took his senatorial oath. Customarily, Senator Alcorn would have escorted his colleague to the president's desk. But when Vice-President Henry Wilson, in routine fashion, called the list of freshman members and asked them to come forward, Alcorn busied himself otherwise. Bruce, somewhat nervous and slightly excited, moved alone toward the rostrum. New York Senator Roscoe Conklin immediately arose, extended his arm and escorted Bruce to the desk. He remained at Bruce's side until the oath had been administered and was the first to offer hearty congratulations.[14] The portly, bearded Bruce drew more attention from the floor and gallery than most new senators except former President Andrew Johnson, who was back at his old desk representing Tennessee.

Presumably, Alcorn's failure to escort Bruce was not racial but political.[15] It should be remembered that it was Governor Alcorn who had appointed Bruce to his first public office, as tax collector of wealthy Bolivar County, a position that Bruce was holding when elected to the U.S. Senate. But subsequently, Bruce had joined with Alcorn's opposition in the election of 1873 and thus helped to defeat Alcorn. Senator Alcorn had not forgotten that act of "ingratitude." Alcorn had not been the regular candidate for the Republican nomination for governor. Instead he had bolted the party leadership and run as an independent. It was rumored that his only aim was to defeat Ames, the regular Republican candidate. Bruce, like many other friends and admirers of Alcorn, simply refused to follow his open rebellion against their own party.

Senator Bruce immediately made a favorable impression in the Senate. Having a magnificent physique and handsome countenance, Bruce was described by a contemporary Mississippi Democrat as "possessing almost the manners of a Chesterfield." Through the influence of Senator Conklin, Bruce was assigned to important committees such as the one on Manufactures, Education and Labor, Pensions and Improvement of the Mississippi River and its tributaries.

During the brief and special senatorial session, the freshman senator from Mississippi usually aligned himself with Republicanism and voted with the party. Yet, he refrained from orations, thus earning the title, "silent senator." Although silent on the senate floor, Bruce engaged in behind-the-scene politicking to have P.B.S. Pinchback of Louisiana seated and his credentials accepted.

While the senate investigated the alleged election irregularities in Louisiana and debated whether to admit Pinchback, the colorful senator-elect waited in the wings of the senate chambers. Had Pinchback's credentials been approved initially, he, not Bruce, would have been the first black to serve a full term.

The controversy over seating Pinchback continued into the regular session. On March 3, 1876, Bruce, addressing the senate, refuted the claim that the Louisiana legislature, which elected Pinchback was an illegal government. For three years, he argued, the President and Congress of the United States had not only recognized but sanctioned it. Louisiana, he reminded the senate, had a black electorate majority of 45,695. Furthermore, he admonished, if Pinchback were not seated, blacks would be forced to negotiate with their former masters and ignore the Republican party. Also, he declared that Grant was not truly concerned about the South; therefore, he would oppose his renomination and re-election as president.[16]

A matter of concern, which caused Bruce even more anxiety, was the 1875 Mississippi election. Consequently, Bruce called for a senate investigation to uncover the "miraculous or extraordinary" means by which the anti-black Democrats gained more than fifty thousand votes in a state with an enormous black voting populous. He cited as an example, the election campaign in Yazoo City, where a Republican majority lost to a Democratic minority. Bruce claimed that the voters were intimidated by violent riots and bloodshed. Furthermore, he stated that on the day of the election the *Yazoo City Democrat*, a newspaper controlled by the Democratic party, carried a news item that boasted the Democrats would win the election either by peaceful means or by force. The newspaper also bragged that fear of lynching prevented Republican candidates from campaigning. During the election campaign, a bloody riot occurred. White rioters killed scores of black voters immediately after voting out of office the Republican sheriff, A. T. Morgan. Four days later, approximately thirty-five to fifty black and white Republicans were murdered in a neighboring town of Clinton.[17]

In his plea for an investigation, Bruce questioned the inability of a Republican controlled government to maintain law and order in Mississippi. He surmised that the key to the problems rested with a reluctant federal government to exercise its power over a lawless state, the inability of local officials to control mob violence, and a governor enjoined by Mississippi courts from using state funds for a militia to eliminate the violence. That blacks could not adequately protect themselves against mob violence did not mean Bruce believed they were cowards or had elected incompetent black governmental officials. The answer, he thought, rested with the enforcement of existing laws and the eradication of the White League's shotgun policy which would prove disastrous for Mississippi and blacks, if it were allowed to prevail.[18]

Bruce convinced the senate to authorize a senatorial investigation of Mississippi's 1875 election. The inquiry began March 31, 1876. The Boutwell Committee in charge of the investigation documented the atrocities that had occurred in Mississippi and labeled the election campaign, "one of the darkest chapters in American history." The committee's report revealed that if the election had been a fair one, Republicans would have won a majority in both houses of the state legislature. Inaction on the part of the senate allowed those who were elected during that "dark chapter" to keep their seats.[19]

Soon afterward, Bruce split with the Republicans in March 1877, when he voted for the admission of Democrat Lucius Q. C. Lamar to the United States Senate, in spite of allegations concerning Lamar's election methods. Lamar and Bruce showed mutual respect for each other during their tenure together in Washington. Yet, they disagreed on virtually every major issue. In other contested elections involving whites, Bruce voted against accepting a challenged Democratic senator from South Carolina and in favor of a Republican one from Louisiana.

Senator Bruce's "maiden speech" in the senate was a vigorous protest against the proposed removal of troops from the South, particularly in Mississippi, where the military authorities were still in control. That speech made a profound impression on the senate and clearly indicated the manly stance Senator Bruce was preparing to take against the injustices practiced against blacks in both the North and South. He was also concerned with the removal of Lieutenant Governor A. K. Davis, who resigned from office because of alleged corruption.[20]

When the Forty-Fifth Congress convened, Bruce sought $100,000 for four hundred of his constituents who desired to migrate to Liberia. Personally he did not approve of such emigration-colonization schemes. In the *Cincinnati Commercial* of February 8, 1878, Bruce advocated a liberal western land-grant policy and federal aid to economically depressed blacks. He adamantly opposed solving the country's dilemma by shipping illiterate poor blacks to Liberia. He argued that "The Negro of America is not African but American—in his physical qualities and aptitudes, in his mental development and biases, in his religious beliefs and hopes, in his political concepts and convictions, he is an American. He is not a parasite, but a branch, drawing life from the great American civilization and adapting himself to the genius of its institutions."[21]

On February 14, 1879, Bruce presided over the senate in the absence of Vice President William A. Wheeler as the senators debated the controversial issue of Chinese immigration to America. Arguing in favor of a motion to exclude Chinese, one senator contended that the nation could not absorb more than two races, and it should be kept "black and white." As a man who had once been bereft of the privileges of citizenship himself, strictly because of color, Bruce entered into the debate and voted against the bill—attesting to his faith in the assimilative powers of the American people.

Newspapers across the country responded to Bruce's remarks in a congratulatory manner. For example, the *Detroit Plaindealer* commented, "This speech was wired to all parts of the country, and before he had taken his seat his fellow Senators crowded around him and congratulated him upon his significant remarks."[22]

The New York Tribune wrote: "Senator Bruce occupied the chair yesterday during a portion of the debate on the Chinese bill. This is the first time a colored man ever sat in the seat of the Vice-President of the United States. Senator Bruce is universally respected by his fellow senators and is qualified both in manners and character to preside over the deliberations of the most august body of men in the land."[23]

Blanche Kelso Bruce, desiring to protect the rights of depositors of the defunct Freedmen's Savings and Trust Company, introduced a resolution for the appointment of a committee to consider all matters pertaining to that institution. The motion passed, and Bruce was appointed chairman. Although Bruce failed to get Congress to reimburse the depositors, his committee ended salaries to so-called commissioners who were rapidly depleting the cash on hand, thus preventing further financial losses to the depositors.[24]

As chairman of the committee on improving the Mississippi River, he was permitted to keep the matter before Congress until it acted to provide adequate facilities for interstate and foreign commerce. Senator Bruce is entitled to a fair share of the credit for the creation of the Mississippi River Commission in 1879. This was the first major step toward the present flood control program which has eliminated much of the flood threat of the Mississippi River.[25]

Senator Bruce was not returned to the Forty-Seventh Congress. However, his impressive record in the preceding three Congresses maintained for him a prominent place among the progressive and constructive statesmen of this country.

Bruce was chosen a delegate to the National Republican Convention in Chicago in 1880, and temporarily presided over that body, one of whose delegates was the future President James Garfield. After the expiration of his senatorial office, Bruce was offered the ambassadorship to Brazil and the Third Assistant Postmastership, both of which he declined.

On May 23, 1881, President Garfield appointed Bruce Register of the U.S. Treasury, the first Negro to hold this position. For four years his signature made worthless paper legal tender. The nomination was confirmed without reference, after a complimentary speech from his associate, Sen. L. Q. C. Lamar. Again, he demonstrated the executive adeptness which his previous life displayed. The former senator performed his work with such dispatch that co-workers and others were loud in their praise of his abilities.[26]

When the Democrats gained control of Congress in 1885, Bruce was replaced at the treasury but still remained active in political and civic affairs. He was in charge of the Negro exhibit at the World's

Cotton Exposition in New Orleans from November 1884 to May 1885. Again in 1888, Bruce was a delegate to the Republican National Convention in Chicago. He was nominated for the vice-presidency on the Benjamin Harrison ticket and received eleven votes. President Harrison assumed office in 1889 and appointed Bruce Recorder of Deeds for the District of Columbia. In 1896, Bruce campaigned for William McKinley. President McKinley reappointed Bruce Register of the Treasury, an office he held until his death.[27]

In later life, Senator Bruce developed his oratorical skills. His services for anniversaries and other special occasions rivaled those of the popular Virginia representative, John M. Langston, and Frederick Douglass. Bruce was made a trustee of the Washington Public Schools and served in this position for seven years. He was elected a trustee of Howard University and was later awarded the LL.D. degree from that school. An old-time Democratic paper stated that Senator Bruce was equal in ability to the average cabinet officer of the day and had a higher character than many. He proved himself personally popular and officially successful.

On June 24, 1878, Bruce married Josephine B. Wilson, a pretty school teacher of mixed ancestry. Mrs. Bruce, the daughter of an Ohio dentist, was culturally refined, wonderfully fitted to command the dignity and respect of her position. Josephine Bruce presided over her residence with true womanly grace, making it a fit rendezvous for the distinguished circle of friends that included the wives of Supreme Court justices, prominent political officials, and Washington's black elite with whom they were so closely identified. Bruce befriended the prominent black leader Frederick Douglass, whom he shared an apartment with while Bruce was a bachelor. The Bruces were the only witnesses to the second marriage of Frederick Douglass.[28]

On May 17, 1898, twenty years from the date of his marriage, Senator Bruce died, a victim of diabetes, at the age of fifty-seven. Washington turned out in force for the funeral at Metropolitan A.M.E. Church, where diplomats mingled with party leaders, professional men, scholars, and clergymen. The Reverend Sterling N. Brown delivered the eulogy. Bruce's eighteen-year-old son, Roscoe, came home from Phillips Exeter Academy in New Hampshire to attend the services. The black-draped casket with silver bars and name plate was born by Congressmen. He was buried with military honors in Arlington Cemetery.[29]

Branch Kelso Bruce, the only black to serve a full term in the

United States Senate until the election of Edward Brooke in 1966, was described by Benjamin Brawley as "probably the most astute political leader the Negroes ever had."[30] Former opponents in Mississippi remembered Senator Bruce as "always the gentleman, graceful, polished, self-assured, and never humble." Senator Bruce himself might have appreciated most the epitaph of the Raymond, Mississippi, *Gazette*, which recalled that he scorned the use of the phrase "colored men," often declaring, "I am a Negro, and proud of my race."[31]

John Roy Lynch
Peerless Statesman

In 1973 the City Council of Jackson, Mississippi, named one of its principal thoroughfares in honor of John Roy Lynch, the first of two blacks ever elected to the Speakership of the Mississippi House of Representatives.[1]

John R. Lynch was born on Tacony Plantation, Concordia Parish, near Vidalia, Louisiana, on September 10, 1847. He was the third son of Patrick Lynch, a rich and respected Irish plantation manager and Catherine White, a slave of the plantation owner. Patrick Lynch, a native of Dublin, Ireland, came to this country at an early age. As a young man he came south and soon found employment on the Tacony Plantation. He also found on that plantation the beautiful young mulatto, Catherine White, who became his mistress and bore his son, John R. Lynch.[2]

Early in life Lynch learned the drudgery of slavery, the despair of a slave mother when the master-father of her children died before completing plans for their emancipation, and the bitter disappointment in a father's friend who broke his promise and kept them all in slavery. He might also have learned how restraining and evasive some states laws were, especially regarding freedom for blacks. In 1863 his family was purchased and taken to Natchez, Mississippi, where he became a house servant with a well-to-do white family.

As a teenager, Lynch saw the Union forces invade the lower Mississippi Valley, where he lived. This was for him a war of deliverance and when the Union forces approached that area, he joined other slaves in the "general strike" and in the enjoyment of freedom long before the cessation of hostilities. This early contact with soldiers—as a camp employee and a waiter on a naval vessel—may have had something to do with his joining the army some thirty-five years later and becoming a major.[3]

At Natchez, through efforts of a friend of his father, young Lynch secured employment in a photographic business. He took advantage of every opportunity to familiarize himself with the details of the business. As a result, in the summer of 1866 the business was turned over to him. He was not only operator and printer but bookkeeper and cashier as well. In fact, he was sole manager of the business and the only employee. The proprietor's other business took him out of town. He returned at intervals to check on financial matters. At no time did the business fail to produce a net profit, or were there any shortages.[4]

Lynch decided to renew his efforts to acquire an education by attending a night school. The school session lasted only four months from the time he began. Being precocious, he also received valuable assistance from the white public school located across the back alley from the photography shop. He would sit in the back room of the business and listen to the lessons from the school. "I was sometimes so much absorbed that I would imagine, that I was a member of the class and was eager to answer some of the questions . . . . The knowledge and information thus obtained proved to be of great assistance to me."[5]

As a young man he read the current newspapers, magazines, and books on parliamentary law. He was interested in the proceedings of Congress, especially the bitter encounter that was going on between Congress and President Andrew Johnson. Thus, in a relatively short time Lynch became quite literate. He developed a capacity for speaking that favorably impressed his listeners. He developed talents and acquired experiences that were to take him successively into politics, public service, the practice of law, and the pursuit of historical studies.

Lynch was scarcely twenty-one years old when he and other freedmen gained the right to vote. As an active member of the local Republican Club he was frequently called upon to address the group. On a mission from the local club to the governor's office, Lynch so impressed Governor Ames that, instead of following the recommendations Lynch brought, the governor appointed John R. Lynch justice of the peace of Adams County.[6]

The twenty-one year old appointee faced the dilemma of raising the required bond of two thousand dollars. There were no Negro bondsmen; besides, few blacks owned real estate. However, Lynch succeeded in finding two blacks who could and did sign notes for a thousand dollars each. He took the oath of office in April 1869. The news was greeted with sarcasm by the local Democratic newspaper: "We are now reaping the ravishing fruits of Reconstruction."[7]

In November 1869 before the expiration of his first year as justice of the peace, Lynch was elected to the Mississippi legislature, where he served until 1873. During his first term he became a member of two important standing committees: Military Affairs and Elections. Immediately he indicated a lively interest in the legislative deliberations; and if he failed in carrying the day for the measures he advocated, he succeeded in serving notice that he would not be ignored. He offered amendments to pending bills, presented riders to measures before the House, and dropped into the hopper his own bills.

In the next session, which convened in 1871, Lynch was a much more important member. He even received one vote for the speakership. Not unmindful of such popularity, the new speaker, H. W. Warren of Leake County, made good use of his erstwhile rival. He appointed Lynch to the special committee on resolutions to express sympathy on the deaths of members of the house and to the joint special committee on printing rules for the use of the house and the senate. Warren also appointed Lynch to the standing committees on education and the judiciary and to the chairmanship of the committee on elections. Lynch soon established himself as one of the most important members of the legislature, frequently offering resolutions, motions, and bills. Actually, Lynch assumed responsibilities tantamount to those of majority leader. He frequently offered the motion to consider the business that lay on the speaker's desk; invariably the motion carried. He offered amendments to pending legislation which were generally supported by a majority of the house.[8]

At the 1871 session of the legislature Gov. James L. Alcorn recommended "that there be created and supported by the state a college for the higher education of the colored boys and young men of the state."[9] Such a bill was drafted and promptly passed. The institution was named Alcorn in honor of the governor and Lynch was named one of the first trustees of the important institution.[10]

When the legislature met in January 1872, John R. Lynch was considered one of its most important members. On the first day he gained a seat on the credentials committee. It was revealed early in the session that the Republicans would control the organization of the house. A movement was made to elect Lynch speaker. His nomination by the house Republican caucus was a foregone conclusion several weeks prior to the convening of the legislature. A preliminary canvass determined that Lynch was not only the choice of the Negro members, but of a large majority of the white Republicans as well. On the first ballot with fifty-eight votes needed for election, the Republicans had a total of sixty votes, but Lynch received only fifty-five. A deadlock developed and continued for several days. Senators Alcorn and Ames made a hurried trip from Washington to use their influence to break the deadlock. Lynch was undoubtedly the best qualified for the position, but a few whites felt unable to vote for him on account of their constituents. But Senator Alcorn countered, "Can you afford to offend the great mass of the colored men that supported you, in order to please an insignificant, small number of narrow-minded whites?" On the following day Lynch received 63 of the 112 votes cast. By substantially the same vote, James Hill, Lynch's political ally, was elected sergeant-at-arms.[11]

With the organization complete, the House was ready for business. Speaker Lynch guided the legislature through a very busy session. One important bill concerned the division of the state into six congressional districts. Unable to agree on a plan for redistricting, the legislature placed the matter in the hands of the speaker. Lynch's plan made five districts safely and reliably Republican and one Democratic. This plan was agreeable to an important Democrat of Lee County. A group of counties in the northeast formed the Democratic district and made possible the election of the Hon. L. Q. C. Lamar to Congress.[12]

Although only twenty-four years of age, Lynch was clearly becoming one of the state's outstanding and influential leaders. That year, 1872, his party sent him as a delegate to the Republican National Convention, where he served on the committee on resolutions. Upon his return he and his friends decided he should run for Congress against the white Republican incumbent, L. W. Perce. Lynch described Perce as a "strong and able man" who had a "creditable and satisfactory record." However, Perce was a New Yorker, a veteran of the Union Army, and the object of bitter attacks by the Democratic press.[13]

Three resourceful Negro Republicans, William McCary, Robert H. Wood, and Robert Fitzhugh, conducted Lynch's campaign. It was a heated and exciting contest, but void of bitterness and any strong racial overtones. His Democratic opponent in the general election was the white Judge Hiram Cassidy. When the returns were in, Lynch had won by a majority of more than five thousand, thus becoming Mississippi's first and only black member of the U.S. House of Representatives. John R. Lynch previously had helped to make Hiram R. Revels the first black to become a member of the U.S. Senate.[14]

Meanwhile Congressman-elect Lynch presided over the 1873 session of the lower house of the Mississippi legislature. That proved to be a busy and productive session, dealing with a wide variety of matters, from changing a person's name to regulating the sale of liquor, to incorporating large banks, industrial firms and colleges. At the close of that session, the house unanimously adopted a resolution complementing and thanking the speaker for presiding "with becoming dignity, with uniform courtesy and impartiality, and with marked ability."[15] J. H. Piles of Pinola, chairman of the Committee on Public Works, got the floor and made a presentation to Lynch:

> The members of the House over whom you have presided so long and so well, with so much impartiality and so much of the *debonair*, irrespective of party, have generously contributed, and complimentarily confided the agreeable task upon me of presenting to you the gold watch and chain, which I now send to your desk by the son of one of Mississippi's deceased Speakers.
>
> Believe me, sir, it is not for its intrinsic worth, nor for its extrinsic show, but rather as a memento of our high admiration and respect for you as a gentleman, citizen, and Speaker.
>
> Indeed, if it were possible to weld into one sentiment, and to emit by one impulse of the voice the sentiments of all, at this good hour, methinks it would be 'God bless Hon. J. R. Lynch; he is an honest and fair man'....
>
> Doubtless we shall not all meet again this side of the All Hail Hereafter. We will miss you, Mr. Speaker. Be it my privilege now, on behalf of the House of Representatives, to bid you a long, lingering and affectionate farewell.[16]

Lynch humbly accepted their accolades, thanking them for their manifestations of confidence and respect. Referring to the gold watch with a yard-long chain, he said, "I shall ever preserve it in grateful remembrance of the generous hearts of those who contributed to it."[17]

Lynch entered Congress as a man of twenty-six years of age, the youngest member of that body. Described as slender and active with light brown skin, black curly hair, broad forehead, soft black eyes, and an obvious aristocratic appearance, he spoke fluently, tersely, and correctly. When he "engaged in a warm discussion," his eyes were "piercing and wild."[18] John Roy Lynch took the oath of office with the members of the Forty-Third Congress, on March 4, 1873, but the house did not start business until December 1. Despite his youthfulness, he had poise, self-confidence and considerable legislative expertise. He immediately became a member of the committee on expenditures in the interior department and of mines and mining.[19]

On the floor, Lynch demonstrated incredible savoir-faire. He made his first formal speech within eight days of the opening of the session. It had nothing to do with discrimination, race relations, or partisan politics. Rather he took a strong hand for the repeal of the pay act of the Forty-Second Congress. That speech demonstrated his ability to organize arguments and propositions, while supporting them with evidence and logical reasoning. He used occasional humor quite effectively. His effective delivery and ready wit appealed to blacks and whites alike. One white author wrote "that he had few, if any, superiors as a stump speaker, and advised Democratic speakers to avoid clashing with him in debate."[20]

Lynch was as aggressive in Washington as he had been in his home state. In December 1873, as a very junior member, he urged a compromise on the move to repeal a twenty-five hundred dollar raise in pay, which Congress had voted for itself, increasing the salary to seventy-five hundred dollars annually. No Congress, he argued, should be allowed to tamper with the pay of its own members; accordingly, any salary increase or decrease should not apply until after the next election.

During that freshman term, Lynch was careful to present the needs of his constituents. He introduced bills for the relief of private persons, for the donation of the marine hospital at Natchez to the state of Mississippi, and for the provisions needed for an additional term of the U.S. District Court for the southern district of Mississippi. He offered a bill to fix the time for the election of representatives to the Forty-Fourth Congress from Mississippi. He succeeded in securing passage of most of these bills, and throughout his tenure his success continued with similar legislation.[21]

In July 1874, John Roy Lynch, U.S. Congressman, sat down at a table in a railroad dining car. An attendant approached him, asking that he leave because the car was reserved for whites. He left without protest. Six months later, however, he arose in the Congress of the United States and stated: "The only moments of my life when I am necessarily compelled to question my loyalty to my Government or my devotion to the flag of my country is when I read of outrages having been committed upon innocent colored people . . . and when I leave my home to go traveling." As the only black ever to represent Mississippi in the U.S. House, Lynch felt certain he had been "elected as a Republican, not as a Negro." The political philosophy that governed his actions was that of a southern Republican. Nevertheless he felt that civil rights for all Americans had higher priority than partisan politics. He was determined to fight for the civil rights of his race. On the floor of Congress he discussed his political opinions with frankness and candor.[22]

Possibly, Lynch considered his greatest speech the one delivered before the Forty-Third Congress in advocacy of the Civil Rights Bill of 1875. Telling the lawmakers to ignore race, color, religion or nationality, he insisted that not all southern whites were opposed to the measure, which after all conferred on blacks no rights they were not already entitled to under the federal and state constitutions. Lynch argued for the bill "not only because it will be instrumental in placing the colored people in a more independent position . . . where their identification with any party will be a matter of choice and not of necessity."[23] He pleaded for the retention of the provision that would open the public schools to children of all races.

He used sarcasm on February 3, 1875, to answer those who said the bill would legislate social equality: "I can then assure that portion of my Democratic friends on the other side of the house whom I regard as my social inferiors that if at any time I should meet any one of you at a hotel and occupy a seat at the same table with you, or the same seat in a [railroad] car with you, do not think that I have thereby accepted you as my social equal." He also appealed to the chivalry of the "gentlemen of the House," asking them to imagine how they would feel if their mothers, wives, daughters, were constantly being insulted in public places.[24]

Addressing himself to an earlier speaker, who rather sardonically had noted that even in bondage blacks excelled in song, dance, and eloquence while lagging behind in other respects, Lynch said: "The answer is an easy one: You could not prevent them from singing unless you kept them continually gagged; you could not prevent them from being eloquent unless you deprived them of the power of speech." Driving home the point, Lynch continued: "But you could and did prevent them from becoming educated for fear that they would equal you in every other respect; for no educated people can be held in bondage."[25]

Because of Lynch's vigorous support of the Civil Rights Act, many whites of his district were determined to unseat him. They were encouraged by the national Democratic trend as seen in the 1874 elections. While Lynch's renomination was assured, that nomination was no longer tantamount to election. Many white Republicans were defecting to the Democrats.

Nevertheless, Lynch was an active, aggressive, candidate for reelection. His Democratic opponent was the popular Col. Roderick Seal. Lynch stood on his record in Congress, pointing out how much he had done for his district and state. During September and October 1875, he campaigned vigorously throughout his district with the assistance of Senator Bruce and others. At Biloxi, the local reporter stated he had been "agreeably impressed. . . . His deportment and bearing were respectful and polite." At Vicksburg, in the course of his speech the lights went out; a stampede ensued. Foul play may have been involved.[26]

Most of the Democratic clubs were armed companies, with funds supposedly supplied by the national Democratic organization. Democratic Club members infiltrated nearly every Republican meeting under the guise "of keeping the peace and preserving order." For the Democrats to win, a Republican majority of between twenty and thirty thousand had to be overcome. This the Democrats were prepared to do by any means necessary.[27]

The race was close, but Lynch again emerged victorious, though by a majority of only two hundred votes. The Democrats, however, made a clean sweep of the other offices. Each side accused the other of misconduct and even fraud. One state newspaper exulted over Lynch's victory: "Notwithstanding the fraud and intimidation practices in Claiborne County to defeat the Republican ticket and the determined opposition against Mr. Lynch on the Sea Coast, we are happy . . . that the Republicans . . . will have at least one representative in the Forty-Fourth Congress in the person of Hon. John R. Lynch."[28] His right to a seat in the Congress was contested, but the elections committee reported unanimously in his favor, and the house confirmed the report by a voice vote.

Shortly after his return to Washington, Lynch called on President Grant to discuss the President's refusal to send troops to Mississippi during the elections. Grant countered that sending troops to Mississippi would have lost Ohio for the party and that he saw no reason to give up Ohio when Mississippi was bound to be lost in any event. Lynch charged that the Democrats were stealing state offices and that they were determined to resist the plans of reconstruction as set forth by the Congress. He also charged that the Democrats had an armed military organization called the White League "for the sole purpose of accomplishing with the bullet that which cannot be accomplished with the ballot."[29] In other words they were determined to rule or ruin. Nevertheless, Lynch expressed a desire for conciliation. He declared, "I have friends there on both sides. My home is there. My interests are there, my relatives are there, and I want to see the state happy and prosperous."[30]

Political control, not reconciliation, was the objective of the Mississippi Democratic legislature that resolved the thorny matter of redistricting. Accordingly, five districts were to be safely Democratic; and a sixth—taking in every county on the Mississippi River and called the "shoe-string district"—was Lynch's district. Most of the voters were Republican, but there was little hope, even on Lynch's part, that he could win in the regular election of 1876. His Democratic opponent, Gen. James R. Chalmers of Fort Pillow fame, was a likely candidate to keep black Republicans in their place.[31]

At the Republican district convention in Vicksburg, a very able and eloquent speech by Capt. Thomas W. Hunt, a brave and gallant ex-Confederate soldier, placed in nomination John R. Lynch for Congress. For the next few months Lynch made an active and aggressive canvass of the district, sometimes at very great personal risks. At Fayette, for instance, the armed Democratic Club took possession of the place where the meeting was held. When Lynch ascended the platform his voice was drowned by the noise, yells and groans of the crowd. After about an hour he abandoned the podium.[32]

Of the election Lynch wrote, "Since the indications were that the Democrats would be successful in the Congressional elections of 1878, the election in the 'shoe-string district' that year was allowed to go by default."[33] Lynch believed, "In any event, the decision had been made that Chalmers must be . . . elected." Accordingly, despite a Republican majority of about 10,000 the official returns showed a Democratic majority of 4,600. Lynch contested the election; but the House committee on elections would not consider the case.[34]

Lynch remained politically active on the state level as chairman of the Republican state committee—an assignment he held for eleven years before resigning. He, Senator Bruce, and political leader James Hill cooperated to control the state party's machinery, with Lynch and Bruce taking turns as chairman of the state convention and Hill generally serving as floor manager. That alliance almost split up in 1880 when they disagreed on whom to support for the party's presidential nomination. Lynch, eager for party harmony, acquiesced, and the team held together.

In 1880 Lynch announced his decision to measure arms with General Chalmers for representative in Congress from the Sixth, or "shoe-string" district. Among four candidates for the Republican nomination, one was his personal friend, Capt. Thomas W. Hunt, the man who had placed Lynch's name in nomination for Congress in 1876. Lynch had since rewarded Hunt by having him appointed U.S. Marshal for the southern judicial district, with headquarters in Jackson. Besides, his political ally and personal friend, James Hill, had been responsible for Captain Hunt's candidacy. These factors made Lynch's campaign difficult and doubtful.

That campaign, filled with various political contrivances, saw the old Bruce-Lynch-Hill alliance destroyed. The district convention was composed of forty-two delegates. After eighty-three ballotings the votes were: Jeffords, sixteen; Lynch, fourteen; Fitzgerald, seven; Hunt, five. On the eighty-fourth a delegate from Warren County, J. W. Short, white, voted for Lynch. A recess was called. A series of agreements led to the following results on the eighty-fifth ballot: Lynch, seventeen; Jeffords, sixteen; Hunt, five and Fitzgerald, four. Hunt's name was withdrawn in favor of Lynch, after which the leader of the Jeffords forces moved to make the nomination of Lynch unanimous.

Learning of Lynch's return to the political battlefield, the *Jackson Clarion* wrote, "The Republicans of the sixth district have nominated Lynch. He was formerly a member of the legislature and is the ablest man of his race in the South." But this praise did not allay the intensity of the kingmakers of the Democratic party. They used every scheme possible—especially intimidation and fraud—to secure the election of their candidate. At Rodney, Republicans were in command and a large Republican vote was polled, counted, certified and returned; but the officer who took the ballot box to the county seat was attacked by a mob and the ballot box destroyed. In Lynch's home county, Adams, he "was informed by a member of the Democratic County Committee that it had been decided to have the county go Democratic."[36]

Col. James Chalmers was seated by the Forty-Seventh Congress, but John R. Lynch filed his protest. The report of the House elections committee was in his favor. The committee invited Lynch to present his case when the fight came on April 27, 1882. Lynch estimated that an honest count would have given Chalmers about five thousand of the twenty-one thousand votes polled. Lynch documented much of his argument. He also cited statements from an interview in the *Cincinnati Enquirer* of Chalmer's boastings. Lynch ended with a quotation from Abraham Lincoln asking for the "considerate judgment of mankind and gracious favor of Almighty God" to bring about racial peace and fraternity. After several days of debate Lynch was seated by a vote of 124 to 84 with 82 abstentions. As he was sworn in, unseating Chalmers, the Republicans cheered.[37]

By then the first session of the Forty-Seventh Congress was half finished. Nevertheless, Lynch introduced measures to amend the election laws, to reimburse the depositors of the Freedman's Savings and Trust Company, to redistrict the Mississippi judiciary, and to clear the way for better rail service to his state.

Having had to fight for a year to win his seat, Lynch had little opportunity to recoup his strength prior to the 1882 election. Meanwhile, the Mississippi legislature had reorganized the congressional districts, using the favored tactic of gerrymandering. Nevertheless, the Republicans insisted that since Lynch was already in the Congress he should make the race in the new district. He and the Democratic nominee, Judge Henry S. Van Eaton, met in joint debate at several places. Lynch said, "The canvass was entirely free from bitterness and excitement, and I was treated with marked courtesy and respect at every point." But he lost the election by six hundred votes; and when the Forty-Seventh Congress expired on March 4, 1883, he returned to Natchez.[38] Yet his political career was not concluded.

1884 was a presidential election year. President Arthur was a candidate to succeed himself, but Sen. James G. Blaine, of Maine, was conceded to be the choice of the Republican National Convention at Chicago. The Mississippi delegation, with a single exception, favored President Arthur. The Blaine forces, in a majority on the national committee, selected Powel Clayton of Arkansas for temporary chairman. The anti-Blaine forces—Roosevelt, Lodge, Fish and others—desired to support another Southerner against Clayton. Lynch's name was suggested. A committee was appointed, with ex-Gov. P. B. S. Pinchback of Louisiana as chairman, to wait on Lynch and to insist on his acceptance. A poll of the delegates revealed that such a movement would have sufficient strength to defeat Clayton by a majority of about thirty-five votes. Thus, Lynch achieved another first of his race as temporary chairman of the Republican National Convention. (Sen. Blanche K. Bruce had briefly occupied the chair at an earlier convention.) Lynch presided for two days before yielding to the permanent chairman. He was later to receive nine out of thirty-seven committee votes for permanent chairman. Lynch was a member of the convention committee, dispatched from Chicago to Augusta, Maine, to notify Blaine of his nomination.[39]

On December 18, 1884, Lynch married Ella W. Sommerville, from whom he was divorced in 1900. He was later to meet Cora Williamson, whom he married in 1911, the year he retired from the army.[40]

Early in the 1890s Lynch began to study law, and in 1896 he passed the Mississippi bar examinations. Shortly thereafter he became a partner in the law firm of Robert H. Terrell in Washington. Terrell had been a clerk in Lynch's office when he was Fourth Auditor of the Treasury. Lynch practiced in Mississippi and the District of Columbia until he went into the army in 1898. Lynch probably had no keen interest in the military; but when President McKinley asked him to serve during the Spanish-American War, from personal regard for McKinley and a deep sense of party loyalty he accepted. In 1901, when he was offered the commission as major in the regular army, he gratefully accepted. As paymaster, Lynch had opportunity to travel to many parts of the world. Everywhere he exhibited that zest for life and the healthy curiosity about people and places that characterized his early years. It was during these travels that he met Cora Williamson who became his second wife.[41]

John Roy Lynch, unlike Revels, Pinchback, and some others, ever remained loyal to the Republican party. Secretary of State Walter Gresham approached Lynch and asked him to go on record as saying that he "was in sympathy with the main purposes of the Cleveland administration as the condition to remain with the treasury department." Lynch replied that he would be happy to stay, but only if there were no conditions. In conclusion, he stated, "The President has no office at his disposal [that] could be a sufficient inducement for me to identify myself with the Democratic party."[42]

At sixty-three he moved to Chicago and qualified to practice law in Illinois. He also dealt in real estate. In 1913 he published *The Facts of Reconstruction*. Though an octogenarian, Lynch was still active and living in 1929 when Oscar DePriest again broke the Congressional color barrier after twenty-eight all-white years. In 1875 he had been asked to deliver a eulogy for Vice-President Henry Wilson. He lived a full rich life and was highly respected. Shortly after midnight on November 2, 1939, Mrs. Lynch, with a premonition that her husband was not resting well, went to check on him. On the bed lay the manuscript pages of his life story. He shifted weakly as his wife entered, lifted his head, then fell back on the pillow. The ninety-two year old Mississippi political leader, historian, lawyer and gentleman was the last of his Congressional contemporaries—white or black.

Lynch was buried with military honors in Arlington National Cemetery. *The New York Times* eulogized him as "one of the most fluent and forceful speakers in the politics of the Seventies and Eighties." The *Chicago Defender* praised Lynch for his achievements, attributing them "to the dauntless spirit he possessed, the seemingly unlimited capacity for the entertainment of useful knowledge and the overmastering desire for unselfish service."[43]

A recent student of the life and achievements of John Roy Lynch described his contributions this way:

> Lynch's career, then, proved that a black could participate and excel within the economic and political structure in the United States, but unfortunately it did not prove that most blacks would be allowed to participate. His election to Congress did not show that society was open, but rather that there were flaws in the theory of black inferiority. Lynch's successes cannot be ignored by those who proclaim white supremacy; nor can his failure be ignored by those who extol the American dream.[44]

James D. Lynch

A Founder of the Mississippi Republican Party

James D. Lynch was the first black to hold a major political office in Mississippi.[1] The Maryland native, a mulatto, who was well educated and very capable, came to Mississippi in 1868 as an official of the Methodist Episcopal Church North. During the next three years Lynch gained a place in the hearts of Negroes and openminded whites that was never challenged by either group. A Democratic newspaper referred to him as "the most popular carpetbagger in the State—the best educated, the best speaker, and the most effective orator of that [Republican] party in Mississippi; and withal, as much of a gentleman as he can be with his present white associations."[2]

A contemporary Democratic leader wrote: "He was a great orator; fluent and graceful, he stirred his great audiences as no other man did or could do. He was the idol of the [N]egroes, who would come from every point of the compass and for miles, on foot, to hear him speak. He rarely spoke to less than a thousand, and often two to five thousand. . . . Imagine one or two thousand [N]egroes standing en masse in a semi-circle facing the speaker, whose tones were as clear and resonant as a silver bell; and of a sudden, every throat would be wide open, and a spontaneous shout in perfect unison would arise, and swell, and subside as the voice of one man. . . . I could not understand it, but in the light of the discovery of the laws of psychic phenomena, I am now sure that it was done by the hypnotic power or influence of the speaker."[3]

James D. Lynch was born in Baltimore, Maryland, in 1838. His father, a free mulatto merchant, early in life accumulated sufficient wealth to purchase the freedom of James's mother. His father provided an elementary education for his son in Baltimore and subsequently arranged for him to attend Kimball Union Academy, Hanover, New Hampshire, one of the several eastern institutions that were opened to blacks by 1860. James's activities at the academy are unknown. He remained in school for only two years, apparently returning to Baltimore at the end of the time. At age nineteen James entered the ministry of the Methodist Episcopal Church North and served congregations in Indiana and Illinois during the late 1850s. He was of medium height, broad shouldered, with a superb head and sparkling brown eyes; his black glossy hair stood profusely on his head "between a kink and a curl." About 1860 Lynch and his bride, whom he had met and married in Galena, Illinois, moved to Philadelphia where he edited the *Recorder*, a popular Methodist publication.[4]

Lynch remained in Philadelphia during the early part of the Civil War, devoting himself to his editorial responsibilities and church-related activities among the free Negro population. When General Sherman's army moved into Georgia in 1864, Lynch followed it as a missionary of his denomination to the downtrodden and confused freedmen. Immediately following the capture of Savannah, the young minister set up a mission for blacks who had flocked to town. On January 12, 1865, Secretary of War Edwin M. Stanton, accompanied by Sherman, paid a visit to Savannah and held a conference with twenty blacks, including Lynch, concerning the aspirations of the Negro freedmen. In this meeting Lynch agreed with his colleagues that their main desire was to secure land, but he sharply took issue with them when they insisted that freedmen wanted to live in their own districts, apart from whites. Lynch insisted that a separate society for Negroes would be disastrous. Accordingly, the proper policy was for federal authorities to push for the integration of the freedmen into the white community.[5]

Soon after the Confederate surrender Lynch returned to Philadelphia. In early 1867 along with a prewar associate, Hiram R. Revels of the A. M. E. Church, and a few other Negroes from the North, Lynch came south again, this time to Mississippi. His purpose was, as he expressed it, "as a religious and moral educator of my race."[6] Such was in striking contrast to white carpetbaggers who swarmed into the defeated areas primarily for economic gain. Settling in Jackson prior to the establishment of rigid racial housing patterns, Lynch and his wife moved into a comfortable neighborhood on West Capitol Street, not too far from the residences of some distinguished whites.

He took his religious mission seriously; and as the leader of the Northern Methodist effort in Mississippi, Lynch reported within a year of his arrival that six thousand blacks had joined the church, twenty meeting houses had been constructed, and numerous schools for freedmen had been established, most of which met in the new churches. Meanwhile, Lynch sought to improve fraternal feeling among freedmen, especially in Jackson. With the assistance of Thomas W. Stringer, who later became a bitter political rival, Lynch introduced Masonry to the blacks of Jackson.[7]

Lynch later expanded his activities to include politics. Soon after his arrival in the state, he saw that political rights were as essential to the elevation of his race as religious instruction, and these required the immediate attention of Mississippi blacks. In 1867 Congress had terminated the old southern governments based solely on white suffrage and had dispatched military commanders to the former Confederate states with instructions to register a new electorate without regard to color. Without neglecting his role as organizer of Negro churches and schools, Lynch joined with other friends of the freedmen to impress upon them the necessity for registering and voting for delegates to a convention that would frame a new constitution for the state.

Lynch firmly believed that Negroes should place their faith in Congress and the Republican party as the means to bring about true and legal equality in Mississippi. Even though it was natural for blacks to support the party of Lincoln and Stevens against Democratic hostility to Negro rights, Lynch and other local Republican leaders faced a difficult task in convincing the mass of plantation blacks that the Congressional settlement would be permanent and that they would be fully protected in the exercise of their new rights. However, Lynch warned blacks against false prophets who promised that rebel lands were to be confiscated and divided among them. He even insisted that freedmen should not become alienated from their former masters, since close cooperation between the races was necessary to insure the success of Congressional Reconstruction in Mississippi.[8]

Meanwhile the Republicans met in Jackson in September 1867 for their first state convention, at which time they rewarded Lynch for his early services to the party by selecting him vice president of the permanent organization. A few days later Lynch threw himself into the campaign to secure voter approval for a constitutional convention and to assure the election of Republican delegates to it, despite the presence of the military and its accompanying dangers for a black political stump speaker.[9]

Lynch and his colleagues' efforts met with success in the 1867 election. Republicans won an overwhelming majority of the one hundred delegates to the constitutional convention, primarily from the unified support blacks gave the party candidates. Of seventy-nine Republicans, sixteen were black. (One black was elected as a conservative.) Of that small group of blacks—certainly not in proportion to their population—eight were preachers.[10] During the organization of the convention, the motion was made that the word "Colored" be added to the name of each Negro delegate; James Lynch then moved to amend it to include color of each delegate's hair also.[11] In response to a barrage of invective and ridicule hurled at them, the Republicans drafted a constitution that, although enlightened in most respects, unwisely disfranchised and debarred from public office many former Confederates. Lynch and many other moderates in the party disapproved of these extreme provisions, "not only as a matter of principle, but also because proscription had provided a windfall for conservative leaders in their efforts to unite demoralized whites for a crusade against the ratification of the Radical constitution."[12]

Unlike the former state constitutions, that of 1868 was to be submitted to the people for ratification. It immediately became apparent that the Democrats and conservatives would oppose its adoption. They were openly against suffrage. A convention of white men of all political groups was called to meet in Jackson. They adopted a plank setting forth white superiority and calling upon "the people of Mississippi to vindicate alike the superiority of their race over the [N]egro and their political power. . . ."[13]

The die was cast. On the one hand the Democrats openly scorned and attacked the aspirations of Negroes, while on the other the Republicans were willing to do little more than grant them the franchise and solicit their votes to put only white Republicans in office. These circumstances called forth the innate abilities of James D. Lynch, who became the leading Negro worker in that bitter campaign. In one of his memorable speeches Lynch directed remarks to both groups, saying Negroes were eager to see political passions abated and that they desired to live in peace with their ex-masters. He said they did not seek "supremacy" or wish to force themselves into social companionship, nor wished to be deprived of their rights. "If local instances indicate a desire on our part to become legislators and administrators of law" he said, "it is because universal hostility among a certain class, to our political equality, leaves us no other alternative."[14] To be sure Lynch was not quite prepared to demand a proportionate share of public offices for blacks, but his statement contained a subtle threat that if whites persisted in their racist politics Negroes in counties where they were a majority would elect their people to office to protect their interests.[15]

The Democratic executive committee issued a rejoinder containing a solemn warning that Negroes should reject the proposed constitution and elect Democratic officials, or "accept the eternal enmity of those upon whom they depended for employment."[16] To make those threats effective Democratic workers at the polls went to great lengths to take the names of all blacks who voted Republican. Gen. Alvin C. Gillem, military governor, dispatched troops to the more important polling places, some of whom joined in intimidating and persuading Negroes to vote Democratic. The constitution was rejected. One editor is reported to have written, "Thank God it is over! and pray His Holy name to remove the sin creating thing, [N]egro suffrage, the most abominable of all abominations. This is a White Man's Government; and trusting in our firm purpose our good right arms and God of Right, we will maintain it so!"[17]

With Lynch in mind, Ethelbert Barksdale, the prominent editor of the *Jackson Clarion*, warned Mississippians to beware of the guile of "African adventurers" from the North who had come to the state to play the part of "black tyrants." He declared, "We would shock the instinct of self-preservation which God has implanted in the bosoms of all his creatures if we invoked a spirit of kindness toward them." Barksdale implicitly invoked a threat of violence: "In assuming the relation of oppressors to a people who have done them no wrong, they must take the chances of their desperate measures."[18]

But the Democrats lost the national election of 1868, which blasted the hopes of the Mississippi Democratic plans. General Gillem was removed. Adelbert Ames, scion of a New England abolitionist family assumed the dual role of provisional governor and military commander. Ames immediately removed many of the Democratic and conservative local officials, replacing them with men sympathetic to the Congressional program of reconstruction. Many of his appointees were Negroes.[19]

The Republican party in Mississippi prior to 1869 was somewhat fragmented—radicals, moderates, and conservatives. The radicals and their proscription position had been repudiated at the polls. The conservatives were charged with keeping company with former secessionists such as Gallatin Brown and Ethelbert Barksdale. Lynch and his associates represented the moderate position. They agreed on the radical principle of equal rights for all. However, they insisted that blacks be given fair representation in all departments of government. Lynch insisted they were not to be dismissed on the grounds of incompetency, since, if given a chance, blacks could prove their competency. He even attempted to set white apprehensions at rest with the succinct comment: "We do not desire mixed schools; a fair division of the school funds will satisfy all."[20]

To promote the cause of moderate Republicanism and black unity, Lynch entered the newspaper business as publisher and editor of the *Jackson Colored Citizen*. In an interview with a correspondent of the *Cincinnati Commercial*, Lynch declared that, though he appreciated the efforts of the radicals on behalf of Negro rights, he opposed their policy of proscription because it alienated a large portion of whites, without whom there could be no success for Republican Reconstruction. It seems his position was "that after the new order in Mississippi had demonstrated black capabilities and had educated both races to a higher level of thinking, racial prejudices would pass away."[21]

The first indication of moderate success was in the state Republican convention of July 1869 when a mild and nonproscriptive platform, reportedly written by Lynch, was adopted. He served in his usual role as vice president of the convention and was selected as one of five, and the only Negro, on the state central committee. Meanwhile, he was appointed by Commissioner Oliver O. Howard as assistant superintendent of education for the schools administered by the Freedmen's Bureau. Later, Superintendent Harry R. Pease, like many other white Republicans who never quite accepted the idea of sharing leadership with blacks, dismissed Lynch, charging drunkenness. Actually Pease and associates sought to checkmate Lynch's growing influence among Mississippi's blacks. However, Lynch's popularity was at its height in 1869, and most white Republicans saw the wisdom of suppressing their hostilities until a more opportune time.[22]

Democrats, conservatives, and national Republicans formed a coalition called the National Union Republican Party. At their state nominating convention they chose two white carpetbaggers to head their ticket and the obscure, ignorant, servile black, Tom Sinclair, from Copiah County, as their candidate for secretary of state. (Thus, Sinclair became the first Negro in Mississippi to be nominated for a major political office.)[23]

The regular Republican nominating convention with the moderates in control met in September 1869 and chose J. L. Alcorn and R. C. Powers to head their ticket. The best known Negro in the state—and probably the most remarkable black who rose to prominence during the period—the Rev. James D. Lynch, was selected as their candidate for secretary of state. Lynch defeated his convention rival, Dr. Thomas W. Stringer, by a vote of 158 to 36.[24]

Again, the silver-tongued Lynch canvassed the state for the Republican cause. His effectiveness on the stump was demonstrated when blacks in the fall election voted solidly for the Alcorn-Lynch-Powers ticket. Supported by Negro votes and a few thousand whites, the state constitution was ratified, minus the offensive proscriptive clauses, and the party of the new order swept to power in Mississippi. Lynch himself ran ahead of his colleagues on the ticket by a majority of 40,612; while Alcorn, with the second highest, led his conservative opponent by some 38,000 votes.[25]

The Republican legislature convened in early 1870 and was faced with the selection of three U.S. Senators—one for the full term beginning in March 1871 and two for unexpired terms. It was clear that blacks should have one of the latter terms and it was equally clear that James Lynch was the undisputed choice for it. John R. Lynch (no relation) states, that James Lynch "was a suitable and fit man for the position" undeniably.[26] However, there were several obstacles.

Lynch himself desired to remain in the state and effect a reconstruction which would secure readmission into the Union. There was also some hostility to his candidacy among several powerful carpetbag members of the legislature, which might have, in combination with Democratic votes, resulted in Lynch's defeat. Finally, because Lynch had just previously been elected secretary of state for a term, his election to the U.S. Senate would have necessitated the holding of another state election, which was undesirable. So Lynch withdrew from consideration, and the Rev. Hiram R. Revels was elected. Lynch then praised Revels's selection as an affirmation of the Republican pledge for equal rights for blacks and optimistically exclaimed, "A glorious sunlight now shines upon the path of Mississippi that leads to a goal of prosperity of which greatest patriots never dreamed!"[27]

As secretary of state in the first Republican government in Mississippi, Lynch demonstrated to the chagrin of many skeptics that blacks were not only capable of participating in politics but were able to serve competently as public officers. He performed his duties without a fulltime assistant and in an unattractive room in the Capitol, which he said was "so unsafe as to imperil life." Such conditions were not caused by Republican discrimination against him; rather it reflected the long neglect of the Capitol facilities and the general belief that very little was required to operate an administrative department. To meet the demands of his office, Lynch was forced to pay some of the expenses from his own pocket.[28]

As secretary of state, Lynch served with distinction as a member of the three-man board of education. He investigated the bewildering situation of sixteenth section lands. The public school system was greatly improved and received the support of an impressive number of whites throughout the state. Lynch's involvement in higher education led to the development of Shaw University at Holly Springs, a small institution founded by the Northern Methodist Church. During his five-year career in Mississippi Lynch was the guiding spirit behind the school. It became a state normal school in 1870. On the other hand, Lynch did not seem keenly interested in the founding and development of Alcorn University, as the black counterpart of the University of Mississippi at Oxford.[29]

About 1871 Lynch became disillusioned with political solutions for the problems of blacks. He continued to insist that blacks' rights should be maintained inviolate, cautioning his followers, however, not to expect too much from their participation in the cauldron of reconstruction politics. Despite his growing disenchantment with politics, Lynch, as the most prominent Negro in Mississippi and possibly the most effective stump speaker of either race in the state, took to the campaign trail in the fall of 1871.[30] Though not a crucial election for the dominant Republicans, Lynch toured the largely white interior of the state in response to a plea that he do so to help change the image of the Negro and the Republican party there. In debate with conservatives he appeared before large white as well as black audiences.[31]

Nevertheless, Lynch's influence among the party faithful was beginning to decline, evident in his failure to win the Republican nomination for Congress in 1872 in the heavily black Jackson-Vicksburg district. Stories of Lynch's affinity for hard liquor began to affect his reputation. On the other hand, many white carpetbaggers and some Negro preachers had long regarded the charismatic Lynch as a threat to their own political ambitions. Meanwhile, rumblings of Negro discontent with the white leadership throughout the predominantly black counties was surfacing. Fear of revolt within the ranks increased. Whites generally believed that only Lynch could successfully lead such a revolt. So, in the district congressional convention, carpetbaggers, at the risk of political oblivion if they failed, struck the first blow by defeating his candidacy for Congress. Emboldened by that success, they next went for the jugular vein. The Reverend C. F. Norris, a Negro minister of Jackson, and Henry R. Pease, the northern-born superintendent of education, hauled James Lynch into court on a trumped-up charge of rape. The accusation was so blatantly partisan that a racially mixed jury quickly acquitted him. But the damage to Lynch's influence among blacks had been done, and his future in Mississippi politics seemed bleak, as new heroes such as Adelbert Ames and John R. Lynch quickly arose to replace him.[32]

With his political career waning, Lynch turned his attention to national politics. As a delegate to the Republican convention of 1872 in Philadelphia, he delivered a speech which the managing editor of the *Philadelphia Press* described as the best made at the convention. Several Mississippi Republicans urged national leaders to use Lynch's oratorical abilities in Grant's campaign. He was subsequently invited to Indiana where he made a spectacular canvass of that state. In New York he made at least one speech before a distinguished audience at Brooklyn.[33]

Lynch returned to Mississippi in late 1872 and was soon stricken with Bright's disease of the kidney, which was complicated by the recurrence of a bronchial ailment. Some Negroes said Lynch never recovered from the earlier defeat and humiliation at the hands of his fellow Republicans.

James D. Lynch died on December 18, 1872, at the age of thirty-four and received a state funeral on December 26, with Governor R. C. Powers and other state officers among the pallbearers. However, out of respect for his unstinted championship of the cause of racial equality, Lynch was followed to his grave in the white Greenwood Cemetery mainly by hundreds of blacks. Editor Barksdale of the *Jackson Clarion*, a political foe, wrote that Lynch, "was one of the foremost Republicans in the State and he had done more than all of them to organize and to build up the party on which they thrived.... It is no exageration [sic] to say that he was the ablest and most influential man in his party in the State...."[34]

One black newspaper commented on his defeat and death, which were close together in time: "As with a magic wand he swayed and moved the masses whilst a candidate for the nomination. But it was snatched from him by the demon of corruption. He never recovered from the blow and when he fell, he fell a victim to the ingratitude of his own race. The arrow hurled against his manly breast and deep into his heart lost nothing of its sting because it was gilded in gold. Shame, shame upon the colored people that they permitted the most gifted orator of his race to be thus stricken down.... the whole race, as a political power, will soon be destroyed by the same instrumentality, and will deserve it, if they continue to follow the advice of the scoundrels who are now filling their pockets and preparing to run off...."[35]

Belatedly, Mississippi Republicans sought to capitalize politically on Lynch by erecting a monument over his remains in Greenwood Cemetery. The Republican controlled legislature of 1874 passed a bill appropriating two thousand five hundred dollars to finance the project. According to a turn-of-the-century historian, James Lynch was the only man for whom a monument had been erected in Mississippi by legislative appropriations.[36] Although opposed by Democrats, the monument produced little controversy until the Vardaman era. In 1900 the Democratic legislature by a vote of ninety-four to zero authorized the removal of Lynch's remains and the monument to the city's Negro cemetery.[37] Governor Andrew H. Longino approved the bill, but there is evidence that the plan was never accomplished. At least the memorial to Lynch remains in the Greenwood Cemetery. Under the bas-relief of Lynch on the monument is the simple inscription: "True to the Public Trust." Buried a few feet away is Ethelbert Barksdale, one of Lynch's most formidable opponents during his career in Mississippi but one who had attested to the truthfulness of the inscription.[38]

James Hill

Politician-Kingmaker

James Hill, Mississippi secretary of state from 1874 to 1878, was born a slave on the J. Hill Salem Road Plantation about two miles from Holly Springs, Mississippi, July 25, 1846.[1]

Hill, a light mulatto, received a rudimentary education, reading and writing, from his master's two daughters. He continued his education while working as a youth in the railroad shops of Holly Springs. Although Hill never obtained any formal education, he financed his younger brother's education at Oberlin College. Hill had no time for diversions, he devoted himself to study and work.[2] With the advent of the Civil War, Hill served his master's sons, John H. and W. B., as a valet.

After the Civil War, Hill joined the Republican party and launched his career in Mississippi politics. Although he did not possess any of the brilliance or oratorical skills of Bruce and Lynch, he became an influential political figure in the state's political machine. In the early 1870s he was elected to the House of Representatives, where he was chosen sergeant at arms and speaker of the house.[3]

After his tenure ended as speaker, the Mississippi electorate chose Hill as secretary of state in the 1874 election, a position he filled quietly and efficiently for three years. During this period, no one ever charged him with dishonesty or malfeasance while in office.

When his term ended as secretary of state, Hill's political career continued. John Lynch appointed Hill as postmaster at Vicksburg and then he served as collector of internal revenues. As collector of internal revenues, he hired a number of blacks his staff. *The Hinds County Gazette* reported, "The indications are that James Hill (colored) now revenue collector in this state, will be the Republican Candidate for congress from this district. A Mississippian by birth, he was secretary of state under the Ames dynasty and discharged his duties faithfully. It is said the few remaining white and colored carpet-baggers of the Ames era will not support him, preferring one of their own number."⁴

After his unsuccessful bid for a Congressional seat, Hill mixed politics with business and civic affairs. For a while he centered his attention on business, acquiring a modest fortune as a successful land agent for the Louisville, New Orleans, and Texas Railroad. He closed his political career as receiver for the Federal Land Office in Jackson and as sponsor of projects directed toward the advancement of the black race. The Republican administrations in Washington held him in high esteem. With the exception of the brief periods when he unsuccessfully ran for Congressional position, Mississippi white Democrats worked with him as a colleague. He also served on the executive committee of the American Citizen's Equal Rights Association, which advocated civil rights and the equality of the sexes.⁵

In 1885, J. J. Spelman and James Hill organized the Colored Fair Association. They received cooperation from state officials and from the white merchants of Jackson, who subscribed over a thousand dollars in premiums. The fair lasted four days. A wide variety of stock, agricultural products, and needle work were displayed, and speeches were delivered by Governor Robert Lowry, state senators J. Z. George, E. C. Walthall, I. T. Montgomery, and ex-U.S. Senator Blanche K. Bruce. The quality of the exhibits and the behavior of the large crowds were highly praised by the press.⁶

James Hill never married. He died in 1901 and was buried in Mt. Olive Cemetery on Lynch Street, Jackson, Mississippi.

Thomas W. Stringer

Physician, Churchman, State Senator

By far the most influential black at the Mississippi Constitutional Convention of 1868 and the most powerful political leader of his race in the state until 1869 was T. W. Stringer of Vicksburg.¹ Stringer, a physician and minister, was born in 1815 in Maryland, later migrated to Ohio,² and ultimately to Mississippi. Of medium height, slightly heavy build, and a light brown complexion, Stringer was a man of many interests, well trained, and a genius at organizing.

Early in life Stringer joined the African Methodist Episcopal Church and was licensed as a preacher at the Ohio Annual Methodist Conference in September 1846, then became prominent in African Methodism in Ohio and Canada. During the mid-sixties, Stringer moved to Mississippi and was instrumental in building schools and Methodist churches throughout the state. Immediately, he joined in establishing Bethel A.M.E. Church in Vicksburg and organizing the Mississippi Conference of the A.M.E. Church in October 1868. He became the pastor of Bethel and was succeeded by the Reverend Hiram R. Revels.

After his pastorate at Bethel, Stringer traveled extensively across the state organizing lodges, churches, and schools.[3] In 1870, two years after the founding of Mississippi Annual Conference of the A.M.E. at Greenville, the conference membership consisted of 4,982 individuals, thirty-five churches, and thirty Sunday schools. This growth was the result of the organizing skills of T. W. Stringer.[4] The first T. W. Stringer Masonic Lodge was organized at Vicksburg in 1867, in the Bethel Hall located at the rear of the church. It was in that same hall that Campbell College was founded in 1890 and its first classes held.

Within the next few years, with the cooperation of James D. Lynch and H. R. Revels, Stringer established another lodge in Jackson and one in Natchez. From these three centers, the movement grew rapidly enough to justify the organization of the Most Worshipful Stringer Grand Lodge at Vicksburg, in July 1876. This grand lodge created in 1880, the Fraternal Life Insurance Benefit which paid to its beneficiaries death claims up to seven hundred dollars. By 1908, this insurance association had fourteen thousand members and owned a thousand acres of timberland on the Yazoo and Mississippi Valley Railroad. In 1907, it reportedly paid its claimants $110,000.[5] In 1975, Grand Master H. M. Thompson reported that lodges with thousands of dues-paying members existed throughout the state.

Stringer, a 33rd degree Mason, served as the first Grand Master of the Ohio jurisdiction of the A.F. and A.M.; District Deputy Grand Master of the territory west of Pittsburgh, Pennsylvania; and the first Grand Master of the Mississippi Grand Lodges.[6] He also founded the Knights of Pythias of Mississippi under the jurisdiction of North America, South America, Europe, Africa, and Asia on March 26, 1880 in Vicksburg. He presided as its first Supreme Chancellor and the first Grand Chancellor of the state. He also belonged to the Knights of Honor of the World.[7]

Stringer was very active in Mississippi politics. One of five blacks elected state senator in 1870, Stringer was among its most prominent leaders, white or black. Stringer exercised his greatest influence at the Constitutional Convention of 1868.[8] Of the one hundred convention delegates, eighty-four were white and sixteen black. Eight of the blacks were ministers. T. W. Stringer of Warren County and the Reverend Henry P. Jacobs of Adams County were the leaders of the black delegates. To be sure, the blacks alone, even with the help of the carpetbaggers, could not control the convention. But by cooperating with the native white Republicans, they were a formidable group.

Stringer's efforts at the convention to secure a provision for compulsory school attendance failed. Black delegates, with the exception of renegade Combash Charles Fitzhugh, bloc voted to table a resolution creating segregated schools in Mississippi. Later, after it had been decided to leave the matter to the legislature, they voted as a group against their colleague Charles Fitzhugh, whose motion would have put the convention on record as opposed to setting up separate schools.

Stringer's suggestion to empower the legislature to legalize marriages between those who had cohabitated together as husband and wife and to prohibit adultery and concubinage were approved by the convention. However, blacks failed in getting Stringer nominated to office at the convention.[9]

Described by personal acquaintances as kind, generous, and patient with those deprived of educational advantages, Stringer was known, respected, and loved by ministers and laymen, blacks and whites, of all denominations. Bishops willingly accepted advice from him. He was remembered by those who knew him as always delightful and an excellent orator.[10]

At the age of eighty-two, after forty-seven years in Mississippi, in the service of the church, the state, and fraternal orders, the Reverend Thomas W. Stringer died as his family and a few friends stood by. His remains rest in the Vicksburg City Cemetery.

Josiah T. Settle
Orator, Lawyer, and Legislator

The Honorable Josiah T. Settle was born September 30, 1850, in the Cumberland Mountains, while his master-father Josiah Settle and slave-mother Nancy Settle were en route from North Carolina to Mississippi. As soon as circumstances would permit, they continued their journey and settled in Mississippi; thus he claimed that as his native state. The father, a descendant of the famous Settles of Rockingham, North Carolina, was a widower when he began raising a family by his former slave. Being devoted to his children and their mother, he manumitted them several years after arriving in Mississippi. After being informed that the laws of the State forbade free Negroes residing therein, Settle left in March 1856 for Hamilton, Ohio, where he relocated and purchased a home for them. He spent summer vacations with his family in Ohio and maintained his Southern plantation the latter part of the year.[1]

Another problem arose concerning his relations with his slave family. His northern neighbor informed him that he had to discontinue the relations with the neighbor's family unless he married the mother. He immediately replied: "That is what I have always desired to do." In 1858 his slave mistress, Nancy, became his lawful wife in a ceremony witnessed by their children, who became his legitimate heirs.

The advent of the Civil War in 1861 brought Settle northward where he remained until he died in 1869. Thus began the Northern existence of Josiah T. Settle, affectionately known as Joe. Because there were no colored schools and only a few colored families in Hamilton, Ohio, Joe attended the white school. Although the law stipulated that black citizens were entitled to enroll in white schools, if the county did not provide a separate school for them, desegregated schools were unacceptable to Ohio whites. Therefore, when Joe enrolled in the white school, he had to learn how to defend himself against the racism of white students and his white instructors.

Finally, relief came when a liberal Christian woman and excellent teacher took charge of the school and took a warm interest in him. Joe soon became deeply attached to her, and he soon began excelling in class. She first inspired him with a desire for something more than a country schoolhouse education. In the spring of 1868, he enrolled in Oberlin College. His freshmen peers chose him as class orator, an honor coveted by most students. Then tragedy struck: during the spring of 1869 his father died. Subsequently, at the end of his freshman year, he left Oberlin and went to Washington where he entered the sophomore class of Howard University. His college years at Howard were rewarding. During his first year there, Joe taught in the preparatory department. Then for two years he clerked for a white man in the educational division of the Freedman's Bureau. Toward the latter part of his senior year, he was elected reading clerk of the House of Delegates, a branch of Washington's territorial government. At the time of his graduation he was performing his duties as reading clerk, teaching two classes a day at the University, and pursuing his own studies. Immediately following his graduation from Howard University in 1872, he joined the law department, took an active part in district politics, and held several public positions, including clerk for the Board of Public Works until its expiration and trustee of the county schools for the District of Columbia.

In the presidential campaign of 1872, Josiah Settle canvassed several counties in Maryland, where his youth and brilliance created a sensation. He delivered speeches in Dayton and Cleveland, Ohio, in support of Ulysses S. Grant's candidacy for president. Soon after the presidential election, Josiah graduated from the Howard Law School. He was admitted to the bar of the Supreme Court of the District of Columbia but decided to relocate in Mississippi. He left Washington for Mississippi in March 1875. After successfully passing the state's law examination in Vicksburg, he was admitted to the Mississippi Bar and located at Sardis, in the northwestern Mississippi county of Panola and formed a law partnership, Settle and Matthews.

He later returned to Washington and married Miss T. T. Vogelsang, a refined and cultivated lady from Annapolis, Maryland, already distinguished for her superior mental qualities. He returned south with his bride and commenced his law practice.

In August 1875 he was unanimously nominated by the Republican convention for District Attorney of the Twelfth Judicial District in Mississippi, in which there was a Republican majority of 2,500 but was unexpectedly defeated. As a member of the State delegation to the National Republican Convention in Cincinnati in 1876, he was elected the State at-large Republican elector for the Hayes-Wheeler ticket. Instead of supporting the Hayes-Wheeler ticket, he voted for Roscoe Conklin as the Republican presidential nominee. At the convention, he seconded the nomination of Stewart L. Woodford of New York for Vice-President. Again in 1880 Settle was chosen as Republican elector on the Garfield-Arthur ticket.

In 1882, at the behest of some party members in Jackson and Washington, he was strongly urged to represent the Republican party as their congressional candidate from the Second Congressional District. At the state convention Settle declined the honor, however, and nominated General James R. Chalmers, who had recently moved to the Second District. Chalmers received the nomination and was elected by a clear majority.

In 1883 a coalition of Republican and Democrats made a fusion ticket for county officers and members of the legislature. Vigorously opposing such a coalition, Settle bolted and became an independent candidate for the legislature. During that campaign he made the most brilliant efforts of his career. Even though he was opposed by the ablest speakers of both parties on every stump in the district, he enthralled the voters and won election by more than a twelve hundred majority vote.

During his tenure in the legislature, Settle was regarded as one of the ablest men in the House, earning the respect and admiration of his colleagues for his oratorical abilities. At the adjournment of the legislature he was presented a gold-headed cane, as a token of his esteem.

After that legislative session, he temporarily abandoned politics and devoted his time to the practice of law. In 1885, he moved to Memphis, Tennessee, and about two months later was appointed Assistant Attorney General of the Criminal Court of Shelby County. On several occasions he received compliments from the court bench. In the meantime, he steadily built a reputable law practice.

One observer commenting on Settle's oratorical eloquence and power of persuasion remarked, "That young man is too eloquent to be a prosecutor for the State, because the jury would be so blinded by his eloquence that the opposing counsel could not persuade them to give a verdict of acquittal."

Roscoe Conklin Simmons

Political Orator

Roscoe Conklin Simmons was a politician, orator, and talented writer in the early years of this century. His oratorical skills earned him a reputation as a flamboyant word artist.[1]

Simmons was born about 1875 at Greenview, Mississippi, and rose from an humble environment to a position of prominence enjoyed by few blacks of his day. He was the nephew of Margaret Murray Washington, wife of Booker T. Washington. By Simmons's own account, Washington sent him at age twelve to live with Senator Mark Hanna of Ohio. Senator Hanna, a powerful millionaire industrialist, gained fame as a "President Maker." Simmons also temporarily lived with Senator Medill McCormick of Illinois. He remained with the Hanna and McCormick families as a "valued employee" all his life.[2]

Many Republicans noticed Simmons's oratorical genius when he campaigned for Theodore Roosevelt in 1910. Following Simmons's eloquent oration on Roosevelt's behalf, William Jennings Bryan, the Populist Party presidential nominee, exclaimed, "Tonight's speech by young Roscoe Simmons has assured him a place among the great orators of the world." Evidently Simmons viewed public oration as his mission in life. When Booker T. Washington offered him a teaching position at Tuskegee, Simmons promptly refused by replying, "I have been called too, to teach, but the rostrum and the public hall will be my classroom."[3]

By 1913, Simmons was recognized as a sensational orator and journalist. He then decided to go to Memphis to espouse Booker T. Washington's philosophy of self-help and to recruit southern blacks for Tuskegee Institute. Consequently, Simmons immediately began publishing a local weekly, The *Memphis Sun*, which attracted financial support and encouragement from R. R. Church, Jr. The *Memphis Sun* shone brightly for six months, carrying Tuskegee releases, success stories, and advice to black farmers, as well as the regular Memphis news. Then Simmons found himself in financial difficulty, and within a year the *Memphis Sun* had set for the last time.[4] Nevertheless, Simmons and Church became close friends.

In 1916 Robert R. Church organized the Church's Lincoln League to promote the election of black Memphians to state and national offices. Though the League's candidates were defeated by the Democrats, they polled enough votes to have Robert R. Church appointed to the national Republican advisory board. Church then sought Simmons's assistance in organizing a national league composed of every important black politician in America. In New Orleans in 1919, the Lincoln League of America was organized, and the members elected Roscoe Simmons, its first president.[5]

Active in three consecutive Republican presidential campaigns from 1920 to 1928, Simmons challenged Oscar S. DePriest for the First District congressional seat in the Illinois Republican primary. He received only token support from the dominant Republican organization, however, and was defeated by 12,000 votes.[6]

In 1932, the Second Ward Republican Club endorsed Roscoe Simmons's candidacy for Illinois state senate. During his campaign, Simmons's oratorical skills captivated an audience of 5,000; however, he was again defeated.[7]

The role of orator made Roscoe Simmons an excellent public relationist for the Republican party. In the election of 1936, the G.O.P. assigned him to the state convention credentials committee when Republicans were charged with driving Negro voters out of the party. Three times delegate from Chicago to Republican national conventions, he seconded the nomination of Herbert Hoover for reelection as President at the national convention in Chicago in 1932 and was invited to second the nomination for Governor Alf Landon for President in 1936.

Unquestionably, Simmons symbolized the leadership of the old order. According to *Ebony* magazine, "he belonged to that era when crafty, conniving Negro politicians out-thought, out-foxed, and out-tricked white politicians in high places."[8] That source admits there was much of the "Uncle Tom" trait in many of the Negro leaders of his day, but their record of accomplishments bespeaks more their stature than latter-day critics often realize. Many people remembered Simmons as a wispy, red-haired, frock-coated wizard of words, the weaver of spells over masses of blacks who followed him like some Pied Piper into the ranks of the Republican party without doubt or question.

But Simmons's hypnotic oratory had magical effects on influential whites as well as blacks. He was the black counterpart to the fire and brimstone Dixie Negro-haters of the school of Cole Blease of South Carolina, Tom Heflin of Alabama and the Vardamans, Bilbos, and Rankins of Mississippi.

Simmons reached the heights of political manipulation between

1920 and 1928 when behind-the-scenes maneuvers, carpetbagging and rubber-kneed diplomacy were the vogue. Then in the thirties Republicanism went down in dismal defeat, and Franklin Delano Roosevelt took over—but not before Roscoe Simmons delivered an eloquent denunciation of Herbert Hoover. In Simmons's address he challenged Hoover: "Speak Mr. President, and tell us Lincoln is not dead. Speak and say there is no higher theme than liberty. Tell us again that our president loves justice and will do it."[9]

Simmons's journalistic flair for writing gave him connections with several newspapers, principally the *Chicago Tribune* and the *Chicago Defender*, for which he worked for more than twenty years. He also wrote a column for the *Chicago Daily News* under the caption, "The Untold Story," in which he revealed the outstanding work done jointly by whites and blacks.

To increase sales and circulation, Robert Abbott, owner and publisher of the *Chicago Defender*, exploited Simmons's oratorical and journalistic talents. He knew that Booker T. Washington's nephew could attract audiences of several thousand. Frequently he made five or six promotional speeches a week. Describing Simmons as "America's Greatest Orator," Abbott sent him on tours of the South as the *Defender's* representative at large. Regularly Simmons wrote a weekly column; nearly every week he was featured on the front page. Simmons eventually became the highest paid employee in the organization and perhaps in black journalism at that time—$125 weekly. One story declared, "With nothing behind him except truth and his amazing genius, this man at thirty-five years, is the ambassador of 12,000,000, the wisest champion his Race ever had, and his country's foremost orator." He made five or six promotional speeches a week. His critics referred to him as "that rascal Roscoe," but Abbott had an undeniable affection for him.[10]

Roscoe Conklin Simmons, the orator, politician and journalist, died on April 27, 1951, after a brief illness. *The New York Times* eulogized him as the "Negro orator, writer and political figure who was a friend of Presidents."[11] His survivors included his widow Althea, former Chicago public school teacher; three sons—William Murray, president of the *Harvard Crimson* student newspaper; Thomas Murray, student at Loyola University; and Roscoe C. Jr., by a previous marriage, of New York City.

Robert H. Wood
Natchez Mayor

Robert Wood was one of several free blacks who lived in Mississippi before the Civil War.[1] According to historian Vernon L. Wharton, Robert Wood and his fellow Natchez resident, William McCary, were "intelligent members of families who had been free and respected residents of Natchez for several generations."[2]

Robert H. Wood was a printer in the photographic establishment in which John Roy Lynch was employed as a messenger boy. In his autobiography, Lynch states, "I rendered such valuable assistance to Wood that I was prepared, after a period of about three months, to take his place as printer while he was promoted to take the place of one of the proprietors as an operator...."[3] Lynch and Wood formed a friendship as colloborators in that photography business that was to be mutually beneficial later on.

Wood, one of the most popular and influential citizens of Natchez, was elected the town's mayor in 1871. Then he served as postmaster and later was elected sheriff of Adams County.[4]

Robert H. Wood presented his credentials as selectman (city councilman) on February 21, 1870. Having duly qualified, he took his seat among the other selectmen and was chosen chairman of the standing committee on Police and Colored Schools as well as a member of the committee on Roads and Public Property.[5]

Later that year Robert H. Wood entered the mayoral contest in Natchez. On January 2, 1871, when the results were tabulated, Wood had defeated his opponent by a vote of 707 to 525. He took office two days later.[6]

In the December 1871 elections, Robert H. Wood was renominated by the Radical Republicans for mayor of Natchez, "his renomination a foregone conclusion. Although the Republicans had a large majority in the county, in the city it was small. (Wood's) reelection was impossible if the Perce men should vote against him or even fail to vote for him." The Perce men bolted the regular Republican convention and formed an independent ticket with H. C. Griffin, a nominee for mayor. Despite campaign manager John R. Lynch's efforts to swing the election to Wood, Griffin won with a vote of 772 to 591.[7]

Many regular Republicans did not support Wood in the mayoral election. Postmaster Costello promised John Lynch that he would support Wood, but Costello campaigned for Griffin, thus violating his agreement with Lynch. Costello seemed convinced that Senator Ames would guarantee his reappointment as postmaster, thus protecting retribution by Lynch. However, Lynch wrote to Senators Ames and Alcorn insisting on his right as Congressman from the district to name the postmaster at Natchez. Both senators replied, conceding Lynch that privilege. Lynch immediately requested Robert H. Wood, the defeated candidate for mayor, to file application for postmaster. According to Lynch's autobiography, the application was protested: "It was publicly known that Wood's name was sent to the senate for confirmation. As soon as the appointment was announced, Costello took the first train to Washington, but the trip was made in vain. The nomination was promptly confirmed and, upon the expiration of Costello's term, Wood took charge of the office, the duties of which he discharged in a creditable and satisfactory manner for several years."[8]

Later Wood voluntarily resigned as mayor to assume duties as sheriff and tax collector-elect of Adams County. Wood was the second black to be elected sheriff of Natchez. (The first one was William McCary, a free black barber and teacher, whose father belonged to the black professional class.) Wood served the people and town of Natchez as a proficient administrator and executive law enforcer.[9]

James Charles Evers

First Black Mayor of Fayette

James Charles Evers, was born September 11, 1922, in Decatur, Mississippi, to James and Jessie Wright Evers. Because his parents were devout affiliates of the Church of God in Christ and strict disciplinarians, drinking, smoking, and gambling were taboo. His father, a temperamental businessman and sawmill worker who could neither read nor write, deplored racism. James Evers boasted that he owned his property and did not rent from whites. Charles's mother of Indian ancestry emphasized the importance of obtaining an education in order for blacks to become independent.[1]

Several racial incidents molded or shaped Charles's stance on civil rights. For instance, at the community store, several white loiterers tried to force him and his brother, Medgar to dance. The racists yelled, "Dance Niggers." On another occasion, the illiterate white storekeeper overcharged their father for several commodities. When he informed the owner, the storekeeper retorted, "Nigger don't you tell me I'm tellin' a lie." A confrontation ensued, the storekeeper pulled a gun, but Jim Evers warded him off with a broken Coke bottle and led his sons to safety. Therefore, Charles and Medgar were warned to watch their steps, to stay in their places, to get off the street when a white woman passed lest they brush her accidentally and be accused of rape. "To be black in this country," Evers chided, "is miserable more often than it's not."[2] But Charles proclaimed, "Medgar and I, right from the start, when we were kids, were determined to prove this wasn't a white man's world—or if it was, we'd at least get our share of whatever there was worth getting and see that some other black folks could too."[3]

In another instance, Senator Theodore Bilbo, a demagogue who advocated white supremacy, saw Charles and Medgar as he espoused pseudo-scientific racism. He shouted to the crowd gathered at the Newton County Courthouse, "You see them two little niggers sittin' down there? If you don't stop 'em, one of 'em will be up here on these steps one day trying to go to Congress." Reportedly, Medgar turned to Charles and stated, "That's not a bad idea."[4] Little did they know at the time that Charles Evers would try to make that prediction a reality.

On yet another occasion, one of their friends and neighbors, Willie Tingle, was seized by a white mob, dragged through the streets, lynched and shot. It was rumored that Tingle had insulted a white woman. Evers's father cut the hanging noose from around Tingle's neck and took the body to the funeral home for burial, but it was too mutilated to be embalmed. Lynchings and other violent mob acts directed against the race were part of the coming of age for black youths in Mississippi, particularly for Charles Evers.[5]

Generally, the Evers felt no hostility toward whites in Decatur. The racially mixed town was such that sometimes black and white children played together. His mother worked for the Gaines and throughout her lifetime she maintained a friendly relationship with that family.[6]

As a youth, Charles enrolled in a rural segregated school in Decatur and graduated from Newton County High School. As customary, blacks attended classes approximately five months per year from harvest to Spring. Ironically, while his mother assisted white children who rode the school bus, her own children had to get themselves ready to walk about eight miles per day to and from school.

Charles painfully recalled that "Those same little kids who'd been taught to hate so long would . . . would spit out the bus on us and throw rocks at us. We'd have to jump in the ditch and dirty up our clothes and go on to school that way."[7]

At school, according to Charles, he was the "loud mouth" Evers boy who was blunt and to the point. He was a hustler. "From the very beginning I could make money," he boasted, "I'd try to find Coke bottles and sell them for a penny-a-piece. I'd hustle scrap iron, scour the fields and nearby towns for old plows and odd pieces of metal. And I'd press cigarette foil out and sell it and make a few pennies."[8]

From childhood to adulthood, Charles Evers remained big, brash, and outspoken. For him life was a rough-and-tumble scramble for existence, and he was prepared to tumble with the best. One observer described Charles as "blunt and direct and there is hardly a toe—black or white—that he has left unstomped."[9]

Charles's brashness helped him to survive in Mississippi's closed society, but he was determined to escape its racism. Therefore, in 1941, like many blacks, he joined the segregated Army only to be confronted with overt racism at Camp Shelby in Hattiesburg. "The white racist officers didn't call us niggers," he stated, "but they did everything but that. They had to call us soldiers, but it was the way they said it. The kind of assignments they gave us, and the kind of restrictions we adhered to, and the kind of punishment they administered."[10] Later in 1943 the army transferred Charles from Camp Shelby to Australia by way of Fort Leonard Wood, Missouri; Camp Claiborne, Louisiana; and Fort Sill, Oklahoma.

After receiving an honorable discharge from the Army in 1946, Charles enrolled at Alcorn A & M College, where he majored in social science. His career objective had been to become a lawyer, but circumstances dictated otherwise. While at Alcorn, Charles engaged in business ventures. He was always hustling trying to make a dollar. Alcorn's president at that time, J. R. Otis, described Charles Evers "as a young man with an eye for business."[11] Evers convinced the Dean of Students to allow him to provide taxi service for the Alcorn community. He transported students and faculty members from Alcorn to Port Gibson for a dollar and charged a dollar and a half for a round trip to Natchez. Also, he withdrew monthly a thousand dollars from a three thousand dollar savings to cash veterans checks for a fifty-cent fee. At night, he sold peanuts and sandwiches.[12]

Business was ingrained in Evers. He inherited his father's and uncle's business acumen. They were businessmen who chased the dollar and squeezed it when they obtained it. His wife, the former Nannie Magee, remembered that when Charles was at Alcorn, "He didn't have much time to study. He was too busy selling peanuts and picking up dry cleaning for a firm in Port Gibson. You know, the businessman on campus who incidentally wants an education."[13]

Before Charles completed his degree requirements, the Army inducted him into the reserves. Later, he returned to Alcorn, graduated, moved to Philadelphia, where he taught history and coached football at nearby Noxapater. In addition, Charles managed his Uncle Mark Thomas's funeral parlor in Chicago.[14]

Several years later, Charles Evers returned to Mississippi where he pursued business ventures and denounced racism. He taught school, operated a taxi company, opened a hotel, and became Mississippi's first black disc-jockey at the white-owned radio station, WOKJ. Evers, the state chairman of the voter registration drive, opened his program with, "Pay your poll tax; register and vote. If you can't register to vote, pay your poll tax anyway." White racists resented his program and eventually the school board fired Evers, the proprietor of his restaurant dwelling refused to renew his lease, and creditors demanded cash for items purchased. Several people filed lawsuits against him, leaving Charles penniless. By 1956, his friends collected twenty-six dollars in pennies to assist him in leaving town. Leaving his wife and children at his mother-in-law's home, he drove toward Flint, Michigan, but decided to stay in Chicago with a sister.[15]

While in Chicago, Charles held odd jobs such as carting carcasses at the stockyard and shining shoes in the men's room of the Palmer House. Later, he opened two nightclubs and eventually obtained an elementary teaching position with the Cook County school system. Afterwards, he quit his odd jobs, devoted his time to teaching and managing his nightclubs, and sent for his family.

Although distantly located from his brother Medgar, the two brothers communicated frequently, and Charles financially supported Medgar's civil rights activities in Mississippi. Both knew that someday Charles would return to Mississippi, though neither knew the return would be under such grievous circumstances. On June 11, 1963, Charles Evers received a telephone call informing him that Medgar had been slain. When he came to Mississippi for the funeral, Charles vowed to stay: "I was born here, and here I'll die."[16]

Through sheer determination, Charles Evers wrought racial change in Mississippi. Charles volunteered to complete the task his brother had left unfinished. The heirarchy of the NAACP questioned Charles's sincerity and were skeptical of this militant, sassy, boastful, profane individual who forced controversial issues. They wondered whether they could control Charles Evers.

In spite of the skepticism, Charles assumed the position as field secretary of the NAACP. When Charles finally settled into his job, he soon became aware that he "had to change Mississippi not by shouting at people, but by giving blacks the courage to get registered and start voting."[17] He teamed with Aaron Henry to strengthen the NAACP in Mississippi. Obviously, many of the black elected officials in Mississippi were either affiliated with or held office within the NAACP.

As field secretary, Charles Evers increased the number of NAACP chapters in Mississippi and protested against all forms of racial discrimination. He urged blacks to register and vote; organized and led demonstrations, boycotts, and selective buying campaigns in Natchez, Port Gibson, Jackson, Vicksburg, and other cities. Evers and his followers desegregated public accommodations as well as campaigned and succeeded in getting blacks hired as clerks, policemen, firemen, salesmen, truck drivers, and U.S. Marshals. He was bent on challenge, and he accomplished the task.

Ten years after Medgar's death the national office of the NAACP reported that Mississippi had 145 black elected officials and that blacks were enrolled in each of the state's public and private institutions of higher learning. This was due in a large part to the efforts of Charles Evers. In 1970, according to statistics compiled by the Department of Health, Education, and Welfare, more than one-fourth or 26.4 percent of black pupils in Mississippi public schools attended integrated schools with at least a 50 percent white enrollment. When Medgar died in 1963, only 28,000 blacks were registered voters. By 1971, there were 250,000[18] and by 1982 over 500,000.

After six challenging and tempestuous years as field secretary of the NAACP, Charles Evers resigned in 1969 to run for mayor of Fayette, Mississippi. He overwhelmingly defeated his seventy-four year old opponent, incumbent R. J. "Turnip Greens" Allen, who had held that office for almost a generation.

On July 7, 1969, Charles Evers was inaugurated as Mayor of Fayette and tackled the race problem. To the utter dismay of the white population, Charles's first project was the erection of the Medgar Evers Memorial in the town's Confederate park. Whites immediately insisted upon its removal. They adamantly argued that since Medgar was not a Fayette native or resident, his monument should not be placed alongside the imposing statue of Marquis de Lafayette, the French mercenary soldier who fought in the American Revolution for whom the town is named. The mayor countered that at least Medgar Evers was a Mississippian whereas Lafayette was a foreigner. Later the monument was transferred from the Confederate park to the front lawn of the city hall.[19]

Evers further antagonized local whites with his integrated staff and his law and order plan to curtail racial discrimination. He succeeded in converting the violent white-controlled town into a safe place for blacks. No longer were blacks afraid to walk the streets or enter a white establishment; no longer did they feel forced to shuffle, grin, and bow in the presence of whites or to respond with "yes-um," "no-um" or "yes sir," "no sir." Moreover, the mayor frequently warned whites against carrying rifles in the cabs of their pick-up trucks while they were within the city limits. "Ain't no rabbits in the streets in town," Evers contended, "so there's no need for guns."[20] Paradoxically, Evers carried a firearm for protection against assasination.

Charles Evers's apparent conflicting social philosophy and political practices drew much criticism from blacks as well as whites. While he staunchly advocated integration, Evers categorically advised an interracial couple—Martha Wood, the city's white attorney, and her husband, Monroe Jenkins, a black policeman—to leave Fayette. Although local white merchants extended credit to blacks, Evers did not. He argued that credit made blacks dependent on whites and that blacks had to learn to be independent. Furthermore, he claimed that "If you buy on credit, then you're obligated to that man."[21]

The two necessary ingredients needed to solve the race problem, Charles Evers declared were the ballot and economic nationalism. "First you get yourself some votes, then you get yourself some money, and people begin to listen to you," he advised the black community. Indeed, it worked for him.

Although Evers failed in his bid for U.S. Congressman from the fourth district, in 1968, he infiltrated the political arena and paved the way for other blacks to enter Mississippi politics. His political task commenced when he helped organize the Mississippi Freedom Democratic Party (MFDP), which was organized to end the uniracial one-party system in the state. Unsuccessful in 1964, but succeeding in 1968, the MFDP challenged and unseated the "regular" segregated Mississippi Democrats at the 1968 National Convention in Chicago.[22]

In 1971, Evers spearheaded an independent campaign in the gubernatorial election in an effort to defeat Democratic incumbent, William Waller. Evers lost, according to the *New York Times*, because "many blacks stayed home and approximately ten to twelve percent of those who went to the polls voted for Waller.... Even the charismatic Evers was hurt by the apparent failure of a black bloc to develop. His 158,000 votes represented little more than half of the registered black voters."[23] As an independent candidate in the 1983 gubernatorial election, Evers lost his bid for governor to Democratic nominee Bill Allain. Nevertheless, this was the first time since Reconstruction a black had sought election as governor of Mississippi.

In many ways, Charles Evers was a catalyst for change. He remained on the battlefront, chiding the establishment for additional political positions for blacks on the city, state, and federal levels. Because he was crafty and frugal, he accumulated wealth and represented the increasing number of black capitalists in Mississippi. Someone observed that Charles Evers was in control of three things that were essential to bring about change—people, politics, and green power.

Change came to Fayette when Evers implemented his "Five-Year Program."[24] Under this plan, Evers acquired an apartment complex, restaurant-lounge (presently a skating rink), and several stores. With the assistance of federal aid, he built the Medgar Evers Health Complex to provide dental and medical care for low income families and he initiated other economic programs to help the needy and the elderly. As planned by the previous mayoral administration, when Evers took office the city treasury had been depleted; therefore, Charles Evers went on national television and solicited thousands of dollars to help the financially troubled city of Fayette. He donated his seventy-dollars-a-month salary to welfare.

Many of the changes Evers sought did not conform to the will of the black community. In the 1980 presidential election, Charles Evers supported Ronald Reagan and Reaganomics, the black voters demonstrated their disapproval in the 1981 mayoral election when they selected Kenneth Middleton mayor of Fayette, thereby ending Charles Evers's twelve year reign. Also, Charles Evers endorsed the 1982 Congressional candidacy of James McBride, a black Jackson minister who ran as an independent in the Fourth Congressional

District. McBride challenged Republican Liles Williams and the Democratic incumbent, Wayne Dowdy, a moderate whom many in the black community supported. By a slim margin, Dowdy was reelected.

Charles Evers knew personally Presidents John F. Kennedy and Ronald Reagan, Senator Robert Kennedy, and Martin Luther King, Jr. Because of his dedication to civil rights, numerous colleges and universities have bestowed upon him numerous honorary degrees. In 1970, his alma mater, Alcorn State University, recognized him as "Alcornite of the Year," and in 1978, Alpha Phi Alpha Fraternity awarded him its Public Service Plaque. When Governor Cliff Finch released his list of "Mississippi Colonels," a distinction formerly reserved for white supporters, James Charles Evers's name was included. In spite of the adversities and disappointments, Charles Evers has carved his place in Mississippi and American history.

Unita Blackwell Wright

Mississippi's First Black Female Mayor

Unita Blackwell Wright, a three dollar-a-day farm worker and native of Issaquena County, Mississippi, was elected mayor of Mayersville in 1977, thus becoming the tenth black mayor in the state and the first black female in Mississippi history to be so honored. *Ebony* magazine described her election as representing, "the inroads women have made in the predominantly male world of politics and signified a change in Mississippi's image."[1]

In 1976, Mayersville, a river town of approximately 500 residents, had no city hall, police department, school, doctor, or even a sidewalk or streetlight. Because there was no city hall, Mayor Wright conducted the town's business from her home. Few jobs were available and those who did work labored as cotton pickers or farm hands. The nearest school was fifteen miles away in Rolling Fork. Mayor Wright was able to alleviate many of these problems by acquiring federal aid and financial assistance from such civil rights activists as, Stokley Carmichael (Kwamé Touré), Robert Moses, and Fannie Lou Hamer.[2]

During the height of the civil rights movement, Unita Wright actively engaged in voter registration drives, which, according to one writer, "served as the high school, college, and graduate school for the articulate eighth-grade dropout."[3] Through the civil rights movement, she acquired organizational skills that enabled her to "function as an SNCC project director for six counties and later as a community organizer for the Child Development Group of Mississippi." She also served as community development specialist with the National Council of Negro Women. As a member of the Mississippi Freedom Democratic Party, she and others unsuccessfully attempted to unseat the regular democrats at the 1964 national convention, but they achieved their goal in 1968 in Chicago. Wright participated in the 1965 march on Selma, a demonstration whose objective was to protest the denial of blacks' suffrage in Alabama. On the trip from Montgomery to Selma, she was riding in the car just ahead of Viola Luizzo, Jewish civil rights activist killed by a sniper's bullet.[4]

Because of her acquaintance with actress Shirley MacLaine and her involvement in the civil rights movement in the 1960s, she was chosen to accompany the women's delegation to the People's Republic of China in 1973. While in China, Wright became increasingly aware of her black identity and, assessing the black struggle in America, she renewed her vow to fight against racial oppression and for racial equality and justice.[5]

Eddie James Carthan

Tchula Mayor

In 1977, the citizens of Tchula, Mississippi, a predominantly black Delta town in Holmes County, elected twenty-seven year old Eddie James Carthan mayor. Campaigning on a reform platform, Carthan promised to serve "all of the people." He believed that being elected mayor was one of the benefits of the civil rights movement. "I thought I could represent those who had come through slavery, knowing nothing about going to a motel, sitting in the front of the bus, or eating in a restaurant."[1]

For over a century this town was controlled by aristocratic white planters and their political allies. Of Tchula's seventy percent black population, two-thirds are on welfare, thirty percent are unemployed, forty-seven percent reside in dwellings without plumbing, and eighty-one percent live in deteriorating housing. No public recreational facilities existed in Tchula, when Carthan assumed his duties as mayor, the town owned one tractor, an old fire engine, and an inoperable squad car. Holmes County is the tenth poorest county in the United States.[2]

To alleviate poverty in the town, Carthan solicited federal aid. As a result of Congressional appropriations totaling three million dollars, the mayor implemented the Comprehensive Employment Training Act Program, a housing rehabilitation program, a program providing child care for working mothers, a nutritional program for the elderly and handicapped, and a medical clinic. The city acquired two new squad cars and a mini bus; a flood drainage and sign construction program was begun.[3]

By the 1981 mayoral election, the four black aldermen had lost their seats and Eddie James Carthan had been sentenced to three years in the state penitentiary on assaulting a policeman. The problem began during Mayor Carthan's fourth year in office when he was reportedly offered a $10,000 bribe to allow the "status quo" white power structure to exist, and a man identifying himself as an FBI agent visited the city hall daily. In a special alderman's election, two of Carthan's loyal black supporters were replaced by two other blacks, Jason Gibson and Roosevelt Granderson, who teamed with John Edgar Hayes, who was already serving as alderman. This triumvirate sought legislation to limit the mayor's authority over fiscal and personnel matters. Subsequently they stopped paying the salaries of city employees' for two months in summer 1979, apparently in order to test their power, closed the city hall for eight weeks, and stationed Police Chief Sharkey Ford at the door with a shotgun and orders to "shoot anyone who tries to enter." They also refused to pay the mayor's travel expenses for trips made on behalf of the town, and the Carthage family began to receive threatening letters and telephone calls. They cut the mayor's salary from six hundred to sixty dollars a month, and they increased property taxes for citizens who openly supported the mayor.[4]

The climaxing incident occurred in 1980 when the Chief of Police resigned, and Mayor Carthan appointed Johnny Dale, a black policeman. The three aldermen—Granderson, Gibson, and Hayes—however, appointed Jim Andrews, brother-in-law of Holmes County supervisor, B. T. Taylor. Andrews dismissed Dale and changed the locks on the city hall door. Mayor Carthan, two loyal black aldermen, and five auxilliary policemen confronted Andrews at city hall informing him that he was acting illegally as police chief since he had not been voted in, sworn in, or bonded. Supposedly, Andrews pulled a gun, a scuffle ensued, and Andrews was disarmed. The mayor filed charges against Andrews; however, Andrews and James Harris, an off-duty black policeman whom Andrews had summoned, pressed countercharges, claiming aggravated assault on a police officer against Carthan. The state dropped Andrews's charges, brought Harris's to the grand jury, and did not hear Carthan's charges at all.[5]

Two months before the mayor's term in office expired, Carthan and six co-defendants were convicted of assaulting a police officer and sentenced to three years imprisonment at Parchman, the state penitentiary. The jury voted eleven to one for a conviction of simple assault—a misdemeanor, however, according to Shelia D. Collins, an educator and social activist within the United Methodist Church, and one of the leaders of the national campaign to free Mayor Eddie James Carthan, the verdict read by the court had been changed to "simple assault of a police officer"—a felony. A jury in Mississippi is not allowed to impeach a verdict that has been delivered to the court. Several months after the conviction, James Harris appeared on TV to recant his story.[6]

Five months after the initial conviction, Carthan was charged by the federal government of "fraud in connection with the purchase of equipment for a day care center he oversaw as mayor." Evidence indicated that Carthan's signature had been forged, and one of the accused admitted to having done so. According to Collins, during the time Carthan was being threatened, he was compiling data on the long history of corruption within the county's white elite—fraud, bribery, kickbacks, the diversion of public funds into private use. Carthan, however, could not obtain a lawyer in the state who would "touch the evidence."[7]

To further compound his problem, the ex-mayor, Eddie Carthan, was accused of capital murder in the June 1981 death of Alderman Roosevelt Granderson, Carthan's political foe. Granderson was shot June 28, 1981, during armed robbery at the Jitney Junior convenience store where he worked part-time. The state also charged David Earl Hester and Vincent Earl Bolden, both of St. Louis, as well as Carthan's brother Joseph, with conspiring with the ex-mayor in the death of Granderson. Bolden pleaded guilty to a lesser charge of murder in exchange for testimony at Carthan's trial.[8]

During the entire episode Carthan received national support

against what was termed by many black civil rights leaders "part of a racist plot by whites to control black elected officials." In an address before a crowd of five hundred in Jackson, Joseph Lowery, president of the Southern Christian Leadership Conference claimed that Carthan was a "victim of a political mob." He proclaimed, "Whether he's hung in a court room or in a smoke-filled room or from a tree, a lynching is a lynching." Another civil rights activist, comedian Dick Gregory warned, "As we walk and think about Eddie . . . let's think about all of the other Eddies that we don't even know about. This case is bigger than just some black and white stuff. It goes all the way to the White House, all the way to the FBI, all the way to the CIA."[9]

As the jury selection process began in the trial of former mayor Eddie Carthan, he drew national support from churches, labor unions, national newspapers, Mississippi legislators, public officials, members of the Congressional Black Caucus and other civic groups throughout the United States as they carried signs and chanted, "Free the Tchula 7" and urged the Reagan administration to halt the trial pending its own investigation.[10] Also, Representative Ronald V. Dellums, a California Democrat, publicly declared Carthan "the victim of an apparent frame-up by the plantation-minded power structure in Tchula."

Over 100 potential jurors were carefully screened by Circuit Judge Arthur B. Clark before a panel of twelve black impartial jurors were selected to hear the capital murder case against former Tchula Mayor Eddie Carthan. The jury consisted of seven women and five men. At issue was "whether Carthan had Granderson killed for his own reasons or if, as Carthan's attorney argued, the former black mayor is the victim of a frame-up plot by whites to remove him from influence in the small Delta town."[11]

During the final days of the Carthan trial, emotionalism took control and racism dominated the issue. In closing arguments, the Assistant District Attorney, Hallie Gail Bridges, argued that the three Aldermen—John Edgar Hayes, Jason Gibson, and Roosevelt Granderson—"took away Carthan's check-signing power, took away his job as city judge, and disputed him at every turn . . . and he just couldn't stand it." Furthermore, she instructed the jury to look Eddie James Carthan squarely in the eye and call him a "murderer." She claimed that the murder was triggered by greed and jealousy. The District Attorney, Frank Carlton, declared that "the trial was not a racial issue but about 'a black man hiring two black men to kill a black man.'"[17]

Taking the witness stand in his own defense, Eddie James Carthan, the black man with high aspiration, pleaded to the jurors in a thirty minute speech that he was on trial because of racism.

> Not because of race. Racism. Racism is behind us. I wonder what would happen to you if one of you tried to register your child in one of the white academies, worship in one of the all-white Baptist churches. I submit to you, you'd find how far racism is behind us ... The use of the court system by the 'power structure' is legally lynching progressive, aggressive black leaders.
>
> I'm here because I'm an illustration to the poor whites and blacks that when you step out of your boundaries and refuse to be a little boy to the power structure, you'll be punished.
>
> Moses died like Martin Luther King without reaching the Promised Land. But God brought Joshua. I submit to you today, we're in the time of Joshua ... We didn't make the Land. But we shouldn't stop here ... I submit that Eddie Carthan is not on trial. Mississippi is on trial.[13]

In his concluding remarks, Carthan reminded the jurors that the Liberty Bell symbolized freedom and that "a 'not guilty' verdict is striking the Liberty Bell ... and let it be heard in the great Delta plains of the South. Strike it! Let it be heard in the hunterlands of Mississippi." Afterwards the courtroom crowd applauded and shouted "Amen! Amen!"[14]

His attorney, Johnny Walls, reiterated Carthan's claim of racism and utilized religious analogy to show Vincent Earl Bolden and David Earl Hester, the District Attorney's key witnesses against Carthan, as agents of Satan. Furthermore he compared Carthan to Jesus Christ: "Jesus was a revolutionary for his time. Jesus was destroyed because he taught new things. And what did they do? They hung Jesus and let the robber man go."[15]

After hours of deliberation, the jury acquitted Eddie James Carthan of capital murder charges. Immediately thereafter he was taken into custody by court officials to begin serving a three-year sentence for assaulting the policeman, James Harris. Because of insufficient evidence, the armed robbery charges against Eddie Carthan were eventually dropped. However, the federal government indicted Carthan for falsifying information used to obtain a loan from a federally insured bank, and he was sentenced to a three-year term in the federal penitentiary in Alabama. Carthan was recently paroled.

Marion Shepilov Barry, Jr.
Mayor of Washington, D.C.

Marion Shepilov Barry, Jr., mayor of Washington, D.C., was born to Marion S. and Mattie B. Barry, sharecroppers, in Itta Bena, March 6, 1936. In 1958 Barry Jr. received a B.S. degree in chemistry from LeMoyne College in Memphis, Tennessee, and in 1960 the M.S. degree from Fisk University, in Nashville.[1]

When the civil rights movement began in the 1960s, Barry abandoned work on a doctorate in chemistry at the University of Tennessee to participate. He served as the first national chairman of the Student Non-Violent Coordinating Committee (SNCC). Because of his involvement in demonstrations and boycotts he was frequently incarcerated; imprisonment, however, did not deter his struggle to obtain justice and equality for black Americans.[2]

In Washington, D.C., he founded in 1967 Pride, Inc., a job-training organization for young people, and in 1968 was co-founder, chairman and director of Economic Enterprises, Inc. In 1970 he moved into the political arena and soon acquired the skills of an astute politician. From 1971 to 1974, he acted as Chairman of the Washington School Board. During election year 1974, city voters elected Barry to a four-year term on the City Council. In 1978 the city's black and white middle class swept the former militant into the mayor's office. Barry, admitting that his role had changed with the times and revealing his astuteness as a politician said,

> I always knew it was better to make policy than to initiate change. If there is a single ideal which has guided and inspired me in both my private and public lives, it is the quest for the uniquely American principle of justice and fair play for all men and women. The promise of this elusive goal took me as a young man, away from my doctoral studies and has since been a major force in the direction my life has taken.[3]

In the 1982 election, Barry was re-elected for a fourth term as mayor. In his campaign, he made Reaganomics an issue, thereby defeating his Republican opponent.[4]

Evan Doss

Claiborne County Tax Assessor and Collector

The youngest and only black elected tax assessor and collector in the state of Mississippi, Evan Doss has been instrumental in Claiborne County's efforts in recent years to equalize property taxes and thereby increase available funds for the public schools and county services.

Doss was born July 6, 1948, in the infirmary at Alcorn A. & M. College, where his mother worked as a housemaid and cook. Her education ended in the fourth grade. His father, a minister and sharecropper, completed only the second grade. As a student at Alcorn College, Doss earned his B.S. degree and was introduced to politics through voters registration drives.[1]

Following his graduation from Alcorn, the Superintendent of Port Gibson public schools hired Doss as a ninth grade history teacher. As a teacher, he submitted educational and community action proposals in an effort to solve the problems confronting Claiborne County. He presented to the governing county board of supervisors several proposals for acquisition of minibuses to transport senior citizens, a multi-purpose building for the community, and recreational facilities. When the board could not fund these projects from the property taxes collected in the county, Doss was perplexed.

Consequently Doss ran and was elected tax assessor and collector of Claiborne County in 1971, polling sixty percent of the votes in a county that is seventy percent black. Despite his sometimes controversial political positions, he is still serving the people of Claiborne in this capacity. Doss's election was a direct result of black bloc voting to elect an official sensitive to black issues: jobs, community projects, land problems, and taxation.[3]

After he selected a competent staff, Doss launched a preliminary investigation of past tax assessment practices and policies. The initial findings were staggering. Doss reported that there were in existence no records of any tax assessment in Claiborne County for previous years, no documentation showing how the former tax assessor had determined property values, and no listings of property for each taxpayer. Thus, Doss concluded that the residents of Claiborne County were being taxed at rates that had been arbitrarily established at some point in history and had never been altered. Absolutely no documents were on file to support any of the property values listed on the tax rolls. Yet the supervisors insisted the figures represented an assessment based on twenty percent to twenty-five percent of the true value of county property.[4]

Doss insisted that the investigation indicated widespread corruption and malfeasance in the administration of the county's property tax. Citizens were paying property taxes according to inconsistent assessment percentages. Low and average income residents (mostly blacks) were paying property taxes based on twenty-five percent of the true value of their properties as listed on the tax rolls. Yet many (mostly white) county residents were paying taxes based on assessments as low as ten percent of the true value of their properties. Investigation showed that in most cases the lowest percentages were being applied to the properties of the county's wealthiest citizens.

According to Doss, "Many residents with homes worth $25,000 were paying less property tax than citizens whose homes are worth $10,000. The homes of many low and average income residents were overvalued in that they were assessed just as much as wealthy homeowners. Large landowners were paying the same amount in taxes as the farmer with a few acres."[5]

As soon as Doss began to review the tax rolls, he received a letter from the Claiborne County Board of Supervisors ordering him not to alter any assessments, or add to last year's tax roll except where new structures had been built or old structures destroyed. Doss interpreted their action in limiting his operating budget and curtailing his authority as an effort to force him to resign; by ordering him to violate the law, the board intended to push Doss into an awkward situation with state authorities.[6]

Doss sought help from the state government. Since Governor William Waller had spoken out in favor of equalization of taxes and a fair interpretation of the laws, Doss on March 10, 1972, wrote to the governor asking for his assistance. He hoped that the governor would respond to his request, thereby demonstrating his concern in the matter. But no response came. Doss then wrote to the State Tax Commission making a similar request. The State Tax Commission refused to act. At one time [the Commission] supported the Board of Supervisors in its violation of the laws. The Tax Commission later retracted its support of the Board's illegal instructions after Doss challenged the commission's views as expressed by a representative sent to Claiborne County.

Doss then took his case directly to the people. In a series of public visitations at the courthouse, he detailed the functions of his office, the inequities of the assessement procedures, and the rights and responsibilities of the individual taxpayer. He also called upon the community to support him in his efforts to overhaul the tax structure. Doss also began holding regular meetings with community leaders to keep them abreast of his difficulties with the supervisors.

The community responded favorably to the assessor's openness and honesty by volunteering to assist his small staff in the preparation of property assessment forms and the tax rolls and by filing objections to the supervisors' assessment. The volunteers claimed that forms and rolls had not been made according to state law.

Forced to submit what he strongly believed to be an inaccurate and illegal tax roll, Doss again called upon the State Tax Commission to act upon this violation of state law. Again the commission refused to act. Doss responded with a statewide press conference. Warning that he would not be intimidated by the Claiborne supervisors, Doss assured residents they would be given a fair and equal assessment and that taxes would be paid according to the law and not according to the needs of the rich and influential.

Doss admitted that he had many trying circumstances during his first term. The Board of Supervisors openly opposed him, cutting the budget for his office. He was even arrested for allegedly refusing to sell car tags to two supervisors. Doss stated that the supervisors arrived on the last day during the rush hour, and sought to get to the desk by cutting in front of the standing crowd. Nevertheless, the public has generally accepted his all-black office staff. Only a few older whites show any resentment. Now that he has been re-elected twice and blacks have a four-to-one majority on the Board of Supervisors, he is optimistic that he will enjoy a more amicable relation with the board and that reappraisal will be forthcoming.

W. E. Mollison

Mississippi's First Prominent Black Lawyer and District Attorney

W. E. Mollison, a lawyer, banker and publicist, graduated from Fisk University in 1880. He was admitted to the bar in May 1881. When Mollison migrated from Tennessee to Issaquena County, Mississippi, in the 1880's, he became actively involved in state politics. In 1881, the Democratic Board of Education appointed him Superintendent of Public Education. After serving two years in that capacity, the voters of Mayersville, a predominantly black town in Issaquena County, elected Mollison Clerk of the Chancery Court, and he was re-elected unopposed in 1887.[1]

In 1892 Mollison temporarily retired from public office to resume his legal responsibilities in his private law practice. One year later, however, a Democratic judge chose Mollison as District Attorney protem, the first black so honored. Later President McKinley appointed Mollison supervisor of the Twelfth Census, a job which entailed supervising or overseeing 165 Census enumerators in Mississippi's largest and most important political district.[2]

Constance Slaughter-Harvey
First Black Female Judge in Mississippi

A Jackson native and graduate of Tougaloo College, attorney Constance Slaughter-Harvey was the first black female to graduate from the University of Mississippi School of Law. In 1976 at the request of Judge Guyton Idom, she served as Scott County Judge in a case in which Idom had previously represented one of the parties involved, becoming the first black female judge to occupy the bench in Mississippi.[1]

Although Slaughter-Harvey is trained to handle various kinds of cases, she prefers criminal ones. For more than eight years she practiced law in Meridian before opening an office in Forest. Her involvement in professional activities includes two years service on the Lawyer's Committee in Jackson.[2]

On February 1980 when she was appointed by Governor William Winter to head the Office of Human Development, Slaughter-Harvey became the third black and the first woman to be appointed to a major post in the Winter administration. She was not new to state government, having served previously with the Health Planning and Development Agency. On 21 January 1980, the day before Governor Cliff Finch left office, he appointed her as one of two non-voting members of the state Health Care Commission.[3]

As Director of the Governor's Office of Human Development, attorney Constance Slaughter-Harvey supervises several programs that services the needs of the state's children and their families, the elderly, handicapped, and low-income Mississippians. The children's program is designed to provide the "delivery of comprehensive child-development services to Mississippi's children and to their families." Also educational programs are implemented that assist the handicapped. The Office of Human Resources also coordinates special programs that impact upon the alleviation of statewide poverty. Senior citizens benefit from assistance provided by the Mississippi Council on Aging which is an arm of the Office of Human Development. In each program, volunteers are utilized in a concerted effort to enhance the quality of life for all Mississippians.[4]

Henry Jay Kirksey

State Senator

Henry J. Kirksey—demographer, lithographer, cartographer, publisher, and state senator—was born May 9, 1915, and grew up in rural Lee County, near Tupelo. He was the fourth of eight children born to Charlie S. and Nettie M. Kirksey, both natives of northeast Mississippi. Farm chores prevented Henry Kirksey from attending school regularly, so, at age 20 he promoted himself to grade nine at Lee County Training School in Tupelo, just as he had done many times previously.

When he reached age 21, Henry Kirksey migrated to St. Louis, Missouri, to live with his older brother, Charles, who advised and urged Henry to "put his age back three years" and continue his public education. Adhering to his brother's advice, Kirksey graduated from Vashon High School in 1939, attended Stowe Teachers College (a St. Louis City College) for a year, and afterwards accepted an athletic scholarship in football at North Carolina College (North Carolina Central University). Following an interruption for military service, Kirksey returned and graduated cum laude with a degree in economics in 1947.[1]

Kirksey entered the military January 4, 1942, as a private in the Medical Corps, United States Army. Upon graduation from the Field Artillery Officer Candidate School in January 1943, he was assigned to the Pacific Theatre—the Philippines and Japan—as unit commander and Tokyo Base Operations Officer. Kirksey was discharged from service in August 1946 in the grade major, field artillery.[2]

In May 1946 Henry Kirksey married Audrie M. Neal of Oklahoma City. To that union was born three children—Henry, Jr., a graduate of Pasadena City College and more recently a Navy veteran with service in Vietnam; Karin Zander, a Phi Beta Kappa graduate of the University of Southern California and Yale Law School and Assistant U.S. Attorney General (Massachusetts) in the Carter administration; and Kevin, presently assigned to the Great Lakes Naval Training Stations.[3]

Upon graduation from North Carolina College, Kirksey came to Jackson, Mississippi, at the request of Dr. Jacob Reddix, president of Jackson State College. However, he only remained there one year and reentered military service in 1948. After completing paratrooper training, he returned in 1949 to St. Louis, Missouri, where he worked for one year as a postal clerk. In 1950 the Kirksey family moved to Los Angeles, California, where Henry learned the trades of printing and publishing as an employee of the California Institute of Social Welfare. From 1954 to 1959 he served as foreman of graphic productions at the Institute.[4]

In 1959 at the urging of the president of Winston-Salem Teachers College, Kirksey left California to develop a newspaper in the Greensboro-Highpoint-Winston-Salem metropolitan area; the venture proved a fiasco. Subsequently, the family separated. Henry Sr. returned to Mississippi where he worked briefly with the Kirksey-Grayson Funeral Home in Tupelo, before becoming editor of the Mississippi Teachers Association (MTA) Journal in 1961.[5]

Henry J. Kirksey, Sr., interpreted his life as an entity for service to his community and to his race. Kirksey left the teacher organization in 1963 and worked with various civil rights organizations throughout the turbulent years of the 1960s. Also, he served briefly as editor of the *Mississippi Free Press* and proprietor of the Kirksey Publishing Company. In 1961, while a member of the board of MTA, Kirksey began a study of public education in Mississippi. In 1971, he correlated his findings with similar studies in state and local governmental operations and the electoral process. Published research in hand, he canvassed the state exposing the gross injustices he saw in the governmental process.[6]

In the sixties many blacks opposed Kirksey, arguing that he was "polarizing the state." When the all-black MTA refused to renew his contract as journal editor in 1963, Kirksey blamed his dismissal on an editorial he wrote eulogizing the slain civil rights activist, Medgar Evers. "I had been warned," Kirksey said, "against involvement with Medgar Evers and when I wrote Evers's eulogy in the journal, I knew that was the end of the line."[7] Kirksey confessed that the termination was rooted in a personal conflict between himself and MTA's executive secretary, the late Ellis Alexander. According to Kirksey, "He didn't want me to question his decisions. His advice to me was to learn how an organization works, find a spot in it, and work toward a goal."[8]

Because of his stance on controversial and unpopular issues and his determination to pursue his own goals, many have called Kirksey a loner. One associate said, "He didn't tell any of us he was running for governor in 1975 until the day before he made the announcement. We were all taken by surprise."[9] Some have called him an unpredictable person who will do almost anything to make a point—for example, lashing out at other black leaders for supporting a bond issue favored by white politicians at City Hall. One adversary accused him of loving the limelight: "He will use the news media to make his charges, to answer his critics, and to champion his causes. He runs for everything, almost every time there is an election. He realizes he has access to the press any time of the day or night."[10]

Certainly, Kirksey lost more campaigns than he won. He sought the political positions of governor in 1975, U.S. Senator in 1976, but withdrew, and again of U.S. Senator in 1978. Like Abraham Lincoln he lost a few, but he won the most important ones. Sometimes he seemed to be fighting alone, but Kirksey somehow managed in the midst of incalculable frustrations to maintain an impregnable sense of hope. For more than fourteen years, Kirksey, practically alone, relentlessly fought to change legislative measures dealing with reapportionment and redistricting that split the black vote. He was victorious on both issues. His triumphant victory led to the election of fifteen black representatives and two senators to the Mississippi legislature in 1979. He was one of the senators.

In 1980 Kirksey ran for the United States Congress from the Fourth Congressional district. In spite of a shoestring campaign waged with less than five thousand dollars Kirksey was impressive at the polls. After winning the Democratic primary, Kirksey captured seven of twelve counties and forty-three percent of the votes in the general election. He won the two largest counties, Hinds and Warren, and finished second in Adams County. Relying heavily on radio advertisements and his name identification that grew out of the legislative reapportionment battle, Kirksey ran well in the vote-rich urban counties and won solid support from black counties. Not since John R. Lynch was elected to the U.S. Congress in 1872 had any black Mississippian advanced this far.

Friends and critics of Kirksey agreed that there are three outstanding or noticeable features: "he is a loner, among blacks as well as whites and he alienates people," said one friend; "he believes so stubbornly in his cause," another friend recalled," that he drives a wedge between himself and his political allies;" and "he has a reputation for comprehensive research that sometimes leads him to complex interpretations of the local political scene."[12] Representative Fred Banks, a Democrat from Jackson, however, is one who is not alienated by Kirksey. Instead Banks says, "Kirksey has a useful role in this society. He's outspoken. I think he also says some things that don't need to be said, but you've got to take the good with the bad."[13]

While Kirksey is proving himself a competent and well informed legislator, he is actively involved in community activities within the following organizations: Alpha Phi Alpha Fraternity, Civic Resource Center, Delta Ministry, National Black Caucus of State Legislators, Mississippi Hunger Coalition, NAACP, National Business League, and the Jackson Urban League.[14]

Robert George Clark

State Legislator

In January 1968, the seating of Robert G. Clark in the Mississippi legislature marked the beginning of a new era in Mississippi politics. Representative Clark, the first black to sit in the state legislature, was elected from District Sixteen, Holmes and Yazoo Counties.

Born on October 3, 1929, in Ebenezer, a small rural town in Holmes County, the grandson of slaves, Clark sprang from a line of earnest school teachers and church workers who farmed their own land and avoided the humiliation of working in the white man's fields. Nevertheless, life had its difficulties for him as for most young blacks growing up in Holmes County. "I had to walk three miles to school in one direction and four miles the other," Clark reminisced. "When it came time to go to high school, we had to board in other towns, for there was no Negro high school in the area and no buses.

The schools were not luxurious, but the teachers did a good job with what little they had to work with."¹

Fortunately, Robert Clark escaped poverty when his parents sent him to Jackson State College where he worked as a custodian for twenty-five cents an hour to pay his tuition. During his second year, he became the institution's first student to be awarded a track scholarship.

After college he taught and served as principal in Louise school for seven years and at Conway-Thomas town school for two years. In addition, he coached athletics, a job which required longer hours without additional pay.

In the meantime (1954) the U.S. Supreme Court overturned the "separate but equal" doctrine, and Robert Clark decided it was time to further prepare himself for the teaching profession. He enrolled as a graduate student at Michigan State University during summers. Upon completion of the requirements for a masters degree in administrative services and education and much of the course work for a Ph.D. at the University of Michigan, Clark "discovered that no matter how much education he had, he was still called upon to be a full-time teacher and coach, or vice-principal-coach. When he balked at such treatment, school officials withheld his contract."²

Sensing it was time to make another move Robert Clark left the public school system in 1966 and took a job as Director of Adult Education and Job Training at Lexington's nearby Saints Junior College, a private school supported by the Church of God-In-Christ. He also became part-time, and later full-time, director of the antipoverty program in Holmes County, in a county that was seventy-two percent black and one in which agricultural jobs were disappearing and industry was utterly lacking.

Clark had an opportunity to inaugurate a job training program funded by the Department of Public Welfare under a half-million-dollar grant, which required use of the facilities of the public school system. The school board and the superintendent refused the offer "on the grounds that they felt it wasn't in the best interest of the children or their parents."³

One year later, 1967, Clark decided to seek a seat in the Mississippi state legislature as an independent. His political strategy was to garner the support of all groups to which he belonged, plus that of all other black factions in his county: ministers, teachers, and plantation workers. He went into the general election of November 7 as the candidate of the black community and emerged victorious over the white veteran incumbent, J. P. Love, a planter who had served in the Mississippi House since 1956 and was chairman of the House Education Committee.[4]

Since then, Clark has been elected to the Mississippi Legislature four consecutive terms. Currently, Representative Clark served on the following house committees as a member or chairman: Agriculture, Education, Labor, Pensions, Social Welfare, Public Health, and Appropriations. Clark was the principal author of the Vocational-Technical Education Act of 1982, passed by the Mississippi Legislature. According to Clark, this bill provides "a system of education that will offer young people of Mississippi an opportunity to become productive citizens of the skill-oriented society of today."[5]

In 1982 Representative Robert Clark, running as a Democrat, lost an intensely close race for Congressman from the Second Congressional District to Republican Webb Franklin. Clark, the favored candidate, who had hoped to become the first black Congressman from Mississippi since Reconstruction, lost by fewer than 2,500 votes. The final tally showed Webb Franklin with 73,238 votes, Robert Clark with 70,674, and the independent candidate William V. Harris with 1,483.[6]

During the campaign Clark opposed most of President Ronald Reagan's economic policy and took a liberal stance on several critical economic issues: he believed that high interest rates were crippling farmers, home owners, and small businessmen; advocated an economic policy that encouraged business expansion and more jobs; supported reduction in federal spending and a balanced budget; agreed with existing Social Security benefits for the elderly. Clark also encouraged maintaining a strong system of public education, an effective and efficient national defense, and adequate health care and medical personnel; opposed foreign aid; and crusaded for anti-crime legislation, equal rights, and agricultural assistance.[7]

The fifty-three year old state legislator employed religious analogies in campaign addresses. At St. James African Methodist Episcopal Church in Leland he told the large congregation, "I've come too far to turn around. Like the Lord said to Moses, 'use what you have,' I say to the people of the Second District, use me, use me like Moses used the rock."[8]

Throughout his congressional campaign, Clark de-emphasized the issue of race and refused the invitation of prominent national Democrats such as Edward Kennedy and Walter Mondale to campaign for him. Instead, he relied upon the endorsement of state Democrats, Governor William Winter and U.S. Senator, John Stennis.

Why Franklin and not Clark? The question was repeatedly asked by blacks and voter analysts. According to the *The Jackson Daily News*, Clark carried, by a slim margin, only eight counties in the predominantly black districts. They were Bolivar, Coahoma, Sharkey, Madison, Tallahatchie, Tunica, Washington, and Issaquena—all of which composed a Democratic majority and most of which Jimmy Carter had carried in the 1980 presidential election. Three significant factors seemed to contribute to Clark's unexpected defeat: a low black turnout in the predominantly Democratic counties of Sunflower and Warren, some blacks in predominantly black Delta counties voting for Franklin, and record numbers of registered whites turning out to vote for the Republican candidate.[9]

Black leadership attributed Clark's defeat to racism and lack of white Democratic support. Aaron Henry, director of the state NAACP Chapter, noted that, although the population of the Second Congressional District is fifty-three percent black, only forty-eight percent are blacks of voting age. In addition to carrying the black bloc vote, Clark needed the support of two of every ten white Democrats to win the election. "Racism is still America's foremost problem," said Henry. Rims Barber, black voter analyst and director of the Children's Defense Fund, said, "A Clark victory would have been an important step in the evolution of our race relations and of the Democratic party, but in the end, racism is what beat Robert Clark." He conceded that Clark "made strides in almost breaking the bounds, and that does count."[11] One Greenville voter summarized the feelings of many: "Race? That's not an issue. The whites are going to vote for the white guy, and the blacks are going to vote for the black guy."[12]

A black political science professor at Jackson State University, Leslie McLemore, expressed his disappointment in the Democratic party for not standing behind the black majority district. Black Senator Henry Kirksey of Jackson stated that the election strengthened his lawsuit that unless the federal court creates a sixty-five percent black majority congressional district in the Delta, where it is presently forty-eight percent; a black candidate will never be elected to Congress. Furthermore, he was "disenchanted with the Democratic party and the AFL-CIO because the groups have not supported the black congressional district."[13]

But Danny Cupit, state Democratic Chairman, responded by saying that racism, not party, was a factor. "When Robert Clark was born, he had black skin. That was the predominant factor in the election. Whenever you lose by that close of a margin, and look back in retrospect, you say you could have and should have done more. But the party made a substantial effort to keep that as a Democratic seat." He refused to commit the party to supporting redistricting. That decision, he commented, would be made by the one hundred-member Democratic Executive Committee.[14]

Despite the Republican victory many black and white Democrats believe that within two years a Democrat will occupy the Second Congressional seat in the United States House of Representatives. As Aaron Henry pointed out, "Yes, I think the white community might just as well make the best of Mr. Franklin: It's his last hurrah."[15]

In addition to participating in state and national politics, Representative Clark is actively involved in civic and community affairs. Presently, he is a member of the Executive Committee of the Mississippi Democratic party, chairman of the Board of Directors for the Children's Center, and Early Childhood Education in Holmes County, an officer in his church and chairman of the Holmes County Advisory Committee on Vocational-Technical Education.[16]

A family man, Robert Clark was married to the late Essie Austin of Belzoni. Their two sons, Robert III and Wandrick, attend the Holmes County public schools.

Aaron Henry

Mississippi Legislator and Political Activist

Born on July 2, 1922, to Edd and Mattie Logan Henry near Clarksdale, Aaron Henry, unlike most of his peers, received a formal education. He earned his B.S. degree with a major in political science from Xavier University in New Orleans. During his senior year in college, he was elected president of the Student Government Association. Later, he received a degree in pharmacy after which he returned to Clarksdale and operated a drug store until 1943. In that year he enlisted in the United States Army as a private and, after a tour of duty in the Pacific Theater, was honorably discharged as a staff sergeant in 1946. Upon his return to Clarksdale, Henry engaged in the civil rights stuggle in Mississippi and actively participated in community affairs.[1]

Henry, leader of the Mississippi Freedom Democratic Party, former president of the Council of Federated Organizations, president of the National Association of Colored People, is the oldest, best known, and most respected civil rights activist in Mississippi. As chairman of the bi-racial Mississippi Freedom Democratic Party (MFDP) he guided the party in its challenge of the regular Mississippi Democrats at the 1964 and 1968 Democratic National Conventions. Although unsuccessful in 1964, the MFDP accomplished its goal in 1968 when the group unseated the regular Democrats and obtained a plank within the party's platform that addressed the economic needs of blacks and other minorities. Moreover, serving as chairman of the Council of Federated Organizations (COFO) during the long hot summer of 1964, Henry directed the activities of the "Big Four" civil rights groups that undertook voter registration drives and operated Freedom schools. COFO membership coalition consisted of National Association for the Advancement of Colored People (NAACP), Congress of Racial Equality (CORE), Students Non-Violent Coordinating Committee (SNCC), and the Southern Christian Leadership Conference (SCLC).

Henry also organized and presided over the Coahoma County branch of the NAACP. In 1960 he was elected president of the Mississippi State Conference of the NAACP, and in 1965 a member of the national board of directors of the NAACP. In addition, the following organizations have elected him as a member of their national board of directors: Southern Christian Leadership Conference, Southern Regional Council, the Mississippi Council on Human Relations, Mound Bayou Mississippi Community Hospital, Mississippi Action for Progress, Coahoma Opportunities, Inc., Medgar Evers Memorial Fund, and the National Council on Aging. He is also an active member of Omega Psi Phi Fraternity.[2]

Because of Aaron Henry's involvement with civil rights activities, he became the prime target of racial harassment. In March 1962, Henry was arrested and sentenced to six months in jail for allegedly making sexual advances to a young white hitchhiker in Clarksdale. Henry appealed the case. Because Henry protested the moral charges and claimed that Clarksdale prosecuting attorney and police chief had conspired against him with trumped up moral charges, the two officials sued him for $40,000 each in damages. The complaints won a verdict in a jury trial, which Henry also appealed and won. Also, the Coahoma School Board fired his wife, who had taught for ten years, for her voter registration activity.[3]

Despite the harassments and lawsuits, Aaron Henry remained faithful in his quest for equality for blacks in the state of Mississippi. He envisions a state void of racial animosity.

In April 1980, Hazel Brannon Smith, formerly the editor of the *Lexington Advertiser*, wrote: "What Aaron Henry is interested in is creating a Mississippi wherein blacks, whites, and other races may live, work, and worship in real peace and harmony." In his own words Dr. Henry declared, "I'm dedicated to the proposition that nothing all-white will sit down at a conference table in Mississippi claiming to represent the state of Mississippi . . . I think that every time a man stands for an ideal or speaks out against injustice, he sends out a tiny ripple of hope."[4]

Throughout the perilous civil rights movement and the apathetic years that followed, Henry navigated local and national storms to improve the quality of life for blacks and poor whites. As a registered lobbyist in the U.S. Congress, he secured congressional support for the passage of the Office of Economic Opportunity Act. This legislative act spawned such programs as Head Start, Basic Adult Education, Community Action, and the Neighborhood Rural Housing Coalition. As chairman of the National Black Caucus on the Aging and the National Rural Housing Coalition and as vice-chairman of National Rural America, Inc., Henry has divided his time equally to bring benefits to the elderly and rural population in Mississippi.[5]

Aaron Henry sought his legislative seat in order to make white Mississippi and the federal government politically responsive to blacks. He asserted that the Negro vote would "make a Javits of an Eastland"[7] and liberate white and black Mississippians to political freedom and economic plenty.

Currently, as veteran representative in the Mississippi legislature from Coahoma County, Henry commented, "I'm truly enjoying my work from inside the government as well as from the outside."[8] His functional role in the legislature entails committee work with the Judiciary, Municipalities, Agriculture, Conservation and Water Resources, and Manpower Committees. He meets frequently with his voting constituents, informing them of legislative decisions that directly affect them as agrarians.[9]

Henry has received over fifty public service awards, including at least two honorary doctoral degrees. Apart from public service, Dr. Henry is active in the Haven United Methodist Church in Clarksdale.

In a 1979 tribute to Henry, his pastor, the Reverend Theo Triplett stated, "He does not have the Goliath mentality; he is a humble man who is not afraid to fight against the giants of our world.[10]

Douglas Leavon Anderson
State Senator

Douglas Leavon Anderson, a native of Hinds County, was elected in 1974 from the 27th senatorial district. He received his B.S. degree from Dillard University in New Orleans and his M.S. degree from Oklahoma University. Presently, he is an instructor at Jackson State University. He holds membership in numerous civic and social organizations, such as the Governor's Judicial Committee, the State Building Commission, State Health Coordinating Council, Alpha Phi Alpha Fraternity, and the Masons.

Fred Lee Banks
Legislator

Fred Lee Banks, a graduate of Howard University, was awarded both the B.S. and Juris Doctorate degrees from that institution. Banks, who is affiliated with the National Conference of Black Lawyers, Urban League, National Association for the Advancement of Colored People, and the National Association of Teachers of Attorneys, wants blacks to receive an equal share in the decision making process and to be accepted as equal partners in American society. "I want to be a part of abolishing harmful legislation and help bring about legislation that will be benefiting," Banks says. Elected to the Mississippi House of Representatives in 1974, Banks, a Jacksonian, represents the 69th district.[1]

Horace Lawson Buckley
Legislator

Horace Lawson Buckley attended Mississippi Valley State University, where the Jackson native received his B.S. degree, and did further study at Tuskegee Institute, Jackson State University, and Mississippi State university. In 1974, Buckley was elected from the 70th district to serve in the state legislature. Buckley's primary interests are education, social services, and economic delivery system. Very active in local and state affairs, Buckley is an involved participant in the Mississippi Teachers Association, Mississippi Personnel and Guidance Association Board, Jackson Housing Authority and the General Baptist state convention.[1]

Credell Calhoun
Legislator

Credell Calhoun, representing the 68th district, where he was elected in 1978, is a native of Louisiana. His educational training include a B.S. degree from Prairie View A. & M. College in Texas and further study at Jackson State University. He has served as administrative assistant to the mayor of Jackson, as auditor for the Governor's Office Job Development Training, and as a counselor. He is a member of the Elks, Masons, Kappa Alpha Psi Fraternity, Hinds County Mental Health Association, and the Mississippi Boy Scouts council. As state representative, Calhoun hopes "to accomplish more and better services for senior citizens, to provide better supervised playground facilities, and to stimulate blacks to become self-sufficient through self-enterprise."[1]

Tyrone Ellis
Legislator

Tyrone Ellis, elected to the Mississippi House of Representatives from the 40th district in 1978, stresses the following legislative goals: "Upgrading the quality of education in Mississippi through an effective school system . . . [using] all influence to see that the people of my district are represented fairly and equally." A Starkville dairy farmer and general contractor, Ellis matriculated at the Illinois Institute of Technology where he received the B.I. degree and later attended East Mississippi Junior College and Mississippi State University. A member of the Oktibbeha County school board, Ellis also holds membership in the National Association for the Advancement of Colored People and the Optimist Club.[1]

Hillman Jerome Frazier
Legislator

Hillman Jerome Frazier is a Jackson native who represents the 67th district in the Mississippi House of Representatives. His main objectives are to "make sure people have a voice in state government and look out for the interest of blacks." Furthermore, he would like to see compulsory education, public kindergarten statewide, and a push for pot-hole legislation in Mississippi. Attorney Frazier is a graduate of Jackson State University and George Washington University National Law Center. He is affiliated with the Prince Hall Mason's, Urban League, National Association for the Advancement of Colored people, Family Service Association, and National Conference of Black Lawyers.[1]

Isiah Fredericks
Legislator

Isiah Fredericks, who represent the 119th district in the Mississippi House of Representatives, "wants to see the public confidence reestablished with the public taking a greater interest in local politics and state issues . . . a stabilized economy and greater economic opportunities for minorities." He believes these things can be accomplished through support of local and state government and cooperative positive attitude of all citizens. A general contractor from Kiln, Fredericks is president of the North Gulfport Civic Club, chief of North Gulfport Fire Department and a member of the board of directors of Harrison-Hancock Community Action Agency and the Southern Mississippi Planning and Development District. Before assuming his legislative seat, Fredericks received his formal educational training at Trace Business College, University of Southern Mississippi, University of Maryland, and the University of Missouri.[1]

David Leo Green
Legislator

David Leo Green, a deputy sheriff and retailer who was elected to the Mississippi House from the 98th coastal district, was born at Rosetta,

Mississippi, and was graduated from Southwest Mississippi Junior College. Green's aim is to help upgrade the overall status of Mississippi government. Green believes the state must improve to meet the challenges of the times and emphasizes that "education is the only way to improve socially and economically." Additionally, Green is interested in improvement in the management of fish and game. Green is associated with the National Association for the Advancement of Colored People, Master Masons, and Multi-Cultural Advisory Council.[1]

Clayton P. Henderson
Legislator

Clayton P. Henderson, state representative from the 9th district and a native of Mound Bayou, graduated from Jackson State University and John A. Gupton College. In addition to serving as a legislator, Henderson is a funeral service practitioner and an insurance agent. He is affiliated with the National Association for the Advancement of Colored People, Falcon Jaycees, Mississippi and National Funeral Directors Association. Because of his concern for the welfare of mankind, poor and rich, Henderson would like to work for improvements in the welfare and educational systems: fight for cuts in Medicaid, get pay raises for teachers, push for higher ADC rates for children.

Leslie Darnell King
Legislator

Leslie Darnell King, a Greenville native, graduated from the University of Mississippi and Texas Southern University Law School. Representing the 51st district in the state legislature, King advocates long range gains as opposed to those more quickly and easily attained. He believes that gains in education and job opportunities, the two most important areas, must go hand in hand: "education prepares citizens for jobs." King actively participates in Phi Alpha Delta, Elks, Mississippi and the American Bar Association.[1]

Barney J. Schoby
Legislator

Barney J. Schoby, a teacher and two-term Adams County supervisor, wants to see more social programs for the poor and less fortunate. The Liberty native received his B.S. degree from Alcorn State University and was elected to the state House of Representatives from the 95th district in 1978. As a staunch supporter of quality education, Schoby emphasizes returning to the basics. He advocates requiring four units of mathematics, a reading program, and English.[1]

Charles Bernard Sheppard
Legislator

Charles Bernard Sheppard, a lawyer and university professor, was elected to the state House of Representatives from the 87th district in 1978. The Claiborne County native is a graduate of Alcorn State University, University of Mississippi law school, Southern University School of Law and Mississippi College School of Law. As state representative, Sheppard wishes to act as spokesman for the people of his district, making them a part of the law making process to guarantee equal opportunities. Sheppard contends that "those deprived should get a double dosage of opportunity." While fighting for the rights of his constituents, Sheppard is actively involved in the Masons, Omega Psi Phi Fraternity, and the National Association for the Advancement of Colored People.[1]

Percy Willis Watson
Legislator

Percy Willis Watson, who is the president of the Forrest County Chapter of the National Association for the Advancement of Colored People, was elected to the Mississippi House of Representatives from the 104th district. The Hattiesburg native received his B.A. degree from the University of Iowa and a law degree from the University of Iowa College of Law. Representative Watson summarizes his legislative priorities as follows: "Individuals who are physically unable to provide for themselves, should be provided for. Voter registration and political participation should become less difficult in Mississippi. The top priority is enforcement of educational provisions. Political change hopefully will lead to economical change." Because Watson believes in community action and involvement, he provides leadership to the following organization of which he is a member: Masons, Phi Beta Kappa, and the Mississippi and American Bar associations.[1]

Charles Lemuel Young
Legislator

Charles Lemuel Young, was elected in 1978 to the state House of Representatives from the 84th district. He is a native of Meridian, Mississippi, and a graduate of Tennessee A. & I. University and did graduate studies at the University of Denver. He firmly believes that the economic incentive of the people must be stimulated and increased and that avenues of small businesses must be promoted. Better veterans programs and veterans' education are two more of his goals. Young is a member of Kappa Alpha Psi fraternity; Elks, National Business League, National Association for the Advancement of Colored People, Mason, Meridian Chamber of Commerce and Lauderdale County Democratic Executive Committee.[1]

Deborah Jones Gambrell
Justice Court Judge

A native of Jasper County, Deborah G. Gambrell became in 1979 the first black elected official in Forrest County when she was chosen Justice Court Judge of Beat 4. She graduated from Stone County Public High School in Wiggins, Mississippi, completed degree requirements for B.S. degree in political science at the University of Southern Mississippi, and received her law degree from Mississippi College School of Law in 1978. Upon graduating, she opened a law office in Hattiesburg.[1]

Since assuming her responsibility as judge, attorney Gambrell has dealt with difficult legal issues including the proposals for Congressional and state legislative redistricting. A current bill introduced in the Mississippi Legislature proposes to divide the area into three districts instead of four. According to Gambrell, "This redistricting would virtually take away a black majority district."[2] Her many duties as judge range from handling criminal misdemeanors to settling civil litigation in her district.

Melvin Redmond
Local Politician

July 1977, when Melvin Redmond was elected city alderman, he became the first black elected official in Vicksburg since Reconstruction. At age 41 he began his official duties July 5, 1977. Under the ward system adopted by the United State Department of Justice, Redmond served the northern part of Vicksburg. The specific purpose of the ward system was to assist with the enhancement of electing minority candidates. On July 6, 1981, Redmond was re-elected to another four year term.[1]

James Winfield
City Solicitor

James Winfield, son of Lawrence and Gertrude Winfield and a Vicksburg native, graduated from the Rosa A. Temple High School. Thereafter he attended Morris Brown College in Atlanta, where in 1967 he received the Bachelor of Science degree in pre-law. Following study at the Emory University Law School, he transferred to the University of Mississippi, School of Jurisprudence, where he received the LL.B. degree.[1]

Attorney Winfield opened offices in Vicksburg and Jackson, and as Vicksburg's only black attorney, handled most of the civil rights and discriminatory law suits for Vicksburg and surrounding areas. He identified with Henry Kirksey and joined in the movement for legislative reapportionment to afford blacks a greater opportunity to hold elective office. He involved himself in Vicksburg municipal equalization lawsuit which would force the city to improve municipal services to the black community.

In 1977 Winfield became the first black to be elected city solicitor for the city of Vicksburg, a position he held for five years. During that same year the National Alumni Association of Morris Brown College, chose him as acting president; in 1980 the Association elected him president.

Eddie Lucas
Mississippi State Penitentiary's First Black Warden

On January 1, 1980, Governor William Winter appointed Eddie Lucas, a Cleveland, Mississippi, native, the first black acting-warden of Parchman State Prison to replace Steve Hargett. Tom Greggory, Department of Corrections Information Director, called Lucas a "mature man, very solid and a good administrator." Others described Lucas as an "extremely efficient and highly competent man."[1]

Following the surprise announcement of his temporary appointment, the fifty-year old Lucas exclaimed, "I have never dreamed that Mr. Hargett would resign and even less that I would become acting warden." Approximately six months later on Monday June 9, 1980, Eddie Lucas, graduate of Alcorn State University and Delta State University in administration and criminal justice, was informed of his appointment as permanent warden of the State penal farm. Lucas, the choice of Corrections Commissioner John Watkins, received the unanimous approval of the seven-member Corrections Board. Watkins, himself a former Parchman warden, had attempted to appoint Lucas as permanent warden two months earlier, but the appointment was blocked at the last minute by Governor William Winter, who "wanted to observe Lucas's performance on the job before he was given permanent status." Upon Lucas's appointment, the governor's press secretary, David Crews, stated, "Lucas's June appointment was done with the governor's full approval now that he had spent some time getting acquainted with Mr. Lucas."

Eddie L. McBride
Minister and Political Activist

The thirty-nine year old black Jackson minister, Eddie L. McBride, sought to force Wayne Dowdy, Democratic incumbent, and Republican challenger, Liles Williams, to discuss critical issues germane to blacks and poor by entering the Fourth Congressional District election as an independent candidate in 1982. During the campaign however, he supported public kindergarten and a lay board of education in Mississippi—two key issues that were of grave concern to the public. He advocated using federal and state funds for programs to improve the education in the state.[1]

Many of his critics accused him of entering the congressional race to siphon blacks' votes from Democrat, Wayne Dowdy. Whatever his reasons for becoming a candidate, he did not receive support from the black communities in the fourth district. When the votes were tallied blacks overwhelmingly cast their votes for Wayne Dowdy who was elected for a second term in office. The election results showed that McBride received only 2,682 votes, Liles Williams 67,613, and Wayne Dowdy 77,680.

In addition to serving as associate minister at Farish Street Baptist Church, McBride owns and operates ELM and Associates, a consulting firm. He sells water purifiers and conducts church workshops and retreats.

Clifford Jennings
Assistant Superintendent of Parchman

Clifford Jennings, 40, was appointed the first black assistant superintendent of Parchman Penitentiary. Jennings, a native of Verona, attended high school at Piney Woods and served in the U.S. Navy from 1951 to 1955. He is a social science graduate from Jackson State University and has done graduate work at Mississippi State University and the University of Southern Mississippi. Prior to joining the staff at Parchman, Jennings served as district executive for the Boy Scouts of America in the Delta Area Council and as deputy director and coeducation coordinator for the Head Start Coordinating Council.[1]

James C. Cooper
Mississippi Highway Patrolman

In 1974, the Mississippi Highway Patrol integrated its unit when the department recruited four blacks to fill its racial quota. Under fire by the Justice Department and the Supreme Court, the Highway Patrol had among its forty-one recruits in 1978, thirty-four blacks. After these recruits completed a fifteen week training program, the graduating class president, James C. Cooper, a black Jacksonian, was class spokesperson at the commencement exercise in April 1978. (Of the twenty recruits who successfully completed the training program, fourteen were blacks.)[1]

Vernon C. Johnson
State Department Official

Vernon C. Johnson, Port Gibson native, is now director of the Agency for International Development (AID) in Tanzania. He attended Port Gibson public schools and was graduated from Southern University in 1948 after service with the U.S. Army from 1942 to 1946. He earned a master's degree and a Ph.D. in agriculture economics at the University of Wisconsin. His AID assignments have included India, Uganda, and Washington, D.C.[1]

Charles E. Pugh
Labor Department Official

Charles E. Pugh, a native of Shubuta and graduate of Jackson State University, was chosen in 1975 to head the U.S. Labor Department's Office of Budget. Pugh a career Labor Department official who was thirty years old when selected, is the first black to direct the overall budget activities of a cabinet-level agency. While at Jackson State University, Pugh twice won the Dansby-Bond Award for outstanding scholarship and student leadership. He was a foreign affairs scholar under a joint Ford Foundation-U.S. State Department program for exceptional students.[1]

William K. Dease, Sr.
Civil Service Commission

August 1973, the Jackson City Council appointed William K. Dease, Sr., to the Civil Service Commission. Dease, a graduate of Lanier High School and Morehouse College, became the first black to hold such a position. Dease, the director of data processing at Jackson State College, was appointed to fill the unexpired term of Joe Kirkland. After the expiration of that term, Dease was elected to a full four year term.[1]

Betty Jones
Postmaster

Betty Jones, a 1970 graduate of Jackson State University, became a postal employee. Her job entailed sorting mail and clerical assignments. Shortly afterwards she was named postmaster for Tougaloo, Mississippi, where she supervised a staff of thirteen.

In the early 1980s Jones was appointed postmaster of Covington, Georgia, where she supervises an integrated staff of thirty. As postmaster, she oversees all operations of the post office, supervises all mail carriers and mail sorting operations, handles customer's complaints, and does the bookkeeping and accounting.[1]

CIVIL RIGHTS

For centuries, the black struggle to obtain civil rights in America, particularly in Mississippi, has been a gradual but continuous battle. The methods of achieving this goal have been modified, but the objectives have remained unchanged. In Mississippi those engaged in the civil rights movement of the 1980s are seeking equal employment opportunities, quality education, and political participation.

The battle began during Reconstruction when the Mississippi Legislature passed a series of acts guaranteeing black people their rights as citizens and invalidating the Black Code which severely limited the civil rights of the newly freed blacks. In order to obtain education, suffrage, and land, petitions were circulated, memoranda written, and speeches published. Subsequently, between 1867 and 1870 blacks obtained certain civil rights such as the rights to vote, to serve on a jury, to serve as witnesses against whites, and the right to use public facilities and accommodations.

A series of decisions by the Mississippi Supreme Court in the 1880s and 1890s reversed the trend toward increased rights. Discriminatory practices in transportation brought about the *Louisville, New Orleans and Texas Railroad Company V. State of Mississippi* case. In that case, the company protested the Mississippi statue that required racially segregated "Jim Crow" railroad cars, which the company contended interfered with interstate trade. The Mississippi Supreme Court ruled the law valid, construing that it applied only to commerce within the state and not to that between states.[1] Upon appeal to the U.S. Supreme Court, the federal judges upheld the decision of the lower court.

In testing the doctrine of separate but equal schools in Mississippi a black man named Chrisman filed suit in 1893 against the mayor of Brookhaven for building a new white school without erecting one for blacks. The Mississippi Supreme Court upheld the law but did not interpret it to require a school established for blacks each time a white school was constructed.[2]

Black Mississippians persisted in attacking segregated laws, but without much success. For instance, blacks asserted that they were entitled to a fair and impartial trial. The case, *Green V. State of Mississippi* involved Green, a black man found guilty of murder by an all-white jury. Green appealed on the ground that one of the jurors had a preconceived verdict before the trial and had stated such during the jury selection. The court disregarded the earlier case and evidence and held that the juror was competent (*Green V. State*, 72 Mississippi 522,1885).[3] A similar case was *Gibson V. Mississippi* in which the accused Gibson was indicted and convicted of killing a white man. Gibson contended that he could not receive a fair trial in his county and requested a change of venue. After reviewing the case, the federal judge refused to remove the case.

The direction established by the court action in the late nineteenth century was not deflected but, in fact, was intensified—for the next three-quarters of a century. The turnaround began in the 1960s with a civil action suit filed by the predominantly black Council of Federated Organizations charging Mississippi law enforcement officers with illegal acts against civil rights of workers and black citizens of the state. The suit, filed in U.S. District Court on July 10, 1964, against L. C. Rainey (Sheriff of Neshoba County), Cecil Price, T. B. Birdsong, and the White Citizens Council of Mississippi, was based on approximately ninety affadavits detailing acts of physical violence including murder, intimidation, unprovoked arrests, prolonged unjustified incarceration, and harassment. The judge for the southern district federal court, Sidney Mize, dismissed the suit without a hearing, but the U.S. Court of Appeals for the Fifth Circuit reversed the decision and a hearing soon followed. As a result, a team of special federal investigators was appointed to prevent violence against black citizens and civil rights workers.

The civil rights movement experienced its most intensely active period in the 1960s. Out of this period came several black Mississippians who made outstanding contributions toward the extension of civil rights for blacks in Mississippi, several of whom achieved national prominence.

Many of Mississippi's civil rights advocates and black politicians supported women's suffrage. Between 1883 and 1900 James Hill, Hiram Revels, and Blanche K. Bruce advocated granting women the right to vote. On February 12, 1890, Hill, a member of the National Executive Committee of the American Citizen's Equal Rights Association, stamped his approval upon a resolution posed by P.B.S.

Pinchback, president of the association. Pinchback instructed the executive committee to involve black females and youth in the struggle for civil rights. He believed they would be "an effective element of success in this grand movement to secure equality of citizens' rights for the colored American;" should women prefer to form an auxiliary association for their sex exclusively, no hindrance should be made to prevent them.[4]

Both Revels and Bruce supported equality of the sexes. At the twenty-sixty annual meeting of the National American Women Suffrage Association held in Washington, D.C., in 1894, Bruce stated his willingness to work toward universal suffrage.[5]

Black females from Mississippi played key roles in the enactment of legislative measures that guaranteed sexual equality. Ida Wells-Barnett, for example, organized the Afro-American Women Suffrage Association. Barnett and Margaret Murray Washington, president of the Federation of Colored Women, viewed suffrage as the necessary safeguard of the nation and the key instrument to fight against racism.

Eventually women, both black and white, gained the right to vote in 1920 with the ratification of the nineteenth amendment to the Constitution.

Once black women had achieved the right to vote, many disappointingly discovered that other legal and illegal disenfranchisement methods still prevented them from voting. Black women were forced to travel under deplorable conditions on street cars, trains and in train stations, denied accomodations in hotels and admittance to restaurants, barred from clerical and management positions, underpaid on jobs. Consequently, these women campaigned against racism for the passage of a national civil rights bill. From 1920 to 1964, black women took the initiative in organizing boycotts, sit-ins, voter registration drives, but they did it with the cooperation of concerned black males and leaders.

In the struggle for sexual equality, black women in Mississippi did not perceive the movement as a liberation from black males but as the liberation of black people. On May 7, 1971, at the NAACP Legal Defense Fund Institute, Fannie Lou Hamer spoke on "The Special Plight and the Role of Black Women." In this speech she asserted, "We have a job as black women to support whatever is right, and to bring justice where we've had so much injustice." Moreover, she chided the black middle class woman for thinking she was different or better than poor women:

Whether you have a Ph.D., D.D., or no D., we're in this bag together. And whether you're from Morehouse, or Nohouse, we're still in this bag together. Not to fight to try to liberate ourselves from the men—this is another trick to get us fighting among ourselves—but to work together with the black man. Then we will have a better chance to just act as human beings and to be treated as human beings in our sick society.[6]

As a result of the efforts of Fannie Lou Hamer, Victoria Gray, Annie Moody, Anne Devine, Joyce Ladner, Lula Dwight, and a host of other black females in the Mississippi civil rights struggle in the 1960s, blacks were able finally to exercise their right to vote. They also gained admission to white colleges and universities, public restaurants, hotels and other public facilities, employment in clerical and management positions, and selection to jury duty.

Black women are still actively involved in the struggle for a better life for black people. The challenges of the 1980s, as expressed by Jennie Young, the president of the Mississippi Southern Rural Women's Network include fair housing, equal employment opportunities, improved health, child care, family living practices, and quality education. The organization seeks to find ways to meet these critical needs and address the issues of racism, sexism, and poverty that black women face.

Ida B. Wells

Crusader

One black woman who typified the struggles of the Afro-American female, defied the obstacles, and achieved abundant success is Ida B. Wells-Barnett. Her birth at Holy Springs, Mississippi, on July 16, 1862, scarcely six months prior to the issuance of the Emancipation Proclamation seemed prophetic of the impatience that was the hallmark of her continuing quest to improve the quality of life of her people.[1]

Ida, the first of eight children born to Jim and Elizabeth Wells, came of age amidst the uncertain and seamy Reconstruction. Her parents had been servants. Her father, son of his master and one of his slave women named Peggy, was apprenticed at eighteen (by his father) to a Mr. Bolling as a carpenter. Her mother, a native of Virginia, was cook for the Bollings.

Ida grew up in a house built and owned by her father, who as a skilled carpenter had plenty of work rebuilding places destroyed during the hostilities. He was a man of independent spirit, even in slavery, who sought and attained his full independence following emancipation. He possessed considerable ability, had much civic concern, and was selected a member of the first board of trustees of Rust College. Her mother was deeply religious and held convictions about the essential dignity of man, developed under the cruelties of slavery.

Both parents stressed the importance of securing an education. At Rust, Ida had the guidance and instruction of dedicated missionaries and teachers who came to Holly Springs to assist the freedmen and was regarded as an exceedingly apt pupil. On Sundays her religious parents would permit only Bible reading, so Ida read the Bible over and over again.

In 1878, a terrible epidemic of yellow fever struck Holly Springs, causing most of its citizens to flee, and killing hundreds of those who remained. In its wake, Ida and her brothers and sisters were orphaned. Though only sixteen, she demonstrated the steadfast courage that characterized her life. Despite offers from neighbors, friends and relatives, Ida determined to keep the family together. With the few hundred dollars her father had left and help from the Prince Hall Masons, who were guardians, she managed for her family.

Meanwhile, Ida passed the teachers' examination and was assigned to a one-room school about six miles from Holly Springs. She lived frugally in order to further her education. At Fisk, for one summer session, she began to write and became intrigued by journalism.

Sometime during the early 1880s, an aunt in Memphis invited Ida to live with her and seek a teaching position there. Ida accepted. Her brothers were apprenticed carpenters, and the aunt took care of the younger sisters.

Ida's next assignment was in the rural schools of Shelby County, Tennessee. Meanwhile, she studied for the teachers' examination for the Memphis city schools. On May 4, 1884, en route to her school in Woodstock, Tennessee, the conductor on the Chesapeake and Ohio Railroad ordered Ida to the smoking car. She refused to move. She had purchased a first-class ticket to assert her right to ride in the ladies car. "He tried to drag me out of the seat," she reported, "but the moment he caught hold of my arm I fastened my teeth in the back of his hand." The conductor returned with two others, including the baggage man; and to the delight of the white passengers, the three dragged her out. She got off at the next stop, returned to Memphis, and filed suit against the railroad. The case attracted much attention because the law stipulated that accommodations should be separate but equal. Railroad personnel continued, however, to insist that blacks ride in the smoking car. This marked the first time that a southern black had appealed to a state court since the U.S. Supreme Court in 1883 declared the Civil Rights Bill of 1875 unconstitutional.[3]

In December 1884, the local court returned a verdict in favor of Wells and awarded her five hundred dollars in damages. However, the victory was short-lived. The railroad appealed, and on April 5, 1887, the Tennessee Supreme Court reversed the lower court.[4]

In her diary Ida Wells wrote: "The Supreme Court reversed the decision of the lower court in my behalf . . . I felt so disappointed because I had hoped such great things from my suit for my people generally. I had firmly believed all along that the law was on our side and would, when we appealed to it, give us justice. I feel shorn of that belief and utterly discouraged, and just now, if it were possible, would gather my race in my arms and fly away with them."[5]

During the fall of that year, Ida passed the qualifying examinations and was assigned as teacher in the Memphis public schools. She became the star of local literary circles and won admittance to black society in Memphis—an aristocracy based on complexion, education, and talent. That society bitterly resented racial discrimination and applauded Wells for her record of vigorous protest against the establishment.[6]

In 1887, she launched her journalistic career, using the story of her suit against the railroad as an initial article. Later, she invested her savings to become part owner of a small Afro-American journal in Memphis, the *Free Speech and Headlight*. Her articles criticizing the Memphis Board of Education for separate inferior black schools led to her dismissal as a teacher in 1891. Dismayed but undaunted, she worked harder on the paper, shortened its name to *Free Press*, and seized every opportunity to speak out in defense of justice for blacks. Circulation of the paper increased, and Ida finally became the sole owner and editor. Using the pen name "Iola," Wells published detailed exposes of white mobs and their dirty work. She supplied to numerous black newspapers articles with stinging rebukes against unfair treatment of blacks by whites. Though often threatened, Wells carried two pistols for protection and fearlessly continued her campaign.[7]

Ida was busily engaged in traveling and writing when on March 9, 1892, three young black businessmen were lynched for committing the crime of being "uppity and too successful." She turned her scathing pen on the lynchers and the white population who allowed and condoned the act. She encouraged blacks to leave Memphis, "a town which will neither protect our lives nor our property, nor give us a fair trial in the Courts, but takes us out and murders us in cold blood."[8] Hundreds took her advice, disposed of their belongings, and left. Those who remained were urged to boycott the street railway. The *Free Speech* was blamed for paralyzing downtown businesses.

An earlier editorial against white backlash in the 1880s had stated: "The old Southern voice that was once heard and made Negroes jump and run like rats to their holes is shut up; or might well be, for the Negro of today is not the same as Negroes were thirty years ago, and it can't be expected that the Negro of today will take what was forced upon him thirty years back. So it is no use to be talking now about Negroes ought to be kept at the bottom where God intended for them to stay."[9]

Weeks later, five Negroes accused of raping white women were lynched. Looking danger squarely in the face, she wrote a series of forceful articles on outrages perpetrated against blacks. In one article she wrote: "Nobody in this section of the country believes the old threadbare lies that Negro men rape white women. If Southern white men are not careful they will overreach themselves and public sentiment will have a reaction; or a conclusion will be reached which will be very damaging to the moral reputation of their women."[10]

The *Memphis Daily Commercial* shrieked: "The fact that a black scoundrel is allowed to live and utter such loathsome and repulsive calumnies is a volume of evidence as to the wonderful patience of Southern whites.... There are some things that the Southern white man will not tolerate and the obscene intimations of the foregoing have brought the writer to the very utmost limit of public patience. We hope we have said enough."[11]

An urgent meeting of the city's white leaders sent a delegation to the *Free Speech* to advise the newspaper "never repeat such ideas or to suffer the consequence."[12] Not surprisingly, no one was there to greet them. The very night her newspaper appeared with a scathing bitter editorial, a mob invaded her offices, wrecked her press, destroyed all the copies of the paper it could find. Mob leaders declared that they would have lynched her if she had been found. A sheriff's sale liquidated any remaining assets.

Unaware of this incident, Ida Wells traveled to New York City to meet with T. Thomas Fortune, editor, of the *New York Age*. But she was astounded and afraid when Fortune showed her an article in the *New York Sun* reporting the destruction of her press and the threats on her life. Immediately, Ida Wells began work at the *New York Age*. With Memphis as her prime target, she told the shameful story of the plight of blacks in the South, exposing the realities of lynchings to the world. She profusely wrote: "White men lynch the offending Afro-American not because he is a despoiler of virtue, but because he succumbs to the smiles of white women."[13] She substantiated her claims with statistics from the *Chicago Tribune*.

Ida Wells toured Europe, where she lectured on the horrors of lynching in the United States. Her first trip in 1893 was financed by the Women's Loyal Union, which consisted of New York black women who supported her crusade. She told her story to members of the nobility and those who had an abiding concern for human dignity. In response to her claims, a prominent British churchman declared, "Nothing since the days of *Uncle Tom's Cabin* has taken such a hold in England as this anti-lynching crusade."[14]

On her second tour in 1893, Wells's lecture dealt with the exclusion of blacks at the World's Columbian Exposition. Petitions sent to the exposition officials from black individuals and groups to participate were denied. With the support of Frederick Douglass and others, she produced an eighty-one-page booklet entitled: *The Rea-*

son *Why the Colored American is Not in the World's Exposition.* In the preface, Wells espoused: "The exhibit of the progress made by a race in twenty-five years of freedom as against 250 years of slavery would have been the greatest tribute to the greatness and progressiveness of American institutions which could have been shown to the world."[15] That booklet refuted the stereotypical distortions printed by most white authors. By describing the achievements and contributions of American blacks, Wells took a giant step in the struggle to rewrite black and American history to dispel the pseudo-scientific arguments concerning black inferiority.

Later Ida Wells took up residence in Chicago and in 1895 published *A Red Record: Tabulated Statistics and Alleged Causes of Lynchings in the United States, 1892–94.* This book contained a hundred pages of the first serious statistical record of lynchings of blacks and others since emancipation. Later Tuskegee Institute compiled and printed records of lynching in America. In the years 1890–1900, 1,217 blacks were murdered or lynched, and none stood trial. Wells presented concrete evidence enumerating each person who was brutally slain by vigilantes for minor offenses. If tried in court and guilty verdicts rendered, the defendants would have received a moderate fine or a light jail sentence. Ida Wells eloquently sought to arouse public sentiment to end brutal mob action. She mercilessly refuted popular misconceptions that most lynchings resulted from assaults and rape of white women. In her argument she said:

> We demand a fair trial by law for those accused of crime, and punished by law after honest conviction. Surely the humanitarian spirit of this country which reaches out to denounce the treatment of Russian Jews, the Armenian Christians, the laboring poor of Europe, the Siberian exiles, and the native women of India will no longer refuse to lift its voice on this subject. If it were known that the cannibals or the savage Indians had burned three human beings alive in the past two years, the whole of Christendom would be roused, to devise ways and means to put a stop to it. Can you remain silent and inactive when such things are done in our own community and country? Is your duty to humanity in the United States less binding?[16]

In 1895, Ida Wells married another crusader, Chicago lawyer-editor, the widowed Ferdinand L. Barnett. Together they campaigned for equal rights for black Americans. She bore him four children. After the birth of their second son in 1897, Ida devoted herself fully to the tasks of homemaker and mother, firmly believing in the importance of a mother in the home during the formative years of her children. "I had to become a mother" Ida Wells exclaimed, "before I realized what a wonderful place in the scheme of things the Creator has given woman."[17]

Nevertheless, Ida Wells continued to fight with voice and pen against every form of injustice, discrimination and racism in Chicago and throughout America. The struggle to end lynching in the United States dominated the writing pad of Ida Wells-Barnett. In 1898, with a five month old child in her arms, she led an outraged black delegation to the White House to protest the lynching of a black postmaster in South Carolina.[18] Speaking to members of the Afro-American Council in Washington, D.C., in 1898, Ida Wells-Barnett denounced mob violence and anarchy north and south. She accused President McKinley of being too busy decorating the graves of Confederate soldiers to defend and enforce laws guaranteeing the rights of blacks. In concluding her presentation, she asserted, "If this gathering means anything, it means that we at last come to the point in our race history where we must do something for ourselves, and do it now. We must educate the white people out of the 250 years of slave history."[19]

Discrimination in the armed forces attracted the attention of Ida Wells-Barnett as the second most critical issue in America's race relations. Upon her return home from Washington, D.C., she journeyed to Springfield, Illinois, to ensure the mobilization of the Illinois Eighth Colored Regiment to Cuba. Eventually, the Regiment was mustered and entrained to Cuba.[20]

Women's rights personally affected Ida Wells-Barnett. As a result, Wells-Barnett established the first black women's suffrage group, the Alpha Suffrage Club. In addition, she served as a director of the Cook County League of Women's Clubs. Twice she marched in suffrage parades in Washington—on the eve of President Woodrow Wilson's inauguration in 1913 and again in June 1918, when she led the five thousand suffragists in a torrential rain to the Republican National Convention where the women demanded inclusion of a suffrage plank in their platform.[21]

In 1901, the Barnetts were among the first blacks to move to eastside Chicago, a predominantly white neighborhood and were subjected to various forms of hostility. When increasing numbers of blacks migrated into the area, white antagonism escalated and white gangs frequently attacked black youths. As a protective measure against such violence, blacks oragnized a tight-knit group that met fistcuffs with fistcuffs. On one occasion when a large white gang followed the Barnett's sons home and stood outside jeering and threatening, Ida Barnett pointed her pistol and dared anyone to cross her threshold to harm her or any member of her family.[22]

When the race-riots occurred during the early 1900's, Ida Barnett, responded immediately. In 1909, after the Springfield, Illinois, race-riot that claimed numerous black lives, Barnett was among the prominent whites and blacks who organized the Niagara Movement that evolved into the National Association for the Advancement of Colored People (NAACP). The goals of the group were the enactment of a federal anti-lynching law, universal suffrage, quality education, and an end to discrimination and segregation. Ida's fiery militancy and constant distrust of whites, however, caused heated controversy within the infant organization. Her intrepid investigations resulted in the removal of lax law officials. And in many instances, her efforts created jobs for blacks in employable areas commonly reserved for whites. In 1913, she accepted the position as probation officer with the Chicago Municipal Court, thus becoming the first black to hold such office.[23]

Two years later, she was elected vice-president of Chicago's Equal Rights League, an advocacy group for universal suffrage. In 1918, Ida Wells-Barnett and Madam C. J. Walker were chosen as delegates by the National Equal Rights League to attend the Peace Conference at Versailles, France. However, the armistice was signed prior to the completion of arrangements. One of her last affiliations was with Marcus Garvey's Universal Negro Improvement Association.[24]

Ida Wells-Barnett was an uncompromising militant who distrusted white involvement in the black struggle for equality. This stance placed her in direct opposition to Booker T. Washington, whose doctrine of compromise and accommodation she publicly and fiercely attacked in speeches before the National Afro-American Council and similar associations. She headed the Anti-Lynching Speakers Bureau of the Council and served as secretary from 1898–1902, when Booker T. Washington's forces took control.[25]

Throughout her struggle for justice and equality for blacks, Ida Barnett remained faithful to the church. While in Memphis Ida joined the African Methodist Espiscopal (A.M.E.) Church. For the first time, she met black bishops, several of whom she later came to know personally. Her associations with members of the clergy were always cordial and respectful. In Chicago her family was active in Bethel A. M. E. Church under the pastorate of the Bishop R. C. Ransom. After Bishop Ransom moved to another congregation, some dissatisfactions developed at Bethel which caused the Barnetts to move their memberships to Grace Presbyterian Church.

In her crusade against racial injustice she generally held meetings in local churches and sought advice and assistance of the ministers. However, she did experience some disaffection with the Methodist Episcopal Church when it would not support her efforts to establish a social center.[26]

In 1910, at the urgence of Ida Barnett, the male Sunday school class at Grace Presbyterian Church organized The Negro Fellowship League created to end racial oppression and discrimination. The League provided dormitories for homeless men at twenty-five cents per night. The League conducted Sunday worship service and established an employment office. She tried to involve middle- and upper-class blacks in this project. Although they admired her dedication, they were unwilling to venture into the area to help the uneducated, unemployed brothers from the South. Langston Hughes asserted that, "Her activities in the field of social work laid the groundwork for the Urban League."[27]

Ida B. Wells-Barnett, the elegant, well groomed, and respectable civil rights advocate, died on March 25, 1931, after an illness of two days, ending a life that spanned nearly seventy years and a career that was devoted to every facet in the process for the advancement of black pride. As a gifted, young black woman, she dedicated herself to the fight for human decency against mob violence, injustice, and inequality; she remained steadfast to the cause throughout her life. In 1941, the Chicago Housing Authority named one of its first low-rent housing developments Ida B. Wells Homes. At the dedication ceremonies, Miss Wells was memorialized as a leader, writer, editor, and crusader for civil liberties. The world will remember Ida B. Wells as a permanent personality in the vanguard of racial and human rights. She was strong in her devotion to her race, strong in the estimation of influential men and women everywhere, who were coworkers with her in the cause for which she so nobly devoted herself.[28]

The breadth of Miss Wells's acquaintances was vast. She knew personally most of the blacks and whites who occupied leadership positions. And she possessed the unique ability to work with peoples of all colors and social classes, especially those of the lower socioeconomic level.

Of Miss Wells's abilities few persons were as qualified to speak as the distinguished T. Thomas Fortune, who said:

She handles her subjects more as a man than a woman; indeed, she has so long had the management of a large home and business interests that the sharpness of wit and self possession which characterize men of affairs are hers in a large measure.

Few women have a higher conception of the responsibilities and the possibilities of her sex than Miss Wells. She has all of a woman's tenderness in all that affects our common humanity, but she has also the courage of the great woman of the past who believed that they could still be womanly while being mere ciphers in the world's broad field of battle.[29]

Margaret Murray Washington
Club Organizer and Civil Rights Advocate

Margaret Murray Washington (Mrs. Booker T.), one of ten children was born March 9, 1865, in Macon, Mississippi. She was a mulatto, with reddish-brown hair, gray hazel eyes, strong features, and a large commanding figure. After completing her early education, she entered Fisk University in 1880 and nine years later graduated. She and another female were the only female members of a predominantly male class. While in school she suffered from poor health, but her ambitious spirit and iron will pulled her through.[1]

After graduation from Fisk, Tuskegee Normal and Industrial Institute employed her as a teacher of English literature. The following year, in recognition of her "exceptional strength of mind and disciplinary power" the trustees of Tuskegee elected her "Lady Principal" and Dean of Women.[2]

In the fall of 1892 Margaret Murray married Booker T. Washington, the founder of Tuskegee Institute and renowned racial accomodationist. In reality, she stood next to him in power and influence, in the home as well as in the public.[3]

Margaret Washington used her influence as a lecturer, teacher, and journalist to assist the less fortunate, to promote social settlement and interracial cooperation, and to organize clubs and movements concerned with elevation of black women. While at Tuskegee, she organized the Tuskegee Women's Club. In 1895 she founded the National Federation of Afro-American Women and served as its first president. She was also involved in the organization of the National Association of Colored Women, formed by an assembly of various women's groups. One of its primary goals was providing educational opportunities for blacks in the United States. It also advocated the formation of a School Teacher's League to protect the rights of black female teachers. The organization was also concerned with wayward girls and infant care. The association established industrial homes for black females in the South, day nurseries, boarding homes, and scholarships. In 1920, the membership totaled 300,000 with chapters throughout the United States, Canada, Haiti, Liberia, and Cuba.[4]

Margaret Washington also became involved with the Committee for Interracial Cooperation, a biracial southern organization concerned with the improvement of educational and social institutions for blacks. In addition, this Committee denounced lynching and promoted education, female suffrage and free press.[5]

On October 7, 1920, at the Women's Interracial Conference, Margaret Washington addressed the Assembly about two issues which affected the stability of the black family: illegal cohabitation of black females with black males and disrupted family life which attributed to social problems within the black community. She also praised white women for their assistance in helping older black females. Because of these comments many of her critics accused her of being an accomodationist with a conservative race policy.[6]

In spite of the criticism Margaret Washington remained one of the South's leading black advocates of women rights and civil rights.

Jack Harvey Young, Sr.
Distinguished Civil Rights Lawyer
(1908–1976)

As a result of sit-ins, boycotts, voting registration, and freedom rides in the 1960s, Mississippi, a hotbed of racial injustice and discrimination, was transformed from a caste-like society into a reluctant pluralistic one. In 1961, for example, a dozen students at Tougaloo College sat in at the Jackson Public Library; when they refused police orders to leave, they were arrested and charged with disturbing the peace. This was Mississippi's first civil rights demonstration case. Attorney Jack H. Young represented the group so well that the NAACP hired him as a full-time staff attorney. Thus began his long and successful career in defense of civil rights.[1]

Another constructive event in the Mississippi civil rights movement that brought Young to the forefront was the May 1961 arrival of 323 Freedom Riders. The Freedom Riders came to Jackson from the North, the East, and the West—via buses, trains, airplanes, and automobiles. They sat in at white waiting rooms, in bus and railroad stations and airports; when ordered to leave, they refused and were arrested en masse and charged with trespassing or disturbing the peace.[2]

The national office of the NAACP authorized Jackson attorney Jack Young to represent the accused. Thus began the long, legal drama that took them before the Jackson Municipal Court where they were convicted of trespassing, fined two hundred dollars each, and given sixty days in the county jail, a judgment which they appealed in Mississippi courts and finally to the U.S. Supreme Court. They refused to post bond, preferring to remain in jail to illustrate their sincerity. Because of overcrowdness in the county jail the offenders were transported to Parchman, the state penitentiary. As many as eight women occupied the same cell, originally designed to accommodate two people. Prison officials placed the convicted Freedom Riders in maximum security cells.[3]

Before posting bond of fifteen hundred dollars each and filing appeals, the Freedom Riders remained in jail thirty-nine days. The Chicago-based Congress of Racial Equality (CORE), who sponsored the Freedom Riders, supplied the bail bonds until the depletion of its funds. Then the NAACP posted approximately three thousand dollars in bond money.

The Freedom Riders who were at Parchman returned to Jackson at night when it was safe to do so. Whites refused them hotel accommodations and no sufficient black hotel facilities existed. Therefore, attorneys Jack Young and Carsie Hall arranged transportation for them to Young's home, where Mrs. Young prepared meals while the attorneys sought overnight facilities for them to sleep. Women Unlimited, an organization composed of black women, found suitable accommodations for the civil rights activists. This was a complicated matter because only a few weeks before, a white minister had been a dinner guest in a black minister's home, for which both were arrested. The black minister was jailed for about two weeks and the other for over a month. The "crime" was that a white man had eaten at the black man's home. Alarmed by the sudden turn of events, the Jackson black community volunteered to take Freedom Riders into their homes without opposition from local whites.

The long litigation proved burdensome. After many delays, the Freedom Riders were brought to trial. At that time only two other lawyers in Mississippi could handle civil rights cases—attorneys R. Jess Brown and Carsie Hall. Meanwhile, demonstrations occurred across the state. Youths sat in at restaurants, and picketed schools. James Meredith enrolled at Ole Miss in 1962, and a white gunman assassinated Medgar Evers in 1963.

The test case regarding the legality of the sit-ins, *Henry Thomas vs. the City of Jackson*, was appealed from the city court to the county court. A new trial was ordered, but Thomas' conviction was upheld. The case was appealed in the U.S. Supreme Court, which reversed the conviction. After the court reversed the original decision in the Henry case the other trespassing cases were dismissed.

In recognition of the role attorney Young played in defending persons who sought their civil rights, the NAACP named him the first recipient of the Ming Award:

JACK YOUNG
THE WILLIAM ROBERT MING ADVOCACY AWARD FOR UNSELFISH, DEVOTED AND COURAGEOUS ADVOCACY IN BEHALF OF THE PROGRAM OF THE NATIONAL ASSOCIATION FOR THE ADVANCEMENT OF COLORED PEOPLE AND THE CIVIL RIGHTS MOVEMENT DURING THE CRISIS YEARS IN MISSISSIPPI. THEREBY ASSISTING HIS PEOPLE TO GAIN RESPECT DIGNITY AND BETTER TREATMENT THROUGH THE COURTS AND ALL BRANCHES OF GOVERNMENT IN THE MAGNOLIA STATE.

June 30, 1975

Commenting later on the civil rights movement in Mississippi, Young said that the movement benefitted from the participation of northern whites jailed for advocating blacks' civil liberties. Prior to that time, black ministers in Jackson only reluctantly supported civil rights and the NAACP, and did not allow civil rights assemblies in their churches. After witnessing the dedication of northern whites, they gradually changed their views. Young highly praised the Reverend G. R. Haughton, pastor of Pearl Street A.M.E. Church, who led the conversion.

Young quickly added, however, that after the courts ruled in favor of civil rights and Congress passed certain civil rights legislations, judicial and executive enforcement of those rights was still necessary. Meanwhile violence erupted and many blacks were beaten and murdered. "It is my opinion," Young concluded, "that after much hassling and haggling with the local establishment, we in Jackson and some other parts of Mississippi achieved an amount of integration in a manner that was more orderly than has been done in many other places." Young also praised Medgar Evers for his "tirelessness and dedication."

In 1963, representing the NAACP, Jack Young successfully defended a black man charged with raping a white woman. An all-white jury acquitted the black defendant. This was a first for Mississippi.

One of three children of Henry H. Young, Sr., a bricklayer, and Jennie V. Young, Jack was born in Jackson March 9, 1908.

Jack's formal education commenced at the St. Mark's Episcopal Church kindergarten. Afterwards he attended Jim Hill Public School, where Professor Sam Brinkley was principal. At Jim Hill he was a schoolmate of author Richard Wright and was personally acquainted with "Biggy," who became the prototype of Wright's Bigger Thomas in *Native Son*. He completed seventh grade at Jim Hill and then transferred to Smith-Robinson School, which went only to the ninth grade. At that time there were no public high schools for blacks in Jackson.

To continue his education Jack Young enrolled in the high school department of Jackson College in 1923. During his first year, he won second prize of an academic scholarship that was established for scholastic achievement, and for the remaining three years in high school he won the first prize. He graduated valedictorian of his high school class. Jack won first place in the academic contest in each of the four years he was in college and again graduated at the head of his class in 1931. In college he was a member of the debating team, played violin in the college symphony orchestra, and worked afternoons at a shoe shop.

Jack's ambition was to enter law school upon finishing college, but he lacked sufficient funds. Like most black male graduates he had a choice of either working for Pullman Railroad or the local post office. Jack took and passed the civil service examination for a letter carrier and during his senior year was employed as a substitute in the Jackson post office.

Working and saving money to enter law school proved an impossible dream because of the Great Depression, but he managed to keep his position as letter carrier until 1951.

Young, still determined to pursue his law degree in spite of economic hardship, persuaded attorney Sidney R. Redmond, a graduate of Harvard Law School and a St. Louis alderman, to tutor him and fellow classmate Carsie Hall. The young Redmond who was the son of the late S. D. Redmond, a Jackson physician and lawyer, arranged special tutoring sessions for the aspiring lawyers whenever he visited Jackson on family related business. Also, he lent Young and Hall his Harvard textbooks and copious law school class notes. Finally, after studying law at night and working all day, Young passed the Mississippi bar on September 25, 1951, and resigned from the post office on the next pay day. He opened his law practice in Dr. S. D. Redmond's former office, where he remained for twenty years.

According to Young, he was at that time the only black lawyer in Jackson. Attorney Burns at Meridian and Ben Green, the mayor of Mound Bayou, were the only other black practicing attorneys in Mississippi. At one time Jackson had as many as thirteen black lawyers in the city, one of whom was Perry W. Howard, the leader of the Black and Tan Republicans, and for many years the National Republican Committeeman from Mississippi.

As in other southern states, black lawyers in Mississippi suffered indignities and racism. Young recalled that throughout the state, court officials disrespected black lawyers. Generally, judges referred to them and their clients by their first names. One judge presiding in Moss Point was the only exception. Blacks, consequently, were reluctant to utilize their services. But during the civil rights movement, things changed.

When asked who or what inspired him to become a lawyer, Young replied, A. A. Latting. Latting, a college professor, spoke of the great need for black lawyers and how they could help blacks obtain their civil rights. Latting's determination and his acquisition of a law degree from Northwestern University greatly influenced Young's decision. His wife, Aurelia Norris, a music teacher from New London, Ohio, whom he married in 1938, also encouraged and gave him moral and financial support. Young recalled that during his first week of practice his total receipts were twenty-five cents for notarizing a paper. Young once said, "During the transition from the post office to the law office, my wife supported me, and without her I doubt very seriously I would have managed to make it."

The walls of his office are lined with various plaques and certificates of awards. In addition to the Ming Award, some others are the National Bar Award, 1961; the Zeta Phi Beta, "Man of the Year," 1962; and the Mississippi Chapter Conference of Black Lawyers, 1962. *Pageant* magazine in 1962 named him one of "Ten Outstanding Leaders"; Jack Young, Carsie Hall, and R. Jesse Brown were awarded plaques and cash stipends by the NAACP Legal Defense

Fund for "Outstanding work in Civil Rights" in 1964. He was named "Attorney of the Year" by Jackson State College in 1965 and received "The Robert F. Kennedy and Martin L. King, Jr. Award" from the Mississippi Council on Human Relations in 1972—"For Compassion, Love of Liberty, Courage, Splendid Service in School Desegregation, with Gratitude and Esteem."

Jack Young "paid his dues" to his people in Jackson and Mississippi. He took cases which other lawyers refused; he represented the underprivileged and the economically deprived. He was a lifelong member of Pearl Street A.M.E. Church, where he served on the board of trustees. During the existence of the Southwest Bar Association he served a term as president. His memberships included Phi Beta Sigma Fraternity, Masons, Knights of Pythias, the Elks, YMCA, and the Jackson Negro Chamber of Commerce. On September 25, 1976, the pioneer civil rights lawyer, Jack Harvey died. After Jack Young's death, his partner-son assumed the major responsibilities of the law firm.

Medgar Evers

Civil Rights Advocate

Born on July 2, 1925, in Decatur, Newton County, Medgar Wiley Evers, the youngest of two sons of James and Jessie Wright Evers, rose to prominence as a civil rights advocate and an office holder in the National Association for the Advancement of Colored People. A timid and soft spoken, yet determined individual, Medgar was greatly influenced by his parents' religious convictions. As members of the Church of God in Christ, a Pentecostal denomination that prohibits drinking, smoking, and gambling, the Evers were very pious people. James Evers, his father, was a rugged migratory sawmill worker who owned his home and property. James, approximately six feet tall, physically strong and mean, could not read or write. Medgar Evers's grandfather, Mike Evers, had been a free black farmer who owned about three hundred acres in Scott County, but local whites illegally confiscated the property.[1]

Described as short, about five feet two inches, with small feet, Medgar's mother, Jessie, of Indian ancestry, frequently went barefoot. She was an industrious woman strong enough to work daily in the field, cook, wash, and iron. In addition, she made all of the family clothing from blue denim. Being very pious, she read the Bible daily and encouraged her children to obtain an education.[2]

Similar to other rural blacks in Mississippi, Medgar attended school four or five months a year. While whites rode the school bus, Medgar and other blacks walked. At school, Medgar was an achiever. He studied regularly and read frequently. After attending the Decatur Consolidated School's eighth grade, Medgar enrolled at the high school in Newton. According to his brother Charles, while in school, Medgar personified the scholar and the diplomat. His suavity and genuine humility made him a popular student.[3]

The draft temporarily interrupted Medgar's education in 1943, when he was involuntarily inducted into the army. While completing his military tour of duty in Europe, he experienced overt segregation. In a correspondence to Charles, his brother, Medgar wrote, "When we get out of the army, we're going to straighten this out."[4]

In 1946, Medgar entered Alcorn A & M College where he majored in business administration and actively engaged in extra-curricular activities. He played football, was a member of the track team, served as editor of the student newspaper, the *Alcorn Herald*, and sang with the college glee club. During his junior year, the student body elected him as class president and vice-president of the student forum. Although he matured to the point that he was considered a leader, Medgar was, nevertheless, a humble young man "whose word was his bond."[5]

While a student at Alcorn, Medgar met the eighteen year old nursing student, Myrlie Beasley of Vicksburg. Medgar, eight years Myrlie's senior, was overwhelmed by her beauty. His introduction to Myrlie led to frequent dates and their marriage on Christmas Eve, 1951. Although Myrlie did not graduate from Alcorn State University, she received her bachelor degree from Pomona College, Claremont, California, on June 9, 1968.[6]

When Myrlie married Medgar, she knew that she had embarked upon a life filled with constant danger because of her husband's involvement with the NAACP. Even as a high school student, Medgar had worked with the NAACP establishing local chapters throughout Mississippi. Because of racism experienced during his childhood, Medgar dedicated his life to the struggle of civil rights. Three years before his marriage, Medgar and other Alcornites traveled to Decatur to register to vote. However, they were confronted with violent white racists. The tenseness of that confrontation was eased by a white woman who pleaded, "It isn't worth it! It isn't worth it!" And the bloodshed was avoided.[7]

Later, Medgar became the official state administrator of the NAACP. His first project was to revitalize the defunct chapters of the NAACP in Mississippi and to create one in Mound Bayou, the all-black town. While he was trying to establish these chapters, as well as sell insurance in Mound Bayou and Bolivar County, Medgar initiated a boycott against gasoline stations that denied blacks the right to use their restrooms. In his struggle against racism, he declared to blacks that "any man with an ounce of pride who works in the Delta wants to do something for the poor black man."[8]

In 1954 when the U.S. Supreme Court declared segregation unconstitutional, Medgar embarked upon another racial struggle when he applied for admission to the University of Mississippi Law School. Surprisingly, there were no reprisals from whites. A few complimented him for his boldness. But, suddenly, negative reactions emerged. Attorney General J. P. Coleman and other state officials held an interview. According to Medgar, "They asked me if I was sincere, I told them yes. They asked me if I was prompted by the NAACP, and I told them no. They asked me where I would stay, and I answered, 'on the campus, sir, I'm very hygienic. I bathe every day, and I assure you this brown won't rub off.' "[9] Coleman informed Medgar that he would notify him concerning his admission to the University. The day after registration, Medgar received a letter stating that he was denied admission because he did not have two letters of recommendation from people in his community.

Following this incident in December 1954, the National office of the NAACP offered Medgar a salaried position as its first field secretary in Mississippi. Since Medgar believed that no blacks could live in Mississippi and die in peace as long as things remained unchanged, he accepted and immediately went to work full time for the NAACP. Conditions changed, but not without repercussion.[10]

As field secretary, Medgar's first task was to investigate, compile, and publish evidence of violent crimes committed against blacks. Often disguised as a farm worker, Medgar collected his data and sent his findings to the New York office of the NAACP, which published the results.

Medgar's goals and objectives as field secretary were impeded or hindered by those blacks "whose major problem was their understandable inferiority complex." For example, in the early days of his crusade, the Mississippi Negro Teachers Association denied Medgar permission to address its assembly. The black press was equally uncooperative. Percy Greene, editor of the *Jackson Advocate*, reportedly labeled him a "young upstart," an "agitator," a man who was still wet behind his ears. His staunchest supporters were the black rank-and-file adults and youths.[11]

Medgar's non-violent struggle for equality frequently led to dangerous risks and bodily harm. While engaged in battles to obtain civil rights for blacks, Medgar was beaten as he participated in sit-ins and lunch counter demonstrations to protest racial discrimination. For instance, Medgar took a front seat on a Trailways bus and refused to move until police seized him and took him to the station house. As soon as he was released, he returned to the same seat on the same bus. A white cab driver saw him, entered the bus, and punched him in the face. Evers did not retaliate.[12]

Because of the dangerous nature of his job, Medgar often discussed and explained his work to his children and tried to teach them how to protect themselves against harm. The children were not allowed outside after dusk; and Medgar and the children played a game called: "What is the safest place if someone starts shooting?" They agreed it was probably the bathtub. His wife, Myrlie, arranged the furniture so that no one ever sat facing the window. After a firebomb was thrown into the Evers home in May 1963, Medgar devised another game called, "This is the way Daddy did it in the army," as he taught them to fall on the floor whenever they heard a strange noise.[13]

Medgar Evers's life was continuously marred by violent incidents. His journeys through small Mississippi towns resembled the flight of a fugitive from justice. It became increasingly unsafe for him to remain in any one place, and he was continuously on guard against being trailed. Even the telephone became an instrument of torture, a reminder of lurking peril. Sometimes it rang all night, and the anonymous caller tapped the cylinder of his receiver with a pistol to let Evers know he had a weapon in his hand. "This is for you," the caller announced. Medgar merely shrugged off the threat and replied, "If I die, it will be for a good cause. I've been fighting for America just as much as the soldiers in Vietnam."[14]

What was it that provoked so much opposition from the local establishments toward Medgar Evers? Basically, it was resistance to change. Because Evers wished to change the lifestyles of poor whites and blacks in Mississippi, he was hated. Daily, Medgar Evers lived in agony, although he was patient, sincere, and unyielding in his opposition to the system. During the trial of the defendants of the first sit-in-demonstration in Jackson, for example, Medgar applauded the protesters for their dedication and sacrifice. Suddenly, a police officer attacked and beat him over the head with a snub-nosed revolver.[15]

Undeterred, Medgar continued his campaign against racial injustice and inequality in Mississippi. He pleaded with Jackson's mayor, Allen Thompson, to appoint a biracial human relations committee to deal with the race issue. "Let's not kid ourselves" the mayor replied, "I believe in the separation of the races and that's the way it's going to be." But Medgar was determined it would change; therefore, he filed suit to force the Jackson public school to comply with the 1954 Brown decision, but to no avail. Next, he organized a peaceful youth demonstration to protest the lack of black participation in the municipal operation of the Jackson government. Lena Horne, a longtime admirer and friend, came to Jackson to encourage the masses.[16]

But change did occur—gradually at first and then with increasing momentum. Medgar Evers succeeded in getting James Meredith admitted to the University of Mississippi and having Clyde Kennard hospitalized, freed, and sent to Chicago with comedian Dick Gregory to work. Kennard had been imprisoned on trumped-up charges of robbery because he sought admission to the University of Southern Mississippi, near his home in Hattiesburg.[17]

On Monday, June 11, 1963, the same day Governor George Wallace admitted two blacks to the University of Alabama, Medgar Evers was assassinated. Evers's premonition that "I'm looking to be shot at any time that I step out of a car" came to fruition. Earlier that day, he telephoned his wife three times to express his love for her and his family. That evening, he listened to President John F. Kennedy's nationally televised address which Evers viewed as a balm to an already depressed soul. At exactly 12:20 a.m., he slowly drove into his driveway. "That's Daddy," cried his two oldest children, as he opened the car door. At the same moment, hidden in a honeysuckle thicket 150 feet across the street, a shadowy figure fired an Enfield army rifle. The bullet caught Evers in the back below the right shoulder blade, ripped through his chest, and smashed into the house. At age thirty seven, Medgar Wiley Evers was dead of an assassin's bullet. "The sacrifice was now complete. This man of spirit, man of love, man of devotion, had given his life so that his fellowmen might someday know justice."[18]

The tensed and saddened days of Medgar's wake in Jackson ignited anger within the black community. Even the black opposition demanded the apprehension and punishment of the alleged killer, Byron de la Beckwith, the avowed racist who was later acquitted of the crime by an all-white jury. This was a travesty of justice not only to the slain leader, but to all blacks who fought and died to overcome racism.[19]

To pay tribute to this now fallen man and slain civil rights advocate, the top black leadership of the nation and about fifty whites came to Jackson. Among those who attended the final rites were Roy Wilkens, Executive Secretary of the NAACP, who gave the funeral oration; Martin Luther King, Jr., of SCLC; Ralph Bunche, undersecretary of U.N.; and Whitney Young, of the National Urban League. By order of President John F. Kennedy, who did not really understand the South and its racist mentality, the interment took place in Arlington National Cemetery.[20]

During the summer of 1969, three years after the assassination of Medgar Evers, the NAACP held its Sixtieth Anniversary Convention in Jackson. The city's best hotels, restaurants, and public facilities were desegregated and utilized by the biracial delegation of more than two thousand. At that convention, Dr. Gilbert Mason, president of the Gulfport branch of the NAACP, unveiled a six-foot marble tablet with the following inscription beneath a huge reproduction of the association seal:

> DEDICATED TO THE MEMORY OF MEDGAR WILEY EVERS, BORN JULY 2, 1925, DECATUR, MISSISSIPPI, FIELD SECRETARY, MISSISSIPPI STATE CONFERENCE OF NAACP BRANCHES, 1954–1963. ERECTED JULY 4, 1969 BY MISSISSIPPI STATE CONFERENCE, NATIONAL ASSOCIATION OF COLORED PEOPLE.[21]

Fannie Lou Hamer

Civil Rights Activist

Fannie Lou Townsend, the youngest of twenty children, was born on October 6, 1917, in rural Montgomery County. When she was two, her family moved to Sunflower County. While still quite young she learned about white domination

> I remember, and I never will forget, one day—I was six years old and I was playing beside the road and this plantation owner drove up to me

and asked me could I pick cotton! I told him I didn't know and he said, 'Yes, you can. I will give you things that you want from the commissary store,' and he named things like cracker-jacks and sardines—and it was a huge list that he called off. So I picked the thirty pounds of cotton that week, but I found out what actually happened was he was *trapping* me into beginning the work I was to keep doing; and I never did get out of his debt again!"[1]

With a production force that included twenty children it was possible for the Townsends to produce fifty to sixty bales of cotton a year. This crop was not for themselves but for the white landowner, on whose land the Townsends labored as sharecroppers. By the time Fannie Townsend was thirteen, she could pick as much cotton as any man.[2]

As a child Fannie Lou could not understand why whites had plenty of food and clothes, big houses, and little work, and those like herself and her family never had enough to eat and had to wrap their feet in rags to keep them warm. When she questioned her mother, Fannie Lou was strongly reprimanded. "There's nothin' wrong with you bein' black, child," her mother scolded, "God made you black. Respect yourself!"[3] Later, her mother bought her a black doll, the only one she ever had.

Fannie's parents were hard workers who sought to improve their economic condition and tried to provide the best for their family. Fannie Lou remembered her mother coming from the fields wearing tattered and torn clothes and too tired to walk. She had worked herself into exhaustion so that the family could survive. Finally, her father saved enough money to purchase three mules and two cows, wagons, cultivators, and other farming equipment. Renting land, instead of sharecropping afforded her father a measure of independence. But success eluded the Townsends. Some whites feared that the Townsends were getting "too uppity" and successful. Therefore, a white neighbor placed poison in the livestock drinking water and killed all the stock.[4]

In a similar incident Fannie recalled that a black plantation worker, Joe Pulliam, was given $150 and ordered to go to the hill country and literally "buy" another black family to add to the white planter's labor force. Instead, the black man pocketed the money and declared he was applying it to what the owner owed him. A heated argument ensued and the black man was shot, but not critically wounded. He entered his hovel, emerged with a Winchester rifle, and killed the landlord instantly. His white companion fled to town to spread the news. Pulliam, knowing he was marked for a violent death, immediately fled to the bayou to make his final stand in a hollow tree stump. Before the mob reached him with gasoline and machine gun fire, Joe Pulliam had killed thirteen men and seriously wounded twenty-six others.[5]

As the flames leaped at him, Joe Pulliam crawled out, and was lying with his head on his gun when they found him. The last bullet in the gun had been snapped twice. According to Hamer's recollection, the mob "dragged him by his heels on the back of a car and they paraded about town with that man and they cut his ears off and put them in a showcase and they stayed there a long, long time—in Drew, Mississippi. All of those things, when they would happen, would make me sick in the pit of my stomach and year after year, everytime something would happen it would make me more and more aware of what would have to be done in the state of Mississippi."[6] Moreover, Fannie Lou Hamer remembered that after the incident, "Mississippi was a quiet place for a long time."[7]

Following the loss of the livestock, economic conditions worsened for the Townsends. Out of despair and desperation Fannie often wished that she was white. "We worked all the time, just worked and then we would be hungry and my mother was clearing up a new ground trying to help to feed us for $1.25 a day." One day Mrs. Townsend was using an ax and a flying object punctured her eye, eventually causing blindness in both eyes. As a result, Fannie Lou grew "sicker and sicker of the system." She watched her mother's strong body weaken under the strain of impoverishment, "and I always said if I lived to get grown and had a chance, I was going to do something for the black man of the South if it cost my life."[8]

Her parents tried desperately to keep their twenty children in school, which proved to be no easy task, despite the sessions of only four months for blacks. At age twelve Fannie Lou joined the Stranger's Home Baptist Church and was baptized in the Queen River. That was also the last year that she attended school. Fortunately, she had learned to read and to write. Although Fannie Lou Hamer never received a diploma, she was awarded an honorary degree of Humane Letters by Tougaloo College in 1969.

Fannie Lou Hamer had great respect for her parents:

My mother was a great woman—poor, ragged, rough black hands—but she still taught us to be decent and to respect ourselves."[9]

From early childhood, our folks taught us to do unto others, and not to hate. It might not matter what you do to me, but it makes a whole lot of difference for my insides what I do to you. If I hate you, then we're just two miserable people. Hate is something destructive. I grew up believin' in God but I knew things was bad wrong, and I used to think, "Let me have a chance, and whatever this is that's wrong in Mississippi, I'm gonna do somethin' about it!"[10]

In the early 1940s when she was age twenty-four Fannie Lou Townsend, herself a physically strong young woman, married Perry Hamer. Her father had died in 1939. Conscious of the needs of her failing mother and a good husband, Fannie Hamer secured a job as sharecropper and timekeeper on a plantation. She held that job for eighteen years—until 1962 when she decided she was going to exercise her right to vote.[11]

In August 1962, civil rights activists such as the youthful Reverend James Bevel from SCLC, a native Mississippian, and James Forman from SNCC, organized a mass meeting at the local church to persuade blacks to register to vote in Ruleville, Mississippi. That was Mrs. Hamer's first mass meeting. The content and delivery of the speeches stirred something deep within her. At the conclusion of the meeting, she and seventeen others immediately signed a list promising to register as voters at the Indianola courthouse on the following Friday.[12] Subsequently, she emerged as the group's leader.

At four-thirty, on August 31, 1962, the eighteen boarded a black-owned bus used to transport local cotton field hands. When they arrived at the Indianola courthouse, police and other curious whites wandered around the bus, casting a hostile eye upon its occupants as they descended.

Inside, the clerk growled, "What do you nigras want?" Mrs. Hamer replied they were there to try to register to vote. The clerk instructed them to go outside and to return two at a time. The registration form requested applicant's place of employment and residence, which were later given to the hostile white Citizens Council. In addition, the applicants were asked to read and interpret sections of the Mississippi State Constitution; it took the entire day for the eighteen to finish the test. White men in boots carrying rifles sauntered in and out of the courthouse saying nothing but casting ominous glances at the black (would-be) registrants.[13] Without learning whether they had passed the test, the group left.

At four-thirty in the afternoon, after a long, frustrating, nerve-racking day, the group reboarded their bus for Ruleville. A few miles outside Indianola they were stopped by police and ordered to unload. Afterwards, they were instructed to reboard the bus and return to Indianola where the driver was fined one hundred dollars for driving a bus of the *wrong color*. The judge later agreed to accept a thirty-dollar fine, which was hastily collected from the group, who were anxious to return home.[14]

At home, Mrs. Hamer's daughter rushed out to meet her and to tell her that her boss, W. D. Marlow III, for whom she had worked eighteen years, "was beside himself with rage" because she registered to vote. Perry Hamer, her husband, confirmed the story before the landowner himself confronted her with, "We're not ready for that in Mississippi now. You'll have to go back there and withdraw that thing, Fannie, or you'll have to leave." Unhesitatingly Mrs. Hamer replied, "I didn't go down there to register for you, I went there to register for myself."

Commenting on the incident Mrs. Hamer said, "You know that was what really did it for me. I just thought to myself, 'What does he really care about us?' I had been workin' there for eighteen years. I had baked cakes and sent them overseas to him during the war. I had nursed his family, cleaned his house, stayed with his kids. I handled his time book and his payroll. Yet he wanted me out. I made up my mind I was grown, and I was tired . . . . I had no choice."[15]

That night Mrs. Hamer left her home, her husband, and children, to stay in Ruleville with friends, the William Tuckers. Ten days later sixteen bullets were fired into the Tucker home, and two local black girls too young to vote were shot by snipers.[16] The next week Perry Hamer took his wife to the home of a niece in a neighboring county.

Undaunted by economic harassment, the Hamers decided three months later to return to Ruleville and become registered voters. Although Marlow refused to pay her daughters for working, fired her husband, and took their automobile, claiming the Hamers owed three hundred dollars on the vehicle, the Hamers established their own home in Ruleville where they were continuously threatened by local officials. One night upon answering a knock at the door, they discovered an infamous local policeman, brother of one of the men involved in the brutal murder of the fifteen-year-old Emmett Till several years earlier. After threatening the Hamers with bodily harm, the man left.[17]

More determined than ever to become a registered voter, Mrs. Hamer returned to the courthouse to take the literacy test. "You'll see me every thirty days 'till I pass," she told the registrar. On her third try, on January 10, 1963, she passed and became a registered voter, one of the first of the county's approximately 30,000 blacks. "But I still wasn't allowed to vote that fall . . . because I didn't have two poll tax receipts." Some were not so fortunate and had to take the test twenty-six times, but they kept going back.[18]

From then on, racial tension and harassment escalated. Her husband and her daughter were arrested, she was harrassed by such things as a $9,000 water bill (her house didn't even have running water), and their church had to be closed because the fire insurance was cancelled and the members were intimidated. One morning before daylight two policemen walked into the Hamers' bedroom with drawn guns and flashlights on the pretense of making a search—without a warrant: "on top of all the harassment we didn't have work. People brought us food, and we were finally able to get commodities from the welfare office . . . . Various people and programs met our every day bills. And SNCC helped a lot—they were the only civil-rights organization that was really interested in doin' somethin' about conditions in the Delta. They started the grass roots movement in Mississippi—people like Bob Moses, Jim Forman, John Lewis. I tried to help them, and the other groups too—SCLC, CORE, and NAACP—and when COFO (the Council of Federated Organizations) was formed, I was a part of it."[19] During those days violence and sudden death lurked behind every bush and around every corner for Fannie Lou Hamer. She had a close call on September 10, 1962, in the form of a quick burst of gunfire from a speeding car, but she escaped. Experience taught her to be careful about burning lights in her modest, frame home; not to stand in windows, nor to open her door to strangers who called at night.[20]

By January 1963 Fannie had become an activist in the civil rights movement. She gathered names for a petition to obtain federal commodities for needy black families and attended various SCLC workshops. She was also elected field secretary for SNCC, and as such, she worked on the voter registration campaign and helped formulate welfare programs. In the spring of 1963 Mrs. Hamer got a job at a Ruleville cotton gin, but in 1964 they did not reemploy her.[21]

By 1963 violence ran rampant throughout Mississippi, and Fannie Lou Hamer became the target of white fury. In June, she joined a group of civil rights workers who traveled to South Carolina to attend a voter registration and training workshop. Upon their return to Mississippi, the violence Mrs. Hamer had anticipated since registering as a voter burst forth in full fury. She was jailed, beaten, kicked. She recalled: "I was nearly out of my mind. In all this my dress had worked up, and I tried to pull it down, and one of them white men—there was five of them in there—he took and pulled it up to my head. They just kept on beatin' me and tellin' me 'You nigger bitch, we gonna make you wish you was dead.' There ain't nothin' like the kind of misery I was goin' through. When they finally quit, they told me to go to my cell, but I couldn't get up, I couldn't bend my knees."[22]

Mrs. Hamer and her coworkers were jailed for three days and charged with disorderly conduct and resisting arrest. When James Bevel and Andrew Young (later U.S. Congressman from Georgia, U.S. ambassador to the U.N., and presently mayor of Atlanta) finally managed to get them released, they had not received any medical treatment. "My body was as hard as this chair. . . . They took us to Greenwood to see a doctor, and then to Atlanta. I wouldn't let my husband see me for a month, I was in such bad shape. Every day of my life I pay with the misery of that beatin'. It was while we was in that jail that Medgar Evers was killed, and one night they offered to let us go, just so they could kill us and say we was tryin' to escape! I told 'em they'd have to kill me in my cell."[23]

But the prospect of death did not frighten Fannie Lou Hamer or lessen her determination to involve black Mississippians in the political processes of the state. She tried unsuccessfully to work with the regular Mississippi Democratic Party on the precinct level but had no luck. Her husband, hired on a new job one day, was fired the following day.[24]

Consequently, she abandoned the idea of working within the tight, traditional political machine in Mississippi and decided along with her fellow cohorts to establish another political party, which they called the Mississippi Freedom Democratic Party (MFDP). The MFDP opened its membership to black and white voters in the state. On the local and state levels, the party affiliates consisted of tenant farmers, laborers, small landowners, clergymen, and other professionals.[25]

The goal of the MFDP was to challenge at the National Convention the legitimacy of the regular Mississippi Democratic party as unrepresentative of the majority of Democratic voters in the state. Therefore, at the state convention in Jackson the newly formed MFDP, well organized and administered, succeeded in getting monetary support and delegates to attend the national Democratic party convention, which convened in August 1964 in Atlantic City, New Jersey. The delegates chose Ed King, a white native Mississippian who was Chaplain at Tougaloo College in North Jackson as chairman of the delegation and selected Fannie Lou Hamer as vice-chairman.[26]

When the MFDP delegation arrived in Atlantic City, they had no illusion concerning their political fate. Without success, the group attempted to unseat the regular Mississippi Democrats. Instead, a compromise was offered. The agreement stipulated that the Regular Democrats would be seated along with two members of the MFDP. Promptly, the MFDP rejected the compromise, and hope of replacing the Regulars withered and died on the convention floor.[27]

Nevertheless, at the Democratic National Convention in front of television cameras, Fannie Lou Hamer told of her horrendous experiences in Mississippi. She also informed the FBI and the Justice Department of the white lawmen who had violated her civil rights. Eventually, the guilty parties were brought to trial in federal court, but an all-white jury found them not guilty. Commenting after the verdict, Mrs. Hamer said, "I used to think the Justice Department was just what it said, justice. I asked one of those men, 'Have y'all got a Justice Department or an Injustice Department?' . . . They didn't investigate what happened to us—they investigated us."

Still determined to obtain equal and fair representation in Mississippi, the MFDP delegation journeyed to Washington, D.C., in January 1965 to challenge the seating of five of Mississippi's United States Congressmen. They failed. However, Fannie Lou Hamer and her colleagues persisted and went onto the floor of the House of Representatives where they aroused Congressional sentiment. Responding to questions with adroitness, Hamer lamented, "You see, this ain't just Mississippi's problem. It's America's problem."[29] Her eloquent appeal moved the House to commence an eight-month investigation that ended on September 17, 1965.

In 1964 Mrs. Hamer announced her candidacy for Congress against white incumbent Jamie Whitten. Local whites laughed and called her "that crazy nigger from across the tracks." Although blacks comprised fifty-nine per cent of the 300,000 persons in the Second District from which she sought election, only 6,616 blacks were registered. Rigid discrimination, Ku Klux Klan terror tactics, and fear of economic reprisals kept most blacks from the polls."[30] Hamer lost the election, but "she demonstrated such overdedication to the cause of civil rights, such tremendous courage and nerve, that tolerance for 'that crazy nigger' vanished in sudden realization that she was a threat to white supremacy, and amusement was replaced by a fierce hatred."[31]

Because of her involvement in the struggle for human rights, the governments in Nigeria, Ghana, Guinea, and other West African countries extended her an invitation as guest of their nations. She recalled caustically that she and her delegation were more cordially received by African heads of state than they had been in Washington in 1963 when they were denied the right to state their case against the lily-white representatives from Mississippi. The delegation had been in Guinea for less than twelve hours when the president, Sekou Toure, called upon them. "With her typical and practical candor she notes the irony of having to go thousands of miles to a so-called land of 'savage heathens' to be personally greeted and made welcome by the head of a foreign nation."[32]

The highlight of her life occurred at the 1969 commencement services at Atlanta's Morehouse College, alma mater of Dr. Martin Luther King, Jr. She cherished the most dramatic moments of the day when the speaker's voice, carrying clearly over the public address system, pronounced:

> Fannie Lou Hamer, you have little formal education and your speech is full of errors of grammar and diction; but you tell your story with a passionate power that is intensified by pain, and you are a natural leader with the capacity to guide and inspire your fellow sufferers. You also have the ability to awaken in your oppressed countrymen your own unquenchable yearning for freedom and equality. We pay tribute to you for your noble example of black womanhood, for your strong defense of human dignity, and for your fearless promotion of civil rights in your native state of Mississippi.[33]

Indeed, Fannie Lou Hamer had done more than talk. She devised a practical plan for feeding with dignity Sunflower County's poor blacks and whites through "Freedom Farm" Co-ops. The Freedom Farm plan called for the acquisition of forty acres of black Delta land and sixty-eight houses, parceled plots for occupants so they could produce their own cotton and canned vegetables and raise hogs and cattle. The first goal was to feed themselves and then to sell surplus goods. Many individuals and organizations assisted Hamer in establishing this project. Her initial goal was three thousand members, each paying three dollars a year.[34]

Until her death of cancer in 1979, Fannie Lou Hamer traveled and lectured across the nation, preaching her unique gospel of freedom and human dignity. She proudly boasted that she had never thought of leaving the South: "I was born here. I watched my folks chop down trees, . . . clean up this land. . . . People who tell me to go back to Africa, I got an answer for them. I say when all the Italians go back to Italy, and all the Germans go back to Germany, and all the Frenchmen go back to France . . . and when they give the Indians their land back and they get the Mayflower and go back to where they came from, then I'll go home too."[35]

William Faulkner, another Mississippian, must have had people like Fannie Lou Hamer in mind when he wrote "The Bear." In this story one character describes the interrelationship between blacks and the South: "two threads frail as truth and impalpable as equators yet cable strong to bind for life them who made the cotton to the land their sweat fell on." But another character responds, "Yes. Binding them for awhile yet, a little while yet. Through and beyond that life and maybe through and beyond that of the sons of those sons. But not always, because they will endure."[36]

It is through such souls as Fannie Lou Hamer that American blacks, the poor whites and blacks of the South, and indeed people throughout the world, will endure and overcome.

Clyde Kennard

Quest for Knowledge at USM

A small farm on highway 59 north in Hattiesburg, Mississippi, was the birth site of Clyde Kennard, the youngest child of Leona Smith and Will Kennard. On July 12, 1927, Clyde became the sixth child and fourth son of the Kennard's. Short in stature (approximately five feet and six inches tall), very thin, dark complexioned, and soft spoken, Clyde was always willing to share, to give, and to help at home. During his early childhood, he was sickly and could not do many farm chores. Frequently, his brothers Lawrence, Albert, and Melvin, or his sisters Dorothy and Sarah would help him pick cotton or other farm produce.[1]

Although physically weak, Clyde had a thirst for knowledge and a burning desire to help others. He completed his elementary training at Bay Springs Elementary School (today known as North Forrest). When his sister Sarah became bed-ridden in 1944 after an accident, his mother sent him to Chicago to help her, and he graduated in 1945 from Wendell Phillip High School in Chicago.

One year after graduation, in 1946, Clyde Kennard enlisted in the United States Air Force, where he remained for four years. Before being honorably discharged, he was promoted to the rank of sergeant. Since the Armed Forces offered educational benefits to veterans, he decided to further his education.

In the early 1950s, he enrolled at Chicago University and remained there until his stepfather, Silas Smith, died; then, he returned to Hattiesburg, Mississippi, to help his mother. His father had died during his childhood.

After returning to Hattiesburg, he decided to continue his education at home by applying in 1956 to Mississippi Southern College (now the University of Southern Mississippi), an all-white institution. Since there was not a black institution of higher learning near his home and since he needed to assist his mother with the family farm, he did not apply to a black college.

As a member of the Forrest County chapter of the NAACP, he discussed his plans to attend Mississippi Southern College with the membership. At that time he was encouraged to apply for admission to the college by the local president, J. C. Fairley and Joseph Otis, a member of the organization. The Admission Office denied him admittance initially because his transcript from Chicago University had not arrived. Later the transcript was received, and the groundwork for his admission laid.

Before attempting to register at the University, Kennard publicly announced his intentions, and the municipal police awaited his arrival at the university. On the date of registration, Kennard was denied admission and then arrested on a bogus charge of speeding and possession of liquor. At that time, liquor was illegal in Mississippi. Later, the Mississippi Supreme Court dismissed the charges. This, however, did not end Kennard's altercations with the local police. On November 14, 1960, the police arrested Kennard "on a charge of inducing a nineteen year old Negro to steal five bags of chicken feed (worth $25), and sentenced him to seven years in jail."[2] Attorneys for the NAACP Legal Defense Fund unsuccessfully tried to free him from the charges.

Medgar Evers, state field director of Mississippi NAACP, solicited the aid of black comedian Dick Gregory in the case. At his own expense, Gregory sent private investigators to Mississippi to determine the innocence of Kennard. Investigative reporting exonerated Kennard and implicated a black youth, who refused to testify for fear of retaliation against his family. Kennard was found guilty as charged by an all white jury and sentenced to seven years at the state penitentiary at Parchman.[3]

During Kennard's brief stay at Parchman, he described segregated life at the prison: "They had fifteen farms at Parchman and no Negro non-inmate employees. We were like slaves. They even fed us leftovers from what the white prisoners ate. The white prisoners had the best jobs, lived in the best buildings. Parchman is just a modernized slave-labor camp."[4]

Because black inmates were close and they were convinced of his innocence, many sympathized with Kennard. He was sustained by the support received from fellow inmates his last night at the penitentiary before his hospitalization for intestinal cancer: "The night I left to come to the hospital, they held a prayer meeting in our barracks. I told them not to do it because it's against the rules and I didn't want them to get whipped because of me. But they sang and sang, and the guards took names and names. In Mississippi in prisons, it's legal to whip prisoners—the law says ten strokes. We called the whip 'black Annie.' I know they were whipped the next day."[5]

Because of his rapidly deteriorating condition, Governor Ross Barnett pardoned him in 1962 at the behest of Robert and John F. Kennedy. At the time of his release from the University Hospital in Jackson, Kennard weighed ninety pounds. Ironically, Kennard spent most of his incarceration at the University Hospital, where he was confined to the "Negro side" of the Jim Crow hospital.[6]

Upon his release from the hospital, Clyde Kennard returned to Chicago to live with his sister Sarah Webb, a nurse. He remained in Chicago until his death July 4, 1962. While he was there Dick Gregory and Sarah paid for his medical treatment.

Clyde Kennard had a tremendous impact upon the lives of many. As a member of Mary Magdalene Baptist Church in Hattiesburg, he started the first Bible class for young people and was also a Sunday School teacher. For those blacks who finally penetrated the racial barriers at the University of Southern Mississippi, Clyde Kennard had weakened the "Colored line" and sacrificed himself.

James H. Meredith

Man with a Mission

"Cap" Meredith, the son of a slave, resented white southern economic domination over blacks. He refused to cooperate with white neighbors who offered to share the cost and maintenance of boundary line fences. Instead, he insisted on moving his fences two feet from the actual line in order to retain control of his property. No white man, he contended, would ever have an excuse to invade the privacy of his eighty-four-acre cotton and corn farm near Kosciusko in the rocky bottom land of Attala County in north-central Mississippi.[1]

James Howard Meredith, the seventh of thirteen children and the first of seven by "Cap's" second wife Roxie, was born on June 25, 1933. Like many of his compatriots, Meredith was baptized "J. H." (initials only), but upon entering the Air Force he enrolled as James Howard. The Meredith's family life was austere. There was no running water in their house, and the open cracks in the exterior provided year 'round "air conditioning." Even though the family slept on beds obtained forty-odd years previously when "Cap" was a sharecropper, Meredith says "that home possessed both pride and order."[2]

His father's concept of independence dominated Meredith's youth to the extent that when he left Mississippi at sixteen years of age, Meredith had never visited a white person's home. "I was taught," he asserted, "to believe the most dishonorable thing a Meredith could do was to work in a white woman's kitchen and take care of a white man's child. I knew that I would starve to death rather than do either."[3] Because of "Cap's" unwillingness to submit to the indignities of white supremacy, Meredith grew up in isolation. If by chance he played with the white neighboring children, they approached him. When he went to Kosciusko, he disregarded the white stores and movies because they were part of another world.

James, a brilliant child with an I.Q. of 141, was one of the brightest pupils in his school. Daily (for eleven years) he walked eight miles round trip to school. And everyday while he walked, a school bus passed him carrying white children to school. Gradually he realized that his world was economically deprived and isolated and that the white world remained "separate and unequal."[4]

At school James devoted his energy to his studies. He was small of stature, approximately four feet and eleven inches, and he weighed ninety-eight pounds; therefore, he shunned athletics. In 1951 when he joined the Air Force he was only fifteen pounds heavier. Nevertheless, after school he performed the regular farm chores—milking cows, feeding hogs, watering the mules, plowing the fields, chopping cotton, pulling corn, and cutting hay. He learned to hunt and fish. At twelve he could strike a match with a .22 calibre rifle. When not engaged in outside activities, he read. He walked four miles to Boy Scout meetings and was a 4-H clubber.

At fifteen, black identity and awareness became apparent, especially in Mississippi. His first encounter with overt discrimination occurred when he returned from Detroit to Mississippi via Memphis. At Memphis the white conductor "rounded up the Negroes and ordered them to a Jim Crow car." Meredith painfully recalled the incident: "It hurt me so much, I began to cry...." I've been crying a little ever since."[5]

As a result of racial discrimination, Meredith resolved to oppose, to fight, and to destroy white domination. In the words of a close friend, he wanted to break "the system that had oppressed him. He was bitter, a real crusader (who) wanted to get back at society. He resolved to fight the battle at all times—on all fronts, in everything he did."[6]

He perceived education as the key to destroying white domination. He fully realized that he had to raise his scholastic record and academic goal in order to compete on equal basis with Mississippi whites. Inasmuch as the level of education he sought was unavailable for blacks in Kosciusko, Meredith went to live with an aunt in St. Petersburg, Florida, where he graduated from Gibbs High School in June 1951.

With an overwhelming desire to attend college but without financial assistance, he enlisted in the United States Air Force. On July 28, 1951, while in the service Meredith quickly gained a reputation for "nursing the dollar." Because he excelled so rapidly, Meredith was promoted to sergeant at the age of nineteen. Within a few years he was earning $180 a month as a sergeant and had banked thousands of dollars. "I knew what I wanted to do when I got out, so I saved," stated Meredith.[7]

In the Air Force, he received numerous medals and awards, including the National Service Award, the Good Conduct Medal, and three Oak Leaf Clusters. Meredith took a series of college extension courses at the University of Kansas and at Washburn University in Topeka, and attended night school at New Mexico Western College. From 1954 to 1960 he enrolled in the United States Armed Forces Institute, spending half the time stateside and the remainder in Japan where he attended the Far Eastern Division of the University of Maryland.

Life in Japan was a delightfully new experience, affording him for the first time "that air of difference about being a Negro that you can never quite touch": he was not confronted with American racism. He shared that experience with his wife, the former Mary June Wiggins of Gary, Indiana, whom he married in 1956. Meredith completed the Officers Candidate Course with honors. During his Japanese tour of duty Meredith also participated in basketball, bowling, golf, and pool.

Toward the end of his military career in the early 1960s Meredith received from his father a one-page letter stating that he was about to die and had built a home in Kosciusko for his wife. He now offered the home to James. To James there was only one answer: "No white man would ever be allowed to buy that piece of land." James purchased the property from his seventy-year old father for $3,000. The money provided some security for the older man during his later years.

After nine years James Meredith was honorably discharged and he drove immediately to Mississippi to engage in a battle against white supremacy. As he stated, "Victory over discrimination, oppression, and unequal applications of the law was my goal." He believed that to accomplish his divine mission meant getting an education. Because blacks were denied admission to the University of Mississippi, Meredith and his wife enrolled at the all-black Jackson State College. While at Jackson State, Meredith was convinced that "only a power struggle between the state and the Federal Government could make it possible . . . to gain admission to the University of Mississippi."[8]

According to Meredith, the decision to apply for admission to the University of Mississippi was an economic one. "When I investigated all areas of business possibilities," he said,

> I learned that there were limitations inherent in the system of white supremacy that would always keep the Negro from going beyond a certain arbitrary level in the economic structure that paralleled the system. Before I could engage in business at the level I desired, the system would have to be broken. Within the limits allotted to the Negro I had no bounds save my own personal capacity, and theoretically I was convinced that a capable and aggressive Negro could rise to the top—as far as a Negro could go in a very short period of time.[9]

Meredith seemed to have had a deft sense of timing. John F. Kennedy narrowly won the presidency against Richard Nixon, his victory generally believed the result of the Negro vote. Meredith believed that President Kennedy would support him in the fulfillment of his mission. On January 21, the day after Kennedy's inauguration, Meredith wrote the university asking for an application for admission.

Five days later, Registrar Robert B. Ellis cheerfully replied, "We are very pleased to know your interest. . . . if we can be of further help to you in making your enrollment plans, please let us know." He sent forms and requested Meredith to enclose six character references from university alumni with the application. Since Ole Miss was "lily-white," Meredith was not personally acquainted with any alumni. But he submitted certificates from six responsible Mississippi Negroes with his application to Ellis on January 31, and the following note, "I am very pleased with your letter that accompanied the application forms. I sincerely hope . . . it (Ellis's) interest) will not change upon learning that I am not a white applicant. I am an American-Mississippi-Negro citizen." He attached a picture of himself to the top of the application. On February 4, 1961, two days before registration for the next semester, Ellis wired his reply: "For your information and guidance it has been found necessary to discontinue consideration of all applications received after January 25, 1961. Your application was received subsequent to such date and thus we must advise you not to appear for registration."[10]

Previously, Meredith had conferred with Medgar Evers, Mississippi Field Secretary of the NAACP. Meredith asked Evers for the support of the NAACP if circumstances warranted such assistance. With no direct authority, Evers agreed to help. And at Evers's suggestion Meredith wrote to Thurgood Marshall, attorney for the NAACP Legal Defense and Educational Fund.

Because Evers knew that Meredith was impatient, he personally called Marshall. The lawyer asked for additional documents to prove Meredith's "legitimacy," at which Meredith became infuriated and simply placed the telephone on the receiver. He felt that his personal integrity had been questioned and later explained, "As far as I was concerned, the case was closed. Other alternatives would have to be pursued." He would not talk to Marshall again. But he later admitted that had it not been for Evers's "expert knowledge of human nature and his ability to deal with people," the matter would have died immediately.[11]

After Meredith eventually sent the necessary documents, Marshall wrote expressing interest in the matter. Fortunately for Meredith, the case was assigned to Constance Baker Motley, who had engaged in legal battles with Mississippi courts for two and a half years before Meredith was admitted to the University of Mississippi.

Certainly the Meredith case was fraught with danger. The system of white supremacy had been unsuccessfully tested by several blacks, who were labeled troublemakers. Black troublemakers were usually "lynched for having a bad or wrong attitude [rather] than for committing a particular crime." Clennon King, a teacher at Alcorn A & M College, was sent to Whitfield's mental institution in 1958 after attempting to enroll during the summer session at the University of Mississippi. His incarceration led to the declaration that "Any nigger who tries to enter Ole Miss must be crazy! Clyde Kennard had attempted to transfer from the University of Chicago to Mississippi Southern near his home in Hattiesburg. He was arrested. On another occasion, he was charged with wreckless driving and illegal possession of whiskey. Finally, he was arrested for stealing chicken feed and sentenced to seven years in the penitentiary.[12]

When it became known that Meredith had similar ambitions, the police of Kosciusko combed the black neighborhood for information about James and his family. The principal of the black high school was called upon to use his personal influence to force Meredith to withdraw his application or face the consequences. His mother courageously replied, "If someone has to die, who is my child more than anyone else's child to die?"[13] At school peer pressure was applied. Friends offered protection as armed body guards, but Meredith refused.

Calculated delays were utilized by the university to discourage Meredith, but they only strengthened his resolve. Letters of application were refused and resubmitted. Attorney Constance Motley drafted a letter which Meredith signed and mailed to Dean Arthur B. Lewis of the college of liberal arts wherein he accused the registrar of racial discrimination. After letter diplomacy failed, Meredith filed a federal suit against the top university officials and the board of trustees for denial of admission.[14]

A series of court delays and appeals followed. A court decision rendered on June 25, 1962—Meredith's twenty-ninth birthday—offered the first real encouragement in more than sixteen months of litigation. The court declared that Ole Miss officials had "engaged in a carefully calculated campaign of delay, harassment, and masterly inactivity, once they discovered Meredith was a Negro." The jurists eliminated each unfair or unjustified admission requirement: the requirement of alumni letters, the policy not to accept transfer students from Jackson State (an accredited institution), and the charge that Meredith was a troublemaker. Summation of 1,350 pages of testimony revealed that "James H. Meredith's application for transfer to the University of Mississippi was turned down solely because he was a Negro."[15]

But more legal maneuvers continued until Motley requested a decision by the U.S. Supreme Court. U.S. Supreme Court Justice Hugo Black, who was assigned to the Fifth Circuit Judicial District during the recess of the Appeals Court, reviewed the facts and ordered the mandate of the Court of Appeals obeyed. Jubilantly, Constance Baker Motley cried, "This is the end of the road for the university."[16]

However, Governor Ross Barnett vowed that he would go to jail rather than submit to the "unlawful dictates of the federal government."[17] After Justice Black's ruling and Judge Sidney Mize's injunction against the university, Meredith sent a telegram to Registrar Ellis stating that he would be arriving on campus. The day of Judge Mize's injunction, Governor Barnett issued a proclamation of defiance, stating that Mississippi would hereafter operate its own schools regardless of what the federal judiciary said about Meredith. His action resulted in a direct confrontation between the governments in Washington and Jackson. Mississippi's Attorney General Joe Patterson scoffed, "It is a sad commentary when the U.S. Attorney General permits his office to become general counsel for the NAACP, Martin Luther King, and other racial agitators and troublemakers."[18]

To enforce the court's decision, federal marshals mobilized in Jackson and Memphis. U.S. Marshals escorted Meredith to the university campus in September 1962, where Governor Barnett stood at the admissions office door to prevent Meredith's entrance. Previously, the university trustees voted to make Barnett registrar so he could deal personally with the matter. The campus was a seething cauldron of conflict. As Meredith stepped from his car, students yelled, "Two, four, six, eight—we don't want to integrate!" And, "Go home, nigger!" In the midst of it all Meredith smiled grimly then entered the Center for Continuation Studies where the registration was supposed to take place. Barnett stymied Meredith and the marshals. As they left the building two thousand students jostled the state troopers, shouting boos and curses.[19]

Another volley of court orders ensued, and another confrontation resulted in Meredith's being kept out of Ole Miss. After three aborted attempts President Kennedy, who had remained aloof, decided to place the full prestige of his office on the line. He personally contacted Ross Barnett in an effort to avoid confrontation. Barnett refused to compromise. Therefore, President Kennedy issued an executive order on Sunday, September 30, directing the Secretary of Defense to take all appropriate steps to enforce the orders of the Fifth

Circuit Court and ordered the Mississippi units of the National Guard into active military service.

At 4:30 p.m., Sunday, September 30, 1962, a convoy of five army trucks arrived at the university's Lyceum Building, carrying a contingent that included Nicholas Katzenback and John Doar of the Justice Department, a group of U.S. Marshals, and James Meredith. University officials ruled that Sunday registration was illegal. Subsequently, Meredith and company were lodged at Baxter Hall.[20]

As darkness descended, the mushrooming crowd of students and anti-black agitators increased, and threatening jeers, Rebel yells, and an occasional gun shot pierced the air. Violence erupted. By 7:45 in the evening, the situation was clearly out of control, and soon James McShane, chief U.S. Marshall, gave the order to use tear gas. He had no other choice.[21]

At ten o'clock President Kennedy appeared on television. He admonished, "If this country should ever reach the point where any man or group of men by force or threat of force could long defy the command of our court and our Constitution, then no law would stand free from doubt, no judge would be sure of his court, and no citizen would be safe from his neighbor."[22]

Nevertheless, the riot raged on unabated. As Monday morning dawned, two persons had been killed, 175 injured, and 212 arrested. According to the *Jackson Clarion Ledger* twenty years later, "It was the *longest night* in U.S. history. And the *darkest*." That Monday morning James Meredith officially registered at the University of Mississippi. He was the first black ever to do so.

A calm and smiling Meredith attended classes on the 114-year-old Ole Miss campus. Referring to students who hurled stones and yelled such insults as "nigger, nigger, nigger, your wife's a black widow," and "go back to Africa," Meredith later admitted that what antagonized him most was hearing someone call him a nigger. He recalled, 'It was the first time in my life, I ever heard a white man call me a nigger in Mississippi.' "[24]

When asked how he felt about Mississippi as he approached the university for the first time, he replied, "As we drove out of Memphis along the highway past the Welcome-to-Mississippi sign, I felt like I always feel when I enter Mississippi. . . . I think it the most beautiful land in the country and whenever I cross the state line, I always look at the soil and think what that state would be like . . . if it had a different way of life."[25]

Significantly, for James Meredith and other black Mississipians, the impenetrable wall of racial segregation and white supremacy was crumbling. According to Meredith, "The barrier of white supremacy has at least been breached. Even if I only had a toe hold in the door, the solid wall has been cracked."[26] Certainly he had stood the test of time and endured abuse. No longer was he troubled by the thought that the system might break him before he blasted the system. Karl Fleming of *Newsweek* reported, "Meredith is so intent on righting wrongs he doesn't care whose head rolls, even among his own people. He is completely dedicated; when he makes up his mind a thing should be done, he does it with a sense of firmness that surprises most people . . . Meredith himself was heard to say, 'Everything that I do, I do because I must; and everything that I must do, I do.' "[27]

In 1962 many of the white religious leaders had denounced racism at the university, Governor Barnett's stance on the admission of Meredith, and racial injustice in Mississippi.[28] But the abuses, the continuous insults, the daily harassments took their toll. Occasionally there were friendly words from a fellow-student or a faculty member, and letters of congratulation from whites and blacks, but the psychological strain unquestionably left its scars. The violent threatening atmosphere was not conducive to studying. Inwardly, Meredith felt doubt and fear. Rumors circulated that Meredith might withdraw from the university. Jack Greenberg, of the NAACP Legal Defense Fund, flew down to counsel with him against such action. A former Jackson College schoolmate from Radcliff-Harvard advisingly wrote, "At this point, I believe, the most important thing to do is to stay at Ole Miss. . . . If you leave now, the students and other Mississippians will think they have won. . . . This must not happen. . . . The nation has the image of a very determined, hard fighting young man aiming at a goal that only he can reach. . . ."[29]

Meredith announced that he would reveal his decision at a press conference in the Jackson offices of the NAACP on January 30. Almost one thousand persons gathered, eagerly awaiting his decision.

At the appointed time, unfolding his message, Meredith read into a forest of microphones: "After listening to all arguments, evaluations, and positions and weighing all this against my personal possibilities and circumstances, I have concluded that the 'Negro' should not return to the University of Mississippi. The prospects for him are too unpromising." Meredith paused and looked out on the crowd. His close friends and supporters gasped, the wire-service reporters ran madly to the telephone, a white Jackson radio station reporter even applauded. After a moment Meredith continued, "However, I have decided that I, J. H. Meredith (using his original name of initials only) will register the second semester at the University of Mississippi." The pyrotechnics caused pandemonium, spectators cheered, reporters hurried back into the room, confusion was obvious, but beneath it all was a heartening note for every man, woman, and child who sees America as "the land of the free and the home of the brave."[30]

In mid-summer the *Saturday Review* expressed what became an increasingly prevalent view:

> There is no dramatic sprint and slambang in Meredith's sort of heroism. He is more nearly the marathoner, a man plodding step by step, pacing himself, not looking to right or left, but just managing to get one foot in front of the other over the long course, and to conserve his energies by keeping the most austere and sustained watch on himself on his every gesture.... How does a man manage to keep himself so rigidly on guard and still listen to lectures, read his lessons, prepare his papers, eat, sleep, breathe, be lonely for his wife, and carry all the irrational powers and persuasions any psyche moves to? How does he keep from punching a wall, or throwing a book through the window, or just standing up in his room alone and howling? Only a terrifying dedication can sustain the man.[31]

On August 18, 1963, after the presence of a federal force that once totaled more than 23,000, a maintenance cost in excess of five million, and numerous incidents of man's inhumanity, James Howard Meredith became the first black to graduate from the University of Mississippi, with a major in government and politics and minors in history and French. In the audience sat his seventy-two-year-old father, "Cap" Meredith, holding his three-year-old grandson on his knee. On the old man's face was a look of deep satisfaction that he had lived to see a day he had hoped for but scarcely believed he would witness. As one writer described the occasion, "As he gazed about, he experienced something he had never known before. White Mississippians actually looking at him without the transparent contempt that he had always seen in their eyes. The fact that his son was graduating with their sons and daughters had given a new meaning to his presence."[32]

James Meredith did graduate studies in economics at Ibadan University in Nigeria and graduated from Columbia University Law School in 1968 with a doctor of law degree, with specialties in corporate, taxation, and international law. After law school he studied finance on Wall Street and completed the Merrill Lynch, Pierce, Fenner & Smith Financial Training School in 1969.[33]

In 1966 Meredith interrupted his law studies to participate in a voter registration march scheduled from Memphis to Jackson. Just inside the Mississippi border he was felled, though not fatally, by three blasts of birdshot from a shotgun. National civil rights leaders rushed to Mississippi to continue the march. Two years later, some of those same leaders chastised Meredith when he announced plans to run for the Congressional seat held by Adam Clayton Powell.[34]

In May 1971 James H. Meredith returned to Mississippi where he maintains an interest in politics. However, he points out that business controls politics, so his goal now is to get control over business.

Twenty years later, in assessing his role in starting the second Civil War, a battle to eradicate racism in its most blatant form in Mississippi, James Meredith contends that in 1962, "the system was separate but equal. Today it is integrated but unequal." He opted that things have regressed and he preferred segregation. He reluctantly accepted an invitation to participate in a program highlighting the racial progress made at Ole Miss since 1962 because he claimed, "there has been little."[35]

The change Meredith perceived consisted of limited black enrollment, a few black athletes participating in sporting events, one black cheerleader, a black studies program, and a few black professors, yet two of the nine black professors are part-time, and only one has tenure. The faculty totals 550. Black student enrollment makes up approximately eight percent or 680 of the total 8,500. The school flag is the old Confederate one and students still yell the Rebel's chant. And James Meredith wonders, has there really been change?[36]

James Chaney

One of Three Lives for Mississippi

Born May 30, 1941, in Meridian, Mississippi, James Chaney, a high school dropout, perceived his involvement in the civil rights movement as an opportunity to make his life meaningful. Approximately five feet and seven inches tall and weighing 140 pounds, James was one of five children of Fannie Lee Chaney. After his father deserted the family, he engaged in manual labor to help his mother keep bread on the table. Like other Mississippi black youths from broken homes, James was raised in dire poverty; therefore, he eventually dropped out of school to assist the family financially.[1]

In spite of his educational handicaps, James Chaney became a dedicated civil rights activist, who worked diligently with the Congress on Racial Equality (CORE) to improve the political plight of blacks in central and southeastern Mississippi. He encouraged blacks to register and to vote. Operating from the CORE headquarters located in the Meridian Community Center, he assisted Michael and Rita Schwerner and Andrew Goodman, civil rights volunteers, with voter registration drives in the area. Also, he helped Matt Suarez prepare for Freedom Day in Canton, Mississippi, where a mass movement was underway to get blacks registered as voters. After the completion of the Canton project, he channeled his energy into scouting counties near Meridian as possible targets for voter registration drives.[2]

In many instances, fearful blacks turned him away; but undeterred, Chaney persisted in his endeavors. His mother recalled a particular event in Canton. James had returned home and told her, "Mother, one-half of the time I was out behind houses or churches waiting to get the opportunity to talk to people about what they ought to do. Sometimes they shunned me off and would say, 'I want you to stay away from here and leave me alone.' But, he would pick his chance and go back again."[3]

James Chaney's involvement in the civil rights struggle was short lived, however, as he was murdered at the hands of law enforcers and the Ku Klux Klan mob. During the summer project of 1964, which was designed to increase the number of black voters in the state, Cecil Price, the deputy sheriff of Neshoba County and sixteen Klansmen lynched James Chaney, Michael Schwerner, and Andrew Goodman while they were doing civil rights work in Philadephia, Mississippi. The three men had gone to Longdale, a little community near Philadephia to investigate a suspicious church burning the day that they were abducted and slain.[4] For weeks before their bodies were unearthed from a dam in Philadelphia, the three civil rights workers were suspected dead by prominent civil rights leaders in the state.

Today, the church has been rebuilt and a plaque decorates the building as a memorial to the three slain civil rights workers. The inscription on the plaque reads:

Out of One Blood God Hath Made All Men.

This Plaque is dedicated to the memory of Michael Schwerner, James Chaney and Andrew Goodman, whose concern for others, and more particularly those of this community, led to their early martyrdom. Their death quickened men's consciences and more firmly established Justice, Liberty and Brotherhood in our Land.[5]

Southern justice did prevail in the case against the perpetrators of these murders. Although no one expected the Klansmen or the deputy sheriff, Cecil Price to be convicted, the grand jury indicted Sheriff Rainey, Deputy Sheriff Cecil Price, and sixteen others. There were two confessions, according to government reports, but these were not made publicly. Seventeen of the eighteen defendants pleaded "not guilty." Eventually Sheriff Rainey was exonerated. The others were bound over for trial.[6]

The murder trial of the three slain civil rights workers took place in Mississippi in 1967. The jurors found Alton Wayne Roberts, Cecil Price, Horace Doyle Barnett, Jimmy Arledge, Billy Wayne Posey, James Snowden, and Bowers guilty of murder. In the case of Reverend Edgar Ray Killen, Jerry Sharpe, and Travis Barnette, the jurors could not agree on a verdict. The other eight defendants were found not guilty. In December 1967, Judge Cox sentenced Bowers and Roberts to ten years in a federal prison. Deputy Sheriff Cecil Price received six years, and the other four defendants were sentenced to four years. The seven appealed their convictions in the Fifth Circuit Court of Appeal.[7]

Prior to this trial civil rights leaders believed that justice would be thwarted; therefore, the NAACP and the SCLC called for a nationwide boycott of products made in Mississippi. Northern industrialists, however, disrupted the plan by opening thirty-four new plants and expanding existing facilities.[8]

Willie Tatum

Acting-Fire Chief and Civil Rights Activist

A prominent black leader is Willie Tatum, acting Chief of the Palmer's Crossing Volunteer Fire Department in Forrest County. The fire department materialized as a result of a community action lawsuit filed against then-Secretary of Health, Education, and Welfare Joseph Califano and the Forrest County Board of Supervisors. In an out-of-court settlement, Tatum obtained enough revenues to build a fire station, to purchase a fire truck, to obtain paved streets, to secure a sewage system, and to construct a recreational center in Palmer's Crossing. Before the suit, there was no fire station servicing the needs of the people in the area. If a home caught on fire, it could burn before city firemen's arrival. Currently, plans are underway to construct a new fire station near a white private school, Beeson Academy. Tatum, who is somewhat skeptical, commented on the plan: "This will move the power from the black area to the white area. Some blacks have been cooperating with the whites. If they'll cooperate and help, then maybe it's better."[1]

The Perry County native, Willie Tatum, migrated in 1954 to Hattiesburg where he worked until his enlistment in the Army. He served for two years, before returning to Hattiesburg, where in 1965, he was employed by the Dow Chemical Company. Because of racism, Tatum believes, he received a demotion in 1973. Consequently, he filed suit with the Equal Employment Opportunity Commission (EEOC), which conducted a thorough investigation, ruled that the company violated black civil rights, and ordered the company to hire blacks and place them in managerial positions. By filing the suit, Tatum paved the way for economic advancement for blacks. Disaster struck in 1975 and Tatum was injured on the job. Today he is disabled, but carries on the struggle for justice and economic equality.

BUSINESS

Lack of capital, training, and clientele have prevented most black Mississippians from entering the business world. During the antebellum period, slavery inhibited the progress of free-born blacks toward economic independence, and racism spurned the evolution of black economic nationalism and self-help during and after Reconstruction.

Paternalism, which existed between slave and master, evolved into individualism as blacks realized their potential for economic success through racial solidarity and self-help. This economic philosophy was espoused and popularized by Booker T. Wasington, the spokesperson for the black race during the late nineteenth and early twentieth centuries. Southern blacks, especially Mississippians, readily accepted his thesis of vocational and industrial training for the masses as well as his theory that economic independence would lead to political and social equality.

Subsequently, black Mississippians engaged in service trades and businesses that catered to the needs of the black community. Many owned and operated beauty salons, barber-shops, restaurants, laundry and cleaning facilities, hotels, taverns, grocery stores, gambling establishments, funeral parlors, insurance companies, and banks. At one time early in this century Mississippi led the nation in having the highest number of banks owned by blacks.

The advent of World War I, World War II, racial injustice, and legal oppression in Mississippi ignited the mass movement of blacks from the South to the North, where economic opportunities afforded blacks the chance to acquire clerical and managerial skills and jobs. This migration drained the South's economy and the black community's resources; therefore, black capitalism dwindled and many black enterprises folded.

The civil rights movement in the 1960s, however, renewed southern blacks' faith in economic nationalism and racial solidarity and contributed to reverse migration, the return of blacks to the south. This migration pattern was also a direct result of northern race riots, high unemployment, housing shortages, lack of recreational facilities, an accelerated crime wave, and southern industrial growth.

Suddenly, the South became the land of political and economic opportunities. Federal assistance programs provided jobs and loans for small black business ventures. Land was cheap. Education had improved. In Mississippi, there emerged a small black professional class consisting of lawyers, doctors, teachers, preachers, and entrepreneurs, who epitomized W.E.B. DuBois's "Talented Tenth"—the missionaries of culture, the merchants of intellectualism, and the mechanics of politics.

William T. Johnson
Natchez Barber-Builder-Diarist

William Johnson, one of America's most remarkable diarist, offered the first known chronological journals kept by a free black person in the antebellum South. His diary reveals much about life in Natchez, a major southern town with a sizeable free black population. The diary also illustrates the extraordinary rise of a black man from bondage to freedom, his success in business, and the respect that he received in his community, and it sheds light on black-white relationships in the South.[1] This essential primary source gives a firsthand account of "a free black man's life, and sets forth another clue in the mystery of what free blacks did in the antebellum South."[2] Author-journalist Hodding Carter, Jr., of the *Delta Democrat Times* concluded that this is the most unusual personal record ever kept in the United States: "not only does the diary depict the more provincial happenings, it also pictures his thoughts and opinions on state and even national and international affairs."[3]

William Johnson was born a slave in 1809 within the Natchez vicinity. His parentage consisted of a black slave mother and white slave master, William Johnson of Adams County. References in his diary and cash books identified a "Capt." or "Cap" Johnson as "Old Dad." A brief notation cited in his cashbook on February 1831 stated: "To a Debt of Father's $7.00" Although this in no way identifies the father, it does indicate something of the character of the son.

Apparently William Johnson, the slave, acquired the name of his master and father. Yet, on several occasions he inserted the middle initial "T". His marriage license was issued to "William T. Johnson." At least one document existed where he signed his signature as William Tyler Johnson.

The emancipation of William Johnson's family commenced when he was age five. His master legally freed Johnson's mother, Amy, in 1814, and promised to support the former slave should she ever need help because of sickness, insanity, or old age. Four years later (1818) an authorized agent of William Johnson carried Amy's daughter, "a mulatto girl named Delia aged about thirteen years," to Philadelphia, with the written authority for her liberation in Pennsylvania and her return to Natchez. Two years later the slave holder, William Johnson, addressed an eloquent petition to the Mississippi General Assembly in session at Natchez requesting the emancipation of Amy's son, William. He certified that William

> was a resident of Mississippi and had no debts that would render the act of emancipation unjust . . . that disposition of his property most agreeable to his feelings and (consonant) to humanity, he claimed, and would give the liberty to a human being which all are entitled to as a Birthright and extend the hand of humanity to a rational Creature, on whom unfortunately complexion, Custom and even Law in This Land of freedom, has conspired to rivet the fetters of slavery.

In 1820, the Mississippi legislature freed William, who became a barber. Upon the emancipation, James Miller, a twenty year old free black from Philadelphia, who married William's fifteen year old sister Adelia, invited Johnson to assist him in his barber shop. Miller's shop was the most patronized in Natchez. He taught young William the tonsorial arts and ethical principles which became a lasting part of his character.

At age 19, William Johnson embarked upon his first independent venture as a businessman when he acquired a barber shop in 1828 at Port Gibson, a town approximately fifty miles north of Natchez. He operated the Port Gibson shop for nearly two years. In 1830, he summarized the profitability and extent of his Port Gibson enterprise: "The amount taken in during my stay in Port Gibson which was twenty-two months was one thousand and ninety-four dollars and fifty cents. This was by Cutting and Saving alone."

Although Miller's successful business was as economically secure as any owned by free black Mississippians during the 1830s, he sold his barbershops to William and moved to New Orleans. Miller had a thriving business in Natchez, owned four slaves, and had nearly $4,000 loaned at interest. Nevertheless, October 14, 1820, he sold the unexpired term of his lease on his Main Street barbershop and other adjourning houses and the furniture therein to William Johnson, his 21 year old brother-in-law for $300.00.

Consequently, young William Johnson finally established himself as a free black Natchez businessman. The first five years of his business career entailed building a debt-free enterprise, which he accomplished. In 1832 the Adams County Court and Police Board licensed him to remain in the state, for he had "Satisfied the Court of his good character." By fall 1833 William accumulated sufficient capital to purchase the property which he was renting. (The property is the present-day site of the post office.) He made a down payment of $2,750 and gave a note for the balance. Less than two years later he paid the note in full. By 1834 the Adams County tax assessor's roll listed him as owning one lot worth $2,700 and three slaves.

Never one to miss an opportunity to make an honest dollar, Johnson augmented his income profitably with numerous enterprises. He made small loans for short periods and carefully bought and profitably sold various merchandise. In 1830–31 he opened a toy shop in one of his vacant rooms. Johnson utilized two of his slaves to haul coal and to sand water barrels. For a brief period, he operated with Henry Melin, a drayman. He also speculated in farm land and acquired a small but steady income from city real estate. He carefully recorded the most minute of his daily personal expenditures, occasionally entering each in two or three different account books. Virtuous yet prone to vice, Johnson was a moderate gambler.

His clothing was indicative of his economic status and his appreciation for the finer things in life. Similar to many men small in stature—less than five feet seven inches—he was meticulous in his dress. On February 26, 1821, he purchased a frock coat for $20.00, a vest and pair of pants for $10.00, and a pair of shoes for $1.50. The following day he paid $20.00 for a suit of clothes and later purchased another for $24.00. His wardrobe also included a pair of "satinet pants," six "Cambrick Handkerchiefs," a white hat and a pair of "Seal Skin Boots." Although Johnson bought expensive items, he consistently noted the expense of mending and "scouring" his clothing. He was not wasteful.

Johnson traveled extensively on business and personal matters, but the theater and women were his favorite diversions. Between 1831 and 1833, he toured New Orleans, Philadelphia, and New York. His trips to New Orleans involved a visit to his sister Adelia and her husband. While in New Orleans Johnson courted many young ladies. One such female was Mary Gatewood, a free black woman whom he corresponded with on a regular basis for a time. Later she came to St. Francesville, Louisiana. Johnson immediately left his friend, Robert McCary, a free black, in charge of his barbershop. For several days Johnson and Gatewood renewed their acquaintance. He lavished luxuries upon her. And before her departure, he gave Mary Gatewood $100.00. Although he failed to mention in his records why he had given her the money, he did write in his ledger: "Francesville, Francesville, good, good."

But the woman Johnson married was Ann Battles of Natchez, daughter of Harriett Battles, an illiterate free black woman who was a friend of Adelia Miller, Johnson's sister. Anne's mother had been the slave of Gabriel Tickernor. In 1822 Tickenor, a resident of Concordia Parish, Louisiana, filed emancipation papers to free Harriet Battles. Under Louisiana law, however, the daughter could not be freed. Therefore, in April 1826, Tickenor, again attempted to free her daughter. Only this time, he hired a Cincinnati lawyer who accomplished the feat in Natchez, Mississippi. In August 1829 Gabriel Tickenor and his wife deeded to Harriet Battles, for a consideration of $2.00, a Natchez lot across the street from Travellers Hall, a hotel.

By 1820 Johnson had begun courting the enterprising Anne Battles; however, he continued to date other girls and maintained his bachelor image. Finally, March 24, 1835, Johnson noted in his cashbook: "To Bon, a Natchez tailor, for my wedding Coat, $48.87½." On April 21, 1835, William Johnson and Anne Battles were united in holy matrimony. Their union was blessed with ten children.

William Johnson wholeheartedly believed that one day character and success, not color, would determine a man's worth in society. During his youth he struggled to maintain high standards of conduct, hoping white citizens of Natchez would, to some degree, accept him socially. That day never came. He did, however, succeed in his attempt to gain a powerful and influential position within the high escheleon of the elite free black society.

Johnson had an abiding interest in people—their activities, triumphs, and perplexities. Free and slave blacks, as well as a few white merchants, professionals, and aristocrats made him a confidant and often sought his advice concerning difficult business, social, and even intimately personal problems. He knew many of the town's most closely guarded business secrets. His position as one of the leading loan negotiators and lenders gave him unusual opportunities to hear harrowing hard-luck tales from potential borrowers. But he safeguarded individuals' secrets—a fact well known and appreciated by his friends and business associates. Even in the privacy of his diary, he recorded few commercial secrets.

Barbershops, taverns, and coffee houses in antebellum Natchez served as commercial meeting centers and informal men's clubs where many business and social contacts were made and unmade. In these places, business deals were initiated, political opinions discussed, and bets laid on impending horse races—all in an atmosphere invariably masculine and more than often rough and profane. For forty years the largest one in town, Johnson's Barbershop, was a clearing house for such affairs and Natchez news. As men waited their turn, they gossiped, talked politics, speculated on the prices of cotton and slaves, discussed the problems of planting, horse racing and other sports, or important visitors in town. Thus he had an opportunity enjoyed by only a few to keep informed of current affairs. Although he constantly listened to off-color news and sly rumors, he was certainly no scandal-monger. Furthermore, he never revealed or utilized information obtained in confidence.

The Natchez entrepreneur's growing enterprise and family responsibilities required the acquisition of slave labor and employment of a few whites. Johnson's apparent affluence made him selective in hiring employees. In securing servants he restricted them to three types: free blacks for skilled employment, approximately twenty-four slaves for household and unskilled jobs, and illiterate whites for farm tasks. Of necessity, therefore, Johnson chiefly used slaves and free black apprentices and journeymen.

Johnson joined in the renovation project of Main Street, which was the business district. His old brick building was neither sound, sightly, nor appropriate for a man who aspired to solidify his economic position and prestige. So in 1838 Johnson contracted for the erection of a handsome new three-story brick building at a cost of approximately $3,400. He carefully examined each brick and timber that went into the structure, unobtrusively watched every move made by the skilled white workmen, and frequently conversed with the construction bosses.

During the 1840s William Johnson's three-story brick home occupied a prominent location in a section of town that bustled with social and business activity. The original deed dated to Spanish occupation of Natchez. Since that time, the title had been acquired by Harriett Battles, Johnson's mother-in-law. Johnson built his first house, a frame building suitable for rental purposes on the site during 1836–1837. This structure burned September 1839. Fire gutted the entire block. A new house was constructed by his slaves who did the menial tasks, while Johnson employed white artisans to do the carpentry, bricklaying and plastering. It was the family home for more than a century.

Today it is listed on the National Register of Historic Places; in nominating the house, the Mississippi Department of Archives and History provided the following description:

> The William Johnson House is a three-bay, two-and-one-half-story townhouse that survives as a typical example of a nineteenth century middle-class dwelling in the Greek Revival style. It is constructed of brick laid in common bond with the facade stuccoed and scored in

imitation of ashlar masonry. Only the pair of pilastered dormers with six-over-six double-hung windows and the raised seam tin roof are thought to be original features of the facade. A two-tiered veranda, with iron supports on the first level and turned wooden columns on the second, was also probably attached to the front (north) elevation at this time. Behind the dwelling is a two-story kitchen comprised of two rooms per floor, each served by fireplaces in a central chimney. Each room has direct access to the outside by means of four-paneled doors painted their original Spanish brown and tan colors. A badly deteriorated catwalk connects the second-floor galleries of each building, and along with the catwalk, a rotting stair gives the only access to the upper level of the dwelling house.

It seems incredible that a black man such as William Johnson lived the kind of life that he did in antebellum Mississippi. Johnson was a man who seized an opportunity and despite all the negative forces imaginable he forged a name for himself in the annals of American history.

In the late 1840s William Johnson became involved in a prolonged quarrel with a white neighbor, Baylor Winn, over the boundary between their property in the swamps. This dispute eventually led to the barber's death. Johnson and Winn, who was about twelve years his senior, had known each other for a long time and had had many business and casual contacts. Frequently they hunted and fished together.

On Monday June 16, 1851, while returning to Natchez from his farm accompanied by one of his sons, a slave, and a mulatto youth, Edward Hoggatt, William Johnson was ambushed and killed. He died early the following morning. According to one document, "While on his death bed, Johnson identified Baylor Winn as his assailant. His death by murder was avenged by the law no more than if he had been a common slave . . . ."

The Montgomerys:

Ben and Isaiah, Father and Son

In 1962 the oldest all-black town in the United States—Mound Bayou, Mississippi—celebrated its Diamond Jubilee Anniversary and paid tribute to its founder, Isaiah T. Montgomery. His father, Benjamin Thornton Montgomery, was born in Loundoun County,

Virginia. Before reaching adulthood, Benjamin was sold to a slave trader, who took him to Natchez, Mississippi, where Joseph E. Davis, a distinguished planter, purchased and enslaved him on his extensive Warren County plantation known as Hurricane. Afterwards Davis sent him to Brierfield, the plantation of former Confederate President, Jefferson Davis, commonly referred to as Davis Bend in southwest Warren County. "The plantation was newly settled, and my father did not take kindly to the change from Virginia town life to plantation life, so he ran away," Isaiah recollected, "but was soon recovered by Davis, who was a man of superior judgment in the selection and management of slaves. He inquired closely into the cause of father's dissatisfaction, and as a result they reached a mutual understanding and established a mutual confidence which time only served to strengthen throughout their long and eventful connection."[1]

Ben Montgomery learned to read and write, at the encouragement of Joe Davis who wanted to give the young slave business latitude and responsibility. As a skilled carpenter, Ben utilized his expertise in building and devised his own instruments. He had a knack for measuring ditches, making levees, and estimating expenses accurately. He excelled as an efficient mechanic, machinist, and civil engineer, which financially benefitted his master.[2]

In *Brierfield*, author Frank E. Everett, Jr., described Ben as "intelligent and quick to learn . . . adept in business and proficient in almost anything he tried."[3] Ben also operated singly a mercantile business. His duties entailed shipping cotton and transacting his master's commercial trade. Ben's store and dwelling house were conspicuously located near the steamboat landing and warehouses. Once his master had guaranteed and vouched for Ben, he bought goods in New Orleans and Natchez in his own name. The ladies of the family shopped at Ben's store, which was supplied with dry goods and staple products.[4] Certainly this was not the usual mode of living for slaves, but Ben Montgomery was an exceptional person who possessed unusual skills and intelligence.

Not only was he endowed with a peculiar entrepreneurship, but he was also an inventor. Ben invented a boat propeller, which Jefferson Davis unsuccessfully tried to have patented. Under confederate law, it was legal to grant patents for inventions by slaves to their owners.[5] (After the Civil War blacks legally secured patents for their inventions without any difficulty.[6])

During his enslaved business career on the Davis Plantation, Ben met and married a female slave, Mary, who was also of Virginia parentage. She was a homemaker and seamstress and sold clothing in Ben's drygood store. On May 21, 1847, Mary Montgomery gave birth to Isaiah, one of two sons born to Mary and Ben at Davis Bend, in Warren County, Mississippi.[7]

Isaiah's educational training began each Sabbath, when George Stewart, a slave, taught him spelling from a Webster blue-covered speller. His father, who owned a private library, taught him the art of writing, recitation, and mathematics. At age ten, when he was summoned to work in the "big house," his father objected believing that his education would be interrupted. Instead Isaiah's opportunities for learning increased. Although Mississippi Black Codes prohibited teaching slaves to read and write, Isaiah received private tutoring in accounting with his master's children. The noted historian Saunders Redding stated that at twelve years old, Isaiah was doing all of the plantation accounts.[8]

In addition, Isaiah had access to Joe Davis's private library, where he frequently read newspapers and periodicals. By constantly reading, he achieved a superior knowledge of history, current events, language, and composition. Often, white visitors to Davis Bend asked Isaiah about current events instead of reading the newspapers. Joe Davis also used Isaiah to copy business and political correspondence as well as articles. Subsequently, Isaiah acquired knowledge of national and international affairs.[9]

The day after Isaiah's thirteenth birthday, on February 11, 1861, Jefferson Davis received a telegram notifying him of his election as President of the Confederacy. Immediately afterwards, Jefferson Davis and Isaiah rode to a landing three miles from Brierfield where Davis waited for the great steamboat, the *Natchez*, to take him to the Confederate capital.[10]

When Jeff Davis assumed the presidency of the Confederacy, his family moved from Davis Bend for safety and Ben managed the entire estate. Despite his limitation, the new master of Davis Bend did all within his power, with reduced labor, to protect and hold the plantation together. By January 1863 he reported that over 300 bushels of corn had been harvested. His primary concern in those perilous days was to produce as much food and firewood as possible. Meanwhile, Union soldiers destroyed farm implements, household and kitchen furniture, and laid waste to "the House that Jeff built."[11]

In the heat of the "Battle of Vicksburg" Captain Porter ordered Davis Bend evacuated. He sent the aged Ben and his family north to

Cincinnati. However, he kept the sixteen year old, precocious Isaiah, as a prize of war. Isaiah served Admiral David D. Porter as a cabin boy on the *Benton* and other ships. He saw skirmishes between Confederate and Union patrols. He witnessed the sinking of the gunboat *Indianola*, as Porter's fleet tried to run through the river defenses. He saw the "Battle of Grand Gulf." His ship stood by at the "Battle of Port Gibson" and made a scouting run from the Red River to Fort DeRussey. It joined in the bombardment of Vicksburg and was there when that city fell, on July 4, 1863. Although he served as a gunner's mate, Isaiah never fired a gun, pulled a lanyard, or breeched a shell. But he was painfully wounded in an accident aboard ship. Captain Porter assigned a nurse to accompany him to Mound City, Illinois, where he recovered in a few weeks and joined his family in Ohio.

But the milieu of Ohio was not for the Montgomerys. Not only were they excluded from the status their superior endowments and training dictated, but they were discriminated against by the mulatto offspring of southern planters who inhabited and controlled Cincinnati and surrounding vicinity. The Montgomerys were of pure African ancestry and had enjoyed under slavery a warm and rewarding personal relationship with the southern master class; here they were free yet lived as peasants among blacks whom they did not understand. Consequently, they returned to Mississippi in 1865.[12]

After the fall of Vicksburg, the plantations Hurricane and Brierfield, known as Davis Bend, were declared by the U.S. government as abandoned lands and reserved for the Freedmen's Bureau. General N. J. T. Dana "consecrated it (Davis Bend) as the home for the emancipated," declaring it to be a "suitable place to furnish means and security for the unfortunate race which he (Davis) was so instrumental in oppressing." Consequently, the "nest in which the rebellion was hatched became the Mecca of freedom."[13]

As a result of the government's actions, the Montgomerys in 1866 leased the plantation from the Freedmen's Bureau. Their cousin Ben Green and several other former slave families joined them at Davis Bend. Their first cotton crop yielded 520 bales the fall of 1867. They had tripled their original investment.[14]

In the meantime, the aged Joe Davis, almost impoverished, was engrossed in legal maneuvers trying to regain possession of the plantations. He was ably represented in Washington by his friend Dr. J. H. D. Bomar. President Andrew Johnson, a personal friend of Joe Davis, granted him a pardon. Davis regained possession of the plantations on January 1, 1867. Realizing the uncertainty of the times Davis immediately sought a purchaser. Quite unexpectedly a prospective buyer appeared in the person of Ben Montgomery. Benjamin T. Montgomery and his sons Isaiah and William agreed to pay Davis $300,000 for 4,000 acres, the asserted total of Hurricane and Brierfield. Interest at six percent ($18,000) would be paid annually on January 1, beginning in 1867. The principal would be payable over a period of nine years, with the final payment due on January 1, 1876. Isaiah signed the purchase notes although he had not reached adulthood.[15]

By 1873 the Montgomerys were the third largest cotton producers in Mississippi. Their cotton crop won every prize at the Cincinnati Exposition. Also in 1873, they paid taxes amounting to $2,447.09.[16]

But all was not well at Davis Bend. Neighboring white planters objected to the Montgomerys and occasionally stopped their tenants and questioned them about activities on the Montgomerys' plantations. Often tenants were jailed on trumped-up charges; therefore, the Montgomerys had to pay their bail or fine. On one occasion their livestock, four mules and a horse, died from drinking water that was poisoned. They also could not maintain steady labor, for some of the freedmen were nomadic. In spite of these racial, domestic, and economic problems the Montgomerys survived.[17]

However, the political appointment of Ben Montgomery as justice of the peace in 1868 by military commander General E. O. C. Ord stirred a wave of negative reactions by local whites. Ben literally held his breath as Isaiah reassured their white neighbors that his father would not hear cases involving whites. Moreover, Isaiah declared that Ben did not really want the appointment as justice of the peace.[18]

Because of his father's age, Isaiah supervised the operation of the plantation. His goal entailed making the plantation self-sufficient; therefore, he built a commissary, purchased merchandise in Cincinnati and sold it to his workers. He maintained a smokehouse and saw and cane mills.

With the help of the Freedmen's Bureau the Montgomerys salvaged some old machinery and built a cotton gin. They loaded their cotton directly onto the steamer from their own dock. In 1869 a disastrous flood swept away their dock, breached the levees, and ruined part of the crop. They had sufficiently recovered by next planting season, but during the harvesting period the dock, stacked with bales of cotton, was mysteriously destroyed by fire. Old Ben attributed the disaster to a careless worker who had dropped ash from his pipe. Ben Green suspected vandalism. Isaiah reserved his opinion but when the dock was rebuilt he invited the white planters to utilize its facilities free of charge.[19]

However, the skilled and tactful Montgomerys could not erect impregnable defenses against all disasters. When the great river heaved and changed its course, Davis Bend became Davis Island and cotton production rose, but the price fell. Agricultural credit soared from fifteen to thirty percent. In 1877 a hundred bales of cotton sold for half its original price ten years previously. After the death of Ben Montgomery in 1878, for many blacks the plantations lost their sentimental value. Even the land petered out. Yet, a thousand acres of good timber still stood and Isaiah had plans for it. He sent his brothers, William and Ben Green, to Vicksburg to build a saw mill. At the mill they produced barrel staves, puncheons, and railroad ties and sold lumber to the steamboats. Nevertheless, the final reign of the Montgomerys at Davis Bend was rapidly coming to its final conclusion.[20]

On May 14, 1867, Jefferson Davis was released from Fort Monroe to prepare for his trial in Richmond, Virginia. In 1868 he returned to Davis Bend and witnessed the habitation of his plantation by former slaves. He returned to Vicksburg depressed but determined to repossess Davis Bend.[21]

On June 15, 1874, Jefferson Davis filed suit in the Chancery Court of Warren County, Mississippi, to establish title and recover Brierfield. He asked that Ben Montgomery be allowed to rescind the purchase and return the property to him as its rightful owner. After a series of legal maneuvers the Warren County Chancery Court, on June 1, 1878, entered a decree authorizing the foreclosure of the Montgomery mortgage which was in default. Enforcement was delayed and foreclosure occurred on March 5, 1881.[22]

Isaiah conceded without a struggle or legal counsel. He merely accepted the thirty-five hundred dollars offered him "partly as a gift, partly as a reasonable share" for the crop left standing in the fields. Perhaps, he voluntarily accepted the offer because he knew that the white business community could financially ruin him. With their worldly possessions the Montgomerys moved to Vicksburg and the ex-master, Jefferson Davis returned to Davis Bend. Afterwards, the mast head of the *Mississippi Register* proclaimed, "A White Man in a White Man's Place. A Black Man in a Black Man's Place. Each according to the Eternal Fitness of Things."[23]

In spite of losing Davis Bend, the Montgomerys were financially secure. By 1883, Isaiah's personal and real properties included six thousand dollars in cash, a new store, and several real estates.

Because of Isaiah's economic and prestigious status, various political parties elicited his support and encouraged him to run for political office. The fusion system, which aligned black Republicans and white Democrats in predominantly black river counties, tried to persuade Montgomery to seek a political position. He refused. When the Republicans, led by the redoubtable Jim Hill, approached Isaiah he flatly declined. Likewise, he adamantly said no to the white Democrats.

Wanting no part in politics and still embittered by his losses at Davis Bend, Isaiah asserted when approached by politicians, "This is a white man's country; let them run it."[24] Former U.S. Congressmen John R. Lynch and Blanche K. Bruce pleaded with Isaiah to politically work with them for the uplift of the black race, but he refused because of their association with Frederick Douglass, whom Montgomery detested. Montgomery resented and blamed Douglass for the 1870s southern black migration to "fool's paradise" in Kansas, and he despised him for marrying a white woman.

Moreover, Isaiah a staunch advocate of segregation and anti-black political participation declared, "The farther you stay away from the white people's politics, the better."[25] In 1886 when the colored Farmer's Alliance co-operated and affiliated with the white Farmer's Alliance, he disassociated himself with the group.

Therefore, Isaiah Montgomery devoted his money and energy to his economic enterprises. In 1886 he and his cousin, Ben, bought eight hundred and forty acres of mostly swamp land from the Yazoo-Mississippi Railroad. This swamp property consisted of cypress, gum, and black trees. One year later, on that property, they built a colony, Mound Bayou. Supposedly, when the first settlers stepped off the train and faced the uncleared wilderness Isaiah rhetorically inquired: "Have you not for centuries braved the miasma and hewn down forests like these at the behest of a master? Can you not do it for yourselves and your children unto successive generations, that they may worship and develop under their own vine and fig tree? Why stagger at the difficulties that confront you?"[26]

Initially the colonists experienced a pioneer and primitive existence. With saw, ax, and dynamite, tools purchased from Isaiah, they cleared eighty scattered acres during that first summer. Montgomery and Ben Green built a saw mill, cut logs for cabins and lumber for railroad ties. When a settler's funds were exhausted, Isaiah either extended credit at fifteen percent or put the settler to work clearing additional land. While men cleared land, women and children worked in the fields. At night bears and coons got in the corn; "deer in herds like cattle" fed upon the sugar cane. Sometimes panthers crawled out of the forest, and "the howling of wolves was common music at nightfall." Until drainage ditches were dug and a levee erected, every rain brought flood. There were swamp fever and death; but eventually a townsite emerged.

Montgomery established a paternalistic government and personal social mores at Mound Bayou, the oldest black town in the United States. Nothing escaped Montgomery's eyes or ears. He was the colony's conscience, its guide and guard. Strangers were not tolerated unless they became residents. Couples had to produce certificates of marriage. Illegitimacy was punished by immediate expulsion of erring mother and child. "Here in this place," Isaiah told the colonists, "we are building a place of safety and refuge."[27] And so they did.

By 1893 Mound Bayou had a population of four thousand spread over twenty thousand alluvial acres and was still growing. As town mayor, Isaiah Montgomery handpicked the three aldermen. Though the sheriff of Bolivar County appointed the Negro deputy for Mound Bayou, Isaiah named him. He chose the town constable, he hired the first school teacher and guaranteed the salary of the first preacher. He owned either in whole or in part the cotton gin and the warehouse, the feed and fertilizer store, the lumberyard, the general merchandise emporium, and the burial business. He held uncounted first mortgages. He grossed a profit of eight thousand dollars per year on lumber. He was reputed to be the only Negro in the United States who could put his hands on fifty thousand dollars "cash money" on an hour's notice.[28]

After his tenure as mayor of Mound Bayou, Isaiah held the positions of postmaster and justice of the peace. Thereafter, he served as "receiver of public moneys," with headquarters in the federal building in Jackson. Later he was elected second president of Campbell College, a religious institution under the auspices of the A.M.E. Church.[29]

On August 23–25, 1900 in Boston, Massachusetts, Isaiah participated in the original creation of the National Negro Business League. At the convention Booker T. Washington was elected president and Isaiah was chosen to serve on the executive committee.[30]

Because the political campaigns of 1888 entailed intimidation, terror, and violence many blacks fled to Mound Bayou for refuge statewide. The Republican grip on municipal governments fell apart, but the Republicans swept the national elections.

The anti-black sentiment and renewed violence forced Isaiah Montgomery to take a political stance. In 1890 Montgomery, the only black present at the Mississippi Constitutional Convention, made a deal with the Democrats. By making property qualification a prerequisite for voting, his goal or objective was to keep blacks out of politics.[31] As a result a literacy test and poll tax were also required for voting.

When John R. Lynch assembled black Republicans together to form a slate of black convention delegates, Isaiah was there. He openly expressed a desire to be on that slate, and the logical inference was that he wanted to "protect the rights of Negroes." Montgomery was easily elected to represent Bolivar County. J. Z. George, the white Democratic leader, "swept Isaiah in, and he was seated in the convention without protest—the only Negro delegate and the lone Republican."[32]

Montgomery's vote helped George and the Democrats elect the temporary chairman, thus gaining control of the convention. One Democrat, W. E. Farr, expressed the prevailing attitude that every feud disturbance or riot could be traced to "the ignorant Negro" thus making him unsuitable to vote or to hold office. Montgomery voiced similar sentiments when he declared that the interests of the state could best be served if blacks were reduced to an inferior status below whites. Consequently, Montgomery postponed the South's commitment to the equality of the races.[33]

While negative reactions emanated from the black community, positive responses oozed forth from the white public. For example, his one-hour speech drew praises from the Democratic press and ex-president Grover Cleveland. The black community felt betrayed and envisioned the negative long-range effects of his remarks upon the struggle for equality, justice, and integration. In the 1920s Montgomery received the blame for the election of a white Democrat instead of a black Republican. Also, he wore the blame for Democratic control of Mississippi politics.[34]

In essence, Isaiah Montgomery was a complexity of contrarieties, though in some organic fashion a product of his times. He was born, educated, and lived at Hurricane plantation, for only one purpose—to serve his white masters. By training and experience he was one thing, but by instinct and temperament another. All his public acts and utterances marked him a believer in the inferiority of his race; yet as a freedman he was sensitive and proud to the extent of vowing he would starve rather than work as a menial for any white man.

He had tremendous self-esteem; but in the face of his own material success also had profound humility. Although Montgomery was generous and 'charitable,' he did not hesitate to demand interest as high as fifty percent on loans, and he was known to take advantage of his workers at Davis Bend by increasing prices on supplies from the commissary by twenty to forty percent.[35]

Isaiah Thornton Montgomery died one year after his deceased wife, Martha Rabb on March 6, 1924, at Mound Bayou, at the age of seventy-two. The couple had been married June 4, 1852. From that union were born seven children which included a set of twins.

Montgomery had witnessed the ending of one era and the beginning of another. In a real sense he had enjoyed the advantages of two generations. Few, if any, other blacks had the economic, political, and social opportunities of a slave and a freedman. Despite it all, Isaiah Montgomery died as he lived—honored and dishonored, revered and despised—when he might well have carved for himself and his posterity an enviable record in the annals of his race.

George Washington Lee

Businessman, Politician, and Author

"Lieutenant George Washington Lee, a black raised on a Mississippi cotton patch, carved out a career of prestige and recognition as an army lieutenant, a wealthy Memphis businessman, a novelist, a fraternal leader of the Negro Elks, and a Republican politician. He was the South's last black patronage boss until he went down to defeat at the Goldwater Republican Convention in 1964."[1]

George W. Lee was born about four miles west of Indianola in Sunflower County, on January 4, 1894—one year prior to Booker T. Washington's "Atlanta Compromise," and lived through Stokely Carmichael's "Black Power" era. His parents, the Reverend George and Hattie Lee, lived near Heathman, a small settlement with a single plantation store. Each Sunday Lee preached at the Crossroads Negro Baptist Church, and on week days he worked the land he had purchased with money from Sunday's collections. However, shortly after George's birth his parents separated; later his father died, leaving his mother to care and provide for George and his older brother, Abner.[2]

After the death of Reverend Lee, a brother seized the family farm; and Hattie Lee, ignorant of hers and the children's rights of inheritance, moved into a sharecropper's shack. In return for planting the land, she received the cabin rent free, enough credit at the store to buy corn meal, sowbelly, and a little molasses for her children. Yet Hattie Lee, the daughter of house servants, strongly motivated to end the family's status as sharecroppers, hitched her wagon behind the mule and took George and Abner several miles to the nearest school.

In a one-room, unpainted segregated schoolhouse George yearned to read and write. At home, George, his mother and brother planted, cultivated, and harvested cotton, hauled it to the gin and hoped the plantation bookkeeper's account would show a profit for them, but the Lees were never so fortunate. Powerless to challenge the bookkeeper's records, but determined to break out of the subsistence cycle, Mrs. Lee sent her older son, Abner, into Indianola to find another type of job, which he did at the cottonseed oil mill. George rode him into town each morning on the plantation mule, until the boss discovered it. Consequently, the mule was taken and the family evicted.[3]

Mrs. Lee moved her family into Indianola which had a population of almost two thousand, more than half of whom were blacks. In 1902 the schools were racially segregated, yet everybody drank Cokes at the same drugstores and mingled in the business community in a manner that was becoming wholly unacceptable to Mississippi whites.

The race issue was practically ignored for more than a decade, then political candidates appealed directly to the race conscious white voting masses. Such conditions spawned racists like James K. Vardaman, a gubernatorial candidate who openly sought to inflame color prejudice by building his platform on the promise to economize or eliminate Negro education in Mississippi. He boisterously proclaimed that black crimes and immorality had increased by one hundred percent since emancipation of blacks in 1865 and that education had spoiled good plantation laborers, making them impudent and worthless. Moreover, Vardaman claimed that "Nigger education" led to rapes and murders, which precipitated the unpleasantries of hanging and burnings.⁴ Subsequently, city officials fired black clerks.

Aware that many blacks had lost their jobs in the business community, young George Lee applied and obtained summer employment in Holmes's grocery store near the railroad depot. Holmes, aged and crippled with rheumatism, hired George to shelve and sell groceries. The money George received from customers was given to Holmes. When the trains stopped, railroad crews quenched their thirst at Holmes's store. Sometimes the engineers allowed George to sit at the engineer's switch. In quieter moments, George overheard white men who sat around the store discussing the weather, crops, and "niggers." Gradually, George felt the sting of race prejudice. Finally, upon suggestion of the white community, Holmes fired George, explaining to his customers "that he had only hired George on the theory that a 'nigger wouldn't have the nerve to steal as much as white boys.' "⁵

Later George Lee became a houseboy for Charlie Klingman, an important cotton planter. Each morning George rode piggy back with Klingman on the master's horse to the cotton office and returned home alone. The Klingmans seemed delighted with George's ability and personality, and George was equally delighted at the kindnesses shown him by the Klingmans. When George grew too old to be a houseboy, the Klingmans helped him to get a job as delivery boy for the Gresham's mercantile store, where he earned more money than ever before. George Lee would have cheerfully remained at Greshams and "waited for luck to make him a success, had his mother not intervened and insisted that he leave dray driving and enter Alcorn A. & M. College to obtain an education like their community leader, Wayne Cox."⁶

According to David Tucker, Lee's biographer, "Judged by white standards, Alcorn offered a limited and inadequate academic education . . . And yet Alcorn was as good as most Negro colleges . . . The school's tuition was free, board was only five dollars a month, and at least one professor encouraged the 'pursuit of truth' and the 'free play of the mind.' "⁷

A. E. Perkins, an Alcorn alumnus and exceptional teacher who took a personal interest in his students, returned to Alcorn the same year that George Lee enrolled. He introduced George Lee to the speeches of the white abolitionist, Wendell Phillips, whose oration on Toussaint L'Ouverture left a permanent impression on the young students, particularly this excerpt: "I attempt, to convice you that the Negro blood, instead of standing at the bottom of the list, is entitled, if judged either by its great men or its masses, either by its courage, its purpose, or its endurance, to a place as near ours as any other blood known in history."[8]

Professor Perkins recognized that George Lee was an achiever, and he encouraged in the boy a radical spirit. Shy and introspective, Lee was a serious student and his prodigious reading set him apart. When Lee delivered his Lyceum oration, "A Defense of Aaron Burr," the faculty, with the exception of Perkins, was shocked that a student would defend the American traitor.[9]

During the summer of 1912, George Lee, like so many other black Mississippians, migrated to Memphis to look for work. In Memphis, a large portion of the labor force consisted of black domestics, common laborers, factory workers, railroaders, loggers, sawmillers, and manufacturing plant hands. In black neighborhoods, a small middle class competed with Italian merchants for the ghetto business. Black Memphians owned restaurants, drug stores, laundries, harness-shops, newspapers, and a gambling saloon-bordello.[10]

Within this prosperous city emerged the black bourgeoisie, a class that George Lee lacked economic credentials to enter. In the midst of black Memphians' economic prosperity, ambitious George Lee found employment as a bellhop at the Gayoso, the city's finest hotel. When hotel manager L. P. Parker died in 1916, Lee composed a tribute to his former boss, at the encouragement of Alonzo Locke, the head waiter. Lee's eulogy was published in the Memphis press, and scores of white Memphians complimented the bellhop. That praise was dampened, however, when a white lawyer pointed out to Alonzo Locke "that the article contained a word used out of context." Lee was anxious to defend himself, and Alonzo, fearful of the lawyer's retaliation, made Lee promise to handle the lawyer with extreme delicacy. With the help of a dictionary "and in his most disarming manner (Lee) forced the lawyer to agree that his use of the word was justified."[11]

When the United States entered World War I, the NAACP called for an end to racial discrimination in the U.S. Army and the commissioning of black officers. The war department yielded to those demands by creating a Negro officer training camp at Fort Des Moines, Iowa, and requested each state to provide its share of one thousand college-educated candidates. Twenty-three years old, George Lee was determined to be one of those candidates, notwithstanding the requirements published by the *Nashville Tennessean* calling for men between the ages of thirty and forty-four. Lee wrote to Alcorn asking Professor Perkins and President L. J. Rowan for letters of recommendation. With his letters of recommendation in hand, George Lee took the night train to Nashville for the qualifying examination. He excelled in both the intelligence and the physical tests, and after adding only a single year to his age became one of the twenty-seven Tennesseans selected to go to Fort Des Moines.[12]

When the camp opened on June 18 under the command of Brigadier General C. C. Ballou, two hundred and fifty Negro corporals and sergeants from the regular army assigned to assist in the instruction competed for commissions with one thousand college-trained applicants like George Lee. Since the army intended to take only half of the men in the group, the competition was fierce, and the pressures were compounded by the candidate's awareness that the black race as well as the individual was being put to the test. Fearing failure, he studied every spare moment. On October 14, George Washington Lee was among the 133 southern Negroes and 506 northern Negroes made officers in the United States Army.[13]

Subsequently, Lee became an important figure within the black community. While at Alcorn, Lee had enviously watched the royal receptions given visiting dignitaries and dreamed that he might someday receive such a reception. That day arrived when he was invited by Alcorn's President L. J. Rowan to speak at the college general convocation and he was given the V.I.P. treatment.[14]

In France, Lieutenant Lee again experienced the insults and innuendoes of American racism, but the 920th Division and particularly Lee's battalion "proved their bravery." After the fighting ended and the medals were handed out, Lieutenant Lee received a citation for bravery in dislodging a German sniper. Lee thought of remaining in the peacetime army; but on his return to Memphis, he found Bob Church, the town's most influential Negro, was more eager to have him in Memphis than in the army. Accordingly, Church advised Lee to return to Memphis and become involved in the fight for racial progress. Lieutenant Lee received his honorable discharge March 27, 1919.[15]

In Indianola, Lee had known the wealthy Wayne Cox, respected leader of the Negro community; in Memphis he knew the wealthy and influential Robert R. Church. Thus, it seemed to Lee that business meant money and money meant power. While he might have become a plain-clothes detective on the Memphis police force,

George Lee accepted a ten-dollar-a-week job as a salesman with the Mississippi Life Insurance Company. After a few weeks George Lee was promoted from salesman to manager. He recruited and trained new agents.[16]

By 1920 the Memphis agency managed by George Lee sold more insurance than any other company office, and Lee was promoted to a vice-presidency in the Mississippi Life Insurance Company. As a vice-president, Lee represented his firm at an annual meeting of the National Negro Business League, where he discovered that the benevolent orders that operated insurance programs controlled the meetings and practically ignored the major profit-making insurance companies. The following year under Lee's urgings, the insurance men created their own National Negro Insurance Association.

For four productive years George Lee watched his salary skyrocket to $6,500 a year and looked forward to an even greater future. But in 1923 two major stockholders, Minnie Cox and her son-in-law, sold their controlling shares to Heman Perry of Atlanta who had organized one of the race's most dynamic insurance companies. Later Perry, involved in financial difficulties, borrowed heavily from a white insurance company which led to his finally selling Mississippi Life to the white Southern Life for $240,000.[17]

Lee, determined to take a militant stand for his race, entered the courts for an injunction to prevent Southern Life Insurance Company from collecting premiums on the old Mississippi Life policies. To protest this injustice, Lee and sales managers from three states picketed the offices of Southern Life and resigned their positions, thereby rendering the old Mississippi Life Company worthless, without agents to collect the weekly premiums. Officials of Southern Life offered Lee a $7,000 yearly salary and two percent of all premiums collected, but he refused and assured the whites he would never help them to take over a business built by his race.[18]

Thereafter, George W. Lee was assimilated into the mainstream of the Memphis black community. He personally attacked the policies and practices of two prominent blacks, the Reverends T. O. Fuller and Sutton E. Griggs, whom he accused of soliciting white philanthropy and for using the pulpits to preach against Negro militancy and for the acceptance of white domination. The *Memphis Commercial-Appeal* generously supported the ministers, but Lee was relentless in his condemnation.

Lee's political career changed when Robert Church invited him to dinner to discuss a business proposition. Church, who had inherited his father's fortune, aspired to be a politician. George Lee became one of Church's foremost lieutenants and spokespersons, thus enjoying the glitter such a position offered him. Lee joined the Republican party and acquired so much political influence that his amiable relationship with Church dissolved. Church accused Lee of acquiescing to "Mr. Crump," white Memphis mayor. At the 1952 National Republican Convention held in Chicago, George Lee made one of the speeches seconding the nomination of Robert A. Taft.[19]

But, Lee's talents extended beyond his insurance office and the speaker's platform. After several rewritings Lee finally found a publisher for his *Beale Street: Where the Blues Began* (1934), the first book by a black author advertised in the Book-of-the-Month-Club News.[20] Local bookstores, however, refused to stock *Beale Street* until Clifton Fadiman, a renowned critic, reviewed it in the July *New Yorker* in which he remarked, "I wish to pin a small but distinctive badge (with ribbons) upon the honest colored breast of Lieutenant George Washington Lee. . . . Mr. Lee's naive Memphis recitals have the authentic color of good cracker-box gossip." After Fadiman's review, the book sold everywhere and George Lee's ego expanded. For fear that some newspaper clippings might be overlooked, George Lee hired a clippings service to collect all of his reviews. He waited for the morning mail, "not to keep a rejected manuscript from being noticed by the office staff, but to read and to show off the complimentary critiques of his published book."[21] His second novel, *River George*, (1937) never achieved the same success as the first book. Later he published stories in *Negro Digest*, *The World's Digest*, and the *Southern Literary Messenger*, and compiled all of his short stories in an anthology entitled *Beale Street Sundown* (1942). Although this book attracted little national interest, it received local praise. The *Memphis Press-Scimitar* raved, "The Boswell of Beale Street has spun the best book of his literary career."[22]

Lee took time away from his literary pursuits to participate actively in civic matters. As an Elk, George Lee was again indebted to his mentor Robert R. Church for the introduction, but it was Lee's ability that catapulted him from one degree of importance to another.[23]

For unselfish committment to community improvement Lee received citations from newspapers, insurance companies, and such organizations as the Elks, R.R. Church Lodge, Lincoln Republican League, Memphis Junior Chamber of Commerce, Omega Psi Phi, and the Tennessee Regular Baptist Convention.

Lee has held such positions as third vice president and director of Atlanta Life Insurance Company; vice president of Tri-State Bank of Memphis; member of the Memphis Port and Harbor Commission; Grand Commissioner of Education for Improved, Benevolent and Protective Order of Elks of the World; member of national board of field advisers of Small Business Administrators under President Eisenhower; member of Regional Export Expansion Council under President Johnson.

George Lee was "Mr. Big" in black business circles in Memphis and the mid-South for more than four decades. In 1969, the respectable *Harvard University Business History Review* published an article "Black Pride and Negro Business in the 1920s: George Washington Lee of Memphis," in which his contributions as business leader were extoled.[24] As "Brown Bomber of Republican party politics in Tennessee and the nation," Lee's name has been known in virtually every noteworthy community-action program launched among blacks in Memphis. He initiated one of the nation's greatest Afro-American-sponsored charities, the "Blues Bowl" football game. His oratory has thrilled and moved thousands. His eloquent eulogy on W.C. Handy was inserted into the Congressional Record, as many of his speeches have been.

Lee, businessman, accomplished author, well-known politician and civic activist, orator, and fraternal leader also provided scholarships for many worthy students, including the late Dr. Martin Luther King, Jr.

Joseph Edison Walker

Banker, Insurance Executive

Tillman, a raw, remote community in the far reaches of Claiborne County, Mississippi, was the birthplace of Joseph E. Walker. He was born March 31, 1880, to a mother affectionately known as "Aunty Patsy Walker." His father is unknown.[1]

Joseph Walker grew up in a meager Christian home. Like other boys of that community, he worked on the farm, went to school a few months of the year, fished, hunted, and enjoyed the bounties of nature. In 1897, at the age of seventeen, Joseph, hopeful of entering Alcorn A & M College, rode the train from Tillman to Lorman and walked the ten miles from Lorman to the college. Upon his arrival he found a meadowlike campus with a student body totaling six hundred boys and two girls. An unofficial and unappointed committee saw the penniless Walker gazing at the college chapel. The group ordered him to go to the chapel steeple to ring the bell and announce his presence. When college officials asked what grade he sought, he promptly replied, 'A Grade.' That, to him, represented the beginning, 'A' being the first letter of the alphabet."

In his effort to secure academic funds to continue his education Walker adhered to the advice of his schoolmate, M. S. Stuart, to apply for summer employment with Port Gibson public school system. He passed the teacher's examination, and was hired as a summer instructor. After teaching several summers in various "back woods" schools, Walker applied for a first grade provisional certificate, becoming the first and only black teacher in Jefferson County certified at that level. Walker acquired the title of professor in Jefferson, Wilkinson, and Adams Counties where he taught during his stay at Alcorn College and during the three years he attended medical school.

In 1903 Joseph E. Walker received the B.S. degree from Alcorn Agricultural and Mechanical College, and immediately entered Meharry Medical College in Nashville, Tennessee. He left Nashville in May 1906, with an M.D. degree and went to Indianola, Mississippi.

Indianola, the county seat of Sunflower County, was unreceptive to professional blacks. In 1905, when President Theodore Roosevelt appointed a black woman, Minnie Cox, as postmistress, white citizens objected, petitioned, and demonstrated. Therefore in May 1906, when Joseph E. Walker took up residence as a medical doctor, one of the old mothers of the town, finding it impossible to restrain her emotions suddenly cried out, "My God, what is dis here town coming to—dese white folks just now getting over habing 'er nigger postmaster and now here comes 'er nigger Doctor—Did Ros'velt send'm 'ere too?"

Wayne Cox, who was the husband of the black postmistress and reputed to be the richest black in the Delta, introduced Walker to the most prominent and respected blacks in the vicinity. These included I. T. Montgomery, founder of the town of Mound Bayou, and Dr. W. A. Attaway, the founder of the Mississippi Life Insurance Company, the first old line legal reserve life insurance company in America."

These business acquaintances assisted Walker in his climb to success as a physician and businessman. When Walker first arrived in Indianola, he camouflaged his destitute condition by pretending to have wealth commensurate with his social status. Consequently, Wayne Cox offered him the presidency of the Delta Penny Savings Bank, and an overwhelmed, but honest, Walker had to confess, "I haven't got any money, Mr. Cox." Appreciating his honesty, Cox promised to buy the necessary stock for him. At the bank board meeting in 1912, the trustees elected Walker president of the Delta Penny Savings Bank, "the first bank operated by Negroes in the state of Mississippi."

Walker possessed all of the administrative acumen to manage a business—initiative, honesty, and investment aptitude. In 1916, the directorate of the financially troubled Mississippi Life Insurance Company offered Walker its presidency. In 1917, Dr. J. E. Walker was installed the third president of that company. In the next six years the assets rose from $48,000 to $60,000, with business in force amounting to approximately $500,000. In 1922, the company grossed in assets, $467,650; Capital Stock, $100,000; and Business in Force, $15,000; this was twenty-five times what it was when Dr. J. E. Walker became its president.[3]

When white resentment toward the expansion of Indianola's black business community escalated and directly affected Walker's enterprises, Walker, and M. S. Stuart, manager of Mississippi Life Insurance Company, agreed to relocate in Memphis, Tennessee—the cotton capital of the world.

Moving to another town did not resolve Walker's business difficulties. His establishment of a competing Insurance Company on Beale Street antagonized the black elite and leadership of Memphis. Having not obtained prior permission or approval from that group, Walker's action was viewed as encroachment. For about three years, the Beale Street opposition endeavored to halt the economic progress of Mississippi Life Insurance Company. The death blow occurred when W. C. Howard, son-in-law of Wayne Cox, gained majority control of the company's stock, displaced Walker, and declared himself president. This was the first in a series of bitter deceptions for Joseph E. Walker.

With indomitable courage Walker searched for machinery to excavate the foundation of another insurance company. This was no easy task. After many restless nights and worn out shoe soles, he met in Nashville, Dr. J. T. Wilson, who needed a young administrative executive. Impressed by Walker's proposition, Wilson promised to purchase $40,000 worth of the proposed insurance stock. Inspired by Wilson's generosity, Walker pushed forward.

When the youthful A. W. Willis, of the North Carolina Insurance Company, Durham, N.C., heard of Walker's proposal, he came to Walker with $5,000 in borrowed money. He took Walker to Newton County, Mississippi, to see his wealthy father, whom Willis persuaded to invest $5,000 in stocks for each of his two daughters. At Nashville, Clarksville, Hot Springs, Meridian, and Crawfordsville, Walker and Willis made meaningful contacts and sold the last share of Walker's proposed life insurance stock.

In 1923 M. W. Bonner, the sole associate from Mississippi Life helped Walker organize the new company and insisted that the new enterprise be named Universal Life Insurance Company. In less than a year, Walker had planned, organized, and established another viable financial institution. The Beale Street hierarchy had mixed emotions about this man from the Mississippi Delta, who had turned disaster into prosperity.

Because of internal strife, the first two years of Universal Life were not as productive as anticipated. Walker's salary totaled only one hundred dollars per month. By the mid 1920s, the country experienced economic prosperity and Universal Life opened branches in Missouri and Texas. Nevertheless, the company was financially troubled and its future uncertain.

However, through honesty and professionalism methods, Walker won for Universal Life the confidence and goodwill of the insurance examiners. For example, one insurance examiner asked Walker to meet him in Nashville and offered to sell him the debits of Mississippi Life for $154,000. After considerable maneuvers with the assistance of the examiner, a sale contract with $10,000 borrowed money was signed for Mississippi Life debits. Universal Life became insolvent, and shortly thereafter a "run" broke the Fraternal Bank. Panic stricken, Walker rushed in to grab some of the securities belonging to his company. He was arrested and held incommunicado, but through the efforts of M. S. Stuart, Walker was released on bond. Immediately, Walker secured from two blacks in Arkansas, collateral of seven hundred acres, amounting to $70,000, and placed it on record as security for the remaining sum of $154,000 debt for Mississippi Life debits. Before the three-year expiraton date, the mortgage against the properties in Arkansas had been cancelled and the cost of Mississippi Life debits fully paid.

During those three years, Dr. J. E. Walker fought adversity, imprisonment, foreclosure, scandals, low wages, alledged embezzlement, and ostracism. But he emerged after the period, fired by propelling ambition.

By 1925, the admitted assets of Universal Life were $135,000, its capital $100,000, and surplus $12,327. Industrial insurance in force totaled $3,568,049. By 1930, the company had increased the industrial, or weekly premium, account to a total of $9,473,704, and it also had $2,087,165 ordinary insurance in force. Assets had grown to $540,495, capital was $108,750, and surplus $48,423. In less than ten years the business grew to more than $15,000 worth of business in force, with an annual collection of premiums and other income of about $900,000, and a surplus of $127,000. The company set aside reserves on its policies in the sum of $300,000. In an article appearing in the *Memphis World*, of September 22, 1932, Dr. Walker was praised for saving the Woodman Union Life Insurance, Hot Springs, Arkansas. Their assets of $100,00 were transferred to the assets of Universal Life. In 1940, Universal Life moved into its new $500,000 home office, a three-story, air-conditioned, brick building of neo-Egyptian architecture.

At a meeting of the Hiawatha Club, the ladies discussed the need for a black owned and operated bank. Mrs. J. P. Johnson, president, asked Mrs. J. E. Walker to get her husband to build a bank. After several days she mentioned the idea to Walker. Nothing was said or done immediately, but one day later Walker asked his wife to get all the children together that night so he could talk to them. That conversation dealt with opening a black-owned bank. Despite the failures of two former black banks in Memphis, the vote was unanimous in favor of opening a new bank.

His son, Maceo Walker, assumed the responsibility of selling the company's stock. He sold $45,000 worth of stock so quickly it quieted the old man's doubt, and J. E. teamed with his son and completed the task. The stock sale opened in April and by mid-August every share had been sold. By October $243,000 had been collected, and the stockholders were ready for the election of their directorate.

December 16, 1946, was a memorable day on crowded Memphis' Beale Street when the Tri-State Bank opened with a capital of $200,000 and a surplus of $40,000. Within two years, its deposits exceeded $1,000,000 and its assets $1,500,000. Within the short span of six months, one man and his son cleared the debris of two ruined black-owned banks and rebuilt a new structure, whose beauty and grandeur symbolized prosperity and endurance. It was the reality of an impossible dream. The organization included Dr. J. E. Walker, President; A. Maceo Walker, vice-president; R. R. Wright, III, Cashier. The board of directors read like a Who's Who of blacks in Memphis and the Mississippi Delta.

Between 1942 and 1948 the Universal Life Insurance Company made fifteen purchases of United States Savings Bonds amounting to $200,000. This was the expression of faith its officers had in their government, the veritable proof of their loyalty. The money used to purchase these bonds represented the toil and sacrifices of millions of black people whose rights of citizenship were abridged and, in too many instances, ignored. Yet, the officials of Universal Life proudly built this monument of patriotism in Memphis, capitol of the mid-South. Standing atop it in mute and solemn form, is the effigy of Dr. J. E. Walker.

Because of Walker's financial achievement, the *Chicago Defender* named him "one of the ten great Americans who had given constructive service to the race in 1948." In addition to his business successes he was the recipient of many honors and awards, a few of which included the following ones: selection as National Chairman of War Bonds Savings Club; citation from Secretary of the Treasury, Henry Morgenthau, Jr., for distinguished service in behalf of the War Finance Program, 1944; listing in *Who's Who in Colored America*; certificate of Honor from Alcorn A&M College in 1947 as Graduate of the Year; Distinguished Achievement Award from the Life Underwriters Association of Washington, D.C. for outstanding contributions to the Community Housing Development of Memphis, Tennessee, and for distinguished accomplishments in banking and insurance; third annual award of the State Fair of Texas, October 15, 1951, in recognition of his outstanding achievement in the field of human relations in the United States; and citation and victory trophy, the highest award of the National Christian Missionary Convention, 1956.

For two years he served as president of the National Negro Business League, founded by Booker T. Washington. He was elected as treasurer of the National Communion of the Christian Church, which included both white and black congregations. He served as delegate to the Republican National Convention, and trustee member of

LeMoyne, Tougaloo, and Jarvis Christian colleges. He was also a delegate to the World's Convention of Disciples of Christ, Leicester, England.

Death came to Dr. Walker in July 1958. His funeral at Memphis' Boulevard Christian Church, which he organized and built, attracted blacks and whites from across the nation—business people, religious groups, civic leaders, and others.[4]

Clarie Collins Harvey

Mortuary Entrepreneur

"I was born in Meridian under the sign of Sagittarius," Clarie Collins Harvey recalled, "the jet propelled arrow, the only child of Malachi C., a mathematics professor at Rust College, and Mary Augusta Rayford Collins, Mississippi's first black librarian." Isaac Collins, her paternal grandfather, was a slave. After the Civil War he married and became a farmer in Hazelhurst. Harvey's maternal forebearers became plantation owners in Lauderdale County, and for more than forty years were merchants in Meridian.[1]

In Meridian, a predominantly white community, Clarie had many white playmates to visit, but she was never allowed at their homes. Sometimes her playmates and classmates would bully her, but she never fought back. Friends often chided, "Why don't you stand up for yourself?"[2] That gentle child grew into a gentlewoman, who involved herself in humanitarian causes.

In 1916 Clarie's father left Rust University in Holly Springs and opened a funeral home and insurance partnership in Hattiesburg. The business successfully expanded into several Mississippi towns, including Jackson. Frequently, however, he stayed awake at night, with shot gun in hand, because whites traditionally buried blacks who threatened to upset the status quo. In 1924 Collins became the sole owner of the family funeral home and insurance businesses at Jackson.[3]

Clarie, who was reading and writing at four, had an unlimited choice of good literature and an excellent guide to help her explore it. She attended public and private schools in Jackson and high school at Tougaloo College. For college she chose Spelman, an all-girls school in Atlanta. Her father had insisted, "You must live in a world dominated by men, and therefore you need to know how to think with them. There is more to be derived from college than what textbooks contain!"⁴

Originally, Clarie hoped to be a medical doctor. In college as she began to think seriously of her future and the family business, she became convinced that business offered black women many more avenues for advancement and service than medicine. After graduating from Spelman in 1937 with a B.A. in economics, Clarie received a certificate in mortuary technique from the Indiana College of Mortuary Science at Indianapolis, where she was the only female in the graduating class. Because of her premedical work she was far ahead of many of the men.⁵

After passing the examinations of the Mississippi State Board of Embalming, Clarie later received an M.A. degree in personnel administration at Columbia University. She also studied at Union Theological Seminary and at New York University Graduate School of Business Administration. Afterwards, for a brief period she taught at the junior high and college levels and engaged in religious pursuits.⁶

As a youth Clarie taught a Sunday school class at Central United Methodist Church and afterwards served for many years as church school superintendent. Later she served as a steward and more recently as a trustee and chairman of the auditing committee. At Spelman College, she was involved in the student Y.W.C.A., and in 1950, she was co-founder and first board member of the Farish Street Y.W.C.A. in Jackson.⁷

Later Clarie Collins gained national and international acclaim for her Christian endeavors. She served as a member of the general board of education of the United Methodist Church, secretary of the National Council of Methodist Youth, and member and secretary of the General Board of Christian Social Concerns. In 1963 the General Board of Christian Social Concerns cited Clarie Collins for outstanding efforts in civil rights and peace. She served on the committee which developed a church center for the United Nations. From 1964 to 1968 she was a member of the Committee on Overseas Relief and of the executive committee commission of structure of the United Methodist Church, 1968 to 1972.⁸

Clarie Collins's involvement in Christian youth work led to her friendship and marriage to Martin Luther Harvey, Jr. She first heard of Martin in 1939 on a train en route to a World Christian Youth Conference at Amsterdam, Holland, at which she represented the national student Y.W.C.A. and Harvey was the African Methodist Episcopal Zion Church delegate. (He also presided as first black president of the United Christian Youth Council of North America, the youth movement of the International Council of Religious Education.) They married in 1943.[9]

When her father and mother died, Clarie C. Harvey, who was general manager of Collins Funeral Home and Insurance Company, assumed ownership of the business. With a staff of fifty employees, the business prospered and by the 1970s its assets were valued at a hundred thousand dollars. Of this venture Clarie Harvey stated, "The result has not been wealth, but it has meant freedom and independence for us and our many co-workers."[10] In 1955 years before "black enterprise" became a familiar term, C. C. Harvey, in association with a group of other blacks, founded the State Mutual (now Federal) Savings and Loan Association, and served on its board of directors until 1968. State Mutual is presently a multimillion dollar all-black institution. She was also vice-president of Investors in Mississippi.[11]

Because of her business acumen, the National Funeral Directors and Embalmers Association chose her as its first "Woman of the Year." From 1956 to 1960, she served as Regional VI Governor of the National Association of Funeral Directors and Embalmers. For two years she presided as president of the Mississippi State Funeral Directors and Embalmers Association.[12]

While expanding her business C. C. Harvey maintained a genuine interest in civic activities and human relations. In 1961 she founded and became president of Womanpower Unlimited, a powerful and first underground interracial human relations group of Protestant, Jewish, and Roman Catholic women who provided housing, prison ministries, and general assistance to the civil rights advocates who came to Mississippi during the 1960 civil rights movement. Through this organization hundreds of women became involved in the struggle for racial good will. They sponsored voter registration and selective buying campaigns. In 1964 she was appointed a member of the Mississippi Advisory Committee to the United States Commission on Civil Rights and served for over ten years. Even when the NAACP was on the black list in Mississippi, Clarie Harvey retained her membership because her father helped establish the Mississippi chapter. She is also a board member of the Southern Regional Council, an agency founded over thirty years ago to improve human relations in the South. She participated in White House Conferences on Human

Relations and advised President Gerald Ford on national plans for women. In 1968, Harvey was elected chairman of the Hinds County Community Service Association sponsored by the Office of Economic Opportunity. However, as the storm of racial confrontation escalated in Jackson, she became reluctant about being involved in the civil rights movement. She confessed, "I thought about leaving, but then I realized I couldn't. I saw that I must get involved totally, seeking God's will for our community."[13]

C. C. Harvey was active with "Women Strike for Peace" during the early 1960s. In 1963 she made a peace pilgrimage to Rome, where she had an audience with Pope John XXIII. That same year Medgar Evers, civil rights activist, was assassinated half-an-hour after he had conferred with Harvey concerning an important tactical matter. She served as his mortician. It was from her establishment that thousands viewed his body before he was taken to Washington for interment at Arlington Cemetery.[14]

Never one to turn down an opportunity to serve, Harvey has given of herself in many educationally related activities. In 1958 she was elected to the board of trustees of Rust College, Holly Springs, Mississippi, and served as its secretary from 1962 to 1965. In December 1971, Rust College honored her with a Doctor of Humanities degree. In October 1972, she began service on the board of trustees of Tuskegee Institute. She was secretary of the Atlanta University Center Board of Trustees for the term 1974–1976, and member of the board of the Children's Defense Fund, in Washington, D.C. Spelman College named her its outstanding alumna in 1966 and invited her to be commencement speaker in 1973. In September 1974, she was the first black elected to the board of trustees of predominantly white Millsaps College, Jackson.[15]

Singly, C. C. Harvey's greatest achievement occurred within the ecumenical movement. She attributed her involvement in ecumenics to her husband's early identification with the movement, her Christian youth work, and her intention "to glorify God." In 1962 she joined women from ten countries at the Seventeenth National Disarmament Conference in Geneva, Switzerland. In July of that year she participated in "The World Without the Bomb" Peace Conference held in Accra, Ghana, West Africa. In March 1971 she was among fifty Protestant leaders who went to Paris to discuss issues with the delegations at the Vietnam peace talks. In August 1971 she was elected to the executive committee of the World Methodist Council. She attended the World Council of Churches' "Consultation on Sexism in the 1970s" and the convocation on evangelism held in Jerusalem.[16]

When not involved in church related matters, Harvey has championed the cause of minorities. In 1972, Governor William Waller appointed her to the Mississippi Commission on the Status of Women. She is a member of the board of the Mississippi Industrial Special Services, which deals with federal public housing in the state. She persuaded Mayor Thompson of Jackson to join her on a tour of the city to discover for himself the great need for housing of blacks. As a result the housing authority and urban renewal came to Jackson. Harvey served on the city's progressive action committee, designed to encourage the economic growth of Jackson. In April 1971 the city council honored Mrs. Harvey with an "Outstanding Citizen of Jackson" award.[17]

In May 1974 Religious Heritage of America selected Clarie Collins Harvey, national president of Church Women United in the U.S.A., recipient of the Churchwomen of the Year Award, and she was "among seven distinguished Americans who made outstanding religious and humanitarian contributions to the nation." Following her return from Nairobi, East Africa, where she was a delegate to the 1975 Assembly of the World Council of Churches, Harvey was named recipient of the 1976 *Upper Room Citation*, becoming the first black American and the second American female to be so honored.[18]

George Johnson

Business Millionaire

George Johnson, millionaire-industrialist, native of Laurel, is president of the Johnson Products Company, Inc., the largest manufacturer of personal grooming products for black consumers. During the initial stage of the Great Depression in 1929, when Johnson was two years old, his mother packed her bags and three sons and traveled to Chicago in search of employment and a better way of life. But it was not until 1954 that Johnson reaped the benefits of improved economic conditions. With $250 in borrowed capital, Johnson founded Johnson's Products and manufactured a single product, Ultra Wave Hair Culture, a chemical straightener for men. Business boomed as a

Hiram Hodes Revels

Blanche Kelso Bruce

James Charles Evers

Margaret Murray Washington

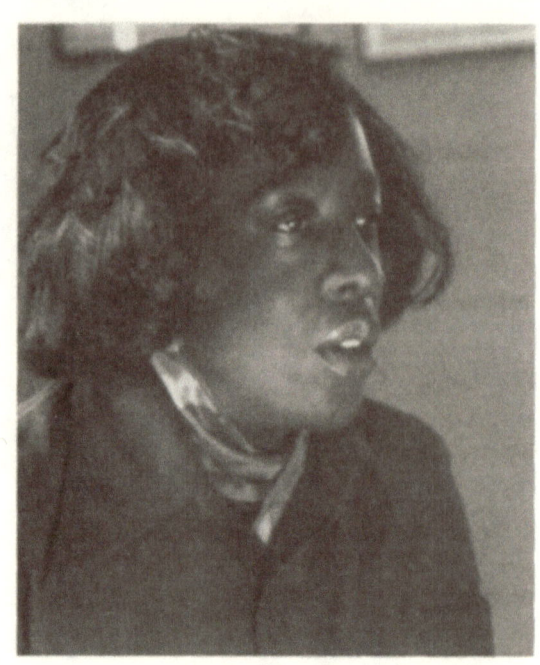

Unita Blackwell Wright

Evan Doss

Charles Bernard Sheppard

Deborah Jones Gambrell

James Meredith

George Washington Lee

Fannie Lou Hamer

Joseph Edison Walker

result of excellent management, capital, advertisement and patronage. Currently, the company manufactures and markets hair products such as dressings, relaxers, conditioners and shampoos, cosmetics, and men's fragrances. Its major brands are Ultra Sheen, Afro Sheen, Ultra Wave, Ultra Sheen Cosmetics, and Black Tie. He has companies in Chicago and Lagos, Nigeria, and employs five hundred individuals.[1]

In 1973, George Johnson returned to Mississippi to acquire property. If not the largest, he is one of the largest black landowners in the state. The Johnson's real estate holdings include two farms: the Louisville property consists of 2600 acres in Winston County, and the Lexington farm consists of 4100 acres in Holmes County. Because Mississippi has, according to Johnson, "the cheapest, good productive land of any state in the country," he decided to purchase property in the state. Farming on the Johnson estate includes raising 1100 head of cattle and producing corn, cotton, soybeans, sorghum, and hay.[2]

In summarizing his success, George Johnson attributes it to the humanistic quality of his personality. He asserted, "I don't think about myself in terms of just being a businessman . . . but I start off with George Johnson the human being . . . Concern for people, I think, is something that isn't often highlighted in describing a businessman. But I start out with that-with people, because I think that's basically what it's all about."[3]

Robert Earl James

Youngest Black Bank President

Robert Earl James, a native of Hattiesburg, became one of America's youngest bank presidents on December 1, 1971, when he was elected at age twenty-five to head the Carver State Bank in Savannah, Georgia, with assets of over four million dollars. In 1980, the bank's assets totaled more than 16 million dollars. The son of the late Jimmie James, Sr., and Mrs. Annie M. James, Robert Earl finished Rowan High School in Hattiesburg and received his bachelor's degree in business administration from Morris Brown College in Atlanta, Georgia, and the M.A. degree from the Harvard University Graduate School of Business Administration in 1970.[1]

James chose banking as a career because he would have exposure to all areas of business, and not be confined to one industry. In addition, he would be exposed to consumer problems as well as the retail aspect of business. Subsequently he engaged in professional and civic activities that would boost his career and provide opportunities to assist the black community. James is listed in *Outstanding Young Men of America* for 1970. He gained experience in several departments of the Citizens and Southern National Banks in Atlanta. Since becoming bank president, he has served as president of the National Bankers Association. He was appointed to the Savannah Port Authority, the Model Cities Evaluation Committee, and Savannah Area Chamber of Commerce Urban Development Task Force. He is an officer of St. Philip A.M.E. Church and a member of Omega Psi Phi Fraternity.[2]

As an advocate of black economic nationalism, James's primary goal is to help blacks move ahead in becoming more economically self-reliant. He asserts, "There needs to be a greater concentration on supporting black enterprises for ideological reasons. If we don't control our own enterprises, we're going to always be parasites on the larger community.[3]

Jessie R. Chambliss

Businessman and Boy Scout Organizer

In Jackson, Mississippi, J. R. Chambliss is a legend. People respect him, love him, and swear by him. He was the fifth of twelve children born in a crude log cabin to Marcus and Susan Claiborne Chambliss July 6, 1885, near rural Tillman, Claiborne County.[1]

His father, Marcus, was a slave, but he soon learned two matters of great importance—the value of a close-knit Christian family life and the need of an education. These he strove valiantly to provide for his children. He sent his daughters and sons to school in Port Gibson. In 1900 Jessie entered Alcorn A. & M. College at Lorman, where he enrolled in the carpenter shop, but later transferred to the shoemaking department, graduating as valedictorian of his class. His instructors were extremely impressed with Jessie's performance, and one teacher promised him a job if he opened a shoe shop in Jackson.

That promise became a reality in 1905. Jessie rode mule-back to the Tillman train station, and then flagged a train to Jackson. From the Jackson railroad station Jessie slowly found his way to the Farish Street shoe shop. There Jessie R. Chambliss commenced a career that bestowed upon him dignity and an income for his family.

Before departing for Jackson, he was given five dollars and the following advice by his father: "If things do not work out, save two pennies to mail a letter back home and I will send your return fare." For the first two weeks Chambliss earned eight dollars a week. Afterwards the owner paid his salary on a commission basis. By Christmas, Chambliss sent twenty dollars home, ten dollars each for his father and mother.

While working in Jackson, Chambliss joined the Pearl Street African Methodist Episcopal Church. On May 30, 1917, he married Norah Robinson, a regular church attendant and choir member. They lived in their home at 624 Rose Street, where their six children—five sons and one daughter—were born.

Three of their sons served in the armed forces. Captain Carroll R. Chambliss, is a career Naval chaplain, whose son Chris is a professional baseball player, formerly with the New York Yankees and presently with the Atlanta Braves. The daughter married a minister, and the other sons became professionals.

In addition to being an ardent churchman, J. R. Chambliss was a pioneer Boy Scout leader in Mississippi. He organized the first Boy Scout Troop for blacks in Mississippi in 1932, at Pearl Street African Methodist Episcopal Church and continued active in the promotion of that troop for forty years. From that troop, No. 51, four Eagle scouts have been honored. In 1954, Chambliss was presented the Silver Beaver Award, the highest award given in scouting for volunteer services.

In 1968 he attended the World Methodist Council at London, England. His church has honored him several times as most distinguished lay-person, most loyal officer, senior steward, and oldest Sunday School member.

Sam Baker

Businessman

The Mississippi branch of the Small Business Administration, a multimillion-dollar agency that assists small enterprise, is supervised by Sam Baker, a graduate of Lanier High School in Jackson and Tougaloo College.[1]

Sam Baker has had a diversified occupational background. Before his March 1980 appointment as director, Baker worked for the SBA for thirteen years until he became vice-president of Commercial Lending at Mississippi National Bank in 1978. He was also a waiter and steward on the Illinois Central Railroad and a letter carrier for the U.S. Postal Service.

Baker highly recommends civil service careers for minorities because of competitive salary ranges, fringe benefits, operational procedures, and opportunities for policy making.

Baker, a native of Jackson, is married to Barbara Willis; they have four children.

Vernon Floyd
Radio Station Owner

Ambition has been a part of Vernon C. Floyd's life. A native of Mobile, Alabama, Floyd established on June 7, 1969, the first black owned and operated radio station in Mississippi—WORV-AM in Hattiesburg. Recently, the station received a license to function on AM and FM frequency. While residing in Mobile, where he cofounded another black radio station, Floyd conducted a feasibility survey—within a 150 to 200 mile radius of Mobile—to determine what heavily populated area did not have a radio station, which catered to the black community. Considering his findings, he decided to lay the foundation for his project in Hattiesburg, one of Mississippi's largest cities that has a large college and black population. Through hard work, prayer, and determination, Floyd opened his radio station. According to Floyd, his strength and drive came directly from his African ancestor, Cudjoe Kazolla Lewis, who arrived in the United States from Togo, West Africa, as a slave in 1859.

Floyd is a graduate of the Mobile public school system and Tuskegee Institute, where he majored in electronics. While a student at Tuskegee, he studied business management as well as architectural and mechanical drawing. This training steered Floyd into the broadcasting industry. He attributes his success in broadcasting and business to "ninety percent perspiration and ten percent inspiration."[1]

Presently, Floyd owns two Hattiesburg radio stations, WORV and WJMG-FM.

Charlene Owens
Business Magnate

One of few black women in Mississippi to discover the key to success and to acquire management skills is Charlene Owens, the youngest daughter of three children born to Josephine Fairley Washington. Her mother, a self-made community storeowner, instilled in her a sense of racial pride and economic nationalism. Charlene Owens proudly boasted that "her parents, despite economic conditions during her childhood, survived, thereby dispelling the myth that blacks can't make it."[1]

The business career of Charlene Owens commenced in the early 1950s when she opened the presently defunct Kiddie Haven Kindergarten, the first black day care center in the Hattiesburg area. Since there were no apartments to accomodate single or married blacks, Charlene erected Schoolview Teacher's Home, a housing unit for single black women. Later, she constructed apartments and acquired trailer units to set up housing for married couples.

Included among her numerous business enterprises and real estate property are Golden Gate Funeral Home, Shopper's World Mini Mall, Jerry B. Owens Business and Professional Plaza Building, and Charlene's Modern Day Apartments in Hattiesburg. She is also the proud proprietor of On The Avenue Mall in Jackson.[2]

Attributing her success to her philosophical belief that anything can be done, she advises aspiring black business leaders, "If you stay with it (business), put God and yourself in it, there's no failure."[3]

Rose Morgan
Beautician

A Shelby, Mississippi, native, Rose Morgan, gained international acclaim as a pioneer in modern beauty culture for black women. Presently, she "supervises a chain of beauty salons operating in New York, Detroit, and Chicago, and has traveled extensively speaking and commentating during fashion and trade shows (television programs), and beauty clinics." She expanded her business through national mail orders.

Her career as a beautician and consultant began in New York after graduation from a cosmetology school in Chicago. She founded and serves as president of the New York based Rose Morgan House which is a subsidiary of her Rodelia Corporation.

In addition to catering to female and male clientel, she actively participates in the following organizations: member of NAACP, board member of Kilimanjaro African Coffee, vice-president of the National Council of Negro Women, and director of Uptown New York Chamber of Commerce, Interracial Council for Business Opportunity and National Bank of New York.[1]

Louise K. Quarles
Managing Officer of
Illinois Federal Savings and Loan-Chicago

After earning a B.S. degree in business administration from Alcorn College, Louise K. Quarles, a Mississippian, accepted a position with the Federal Wage Stabilization Board before assuming her present title as secretary and managing officer of the Illinois Federal Savings and Loan Association. The Chicago-based company's assets total more than $27 million. According to Louise K. Quarles, "the field of business is opening wider for women executives and it is most necessary that we (black women) take the opportunity to prove ourselves capable of handling any position we accept."

Indeed Quarles's election to the board of directors for Illinois Federal in 1968 attests to that fact. She was the first women ever to serve in that capacity. Also, she is a member of the board of directors of American Savings and Loan League, Community Renewal Society, and Community Renewal Foundation as well as trustee of Chicago Theological Seminary. She is a member of Alpha Gamma Sorority, a business and professional women's organization. And, she has obtained a graduate degree from the American Savings and Loan Institute.[1]

Randolph T. Myrick
Banker

Another prominent black in banking is Randolph T. Myricks, Mississippi native, who was appointed personal banking officer at M & I (Marshall and Illsley Bank) in Milwaukee, Wisconsin. Myricks, twenty-eight joined M & I in 1968.[1]

Emorrie Jenkins
Milwaukee Businessman

Emorrie Jenkins, president of Milwaukee's first black-owned and operated cab firm, Apex Cab Cooperative Association, Inc., employs one hundred drivers and gives them an equal share in company profits. He predicted that Apex will generate some 175 to 200 full- and part-time jobs at its peak of operation and a minimum cash flow of $1.5 million its first year. Originally from Mississippi, Jenkins is also a mechanic in the Air Force Reserve, having served twelve years of active duty in the Pacific.[1]

E. W. Green
Successful Farmer

E. W. Green, a wealthy and independent farmer in Jefferson County, began working for ten dollars a month. Ten years later, Green earned sixty dollars a month. Through thrift and budgeting, he acquired one thousand acres of land, eighty head of livestock; his personal and real property was valued at eighty thousand dollars in 1912. He employed seventy workers to harvest his crops, which yielded in 1912 five thousand bushels of corn and forty bales of cotton.[1]

Thelma Sanders
Fashions and Business

Thelma Sanders, a Jackson native, was one of the pioneers in black-owned retail clothing stores in Jackson. After graduation from

Tougaloo College, she did further study at the University of Southern Mississippi, where she earned a certificate in Business Management, Business Law, Principles of Accounting, and Marketing. She is married to Dr. I. S. Sanders, prominent educational, business, and civic leader. Her shop became a mecca for black women interested in the latest fashions. Thelma operated Sanders Women's Apparel for more than twenty years. She has conducted workshops and career clinics across the state in "Charm and Fashions."[1]

Naomi Sims
Model-Businesswoman

Mississippi-born Naomi Sims, is hailed around the globe as one of the world's most beautiful women. A famous model, Naomi has appeared as "cover girl" and on editorial and advertising pages of many fashion publications. She also has appeared on several television commercials. She began her modeling career in New York in 1967. She retired from modeling in 1973 to devote her time to the Naomi Sims Collection, which consists of cosmetics for black women. In addition to articles in women's magazines, she wrote a comprehensive illustrated encyclopedia, *All About Health and Beauty for the Black Woman*, published by Doubleday.[1]

EDUCATION

Education was of paramount concern and the motivating force within the Mississippi black community before and after freedom. It was the key to enlightenment, the eroding agent of ignorance, and the catalyst to uplifting the black race—economically, socially, and politically. Black leaders viewed education as the economic vehicle to wealth, power, and freedom and as a survival mechanism that would eventually lead to the assimilation of the race into the mainstream of "Dixie America."

The unequal distribution of wealth, a disproportionately large rural population, and a racial caste system made universal free public education non-existent in Mississippi before the Civil War. Consequently, few Mississippians, black or white, received an education. Those belonging to the aristocracy were generally educated either outside of the state or at home by private tutors. The illiteracy rate, therefore, was extremely high, and it did not decline until the era of Reconstruction.

Reconstruction wrought change within the state's political system and brought about new political leadership that directly affected education. The election of black public officials to key positions in Mississippi—the state superintendent of schools, state legislators, and U.S. Congressmen—brought to the forefront competent, enlightened, and ardent supporters of a comprehensive public-school system. Their efforts were enhanced by petitions from the black community to the state legislature and the federal government. As a result, an education bill was enacted that provided for a common school education for both blacks and whites. However, the lack of school buildings, inexperienced and indifferent school officials, poorly prepared teachers, and inadequate funding hampered black education. Subsequently, in order to receive an education, blacks organized benevolent societies, relied upon the Freedmen's Bureau Schools, and accepted philanthropic assistance from northern whites. The greatest assistance, however, came from black parents who were willing to endure oppression and to make financial sacrifices so their children could get an education and escape the "increasing proscription and indignities that a renascent South was heaping upon the Negroes."

Although blacks made financial sacrifices to pay property taxes in order to support free public education in Mississippi, white school officials appropriated only small sums to educate blacks, to pay black teachers, and to maintain black institutions. For example in 1900 in Adams County, the per capita cost of education per school population was $22.25 for each white child and only $2.00 for each black child. The disparity in black and white teachers' salaries was also significant. Generally, a white teacher earned approximately one and a half to twice as much as his black counterpart. Little or no money was allotted for textbooks, equipment, or building repairs. Regardless of these disadvantages, black teachers persevered and black children were educated.

The stagnated and segregated black public schools existed in Mississippi for several years after the United States Supreme Court ruled in *Brown vs Board of Education* (1954) that "separate and unequal" schools were unconstitutional and shall no longer exist. In the second Brown decision of 1955, the court ordered the desegregation of schools with "all deliberate speed." The die had been cast. These cases marked the beginning of a new era in race relations in Mississippi.

White Mississippians resisted desegregation of the schools. Discriminatory roadblocks were erected by racist demagogues and the Mississippi White Citizen's Council. White legislators and Congressmen ratified the "Southern Manifesto," a document denouncing the Brown decision and calling for open defiance to government intervention to achieve desegregation. The white backlash of Mississippi viewed the issue as an infringement upon states' rights, and the controversy became an alignment of states' rights versus federalism, positions which are still held by some. By the early 1970s, however, most public school districts in Mississippi had been desegregated by court order.

For the past century, predominantly black institutions have been the major source for providing higher education to black Americans. Many black leaders received their baccalaureate degrees from these institutions. Now the existence of black colleges is being jeopardized. Presently, the central issues in the plight of historically black institutions are decreased enrollment, inadequate funding, deletion of curricula, and merger with predominantly white colleges and universities.

Since 1974, the peak year of black educational opportunity, enrollment at predominantly black institutions has declined because of inadequate financial assistance, outdated physical and research facilities, and insufficient staff. Although these causes can be cited as potential threats to the survival of black colleges, the most threatening cause is the drainage of students from black institutions into white colleges and universities. According to an article in the *Black Collegian*, the decline in enrollment at black colleges is attributed to the recent growth opportunities in white colleges.[1]

Added to these concerns is the problem of depleting state funds available to publicly-supported institutions. The proposed remedy, advocated by many state officials, is to merge predominantly black institutions with predominantly white ones.

A challenge to the legitimacy of publicly-supported black colleges and universities is another area of concern. Some opponents contend that black colleges create a dual system of education which is unconstitutional. Moreover, some believe that only white institutions can guarantee equal educational opportunity for blacks.[2] A recent court case which challenges the existence of publicly-supported black colleges is *Adams v Califano* which is still being litigated. The results of this case will significantly impact upon the survival of black institutions. As Milton Morris stated:

> ... federal officials tend to view black colleges as parallel but inferior to white ones; they view them as simple vestiges of segregation ... that perspective leads to a clear and present danger for black colleges. The important understanding of black colleges as a unique creation of blacks to promote equality and educational progress beyond segregation and desegregation has yet to be insinuated into the rulings.[3]

The continuing existence of historically black public and private institutions in Mississippi and the service they are rendering to the black race is unquestionable. The number of blacks who have achieved in science and in the arts and humanities attests to the fact that these institutions are achieving their goals and producing achievers who are competitive in the market place. One can judge the worth of any institution by its reputation, its leadership, and its student population.

The educators considered in this section have made contributions to the development of black schools and institutions of higher education. In spite of Mississippi's dual system of education and inadequate funding of black institutions, the state has produced some of the most outstanding educators in the nation.

John Dewey Boyd
President of Alcorn College
1957–1969

Dr. J. D. Boyd, the fourteenth president of Alcorn A. & M. College, was born in Dolorso, a community in rural Wilkinson County, to John and Elizabeth (Fry) Boyd, on September 3, 1899.[1] As a youth, he liked the out-of-doors and spent much time in the fields, woods, and streams. He reports that his father often took the time to encourage him to get an education as a necessity for achieving some security.

After completing high school, Boyd taught elementary school, and later entered Alcorn College, from which he received the B.S. degree in 1931. Following his graduation from college, he was appointed principal and agriculture teacher in Sunflower County, a position he held for five years. In 1936 he accepted similar employment at Lampton Institute in Marion County. He remained at that post for eleven years and was successful in upgrading that school to a four-year high school with a model home economics cottage, a first for that county.[2]

While at Lampton, Professor Boyd convinced the school's trustees of the necessity of a Rural Life Center. Later he was appointed to the committee which selected a site for the center, which was financed by the Women's Division of Christian Service of the Methodist Church. The Center consisted of a library, health clinic, gymnasium, and club rooms, the first such in the state for blacks.[3]

In 1941 Boyd was named president of Utica Institute. During his administration, Utica's status was elevated from agricultural high school to junior college, and it became a state supported institution. The enrollment increased from three hundred to more than a thousand, and the college was accredited by the Southern Association of Colleges and Secondary Schools.[4]

Professor Boyd returned to Alcorn in 1947 as professor of agronomy and manager of the college farm, and remained in that position until 1951. In the meantime, he studied during summers at the University of Illinois, where in 1949 he received the M.S. degree.

In 1952 Professor Boyd was elected president of the Mississippi Teachers Association, the only professional organization for Negro teachers in the state. Prior to his election to that office, a suit had been filed by the Negro teachers for equalization of teachers' salaries. Boyd pursued the litigation to a favorable conclusion and succeeded in inaugurating several improvements in the education system for Negroes.⁵

The 1954 Brown decision striking down the "separate but equal" doctrine created much controversy within the state. Some high-ranking officials considered abolishing public education in Mississippi. Boyd played a prominent role in meetings with members of the legislature, the governor, and others in order to save public education.⁶

Dr. Jessie R. Otis had been elected president of Alcorn College in 1949, but resigned that position in 1957. At that time Boyd was elected to the presidency of Alcorn A. & M. College and became the third alumnus so honored.⁷

He succeeded in changing an $85,000 deficit to a $50,000 surplus within a few years. A high priority was to obtain an "A" rating by the Southern Association of Colleges and Schools. To that end President Boyd recruited a trained and dedicated faculty, established a varied curriculum, and improved the physical plant. The student enrollment reached the highest peak in the history of the school.⁸ The college received the "A" rating by the Southern Association of Colleges and Schools in December 1961.

Other accomplishments of his administration included the renovation and refurnishing of Oakland Chapel, the President's Mansion, and Bowles Hall. A fine arts building, a student union building, a million dollar library, some thirty-odd faculty apartments and cottages, a mechanical arts facility, a health center, and a dairy barn were among the new constructions of his administration.⁹

President Boyd has been active in civic, political, and professional organizations. In the 1920s J. E. Johnson of Prentiss Institute organized the Committee of One Hundred—an organization to promote civic responsibility among Negroes. Upon invitation President Boyd joined that group and worked diligently "to keep politics alive among Negroes."¹⁰

In 1960 the land-grant colleges decided to celebrate their centennial. President Boyd was the only black named to the planning committee for the celebration. The events took place over a period of two years, ending with a final meeting in 1962 in Kansas City.

In spite of the college's and Boyd's many successes, Alcorn College had its problems. Plagued with student unrest since the days of its first president, former U. S. Senator Hiram R. Revels, Alcorn had a series of marches, demonstrations, and strikes in the 1960s, the turbulent years of the civil rights movement, a decade filled with student demands for African-American studies, racial equality, and justice. Yet, during that period Alcorn College also produced the school's first Woodrow Wilson Scholar and the first Rockefeller Scholar and was the only predominantly black state college to have a Danforth Fellow. The state's first Olympic gold medal winner was an Alcorn student, Mildrette Netter, who performed at the 1968 Olympics in Mexico City.[11]

When asked in the 1960s by one of Mississippi's leading editors what he thought Negroes wanted most, Boyd replied that "the Negro wanted political freedom and rights as citizens, that he would not settle for less, and that he would get it one way or another." Furthermore, he stated, it would be better for all should these be granted, for that which is taken by force will not easily improve by discussion.[12]

In 1962 President Boyd was invited by President John F. Kennedy to attend the White House Conference on Education. In 1964 President and Mrs. Boyd attended the World Food Congress in Amsterdam, Holland, following which they toured western Europe with their granddaughter, Johnetta Dockins.

Late in life President Boyd took up the hobby of painting and has been acclaimed as a primitive artist. He retired from the presidency of Alcorn A. & M. College in 1969 to his rural home near Lorman.

He maintains an interest in politics and was a delegate to the 1972 National Republican Convention at Miami, Florida. Dr. Boyd is a member of Phi Beta Sigma, Phi Delta Kappa, a Mason, an Elk, and a Baptist. He was married to the former Cleopatra Carter on August 14, 1921. They had one child, a daughter, Katye Carlotta.

Walter Washington

President of Alcorn State University
1969–

Since becoming president of Alcorn State University, the oldest predominantly black land-grant university in the United States, Walter Washington has adhered to its original objective—that is, the maintenance of a first class institution that stresses the pursuit of academic excellence while imparting scientific and practical knowledge in the liberal arts, vocational and industrial technology, and agriculture.[1]

Alcorn State University has experienced academic expansion and physical growth through a $20,000,000 capital improvement plan. To Washington's credit, positive changes have occurred, including the following: construction of a dairy, swine research center, truck crops research center, biological research buildings, health and physical education complex, water plant, administrative classroom building, recreational park, industrial technology building, faculty garden apartments, agriculture science building, and a landing strip for small aircrafts.[2]

President Washington insists that research, creativity, and academic excellence are essential to the institution's development and growth; therefore, he established three new divisions of study—nursing, business, and graduate studies. In addition, Washington instituted an Army ROTC unit, ASU branch of the Mississippi Agricultural and Forestry Experiment Station, ASU branch of the Mississippi Cooperative Extension Service, and a communication program. Also Oakland Memorial Chapel was entered into the National Register of Historic Places. Alcorn's president strongly encourages the faculty to research and publish. In addition, he urges faculty involvement or rendering of service to the local communities as well as the university. As a result of these accomplishments, Alcorn A. & M. College was converted to Alcorn State University on March 15, 1974.[3]

Because of President Washington's concern for faculty, staff, and student welfare, Alcorn for the first time has a faculty assembly and senate insuring faculty participation in the decision policies of the institution. Also, the president has involved students in the making of the university's policies and regulations. As a result of the liberality of the president's plans, policies, and capital improvements, student enrollment has significantly increased.

Walter Washington's background and training prepared him well for administrative leadership. One of three sons and two daughters born to Reverend and Mrs. Kemp Washington, he completed his elementary and secondary education in the Hazelhurst and Copiah County public schools. A native of Hazelhurst, Walter Washington is a man of deep convictions and religious beliefs. Washington was graduated from Tougaloo College, with a B.A. degree in secondary education. He received a M.S. degree from Indiana University and an

Education Specialist certificate from George Peabody College. He was also awarded a certificate in Alcoholic Studies from Yale University. He was the first black to earn a terminal degree in school administration at the University of Southern Mississippi.[4]

Washington's professional career began in 1948 with a teaching position at Holtzclaw High School in Crystal Springs. Afterwards, he accepted an appointment as instructor and assistant principal at Parish High School in his native Hazelhurst. Two years later, the Board of Trustee of Utica Junior College appointed him Dean of Academic Affairs. He remained at Utica for four years before leaving to assume the principalship of Sumner Hill High School in Clinton. In 1957, the Board of Trustees of Mississippi Institution of Higher Learning named him President of Utica Junior College, where he remained until July 1, 1969, when he became President of Alcorn State University.[5]

During the course of his academic career, President Washington became affiliated with numerous professional and civic organizations. He served as president of the Mississippi Teachers Association, National Pan-Hellenic Council, National Alumni Council of the United Negro College Fund, and Alpha Phi Alpha Fraternity. He has acted as chairman of Secondary Commission of Southern Association of Colleges and Schools, a member of the Board of Directors of Mississippi Mental Health Care, the Advisory Board of the State Vocational Education Program, Mississippi Economic Council, Mississippi Commission on Hospital Care, Mississippi Heart Association, Andrew Jackson Council of Boy Scouts of America, and member of the Board of Directors, First Natchez Bank.

He is a member of Phi Delta Kappa Educational Fraternity, Kappa Delta Pi Honorary Society, Alpha Kappa Mu Educational Honorary Society, and the American Association of School Administration.[6]

Washington is listed in *International Men of Achievement, Who's Who in the South and Southwest, Who's Who in American Education, Who's Who in American College and University Administration, Personalities of the South,* and *Outstanding Educators of America.* Ebony magazine has named him for two years among the "100 Most Influential Black Americans." Among his special honors are Silver Beaver, Boy Scouts of America; honorary doctorate, Tougaloo College; and the Distinguished Achievement Award by Peabody College.[7]

Walter Washington is married to the former Carolyn Carter of Canton, a former schoolmate at Tougaloo College. Carolyn holds a doctorate degree in education and is a professor of sociology at Alcorn State University.

B. Baldwin Dansby
President of Jackson State College
1927–1940

Dr. B. Baldwin Dansby was a native Georgian who graduated with a bachelor's degree in mathematics from Atlanta Baptist Seminary, now Morehouse College, in 1906 as valedictorian of his class. Before accepting the position as dean and professor of mathematics at Jackson College in 1911, he had taught high school mathematics at Morehouse and at Florida Baptist Academy, now Florida Memorial College. During his tenure as a teacher at Jackson College, he was granted a year's leave for graduate study at the University of Chicago under a fellowship grant by the General Education Board of New York.[1]

On October 1, 1927, Dansby was appointed the fourth president of Jackson College, then a struggling private school supported by the Baptist Home Mission Society. For more than ten years Dansby strove valiantly to keep the school's doors open. He is credited with bringing the school through its most severe financial crisis from 1927 to 1940.

In 1940 the state took over the institution and changed the title of the school to Jackson State College. The new president, Jacob Reddix, retained Dansby who served in the dual positions of registrar and assistant to the president, from 1941 to 1951. Although he officially retired in 1951, Dr. Dansby continued to teach mathematics for two years.

Dansby became a Mississippi citizen in every respect. He was State Rosenwald Building Agent and Supervisor of Black Schools from 1923–1926; founder and editor of *Mississippi Educational Journal*, the official organ of the MTA-NEA; director of summer school for in-service teachers at Alcorn A. & M. College, 1924–1926; president of the Mississippi Teachers Association, 1930–1932; treasurer, Mississippi Council on Interracial Cooperation; one of the founders of the Farish Street YMCA; organized Jackson State University alumni chapters in Chicago, St. Louis, Washington, D.C. and Memphis, and was a member of the board of deacons of College Hill Baptist Church. Jackson State University's Hall of Expressive Arts is named in honor of Dr. B. Baldwin Dansby.

He died in 1975 at the age of ninety-six, after forty-two years of service to Jackson State University and to Mississippi.

Jacob L. Reddix
President of Jackson State College
1940–1967

On May 2, 1897, to Nathan and Frances (Brown) Reddix was born Jacob Reddix, the youngest of nine sons. Each of the nine was born on the family's homestead in Vancleave, Mississippi, which the Reddix clan have owned since August 1877. The family roots consist of a racial mixture of Africans, Creoles, and Cajuns.[1]

Race relations in Vancleave, located on the Gulf Coast, contrasted with those in the Natchez area and other parts of the state. In Vancleave slave labor was not utilized to cultivate cotton, tobacco, or sugar cane. The timber industry attracted free black and white workers, who frequently lived in the same camps. In fact, a black man was appointed postmaster of Ocean Springs, a town located twelve miles from Vancleave, without any racial confrontations.

The economy of Vancleave was intertwined with the lumber industry, which employed a majority of the town's population. At one time, Jacob's father burned charcoal for a living and cut timber for the sawmills. He simultaneously operated a subsistence farm and raised sheep and cattle.

Since money was scarce and most families owned land, the people displayed a kind of backwoods independence. By the turn of the twentieth century, Jacob's paternal step-grandfather, Henry Galloway, had bought 160 acres of land from his ex-slavemaster, who sold land to more than twenty-five black and white families in Vancleave.

Although blacks and whites lived within close proximity of each other, the Vancleave school system was segregated. The first public school in the area was the Vancleave Public School built for whites in 1880. Two years later, the town erected Bluff Creek Public School for blacks. Both institutions were basically as separate but equal as they could physically be—one-room schools with little or no furniture and equipment, and with teachers in both schools receiving a salary of fifty dollars per month. The Reddix clan attended Bluff Creek Public School.

Because Jacob cried to go with his older brothers, he started to school before he was five years old. The teacher allowed him special privileges because he was the youngest among thirty-five pupils. By the time he was seven Jacob had learned to read and to write and had read every book he could find. But by the time he was nine, he had little or no admiration for academic excellence or for any proficiency in the liberal arts. In an environment that produced only lumberjacks, graduating from the elementary school was not a necessity.

However, Jacob's desire to learn was whetted by formal training in the local Baptist Church. At Sunday School, Jacob became fascinated by the stories of Moses and the Children of Israel in Egyptian bondage, the Exodus from Egypt and their journey to the "Promised Land." Indirectly he acquired an appetite for history which he nurtured throughout his life.

In 1907, a relative who had attended Miller's Ferry Normal and Industrial Institute at Miller's Ferry, Alabama, urged Jacob's mother to enroll her children at the Institute. At the time his mother decided Jacob was too young to go so far away from home. But Reddix remembered, "In the fall of 1909, my mother persuaded my father to send my brother Eugene and me to school at Miller's Ferry Institute." Miller's Ferry was founded in 1896 under the auspices of the United Presbyterian Church of Pittsburgh, Pennsylvania. One of the unique features was that the faculty members were all blacks.[2]

After his parents had saved forty dollars to pay their expenses, Jacob and his brother left for Ferry Institute. The thirty-acre campus was located in a beautiful grove of pine trees between a large cotton plantation and a swamp. There were about fifteen buildings and a student body of one hundred, approximately half of whom lived on campus.

Miller's Ferry Institute operated on the principle espoused by Booker T. Washington: all students were required to learn a trade. Jacob worked in the general shop and was paid ten cents an hour. He advanced to foreman during his high school years and earned fifteen cents per hour. He remained there for seven years.

The advent of World War I in 1914 coincided with the completion of Jacob's study at Miller's Ferry Institute. The outlook for jobs was precarious. A classmate invited Jacob to accompany him to his home at Mobile, Alabama, and Jacob accepted, arriving there with a total of thirty cents. With no money to pay for the transfer of his trunk, he left it at the train station. The next morning after breakfast Jacob informed his hosts of his plans to seek employment at the Mobile and Ohio Railroad shops, to which they offered no encouragement.

Dressed in his Sunday clothes—neat blue serge suit, collar and tie, black shoes, and a white straw hat—Jacob Reddix boarded the street car for the three-mile ride to Whistler, where the shops were located. As he approached, he noticed thirty or forty men being turned back from the gates. Nevertheless Jacob found the foreman and overheard him tell another youth, "You're too young. We don't hire anybody under twenty-one." Turning to seventeen-year-old Jacob, whom he carefully inspected, he said, "I'm going to hire you, but you're not dressed for work now. Give me your name and report for work at the yard office tomorrow morning at seven o'clock." Jacob worked at the sawmill until 1917.

In 1917 Jacob returned to Miller's Ferry Institute, and on December 6, 1917, Jacob and four classmates enlisted in the U.S. Army. From the enlistment center in Atlanta, Georgia, they were shipped out to Camp Alexander, a new camp for blacks near Newport News, Virginia. Construction at the camp had not been completed; besides, the worst winter storm in fifty years hit the area, making living conditions almost intolerable. Eventually, Jacob was assigned to the band and enjoyed some very profitable experiences. The band was discharged on August 19, 1919, at Camp Shelby, Mississippi. The Army gave the band members their instruments, some of which Jacob arranged to purchase for Miller's Ferry Institute. He returned to school that fall and reorganized the Institute Band, for which he was director until he completed high school in 1920.

Jacob Reddix, who wanted to go on to college but did not have the means to do so, worked as a teacher in Birmingham, Alabama. Jacob arrived in the late spring of 1921 in Birmingham to visit a former schoolmate. As usual, he was virtually without means of support. To assist Jacob in obtaining employment, his friend introduced him to the principal of Council Elementary Schools, W. R. Wood. Afterwards Wood invited Jacob to his office where he inquired regarding Jacob's background, training and plans for the future. Wood revealed that he needed a faculty member who could qualify to teach crafts and elementary shop under the Smith-Hughes Act and also serve as assistant principal.

With a letter of recommendation from Wood, Jacob went with haste to the board of education office. The superintendent gave Jacob a provisional license, a temporary teacher's permit for the remainder of that school year, and a conditional contract for the following school year at an annual salary of one hundred dollars a month for ten months.

The following evening the Woods invited Jacob to their home for dinner; and inasmuch as their only child, a son, was away at medical college, they invited Jacob to live with them until the opening of school in the fall. In the meantime, Wood succeeded in finding summer employment for Jacob. Also during that summer, he passed the teacher's examination and received a permanent teacher's license.

After an exciting year as a teacher and assistant principal, Jacob Reddix went to Chicago the following summer to work and to visit a young lady, Daisy Uvasine Shirley. A British subject, she had lived in the United States for a year while attending high school in Evanston, Illinois. Jacob was impressed with her meticulous speech and soft English brogue, which was so different from his southern patois. Thus began a romance which eventually led to marriage.

After that summer, he taught for two years in Birmingham at Council Elementary School, before informing Principal Wood of his plan to return to his studies. He went to Chicago, where he passed the examination for postal clerk. He soon learned that he was just one among many blacks who were attempting to work the eight-hour midnight shift and attend college during the day; most became bitterly disappointed and gave up in defeat. Reddix did not.

In 1924 at age twenty-six Jacob Reddix entered Lewis Institute as an engineering major and won the La Verne Noyes Scholarship for veterans. In the summers during his schooling at Lewis Institute Jacob worked as a Pullman porter. In June 1927 at age thirty, Jacob was graduated from Lewis Institute. Three months later, Reddix became a member of the first faculty of Roosevelt High School in Gary, Indiana, and served there for seven years.

In 1939 Professor Reddix was awarded a Rosenwald Graduate Fellowship and enrolled at the University of Chicago to study economics. Toward the end of that year of study, Dr. Will W. Alexander, vice-president of the Julius Rosenwald Fund and administrator of the Farm Security Administration (FSA) of the U. S. Department of Agriculture, appointed Reddix "Advisor of Cooperatives" in Washington, D.C. That position involved providing supervision, counsel, and advice to resident tenant-purchasers regarding the problems of managing cooperatives. Reddix resigned his position at Roosevelt High School and reported within two weeks to his Washington post.

At the end of the first month in Washington he took a short leave to visit his wife in Gary and to discuss plans for moving to Washington. While he was there, the trustees of the Rosenwald Fund, who had recently awarded a grant to convert Jackson State into a teachers college, informed Reddix that they would nominate him as president. Reddix was invited to appear before the Board of Trustees of Institutions of Higher Learning of the State of Mississippi in Jackson, on Monday morning July 22. After Reddix told the members something of his early life and schooling in south Mississippi, Judge Jeptha Barbour of Yazoo City, chairman of the board, announced: "This board has just elected you the new president of Jackson College. The members felt that anybody who was born in the poorest county in Mississippi under the conditions of the schools at that time, but who could get a good education and achieve what you have in spite of these handicaps, should be the president of our new college."

On Monday, August 5, 1940, President Reddix flew from Washington to Jackson to begin his work at Jackson College. The summer school graduation was on August 8, and at that program Reddix was presented the keys of the college. The new president employed all but one of the old faculty and staff—fewer than thirty persons. Because of the extensive repairs of campus facilities, all faculty, staff, and students lived in the city that first year. On October 2, 1940, Jackson College began a new era in its long history, with an enrollment of 108 students. President Reddix took seriously his mandate to upgrade the teacher-education function of Jackson College, and he called upon the services of a number of able people to assist him in this work.

After more than twenty seven years of dedicated service to Jackson College, President Reddix resigned in 1967. A report by the Carnegie Foundation of Higher Education in February 1971 revealed the progress made during Reddix's administration:

> The growth and development of Jackson State College during the past thirty years has been phenomenal. The regular full-time enrollment has grown from 108 students to 5,000 while the annual state appropriation has been increased from $10,000 to $5,400,000. The college is now probably the second largest predominantly black college in the nation. Rapid growth has created many special problems for Negro colleges. Jackson State has experienced its share of such problems as securing qualified faculty and staff members as well as buildings, equipment, and operating budgets.

The College advanced steadily in the initial years under President Reddix's administration. Then came a period of rapid expansion both physically and academically, matched by increased student enrollment. This period was highlighted by the structuring of curricula leading to the Bachelor of Arts degree in liberal studies, the organization of a program of graduate studies, and the purchasing of a tract of land to aid expansion.

During these years of activity, Reddix maintained his interest in cooperatives and teacher education. He was a vigorous force in the organization and development of the Hinds County Educational Federal Credit Union and State Mutual Federal Savings and Loan Association. In 1948, he served as a consultant to the Phelps Stokes Fund for which he studied the feasibility of an effective teacher-education program in the Republic of Liberia, West Africa. While in Liberia, he served as a consultant to the Booker T. Washington Institute at Kakata.

Reddix was active in many civic and religious organizations. He served as chairman of the trustee board of the Farish Street Baptist Church, president of State Mutual Federal Savings and Loan Association, vice-president of the Central Mississippi Development Corporation, and was a member of Mu Sigma Chapter of Phi Beta Sigma Fraternity and a 33rd Degree Mason in the M. W. Stringer Grand Lodge. He also served on the Governor's Commission on Law Enforcement Assistance. His memoirs, *A Voice Crying in the Wilderness*, were published posthumously by the University and College Press of Mississippi in November 1973.

Dr. Reddix departed this life on May 9, 1973. His survivors included his widow, Daisy Shirley Reddix; a daughter, Shirley Reddix Vanderpool and a granddaughter, Dawn Constance Vanderpool of Nassau, Bahamas; a brother, Joseph Reddix of New Orleans, Louisiana, and numerous nieces, nephews, and other relatives.

John A. Peoples, Jr.

President of Jackson State University
1967–1984

John Arthur Peoples, Jr., the son of John A. and Maggie (Rose) Peoples, was born at Starkville on August 26, 1926.[1] After receiving his high school diploma from Henderson High School, he enrolled at Jackson State College where he received the bachelor of science degree in 1950," with highest honor."

In 1951 John Peoples joined the faculty of Froebel High School, Gary, Indiana, as a teacher of mathematics, where he remained for the next seven years, serving as principal of the evening school in 1957–1958. In 1958 he was elected assistant principal of the Lincoln Elementary School at Gary and principal of the Banneker Elementary School from 1962 to 1964.

Meanwhile, Peoples engaged in graduate studies at the University of Chicago, where he received the master of arts degree in 1951 and the Ph.D. in 1961. In 1964 he accepted a position on the faculty of Jackson State College as associate professor of mathematics and vice-president. In 1965 he was elected a post-doctoral fellow in the American Council on Education Academic Administration Internship Program. He interned as assistant to the president of the State University of New York at Binghampton from September 1965 through May 1966.

On March 2, 1967, Dr. Peoples assumed duties as the sixth president of Jackson State College and the first alumnus to be so honored in the ninety-nine-year history of the college.

Dr. Peoples is listed in *Who's Who in American Education*, 1952, 1967; *Outstanding Young Men of America*, 1965; *Who's Who in American College and University Administration*, *Who's Who in the South and Southwest*, 1967–1968, 1969–1970, 1971–1972; and *Who's Who in America*, 1972–1973.

He is a member of Alpha Kappa Mu Honor Society and a recipient of the prestigious Danforth Foundation Short-Term Leave Grant, 1971. Among his awards are alumni awards from Jackson State; Mississippi Teachers Association Outstanding Native Son Award, 1968; Omega Man of the Year Award, 1966, Sigma Omega Chapter; Omega Psi Phi Fraternity; and Phi Delta Kappa Award, Utica Junior College Chapter, 1971.

A few of his commissions and committee assignments are: Administrative Affairs, American Council on Education—December 1967–December 1970 (chairman, 1970); Southeastern Regional Council, American Association for Higher Education, November 1970–November 1971; Committee on Studies, American Association of State Colleges and Universities, 1969–1972 (chairman, 1969); Advisory Committee, Office for Advancement of Public Negro Colleges, National Association of Land-Grant Colleges and Universities,

1968–1971; President's Council, Institutions of Higher Learning, State of Mississippi, 1967 (chairman, July 1972); Mississippi Committee for the Humanities, National Endowment for the Humanities, 1972, 1974; and governor of Mississippi Crime Commission, 1967–1968.

Jackson State University was the first predominantly black institution in the state to offer courses leading to a graduate degree, and the only supported university in the capital city.

In spite of the many achievements of John A. Peoples, he was forced to resign as president of Jackson State University in August 1983. Citing declining enrollment, deficit and other financial problems, the Board of Trustees for Higher Learning called for his resignation, effective June 30, 1984.[2]

Earnest A. Boykins, Jr.
President of Mississippi Valley State University
1971–1981

Ernest A. Boykins, Jr., was born in Vicksburg on October 5, 1931, and grew up in a family of five children. His early education was obtained at Vicksburg's St. Mary's Parochial School where he finished high school in 1949. He received his B.S. in biology from Xavier University (New Orleans) in 1953, and in 1954 accepted a teaching position at Alcorn A. & M. College, where he remained until his election to the presidency of MVSU.[1]

Meanwhile, during that period he traveled and studied intermittently. His studies included receiving the master of science degree in biology at Texas Southern University in 1958, pursuing graduate work in cell biology at the University of Connecticut in 1959–1960, and earning a Ph.D. in zoology at Michigan State University in 1964.

His outstanding contributions to Mississippi institutions of higher learning began in 1958 when Professor Boykins was selected as acting head of the Department of Science at Alcorn. On July 1, 1970, he became director of the Division of Arts and Sciences at Alcorn. Later in 1971, he was appointed director of Cooperative College School Science Program. On May 20, 1971, Dr. Ernest A. Boykins was elected the second president of Mississippi Valley State College and assumed the office on the following July 1.

Dr. Boykins is listed in *American Men of Science, Outstanding Educators of America, Outstanding Citizens of Mississippi, Personalities of the South* (1973), *Distinguished Young Black Americans* (1973), *Leaders in Education* (1973), *Contemporary Notables* (1974), and *Who's Who in the South and Southwest* (1975).

Dr. Boykins is frequently sought to serve as a consultant and committee member. Among those he has accepted are the following: Mississippi Regional Medical Program (Regional Advisory Group); Mississippi Economic Development Council; WABG Television Advisory Board; Development Panel of the United National Association for the Ralph Bunche Awards Program for the State of Mississippi; Mississippi Catholic Foundation; Inter-Institutional Cooperative Program for College and Public School Teachers of Disadvantaged Youth (1968–1970), University of Mississippi; Regional Older Persons Advisory Committee for the Office of Economic Opportunity; and Special Health Career Opportunity Program Consultant of the Department of Health Education and Welfare (1973).

Dr. Boyd has also been a member of Delta Council; Boy Scouts of America, Executive Board Member (1973); Leflore County Chamber of Commerce (1974); Leflore County United Givers Board (1974); Postsecondary Education Planning Board (1974); Criminal Justice Council for Greenwood and Leflore County (1975); National Science Foundation's Science Education Advisory Committee, (1975); Minority Medical Education Foundation, Board of Directors (1975); Board of Trustees of Xavier University in New Orleans, Louisiana (1975–present); and Phelps Stokes, National Health Service Corps Project Advisory Committee, (1975–present).

His professional and fraternal memberships include American Council on Education, American Association for Advancement of Science, American Institute of Biological Science, National Council on Higher Education, Mississippi Conservation Educational Advisory Council, Association of Southeastern Biologists, Sigma Xi Scientific Honor Society, National Collegiate Honors Council, Phi Delta Kappa, Beta Kappa Chi, Omega Psi Phi Fraternity, Alpha Kappa Mu Honor Society, and American Association for Higher Education.

While at Alcorn State University Boykins distinguished himself as a biology scholar in both research and publication as well as teaching and administration. Several proposals written by Boykins were funded by the National Science Foundation.

Joe Louis Boyer
President of Mississippi Valley State University
1982–

Born January 20, 1940, in Florida, Joe Louis Boyer has implemented progressive and traditional programs since assuming the presidency of Mississippi Valley State University. According to Boyer, his main objective is "to provide MVSU students with a better education." To meet these objectives, he advocates "upgrading entrance requirements for state universities, emphasizing academic achievement by limiting the number of hours students can take when assigned to remedial courses, and activating a fund-raising campaign among MVSU alumni and supporters."[1]

Boyer promised to improve MVSU's academic standards and educational programs by instituting a campus curfew for students and by eliminating week-night dances on campus. His curfew policy enforcement requires that students vacate the lobbies of dormitories of the opposite sex by 10:30 p.m., that dorm managers lock the doors at 11:30 p.m., and admit students until midnight. After that time, students will be admitted by security personnel, and their names submitted to the president.[2]

He rejects as a current goal the main purpose of the university when it was created: "to serve the large number of under-educated black young people whose opportunities for advanced education were seriously limited by economics, geography, and segregation." Today, he believes, conditions have changed and students have a choice of either attending a predominantly black institution such as MVSU or a predominantly white university. Subsequently he proclaimed, "I'm not going to accept deprivation, I'm not going to accept 'black,' I'm not going to accept 'poor' as an excuse. This is a first class institution. Once the standards have been set, we're going to meet them . . . I think it's imperative that we increase the quality of education.[3]

In preparation for an administrative role as the president of Mississippi Valley State University, Joe Louis Boyer graduated from Roger Hungerford High School in Eatonville, Florida. He received his B.S. degree from Tennessee State University, the M.S. from the University of Illinois-Champaign-Urbana campus, and the Ph.D. from Ohio State University. Boyer's academic and administrative experiences include teaching at Westhighland High School, Alabama; Stillman College, Tuscaloosa; and Ohio State University. He also served as Chairman of the Department of Education Foundation at Auburn University in Alabama.[4]

Because of his expertise in education and oratorical skills, he has spoken before numerous academic, religious, civic, and social groups; served on numerous academic committees; acted as educational consultant for schools in Alabama, Tennessee, Florida, South Carolina, Mississippi, Kansas, and Ohio; and chaired several accreditation teams in the Southern Association of Colleges and Schools.[5]

Included among his publications are articles in Theory Into Practice, Educational Leaders, and They Came and They Conquered. He co-edited Curriculum and Instruction: After Desegregation and co-authored Inside Today's School: An Instructional Manual. He has submitted and had published book reviews in the following journals: Educational Leadership and The Educational Forum.

He is affiliated with Phi Delta Kappa educational fraternity and the Association for Supervision and Curriculum Development.[6]

George A. Owens
President of Tougaloo College
1965–

George Owens, son of sharecroppers, was born near Bolton in Hinds County, on February 9, 1919. Despite the usual vicissitudes of black children whose parents were in that particular economic group, George managed to complete the local public schools and attend Jackson College High School. He worked his way through Tougaloo by doing such jobs as chauffeuring the president's wife and earned an A. B. in economics in 1941.

Immediately after graduating from Tougaloo, Owens enlisted in the U. S. Army as a private and was honorably discharged in March 1946 as a captain of the Corps of Engineers. In 1944, he married Ruth Douglas. He returned to Jackson in 1946 and was employed as a clerk in the office of Security Life Insurance Company.

In 1947, Owens migrated eastward to Jersey City, New Jersey, and worked for two years as bookkeeper at Gladstone's Hardware Store. Later, he moved to New York and became a junior executive at Saks

34th Street. Taking advantage of educational benefits provided by the G. I. Bill, he left Saks and enrolled in 1948 at Columbia University, where he was awarded the master's degree in business administration with a major in accounting. Then, he returned south to Talladega, Alabama, as business manager of Talladega College, where he remained until 1955.[1]

In 1955 Owens returned to Mississippi as business manager of Tougaloo College, a position he held for nine years. In 1964 he was named acting president of Tougaloo and in June 1965, was unanimously elected the first black to head that institution. "I took over," said Owens, "at a time when new opportunities for Negroes in American life were really coming about. We knew we had to educate our students for a new day of equal opportunity."[2]

Subsequently he instituted a three-fold plan: campus development and financial stability; academic excellence and post graduate placement; and intellectual and ideological stimulation. President Owens's first accomplishment as president was the establishment of a cooperative program with the Ivy League's Brown University that included the exchange of both students and faculty. Because so many black students have inadequate training in basic courses, President Owens inaugurated remedial courses in reading, writing, and speaking for at least one-fourth of the students. And he initiated a program he calls "a poor man's Antioch plan," in which students are helped to find course-related summer jobs, many of them in urban ghettos.[3]

One striking result of these innovations has been that more Tougaloo graduates have opted for graduate school and government careers than for the traditional public school teaching. Tougaloo's history as a "hot bed" of civil rights activity has not endeared that institution to many white Mississippians. Despite serious efforts of the Mississippi legislature to revoke Tougaloo's charter "in the public interest," President Owens has often indicated he has no intention of changing: "We could do it the other way, give in a little, but we'd pay more in human dignity and self-respect. The price is simply too high."[4]

President Owens holds membership in a number of professional and fraternal organizations including: College Placement Services, Inc., Bethlehem, Pennsylvania; Communications Improvement, Inc., WLBT-television station, Jackson, Mississippi; Higher Education Compact, New York; Institute of Politics in Mississippi, Jackson, Mississippi; National Council of Churches, New York; Southern Regional Council, Atlanta, Georgia; United Church Board for Homeland Ministries, New York; United Negro College Fund, Inc., New York; The Academy of Political Science; Advisory Council to Board of Trustees, National Association for Advancement of Colored People; National Urban League; and Phi Delta Kappa Educational Fraternity.

Among his honors are LL.D., 1967 from Bethany College, Bethany, West Virginia; LL.D., 1967 from Houston-Tillotson College, Austin, Texas; LL.D., 1967 from Brown University, Providence, Rhode Island; L.H.D., 1970 from Wilberforce University, Wilberforce, Ohio.[5]

Laurence C. Jones

"The Little Professor"

Laurence C. Jones, founder of Piney Woods Country Life School, came to Mississippi from the mid-west. He explained his decision:

> During my sophomore year I heard our President, Dr. George E. MacLean, use the phrase, *Noblesse Oblige*, and one day in the botany class Professor Thomas H. MacBride explained to me its meaning. More than ever I realized that because of the superior advantages for schooling that had been mine, I was morally obligated to pass the opportunity on to those less fortunate than myself. I believe I had always had a subconscious desire to engage in the poultry business. One of my fondest dreams was to realize money enough from this business some day to cross the ocean and see the countries of the Old World. *Noblesse Oblige*, however, taught me that my duty was down in the black belt among the less fortunate of my people.[1]

Born on November 21, 1882, Laurence Clifton Jones grew up in the picturesque setting of St. Joseph—a pretty city, the busiest and richest of its size in the state of Missouri. His father, a porter at the Pacific Hotel, was a native of Alabama and had seen service in the United States Army, Company K, from 1867 to 1876, after which he was honorably discharged. The very sight of "Ole Glory" waving in the air always exacted from him an emotional response. Despite many hardships and temptations, he developed the personality that made him a great reader and the character that earned for him the title "Honest John."[2]

His mother's creed was somewhat more sophisticated: one was not merely to be content in whatever place he chanced to fall; rather one must do well according to one's strength; that was his reason for being. ". . . so that aside from the sweetness of her personality, there was a strength, an irresistible something about her that made her very presence a power for good." By occupation, she was a laundress and seamstress. She nevertheless managed to be an excellent homemaker for her husband and her children. But always she demanded a full report of the children's behavior during her absence. If it had been good there were delightful rewards, the greatest being one of the wonderful stories she would tell.[3]

Laurence was the only boy in the family, and all the maternal hopes and ambitions were centered on him. He was expected to possess all the commendable traits of his ancestors, to emulate all the men of the race who had achieved prominence since the founding of America, and add something of his own. The family fondly hoped he might become a lawyer, doctor, editor, minister, businessman, or a professor. He considered politics; but he knew regardless of occupation, he had to be a gentleman.[4]

Laurence's maternal great-great grandfather, a native of Virginia, purchased his freedom and moved to Pennsylvania. There Robert Foster, Laurence's mother's father was born. Grandfather Foster moved to Michigan and in 1848 founded an educational institution that was open to all regardless of color, sex, or religious affiliations. Incorporated under Michigan law as a manual labor institute, it was possibly the first school to be established in this country for industrial training of black boys and girls. Once a year Foster would go east to solicit funds and make friends for the race, which reminded Laurence in later years that in more ways than one he "took after his grandfather."[5]

As a boy Laurence read *Robinson Crusoe* and the Bible. Laurence believed that what he was taught in high school was futile; therefore, he became a regular customer at the public library. He had read and heard his mother speak of Boston and its wonderful schools. He managed to save eighteen dollars and purchased a ticket to Rock Island, Illinois, to tell his Aunt Sally and Uncle Charley goodbye before going to Boston. His parents, suspecting his destination, wired his uncle and informed him of Laurence's plan. Soon after his arrival, Laurence moved with his relatives to Marshalltown, Iowa, where Laurence was the first black graduated from Marshalltown High School. He attended University of Iowa at Iowa City and received the bachelor of philosophy degree in 1907.[6]

Jones recalled:

> In 1907, the year of my graduation, comparatively few Negroes had a similar chance at formal education. Although I had tempting job offers which ranged from the insurance business to a subsidized career in musical comedy, it seemed to me that if I used my education for selfish profit, [it] . . . would be a form of 'willful waste.' I decided to share my advantages with the neediest people of my race in the Black Belt of Mississippi. There was the most shocking waste of all: the waste of the human mind and soul. Men, women and children exhausted their bodies in the fields, making their living as farmers but having no knowledge of farming beyond the drudgery of chopping and picking cotton. Unable to read, write or figure, they had no way of knowing if what they were charged at the store was correct, or if their wages were paid in full. Winter diets were corn meal and dried peas because the women had never learned how to can or preserve the summer yield from their gardens or the wild berries that grew at their doors.[7]

Despite his more lucrative offers, Jones accepted a teaching job at Utica Institute (now Hinds Junior College). During his second year at Utica he spent Christmas with one of his students in the Piney Woods area near Braxton—a community just south of Jackson. For them "taking Christmas" was a continuous round of fireworks, frolicking, feasting, and preaching services that lasted throughout the day and were interrupted only by summons to heavy laden tables of food.[8]

While in Braxton, he attended a session of a District Sunday School Convention, whose aim was the building of a high school, but in its twenty-five years of existence little had been accomplished.

> On my last night [Jones remembered] I sat among a group of these people and in the soft glow of a great pine-knot fire I told them of how the people farmed and lived in Iowa, of how the boys and girls were educated, how they celebrated Christmas; and I promised that later I would come back and see if in any way I could help them."[9]

The next May, after the closing of school at Utica, Dr. Jones set out again for the Piney Woods. At Jackson he pawned a gold watch given him by a white fraternity group where he waited tables at the University of Iowa. With the money from the watch he bought a ticket to Braxton for eighty-five cents, and with $165 in cash he arrived in the Piney Woods to begin his memorable work.

The natives welcomed Dr. Jones, and immediately he went to work, visiting homes, churches, neighborhood gatherings under trees at noontime or anywhere he could get an audience. Sometimes astride a mule, sometimes in an ox-wagon, but more frequently afoot, walking eighteen or twenty miles a day, Jones travelled across Rankin and Simpson counties. Early he discovered that the future of the majority of the people would be as rural dwellers, and thus his task would be to make them better country-folk. His modus operandi was to teach diversified farming and to discuss the cost of raising ten-cent cotton and buying fifteen-cent bacon and ninety-cent corn from meat houses and corncribs of the North. He demonstrated the folly of saving the worst land for corn, their cash crop, and of going to the crib in the spring and picking up anything left for seed corn, instead of selecting their seed corn in the field. Together they "read" all available farm journals and decided that the base of operations was in the kitchen, the household, the garden and the farm. To the women he directed advice about sanitary cooking and whitewash, sometimes applying the whitewash himself.[10]

By October 1, 1909, Jones had journeyed many miles before returning to Braxton with renewed determination to establish a school. Skepticism expressed by blacks and whites did not deter Jones. But, a poor crop yield and the scarcity of money impeded his efforts. The bank president promised financial assistance and a lumber company offered building materials. After the initial stage of the project had come to fruitition, little or no assistance came from the black community.

Confronted with financial barriers and skepticism, Jones decided to teach these illiterate boys and girls without the formality of buildings and blackboards. So the inspiration came to him to open his school under the old cedar tree, on the old Mordecai Harris Place. On Monday morning three boys and a few old men assembled under the tree, sitting on pine logs, and after singing "Praise God from Whom All Blessings Flow," reading lessons from the Bible, and offering prayer, Laurence Clifton Jones, declared that the school was officially opened.[11]

Near the cedar tree school, Jones discovered an old cabin in which a drove of sheep took nightly shelter; it also housed lizards, snakes, owls, and weeds. Jones found the owner, an aged colored man, who promised to give forty acres and fifty dollars—a substantial beginning for the school. The following Saturday the property was deeded to the trustees of the Piney Woods Industrial School. During the following weeks, money and promises of lumber and haulings were made. The first building was dedicated and named Taylor Hall in honor of the man who had given the first money toward its erection.[12]

On May 17, 1913, a charter was formally granted to The Piney Woods Country Life School. In the second year of the school's existence, a friend sent money toward the purchase of a small hand press and type, and the school published a paper, *The Pine Torch*, which continues to this day.

Little by little—or in the Jones tradition, "inch by inch"—the school prospered. Donations came in the form of money, an old piano, a typewriter, tools for a blacksmith shop, farm implements, a mule, a plow, an old broom-making machine, more buildings, a barn, and a growing student body, all of which symbolized a growing institution.

During the fifth year, Jones addressed the student body:

> Today marks the beginning of the fifth year of this little school in the Piney Woods. In the glow of a bonfire five years ago, before we had adequate shelter, I saw many of your faces light up with a new understanding of the meaning of education as we studied our books and practised our manual training.... A song you have just finished typifies the spirit of this institution more than anything; 'Keep Inchin' Along; Jesus Will Come By and By,' today, we need such a sentiment to guide us over the rough and rugged road we must travel if we are to reach the sunlight.[13]

The tranquility of Piney Woods came to an end when disaster struck. One morning a barn, whose loft had served as living quarters for boys, burst into flames. A few years later Harris Hall, which housed more than fifty boys, went up in smoke. Another blow came when a cyclone totally destroyed the town of Braxton, the business and banking center for the school. Not a year has passed without some crisis in which only faith could point the way.[14]

One of the most fearful incidents of all occurred when a minister friend had invited Dr. Jones to help him in a revival in a state west of the Mississippi River. One night during the revival, Dr. Jones exhorted, "life itself is a battle, we must stay on the firing-line, and battle against ignorance, superstition, poverty and all the evil elements of earth and air." Some white boys passing the church stopped for a few minutes and heard a few of the words and hastened off to spread the news that the preacher was "urging the Negroes to rise up and fight white people."[15]

The following day about noon, half a hundred men rode up and called for the preacher. Dr. Jones hurried to the door and announced, "I guess I'm the one you're looking for." In a harsh voice their leader ordered Dr. Jones out into the center of the crowd. One threw a rope over his head, drew the noose, and away they went to a place free from trees, except for one with a jagged branch reaching out from it. Wood, branches, and sticks had been piled underneath. Jones was bodily thrown atop the pile of wood, guns were cocked in various parts of the crowd, and random shots were fired. One published account described the incident:

> Then a strange thing happened. One man demanded that Jones speak. Jones explained to the satisfaction of the crowd the context of his speech on the previous evening. Then an aged man wearing a Confederate button pushed his way through the crowd waving his hand for silence and said, 'I know these men, they're all right folks; this must be a good darky.' Turning, he grasped Jones hand and said—'Come on down, boy,' and took the rope from around his neck, then others reached out and shook hands with him. God had delivered.[16]

Subsequently, Jones was able to return to Piney Woods and witness its growth. Eventually, there were gardens for food and a dairy at the school, students made brick for dormitories and classroom buildings. Athletes competed in baseball games, and voices for the Cotton Blossom Singers toured the United States raising money and spreading the message from the Piney Woods. They were enrolled in Piney Woods Junior College, which provided the first unique opportunity for blacks in Mississippi. Finally, there were students with hopes and no money, but Laurence C. Jones turned none away.

As early as 1925, Dr. Jones had to raise $30,000 to operate Piney Woods School. He travelled across the United States making friends for the school. These friends donated clothing for children and money which was utilized for buildings, such as the gymnasium and the Chandler Auditorium.

Laurence Jones worked with many other schools in the area, and in the 1930s Piney Woods became a home and school for blind students in Mississippi as well as the regular enrollees.

Piney Woods School continued its struggle for survival and existed on a "hand to mouth" basis with gifts of clothing, seeds, equipment, and money from donors throughout the United States. Finally, in response to continued appeals from whites in and around Jackson, Ralph Edwards honored Dr. Jones in 1954 on his television program, "This Is Your Life." Six bags of mail and $21,000 came the first day, twenty-two bags and $73,500 the second day, and by the third day $245,000 had poured into Piney Woods. One little girl sent a nickel; a little boy sent a pig. Contributions received from that television program began a permanent endowment for Piney Woods

School, and it became a truly national institution. Still, support for Piney Woods totals only thirty percent from the endowment while sixty-five percent comes from the donations of friends and alumni.[17]

Laurence C. Jones built a family in the same way he built Piney Woods School. Grace Allen joined his efforts in Mississippi and labored as his untiring and loyal wife until she died in 1928. Dr. Laurence C. Jones, after ninety-two years of life, died early on Sunday morning, July 13, 1975. He died quietly, as quietly and as deliberately as he had founded and built Piney Woods School, by just "inchin' along." Three children survived him, two sons and a daughter. Dr. Jones's sister, Mrs. Nellie Bass, has long worked at Piney Woods and remains there.[18]

Jones was an avid reader, and he also wrote books, among them *Piney Woods and Its Story* (1922), which was used to raise funds for the school, and *The Bottom Rail and Up Through Difficulties*.[19] Yet at heart he was a teacher and a human being who enjoyed others while pursuing his vision—a vision that was directed by the belief that divine guidance would enlighten and protect his path.

Dr. Jones and Piney Woods School are the subject of three books—Beth Day's *The Little Professor of Piney Woods* (Messner), Leslie Harper Purcell's *Miracle in Mississippi* (Carlton Press), and Alferdteen Harrison's *Piney Woods School* (University Press of Mississippi).

Friends, associates, and dignitaries numbering over twelve hundred attended the funeral service for Lawrence Jones in Chandler Auditorium on the Piney Woods campus on July 17, 1975. He lies buried in the Piney Woods Cemetary alongside his wife and only a few steps from the cedar tree and log cabin where Piney Woods School began.[20]

Jane Ellen McAllister

Pioneer in Black Education

Jane McAllister, the first black woman in the United States to earn a Ph.D. in education, was born October 24, 1899. She was the daughter of Richard McAllister, a postman, and Flora McClelland McAllister, an 1891 graduate of Jackson State College and a Vicksburg public school teacher for forty-two years.[1]

Reflecting on her childhood, Jane said, "[Jackson State College]

President and Mrs. [Charles] Ayer kept in touch with my mother all their lives and guided her in her teaching, and she in turn guided me. They fed her and she fed me—the Bible, Lamb's *Tales from Shakespeare,* the *Tanglewood Tales,* and Louisa May Alcott."[2] She recalled her mother admonishing, "you must dream the impossible dream and beat the unbeatable foe."[3]

As a student, Jane achieved academic excellence in school. Even as a second-grader she helped teach first-graders. The precocious Jane finished the Cherry Street High School in Vicksburg while still in her early teens. Her high school was poorly equipped and staffed and did not offer Latin or geometry. But those two subjects were needed for Jane to enter college. So her father borrowed the necessary books from a wealthy white family on his mail route. Her mother taught her at night—Latin and mathematics—thereby fulfilling the admission requirements.[4]

At sixteen Jane entered Alabama's Talladega College where she compiled an enviable academic record and was graduated with honors in 1919. Encouraged by her parents, she enrolled at the University of Michigan and received the M.A. degree in 1921. Meanwhile, she served as instructor of education at Southern University at Baton Rouge, Louisiana, from 1919 to 1922. Afterwards, she earned her doctoral degree at New York's Columbia University. She recalled, "It was a grand day in 1929 when my mother learned that I had been awarded a Ph.D. I was the first Negro woman in the United States to earn a doctorate in education. My doctoral thesis considered the question of the training of Negro teachers in Louisiana."[5]

"The real history of the study of American Negro education on the advanced level in Teachers College," according to Mable Carney, "began with the pioneer achievement of Doctor Jane Ellen McAllister in 1929."[6] Jane McAllister became not only the first black candidate ever to receive the doctor's degree from Columbia University, but the first black female doctoral candidate in education in the world.

Jane McAllister's distinctive academic career included leadership and professional positions at Miner Teachers College, Washington, D.C.; Consultant in Rural Teacher Education for the General Education Board and the Rosenwald Fund at Grambling and Jackson State Colleges; Director, Training School, Virginia State College, Petersburg; Director, Teachers Training, Southern University, Baton Rouge; Chairman, Department of Education, Fisk University; Professor of Education, Director of Summer Institute for Disadvantaged Youth; and Professor Emeritus at Jackson State College.[7]

McAllister's dedication set her apart from other scholars. Nevertheless, she has remained a humanitarian—"gifted with a brilliant mind, highly sensitive to others' needs, possessing a rare quiet charm, gentle and warm hearted, firm, serious and confident in her work, at times humorous and even playful."[8]

She discovered early that in southern institutions, "Poorly prepared teachers teach poorly prepared students to be poorly prepared teachers." So she resolved to eliminate the dilemma. Her foes were poverty, educational neglect, and anti-black education sentiment. Her task was to inject verve into the education of the southern black teachers; therefore, she challenged them to "dream the impossible dream." And thanks to Jane McAllister, many did just that.[9]

She considered the South the ideal setting for training black teachers. Therefore, she readily agreed to Jackson State's President, Dr. Jacob Reddix's offer to become professor of education.

Five mornings a week, for eighteen years, Jane Ellen McAllister boarded the bus in Vicksburg for the ninety-mile round trip to Jackson—a long trip indeed for one who was not compelled to work, and certainly not a pleasant one with racial tensions as they were. According to McAllister's secretary, she never failed to hold classes. If she were late, it was because the bus was late. "Moreover, in all those years, I never knew her to be ill a single day," the secretary stated.[10]

When McAllister embarked on her mission at Jackson State, she possessed an arsenal of talents and qualities uncommon to most of her colleagues—a superior academic background, a highly successful and competitive career, a national reputation in educating disadvantaged students, administrative skills in conducting a teacher-education program, and fund-raising skills. Her wide experiences had freed her from the emotional debilities frequently the heritage of many blacks of the region.

Jackson State College was the academic showcase for McAllister's accomplishments. She plunged into an intellectual safari that brought men, money, and movements to the campus. As an excellent organizer, she invited renowned individuals such as Dr. Faust, president of the Ford Foundation, Judge William Hastie, and U.N. undersecretary Ralph Bunche to participate in a lecture series. On another occasion, she succeeded in having one of the Time Life series, "Time Marches On," programmed from the Jackson campus. Also she acted as consultant and developed the education curriculum at Jackson State College.[11]

Using telelecture equipment to give the students exposure to the outside world, McAllister created a program of telephone interviews with famous people throughout America. Not only did isolated students get a look at the "outside world" through their visitors and telelectures, but the "outside world" discovered Jackson State College. The Ford Foundation heard of the brave, shoestring venture and provided funds for a series of combined television-telephone lectures on Greek drama with Moses Hadas of Columbia University. The students also sponsored a humanities course by telephone, taught by members of the Stephens College faculty in Missouri.[12]

As a result of these programs the Southern Education Foundation supported a college readiness program which brought promising high school students to the college for "enrichment," a necessary first step in improving precollege education. At first, the program participants included only promising ninth, tenth, and eleventh grade students living near the college. This "reservoir of talent," according to McAllister, "expanded and evolved with the help of federal funds into a summer resident program for students outside the Jackson commuting area."[13] Her ingenuity led the Ford Foundation in 1965 to provide a major grant of $120,000 for a college readiness program and a three year seminar series for continuing enrichment courses.[14]

McAllister also provided in-service training for teachers with financial assistance from the Field Foundation, the Southern Education Foundation, and the National Science Foundation. During the summer of 1962, twenty-two competent secondary teachers and twenty-six high school students from across the state participated in "Project Enrichment," an in-service workshop designed to eliminate cultural deficiencies. McAllister thus devised programs to improve teacher education.

Commenting on the project, McAllister stated, "The thirty teachers who participated in the institute, themselves the product of disadvantagement, living in the small towns that dot rural Mississippi, were to become the 'textbooks' to describe, in a manner no book has ever done, the disadvantaged Mississippi child."[15] Through the practicum, each discovered, through close contact with one child and his community, how this individual child thinks, plays, and learns, and how his parents think, feel, and learn."

Under the direction of McAllister, the state department of education and the Statewide Superior and Talented Student Project (STS) co-sponsored "STS Day" on August 3, 1962. This was the first step in establishing an STS in black accredited high schools.

The following October Dr. Robert E. Cousins, Director of Field Services for the Southern Education Foundation, held an exploratory conference with the administration and faculty of Jackson State. Cousins praised Dr. Jane E. McAllister as the originator and principal "moving spirit" behind enrichment instruction for superior students in the South and the Continuing Education Enrichment Project (CEEP).[16]

In 1965, McAllister received support for an institute for teachers of the disadvantaged under Title XI of the NDEA. Based on innovations developed by McAllister and her staff through previous in-service classes and summer programs, the institute touched 1,200 teachers. A team from New York's Bank Street College of Education evaluated the NDEA institute and reported, "despite the reluctance of some, Dr. McAllister's programs had become a symbol of change and hope, a force in the attack on disadvantagement and disintegration that is the result of poverty and bias."[17]

Dr. McAllister also organized and served as consultant and contact person for the following summer projects: Self Help Opportunity Project (SHOP) for unemployed high school dropouts (The training of indigenous persons for subprofessional occupations); Self Help Elementary Program (SHEP) for low-income family children; and the Office of Economic Opportunity (OEO) institute for principals, teachers, and auxiliary personnel.[18]

Therefore, in the summer of 1966 Jackson State was bristling with workshops, institutes, and seminars, many the result of Professor McAllister's patient labor. These were all made possible through "grants which didn't need the signature of the white superintendent of schools or the white Department of Education . . . Locally, such grants would never be approved; the papers would be lost or unsigned."[19] Under the National Defense Education Act the money could be given directly to the institution. One grant helped her send teachers to visit innovative schools in northern cities. Another allowed her to buy paperback books for students who had never owned a book before. Others allowed teachers and students to visit nearby cities, factories, museums, and parks.

In 1967, McAllister took a sabbatical, the first and only leave during her teaching career of forty-eight years. In 1969, she retired from the classroom and devoted her life to traveling and writing.

McAllister's publications included a book, *A Handbook For Students and Teachers* and numerous articles in such publications as the *Journal of Negro Education, Teacher Education Quarterly, Educational Administration and Supervision, School Executive,* and *The Journal of Teacher Education.*[20]

The numerous awards or honors bestowed on Professor McAllister include the following: delegate to 1949 Conference on Education Problems of Special Cultural Groups, Columbia University; observer, White House Conference on Education, 1955; delegate, U.S. Department of State to UNESCO, in Prague, Czechoslovakia; and Trustee of Talladega College in Alabama.[21]

In 1970 the SNEA and the School of Education of Jackson State University established the Jane Ellen McAllister Lecture Series in honor of Dr. McAllister, Professor Emeritus of that university. The campuswide convocation is held annually in observance of teaching as a career and attracts a large number of professionals from throughout the area.[22]

Dr. McAllister is completely dedicated to teaching, has an uncompromising devotion to her family, and adores children. She once read in the Vicksburg press of a black teenager accused of a murder who was to be tried in the criminal court (a legal procedure in Mississippi). Although she was not acquainted with the youth or his parents, she immediately assumed the responsibility of securing legal counsel. After a long and diligent fight to keep the case out of the criminal court, she succeeded and thus kept the youth from going to the state penitentiary at an early age.[23]

Dr. McAllister's philosophy of life, developed in the stormy racial climate of her native South, is simply stated: "Living without bitterness is not easy; but education, not fighting, is the only way out of blackness, poverty, bias and ignorance"—her way of dreaming the impossible dream.[24]

Florence Octavia Alexander

Educator

Florence Octavia Alexander has been called the "most influential pioneer woman who dedicated her time and talents in the improvement of educational opportunities for blacks in Mississippi." Born in Lincoln County, eight miles east of Summit, the third of eleven siblings of Mr. and Mrs. Columbus Alexander, she entered Jackson College as a ninth grade pupil and was graduated as valedictorian in 1912. She worked her way through Hunter College, Columbia University, where she received the bachelor of arts with a major in science. Miss Alexander had previously received the B.S. in education from Hampton Institute and the M.A. in supervision and teacher training from Columbia University."

"Miss F. O.," as she is affectionately known, began her career in a one-teacher school in rural Lincoln County. For the next nine years, she served as a teacher trainer at Jackson College and three years as a teacher trainer at Langston University, Oklahoma. Other teaching experiences include work at Rust College and Piney Woods School in Mississippi, Southern University and Grambling College in Louisiana.

In 1932 she became the first black female to serve in the Mississippi Department of Education. She worked there as a state supervisor for twenty-six years with teachers, pupils, and Jeanes Supervisors (county home economic and agricultural teachers) throughout the eighty-two counties of the state.

She was the first female to be elected president of the Mississippi Teachers Association and held many professional, civic, and social positions. She also presided over the Woman's Baptist State Convention and the State Federation of Colored Women's Clubs for several years.

Cleopatra D. Thompson

Renowned Educator

From the Mississippi Delta has come an internationally prominent educator. Born in Egypt, Mississippi, Cleopatra Davenport Thompson set her sights at an early age on navigating the "Red Sea of ignorance" and entering the "Promised Land of knowledge."

After graduating from Aberdeen High School, her parents, the late Alonza and Lizzie Blanchard Davenport, and friends encouraged Cleopatra to enter Alcorn A. & M. College, where she received the bachelor of science degree in education in 1932. That same year Thompson embarked on an enviable career that began as an instructor in English and mathematics, basketball coach for boys and girls, and assistant principal at the Walthall County Training School, Lexie, Mississippi.[1]

The next year she moved into the administrative phase of her profession by becoming director of teacher education at Okolona Junior College, a position she held for nine years.

Meanwhile, she was busy preparing herself for further service. In 1937 she received the M.A. from Atlanta University. In 1942 Professor Thompson assumed responsibilities as principal of the laboratory school and director of off-campus workshops at Alcorn.

After four years at Alcorn, Professor Thompson taught at Jackson State, Rust, and Tougaloo Colleges, Cornell University, and the University of Liberia, West Africa. In 1960 Cleopatra D. Thompson received her doctorate of education from Cornell University. She did post-doctoral studies at the University of Chicago and the State University of Iowa.

Upon completion of the requirement for the doctorate degree, Thompson returned to Jackson State and transformed the School of Education into a reputable department of achievement. Thompson's thirty-one years tenure at the university began in 1946 when she organized and served as the director of the Jackson State College-Meridian Residence Center. Later, the president of the college appointed her as the first dean of the School of Education in 1967. She served in this capacity for approximately ten years.

Under her leadership and supervision as dean, the School of Education manifested tremendous growth and achieved many noteworthy accomplishments. Among these were the university's initial professional accreditation by the National Council for the Accreditation of Teacher Education programs. While she was dean, the student enrollment increased from 422 in 1965 to 1,162 undergraduate and 856 graduate students in 1977. The faculty increased from 19 to 108 during that period. Educational and research centers were established including an early childhood center, curriculum center, psychology and reading laboratories and special education-psychology learning center. Meanwhile, approval was granted for the establishment of a reading clinic and a Metrication Center laboratory for the Department of Guidance. In 1977, after ten years of service as dean, Thompson was appointed as the university's first Distinguished Professor of Education.[2]

As one of those rare individuals dedicated to professionalism and civic responsibility, Thompson became actively involved in civic, religious, and social organizations. She is an participatory member of Farish Street Baptist Church, National Council of Negro Women, National Federation of Colored Women's Clubs, and a Golden Life Member of Delta Sigma Theta. In addition, she has participated in professional organizations such as American Association of University Women, American Association of University Professors, National Education Association and affiliates, Association of Teacher Educators (local, district, and national), Phi Delta Kappa (national educational fraternity), Pi Lambda Theta (national honor association).[3]

Dr. Thompson has received numerous fellowships, scholarships, honors and awards, including graduate assistant, Department of Child Development and Family Relations, Cornell University; General Educational Board, Atlanta University; and fellowship recipient, Southern Fellowship Fund. In 1978 she was appointed to the Governor's Commission on the Status of Women. She was a delegate in 1960 to the Golden Anniversary White House Conference on Children and Youth and a member of the Press and Radio Committee of the Women's Auxiliary to the National Baptist Convention. Biographies of Cleopatra Thompson appear in several national and international yearbooks, including *Who's Who of American Women, 1970-1971*; *Two Thousand Women of Achievement, 1972*; *World's Who's Who of Women, 1973*.

Some of her awards have been Woman of the Year, Jackson alumnae chapter of Delta Sigma Theta; Alcornite of the Year, 1961; Mother of the Year, 1960 and 1967; Delta of the Year, Jackson alumnae chapter, Delta Sigma Theta, 1973; Distinguished Service, Southern Regional Educational Board; Meritorious Award, Atlanta University National Alumni Association; Teacher of the Year, Mabel Carney Chapter, Student National Education Association, Jackson State University, 1977; Distinguished Educator's Award, School of Education, JSU, 1976; Distinguished Club Woman of the Year, Mississippi State Federation of Colored Women's Clubs, 1978; and the Mary McLeod Bethune Award, National Council of Negro Women, Jackson Section, 1976.

Internationally renowned, Cleopatra Thompson worked in West Africa, and participated in international educational conferences and assemblies in Africa, Asia, Europe, and South America, including seven international assemblies and educational seminars in twenty-six countries. She has also traveled with international tours in Canada and Mexico. She presided at plenary sessions for the International Council on Education for teaching at world assemblies in Washington, D.C.; Lagos, Nigeria; and Rio de Janeiro, Brazil.

The venerable educator is also the author of innumerable articles and papers and a frequent contributor to various magazines and professional journals. Her most recent publication, *The History of the Mississippi Teachers Association, 1973*, was one of three treatises selected and promoted by the Association for the Study of Afro-American Life and History, during the American Bi-Centennial.

Although Dr. Thompson retired from Jackson State University in 1978, she is in constant demand as a lecturer and consultant in educational and related symposia. She is married to H. McFarland Thompson, also a retired professor at Jackson State.

Mrs. Aurelia N. Young, Assistant Professor of Music at JSU and Member of Delta Sigma Theta Sorority, says, "Soror Thompson has been an instrument of change throughout her entire life wherever she has gone . . . not only in Mississippi, but throughout this country and in others. She has never been content with conditions as she found them, but rather, she has set the highest goals and dedicated her life to achieving them."

Hazael McFarland Thompson

Educator, Civic and Fraternal Leader

Black civic leaders organized fraternal orders to build schools and churches, to assist the poor, and to provide burial services and benefits to its membership and their dependents. One of the most active fraternal orders in Mississippi is the Prince Hall Masons, established by the Reverend Dr. Thomas W. Stringer, a famous churchman, politician and physician. The survival of the fraternal order has been dependent upon consistent and exceptionally capable personalities as the Grand Masters of the group. That was true with Dr. Stringer, the first one, and is signally true with the incumbent, the Honorable Hazael McFarland Thompson.[1]

Born into a family of educators, H. M. Thompson was graduated from the Greenwood Public School System. He received the bachelor of arts degree from Tougaloo College, the master of science from Atlanta University, the master of arts in teaching from Cornell University and completed further study at Colorado State and Yale Universities.

The achievement of his educational goals as a teacher has been both extensive and fruitful. He began that career at Harris High School in Meridian and later taught at Lanier High School in Jackson, Okolona Junior College, Alcorn State, and the University of

Liberia. He has served as an educational consultant to Mississippi State University and Guttington College, West Africa. In 1978 Professor Thompson retired from Jackson State University as professor of mathematics. Presently, he is serving as visiting professor of mathematics at Tougaloo College. He is married to Dr. Cleopatra D. Thompson and they have two children, a son and a daughter.

Mr. Thompson's professional affiliations are numerous. He served as president and vice-president of the Mississippi Teachers Association-National Education Association prior to the integration of the state teachers organization into the Mississippi Education Association and was formerly the chairman of the National Council of Teachers of Mississippi. Presently he is actively involved as a member in the following organizations: the American Association of Higher Education, the American Association of University Professors, and Phi Delta Kappa, an educational fraternity.

In his scholarly pursuits Thompson has published in leading academic journals and delivered and read innumerable speeches and papers in his professional fields. One of his popular discourses has been his travelogues on Africa, Asia, Europe, North America, and South America. His travels have covered forty-four countries on five continents.

Honors bestowed upon Thompson include a Shell Oil Fellowship to Cornell University; National Science Foundation Fellowships to Cornell and Yale; "Alumnus of the Year," from Tougaloo College, 1967; "Omega Man of the Year," from Omega Psi Phi Fraternity, 1969; Mississippi Teachers Association Award, "Outstanding Service to Education,"1976; National Business League Merit Award, 1977; Atlanta University National Alumni Association Meritorious Achievement Award, 1977; and a citation as Outstanding Teacher by the Mabel Carney Chapter, SNEA, Jackson State University.

Not confining his interests to education and fraternal orders, Thompson has generously given of himself to civic and community affairs. He served as Boy Scout Master in Okolona and Alcorn, Field Executive of the Choctaw Area Boy Scouts, and District Boy Scout Commissioner in Jackson and Liberia, West Africa. His activities have also included being an official and commissioner of high school and college athletic conferences, president of the Tougaloo National Alumni Association, and co-chairman of membership and financial drives for the YWCA and the United Way. He has also been president of the Central Mississippi Planning and Development District, and a member of the boards of directors of Jones Community Center, Bethlehem Center, State Mutual Savings and Loan Association, Jackson Urban League, and the Jackson Opportunities Industrialization Center. Other community involvements by Thompson include membership on the Arts-Planetarium Commission for the City of Jackson, the Oakley Training School Advisory Committee, and the Governor's School Finance Committee.

William H. Holtzclaw

Utica Junior College Founder

Professor William H. Holtzclaw was born June 1870 in Roanoke, Alabama, but like many others he made his mark in Mississippi. His studies at Tuskegee Institute provided an opportunity to demonstrate his exceptional abilities and brilliance which distinguished him for an outstanding career in educational leadership. He became a protégé of Booker T. Washington, whose encouragement and assistance aided him in his chosen labors. After completing his studies at Tuskegee, Holtzclaw continued his studies at Harvard University.[1]

Afterwards he returned south and in 1903 founded Utica Institute, at Utica, Mississippi. Holtzclaw traveled and lectured in interest of the institution gaining wide acquaintance and respect of the nation's leading philanthropists whose financial aid led to the development of Utica Institute, where hundreds of young Negroes from many states obtained an education, which otherwise would have been denied them. The Utica Singers traveled throughout the United States and in Europe collecting revenues for the school. Utica is now an accredited junior college that has recently become a branch of the predominantly white Hinds Junior College.

Professor Holtzclaw developed a deep love and interest in the state, while at the same time enjoying the highest respect as a Negro leader. Possibly, his greatest contribution was the organization of the Farmer's Conference, through which much was done to raise the standard of Negro farmers. He was one of the founders of the Mississippi Association of Teachers in Colored Schools and a member of the board of directors of the *Mississippi Educational Journal*. The high school at Crystal Springs is named in his honor. He died in September 1943.

Willa B. Player
Educator, Librarian, College President

Born on August 9, 1909, in Jackson, Mississippi, to Clarence C. and Beatrice Day Player, Willa B. Player grew up and achieved outside those confines. Player is best known for her outstanding record at Bennett College, Greensboro, North Carolina, where she began a long and impressive career as instructor of Latin and French and vice-president of instruction, before being promoted to the presidency in 1955.[1]

Her unusual preparation for service in academe commenced in 1929 when she received the B.A. at Ohio Wesleyan University; M.A. from Oberlin (1930); a Certificat d'Etudes from the University of Grenoble, France (1935); a doctorate in education at Columbia University (1946), where she had been awarded a Frank Ross Chambers fellowship. She did post-doctoral studies at the University of Chicago and the University of Wisconsin. Other fellowships included one from the General Education Board in 1945–1947 and another from Ford in 1953–1954.[2]

Educational honors bestowed upon her included Doctor of Laws, Ohio Wesleyan University, 1953; Doctor of Laws, Lycoming College, 1962; Doctor of Laws, Morehouse College, 1963; Doctor of Laws, Albion College, 1963; Doctor of Humane Letters, Keuka College, 1967; Doctor of Humane Letters, University of North Carolina at Greensboro, 1969; and Doctor of Public Service, Prairie View Agricultural and Mechanical College, 1971.[3]

As a professional and civic activist, Player maintained membership in the following: Kappa Delta Pi and Pi Lambda Theta, National Honor Societies; President of the National Association of Schools and Colleges of the Methodist Church, 1962; South Atlantic Regional Philosophy of Education Society; North Carolina and National Teachers Associations; St. Matthews Methodist Church; Young Women's Christian Association; National Council of Negro Women; the Commission on Liberal Learning of the American Association of Colleges; Women's Planning Committee; and Japan International Christian University Foundation, Incorporated. She served as secretary to the board of directors of Piedmont University Center Incorporated; as a member of the National Commission on Religion and Race; on the board of trustees, Ohio Wesleyan University; and the board of directors, Southern Fellowship Fund.

She is listed in *Who's Who in American Education; Who's Who of American Women; Leaders in Education; Who's Who in Methodism;* and *Who's Who in America.*

Among her numerous awards were Superior Service Award, Department of Health, Education, and Welfare, June 2, 1970; Distinguished Service Award, Department of Health, Education, and Welfare, April 13, 1972.

She traveled extensively in England, France, Italy, Switzerland, East and West Africa, and Japan. During the Nixon and Ford Administrations Dr. Player served as director, Division of Institutional Development, Bureau of Postsecondary Education, U.S. Office of Education, Washington, D.C.

William Arthur Butts

University President and Author

William Arthur Butts was born on April 25, 1933, at Kilmichael, to Mr. and Mrs. Sylvester Butts. After receiving his elementary and secondary education, he entered Mississippi Valley State College (MSVC) at Itta Bena, where in 1957 he earned the B.S. degree in political science. His college education was interrupted in 1953 by service in the U.S. Army. He was honorably discharged in 1955 with the rank of sergeant.[1]

After two years as a high school teacher, Butts enrolled at Southern Illinois University where he was awarded the master of arts degree in political science in 1962.

In 1963 he was employed as assistant professor at Mississippi Valley State College where he remained until his election as president of Kentucky State in 1975. In 1969 he became a visiting professor of history at the predominantly white Delta State College, Cleveland, Mississippi. In 1973 Butts studied African culture in West Africa for six weeks. As an administrator and professor, Butts was actively involved with many facets of university instruction and administration at Mississippi Valley State College such as chairman, Division of Arts and Sciences, 1967–75; chairman, Department of Social Science, 1971–1975; special assistant to the president, 1967–

1969; special assistant to the president, Delta State University, 1969–1971; Director, Upward Bound, 1968–1969; Director, Law Enforcement Program, 1971–1974; and Campus Director, Consortium on Research Training, 1974–1975.

He has held memberships in the Greenwood Voters League and Turner Chapel African Methodist Episcopal Church. In the latter he was a member of the Trustee Board and Director of Christian Education. He is a member of Omega Psi Phi Fraternity, a 32° Mason, a Shriner, past president of the Mississippi Valley State University Alumni Association, and past executive secretary of the Alumni Council of Public Colleges, State of Mississippi. He is also a Danforth Associate and a Kiwanian. Butts is affiliated with numerous professional and learned societies such as Phi Delta Kappa, American Political Science Association, and Association for the Study of Afro-American Life and History. He is listed in *Outstanding Educators of America*,1972 and *Personalities of the South*, 1972.

His publications include *The Relationship of Economic and Social Variables to Population Change* and *Black Voter Registration in Mississippi, 1940–1966*.

Edward Allen Jones

Linquist, Scholar, Diplomat

The Mississippi Delta is world renowned for the fertility of its soil. Its products are numerous and varied, and so are the talents of its blacks. But none is more gifted and honored than Edward A. Jones, born in 1903 to George H. and Carrie Cox Jones of Indianola. When that family left its traditional moorings, it was Edward's grandmother that protected him from the ravages of a broken home.[1]

Grandma Ella Lamb owned a small farm. She determined that Edward should have more formal training than that offered at the grammar school of his native Indianola. But, it was not to be Tuskegee as his grandma had wanted. Rather, Edward under the influence of his school principal, Ira Gentry, Sr., enrolled at Morehouse Academy in 1918.

At Morehouse he opted for the classical rather than the scientific course. At the impressionable age of fifteen Edward encountered

Latin and Greek. He discovered that those languages held for him a peculiar interest. Upon graduation he entered Morehouse College and continued to pursue the classics, graduating valedictorian in 1926.

That fall Jones began his teaching career at Edward Waters College in Jacksonville, Florida. Conditions there were not to his liking, so he decided to go into insurance. While visiting his alma mater that summer, Edward had a session with Dr. Samuel H. Archer, his academic mentor, who invited Edward to join the Morehouse faculty. He had observed Jones teaching math classes during his senior year. Thus began a career of teaching at Morehouse and a variety of scholastic activities. He came up through the ranks from instructor to full professor and chairman of the Department of Modern Languages.

During the summer of 1929 Jones studied at Grenoble, France, where he received the Certificat d'Etudes Francaises (with special mention). That following school term Jones was awarded a fellowship by the General Education Board to complete his master's degree at Middlebury University (Connecticut). He recalled with a chuckle that he had to borrow his fare from New York to Middlebury. He was, however, delightfully surprised upon arrival to find a check awaiting him.

There was no room for him on campus. However, in the list of private homes he did find a room with a white family. The wife cordially welcomed him, but when the husband came in he was "inflamed." The next day he reported his situation to the president, who personally helped to find him a nice place.

After receiving the M.A. in French in 1930, Jones began making definite movements toward scholarly pursuits in the modern languages. Toward that end he began studies at Cornell University toward the Ph.D. degree, which he was awarded in 1943.

Dr. Edward A. Jones was not satisfied just to be a holder of the highest degree any American university could bestow; he moved to justify having that degree by further research and scholastic participation. Following are a few of his honors and distinctions: 1942 co-winner, Corson French Prize at Cornell University, for essay on Moliere; 1942–43 Romance Language and Literature Department Scholarship holder at Cornell; election to membership at Cornell, National French Honors Society, 1943; election to membership, Phi Kappa Phi Chapter, 1944; Phi Beta Kappa Chapter, as alumnus member, 1960; member of Committee of Qualifications, United Chapters,

Phi Beta Kappa (the committee responsible for appraising and visiting institutions seeking chapters) since 1969; recipient, Ford Foundation grant for Sabbatical Research, 1968; editor, College Language Association (CLA) Journal, 1977; and Honorary Consul to Senegal, 1970, by appointment of Senegal's President Leopold Sedar Senghor.

Jones has written numerous professional articles for journals in this country and abroad. His published books include, *A Candle in the Dark: A History of Morehouse College*, Judson Press, 1967, and *Voices of Negritude*, 1971. He is listed in *Who's Who in the South and Southwest, In Colored America, Among Black Americans, Directory of American Scholars, Outstanding Educators of America, Contemporary Authors, Men of Achievement,* and other publications.

Dr. Jones volunteered this bit of philosophy, especially for young blacks today: "Stop complaining about what has been done (to us blacks), and get down to the business of doing something yourself. Get out and make something of yourself. Force yourself into the mainstream. Be competitive. Instead of expecting handouts and special considerations, exploit your own abilities."[2]

At the Atlanta Hilton, Saturday, April 5, 1980, Dr. Jones was honored with a testimonial dinner, for fifty-two years of outstanding service to his alma mater. Forty of those years he served as chairman of the Modern Language Department. Dr. Jones served under four presidents and is now "quasi retired."[3]

Romeo Benjamin Garrett

Educator, Minister, Author

Bradley University held a testimonial dinner, Saturday, October 14, 1972, in its student center, honoring a quarter-century of service to the university and the Peoria Illinois University for Dr. Romeo B. Garrett, Associate Baptist Minister, Professor Emeritus, and Second Vice-President NAACP (Peoria Chapter).

Beginning in 1977, Bradley University designated the third week in April Romeo Garrett Week as "one of the expressions of the high regard that the black students, professionals, and the communities of Bradley University and Peoria, Illinois, hold for this remarkable man."[1] Garrett Week celebration consists of a seven-day series of educational, cultural, and social activities. To further honor a man of such high esteem, Peoria's black community named its recreational facilities, a newly constructed edifice, the Romeo B. Garrett Culture Center, as a permanent memorial to Garrett for his "works in and for the black community and as a lasting tribute to one of the pioneers of black studies."[2] The center is utilized by black students, fraternal organizations, social groups, and the Peoria community.

Such a renowned figure as Romeo B. Garrett had a humble beginning. Born February 2, 1910, in Natchez, he was the son of Charles Edward and Ponkie Duncan Garrett. His grandparents had been slaves, and his parents were poor. There was little prospect for an education for him in Natchez, but Romeo was undaunted by the barriers of poverty and unequal opportunity. He barely managed to keep body and soul together until he completed the local public schools. He had heard of Straight (Dillard) College in New Orleans and after some difficulties he arrived in New Orleans and found a job as a porter. In 1932 he proudly received Dillard's B.A. degree in social science.

Following graduation, Garrett began compiling a distinguished record of service to the black community. For two years, the New Orleans Welfare Department employed Garrett as a social worker. He then served as supervisor of adult education for blacks in New Orleans for approximately eight years. During his tenure as administrator, the illiteracy rate decreased, and he gained a reputation for educating people in a land where officials said he was unqualified educationally.

Because of the outbreak of World War II, Garrett's humanitarian service to New Orleans's blacks was permanently disrupted. In 1942, Garrett answered his country's call to military service. While stationed at the Victorville Army Flying School, Victorville, California, he was selected "Soldier of the Month" and awarded a trip to Hollywood.

After a stint with the army, Garrett went to Peoria, Illinois, to continue his education at Bradley University, where in 1947 he was awarded the master of arts degree. The summer after receiving his M.A., he was invited to join the faculty at Bradley University. Because of his ability and his eagerness to prepare himself for service, Garrett entered the doctoral program first at Illinois University and then at New York University; he attained the Ph.D. degree from New

York University in 1963. Previously in 1949 Natchez College in the city of his birth awarded him an honorary LL.D.[3]

Because of his deep religious convictions and his concern for the plight of the black race, he was ordained a Baptist minister and pastored Peoria's Zion Baptist Church for more than twelve years. Thereafter, he was appointed to his present position as associate minister. He believes the solution to the racial problem lies within the church. "The main solution to the racial problems lies within the scope of our churches," stated Garrett. "Because they are committed to the brotherhood of man, they can work to promote goodwill."

Numerous honors were bestowed upon Garrett for his unselfish religious, educational, and cultural endeavors to improve the quality of life for mankind. In 1966, Dillard University named Garrett, "Alumnus of the Year," and he was presented the "Distinguished Alumni Award." At the banquet, he was the keynote speaker. In his presentation, he warned the audience against the pitfalls of material progress when he declared that, "Let us not forget the age-old values beyond the material and temporal. Let us ever strive to transform fear into faith; bigotry into benevolence; prejudice into justice; hostility into hospitality; and antipathy into sympathy. Then and only then shall we realize a bright new tomorrow."

Honors include the Romeo Garrett Scholarships, approved in 1964 by the Board of Trustees of Bradley University and awarded annually to five potential young Negro leaders graduating from high schools in the central Illinois area. In making the announcement of the scholarships, Executive Vice-President A. G. Haussler stated, "Dr. Garrett has contributed outstanding leadership to the advancement of the Negro race in this community . . . the ambassador of goodwill for his race."[4]

Also in 1964 Garrett was the recipient of New York's University's Founders Day Award for consistent evidence of outstanding scholarship. The City of Peoria named Garrett "Peoria's Outstanding Citizen," and in 1974 Bradley University's National Alumni Association named him the second recipient of the Mergen Award, in recognition of his "contributions in the area of church, professional groups, human relations, public service, and volunteer organizations."

Garrett's publications include the following: "The Negro in Peoria—1773–1905," *Negro History Bulletin*, April 1954; "African Survivals in American Culture," *Journal of Negro History*, October 1966; "Our Heritage from the American Indians," *Journals of Illinois*

Archeological Society, January 1954; "The Bible and the Negro," *Negro History Bulletin*, April 1973; "Social Aspects of the Aging Process Among A Selected Older Population," *Clinical Medicine*, March 1974; *Famous First Facts About Negroes*, Arno Press, New York, 1972; and "The Role of the Duryea Brothers in the Development of the Gasoline Automobile," *Journal of the Illinois State Historical Society*, April 1975.

Dr. Garrett was married to Naomi Sanders on November 29, 1945.

Melerson Guy Dunham
Educator, Author

A woman endowed with many talents, Melerson Guy Dunham, a native of Walthall County achieved a measure of success in several areas—education, religion, federated clubs, social, civic, and political affairs. After finishing the public schools of Walthall County, she ventured forth to Rust College where she was awarded the bachelor of arts degree. She then taught public school for several years. She returned to studies at Indiana University, received the M.A. in history and subsequently became assistant professor of history at Alcorn A. & M. College, remaining in that position for several years.[1]

Dunham engaged in activities relating to the advancement of the church and women. She remained active throughout her adulthood in the affairs of the Methodist Church, where she held positions of responsibility on local, jurisdictional, and national levels. As a member of the Federation of Colored Women's Clubs, Melerson Dunham served as president of the seventh district, vice-president of the state federation, statistician of the Southwestern Area, member of the Credentials Committee of the National Federation, and president of the Mississippi Federation.

In 1971, she authored *The Centennial History of Alcorn A. & M. College*. Presently, she is writing a history of the Mississippi Federation of Colored Women's Clubs.

Melerson Dunham holds membership in several professional organizations, including The Southern Historical Society, Association for the Study of Afro-American Life and History, Mississippi Historical Association, Association of Ministries to Blacks in Higher Education, and is the Mississippi Director of the Association for the Study of Afro-American Life and History. She is listed in *Personalities of the South* and *Who's Who in Methodism*. In 1975 she received the award from the National Concerned Black Women of the United Methodist Church.

After retiring from Alcorn, Dunham taught part-time at Prentiss Institute as well as traveled, lectured, and published. She is an active Democrat and political participant.

Charlemae Hill Rollins

Librarian, Author

Charlemae Hill was born in Yazoo City, Mississippi, on June 20, 1897, to Allen G. and Birdie Tucker Hill. On April 8, 1918, she married Joseph Walter Rollins of Topeka, Kansas. From that union, one child was born, Joseph Walter Rollins, Jr.[1]

As a part of her advanced education, Charlemae Rollins engaged in special studies at the University of Chicago, and later enrolled in special courses in library science at Columbia University.[2]

Pursuing a career in library science, Charlemae Rollins compiled an impressive record of dedicated teaching and librarianship. From 1946 to 1960, she taught children's literature at Roosevelt University. Previously, she taught at Fisk University, Rosary College (Illinois), and San Francisco State College. Prior to teaching at Roosevelt University, the George C. Hall branch of the Chicago Public Library employed her as Children's Librarian from 1927 until her retirement in 1963. Upon retiring, the Chicago Library awarded her a meritorious plaque.[3] At that time Gwendolyn Brooks, the only Negro Pulitzer Prize winner, wrote this poem as a tribute to Charlemae Hill Rollins:

>Her gift is long delayed.
>And even now is paid
>In insufficient measure.
>Rhymeful reverence,
>For such excellence,
>Is microscopic treasure.
>NOTHING is enough
>   Who gave us sentience—
>   Who gave us definition—
>Who gave us her vision.[4]

Among her professional associations, Rollins served as president, Children's Services Division, American Library Association, 1957–1958; chairman, Children's Section, Illinois Library Association, 1954–1958; chairman, Elementary Section, Illinois Unit of Catholic Library Association, 1953–1954; honorable member, Phi Delta Kappa (teachers sorority), 1959.[5]

Her honors include American Brotherhood Award of the National Conference of Christians and Jews, 1952; Library Letter Award of ALA, 1953; Grolier Society Award, 1955; Woman of the Year of Zeta Phi Beta, 1956; honorable member, Phi Delta Kappa, 1959; Good American Award of the Chicago Committee of One Hundred, 1962; Negro Centennial Awards, 1963; Children's Reading Round Table Award, 1962; Woman of the Year, Woman's National Book Association, February 1970.[6]

In addition to articles in various professional journals, Rollins published *Danger Son*, 1967; *Goin' Down Slow*; *Christmas Gift*, Follett, 1963; *They Showed the Way*, Crowell, 1964; *Famous American Negro Entertainers of Stage and Screen and TV*, Dodd, 1967; *We Build Together*, National Council of Teachers of English, 1947 and 1951; and *The Magic of Books*, Science Research Association, 1952.[7]

Ruby Stutts Lyells

Mississippi's First Black Professional Librarian

Ruby Stutts Lyells, the daughter of T. F. and Rossie Cowan, is a professional librarian and retail druggist. The Yazoo County native graduated from Alcorn State University and later studied at Hampton Institute and then the University of Chicago Library School where she received the B.S., L.S., and M.A. degrees respectively.[1]

Upon leaving Chicago, Lyells returned to Mississippi and became its first professional black librarian. As head librarian at Alcorn and Jackson State universities and at Atlanta and Jackson (Mississippi) public libraries, she contributed articles to several professional journals, lectured at prominent institutions, and presented papers at professional conferences.

Ruby S. Lyells maintains active membership in Church Women

United, League of Women Voters, Alpha Kappa Alpha Sorority, American Association of University Women, and Hinds County Republican Women's Clubs. She is a past-president of the Mary Church Terrell Literary Club and former director of Mississippi Council on Human Relations.

Probably, her most outstanding affiliations have been with the Mississippi State Federation of Colored Women's Clubs, where during her long tenure Ruby Lyells served as president, vice-president, treasurer, chairman of the financial committee, director of publicity, and lobbyist for many important legislative bills. One of her most recent community involvements was hosting "Learn With the League," a public affairs television program co-sponsored by the League of Women Voters.

Joffre T. Whisenton

Education Specialist

Joffre Trumbull Whisenton was born in Hattiesburg, on August 25, 1934. He received his high school training at the Magnolia High School, Moss Point, Mississippi, after which he was graduated from Tougaloo College in 1955. In college his major interests were biology, health, physical education, and recreation. In 1956 he received the M.S. degree in health, physical education, and recreation from Springfield College, Springfield, Massachusetts. In 1968 he was the first black to be awarded the Ph.D. from the University of Alabama, with concentrations in physical education, special education, administration, and curriculum development.[1]

His professional experiences include teaching and administration at Stillman College, Tougaloo College, and the University of Alabama. From 1969 to 1974, Whisenton was associated with the Southern Association of Colleges and Schools, as director of Special Studies, Commission on Colleges, and Associate Executive Secretary, Commission on Colleges. Whisenton is presently with the Division of Colleges in the Department of Health, Education, and Welfare.

Among his publications are *The Use of the Q-Sort Technique in Revising the Philosophy and Purpose of Stillman College for Its Institutional Self-Study;* summary and findings of a doctoral study—

A Comparison of the Values, Needs, and Aspirations of School Leavers with Those of Non-School Leavers; From Tragedy to Promise: Progress Made By Black Colleges in the South.

Whisenton is the recipient of graduate fellowships from several philanthropic organizations: the Congregational Church of the American Missionary Association; the Board of Christian Education of the Presbyterian Church in the United States; the United Negro College Fund; and the Southern Education Foundation.

His professional memberships and activities include Phi Delta Kappa, American Psychological Association, American Personnel and Guidance Association, American Association for Health, Physical Education and Recreation, The Urban League, Life membership in the NAACP, and Young Men's Christian Association. He is listed in *Outstanding Young Men of America,* 1968.

Whisenton is married to the former Zadie Elizabeth Beford of Grenada. They have one son, Joffre Conrad.

William Smith Demby

Educator, Agriculturalist, and Civic Leader

William S. "Jack" Demby, one of five children born to William Clarence Demby and Allene Smith Demby of Rodney, Mississippi, grew up on the former campus of Alcorn University, now Alcorn State University. There he finished elementary school, high school, and college, receiving the B.S. in agriculture education in 1927. In 1928 he enrolled at Meharry Medical College's School of Dentistry but after his first year was forced to withdraw because of financial circumstances.[1]

In 1929 he returned to Mississippi and accepted a position as vocational agriculture teacher. He was later to serve as Farm Security Supervisor, Associate County Agriculture Agent, Vicksburg Housing Authority Agent, and as principal of Curve Junior High School near Clarksdale until his retirement in 1967.

Currently, Demby is serving as part-time voting rights examiner for Mississippi, Louisiana, and Alabama. He is vice-president of the Port City Cooperative of Vicksburg, a bi-racial group of entrepreneurs who seek and assist businesses locating in Vicksburg.

For most of his adult life he has been active in fostering and supporting meaningful youth organizations. He has been a Scout Master for a Vicksburg Boy Scout troop. For more than thirty years, he has been a member of the Board of Management of the Jackson Street Branch of the Y.M.C.A., which in the absence of a Y.W.C.A. initiates programs for boys and girls.

William S. Demby has been described as a man with three loves—his family, his church, and his school, Alcorn. He is married to Melissa Pope Demby and they have two children, Dr. Allene D. Gayles and William S. Demby, Jr. He is a member of Bethel African Methodist Episcopal Church, where he is active as a lay-leader. He serves as a steward, church treasurer, president of the senior choir, and District Steward; he was formerly president of the local and district lay organization. In 1960 and 1964 he was elected a delegate to the General Conferences of the A.M.E. Church. Subsequently, he was elected a member of the Episcopal Committee, the General Board of Education, and the Inquiry Committee. Numerous plaques and certificates have been awarded him by various church, civic, and community organizations. In 1963 he was voted "Outstanding Layman of the Year" by the Lay Organization of the Eighth Episcopal District of the A.M.E. Church. That district comprises Mississippi and Louisiana.

Demby has personally recruited some of Alcorn's finest athletes from Warren and surrounding counties and is an avid supporter of Alcorn State University. He served as president of the Alcorn National Alumni Association for nine consecutive years. He considered the two highlights of his life being chosen "Alcornite of the Year" by the National Alumni Association in 1959, the highest honor bestowed an Alcorn alumnus, and being invited to deliver the Centennial Address at his alma mater in 1971. He views with humility and great pride a large plaque presented by the Alcorn State University National Alumni Association, upon his retirement in 1967, which is inscribed: "In recognition of a lifetime of unselfish and meritorious service and devotion to the promotion of good will and the general welfare of your Alma Mater above and beyond the call of duty. We, including the hundreds of students you have helped, today, hail you Mr. Alcornite."

Other honors he has received include the following: United States Department of Agriculture Award for twenty years of service as a federal employee, 1961; County Agriculture Agents Award for twenty years of meritorious service to Warren County and the state, 1963; Distinguished Service Award for long and efficient service in agriculture Industry, by the Mississippi Negro County Agriculture Association, 1963; Certificate of Recognition for outstanding accomplishments in the field of agriculture extension by W. M. Bost, Director of Mississippi Cooperative Extension Service, 1963; a plaque for outstanding service to the Community Organization of Warren County, 1967; The Ebonaire Bridge Club's Annual Award "for outstanding contributions to the development of youth in Vicksburg," 1975; and Theta Sigma Lambda Chapter of Alpha Phi Alpha Fraternity, Inc. "Man of the Year" for outstanding service to the community, 1978.

The J. E. Johnsons

Leaders in Education and Racial Advancement

There is an old saying that no matter how far a turtle moves his front feet, his body will not move an iota until it brings up its rear feet. The fact is Mr. and Mrs. J. E. Johnson of Prentiss Institute were totally committed to bringing up the disadvantaged youth of Mississippi long before it became fashionable.

Jonas Edward Johnson, cofounder of the Prentiss Normal and Industrial Institute, a private junior college, and of Oak Park Vocational School, black high school in Laurel, Mississippi, was born on May 7, 1879, to Charlie and Ella Kaigler Johnson in a rural community, five miles from the town of Magnolia, in Pike County. Jonas, eldest of fourteen children, developed early in life an obsession for securing an education. He attended the local public schools until age sixteen and then entered Alcorn A. & M. College in 1895, from which he graduated in May 1902 as valedictorian of his class.

Coincidentally, on May 7, 1882, Bertha La Branche, daughter of Jules Alcee and Onie Smith La Branche, was born at Wesson, Mississippi. She attended Tuskegee Normal and Industrial Institute and was graduated in 1902. That same year J. E. Johnson was elected principal of the Magnolia Public School, a post which he held for four years. In the meantime, Miss La Branche came to Magnolia as teacher and assistant to the principal of the Magnolia Industrial College.

J. E. Johnson and Bertha La Branche were married on August 3, 1904. Mr. and Mrs. Johnson, not only had the same birthday (three years difference, they had the same ambition in life—serving the Negro youth of Mississippi. In May 1907 the young couple with two babies in their arms, and penniless, but determined to surmount all obstacles through faith and prayer, came to Prentiss and founded Prentiss Normal and Industrial Institute. Prentiss, an infant town where the folk were busy carving their homes from the forest, was located forty miles from any railroad, and had a population of less than 200.

On the basis of that faith, Johnson told L. Tyrone, president of the Bank of Blountville, of their ambitions. The banker was so moved that he encouraged Johnson and lent him six hundred dollars to purchase the original forty acres just outside the corporate limits, for the humble beginnings of Prentiss Normal and Industrial Institute.

The school was described in a 1950 publication:

> The property on which the school is situated was once a plantation, and the antebellum big house, one hundred and forty years old, is now (1950) used as a music studio. It is said that several grandchildren of slaves who belonged to the plantation have graduated from the school. The Prentiss Jubilee Singers have been used to publicize the work of the institution for more than forty years, a third of the operating-expenses usually being met from funds raised by the traveling singers. They have toured every section of the United States.[1]

In assessing the Johnsons' contribution to education, Mrs. C. C. Mosley remarked, "The advancement of education in the state for the past forty-seven years is due in a large measure to the long-range planning of its founders, Principal and Mrs. J. E. Johnson."[2]

Although Johnson had been a principal for four years, he did not possess a teacher's license. He took the examination, making the highest average ever made by a Negro in the county, and became the first Negro in the county to acquire a first-grade license. In 1912 the Johnsons succeeded in getting the U.S. Department of Agriculture to place the first local agent at Prentiss Institute, and later succeeded in getting the state's first Jeanes Supervisor.[3]

Johnson was a natural leader of men. In the 1920s he had the tenacity to organize the Committee of One Hundred "to promote civic responsibilities among Negro people."[4] That organization was the forerunner of modern politics among Negroes in Mississippi. Anselm J. Finch declared that the number of "Negro teachers in Mississippi could be put in a 'T' model Ford who would even discuss voting, [while] J. E. Johnson was preaching citizenship through voting. Instead of the white people in Prentiss running Johnson away, they praised him for his manhood and spirit of true Americanism. J. E. Johnson was the first Negro to tour the state openly and courageously in the interest of a home for delinquents. Twenty years later, Mississippi felt the dire need of such an institution by creating Oakley Training School.

Because of his hard work, organization skills and prophetic vision, Johnson proved to be an efficient administrator. Prior to a two-year term as president of the Mississippi Teachers Association in 1924, Johnson had served as president of the Sixth District Educational Association. During his administrative leadership, the *Mississippi Educational Journal* began publication, and the state was divided into school districts.

His mate, Bertha Johnson, worked as diligently as her husband to accomplish their shared goals. Preston Sewell Bowles, an Alcorn A. & M. College graduate who became a member of the faculty and later president, paid a tribute to Mrs. Johnson:

> when [J. E. Johnson] left college to seek a mate in life, he didn't seek the companionship of a Hollywood star, or a Chicago faddist, but a woman whose heart beat in unison with his own, in their cooperative purpose to go out into the rural districts, where opportunity was rare, and to lift up a light for those who sat in darkness. . . . And they, together opened many a door of opportunity to boys and girls, young men and women, that would have remained forever closed but for them.

Bertha Johnson was distinguished in her own right. As a prominent member of the Federation of Colored Women's Clubs, she directed her energies toward interracial activities and youth education and rehabilitation. Mrs. Johnson was honored with a "This is Your Life" program at the Twenty-second Bicentennial Convention of the Southeastern Association of Women's Clubs in July 1963. Participants extolled the honoree for her dedicated service and humanitarian achievements, as co-founder of Prentiss Institute; joint organizer of the first high school for blacks in Jones County (Oak Park Vocational High School); past-president of the Mississippi State Federation of Colored Women's Clubs; past-president, Southeastern Association of Women's Clubs; and President Emeritus of the Southern Association of Women's Clubs.[5]

Even more significantly, she was instrumental in the establishment of the Oakley Training School which climaxed twenty years of effort on the part of black Mississippi women who worked with Mrs. Johnson on the steering committee. Their endeavors came to fruition when the state legislature passed a bill establishing the school.

Tuskegee Institute awarded Bertha Johnson the honorary master's degree in 1942, for outstanding service. She was photographed and listed in NAACP's *Crisis Journal* and in *Who's Who In America*."[6]

Arenia C. Mallory
Saints Junior College Founder

Dr. Arenia C. Mallory, founder of Saints Junior College, Lexington, Mississippi, headed that private institution for approximately fifty years. Saints Junior College presently called Saints Academy was established by the Board of Trustees of the Church Of God in Christ (COGIC) in the early 1900s. Mallory guided the college through its formative years and made it a respectable private and religious institution for black youth. Although the college was under the auspices of COGIC, it accepted students of other denominations. Many blacks from throughout the United States received a two-year associate degree from Saints Junior College before it was converted into a private secondary school in the 1970s.[1]

Mallory proved an efficient and scholarly president as well as an active civic leader. During her tenure in office, several buildings were erected and the choir gained national fame as performers of gospel music and song. During the late 1960s, she became the first black and the first female ever elected to the Holmes County Board of Education.[2]

McKinley Charles Martin
Coahoma Junior College President

Dr. McKinley Charles Martin, 1962 honor graduate of Jackson State University and native of Clarksdale, was appointed in 1979 president of his alma mater, Coahoma Junior College, where he had previously served as director of continuing education and registrar. Dr. Martin received his M.A. degree from Delta State and his Ph.D. from Florida State University with a perfect (4.0) grade point average.[1]

Joyce Ladner
Sociologist and Author

Joyce Ladner, sociologist and author, was born in Waynesboro, but she attended and graduated from Earl Travillon Attendance Center in Forrest County. She received the B.A. degree from Tougaloo College in 1964. She continued her education at Washington University, where she received both the M.A. and the Ph.D. degrees.

She published many articles in newspapers, anthologies, and professional journals. Her best known books are *Tomorrow's Tomorrow: The Black Woman* (1971); and *The Death of White Sociology* (1973). Presently she is professor of sociology at Hunter College in New York. Previously she taught at Howard University, Washington University (St. Louis), and Southern Illinois (Carbondale). In addition, she traveled and lectured extensively abroad, particularly in Africa.[1]

Gladys Noel Bates
Educator

Gladys Noel Bates, Jackson native, influenced the quality of the profession for public school teachers in Mississippi. After graduation from Tougaloo with honors, she earned the M.A. at West Virginia University. For more than a decade she served with superior distinction as editor of the *Mississippi Teachers Association Journal*. One of her greatest achievements was the suit filed in her name for the equalization of salaries for white and black teachers based upon qualifications. That suit generated the legal climate that eventually enabled black teachers in Mississippi to receive the same salaries as their white counterparts. The Jackson Board of Education, however, refused to issue contracts to Gladys Bates and her husband, J. M. Bates. They left the state and joined the Denver, Colorado Public School System.[1]

Lou Emma Holloway
Historian

Professor Lou Emma Holloway, associate professor of history at Tougaloo College, was appointed in 1974 to the Consolidated Regional Archives Advisory Council of the General Services Administration. Professor Holloway, a native of Rankin County and a graduate of Tougaloo, received her M.A. in history from the University of Denver, a certificate of advanced study in American/Afro-American Studies as a Rockefeller Foundation Fellow, and a Wesleyan University Fellow from Wesleyan University. Also, Holloway engaged in graduate work in African studies as an African-American Institute Fellow in Ethiopia, Kenya, Tanzania, Uganda, and Zambia. She was the first female Tallman Professor at Bowdoin College. In addition to receiving other numerous awards, she is listed in the 1973 edition of *Outstanding Educators of America*.[1]

Janice White Sikes
Curator

Janice White Sikes, a native Mississippian, migrated to Atlanta, Georgia, and became curator of special collections at Atlanta Public Library. Born to Willie J. and Bonnye Moore White in Meridian, Janice was graduated from Spelman College in 1973 and received her master of library science degree from Atlanta University in 1975. Janice began her career as a librarian at the Atlanta Public Library as a library aide, and was soon promoted to the position of Curator of the Special Collection Department, which houses an extensive collection of rare books, magazines, periodicals, films, newspapers, and other items that re-create the black experience from pre-colonial Africa to the present. When the multi-million dollar Atlanta Public Library opened May 25, 1980, Janice Sikes ended seven years of service in the Atlanta Public Library. Presently she is authoring a book on the black experience.[1]

When asked what forces shaped or influenced her life, she unhesitatingly responded: "Besides my own parents, my grandparents have been the *élan vital*." Her paternal grandparents are Mr. and Mrs. James R. White of Kemper County and her maternal grandparents are Mr. and Mrs. Caesar Moore of Hopewell, Neshoba County of Mississippi.

Dorothy Gordon Gray
Education and Religion

Dorothy Gordon Gray, pioneer and a past-president of the Negro Home Economics Association, was the first black to hold elective office in the integrated Mississippi Home Economics Association. Formerly, she was chairman of the Home Economics Department at Alcorn State University and previously head of the Home Economics Department at Tougaloo College. She also holds prominent positions in the Wesleyan Service Guild of the United Methodist Church and the Mississippi Religious Leadership Conference.[1]

Julius Eric Thompson
Educator

Julius Eric Thompson, a native of Natchez, a graduate of Alcorn State University, with a Ph.D. from Princeton, was a Danforth Fellow in 1969, a Princeton Fellow in 1970, and a Ford Fellow in 1972. He is listed in the 1971 edition of *Outstanding Young Men of America*, *Living Black American Authors* (1974), *Community Leaders and Noteworthy Americans* (1974), *Personalities of the South* (1974), *The Writers Directory* (1974), and *Contemporary Authors* (1974). He is assistant professor of history at Jackson State University and a prominent young scholar.[1]

LITERATURE AND JOURNALISM

Beginning in the late eighteenth and early nineteenth centuries, an embryonic black bourgeoise, expressed disdain for mores and customs of African origin. Prior to that time black writers in the United States had imitated the writing style of white authors and chosen non-racial subject matters for commercial appeal. By the turn of the century the traditional plantation roles of blacks were deplored by many black writers. These writers refrained from using dialect and the mythical images of blacks as Sambos and Uncle Toms. They sought neither to amuse nor to inform their white audiences about the legacy of the African-American experience. Psychologically, the institution of slavery had instilled in them a sense of racial inferiority and negativism, which were reflected in their writings.

Not until the 1920s did black writers view their past, their sufferings, and their survival as a part of their culture. These writers focused upon racial propaganda and protested the American experience in their works. As Langston Hughes, black poet of the twenties, wrote, "We younger Negro artists who create now intend to express our individual dark-skinned selves without fear or shame. If white people are pleased we are glad. If colored people are pleased we are glad. If they are not their displeasure doesn't matter either." Yet there were still those few who rejected "the flamboyance and defiance and the glorification of the lowest straits of Negroes."

The Great Depression marked a turning point in black literature as writers were confronted with the harsh realities of ghetto life and social injustice in America which were intertwined with the black experience. For example, Mississippian Richard Wright's novel, *Native Son*, an instant success when it was published in 1940, dealt with racial conflict and protest as well as the white rejection of blacks as human beings.

With the technological advances that followed came the search for identity. Black writers examined an inner conflict within the black man that had to be resolved. Assimilation was perceived as the key to the dilemma.

Since the 1960s some black literature, television, radio, and newspapers have espoused nationalism and revolution. Emphasis is placed upon "Mother Africa." The black media is torn between assimilation/integration and separatism/nationalism. A new style of writing emanated, and to understand black literature accurately, readers must interpret it from the black perspective.

Much of the literature written by black writers from Mississippi has dealt with the racial, social, and economic exploitation and injustice suffered by the black race. Imitating the writing style of whites, they disfused or saturated black literature with southern dialect and mores. Although some departed from the traditional historical practice of projecting blacks as inarticulate and poorly educated, many did not. Contained or incorporated within the published works of the writers cited are black songs, folktales, proverbs, aphorisms, jokes, verbal games, and narrative poems. In these the writers tried to reconstruct the black past through written documents and oral history. Through their works, one can recreate the background, thought, action, and culture of blacks.

Three major themes are expressed in these writers' works: oppression, resistance, and survival. From slavery to the present, blacks have been confronted with racial oppression and discrimination. In some instances, blacks organized lobbies, revolts, protest organizations, and movements or remonstrated through written communication, such as petitions or elections. Blacks' survival depended upon the condition and circumstances under which they lived; therefore, they devised survival mechanisms such as accomodation, assimilation, separatism, or protest. Examples of each are contained within the biographical sketches of the authors and publishers mentioned in this section. Mississippi can lay claim to two of the nation's major black literary talents of the twentieth century—Richard Wright and Margaret Walker Alexander.

While literary endeavors are often set apart from the mainstream of American life, the press is very much a part, directly reflecting and affecting politics, economics, and day to day living. Such is the case with the black press. As early as the 1700s, the black press in the United States was created out of the protests of blacks mistreated under southern Jim Crowism, an undemocratic legal system, and prejudiced politicians. Editors and publishers were crusaders against discrimination and advocates of racial equality and voting rights. They informed black citizens about important issues and advised them concerning political, economic, moral and social activities, and problems.

In the 1960s the black press—established, owned, operated, and controlled by blacks was the unifying instrument of the community, reflecting the hopes, aspirations, and protests of black people. In essence, it was the voice of the black community, speaking for and to the black man.

This section presents a few of the black Mississippians who, as writers, publishers and editors, voiced the concerns of blacks in Mississippi and in the nation.

Richard Nathaniel Wright
Novelist

Richard Wright achieved the unique distinction of being the first black novelist to acquire fame and fortune in the United States.[1] When one peers into his background and early life, it seems improbable that he would have so nobly achieved. The Wrights were plantation slaves in northwest Adams County, their blood a mixture of white, Indian, and African. When the Civil War ended, Nathaniel Wright, his paternal grandfather, was emancipated and given a plot of land. From the rich soil in Stanton, situated about twelve miles east of Natchez,[2] his grandfather was able to sustain his family.

Wright's illiterate sons became disillusioned with working in the fields. They hired themselves out as day laborers on various plantations. Nathan, Richard's father, left home during his early twenties to become a sharecropper in a nearby village.[3]

Richard's maternal grandfather, Richard Wilson, was born of unknown parentage, about March 21, 1847, on a plantation near Woodville in Wilkinson County, Mississippi. On learning of the assassination of President Lincoln, Richard escaped from his owner and traveled until he reached Mound City, Illinois. In Mound City he enlisted for three years, but he served only ninety-seven days in the federal navy because the war ended. With an honorable discharge he returned to Wilkinson County, where the radical Republicans had established a black militia to insure free elections.[4]

Richard Wilson's few months in battle rendered him blind in his right eye, and he suffered from chronic rheumatism that warped his body. When applying for a veteran's disability pension, he discovered his record could not be found. He persisted, and an investigation revealed that his last name had been spelled "Vincent" instead of Wilson. The decades of correspondence caused him to live under the delusion that the War Between the States would be resumed. It has been written that "he hated whites so passionately that no one ever heard him speak of them except as 'goddam rebels.'"[5]

On February 26, 1871, Richard Wilson married Margaret Bolden of Woodville. Margaret, born about 1853, took the surname of her master. Because of her mulatto complexion she worked as a house servant. After emancipation, even though she could neither read nor write, she learned the trade of midwifery. When the family moved to

Natchez in 1895, she became an assistant to a white doctor. Competent, honest, and a hard worker who frequently preached morality to others, she held an indisputable prestige among her friends and acquaintances.[6] Although her grandson Richard came to loathe her tyrannical authority, he was able to recognize that she was the most influential and impressive member of the family.

The Wilsons had nine children, all of whom were influenced by their mother's powerful personality. Eight reached maturity and obtained a formal education, which qualified them as teachers, preachers, and a carpenter-contractor. Ella, born in 1883, was the second, oldest girl and fourth child. She was elegant, pretty, intelligent, and courageous.[7]

In 1907, twenty-four year old Ella Wilson, a Cranfield school teacher, met an illiterate sharecropper, Nathan Wright, a handsome man with high cheekbones, a long narrow-bridged nose, deep wide-apart eyes, and reddish brown skin. Despite her parents' disapproval, Nathan and Ella were married. The Wilsons, status conscious mulattoes who had set themselves apart from the farmers in the vacinity, considered their daughter's marriage an uneven yoke. Nevertheless, Ella and Nathan settled as sharecroppers on a farm twenty-two miles east of Natchez in the village of Roxie.[8]

On September 4, 1908, in the midst of the unending financial difficulties, Ella Wilson Wright gave birth to her first born, Richard Nathaniel Wright. A little more than two years later, Ella bore a second son, Leon Alan. Nathan abandoned farming and became an itinerant laborer. Thus, he lived apart from his family for a while before finding a job in the city at a sawmill. In 1911, unable to take care of two small children and the farm, Ella went to live with her parents in Natchez. In Roxie, Richard had experienced the horrors of rural poverty; however, in Natchez, he saw another side of life.[9]

Nathan decided to take his family to Memphis, where he had found a job as night porter at the Lyle Drug Store. But father and son clashed over the restrictions on keeping quiet during the day when father was to sleep. "I cannot even remember having established any kind of relationship with my father at all." Richard reminisced, "Though he was real and tangible enough, he always seemed, in my mind, to exist far away. He was the lawgiver in the family, I felt. I do not recall his ever having said anything kind. His voice was loud. He was a big man and I still have memories of his drinking beer and eating long and hard at the kitchen table."[10]

The unsavory characters in his low socio-economic neighborhood and his peers initiated Richard into a survival environment. His mother forced him to assert his rights with his fists, but his underlying timidity remained. While his mother worked, Richard and his brother took to the streets. Richard discovered Beale Street in Memphis with its disreputable adults. He peeped under saloon doors, followed drunks, used four-letter words, began to taste alcohol, and became drunk on at least one occasion.[11]

Richard's father consistently stayed from home until he eventually deserted his family for a "strange woman." With that desertion, Richard experienced for the first time the gnawing pangs of hunger that were to become an integral part of his existence. His mother had sacrificed her teaching career, first to work on the farm and then to work in white folks' kitchens. Despite her pride, she took Nathan to court for family support. There Richard witnessed his father smiling and falsely stating that he was doing all he could for his family. On another occasion when Ella desperately sent the children to Nathan to ask for money, Nathan offered Richard a nickel.

Because of their destitute condition, Richard did not attend school. One day, the coal deliveryman taught him to count to a hundred within a few minutes. With his mother's help he learned to read, thus developing an increased interest in reading instead of drinking. At eight he entered Howard Institute in Memphis. School seemed to intensify his emotional problems and emphasized the shame of his being poor and fatherless. He also broadened his knowledge of swear words and obscenities and proudly displayed such vocabulary one day by scribbling on windows along the way home. When his mother discovered the prank, she forced him to wash the profanity off under the humiliating gaze of the neighbors.[12]

In 1915 Grandmother Wilson visited. The boys started going to Sunday school, and Ella began to seek refuge in religion. Soon after Grandmother Wilson left, Ella fell suddenly ill, and everything fell apart immediately. Besides facing the winter's cold and living on the charity of neighbors, Richard took care of his mother and brother.

Eventually, Richard and his brother were sent to a Methodist orphanage where the directress, a Miss Simon, terrified Richard with her advances. Constant hunger, the strict discipline, the tricks and intrigues of the other children, and the separation from his mother induced in him constantly the idea of running away. He escaped one evening only to be caught by a white policeman, who returned him to the home where he was whipped by Miss Simon. As soon as Ella was able to save enough money, she took her sons out of the orphanage.[13]

Thereafter, Ella visited her parents in Jackson, where Richard enjoyed the most glorious days of his childhood. His grandfather took him and his brother on long walks and fishing trips. The boys picked blackberries, peaches, and nuts. For the first time in Richard's life, he experienced contentment. At his grandmother's home, he met a boarder and young teacher, Eloise Crawford, who introduced him to the fascinating world of fiction.[14]

However, Grandma Wilson, in true character of her strict Seventh Day Adventist religion, warned Eloise to refrain from conversing or reading stories to Richard. So when she suddenly discovered Eloise and Richard engaged in story telling, which she considered "works of the devil," Eloise was evicted. The interrupted fictional session left a void, which Richard was determined to fill or satisfy. This visit afforded Richard an opportunity to analyze and to better acquaint himself with his grandparents. He viewed his grandfather as an easy going playmate. On the other hand, he associated his grandmother with whiteness, authority, and terror. Her whiteness confused Richard about her race. For example, he experienced "the bitter amusement of going into town with Granny and watching the baffled stares of white folks who saw an old 'white' woman leading two undeniably Negro boys in and out of stores on Capitol Street."[15]

So another facet of Richard's world included white folks and the confusing position they occupied in relation to blacks. For most southern blacks, racial segregation and discrimination was a daily occurrence. But the isolated village of Roxie, the semi-exclusive upper-lower class neighborhood of Natchez, and the ghetto of Memphis had practically shielded Richard from contact with whites. Now the eight-year old Richard had to cope with the fear of whites along with the familiar specters of hunger, emotional insecurity—all burning, unresolved issues.

After a short visit with her parents, Ella Wright journeyed to Elaine, Arkansas, where she resided with her sister Maggie and her brother-in-law, Silas Hoskins, a saloon keeper. To Richard's delight there was always plenty of food. At first he would stuff his pockets with biscuits for fear he might not have any for the following day. Uncle Silas took a genuine interest in his nephews as he often took them on tours of the town in his buggy. For once Richard felt at home without the endless prohibitions of Grandmother Wilson.[16]

But this peacefulness was short-lived. Envious whites killed the successful Silas Hoskins and threatened to murder the entire family. Again, Richard was consumed with fear. "This was as close as white terror had ever come to me and my mind reeled," said the terrified Richard. When Richard asked his mother why Uncle Hoskins had not fought back, "the fear in her made her slap (him) into silence."[17]

The penniless, heartbroken, and now horror-stricken Ella and her brood journeyed to Jackson, but later returned to West Helena, Arkansas, to stay with Maggie. The two sisters rented one-half of a double tenant house, in front of which ran a sewage ditch. In *Black Boy*, Wright described the scene: "The neighborhood swarmed with rats, cats, dogs, fortune-tellers, cripples, blind men, whores, salesmen, rent collectors, and children."[18] The landlady lived in the other portion of the house and operated a bordello. One day Richard unaware of these activities peeped through a crack in the wall and saw a nude man and a woman lying on a bed. He giggled. The couple saw him, got up, dressed and left, but not before telling the landlady about the incident. She severely scolded Richard and accused him of driving away her customers. Now sex became one of his major concerns.

Another terrifying incident beset the Wright clan. When his aunt Maggie announced that she intended to marry and live with a Professor Matthews in Detroit, Richard was saddened for she was his "other mother." Because Professor Matthews usually visited Aunt Maggie at night during their courtship, Richard suspected him of unsavory activities. True to form, his new uncle was having a love affair with a white woman. When he tried to end the relationship, she cried rape. To silence her, Matthews knocked her unconscious, stole her money, and set her home afire to destroy the evidence of assault.[19] Consequently, he and Maggie hurriedly left town.

With Maggie gone, the Wright family again suffered hunger pains. To acquire money Richard sold his dog, Betsy. After several months Ella found employment in a doctor's office for five dollars a week. While she worked, her sons roamed the streets and engaged in cinder-throwing wars with white boys. On one occasion a white boy threw a broken bottle at Richard, causing a deep gash behind his ear that required three stitches. When Ella learned of the fight, she stripped Richard nude, whipped and lectured him concerning "gems of Jim Crow wisdom." He was never, never to fight white folks, she admonished. For Richard, white symbolized fear.[20]

Another racial incident occurred in November 1918 at the conclusion of World War I. As the soldiers returned home, Richard witnessed whites and blacks laughing, singing, dancing, and shouting together. There was much praise for the "Fighting Black Devils," the black soldiers who had broken through the Hindenburg Line. But the holiday spirit was short-lived. In a few months newspaper headlines reported widespread lynchings of returning black soldiers. Again Richard experienced fear.[21]

During this time, Ella's health declined. A halting, lisping quality, crept into her voice—an omen of future illness. Yet, she forced herself to work whenever possible. Sometimes she lay in bed weeping, praying and talking to Richard about her mother's house. Meanwhile, Richard was fearful, hungry, and anxious. One morning the shouting, excited Richard shook his mother to see whether she was still alive, Ella moved slightly and groaned. Immediately Richard summoned a neighbor. A doctor was called, who informed Richard that his mother's entire left side was paralyzed, and she would need constant care.

Subsequently, Richard wrote his grandmother and asked her to come at once. In the meantime the neighbors nursed Ella, fed the children and washed their clothers. Richard, though hungry, was too proud to eat, ashamed to accept charity. Grandmother Wilson arrived and dictated letters to Richard to send to her children requesting money so she could take Ella home. They responded, and Ella and the children were taken to Jackson.[22]

Finally a family conference was held, and it was decided that Alan would go to Detroit with Aunt Maggie, and Richard would live in Greenwood with Uncle Clark. Richard was disappointed; he had wanted to go with Aunt Maggie. Richard did not stay in Greenwood very long before he returned to his grandmother's home in Jackson.

At age twelve, Richard virtually a nomad had not attended school a full term. He had drunk deep of the dregs of the ghetto—rats, filth, liquor, hunger, anger, and despair. Though a child, he often participated in the undesirable aspects of adult life. His only hope was his mother, the only person to whom he belonged, and now she was very ill. Fate seemed against him! Not only did constant hunger keep him too weak to earn any money, but he also was unable to prevent bad fortune and illness. He was an emotional wreck; he walked in his sleep and was on the verge of a nervous breakdown.[23]

His position in the Wilson household was a tenuous, delicate one; he was a minor, who had not accepted his grandmother's religion. Richard was baptized, although he refused to accept religion. It was the church that became the setting for his awakening sexuality. He fell idealistically in love, as is usual for that age, with an elder's wife, who sang in the choir.[24]

His grandmother equated Ella's illness with Richard's faithlessness, thereby forcing Richard to live with a feeling of guilt. Richard described the effects of his mother's illness:

> My mother's suffering grew into a symbol in my mind, gathering to itself all the poverty, the ignorance, the helplessness; the painful, baffling, hunger-ridden days and hours; the restless moving, the futile seeking, the uncertainty, the fear, the dread; the meaningless pain and the endless suffering. Her life set the emotional tone of my life, colored the men and women I was to meet in the future, conditioned my relation to events that had not yet happened, determined my attitude to situations and circumstances I had yet to face. A somberness of spirit that I was never to lose settled over me during the slow years of my mother's unrelieved suffering, a somberness that was to make me stand apart and look upon excessive joy with suspicion, that was to make me self-conscious, that was to make me keep forever on the move, as though to escape a nameless fate seeking to overtake me.[25]

In Jackson, he once again, knew "biting hunger, hunger that made my body aimlessly restless, hunger that kept me on edge, that made my temper flare, hunger that made hate leap out of my heart like the dart of a serpent's tongue, hunger that created in me odd cravings."[26]

A classmate at Jim Hill discovered his plaguing hunger and suggested that Richard sell papers. That idea was exciting because he liked to read. For a brief period it was a financial success, but Richard returned to school and to the usual fare of mush and lard gravy for breakfast and boiled collard greens for dinner. There was no lunch. His mother's health improved a bit, but she was crippled for life. Soon Grandpa Wilson's health worsened and he died. "My clothing became so shabby that I was ashamed to go to school." Although unprepared for school, he did enroll at Smith-Robertson.[27]

One day at school he wrote a story and called it "The Voodoo of Hell's Half-Acre." It was published in three installments in the local Negro newspaper, the *Southern Register*. His schoolmates were baffled, his gang outraged, the editor encouraged; his mother was worried, Uncle Tom was highly critical, and Aunt Addie called it sinful.[28]

When he was about fifteen, while working in a white home, a lady asked him why he still attended school and what he wanted to be when he grew up. Almost without volition Richard answered, "A writer." "You'll never be a writer," she said; "who on earth put such ideas into your nigger head." On May 29, 1925, he graduated from grammar school as valedictorian and gave a speech he had written himself.[29]

Knowledge of beatings and lynchings of blacks by whites caused him and his young comrades to boast about being black and increased their hatred of whites. These events supplied him with a wealth of experience of legends, proverbs, folk tales, and superstitions ranging from voodoo to Christianity. They also laid the foundation for his novel, Native Son. His biographer, Constance Webb explains:

> For a long time Native Son had been germinating in Richard. From the first Biggy Thomas, a Jackson classmate, who defied all Jim Crow laws and taboos, to the hundreds of people he had met in Chicago, Richard had unconsciously stored away their actions and emotions . . . that crystallized and coagulated into clusters and configurations of memory, attitudes, moods and ideas. . . ."[30]

Despite his hunger, his loneliness, his despair, his hate, and all his unpleasantness, Richard dreamed of going north and writing books. Meanwhile, he bought clothes, shoes, and a cardboard suitcase and hid them at home. Although his mother protested, he soon sped away on a Jim Crow coach. Richard went as far north as Memphis. Immediately he found a job as dishwasher in a cafe that paid ten dollars a week, with two meals. Richard concluded this would offer him a good opportunity to save money for his anticipated trip to Chicago.[31]

Richard found another job with an optical company where he met other blacks most of whom were uneducated. However, he conversed with them about their jobs, white folks, sex, and religion. He bought second-hand magazines, read and re-sold them. Going to work early allowed Richard time to read the morning *Commercial-Appeal*. One day he was struck by an editorial dealing with H. L. Mencken, editor of the *American Mercury*. "The article was a furious denunciation of Mencken, concluding with one, hot, short sentence: Mencken is a fool."[32]

He wanted to read more about Mencken. He borrowed a white man's library card and forged notes to the librarian for books by Mencken. That night he read *A Book of Prefaces* and was "jarred and shocked by the style, the clear, clean, sweeping sentences." Mencken was consumed with hate, denouncing everything American, extolling everything European or German, laughing at the weaknesses of people, mocking God. Suddenly a whole new world opened up for Richard, a world of writers, of reading, of moods and ideas. More than ever, he yearned to go north, to escape Jim Crowism, to express the thoughts that burned in him, to fight the southern way of life. He read Dreiser, Sinclair Lewis, Masters, Anderson, and whatever he could get his hands on.[33]

He sent for his mother, but Aunt Maggie, whose husband had deserted her, came to Memphis casting about for a job. They talked and planned the trip to Chicago. He and Aunt Maggie arrived first and then his mother and his brother. Prior to leaving he broke the news to his white employer and co-workers; there were admonishments not to leave. Only Mr. Falk, whose library card he had used secretly, encouraged him to go.[34]

In December 1927, at the age of nineteen, Richard Wright, tall and strong, lean and hungry, arrived in Chicago. He was eager for a job that would in some manner contribute to his hunger for personal fulfilment and freedom. After working briefly as a porter and a dishwasher, he took a temporary job with the post office. With a salary of seventy cents an hour, or approximately twenty dollars a week, his confidence grew. A permanent position, though, depended on a physical examination with a minimum weight of 125—fifteen pounds above his 110. Although he undertook an increased calorie diet, when he was called in for the physical, he did not push the needle of the scales to the required 125. So, despite his score of 94 out of a possible 100, Richard was denied a permanent position at the post office.[35] Taking it in stride, he went back to a part-time job as a dishwasher at the Northside Cafe.

Richard and his Aunt Maggie clashed over Richard's incessant reading. With the promise of steady employment and no savings Richard moved his mother, Aunt Cleo, and brother into a three room apartment, where "Cockroaches ran out of every crack and corner and the odor of grease hung in the air at night." But Richard was the man of the house, and at night the kitchen became his private room. Writing was becoming his only reason for existence.[36]

Richard became so involved in writing that he failed to recognize what was happening to the economy of the nation. But when time came for the verification of his appointment as permanent clerk, he was told it would be temporarily delayed because of a drop in the volume of mail. His hours were cut, and his wages decreased. The volume of mail fell so low that he worked only one or two nights a week. Finally the post office job ended, and once again Richard was unemployed.

Suddenly things began to cave in around him—Aunt Cleo had a heart attack, his brother developed stomach ulcers, and his mother became ill. In addition to looking for work he had to pay the hospital bills and do the cooking, cleaning, and shopping. It helped somewhat when Alan went to live with an uncle in Toledo. Richard swallowed his pride and went to see a distant cousin of his mother's who was superintendent of a burial society; he was hired as an insurance agent. This fell short of Richard's expectation and he was somewhat sickened by the racketeering enterprise, which exploited poor people. But the cousin shrugged his shoulders and, "Well, if you don't sell them, somebody else will . . . you've got to eat, haven't you?"[37]

For each new policy he wrote, Richard received fifteen dollars, but for every policy that lapsed he was penalized fifteen dollars. There was also an incentive ten-percent commission on new premiums. Every day he visited flats filled with hungry men, women and children, most of whom were broken and defeated in one way or another. He returned home at night with nerves so taut and body so exhausted that he could neither read nor write. Each morning he awoke feeling he had not slept the previous evening. Every day some attractive housewife made a desperate effort to maintain her insurance premiums by prostituting herself.[38]

To improve his financial condition, Wright also engaged in political affairs. When a Republican precinct captain asked Richard to assist in getting votes for William Hale Thompson, a political candidate, commonly referred to as "Big Bill, the Builder," Richard, disinterested in Thompson or politics, readily agreed. He needed the money and hoped to receive a clerical position on Thompson's staff.

Relief kitchens were established throughout Chicago, but Richard and his family avoided them because they felt charity would rob them of their self-respect. But one morning Ella awakened Richard and told him there was no food. Shame and pride kept them from looking each other in the face. Richard soon dressed and went to the county bureau of public welfare, where he waited in line several hours for an interview. While he waited he saw hundreds of blacks for their first time conversing and sharing their grief and sentiments. "These people now knew that the past had betrayed them, had cast them out; but they did not know what the future would be like, did not know what they wanted." Wright recalled, "I was slowly beginning to comprehend the meaning of my environment; a sense of direction was beginning to emerge from the conditions of my life."[39]

The Wright family qualified as welfare recipients. Once a week their caseworker, Mary Writh, visited the Wright's apartment. At first they resented the white official invading their privacy. However, Writh did not snoop but simply asked perfunctory questions and noted the answers in her notebook. When she discovered that Richard wanted to be a writer, she was enthusiastic and used her position and influence to get him several profitable assignments. Finally he got a job with the Writer's Project of the W.P.A. Since he had prior publications, he was classified as a "professional writer temporarily out of work."[40]

Following this job, the welfare office assigned Wright as publicity agent for the Federal Negro Theatre. This position afforded him opportunities to meet and mingle with famous artists and writers. Most were affiliated with the University of Chicago and the Communist party. These intellectuals participated on forums dealing with literature, music, art, and politics. Richard learned from their writing style and content.

The John Reed Club founded by the Communist party in New York in 1929 published several magazines which featured the works of unknown writers and artists, providing a stimulating milieu for talented young people. At the Chicago chapter, Richard read back issues of *The Masses*, *Anvil*, *Left Front*, and *International Literature*, all publications printed by the Communist party. At home as he lay across his bed reading, he discovered that there "did exist in this world an organized search for the truth of the lives of the oppressed and the isolated."[41]

Always, after reading the magazines, Richard was obsessed with an immense feeling of freedom, followed by ripples of energy and a desire to write, to compose poems, several of which were published in the *Anvil*, the *Left Front*, and *The Masses*. However, he did not wish the editors to publish his poems as bait to get him to join the party. The scope and seriousness of the Club's activities impressed Richard, and its optimism in the midst of the Depression was a sharp contrast to the Republicans and Democrats. He had many reservations, but he perceived "the Communists as the only political organization that was expressing the country's widely felt need for a drastic change."[42]

Richard attended regular meetings of the John Reed Club and they published some of his poetry. In January 1932, Richard joined the

Club and committed himself wholeheartedly to its principles.[43] Secretly Richard vowed to make blacks understand Communism and accept its philosophy through his writings. Shortly afterwards at a special meeting of the Club, Richard was elected executive secretary. (He later learned he had been used in a factional fight between the writers and the painters.) Subsequently he became an official member of the Communist party.[44]

At the First National Conference of the John Reed Club, held in Chicago in 1932, Richard met a black Communist, David Poindexter, native of Tennessee. "Distrustful but aggressive, he (Poindexter) was a bundle of the weaknesses and virtues of a man struggling blindly between two societies, of a man living on a margin of culture." Richard saw Poindexter's story as a viable biography of a folk people in their adjustments to an urban environment. "If he could show this, then each stage of development would reveal the dramas of hope, fear, love and hate that existed in the Negro people."[45]

Poindexter agreed to have his biography written by Richard Wright. Richard visited David every morning for two hours and took notes. This worked well until word spread within the Party that the two men were meeting, talking, and taking notes. A member of the local and Central Committee questioned Richard about the matter. Richard became circumspect. He felt frozen; but the Club needed his attention, and he pushed the episode aside.

Local party leaders made many demands upon the Club for speakers, sign painters, and money, to the extent that little or no time or energy remained for publication of its magazine, *Left Front*. Richard tried to mediate between the opposing groups because he wanted the John Reed Club to continue as a source of encouragement to young writers. But the Party soon proposed that the publication of *Left Front* cease. When Richard asked what was expected of writers—books or political activity—the answer was *both*. Eventually, the Club was abolished, and Richard witnessed the ruthlessness of the Party's policy.[46]

Freed from the routine of Club responsibilities, Richard worked on a series of short stories and a novel about post office workers. Working practically all day and writing at night caused Richard to suffer a serious case of pneumonia. After his illness, the editorial staff of *New Masses* journals asked him to write an article on the Joe Louis-Max Baer fight. Immediately after the fight Richard stood on the street, stared all around him and was touched to his depths by the exultation that burst from the black community at Louis's victory.

When he sat at his writing table later that night, words poured almost as fast as he could move his hand. He spoke directly to fellow Communists, laying bare the unharnessed dynamism that lay close to the surface of the black community.[47]

Not long afterwards, James W. Ford, a member of the Party's hierarchy, the Communist International, ordered Wright to complete a task. When Richard objected because he was in the midst of a novel and needed six months to finish it, Ford was not impressed. "The Party can't wait," Ford said. He even implied that if Richard did not accept Party law, he would be branded a counterrevolutionary. Continuing, Ford said, "The role of the creative writer is to serve the interests of the people by inspiring them and helping them to prepare and organize their struggle. The Party has made its decision; you are to accept this task."[48]

Richard saw the seamy side of Communism and rebelled against it. On the one hand he accepted Communism as the most viable socio-political force for blacks, and on the other he was repelled by the authoritarianism of leading Communists. Because such action seemed the opposite of freedom, Richard was unable to resolve this obvious dichotomy. "But, regardless of tactics," Richard rhetorically asked, "what is there to go back to?"

During this period Richard enjoyed some distinction as a poet. In the name of the Central Committee, James Ford and Benjamin Davis offered Richard the position as Harlem editor of the *Daily Worker*. With three unpublished novels, a half dozen short stories and several poems tucked in a briefcase, a portable typewriter and a cardboard suitcase containing his meager wardrobe, Richard left Chicago for New York.[49]

In New York, Wright not only served as editor of the *Daily Worker*, but he also edited a new literary quarterly, *New Challenge*, whose focus was the black writer and his problems. To delineate the objectives of *New Challenge* to other black writers, Wright composed an important article, "Blueprint for Negro Literature," in which he spoke of the value and function of black folklore, black nationalism, Marxism, and art as instruments for changing the structure of society. "It was important," he said, "that the black writer not isolate himself; he must work as part of a collective power, neither forsaking professional autonomy nor forgetting the strength that comes from a united effort."[50]

Wright tried hard to heed his own advice, but there existed an abyss between Wright's personal goals and those the Party had for him. Wright found himself becoming disillusioned.[51] But as long as the Party did not interfere with his fiction-writing, he was reasonably content to endure the uncertain ideology.

In 1938 his short story, "Fire and Cloud," won a *Story* magazine prize, and his first collection of fiction, *Uncle Tom's Children*, was published, not by the leftist press with its limited audience, but by the prominent mainstream house, Harper Brothers. A second edition in 1940 added a fifth story, "Bright and Morning Star," and, as a preface, the autobiographical essay, "The Ethics of Living Jim Crow." In 1941 he permitted the Marxist house, International Publishers, to reissue "Bright and Morning Star," as a separate volume that included a special preface entitled, "A Letter to International Publishers." As may be surmised, at that period Wright was firmly rooted in Communist idealism and was eager to use the story to assist the movement.[52]

In 1939 shortly after the first publication of *Uncle Tom's Children*, Wright received a Guggenheim Fellowship that helped him complete work on *Native Son*. That same year he married Rose Dhima Meadman, a Russian-American dancer, with Ralph Ellison as his best man. The next March, when Harper Brothers published *Native Son*, the Wrights were overwhelmed by publicity as the sales soared. Approximately a month later, sales totaled a quarter of a million copies. According to a Harper's executive, it was their best selling novel in twenty years. *Native Son* was chosen as the Book-of-the-Month-Club selection for March. The next year Wright was awarded the Spingarn Medal, the NAACP's annual award to a black American for high achievement. A few months later he was honored at a gathering of Marxist writers, at the fourth biannual American Writers Congress.[53]

Actually the book generated a prodigious amount of polarized comment. There was almost universal acclaim from the mainstream and the Marxist left; however, some prominent critics considered the book's credibility damaged by excesses of hatred and violence. A few Marxists complained that too much emphasis was placed upon Negro's rebellion and not enough stress on constructive group action. Over 300,000 copies were sold in this country, it was translated into six languages, and made into a Broadway play. Wright refused a $50,000 offer by a film studio to cast the characters in *Native Son* as white people.[54]

He began to perceive his wife as indolent, slothful, and bourgeois. His anger and distaste for her grew, and he divorced her. On March

12, 1941, Richard married Ellen Popular, a white party organizer, at Coytesville, New Jersey. Her parents disapproved of the marriage, but Ellen decided to make her marriage work. The next year in April their first child, Julia, was born.[55]

Wright's literary genius uninterrupted by marital problems led to his writing of his autobiography. On December 17, 1943, Richard Wright sent his autobiography to his literary agent. He called his autobiography *American Hunger*, but finally changed the title to *Black Boy*. Among Wright's most moving works, *Black Boy: A Record of Childhood and Youth*, according to Michel Febre, best recaptures "the pain and fear, the pleasures and hopes, innocence and growth, the metamorphosis toward an uncertain adulthood."[56]

By March 1945, sales of *Black Boy* had reached over 400,000, it had been chosen a Book-of-the-Month-Club selection, and was listed in every New York newspaper at the top of its best-seller list. White reviewers seemed to have gone mad, Richard thought. Critics declaimed, "Genius defies explanation; great literary talent; outstanding literary achievement of the last few years." Mississippi banned the book. Mississippi Senator Theodore Bilbo attacked the book and its author on the floor of the U.S. Senate.

> Black Boy should be taken off the shelves . . . , sales should be stopped; it was a damnable lie, from beginning to end; it built fabulous lies about the South. The purpose of the book was to plant seeds of hate and devilment in the minds of every American. It was the dirtiest, filthiest, most obscene, filthy and dirty, and came from a Negro from whom one could not expect better.[57]

Meanwhile, Wright's ideological conflicts with Communism continued to widen until 1944 when he left the Party. The years 1946 and 1947 were critical for Wright. Having left the Communist party, Wright realized that he could not broaden his artistic and personal freedom without leaving the oppressive soil from which he had sprung. Neither Chicago nor New York had proven any better than Mississippi as places where a black man and his white wife could be treated as free people. In August 1947, he packed his books, recordings and other belongings and moved to Paris, where, except for a brief stay in London, he made his home for the remainder of his life.[58]

On November 20, 1960, Wright was admitted to the Clinique Chirurgicale Eugene Givez, a small Parisian hospital. At eleven p.m. on November 28 at age fifty-two, he was found dead. The cause of death was listed as a heart attack. On December 3, his body was cremated and the urn of ashes deposited in a small columbarium in Paris' Pere Lachaise Cemetery.[59]

Of his works, *Native Son* and *Black Boy* were the most outstanding. *The Outsider* and *Black Power*, preceded by thirteen years "the anguished resolution of the black community to stand up as men, to die if need be, and warned ex-Premier Kwame Nkrumah of his nation's vulnerability seven years before Ghana's first independent government was overthrown."[60] Also included among his writings were *Savage Holiday*, (a counterpoint to *The Outsider*), "Pagan Spain," "White Man, Listen!," "Color Curtain," "Island of Hallucinations," and a large number of poems.

Margaret Walker Alexander

Educator and Author

The prize winning black author, Margaret Abigail Walker, was born on July 7, 1915, in Birmingham, Alabama, to Sigismund Constantine Walker and his wife Marion Dozier. Walker, a West Indian immigrant, converted to Methodism and became a minister. Her mother, Marion, the daughter of a Baptist minister, was a gifted musician. When Margaret was ten years old, her father accepted a teaching position at Dilliard University and her family moved to New Orleans.[1]

While in New Orleans, Margaret A. Walker launched her literary career. One year after graduating from high school at age fifteen, Margaret published her first poem, "I Want to Write," which appeared in the 1934 edition of *Crisis Magazine*, then edited by the Brahmin, W.E.B. Du Bois.[2]

After graduating from high school, Margaret Walker enrolled in Northwestern University. Upon completing her requirements for the baccalaureate degree, she accepted her first job with the WPA Federal Writer's Project in Chicago. While there, she renewed her acquaintance with Richard Wright. She continued to pursue a career in journalism and in English as she published poetry, edited a magazine, and honed her writing skills with help from her peers. She became recognized as an expert on the Harlem Renaissance, a black cultural revolution of the 1920s.[3]

Several years later, she continued her educational training at the University of Iowa, where she obtained an M.A. and a Ph.D. Soon thereafter, she accepted her first teaching job at Livingston College in Salisbury, North Carolina. During that time, she traveled to New York for the publication of her poetry collection, *For My People*, which charted new paths in black poetry. While in New York, she was hired by the National Concert Artist Corporation as a tour speaker. While on assignment in Pine Bluff, Arkansas, she met her husband-to-be, Firnist James Alexander. Margaret and Firnist were married on June 13, 1943. From this union were born two sons and two daughters.[4]

The Alexanders moved in 1949 to Jackson, Mississippi, where she taught at Jackson State College. For more than thirty years, she has enlightened and inspired young Mississippians. Presently, she is professor emeritus at Jackson State University. Although Margaret Walker resided in Illinois, North Carolina, New York, West Virginia, none of these places captured her heart as Mississippi has. She calls Jackson home.[5]

To show their appreciation for her work, Mississippians, black, and white, have bestowed on her numerous honors. On July, 12, 1980, Governor William Winter issued a proclamation declaring that date Margaret Walker Alexander Day throughout the state. Mayor Dale Danks of Jackson presented her with a key to the city. President Jimmy Carter and other prominent leaders sent telegrams of admiration and appreciation for her outstanding contributions in the fields of education and literature. The day was replete with a "This is Your Life" presentation, featuring such notables as poet Nikki Giovanni and Pauline Saxton, a former classmate and roommate. Also highlighting the day were a press conference and a parade through downtown Jackson. The affair was an unprecedented event honoring a black Mississippian. That evening the Jackson Urban Guild hosted a banquet in her honor with Lerone Bennett, senior editor of *Ebony* magazine and a native Mississippian, as the keynote speaker.[6]

Throughout her life, Margaret Walker Alexander, a remarkable woman and a giant in American fiction and poetry, has received numerous honors and awards for her outstanding literary works. Among many were Yale University's Award for Younger Poets, 1942; Rosenwald Fellowship, 1944; Ford Fellowship at Yale University, 1953–54; and an honorary doctoral degree in literature from Tougaloo College.[7]

Writing has been the Promethean spark for Margaret Walker Alexander. *For My People*, written when she was twenty-one years of age, has become a classic. Her *tour de force* is the novel, *Jubilee*. Without question, *Jubilee* added a new dimension to the historical novels of the Old South and the Civil War. In this book, which was written out of gratitude for her grandmother, Margaret Walker drew upon the rich resources of black folklore and folk idiom to give acceptable literary expression to the untapped historic tradition of the black experience in the South. Other published works include: *Prophets For A New Day, October Journey, How I Wrote Jubilee*, and co-authored with Nikki Giovanni, *Poetic Educations: Conversation Between Nikki Giovanni and Margaret*.[8]

Currently Margaret Walker Alexander is composing two novels, her autobiography, and a cookbook. Recently, she completed a definitive biography of her friend and long time associate, Richard Wright. She revealed some unpleasant tidbits about Wright's supposedly close friends and clandestine activities. According to Walker, "I just wish to set the record straight." And she has.[9]

The vision of Margaret Walker Alexander is reflected in this excerpt from, "For My People":

> For my people everywhere singing their slave song repeatedly:
> ... Let a new earth rise
>   Let another world be born
>   Let a bloody peace be written in the sky
>   Let a second generation full of courage issue forth;
>   Let a people loving freedom come to growth.[10]

Anne Moody
Author and Civil Rights Activist

Anne Moody (Mrs. Austin Straus), was born in Centreville, Mississippi, where she attended the local public schools. Later she enrolled at Natchez Junior College but received the B.S. degree from Tougaloo College in 1963. While in college she engaged in civil rights activities and worked with the NAACP, CORE, and SNCC on voter registration projects, desegregation of Jackson's Woolworth Store, and the organization of freedom schools. In 1964 she became a public speaker and fund raiser for the national CORE, and was civil rights project coordinator for Cornell University in 1964–1965.

Since, she has devoted herself to being a full time writer-lecturer. Her *Coming of Age in Mississippi* received the American Library Association "Best Book of the Year Award," the "Gold Medal Award" from the National Council of Catholics and Jews, and a citation from *Mademoiselle* magazine. Recently she has turned to writing children's books.[1]

Percy Greene

Editor, Publisher

"Percy Greene, despite a lot of other things," asserted one university professor, "must be given the credit for politicizing the Negro in Mississippi, in these modern times." A historian of the mid-twentieth century wrote: "Mr. Percy Greene, editor and publisher of the *Jackson Advocate*, was the organizer of the Mississippi Negro Democratic Association. He now (1950) serves as its chief executive. He has been tireless in his effort to bring the Negro of Mississippi into full political participation."[1]

Percy Greene, one of twelve children, was born in Jackson on September 7, 1898, to George Washington and Sylvia Stone Greene. He attended the Jackson public elementary schools, after which he entered the Catholic high school for one year and then transferred to Jackson College High School. In 1915, Greene left home and journeyed to Illinois, Ohio, and most of the midwest.

Two years later in 1917, the United States entered World War I and Percy Greene enlisted: "Not because I was interested in fighting, but because I wanted to see the world," he said.[2] While in the army, he spent a year in England, during which time he traveled throughout the British Isles, crossed the English Channel, and spent two years in France on special assignments.

Prior to Greene's discharge from the army, he took a competitive Civil Service examination. As a result of his high score on the test, he won a scholarship and received a certificate in bookkeeping and accounting. When the army released him from military duty, he returned to Jackson and pursued academic studies in business. To finance his education, Greene took employment as a mail carrier.

While a part-time employee and student at Jackson State College, Greene budgeted his time and played football for three years. During that period, the football team never lost a game. In fact, in one game he made nine touchdowns to lead the team to a 150-0 scoring victory, which ultimately led to his induction into the Jackson State Athletic Hall of Fame.

Upon graduation from college, Greene became an apprentice in Dr. S. D. Redmond's law office. For approximately four years Dr. Redmond instructed his son Sidney, a student at Harvard Law School, to send Greene his notes weekly. "I studied those notes," Greene recalled, "and Dr. Redmond tutored his son and me each summer."

Sidney, one of the top ten graduates from Harvard, and Greene took the bar examination. This occurred in 1927 when there was public outcry against white women and blacks practicing law in Mississippi. Sidney passed. The secretary conducting the examinations, Miss Lucy Summerville, informed Greene that he scored 69 (the passing score was 70). Subsequently, she wrote Greene that he was deficient in commercial law and suggested that he re-take the examination at a later date. Greene remembers the later incident:

> At that time I was also a messenger for the clerk of the Mississippi House of Representatives, and by appointment served as liaison officer between the whites and blacks for the Selective Service Board. Just prior to taking the bar examination the second time, I had an altercation in the Capitol Building with a white gentleman, whom I handled very roughly. The Honorable Walter Wood was Secretary of State at that time, and when the result of the examination was published, my name did not appear.

Dr. Redmond succeeded in getting young State Senator Walter W. Capers, son of the rector of St. Andrews Episcopal Church, to investigate the matter regarding the bar examination. Senator Capers told Dr. Redmond that Walter Wood said, "Yes, that 'nigger' made the highest mark on the list . . . but as long as I am Secretary of State he [Greene] will never be a lawyer in Mississippi."

In spite of Wood's remarks and his determination to prevent Greene from practicing law in Mississippi, Sidney Redmond encouraged him to pursue a law career. Greene's parents and other mentors wanted him to be a preacher; however, Greene claimed that God planned for him to be a newspaper publisher. Greene later declared about his decision: "Since I have become a newspaper man I can truly say that I have been to the top of the mountain."

As a newspaper publisher and editor, Greene counseled with presidents of the United States about problems confronting the black race. Lining the walls of his office were pictures of Greene with mayors, various government officials, and at least three presidents.

His first publication was *The Colored Veteran*, which he founded in 1927. This newspaper was co-sponsored by the National Association of Negro War Veterans, whose main concern was denial of black memberships in the American Legion, the Disabled Veterans, and the Veterans of Foreign Wars. Greene organized the Association of Negro War Veterans, and *The Colored Veteran* became a spokesman for veterans' causes. In 1939, Percy Greene founded the *Jackson Advocate* which at one time had a substantial paid circulation, but today is mostly an advertiser-distributed organ.

In 1946 Greene organized the Mississippi Negro Democrat Association to give Negroes a viable political vehicle. "The Negro Republican leaders were doing nothing and had almost justifiably dedicated themselves to the charge that they were only a vest pocket organization," Greene argued. "But, when I organized the Democratic Association they put me out of the lodges and almost out of the church. The irony is that the very persons who were instrumental in trying to drive me out of the councils of the race now proclaim themselves bigger Democrats than I am."

Greene was a civil rights advocate long before such Johnny-come-latelys as Eldridge Cleaver and Dr. Martin Luther King, Jr. "When the final story of the civil rights movement is written," Greene asserted, "they are going to say it was started in Mississippi in 1927 and 1928 by Percy Greene, the editor and publisher of the *Jackson Advocate*."

In 1924, Percy Greene married Frances Reed. They had met during the days of his football career at Jackson State. To that union were born two daughters—Dr. Frances Lorraine Parker, B.A., Dillard; M.A., University of Chicago; and Ph.D., Smith College; presently head of the department of psychiatry and social training at the University of Georgia in Atlanta; and Gwendolyn Greene Kelley, public school teacher.[11]

Greene believes that the "solution to racial betterment is to be found in the ability of the Negro to look inward. He is not going to be worth anything as long as he awaits the contributions of foundations and the federal government." When asked if he thought leaders in education would agree with that, Mr. Greene replied, "I have never been concerned about what folks thought about me. They have called me 'Uncle Tom,' 'Buzzard,' 'White Folks' Nigger' and everything you could imagine. However, I remain undaunted in my interest and concern with the plight of my people."

Greene, though somewhat given to self praise, has merited recognition for his contributions. For his services the *Chicago Defender* has given him three awards. He was listed on Drew Pearson's 1947 roll of democracy, and he has received a citation from the Schomburg collection of the New York Public Library for his contribution to democracy in the United States. He has been honored by the Mississippi Association of Teachers in Colored Schools and by the Jackson Community Chest. In addition to these the L.L.D. degree was conferred upon him by Campbell College."

The William A. Scott Family
Printers and Publishers

Emmeline Southall, the eldest daughter of Daniel and Amanda Southall, was born in East Liverpool, Ohio, on October 3, 1878. As a child, she was shy, obedient and conscientious. The only black enrolled in Latin class, she maintained the highest grade point average throughout her high school tenure. Soon after her graduation from East Liverpool High School, she met and married in 1899 Reverend William Alexander Scott, a graduate of Hiram College in Ohio and a religious, fraternal, and business leader. Thereafter, they moved to Reverend Scott's hometown, Edwards, Mississippi, where they purchased a printing business in 1900.

Together, the newlyweds worked diligently and harmoniously to make the printing company a successful enterprise. When Scott, who was also minister of the Christian Church, was elected Grand Worthy Counselor of the Court of Calanthe, Emmeline became his business assistant. As business assistant, Emmeline supervised the operation of the Progressive Printing House, the family business. In 1910, Scott relocated in Jackson, where he pastored the Farish Street Christian Church and bought another printing company. As the business prospered, the Scotts built the two-story brick W. A. Scott Building to house the printing company and to serve as a home for their expanding family, which included William Alexander II and C. A. Scott.

By the 1920s the Scotts owned an eighty acre farm and a printing company, and their reputation as printers and business leaders had spread throughout the Mississippi Delta, central Mississippi, and the other southern states. Consequently, the Scotts decided to move to Johnson City, Tennessee, in 1923 to further expand their holdings; but in November 1928 Reverend Scott succumbed to a serious illness.

To assist with the family's expenses and to further her education, Emmeline taught in the Johnson City public schools and attended Tennessee A. & I. College. Later, she matriculated at Atlanta University. By this time, the Scott family included six sons and three daughters.

Two of the Scott's sons, W. Alexander II and Cornelius Adolphus, eventually joined the family printing business. W. Alexander Scott II, the eldest sibling, who was born in 1902, attended Morehouse College where he played football and was inducted into the Athletic Hall of Fame. From 1925 to 1928, he worked as a railway mail clerk in Jacksonville, Florida. In the meantime, he maintained a keen interest in printing, and in 1927 he published a black business directory which listed all of Jacksonville's black-owned businesses.

W. Alexander II and his brother, Cornelius, who studied journalism at the University of Kansas launched their printing career in 1928 with the opening of a newspaper in Atlanta, Georgia. They purchased the Herman Perry's Service Company Printing Office, a holding of Standard Life Insurance Company. They converted the printing office into the headquarters of *The Atlanta World*, a daily newspaper. The newspaper venture grew and they published other newspapers such as the *Birmingham World* (Alabama) and the *Memphis World* (Tennessee). This was the beginning of the first chain of black-owned-and-operated newspapers. By 1933, the Scott's Newspaper Syndicate included over fifty publications servicing Ohio, Illinois, Missouri, Texas, and Arizona as well as other southern states. These newspaper chains were the first and largest in black journalism history with a circulation well over 80,000.

The Scott brothers' main goals or objectives in creating or printing these newspapers were "to give constructive and inspiring news to black people, to create jobs, and to prove that the black race could produce an important business. The idea of removing racial barriers and eliminating racial injustices were also driving forces."

However, for the youthful W. A. Scott II, who developed a keen interest in real estate and broadcasting as well as journalism, life was short circuited by an assassin's bullet February 6, 1934. Three days later, he died at the age of thirty-one. A writer and a journalist eulogized: "With the taking of his [Scott's] life, Atlanta and perhaps the nation lost one of its brightest young entrepreneurs.... Throughout his brief life, those who knew him said, few men surpassed him in competitive spirit. And this included sports, college debating, piano playing, billards, or succeeding in business."

Upon the death of W. A. Scott II, Emmeline rallied the family together and the presses continued to roll, newsstand and home deliveries were on time, and Cornelius Scott assumed the position of general manager. As such, Cornelius vowed in an editorial, "We will carry on. It is the iron-clad determination of his (W. A.'s) relatives and those who knew him through daily contact as members of his staff to carry on." And carry on they did.

Cornelius continued the tradition of hiring capable and aspiring personnel. Included among the best was Cliff McKay, managing editor, who resigned to accept a position with the *Afro-American*. Later Governor Agnew of Maryland appointed him as the first black director of Maryland Public Works. Another managing editor, William Gordon, a Neiman Fellow at Harvard University, became Senior Foreign Service Officer, for the U.S. Information Agency. Others who worked with the Scott's newspapers have included Lerone Bennett, senior editor of *Ebony*; Robert E. Johnson, editor of *Jet* and vice-president of Johnson Publishing Company; Ariel Perry Strong, former linotypist, now editor of *Black Stars*; Eddie Williams, reporter, now executive director Joint Center for Political Leaders, Washington, D.C.; Paul Delany, reporter and now senior staff member *New York Times*; and Stanley Southall Scott, reporter, member of the White House press staff under President Richard Milhouse Nixon and Gerald Ford, and more recently a vice-president of Phillip Morris Company. Harmon Perry, Atlanta Bureau Chief of *Jet* Magazine, stated that his eighteen years with the *World* provided invaluable experience and credentials that led to a job with the *Atlanta Journal* and *Jet*.

For forty-six years C. A. Scott has been the editor and general manager of the *Atlanta World*. Although the paper allegedly has a non-partisan editorial policy, Scott is an unabashed Republican. In 1976 *Time* magazine, reporting on an annual meeting of the National Newspaper's Publishers Association, chided Scott for not designating other capable individuals as editor. Nevertheless, it must be acknowledged that the Scott family, C. A. Scott in particular, has maintained and achieved W. A. Scott's objective to render service to the black community and the nation.

August 13, 1980, the *Atlanta Daily World* commemorated its

fiftieth anniversary. Greetings and accolades were numerous. It was a first for a black daily. C. A. Scott cited some of the more prominent accomplishments during those years. "Our first big honor," he said, "was to get President Franklin Roosevelt to accept Harry S. McAlpin as the White House Correspondent for the *World*. For the first time in history a black reporter could ask a President a question at his press conference. . . . We shared reports from this correspondent with members of the Negro Newspaper Publishers Association. That history making year was 1944."

However, John L. Calhoun, former city councilman and fellow Republican opted that C. A. Scott's greatest achievement was in the civic-political arena. He recalled the personal as well as organizational support C. A. gave the Atlanta Civic and Political League, the Republican Party, the All-Citizens Registration Committee, and the National Newspaper Publishers Association. The *Atlanta World* made extraordinary contributions, Calhoun said, in getting elected Mayors Hartfield, Allen, Massell, and Jackson; State Senator Leroy Johnson, the first Georgia black elected since Reconstruction; the first black members on Atlanta's Board of Education, Dr. Rufus Clements and city alderman Q. V. Williamson; and the first black police officers.

Columnist Charles E. Price in the "50th Anniversary Edition" declared:

> The presence of a daily Black newspaper has made the difference. The *Atlanta Daily World* has made that difference. From its beginning in 1928, it had been a "newspaper with a constructive policy," it has printed the news while it was still news about and for Black folks.
>
> The *World* has been the voice of Blacks in making its case to the nation and the world. The importance has not been mainly in the truth of its editorial position but in its very existence and the source of communication that it provided for people who were left out or isolated from the mainstream of American life.
>
> The paper provided a record for Blacks for all to see and it kept in focus the doings of aspiring Blacks. It made it impossible for those who would push under the rug the progress of Blacks to do so, rather it told the story of Blacks and in doing so tended to force others to give some spaces to the news about Blacks.
>
> In making known the achievements of Blacks and by keeping in proper focus the doing of Blacks, the *World* has offered a great service to the nation's Blacks and when racial pride became a byword of the period of Black pride, the *World* became the source of historical data on the achievements of Blacks. The pages of the *World* give a running

account of the living of people who had been virtually ignored by the White press.

Unprecedented recognition for a black newspaper was accorded by its induction into the society of professional journalism—Sigma Delta Chi—on Sunday, March 16, 1980. The *Atlanta Daily World*, the fifty-two year-old black-oriented journal, received the journalistic award for its "years of distinguished leadership" to the community, the city, and the nation. Howard Graves, president of Sigma Delta Chi asserted: "I am proud to have the *Atlanta Daily World* as a part of the Society . . . A Champion of the people over the years, the *Daily World* has a heritage of outstanding people and distinguished leaders who have insured their readers that their First Amendment rights won't be violated."

Lerone Bennett, Jr.
Well-known Journalist

The fertile Mississippi Delta has produced a prodigious amount of cotton and blues; it has also produced many of Chicago's blacks, one of the most distinguished being the articulate, prolific, urbane, Lerone Bennett, senior editor of the nation's most prestigious black magazine, Ebony. Bennett, often referred to as "resident historian of the Johnson Publishing Company," was born in Clarksdale, on October 17, 1928, to Lerone Bennett, Sr. and his late wife, the former Alma Reed.[1]

Bennett's writing career commenced as staff writer with his high school newspaper in Jackson. Also, he edited the race weekly, *Mississippi Enterprise*. At Morehouse College, where he was a schoolmate of Dr. Martin Luther King, Jr., the newspaper staff elected him editor of the *Maroon Tiger*. After graduation from Morehouse in 1949, Bennett launched his journalism career when he became a reporter for the *Atlanta Daily World* and was later promoted to city editor.[2]

In 1953 Bennett joined the Johnson Publishing Company as associate editor of *Jet* magazine. One year later, he was named associate editor of *Ebony*, a position he held until 1958 when he was promoted to first senior editor of *Ebony*, a position he presently occupies. In 1968 Northwestern University hired him as visiting professor of history and later chose him as chairman of the Departmnent of African-American Studies in 1972. While still chairman of African-American Studies at Northwestern he was selected as Senior Fellow of the Institute of The Black World, a black publishing and clearing house.[3]

Lerone Bennett's articles in *Ebony* served as a springboard to his becoming a freelance writer for international publications. Many of his essays, poems, short stories, and articles have been translated into French, German, Japanese, Swedish, and Arabic.

Included among his many publications are: *Before the Mayflower*, 1962; *The Negro Mood and Other Essays*; *What Manner of Man* (a biography of Dr. Martin Luther King, Jr.); *Confrontation: Black and White*; *Black Power, U.S.A., the Human Side of Reconstruction 1867-1877*; and *Pioneers of Protest*. Also, he has contributed to *New Negro Poets: U.S.A.*, edited by Langston Hughes; *The Day They Marched*, Doris Saunders, editor; *American Negro Short Stories*; and *The White Problem in America*, editors of *Ebony*.[4]

Before the Mayflower, his first major publication, grew out of a series of articles originally published in *Ebony*. In the preface to the book, Bennett wrote, "*Before the Mayflower* deals with the trials and triumphs of Americans whose roots in the American soil are deeper than those of the Puritans who arrived on the celebrated Mayflower a year after a 'Dutch man of war' deposited twenty Negroes at Jamestown."[5]

As a social historian, biographer, author, poet, and world traveller, Bennett focused attention upon the irony of the black man's participation in the American Revolution as "one of history's greatest paradoxes." Furthermore, he asked his readers to "consider the background of the great event. A colony with a half-million slaves decides to go to war in support of the theory that all men are created equal, are 'endowed by their Creator with certain inalienable rights.'" He cited the heroic deeds of black patriots such as Crispus Attucks who becomes the first martyr and the blacks, some of them slaves, who entered the firing lines and thus "signed the Declaration of Independence with their blood."[6]

To further demonstrate his commitment to the black struggle for equality, Bennett participated in the historic 1963 March on Washington. Later he wrote about the march in an introductory statement of a book edited by Doris E. Saunders. According to Bennett, the march was the beginning of something and the ending of something: "It came 100 years and 240 days after the signing of the Emancipation Proclamation. It came like a force of nature. Like a whirlwind, like a storm, like a flood, it overwhelmed by its massiveness and finality. A quarter-million people were in it, and of it; and millions more watched it on TV and huddled around radios. There had never been anything quite like it."[7]

Similarly, each of his publications is an indictment of racism, inequality, and injustice in America and an advocacy of black protest and its significance. In *The Negro Mood*, for example, Lerone Bennett accurately interpreted, "The Negro rebellion is an outgrowth of migration, urbanization, increasing self-consciousness, and increasing alienation. In order to make an adequate response to that rebellion, we must view it within the context of a long history of developing protest and social contention."[8]

"Lerone Bennett's importance as a writer," noted historian John Henry Clarke, wrote, "is accentuated by his ability to bring new insight to old subjects on the agenda for discussion. His writing is consistently sharp and clear." According to Clarke, Bennett's article, "SNCC: Rebels With a Cause" (*Ebony* magazine, July 1965) exemplifies his analytical ability. He appraises the Student Non-Violent Coordinating Committee as "the most radical, the most controversial and perhaps the most creative of all the civil rights organizations."[9]

In 1975 *Ebony* published an article, "Should Blacks Celebrate the Bicentennial?" which presented three different interpretations. Two respondents were native Mississippians—one of whom was Lerone Bennett, Jr. Bennett adamantly responded "No!"

> No for all those who believed, and did not see.
>
> No for all those who said it and did it, and died broken and betrayed.
>
> No for W. E. B. DuBois whose body lies "a-moulderin," in a Ghana grave because we didn't believe it.
>
> No for Martin King and Malcolm X and Medgar Evers. No for Harriet Tubman. No for Nat Turner. No for James Earl Chaney. No for Morning Cloud and Osceola and Morning Dew.
>
> No for the millions of slaves, and the millions of sharecroppers, who lived through two hundred years of Hell and sleep now in moonless nights in unmarked graves.
>
> No for all the black men who died for the freedom of white folk, for all the black men who died for General Washington and General Jackson and General Pershing and General Eisenhower.
>
> No for the Americans, for the *real* Americans. And yes, No for the whites who believed it and tried to live it.
>
> No for the dead.
>
> And No for the Living.

No for the hungry and humiliated and despised, for all those out of work and out of hope.
For the Living, for the Dead, for the Unborn: No. No. No.[10]

He has lectured extensively in colleges and universities at home and abroad. He holds memberships in the following organizations: Fellow, Black Academy of Arts and Letters; Board of Directors, Race Relations Information Center, Institute of the Black World; Board of Trustees, Martin Luther King Memorial Center; and Kappa Alpha Psi, fraternity.

Among the numerous awards and honors bestowed upon Bennett are: Patron Saints Award, Society of Midland Authors; Book of the Year Award, Capital Press Club; Honorary Doctor of Letters, Morehouse College; and listing in Who's Who in America as well as Who's Who in the Midwest.

He is married to the former Gloria Sylvester, daughter of Mr. and Mrs. Elliott Sylvester, of Mobile, Alabama. They have four children: Joy; twins, Constance and Courtney; and Lerone III.[11]

William Dilday
Television Manager

In 1964, the United Church of Christ filed suit with the Federal Communication Commision against the Jackson NBC affiliate, WLBT-TV, which was managed by the Lamar Broadcasting Company. The suit was initiated after the reporting of a news segment of the 1960 civil rights demonstration in which the anchorman, laughing, broadcasted, "Look at those nigras run."[1]

In a landmark decision, the Federal Communication Commission outlawed exclusion of blacks from jobs, and in 1969, the FCC stripped Lamar of its license; thereby paving the way for the sale of the station, WLBT-TV. Communication Improvement, Inc. (CII), an interracial non-profit group appointed by the FCC, has operated the station since 1971. Fifty-one percent of the stock of the station is owned by blacks. One of the principal owners is Aaron Henry, well-known civil rights activist who is also the chairman of the board. Another board member includes William D. Mounger, part owner of the all-white Jackson Academy. Other members of the board include Alvin Flannes, Charles Young, Judge Reuben Anderson, Dr. Albert Britton, Robert Neal, and Walter G. Hall.[2]

To oversee the management of the station, the board named William Dilday, Boston University business school graduate, as general manager. Subsequently, he became the first black television manager in the country. As a result of Dilday's excellent supervision, the station is becoming the second television station in the "Top 100" market. It also has one of television industry's highest percentages of black employees.[3]

Jessie Mosley
Author, Community Leader

Jessie Mosley (Mrs. C. C. Mosley, Sr.) of Jackson, is well-known as a community leader and author. She holds memberships in the NAACP and the National Council of Negro Women and is a charter member of the local branch of the National Association for the Study of Negro Life and History. Her publication, *The Negro in Mississippi History*, published in 1950, is a well documented and resourceful, though sketchy, account of Negro life from territorial days through the first quarter of this century.[1]

Sarah Harvey Stevens
Journalist

Sarah Harvey Stevens is a graduate of Lanier High School in Jackson and the Henderson Business College, Memphis, Tennessee. In the early 1960s she became the first woman editor of a newspaper in Jackson, the *Mississippi Enterprise*. Meanwhile, she became a contributor of the *Jackson Daily News*. The Jackson Business and Professional Women's Club named her their Woman of the Year and nominated her to *Who's Who Among American Women*.[1]

William Gordon
Foreign Service Correspondent

William Gordon, Senior Foreign Service Officer for the United States Information Agency, headed a group of twenty-five foreign correspondents who toured fourteen different countries in 1974. Their itinerary included six southern states. During their visit to Mississippi, Governor Waller presented Gordon, who was born in Bentonia, the Governor's Outstanding Mississippian Award for outstanding achievement in journalism.[1] Prior to entering the foreign service Gordon was managing editor of the Atlanta *Daily World*, a daily newspaper founded by W. A. Scott II, and maintained by the Scott brothers, natives of Mississippi.

THE PERFORMING AND VISUAL ARTS

The history of black music in Mississippi can be traced to its African origin. The ballad, for example, gives a history of black people or ceremonious occasions. Southern blacks utilized musical instruments similar to those of Africans—the banjo, fiddle, drum, rattles, tambourine, and harmonica. Singing became a daily ritual, expressing depression, oppression, resistance, and survival. Gospel music offered inspiration, hope, and escape from enslavement.

White southerners popularized minstrel shows to project negative images and the inferiority of the black race. White men blackened their faces with burnt cork, used black dialect, and imitated the Sambo plantation slave personality. When freedom came in 1865, true black minstrels tried to eradicate the negative stereotype of blacks. Because they projected an intelligent black who satirized the dual role of whites, these minstrel shows were banned in certain southern states and the performers beaten or incarcerated. Blacks sang songs of victory, when they gained their freeeedom, became citizens, obtained the right to vote, or won a major court battle. Nationalistic songs were sometimes performed at solemn occasions and at festive celebration.

With the advent of World War I, blacks produced impromptu campfire songs that dealt with the war. After the war, black music and other art forms found an exciting new life in the Harlem section of Manhattan. This artistic explosion in the 1920s, known as the Harlem Renaissance, emphasized the "New Negro," a militant who protested racial injustice and demanded immediate equality. During this period many southern blacks moved to northern cities, seeking refuge from lynchings, economic exploitation, suppression of education, and denial of political rights, thereby enhancing the cultural explosion underway. The music of this period included ragtime, jazz, blues, and spirituals. Mississippi's William Grant Still emerged as a classical composer.

The black cultural revolution in the performing arts reached its apex in the civil rights movement of the 1960s. There were songs and music of protest and liberation. Black actors and actresses received featured roles on television and on the stage. This time marked the end of an era of segregation and with it an end of stereotypical projection of blacks, and it symbolized the dawning of a new day for black musical performers.

Until recent years white motion picture industries generally excluded blacks. When blacks were accepted, they were cast in demeaning roles. Realizing that black film production was a lucrative trade, filmmakers began to design films primarily to attract black audiences. To increase ratings on television and on radios, blacks were hired as newscasters, talk show hosts, and guests on many specials. Many talented black Mississippians reaped the benefits of this new discovery.

The creativity of Mississippi's African-American visual artists is rooted in traditional African abstract painting and sculpture. These artists are concerned with expressing philosophical concepts rather than with accurately representing physical characteristics of what they actually see. Most sculptures have sharp, angular, flat shapes. Distortion is another characteristic of this type of art form. The beauty and power of works by black artists lie in their inner or hidden meaning. These tangible forms represent the abstract autonomy of the universe, the spirits and mythological beings which inhabit the environment of the African. The incalculable influence of primitive African art is evident in twentieth century African-American art, such as that of Barthe and La Vern Hamberlin.

Elizabeth Taylor Greenfield

Operatic Performer

Born a slave in Natchez, Mississippi, in 1809, Elizabeth Taylor Greenfield gained critical acclaim for her performance in "The Black Swan." Critics praised her for her "remarkably sweet tones and wide vocal compass."[1] While still an infant, she was taken to Philadelphia, Pennsylvania, where she was adopted by a Quaker, Mrs. Greenfield, who paid for her musical training.

Elizabeth made her first musical debut in 1851 in Buffalo, New York, where she sang before the Buffalo Musical Association, thereby establishing her reputation as an artist. She was in demand as a performer nationally and internationally. In 1854, she performed before Queen Victoria at Buckingham Palace.[2]

After a brief concert career, she retired and opened a voice studio in Philadelphia.

William Grant Still

America's Greatest Black Composer

One summer evening in 1936 a black man stood before the Los Angeles Philharmonic Orchestra and conducted two of his original compositions in the Hollywood Bowl, marking the first time a black American had ever led a major symphony orchestra in the performance of serious music. Again, that same man made history when he became the first to conduct a white radio orchestra in New York City. In 1949 when the New York City Center Opera Company, celebrating its fifth anniversary, presented his opera, *Troubled Island* (1937), it was the first time an opera composed by a black was performed by a major American opera company.[1] The man, the conductor, the composer was William Grant Still, a native of Woodville, Mississippi.

William was born on May 11, 1895, the only child of William Grant and Carrie (Frambo) Still, both of whom were brilliant musicians and talented and versatile school teachers. His ancestry included Scotch-Irish, Spanish, Cherokee, and African. Before moving to Mississippi his parents taught at Alabama A. & M. College, Huntsville, Alabama. Besides mathematics, his father taught music, played a coronet, led a Woodville brass band, and tried composing.[2]

His father, a graduate of Alcorn A. & M. College, died when he was three months old, after which his mother took him to Little Rock, Arkansas, to live with her mother and sister, and where she taught school until her death in 1927. It was not strange when, as soon as the child realized what music was, his thoughts turned to it so unerringly that no scoldings, no arguments nor pleadings could shake his eagerness to become a composer.[3]

Frequently, when he wished to amuse himself, he made toy violins. He varnished and equipped them with strings, and some even succeeded in producing tones! Later, his mother decided he should have violin lessons. No sooner did he learn to read notes than he wanted to write them. He produced his own manuscript paper, jotted down little melodies, and often took his new concern with him to school. While other students were aimlessly scratching, William was scribbling musical notes. He organized schoolmates into little bands to play his melodies.[4]

At home his grandmother often sang hymns and spirituals. "Little David Play on your Harp" was one of her favorites. Such experiences helped him to acquire a knowledge of the songs of his people. He came to love these, which he learned to play with such exquisite harmonies that they assumed unsuspected beauty. A communal pastime of his childhood days was serenading. William enjoyed that activity and regretted the passing of the custom. He often sang in the aisles of trains, the passengers giving him candy and money in return. He began to sing everywhere.

When William was nine or ten years of age, his widowed mother married Charles B. Shepperson, a postal employee and a lover of operatic music who spent much of his salary to purchase a phonograph and the best Red-Seal records on the market. Young Still had opportunities to hear the kind of music that pleased him far more than any he had ever heard before. He played each record over and over again, to the utter neglect of whatever work was to be done. In addition, Shepperson took him to good musical shows and told him stirring stories that fired his romantic imagination. At home they often sang duets and discussed the plays they had seen and the music they had heard.[5]

His mother's personality was so dynamic she could command attention merely by entering a room. Her determination, good sense, talent, and high moral character strongly influenced her son's life.

Her students adored her and learned more from her than from any other teacher; and so did her young son, for he too was in her classes. However, she was stricter with him than with the others, lest she be accused of favoritism. At sixteen, William was graduated from high school as class valedictorian.[6]

At heart, his mother sympathized with his desire to become a composer, but she openly avowed her disapproval, simply because she and her husband felt that there was no future for a colored musician. Insisting that he train for a secure profession, they sent him off to Wilberforce University in Ohio in 1911 to major in science. But music absorbed him. Eventually, he arranged, orchestrated, led, and composed for the school band. A concert was given solely of his compositions. The approbation accorded him meant much at that time. He heard of the Conservatory at Oberlin College and wanted to transfer there, but his mother was unyielding in her desire for him to become a physician.[7]

Every month before his allowance came, the music books he wanted were checked off; as a result music publishers and dealers took practically all his spending money. When he began to buy opera scores, his first acquisition was Weber's *Oberon*, the second Wagner's *Flying Dutchman*. His French class became more interesting when he took to class a music book containing stories of all the famous symphonies and read it during the class period.[8]

In addition to playing the violin, he learned how to play all the reed instruments. Later he played for the college choir and thus learned to transpose easily, because at that time separate parts were not written. In his capacity as bandleader, he had to learn to play different instruments such as piccolo and saxophone so he could teach the other players. This intimate knowledge of orchestral instruments later meant much to him and to his career as an orchestrator.[9]

At Wilberforce some members of the faculty went with him to operas and concerts in Dayton, Ohio. Others encouraged his efforts at composition. It was then that Still decided to emulate the famous Coleridge-Taylor in every way, spending many months in a fruitless attempt to make his hair grow straight upward, as did that of his hero. Failing that, Still decided that someday he would be "greater than Coleridge-Taylor" and wear his hair in his own way.[10]

At home during summer vacations Still worked during the night to hide his efforts at composing from his parents. He entered several national contests for composers. In one contest for a three-act opera, he ambitiously mailed out a score of some twenty pages, and in another the judges wrote telling him that his music had merit but that they were afraid they did not completely understand it.[11]

Back at Wilberforce for his senior year, he felt absolutely unwilling to give up a career in music. He was thoroughly uninterested in his courses and mischievously broke the rules. He stayed in trouble with the authorities and was finally expelled a few months before graduation. However, in 1936, more than thirty years later, Wilberforce awarded him a diploma of honor and the honorary Master of Music degree, "in recognition of his erudition, usefulness, and eminent character." Howard University, Oberlin, and Bates College have also awarded him honorary degrees.[12]

Lean years followed the Wilberforce days, but Still began the long hard struggle to achieve his life's ambition. Lacking a degree, he did odd jobs for little pay. He married. He played oboe and cello with various orchestras, nearly starved, and always wondered how he could crash into the business of making music and getting paid for it.[13]

In 1916 at age twenty-one, he received a small legacy from his father and promptly enrolled at Oberlin College's Conservatory of Music, taking private lessons. Meanwhile, he worked as a waiter and janitor to stretch his meager funds. He made enough to return to school for the regular session. After completing one semester's work in theory and violin, Still had thoroughly impressed his teachers. Professor Lehmann, moved by his talent and sincerity, asked Still why he did not study composition. He replied frankly that he had no money. A few days later, Lehmann informed Still that the theory committee had decided to give him free tuition and to have Dr. George W. Andrews teach him composition. Thus a scholarship was created for him where previously none had existed.[14]

In 1918 Still joined the navy and served in World War I as a messboy. Afterwards, he joined W. C. Handy, "Father of the Blues," working daytime in Handy's music publishing firm in Memphis and playing nights in Handy's band. Hating the sordid night life of Memphis and other southern towns where Handy's band played, Still tasted the dregs his mother had warned him awaited black musicians. However, his prospects improved when he moved to New York City in the early 1920s. There he not only worked in Handy's new music publishing firm but also arranged for and played in jazz and theater orchestras at much greater pay than in Memphis. To this day, Still is grateful to Handy for this early help, as well as for his unwavering generosity and support.[15]

In 1921 Still played oboe in Eubie Blake's orchestra for the successful black musical *Shuffle Along*, featuring Florence Mills. While *Shuffle Along* was playing in Boston, Still, aware that he could now afford to pay for musical lessons, applied at the reputable New England Conservatory of Music. He was informed that George W. Chadwick would teach him free of charge. Still protested that he could afford to pay, but generous Chadwick refused to take his money.[16]

In New York, Still accepted a position as recording director with the Black Swan Phonograph Company. There he discovered a man preparing to respond to a request from Edgar Varese for a talented young Negro composer to whom he could offer a scholarship in musical composition that he knew of no one suitable. Still hastily advised, "I want that scholarship. You can just tear up that letter!" Subsequently, he was introduced to Edgar Varese and modernism. Later, Still declared, "When I was groping blindly in my efforts to compose, it was Varese who pointed out to me the way to individual expression and who gave me the opportunity to hear my music played. I shall never forget his kindness, nor that of George W. Chadwick and the instructors at Oberlin."[17]

Meanwhile, Still played in vaudeville and in the pit for many musical shows. He became band leader at the Plantation Club and wrote arrangements for a coterie of entertainers including Sophie Tucker and Don Vorhees; he also orchestrated several editions of Earl Carrol's *Vanities* and one edition of J. P. McEvoy's *Americana*, *Runnin' Wild*, and *Rain or Shine*. Later he arranged music for Paul Whiteman, who played some of Still's compositions for the first time in public and commissioned several notable works from him. Still was the first to arrange and record (with Don Voorhees) a fantasy on the famous *St. Louis Blues*; that was in 1927 on a Columbia disc.[18]

By 1926 at the age of thirty, Still felt he had achieved maturity. He had played every kind of instrument in every kind of band, in theaters, night clubs, and touring troupes. He had a thorough grounding in harmony and musical theory. He had twelve years of experience in arranging and composing in many forms, ranging from classical symphonies to jazz and "modern." He decided then to write neither as a conceited individualist nor as a slave to the old patterns, but as a modern American, building on the feeling of his own Negro-American background. He retired from professional orchestra playing and occupied himself solely as arranger and orchestrator.[19]

When CBS first started, Still arranged Don Vorhees's music for the network broadcasts. Later he was arranging at NBC when Willard Robinson sang on the Maxwell House Hour. Soon Still was making arrangements for Robinson's "Deep River" program at radio station WOR. Without Still's knowledge, some of the orchestra members quietly suggested to Robinson that Still be allowed to conduct their orchestra. The management agreed. Thus, Still became the first black man to lead a radio orchestra of white men in New York City, a post he held for several months.[20]

Still then began drawing themes from Afro-American folk and jazz idioms. His early works included a symphonic poem, *Darker America* (1924), the lively *From the Black Belt* (1926), and a ballet with a West Indian setting, *La Guiablesse* (1927). Howard Hanson, director of the Eastman School of Music and Rochester Symphony, encouraged Still and performed his works. One of Still's best known works is his symphonic poem, *Africa* (1930), but his *Afro-American Symphony* (1930) is generally regarded as the greatest work. Dedicated to Irving Schwerke and premiered in Rochester, it was soon played by the New York Philharmonic, the Philadelphia Symphony Orchestra under Leopold Stokowski, and the Berlin, Leipzig, and Stuttgart symphonies. One reviewer said, "There is not a cheap or banal passage in the entire composition." Another called it, "honest, sincere music . . . developed without recourse to theatrical invention."[21] An audience in Berlin broke a twenty-year tradition to encore the *scherzo* from this symphony; several years later, a Budapest audience did the same thing.

His *New Symphony in G Minor* (1937), subtitled "Song of a New Race," was premiered by Stokowski, who places Still among the American composers whose work he most likes to conduct. The Rochester Symphony and the Philadelphia Orchestra, under Hanson and Stokowski respectively, are among orchestras that have made recordings of Still's works. Still settled permanently in Los Angeles before World War II. He composed for several Hollywood movies, but gave up his most lucrative contact in 1943 when a director insisted on coverting a film on blacks into the traditional degrading Hollywood "darky" stereotype.[22]

He has won many honors, including two Harmon Awards, for contributions to American culture, Guggenheim Fellowships (1934 and 1935), and Rosenwald Fellowships (1939 and 1940) in composition. Millions attending the World's Fair in New York in 1939 heard Still's musical accompaniment for the continuous six-minute showings of "Democracity" at the Perisphere, performed 120 times a day, without realizing a black composed it. The jury that selected the composer for this World's Fair theme played many recordings without knowing their composers. Of all the works heard, the two they liked best were a suite, *From a Deserted Plantation* (1933), and a ballet, *Lenox Avenue* (1937), both by Still. The latter had been commissioned by CBS Radio in its first American Composers Series. Still's *Plain-Chant for America* (1941) was commissioned for the one hundredth anniversary of the New York Philharmonic. In 1944, in competition against thirty-seven other composers, Still's *Festive Overture* was selected unanimously for the commemoration of the Cincinnati Orchestra's fiftieth anniversary, and was awarded a $1,000 War Bond. His opera, *Troubled Island* (1937), set in Haiti with a libretto by Langston Hughes, was presented by the New York City Center Opera Company in 1949 for its fifth anniversary celebration. This was the first time an opera composed by a black was performed by a major American opera company.[23]

Still's other operas include *Blue Steel* (1935), *A Bayou Legend* (1940), *Costaso* (1949), and *Highway No. 1. U.S.A.* (1963). Among his other ballets are *Sahdji* (1930), with an African setting, and *Miss Sally's Party* (1940). Two of his works frequently performed for chorus and orchestra are *And They Lynched Him on a Tree* (1940), from a poem by the wife of Attorney General Francis Biddle, and *Those Who Wait* (1943). Such concertos as *Kaintuck* (1935) and *Pastorela* (1946) are performed often, as are the short orchestral works *Ebon Chronicle* (1936), *Caribbean Melodies* (1941), *Poem for Orchestra* (1944), and *To You, America* (1952). His third and fourth symphonies were composed in 1945 and 1949. Among his best known songs are "Levee Land," written for Flo Mills; "Winter's Approach," setting a poem of Paul Laurence Dunbar; and "Breath of a Rose."[24]

Many people have begun to regard Still's greatness. He hears the things they say and is grateful for them, but he is never impressed with his own importance. At a meeting of the NAACP, after the speeches had been unusually long, someone noticed that the renowned composer, William Grant Still, was in the audience. Would Still, they asked, consent to speak to them on some matter of moment? He arose in an impressive silence. Then, with all eyes focused on him: "I wonder," said he quietly, "whether everyone is as hungry as I am?" Then he sat down, and the meeting was adjourned. One of his biographers states, "William Grant Still, a genuine American composer, will become world famous. When he does, he will be the last person in the world to know it, or to believe it if the knowledge is thrust upon him!"[25]

His first marriage ended in 1932 when his wife deserted him. He would be the first to say the failure was not all her fault. "It was just that these two people had too little in common, lived in separate worlds, had small appreciation of each other's ideas and ideals. Anyway, when she went sailing off Still cried, 'I've finally begun to live.' "[26]

In 1939 Still married Verna Arvey, a Russian Jewish musician and a well-known music critic, who is also "lady of all work" in the Still household. The seventy-nine year old Dr. William Grant Still and Mrs. Still came to Jackson, Mississippi, in November 1974 to witness the world premiere of his opera *A Bayou Legend*, presented by Opera-South, a black company with white backing and a mixed following.[27]

A kind of musical poet laureate, he has written the music for many national festivals. He is a member of national and international associations of composers, and receives a part of his income from radio royalties as a member of ASCAP (American Society of Composers, Authors and Publishers). Dr. Howard Hanson, famed international conductor and music critic, has named Still "one of the four leading composers living in America today."[28]

Still is somewhat a recluse. He is not a member of any lodges and does not frequent night clubs. He does not even attend church anymore, "though he has a deeply reverent feeling about God and a mystical attitude toward his music as a sacred mission for expressing and interpreting the beauty and rhythm of God's universe."[29] But Still has been described a religious man who writes at the end of every new composition, "With humble thanks to God, the source of inspiration."[30]

Leontyne Price

Diva

Leontyne Price's parents, James Anthony and Katherine Baker Price of Laurel, Mississippi, were childless for thirteen years. James, an erect, dignified, sparrow-thin man, worked as a laborer in local sawmills and as a part-time carpenter. Kate, an iron-willed woman, took to midwifery to increase the family income, working at first for ten dollars per delivery and frequently for a side of bacon or a barrel of peas. On Sundays Kate sang hymns in the choir of St. Paul's Methodist (Episcopal) Church, where they were regular worshippers. One Sunday morning while so engaged, Kate felt the initial pangs announcing the impending birth of their first child, Mary Leontyne Violet Price, who was born on February 10, 1927.[1]

Leontyne and her brother George were reared by "old fashioned, God-fearing parents." Both of their grandfathers were Methodist ministers. Leontyne was later to play the piano and sing in St. Paul's church choir. She and George grew up amidst the conventional parochialisms of northeast Mississippi of the thirties and forties. Leontyne has described her upbringing: "The color bar was as strong in Laurel as anywhere in the South, but the children were not aware of it at that time: We were taught to judge people as individuals, not on the pigmentation of their skin."[2]

One day at the age of two, sitting on her mother's knee, Leontyne listened to a local school teacher singing a ditty called "And the Little Brown Bear Said, 'Bo.'" Her mother recalled, "Each time the lady would sing, Leontyne would bat her eyes and say, 'Bo, a bo.'" When the teacher finished singing she told Mrs. Price, "You have an armful of music there!" The proud mother answered, "Well I have prayed for it, and if she wants music, I guarantee she'll get it."[3]

Leontyne's first memory of music was hearing her mother sing in "a lovely lyric soprano voice" while hanging out clothes in their backyard. Leontyne had a toy piano at three and "ran her mother crazy giving concerts." At three and a half years old, Leontyne took her first piano lessons from Hattie McInnis, Laurel's black music teacher, at two dollars per lesson. Often her mother did not have the fee and would do the teacher's laundry.[4]

Her music teacher, Hattie McInnis remembered: "When one tiny girl was brought to me, I might have wondered if she was four (the youngest I accepted) had she not had such talent. As it was, months later I learned my little prodigy had started at three."[5] A few months after Leontyne began studying piano, her parents traded their Victrola as down payment on a real piano. However, her father was not enthusiastic about the lessons. But when Leontyne performed in a piano recital at age five, he was convinced. The mother proudly boasted, "Her feet couldn't even touch the floor, but she had committed the piece to memory. From then on, her father has seen what I had seen long before then."[6]

For more than twelve years, McInnis and Leontyne were teacher and student. The student joined the Oak Park High School choral group as first soprano. After Leontyne's solo recital at age sixteen, the *Laurel Leader Call* observed: "She is exceptionally gifted, with the ability to produce beautiful music both on the piano and by voice; that rare musician who can reach the hearts of her hearers with her interpretation of the classics, as well as make their feet restless with her unique rendition of modern music."[7] In 1944 Leontyne graduated from Oak Park High where she actively participated as cheerleader, majorette, and soloist.

During high school, "Big Auntie," Everline Greer, a longtime servant and cook for the Chisholms, a white family, gave Leontyne the opportunity to play with Jean and Peggy, the two older Chisholm daughters and to advance her musical career. Leontyne labeled the Chisholms her "other family," and herself their "chocolate sister." In those days Leontyne was "forever" singing and Mrs. Chisholm often accompanied her at the piano and had her perform at informal musicales. Consequently, an affinity developed between Leontyne and the Chisholms, who subsequently helped her. In later years Leontyne commented, "Everyone finds it so amazing that two families should love each other in the middle of Mississippi which is, let's face it, a red-hat (sic) state where my ancestors were not so high on the social scale. Well, that hasn't got a cotton-pickin' thing to do with it. There wasn't anything in the world Mrs. Chisholm wouldn't have done for me. But she was my friend first and my benefactress second—whatever I turned out to be and even if I didn't turn out to be much of anything."[8]

As a teenager, Leontyne was always a popular soloist at the black community's civic and church events. These engagements persuaded her to consider a career as a music teacher. Therefore, she applied to the College of Education and Industrial Arts (now Central State College) in Wilberforce, Ohio. On her application, she wrote, "I'm worried about the future because I want so much to be a success."[9]

Leontyne's introduction to Central State College was arranged by an army chaplain at Camp Shelby who had heard her sing and helped arrange a partial scholarship. So, at age seventeen, with her first piece of luggage and two coats, Leontyne left Laurel for Wilberforce, Ohio, a little apprehensive of her ability to move from center stage at Laurel to the outside world. At Central State she enrolled in a teacher's training course, and she continued singing—in the glee club, the choir, and the dormitory shower. Even as a freshman she had what a friend remembered as "a star quality." Once she was stopped by hazing upperclassmen and ordered to sing. Immediately she began singing "Because," and when she finished everyone just stood by amazed. Her voice so surprised them that they stopped hazing her and the other freshmen.[10] During her senior year, Leontyne considered specialized training at Julliard School of Music in

New York. Such plans were initiated by Charles Wesley, president of Central State, a musical minded historian whose daughter Charlotte became an opera singer. He encouraged Leontyne to become a professional singer and also suggested she apply for a scholarship at Julliard.[11]

But Leontyne knew that even with a scholarship neither her father nor she had enough money for Julliard; therefore, she was tempted to sing in night clubs.[12] Fortunately at a concert at Antioch College Paul Robeson heard her sing, decided that she was "marvelous," and agreed to a singing benefit to finance her musical education. That concert raised $1,000. Meanwhile, her friend Mrs. Chisholm offered to pay Leontyne's living expenses, so she could accept the scholarship.[13] Leontyne insisted, "I love her more for that—for asking—than for any check she gave me." When acknowledging those responsible for her success, not only does she mention that "wonderful Caucasian family," but also "the Omnipotent" for providing talent, and "my parents for having birthed me."[14]

In 1948 with a B.A. degree from Central State, she enrolled at Julliard and studied under former concert singer, Florence Page Kimball, which proved advantageous for Leontyne. Kimball's first impression was that she was a "gawky very simple child—just another student." But after hearing Leontyne sing Mistress Ford's role in the student production of *Falstaff*, Kimball realized that Leontyne was more than "just another student." Professionally, Kimball was her voice teacher; personally, she counseled her on how to dress, how to act, and how to handle the social perplexities of a northern city. After Leontyne left Julliard, Kimball remained her teacher, advisor, and friend.[15] "Lee used to go to Miss Kimball," Leontyne's friend observed, "the way other people would take to a psychiatrist or a priest."[16]

For four years, Leontyne labored at Julliard, appearing in student productions and singing for anybody who cared to listen. Composer Virgil Thompson selected Leontyne to sing the role of St. Cecilia in a revival of his *Four Saints in Three Acts*, which was presented on Broadway for two weeks in April 1952. From that performance she received her first professional check, and later said, "everything started to happen at once for some weird reason or another."[17]

That brief Broadway appearance was so successful that George Gershwin granted her an audition and, after hearing her sing "Summertime," gave her the feminine lead in *Porgy and Bess*. In that opera Leontyne Price sang before a packed house for two years, 1952 and 1953, in American cities and then abroad in Berlin, Paris, and

London under the sponsorship of the state department. Peter Hume of the *Washington Post* wrote, "Leontyne Price sings the most exciting Bess we have heard and will no doubt spend a long time in this role. But when she is available for other music, she will have a dramatic career. Her acting is as fiery as her singing."[18]

Meanwhile, Price was laying the groundwork for a career in grand opera by studying and giving concerts. The producers of *Porgy and Bess* arranged her schedule so that she could accept invitations from such composers as Igor Stravinsky, Henri Sauguet, and Lou Harrison to present their works at the Metropolitan Museum of Modern Art in New York and at Constitution Hall in Washington, D.C. In October 1953 Sam Barber asked her to sing his "Hermit Songs" at the Library of Congress, an event that was a huge success. She then flew to Rome to sing at the International Conference of Contemporary Music, the only American invited.[19]

On November 14, 1954, Price gave a Town Hall recital to an enthusiastic audience and press. One writer, Jay Harrison of the *New York Herald Tribune*, criticized her "consistent tremolo" and unevenness of tone, but he praised her ability to project "a personality that literally spills charm over the footlights."[20]

In February 1955 Leontyne Price became the first black American chosen to sing a title role in a television-produced opera. The announcement of the forthcoming appearance caused controversy and criticism all over the country, but most of it evaporated when her performance of Puccini's *Tosca*, which was viewed by millions, demonstrated her absolute mastery of the role.[21]

Following the *Tosca* success Leontyne sang leading roles in NBC television productions of Mozart's *The Magic Flute* in 1956, Francis Poulenc's *Dialogues of the Carmelites* in 1957, and Mozart's *Don Giovanni* in 1960. Under the sponsorship of the State Department and the American National Theatre and Academy, she went to India in the summer of 1956 to sing in four major cities. On September 20, 1957, she made her grand opera stage debut at the San Francisco Opera in Poulenc's *Dialogues*.[22]

Miss Price once confided to a friend, "Since I first began to train as a singer my special goal and ambition has been to sing at the Metropolitan Opera in New York."[23] But when Leontyne Price entered the venerable Julliard no black had ever sung a solo role at the Met. The first was Marian Anderson, who long past her prime, appeared in 1955 in the minor part of the fortune teller Ulrica in Verdi's *A Masked Ball*. Between Anderson and Price were baritone Robert McFerrin and sopranos Mattiwilda Dobbs and Gloria Davy.[24]

En route to the Metropolitan Leontyne Price, the fifth black to appear at the Metropolitan, did her homework and did it thoroughly. Meanwhile, her band of followers steadily increased all across America and even in Europe. In succeeding seasons she returned to San Francisco to interpret the title role in Verdi's *Aida*, Leonora in Verdi's *Il Trovatore*, and the leading part in Carl Orff's *The Wise Maiden*. With the Lyric Opera of Chicago she sang in Massenet's *Thais*, the part of Liu in Puccini's *Turandot* in 1959, and *Aida* and *Madame Butterfly* in 1960. In 1956 she sang in Handel's opera *Julius Caesar* and the role of Poppea in Monteverdi's *Coronation of Poppea* in 1958, both presented in concert form by the American Opera Society.[25]

Internationally, Leontyne Price was a smashing success. At the request of Conductor Herbert Von Karajan, Miss Price took the role of Aida at the Vienna State Opera. This was followed by a performance at the Verona Arena, a tour of Yugoslavia, and recitals at the Brussels World Fair. She was also soloist in Beethoven's *Missa Solemnis* at the Salzburg Festival, and sang in Covent Garden in London. After vowing never to enter Milan's Theatro alla Scala until she could sing there, in May 1960 Leontyne sang *Aida* without rehearsal. She was awarded "bravas" by her demanding audience, and one Italian critic wrote, "Our great Verdi would have found her the ideal Aida."[26]

Miss Price's unremitting hard work in concert halls, opera houses, recording studios, and practicing and coaching sessions was rewarded by her first offer from the Metropolitan Opera in 1959. Her lifelong ambition was realized! But she turned it down because it was the wrong kind of contract and at the wrong time: "I was doing something else at the time and said to myself, Oh, well, I can't go now, so I guess I'll never make the Met."[27]

On January 27, 1961, Leontyne Price of Laurel, Mississippi, made her debut at the Metropolitan Opera. After she sang *Donna Anna* in Salzburg, she was again invited to sing at the Metropolitan and offered a "decent" contract.[28] This time it was in the difficult role of the Countess Leonora in Verdi's *Il Trovatore*. To Miss Price it was the fruition of her dream—"to star at the Metropolitan Opera, almost universally regarded as the culmination of any operatic ambition."[29] To her friends in Laurel it was the "pinnacle." A score of friends and relatives from Fifth Avenue were in the audience. Her triumph monopolized the front page of the *Laurel Leader-Call*. That night the local Western Union operator struggled under the weight of well-wishing wires. "I know where to reach her," the operator snapped to callers; "just tell me what you want to say."[30] To the critics she had "scored one of the greatest operatic triumphs in recent years."[31] To the audience it was a thrilling experience that moved them to "give her the longest ovation ever witnessed at that house, a full forty-two minutes of unrestrained admiration."[32]

Miss Price had not wanted her first role at the Metropolitan to be that of the Ethiopian princess Aida in the Verdi classic. She insisted on starting in a role where skin pigmentation played no part in the selection of the artist. After her debut, the impresarios were the first to admit the soundness of her judgment. She contracted to sing five roles that first season: Leonara in *Il Trovatore*, Aida, Cio-Cio-San in *Butterfly*, Ionna Anna in *Don Giovanni* and Liu in *Turandot*. *Time* magazine praised her performance: "Her Leonora proved to be a remarkable portrayal of a woman in whom dignity struggled with desperation and in whom grief somehow shone more movingly through a profound sense of repose. The amalgam of qualities made her fourth act aria "D' amor sull'ali rossee" a dramatic as well as a technical triumph. It was perhaps the most widely applauded moment of the present season. Sustaining all of the performances was a voice unfurling like a bright banner from the stage and throughout the opera house."[33]

One music critic commented, "Leontyne's (voice) is known technically as a lyric *spinto*—a high soprano voice with dramatic feeling. No singer today is better capable of straddling both the lyric and the dramatic moods than she is, and none possesses a voice that is more secure throughout its considerable range—the G below middle C to the D above high C—and with it the feather-lightness of a much smaller voice."[34] She can send her soprano flooding through a house the size of the Met without straining and with the marvelously reassuring suggestion that she has power to spare. Her special glory is a legato line of floating, five-span phrases. A most demanding critic passed judgment on her voice when he heard it for the first time: "it gave him goose pimples, said Conductor Herbert von Karajan."[35]

One would not describe Leontyne Price as a beautiful woman; though her clear, brown skin, high cheekbones, and compelling eyes set in charcoal shadows give her a most memorable face. Her height is medium yet commanding; according to one review, "she animates any costume she wears; and she can whip a train or thrust a sleeve with regal authority." But what really distinguished Leontyne Price as an artist was obviously talent and training. To paraphrase Jackie Robinson's oft-quoted phrase, she never felt she had it made. Though amply talented, Leontyne Price continued to train under the guidance of her teacher, Florence Page Kimball. She frequently studied other singers' versions of her role. Like many performers, she did not peak until after thirty.[36]

A close observation of Price's career revealed that her preparation for each performance was a low-key ritual. Before each performance, she drank hot bouillon with steady swigs prior to particularly difficult scenes that might "tensify" her. She never entered the stage without saying a prayer which enabled her to face any difficult or disappointing situation. Therefore her performances reflected an inner strength of strong character. In 1959, when she performed *Thais* in Chicago, the reviews were not good, so Miss Kimball stayed to read them with her, warning that they were disappointing. "What do they say about my voice?" inquired Leontyne. "They say you have a great voice," replied Miss Kimball. "All right then," said Leontyne. "The rest I can learn; and I will." Of the debut she recalls, "I just stood there in the wings and thought; 'Dear Jesus, you got me into this now you get me out.' "[37]

Unspoiled by her amazing success, she always returned home to Laurel, where she'd truly relax and just be Leontyne. Her homecoming performance at Laurel in 1963 was one of her greatest and memorable experiences. More than two thousand persons from at least ten states, but mostly from Mississippi, overflowed the Oak Park School auditorium and cafeteria. That unsegregated audience, one of the first in Mississippi, gave a tremendous response to the program which included a full repertoire to demonstrate the great range of "the girl with the golden voice." There were repeated encores and standing ovations.[38]

As an opera star who has made musical history, she is often honored for her achievements. The Metropolitan paid her a supreme tribute by asking her to open the 1961–1962 season with a performance in the starring role of Puccini's *Girl of the Golden West*. Thus she became the first black ever to open a season at the Met. On January 2, 1966, the NAACP awarded her the Spingarn Medal, "in recognition of her divinely inspired talent, in tribute to her extraordinary achievement as the outstanding soprano of our era, and in appreciation of her priceless contribution as artist, citizen, and person, to the continuing crusade for justice, equality, and understanding among the peoples of the world."[39]

On September 16, 1966 the Metropolitan Opera, after three years of planning and decades of disappointments, opened its new $45.7 million super-house in Lincoln Center. That occasion was also the world premiere of a new opera based on Shakespeare's *Anthony and*

Cleopatra, and the premiere of Leontyne Price singing the lead role. Never in musical history had there been an event with such fanfare and publicity as that opening night. The ticket supply was quickly exhausted, even though seats sold for as high as $250, and thousands were turned away.[40]

"As the giant curtains parted to a first-night audience of luminaries, Miss Price stepped not only onto the stage, but into history. This was the climax of a career that had seen her lauded, applauded and decorated, both at home and abroad. For this woman, who has been called 'the voice of the century,' it was a personal triumph."[41] Incidentally, when the curtain dropped for the last time at the historic old Metropolitan Opera House in April 1966 it was Leontyne Price as prima donna of the company that rang down the curtain at that farewell gala. "Her costume of golden cloth and jewels was designed to evoke the riches and opulence of Cleopatra's court. She was so heavily costumed, said *Time,* that 'it was a wonder she could sing at all, though sing she did, and her burnished voice never sounded better.' "[42]

In 1967 Miss Price returned to perform in Mississippi, this time at Jackson's Coliseum in a benefit for Rust College; and she received a standing ovation from an integrated audience. That crowd interrupted her repeatedly with applause in the middle of song cycles—until she gently asked them to wait until the cycles were over. *The Jackson Daily News* raved, "Lustrous, shining, glowing, majestic, lush, delicate, brilliant, glorious!"[43] After that performance, she traveled to Atlanta and sang to a packed house in the Municipal Auditorium with the Atlanta Symphony. Shouts of "Bravo!" and "More, more!" followed each of her three encores. At the end the orchestra laid down its instruments and joined in cheering "fortissimo."[44]

In 1972 during an interview concerning her future, she stated, "But, let's face it. I'm forty-five and not ashamed of it. I made my Met debut more than a dozen years ago, and I put in a lot of hard years, there and around the world. I feel the time has come to protect what I've got in here—pointing to her throat—and I'm not so greedy as to pile up everything I can get this year or next. I'd rather do what I can do comfortably for some years to come, set a goal each year of what I want to earn, which engagements give me the best balance of the kind of singing I want to do, and keep going that way for however long I can. Poor as I was when I started, I realize now I've gotten to the point where I know I will have a roof over my head, clothes to wear, and food to eat on what I have earned. Isn't that really what life is all about, anyway?"[45]

During the Broadway run of *Porgy and Bess* on August 31, 1952, Leontyne Price married her "Porgy," baritone William Warfield, in Harlem's Abyssinia Baptist Church, with one of the Chisholm daughters attending and with six members of the cast as bridesmaids. She makes her home in a twelve-room house on Vandam Street, a narrow thoroughfare on the southern fringe of New York's Greenwich Village, where she enjoys entertaining her family and friends. Her hobbies are interior decorating, record collecting, and walking her pet poodles. She has also refurnished the Prices' home in Laurel and built a room to accommodate Big Auntie.[46] Leontyne Price has made numerous recordings of her operatic arias, as well as her French and German art songs, and was selected by *Mademoiselle* as one of the ten outstanding women in 1955, for her performance in *Tosca*. Her RCA Victor recording of Bizet's *Carmen* was named "Record of the Year" by newspaper and magazine record review critics representing Italy, Germany, and the United States. She is a member of the American Guild of Musical Artists, Actor's Equity Association, and The American Federation of Television and Radio Artists, as well as Sigma Alpha Iota and Delta Sigma Theta. In April 1965 the Italian government conferred upon her the Order of Merit of the Italian Republic.[47]

"From time to time Leontyne Price has made it clear that she prefers to stress her achievements as an American singer rather than an American Negro singer.... 'It is incidental that I am pigmented. I am a relaxed American. I am living what I have to say and singing what I have to say. I'm not out in front of any groups. I am what I am.'"[48] "'I am not a crusader in anything except my career.' Often when she talks about her race it is in joking fashion. The dusky Aida she refers to as her 'makeupsaver role.' Once a wardrobe mistress forgot and warned her about soiling her light costume with the dark Aida makeup. Leontyne pointed to her skin and said, 'Honey, you'd be surprised; that won't come off.'"[49]

B.B. King
"King of the Blues"

The Mississippi Delta has produced a lion's share of Blues alumni. But perhaps none is more celebrated than B. B. King—"Bossman," "Chairman of the Board," "The Main Man," "King of the Blues."

Riley B. ("I never knew what the B was for") King, the oldest of five children of Mr. and Mrs. Albert King, was born on September 16, 1925, on a cotton plantation between Itta Bena and Indianola, Mississippi. His parents separated when he was about four years old. His mother went to live in the Mississippi hill country and took him with her. She died when Riley was nine, leaving him to care for himself.[1]

For the next five years he remained with the whites for whom his mother had worked, near Kilmichael. Even though living alone afforded freedom, he complained, "The hard thing for a growing boy is when you have no one to talk to. Many things were shut up inside me. I learned to bottle quite a few things inside."[2] His father did not know where he was. However, he says the whites were nice to him. Though they were poor, they fed him, paid him about fifteen dollars per week, and allowed him to attend school. That school was a one-room shack with eighty-six pupils and one teacher. He walked ten miles to and from school, while a school bus picked up Wayne, his boss's son. Riley's duties were to work after school and milk ten cows morning and evening.

"Now believe me, it was one of the happiest parts of my life, because there, then, they were just simple people. Today, I find people are different."[3] Riley's father found him when he was fourteen and took him back to the Delta, near Lexington. There he experienced the long hours and hard work of the plantation—ploughing six months, always working five and a half to six and a half days a week, and never having a vacation. But, Riley recalled, there was a difference. His father had remarried, and the new brother-in-law was a guitar-playing Holiness preacher. There was also a young aunt who, besides being a blues fan, had a collection of early blues records. The young Riley King was fascinated by the guitar, and perhaps less so at the time, by the blues records. He persuaded his plantation boss to buy him an eight dollar Sears and Roebuck guitar and take the cost out of his wages.[4]

As important as this experience proved to be, King's musical career began much earlier. At four or five he sang spirituals with his mother. They formed a duet and sang at church, in the cotton fields, on the way back and forth from home, or anytime they were alone. His mother was a churchgoing Christian. Of the traditional black churches in the community, the three he remembers are Methodist, Baptist, and Church of God in Christ. It was the Church of God in Christ (Holiness/Sanctified) that he liked most, "because they used instruments."[5] The trips to church every Sunday influenced him in a way even the spirituals that were sung every day could not match.

At church Riley became intrigued by the preacher-guitar player; therefore, on pastoral Sundays when the preacher dined with the King family, Riley would slip into the room where the shiny guitar was lying on the bed and pluck a few strings. That was the first electric guitar he had ever seen. When the preacher finally discovered King's unamplified plucking, he began giving Riley guitar lessons. The Church of God in Christ never had a more faithful member of its congregation.[6]

At that time Riley was not attracted to the blues. Generally, blacks consigned the blues to workers of iniquity. They were ashamed of the blues. "Reels," as they were commonly called, were decidedly immoral, "low down." Riley, a cousin, and two other fellows formed a quartet and sang spirituals, calling themselves the Elk Horn Jubilee Singers. The Golden Gate Quartet, whom they heard on the radio, became their idols. The school teacher encouraged them to continue singing, saying that one day they just might be as good as the Golden Gate group.

Of course, King could attend school only during the rainy season, when he was not needed in the cotton fields. In the tenth grade he became a drop-out. The money he made in the fields had become more important to his livelihood than schooling.[7] There was nothing to do but plantation work. King once explained, "We worked from 'kin to can't,' which meant from the first hour of daylight when you can see, til the last hour when you can't see, chopping cotton and working when it was too cold for the mules to get out."[8] The pay was from eight to ten dollars a week. During this time, however, he was continuously pickin' on his guitar.

But blues were in the air, or at least in the jukes and joints where plantation workers gathered for relaxation—drinking, dancing, and gambling. There King met other boys who were playing guitar, and before long he was hitch-hiking the eight miles to Indianola to hear Charles Brown, Louis Jordan, Robert Junior Lockwood, and other significant bluesmen demonstrating both the older rural and newer urban styles.[9]

His aunt strictly forbade the singing of blues around the house, so he made himself content to sing spirituals. But there was a longing deep within him, a yearning for an expression that was more real and more meaningful for Riley King. Besides, he discovered many people liked to hear the blues.

In 1943 when King was inducted into the army, he began to sing the blues. "It was a funny thing," he recalls, that while most fellows tended to get religious and sing spirituals in the army, he sang the blues. When he returned to the Delta, he realized people were making a living by singing the blues. But he remained on the plantation until after the end of the war to avoid reinduction.[10]

Later on he would slip off to nearby towns on weekends, stand on the corners picking and singing blues. Passersby would gather around, listen a while, leave him some change, and move on. Some Saturdays King would visit three or four towns. King began to gather in twenty-five to thirty dollars for just one day—far more than he earned for a whole week's work in the fields.[11]

He had long admired the recordings of Blind Lemon Jefferson, Booker T. Washington White, Lonnie Jackson, Charlie Christian, and T-Bone Walker, whose "Stormy Monday" he calls his greatest inspiration. Of Blind Lemon he says, "I idolized him . . . he was more an original than the rest—he followed no guidelines . . . to me he was true. He was sayin' only what he believed and thought and it wasn't phony. And today, just to charge my batteries, I carry tapes of his records around . . . to play whenever I can."[12]

In 1946 at age twenty-one, Riley B. King laid down his hoe in the Mississippi Delta and headed north. It was not too many miles from the cotton fields of Itta Bena, Mississippi, to Memphis, the blues capital of the world; but for a country boy with mud still clinging to his shoes, it was the longest journey he would ever make. For King, it was going from one world to another; it was swapping his seventy-five-cents-a-day cotton chopping job for the unknown.[13]

With his battered guitar and a hat full of memories—of poverty and pain, of hunger and hurt—King placed his stake on a musical future. "He'd heard that whistle blow." But he knew that as a black blues man he had first to find acceptance among his own people. For three generations they had turned their backs on blues. Whites were the ones who wanted to hear wailing, mournful sounds. But, a hopeful King hitch-hiked to Memphis. He stayed with his cousin, the legendary blues singer-guitarist, Bukka White, who was able to get King a ten-minute spot singing commercials for patent medicine on radio station WDIA and playing one night stands in local night clubs.[14] Nat Williams, popular WDIA manager, said that when he first heard King perform, he realized that before him was the 'spirit of Beale Street personified.'[15]

Some time later Sonny Boy Williamson, who had a radio program in West Memphis, and King reminded him of their meeting in Indianola, Mississippi, when Sonny Boy played plantation halls. Williamson allowed King to sing a number on his program, and from that appearance King landed a five-nights-a-week job at the 10th Street Grill for twelve dollars a night plus room and board.[16]

Later when one of the disc jockeys left WDIA, King took over the slot. On the air he sang his blues songs, representing the spirit of Beale Street, the Memphis street previously made famous by W. C. Handy. Because he specialized in playing the black music of Beale Street, he was first billed as Riley King, the "Beale Street Blues Boy." This was later shortened to "Blues Boy," which finally came to be just "B. B." As his popularity began to grow, his show was expanded, and record companies began to take notice of him.[17]

King got together a trio of instrumentalists, and the four of them had a fifteen-minute live spot on WDIA daily. He also brought in a number of other performers to fill the two-hour show that had previously been made up mainly of recordings. Because the program offered newcomers an opportunity to display their talents, it became very popular.

About 1949 B. B. King began recording his own music on RPM, a minor label. After several releases he came up with a hit, "Three O'Clock Blues," which made the top of rhythm and blues charts in 1950 and remained there for four months, and launched his professional career. Immediately King sallied forth on travels that would lead him eventually into the "Big Time."[18]

> Everybody wants to know why I sing the blues,
> I've been around a long time;
> I've really paid my dues.[19]

By any standard of our time Riley B. B. King has paid his dues. For over twenty years he played the grueling Chitlin' Circuit—some three hundred one-night stands a year, in run-down Negro night spots from Oakland, California, to Charleston, South Carolina; in smoky backrooms in the Mississippi Delta, where the whiskey was raw and was poured out of Mason fruit jars; in bigtime Chicago, where shabby clubs bunched together on the seamy South Side became meeting places for people who spent lifetimes waiting on tables and losing hope. Many times he did not receive the promised fees. In 1956 King and his band played 342 one-nighters. About once a year he played week-long engagements at the larger urban black theaters—the Howard in Washington, the Regal in Chicago, and the Apollo in Harlem.[20]

One evening in the mid-1950s King was playing for a dance in Twist, Arkansas. The dance hall was heated by a large container filled with kerosene, placed in the middle of the floor. Two men got into a fight, upset the container, and set the hall afire. Everyone made it for the exits. King dashed to safety, but suddenly remembered that he had left his thirty-dollar guitar. He rushed back to retrieve it, narrowly escaping death. The next day he learned that two men, who had burned to death, had been fighting about a lady named Lucille. "So I named my guitar, Lucille, to remind me not to do anything silly like that again."[21]

In 1954 B. B. King hit big with "Everyday I Have the Blues," now his theme song. During the next few years, King succeeded in building up a limited but intensely loyal, blues-conscious following. In between live appearances he reached them through his recordings issued on Crown and Kent labels, both of which were owned by the same small company that put out his first RPM recordings. But by the early 1960s King's career was in a slump. The top disc jockeys did not play his recordings, and a large portion of blacks spurned his music, finding it uncomfortably reminiscent of their "down home" roots. The folk revivalists considered him too urban and commercialized.[22]

When the Rolling Stones and other British rock groups hit the American entertainment circuit in the mid-sixties, scholars began researching the origins of rock music. This led them inevitably to the blues, to the most prolific and most profound purveyor of the blues, Riley B. B. King. About that time King heard of Sidney A. Seidenberg, a businessman who had been involved in the careers of several major artists and in 1968 persuaded Seidenberg to become his manager. Immediately King's career began to soar as he penetrated the college and white night club markets. Over the next eighteen months King played at 134 universities and colleges, establishing a reputation with white audiences. In 1969 the Rolling Stones, who had discovered the relationship of rock to blues, invited King to join their American tour; they played eighteen dates before a million people. Prior to 1968 King had not appeared on any television shows. Blues-rock star Mike Bloomfield helped to give King a big personal boost into the limelight, by making his contemporaries aware of B. B. King and his influence on rock music. Since then King has appeared on all the major television talk shows in the country, including the Ed Sullivan, Merv Griffin, Dick Cavett, Johnny Carson, Flip Wilson, and David Frost shows.[23]

The "King" has played all over—England, Canada, Australia, Israel, Africa, New Zealand, and Asia. In a small town named Toronto he played at the Shakespearean Festival. He was the very first blues artist to play Flamingo Club in Las Vegas. The happiest time of his life was when he played the Fillmore West in 1968, after returning from his first European jaunt. Formerly, the Fillmore had been a black nightclub, but when King walked on stage and saw that sea of white faces, "I thought I had made a mistake," he said. Bill Graham walked up, shook his hand and announced, "B, we're awful glad to have you here." After regaining his composure he stood by the bandstand, and Mike Bloomfield introduced him: "Ladies and gentlemen, the greatest blues guitar player in the world—the Chairman of the Board—B. B. King." They all stood up. "I couldn't believe it. My first all-white audience and my first standing ovation in my whole life."[24] Since then there has been no looking back for him. On May 2, 1970, he made his Carnegie Hall debut as the main attraction at an all-blues performance.

In 1971, B. B. King became "Professor King," and not without good reason. In May of that year he delivered his second lecture at a major university, Yale University's Stiles College. A packed room of three hundred students—with an overflow turned away—waited patiently, milling around the room. The richest, brightest, scraggliest, most privileged white kids in the world gave a standing ovation when King entered. Visibly nervous, King apologized for his lack of formal education which, mistakenly, he assumed was a handicap. Adoringly, they hung on his every word and every note he and "Lucille" sang. King had been invited by Yale writer-composer-critic, Carman Moore, an assistant professor in the graduate school of music. According to Moore, King "gave one of the most interesting lectures on the history of blues heard in many years. He got a rising ovation when he came in and a longer, warmer one when he left."[25] However, in July 1973 when Lynn "Cato" Goodwin was interviewing King for *Club Calendar* and asked him about his forthcoming college dates, King replied, "It disturbs me, that I am not invited to more black colleges. As you know I was given an honorary degree at Princeton University. I treasure that, but I feel more at home getting the blues message to black college students."[26]

In 1972 B. B. accepted an invitation to play, sing, and lecture at Marymount College, Los Angeles. He was the guest of Professor Leonard Feather, who one day inquired, "Did you study the blues—

why the blues?" In true slow, studied, southern fashion, B. B. replied: "I think I've had the blues all my life. I was born in poverty and hunger, on a Mississippi plantation ... a super farm hand ... all this built up inside, questioning, does it have to be like this? I wanted to be like Joe Louis, 'till one night one of the guys stopped me from thinking like that! ... The death of my mother when I was nine, and my grandmother, the death of my first childhood sweetheart when I was eleven—all building up within me. Living alone for five years. I got relief from all those things by playing and singing the blues. It was a natural progression. I have only one thing to do—to play and sing the way I feel. At one time I was sort of ashamed of music, of what I was doin' because friends and those around me didn't seem to dig what I was doin' or understand my feelings. For a long time after I became professional I had to play with a great deal more sadness than I had in the beginning ... but then one day I had to say to myself: I didn't go to Harvard, I didn't finish high school. I'm B. B. King, a blues singer, and I have to sing what I believe and feel. ... I wish everybody could like it, but if they don't, it's the same anyway."[27]

Recently B. B. has given many concerts for prison inmates. His first prison concert was arranged by Cook County (Chicago) Jail Warden Winston E. Moore, a black psychologist and an enlightened and dedicated official. Moore observes that of a long list of entertainers approached to do prison concerts, King was the first to agree, simply asking, "When do you want me?"[28] In 1975 he had played in more than thirty prisons. Prison performance has become a reform crusade. He and F. Lee Bailey formed a partnership and in 1970 organized the Foundation for the Advancement of Inmate Rehabilitation and Recreation (FAIRR).[29]

In April 1974 King expounded on the blues to more than seven hundred Harlem schoolchildren who wriggled happily in their seats at the Apollo Theatre. He had asked the management for permission to do a free program because of his concern for black children who were denied exposure to a musical form that was an important part of their heritage.[30]

One writer observed in the mid-seventies that there had been an obvious cultural shift in the blues during the previous ten years. He felt that in the past blues had been usually related to love affairs, heartaches, and pain, often relating to a man and his woman, while the newer blues songs concerned social conditions—for instance, King's, "Why I Sing the Blues."

King responded: "You see, years ago, you could not say or sing

Elizabeth Taylor Greenfield

Lucia Hawkins

William A. Scott

Percy Green

William Grant Still

Moorland-Spingarn Research Center, Howard University

Margaret Walker Alexander

B. B. King

Leontyne Price

Charley Pride

James Earl Jones

Richard Nathaniel Wright

Special Collections, John Davis Williams Library University of Mississippi what you wanted to say, and the blues served as a vehicle to relay a message, and that message in fact was social, and it was about conditions, and very often when I sing about a woman, I—in reality would be singing about a social situation. A situation which was in essence describing my state of being. So I would have to say, yes, it is the same blues.

"Very often being black and being a blues singer too, there is a commitment to relay a message to the people. I happen to recall a song by Blind Lemon, a man whom I have a great deal of respect for and grew very fond of, . . . that went something like, 'White folks in the parlor fighting over ice cream, while black cooks in the kitchen are fighting over collard greens.' So you see, the blues has always had some kind of social inference."[31]

Traditionally King lapses into a homily during his concerts. On one occasion he defined blues as, "Lyrics dipped in melancholy and stirred with heartbreak." Again, "Blues has a language of its own—the deep stabbing hurt that only the lost, lonely, and down-trodden can know." Then with "Lucille" he peals out its language—each note and each word representing a slice of anguish in B. B.'s life. (In addition to the hurts of his youth, there have been two marriages and two divorces. He has eight children and several grandchildren.[32])

When asked how he thought whites related to his music as compared to black audiences, King hurriedly replied: "True enough the blues is our cultural heritage, but when you pinch a man, he says ouch, no matter what color his skin, and the same applies to his ability to feel and appreciate a particular sound, because in either situation the individual's senses are being activated. What I am saying is that much as we [blacks] love and appreciate our heritage, we are all human beings, black and white; therefore, I would imagine that even though whites don't relate directly to our situation, they still feel the expression in the art for itself."[33]

B. B. believes that the blues is very much a universal language, with its subject matter the problems that occur all over the world. One day he asked his audience: Have you ever felt lonely? Have you ever felt hungry? Have you ever wanted something you couldn't get? Have you ever been worried? The answer to each was yes. "Then" he replied, "you have had the blues."[34]

His style is intensely personal. B. B. is an intimate communicator from his heart to his listeners through the chords of "Lucille," which he says actually sings to him. His fingers move along the strings speaking a language all his own, yet universal, to anyone who will allow himself to be immersed in mood. He confides, "I work most of the time with my eyes closed, I don't do it purposely, but in early years I used to get booed a lot and people threw tomatoes and eggs at me. So I learned to close my eyes so I wouldn't see 'em comin'."[35]

Some very impressive superstar guitarists have been influenced by B. B. King, including Jimi Hendrix, Eric Clapton, Jeff Beck, Mike Bloomfield, and Elvin Bishop. Indeed King himself is a superstar who spent more than twenty years en route. With such credentials one would expect a massive ego, a pretentious personality, or even artistic posturing. To the contrary B. B. King is prompt, sincere, hardworking, and totally professional. One author states, "His identity is unrehearsed and honest, and the impression lingers that his music comes from the same source. Everything about his presence seems personalized, from his songs to his melody lines. Even his guitar has a name. . . ."[36]

Certainly B. B. has made the blues respectable. He does not make lousy records or appear in work shirts and coveralls. Nor does he chase experience capriciously, or drop-kick his guitar from the dressing room to the stage. His entire career has been a personal triumph. It exemplifies the achievement of respectable status by the blues: "I don't mind being called a blues singer," he once told an interviewer, "just as long as the tone of voice is right."[37] *Music Week* put it this way: "B. B. King wants to legitimize the blues."[38]

B. B. remembers another day. He remembers the unpleasant things people used to say about blues singers: "They spoke of them as if they were all illiterate and dirty. A few whites gave the blah-blah about blues singers, but mostly it was Negro people, and that was why it hurt."[39] King confesses that really, he believed, they were trying to lift the standards of his race and did not wish to be associated with something that was "low down." But, he says, "I'm me. . . . Blues is what I do best. If Frank Sinatra can be tops in his field, Nat Cole in his, Bach and Beethoven in theirs, why can't I be great and known for it, in blues?"[40]

From this writer's vantage point, B. B. King has achieved greatness as a bluesman. Indeed, as one writer succinctly stated, "Superlatives cannot do justice to the magnificence of B. B. King's playing. His range—from traditional mournful, crying, angry blues to the more jazzy Django Reinhardt brass sound—is vast and his style impeccable."[41] The incredible fact is that this man, born amidst the most unpretentious circumstances, literally taught himself to play the guitar.

His 1970 honors included two Grammys from the National

Academy of Recording Arts and Sciences (NARAS) for the best vocal performance in "The Thrill is Gone." He also won *Guitar Player* magazine's poll as top blues artist, and top album, "Completely Well," in *Jazz and Pop* magazine's eighth annual International Critic's poll. In 1971 King was named a founding member by the board of the John F. Kennedy Performing Arts Center and won top honors as best blues performer in polls conducted by *Downbeat*, *Guitar Player*, and *Billboard* magazines.

Again in 1972 he won polls by *Guitar Player* and *Downbeat*. B. B. King was also given the Humanitarian Award by the director of the Federal Bureau of Prisons. In 1973 he was given a similar award by B'nai B'rith Music and Performance Lodge of New York City.[42] That same year B. B. King became Dr. B. B. King, L. H. D., when George A. Owens, President of Tougaloo College, presented him with an honorary Doctorate of Humane Letters. The citation reads:

> From Indianola and Itta Bena, Mississippi, with an $8.00 guitar and from the Beale Street of W. C. Handy of Memphis, you have become the "Main Man" of the blues idiom. Your life represents a high standard of what hard work, intelligence, and perseverance can do. You and your guitar, Lucille, have caused to be recognized the respectability of a language of humanity that all people understand and love. The blues idiom is no longer "low down" music. As we listen to your great single "The Thrill Is Gone," the blues is as the title of your 1970 LP album, "Completely Well." You honor us with your acceptance of this honorary Doctorate of Humane Letters.[43]

In it all, Dr. B. B. King has remained a gentle man. For several years he has come to Mississippi to cohost with Charles Evers the "Mississippi Homecoming," in honor of the slain civil rights worker, Medgar Evers. He is never too busy or too big to serve wherever or whenever he can.

B. B.'s constant female—a polished gilded Gibson, with golden frets, that responds to his powerful fingers with the most exquisite anguished notes this side of death-row—rests in her black leather case in the corner of the dressing room, always within loving view of the only man who can tame her. Printed on the outside of the case in white block letters is "My name is Lucille. Please handle me with care."

Ellas "Bo Diddley" McDaniel
Rock 'n' Roll Pioneer

"Bo Diddley" was born Ellas McDaniel, December 30, 1928, in Magnolia, Mississippi, to a mother only sixteen years of age. His father, he never knew. While he was an infant his mother moved to McComb. Unable to support a family, she gave permission to a cousin, Gussie McDaniel, to raise her son. In 1933 McDaniel and young Ellas moved to Chicago.

Ellas "Bo Diddley" McDaniel's musical inclination commenced during his youth. At age seven he began violin lessons. When he was thirteen his half-sister gave him his first guitar, to the horror and disappointment of his adopted mother, who wanted him to become a concert violinist. "I played the violin 'til I was fifteen," Daniels recalls; then, "I'll tell you what put the brakes on me. I looked around and didn't see too many black violinists. That's when I grabbed the guitar, 'cause I seen plenty of black guitarists."[1]

At age fifteen, Daniels dropped out of school and earned nickels and dimes by strumming his guitar on street corners with a cousin who played the washboard. Throughout his teens, he played with friends at parties, contests, and clubs, but he acquired most of his money working construction, driving trucks, and unloading boxcars. He temporarily pursued boxing as a light-heavyweight. He trained regularly in neighborhood gymnasiums before retiring at nineteen because, "I was getting whupped."[2]

Physically, at age fifty-seven, Bo Diddley appears to be in his youthful thirties. He is a huge, hulking man, with large shoulders, thick, tree-trunk arms, and hands like those of the construction worker—coarse, cracked and strong. His grey-tinged hair, wet and matted, is combed straight back. The brown tortoise-shell glasses with their tinted lenses can't hide his eyes. They are young eyes, and when he talks, they shine with childlike intensity.[3]

The rise and decline of Bo Diddley came quickly. During the mid-fifties, when rhythm and blues united with country music to create a new art form called rock 'n' roll, Bo Diddley delighted the musical world's most influential performers. He was an original, one of the first artists to explore the potential of a purely electric sound on his tremoloed guitar. His tunes were powerfully charged, rhythmic and raw, yet simple in structure. In the melting pot of rock music, however, many music critics ignored the contributions made by Daniels.

One critic who did not ignore him says "Bo Diddley's influence is so pervasive and prevalent, it is often taken for granted. Today, his records are found in the cutout bins of record shops and none of his albums are in the catalogs."[4]

Bo Diddley's music consists of "combinations of jazz, blues and gospel," reflecting the compositions of people such as John Lee Hooker and Muddy Waters. The religious tunes and rhythms of the black church—the tamborines, the gospel choruses, and ascending and descending chords—greatly influenced the musical genius of Bo Diddley.

Hoping that a record would increase his popularity, and at the very least provide higher paying night-club work, Bo, along with a friend, made a demonstration recording of two original tunes. At that time he had a wife and two young children. In 1951, the 708 Club in Chicago hired Bo Diddley and provided him with his first night club performance. Playing with various groups, he held day jobs that allowed him to perform in low-paying night clubs. He was going nowhere fast, making about thirty dollars a week.[5]

In 1955, Bo Diddley's luck changed. He played one of his tunes, "Uncle John," for Phil and Leonard Chess of Chess Records. They liked it, signed Bo to a contract, but suggested he change the title of the song. He renamed the tune after himself—Bo Diddley. The record was recut with Bo doing the vocals and guitar, Jerome Green on maracas, and an assortment of studio musicians. "Bo Diddley," his first record released in 1955, along with the flip side, "I'm a Man," established him as a major rock talent.[4]

Both songs were simple autobiographical tunes that emphasized strong, direct, infectious rhythm, with Jerome Green's maracas helping to bring out the beat. The record "Bo Diddley" was roughly a self-portrait sung in the form of an old folk tune. "Bo Diddley bought his baby a diamond ring/If that diamond ring don't shine/I'm gonna take it to a private eye/If that private eye can't see/He ain't gonna get the ring from me." The song became Bo's personal signature and symbolized the lifeline of his music. The other tune, "I'm a Man," was more than a proclamation of gender. The song conveyed to white America that Bo Diddley was a man. And if there were any doubt he spelled it out, "M-A-N, MAN." His list of innovative compositions increased. In 1955 there were "I'm Sorry" and "Crackin' Up," "Say Man" in 1959, "Road Runner" in 1960, and his last big hit, "You Can't Judge a Book by the Cover," in 1962.

Bo Diddley's singing and musical composition established him as one of rock's greats, and his stage show was equally dynamic. His favorite musical instrument was an oblong, square-shaped guitar. A true showman, he electrified his audience when he flaunted his guitar, playing it behind his back or picking it with his teeth.

His lyrics and rhythms had a resounding effect on English music. The Rolling Stones recorded Diddley's "Mona" on their first album and used Bo's beat on other tunes, notably "Not Fade Away" and "Empty Heart." The Yardbirds owed one of their biggest hits to Bo Diddley when they recorded "I'm a Man." Eric Burden and The Animals revised "The Story of Bo Diddley." And one English group, The Pretty Things, took their name from Diddley's tune, "Pretty Thing."

In the early 1960s Bo retained his recording contracts with Chess Recording Company. Since his most productive days were behind him, he guarded his finances more closely. That led to monetary conflicts with the Chess brothers. He earned about $250 per concert. Even when his albums were a booming success, he received the same amount. With rising costs, a band to pay, and traveling expenses, Bo experienced financial difficulties. "When I found out what was happening, I was shocked," says Diddley.

> I had an album called *Bo Diddley is a Gunslinger*, that went gold (sold over a million) in 1962. I have yet to receive a dime for it. I think I've made about thirty-two or thirty-four records. I don't remember, but I would have starved to death if I had to rely on the money I made from records. Most of my income today is from live shows. The amount of money I've earned from all the records combined wouldn't have supported me for one year. I'm not much in demand now, but I can still make good money performing. People still recognize me. I stayed a little bit. People say, "Oh, yeah, I remember that dude, I listened to him years ago."[6]

To please the crowds that stop by his place, Bo walks over to his van, takes a guitar he has owned since 1958, and treats the visitors to an impromptu concert. He sits in the doorway of the van, wraps time-worn hands around the guitar's neck, and plays bits from "Bo Diddley." As he plays, he smiles, lost in the joy of his music.

His wife comes outside, seeing the crowd, and the photographer says, "Bo, you didn't get dressed for them. Look at you, in a t-shirt, boots, and jeans. Look at how you look." Bo stops. "Oh, yeah, here I am sitting in my $15,000 van, playing my $3,200 guitar, all on my $100,000 ranch. I don't think too many people could say anything about that." Bo Diddley fingers his guitar once again and sings the tunes that gave him the van, the guitar, and the ranch, a medley of rich echoes from the glory days of his past.[7]

Bo Diddley and Kay, his third wife—a white woman—have been married for nineteen years. They live near Hawthorne, Florida, on their seventy-two acre farm along the shore of a lake. Three trailers dot the landscape. Bo and Kay live in one, Kay's two daughters in another, and Bo's daughters in the third. Pointing to his daughter's home, Bo says, "This trailer was left on the property. The man that I bought the property from, he just threw it in. Said it would cost too much to move it. I'm going to turn it into a studio as soon as I get my house built." So lives the man who almost single-handedly invented rock 'n' roll—Bo Diddley.

"I got a surprise for the music world," he chuckled: "You tell 'em Bo is back."

Charley Pride

Pioneer Black Country Music Superstar

One of the Mississippi Arts Festival's biggest attractions was Charley Pride, the handsome, sleepy-eyed, six-foot superstar, who thrills his fans at home and abroad with rich, soulful sounds of country and western music. Numerous journalists and commentators compare him with Jimmie Rodgers and Hank Williams, but country music fans and the industry claim that "Charley Pride, the first of his race recognized as a major talent in the world of country music, has no comparison." In 1975 he had ten gold albums, as public testimony to his popularity.[1]

Charl Frank Pride was born on March 18, 1943, in the Delta town of Sledge. There on a farm, his sharecropper parents had eleven children—eight boys and three girls. Although his mother died in 1956, his father, a retired school bus driver and barber, still lives in Quitman County.[2]

Charley Pride recalled that at age six his happiest moments were spent listening to the Grand Ole Opry country music broadcast. Subsequently, his admiration for country and western music soared and eventually made him nationally and internationally famous and financially secure.

Some members of his family did not understand his devotion to country music and regarded him as strange. Traditionally, country music was linked with white musicians and audiences. Blues was the medium for blacks. A few family members and friends *liked* hillbilly, but Charley *loved* it. A neighbor nicknamed him "mockingbird" because each morning he sang when he performed his daily chores, went to school or played baseball.

At fourteen, his love for that music was so great he saved money from his meager earnings in the cotton fields and purchased a guitar from Sears and Roebuck. "It was a Silvertone—a cheap one—not a Stradivarius type," Pride recalled. "It got rained on and cracked all to pieces. I cried about that. But then I taped it up and played it anyway."[3]

Pride taught himself how to play the guitar. He did not know how to read music; therefore he tuned his guitar by the radio. "I sat by the radio and tuned it straight across E Chord, and barred every change I made," Pride reminisced. "I played guitar like that until I started to record."[4]

In 1954 at the age of seventeen, with a music career lurking in his subconscious mind, Charley Pride tucked his guitar under his arm and worked through a maze of odd-jobs, while persistently seeking a break into professional baseball. In the meantime, he lackadaisically entered a talent contest at Lowe's Grand Theatre in Memphis. Chosen as a semifinalist, he was to appear in the finals the following evening. Instead he left the next day for a baseball training camp.[5]

For several years, Pride's career was a mixture of music and baseball. He stated that "Many a time I've walked from Sledge to Birdie—seven miles—and pitched nine innings and walked back home. I just love the sound of the crack of the bat."[6]

He made an impressive record in the sports world, playing ball in the Negro American League, with Detroit and the Memphis Red Sox. "We were playing on percentage," he said, "and lots of times our games were rained out. I was hungry many a day." However, he interrupted his baseball career for a two-year military stint, during which time he married Rozene Cochran of Oxford. They now have three children, two boys and a girl—Kraig, Dion, and Angela.[7]

In 1958 he returned to baseball, playing once again in the Negro American League for the Birmingham Black Barons. But breaking into the majors proved very difficult for Charley Pride. Consequently, he returned to Memphis in 1959 and spent his time unloading lumber and playing baseball with the Red Sox. After being dropped from that team in 1959, he wrote to the Missoula Timberjacks and was invited to make the move to Montana. They, too, let him go after he had pitched a few innings in Pocatello, Idaho.

Refusing to be discouraged, Charley sent his newspaper clippings to the Los Angeles Angels in February 1961. "I looked real bad," he said of his two-week performance at their training camp. Then someone suggested he go to San Bernardino, California, to work out. When he arrived there, he declared, someone told him to go to Arizona, so he took a plane back to Montana. There he took a job at a zinc smelter with Anaconda Mining Company for twenty dollars a day and played semi-professional baseball with the Pioneer League in Helena, Montana. Occasionally, the team traveled to other cities. One night at a ball park in East Helena, "just for kicks," Charley sang over the park's public address system a novelty song, Lonzo and Oscar's "There's a Hole in the Bottom of the Sea." The next day a local newspaper praised his outstanding performance, both on the field and off. His landlady talked the manager of a local establishment featuring country music into giving Charley an audition. He was a hit at the club and became much more aware of his fondness for the music.[8]

Continuing to hold down his job at the zinc smelter, Charley began working two nights a week at clubs in Helena. Once, he appeared on the same show with Red Foley and Red Savine. They advised him to try Nashville. But he continued to carry in his breast a compelling desire to make one last attempt to become a famous baseball player. From his modest earnings, he bought six W 166 Brooks Robinson bats with his name engraved on each. He sent his bats and several telegrams, to the New York Mets training camp at St. Petersburg.

Then, he went to the hotel in Petersburg where the Mets were staying, introduced himself to Manager Casey Stengel, and told him he wanted to join the club. Afterwards, Pride overheard the director of the minor league operations say to Stengel, "He saved his money and came all this way. At least we can take a look at him." To which Stengel replied, "Well if you want to look at him, take him out to a pasture somewhere. We're not running any tryout camps here."[9] That ended Pride's baseball career.

A broken-hearted Charley Pride decided to return to Montana, but en route he stopped in Nashville, where he met two men who changed his lifestyle: Jack D. Johnson and Jack Clement. Impressed with a wax disc that Pride had made, Johnson auditioned him and then took Charley to see Jack Clement, a well-known Nashville songwriter and record producer. Clement instantly recognized Charley's sincerity and talent, therefore he set up a recording session for Pride. However, Johnson and Clement wanted Pride to dress comically and be billed as George Washington Jones, III. He refused.

However, the result of his first recording session proved to Chet Atkins, vice-president of RCA in Nashville, that Charley Pride possessed extraordinary country music talent. After a brief wait, Atkins made the monumental decision that led to Charley's recording contract with RCA Records. Jack D. Johnson became and remains Charley's very capable manager, and Jack Clement still produces Charley's records.[10]

In 1965 his first single, "The Snakes Crawl at Night," did moderately well, but when "Just Between You and Me" was released, Charley Pride was on his way to fame and fortune. From that point onward, he had hit after hit, including "Does My Ring Hurt Your Fingers," "I Know One," "Kaw-Linga," "I Can't Believe That You've Stopped Loving Me," "Let The Chips Fall," "I'm So Afraid of Losing You Again," "Is Anybody Goin' to San Antone," "I Wonder Could I Live There Any More," "I'd Rather Love You," "Let Me Live," "Crystal Chandelier," "Kiss An Angel," and "Oh Lonesome Me."

His recording of "Just Between You and Me" won him a Grammy nomination in 1966 for the best Country and Western Male Vocal performance. Since then he has recorded thirteen top-selling albums. By 1975 Pride had twenty-two record albums, twelve of which (plus one single) were Gold. He won three Grammys exactly ten years after first meeting Savine and Foley.[11]

Pride dreams of writing hit songs and operating successful enterprises. He has written some songs and coauthored "Santa and the Kids" and "Happy Christmas Day," which met with moderate success. "In songwriting, you have to say as much as possible with the least amount of words and that isn't always easy," Pride asserted. "I would like to write songs about people, music from the soul, the joys and happiness of life. I wouldn't want to be a writer of message songs and go too far out of the entertainment arena."[12] Businesswise, the popular singer invested in five corporations, bought land in his home county where his old school once stood, and wants to buy the farm where he lived as a child.

The fact that he has sung from the stages of practically every well-known city in Europe and America has not turned his mind away from his origins. "I always ask my audiences for a round of applause for my hometown, Sledge, Mississippi. I love my home state." Presently he makes his home in the prestigious Highland Park area of Dallas, Texas.[13]

Charley maintains that the only difference between him and other country and western music singers is "pigmentation." Of course, Pride prefers to have his color forgotten but admits there are not enough black country singers for that to occur. He recalls several anti-black incidents in Nashville. For example, when Jack Johnson played Pride's tape at various recording companies, the management remarked, "a pretty good voice." Then Johnson showed them Pride's picture, and they shouted, "Man you must be out of your mind."[14]

On one specific occasion in 1965 Johnson and Chet Atkins set up an independent recording session with RCA representatives. They liked the tape. But when Atkins stated, "First of all, before we sign him, I want you to know he's a Negro," they had to have time to think about it before reaching a decision. "I was something new and they checked me out like they were the Central Intelligence Agency," said Pride.[15]

RCA released the record without hope. They wanted the people to decide. When articles appeared about Pride in magazines, the company was surprised. "They associated a white voice with a white skin." The "skin hang-ups," as Charley calls them, caused him some problems at first, but no more. "I have African, Caucasian, and Indian ancestry. I'm a genetic man, Charley Pride, American. I operate all around those little hang-ups I have to face, because while others are thinking whether they're pink or green, I have to think of something constructive to keep moving. I'm just an old cotton picker trying to hustle."[16]

His racial problems were never with the fans, but with the promoters and club-owners. "I had the number three record in the nation and couldn't get bookings. One promoter would wait for another to book me to see how I'd go over. Once I drove all the way from Chicago to Montana for a two-night stand at fifty dollars a night just to play a club where all the big stars played."[17]

Ever since Charley Pride first stepped before the microphones at the Grand Ole Opry in January 1967, he has commanded a permanent place in that sphere of music. As a stage performer he is one of the hottest tickets in country music, drawing sell-out houses on completely booked-up tours and in the top country music rooms in this nation and abroad. His first major personal performance was in Detroit where he drew 10,000 fans, mostly the "brothers and sisters."

With more than twenty albums in his catalogue and a steady stream of chart-topping country singles including the million-selling "Kiss An Angel Good Mornin'" Charley Pride is one of the industry's biggest-selling country artists. His popularity has overflowed into the mainstream of popular music. He has sold more records for RCA than any singer since Elvis Presley.[18]

As an insight into Pride's talents, one need only ponder some of his achievements. He was chosen Artist of the Year and Best Male Country Vocalist of the Year by the Country Music Association (CMA); Entertainer of the Year by the Music Operators of America (MOA); Top Country Artist on albums, Top Male Vocalist on singles, and Top Male Vocalist in *Cashbox's* Country Music award list. In addition, he has Grammies for Best Sacred Performance for his RCA album "Did You Think to Pray," for Best Gospel Performance for his single, "Let Me Live," and for Best Country Performance, Male, for his album "Songs of Love By Charley Pride."

In his first appearance with the Grand Ole Opry in January 1967, Charley Pride assumed a permanent place in the field of country music, and became the first black performer to be recognized as a major country talent. He remains one of the very few black country artists to achieve stardom.

According to Charley Pride, country music is the basis of all American music. People have become more exposed to it and to what they previously thought it might have been and sounded like. They used to call it hillbilly, but it is now Country-Western. He thinks audience objectivity is what matters: "It's a matter of relating and listening to it objectively. This is what's happening. I just love to sing and make people happy. It's a beautiful thing."[19]

Arthur Crudup

Blues Musician

Arthur "Big Boy" Crudup, the Forest, Mississippi, native, epitomized blues music. He was the "premier blues man of his time," according to Charles W. Tisdale. Without him seventy percent of the popular music today would have a different rhythm, and without his contribution many of the legendary rock idols such as Elvis Presley would have remained in oblivion. According to Tisdale "it was the singing, lyrical, derisive, impudent, high riding style of "Big Boy" Crudup, which catapulted Presley to fame with "That's Alright" and "You Ain't Nothing But a Hound Dog." Both songs were written by Crudup.[1]

Although dubbed "the father of rock and roll music," musical historians generally term Crudup a "country blues" artist. However, Crudup's basic style was always less strident than "country blues"—softer, more subdued, an almost lyrical style, and should thus be more closely identified with the more sophisticated urban, midwestern, or "Kansas City" blues style. Furthermore, Crudup affected certain personal innovations in style affected by no other blues artist, with the possible exception of Lightning Hopkins.

Frederick O'Neal

Actor

Frederick O'Neal was elected the first black president of the professional union, Actors' Equity Association, a "fitting tribute for his long years of service to the American Theater as both actor and teacher."[1] Presently, O'Neal is president of the Associated Actors and Artists of America, AFL-CIO and vice-president of the A. Philip Randolph Institute.

O'Neal was born August 27, 1908, in Brookville, Mississippi. Following his father's death in 1919, he migrated with his family to St. Louis, where he completed high school and afterwards appeared in several dramatic productions for the local Urban League.

In 1927, O'Neal founded the St. Louis Aldridge Players, a community theater. During the subsequent nine years, he performed in thirty of its productions. Then in 1936, he moved to New York City and four years later with Abram Hill founded the American Negro Theater. Today its alumni include such renowned artists as Sidney Poitier, Earle Hyman, Harry Bellafonte, Ruby Dee, Ossie Davis, Hilda Simms, and others.[2]

O'Neal has starred in several stage productions and television drama and comedy. He was featured in "Take a Giant Step," and "The Winner;" and he was cast in the starring role of "Anna Lucasta." During the 1944–45 season, he won the Derwent Award and the Drama Critics Award for best supporting performance by an actor on Broadway. Among his most noted film performances were "Pinky" and "The Man With the Golden Arm."³

During his dedicated acting career, O'Neal "initiated and helped organize" the British Negro Theater in London in 1948. As an actor, director, university lecturer on the theater, films, radio, and television, O'Neal wrote and published many articles that dealt with the African-American's role and impact upon American theaters.⁴

James Earl Jones

Actor

James Earl Jones was born in Arkabutla, Tate County, Mississippi, on January 17, 1931. His father was Robert Earl Jones, the actor, who deserted his pregnant wife to follow first a prize fighting career and afterwards a career on the stage. His mother, Ruth Williams Jones, eventually divorced her son's father and remarried, taking her six-year-old son to live with her parents, John and Maggie Connolly, on a farm near Manistee, Michigan. James Jones's grandparents adopted him, and he saw his mother only occasionally.¹

For some reason soon after he arrived in Michigan he began to stammer. His speech problem became so acute that his only means of communicating with his teacher and schoolmates was by writing. In spite of this handicap, he finished elementary school and enrolled at the Norman Dickson High School. There he forced himself to join the debating teams and to enter oratorical contests. When he graduated in 1949, he had overcome his speech impediment.²

James Earl Jones entered the University of Michigan on a scholarship in 1949. In search of some identity he joined the drama group. He first chose premedicine as a major, but he later changed to drama, graduating in 1953 with a B.A. degree.

In college he joined the Army ROTC, and after graduation he was sent to Ranger Training Camp at Fort Benning, Georgia, to fulfill his military obligation. He recalled: "I was in with a bunch of [white] southern boys. It was a test of manhood and to them a black man could not be a man. They washed me out."³ His next assignment, with the Cold Weather Training Command in Colorado, proved so successful that he almost decided to make the army his career. After his release from the army in 1955 First Lieutenant James Earl Jones went to New York City, where he lived and became acquainted with his father for the first time.

Utilizing benefits from the G.I. Bill, Jones studied acting in New York at the American Theatre Wing, from which he was graduated in 1957.[4] He also studied under the tutelage of Lee Strasberg and Tad Danielewski, who helped him obtain his first small role in an off-Broadway production, *Wedding in Japan*. Although many of his early roles were inconsequential (walk-ons) and the pay was meager ($125 per week), seldom did James Earl Jones need an acting job. As one critic explained, "Jones was called to read for *The Blacks*, and bulled his way to success."[5] To supplement his income, he scraped and polished floors or worked in night clubs.[6]

Among his early roles were *Sunrise at Campobello*, *The Cool World*, both Broadway productions of 1959, and *The Pretender* (1960), an off-Broadway production in which he played a starring role. From 1955 to 1959, Jones performed in summer stock at the Manistee, Michigan Summer Theatre. In 1960 he joined Joseph Papp's New York Shakespeare Festival, where he made a landmark portrayal of *Othello* in 1965. The next fall the production moved to the off-Broadway Martinique Theatre, where it ran for nearly a year. Jones's performance as *Othello* won him the Drama Desk-Vernon Rice Award for best actor of the year in an off-Broadway production.[7]

Jones's physique made him idealy suited for the role as *Othello*. One observer described Jones as having butterscotch skin and eyes the color of jade. He stands six feet and one-half inches tall and weighs 200 pounds. Metaphorically, he has the locomotive look of Sonny Liston in his best days.[8]

James Earl Jones has achieved success as an actor on stage and screen. He performed several brilliant portrayals of Shakespearean characters on television, and he made several movies with considerable box-office success. He has been a frequent performer in various stage roles and is an off-Broadway favorite. But probably his greatest performance was his portrayal of Jack Jefferson (Johnson) in the Broadway smash hit, *The Great White Hope*. Jones said of that role: "No other play has drawn as much out of me; no other play has demanded so much. It's like a birthing."[9] For that tremendous outpouring of creative energy, Jones won the 1969 Tony Award as Broadway's Best Actor of the year.[10]

Commenting on *The Great White Hope* James said: "For many people it represents a sort of milestone, in that, after a long search, American theater has returned to its own roots."[11] Quoting John O.

Killens, Jones declared that blacks will never feel their identity until they elevate their folk heroes to a status above the current quiet legends and that Jack Johnson was one of the first to be canonized successfully by the theater.[12]

However, "Jones feels that the turning point in his life, both as an actor and as a person, came in 1961 when he was cast as Deodatus Village in Jean Genêt's *The Blacks*."[12] In that dramatic role Jones was forced to face all the hatred, disaffections, and distrusts that exist between whites and blacks. "Through that role," Jones recalled, "I came to realize that the black man in America is the tragic hero, the Oedipus, the Hamlet, the Macbeth . . . even the working-class Willie Loman, the Uncle Tom and Uncle Vanya of contemporary American life."[13]

One of James Earl Jones's most outstanding and well known performances was his portrayal of Alex Haley in the widely acclaimed television movie, *Roots*, adapted from Haley's best-selling novel. Jones also starred in a television detective series, *Paris*, a show that received critical praise, but was not a success in the ratings.[14]

James Earl Jones was not involved in the "money game." He believed money had only two functions—to buy land and real estate and to purchase novels to film. For several years before his marriage to Julienne Marie who played Desdemona to his Othello, he lived in a $13.80-a-month cold water flat in New York's Lower East Side, and it is reported that he often appears for interviews in faded blue denims and workmen's shoes.[15]

"He is immensely well read, full of curiosity, and highly self-disciplined, a wholly engrossing conversationalist . . . and a good listener." Among his heroes are Malcolm X and Mohammed Ali; even though Jones was not active in the movement of the sixties, he has repeatedly said that if he had not become an actor he would have been a revolutionary. Instead, he has found an opportunity to make his statements about race through the parts he has played. He once told a *New York World-Telegram and Sun* reporter: "A lot of actors would prefer to ignore their Negro-ness, as if it were a limp that you hope people won't notice onstage. I don't want the audience to forget I'm a Negro. Acting is a visual art, and you want everything to count. . . . I ask an esthetic response to my color."[16]

Richmond Barthé

Sculptor

Richmond Barthé, born in Bay St. Louis, Mississippi, in 1901, was educated at the Chicago Art Institute from 1924 to 1928. His first love was painting, but it was through his experiments with sculpture that he initially gained critical acclaim in 1927. Barthé's honors continued to accumulate for the next forty years. Shortly thereafter he became renowned as the best known black sculptor living in the United States.[1]

Barthé's first commissions were busts of Henry O. Tanner, black artist, and Toussaint L'Ouverture, black liberator of Haiti people from French colonialism. The resultant acclaim led to a one-man show in Chicago and a Rosenwald Fellowship for study in New York City.[2]

In 1946 Barthé received the first commission given to a black for a bust slated for inclusion in New York University's Hall of Fame. A year later, he was one of a committee of 15 artists chosen to help modernize the sculpture prevalent in the Catholic churches within the United States. His work has been exhibited at several major American museums, including the Metropolitan in New York City. In 1971 Barthé was the only black sculptor to hold membership in the National Academy of Arts and Letters.[3]

Sam Gilliam

Painter

Sam Gilliam, a Mississippi-born painter, has produced hanging canvasses which are laced with pure color pigments rather than shades or tones. He combined these pigments in weird configurations on drooping, drapelike canvasses giving the effect, as described by Time magazine, of "clothes drying on a line" . . . his canvasses are designed "like nobody elses, black or white."[1]

Gilliam, a native of Tupelo, was awarded his M.A. degree from the University of Louisville and in 1966 was the recipient of a National Endowment of Humanities and Arts grant. Subsequently, he has had one-man exhibits at the Washington Gallery of Modern Art, Jefferson

Place Gallery, and Adams-Morgan Gallery in Washington, D.C. His artistic collections have been exhibited at the First World Festival of Negro Arts in Dakar, Senegal (1966), in "The Negro in American Art" at University of California at Los Angeles (1967), and in the reputable Whitney Museum's American Art Annual (1969). He is an art professor at the Maryland Institute of Art in Baltimore.[2]

Lavern Hamberlin

Painter, Woodcarver, Sculptor

Lavern Hamberlin, a thirty-four-year-old native of Fayette and mathematics teacher in the Jefferson County School system, is a popular self-taught artist. Hamberlin creates from cypress logs lifesize woodcarvings that are derivatives of African and African-American culture and heritage. With raw wood and his special tools, he chisels away at the woodlogs to create such sculpture as the six foot "Gospel Singer," purchased by a Woodville, Mississippi, attorney who observed Hamberlin's art work at a Jefferson Military College crafts show. Another impressive piece of art is his tall sculpture of an African woman carrying a basket on her head. Hamberlin has completed approximately six lifesize sculptures and dozens of smaller masks and woodcarvings.[1]

Obtaining his wood from various local sawmills, Hamberlin prefers to work with cypress because it is plentiful, climatic durable and easy to work with in creating objects. Most of his artistic creations can be viewed from his front yard which is his exhibition site. His carport serves as his studio and a chisel and mallet are his tools. Before carving each piece, Hamberlin shapes the model from clay and then precedes to design his lifesize sculptures.[2]

Hamberlin, a graduate of Jefferson County Public School System and Alcorn State University, was motivated by his university's art teacher whom he observed working with simple tools and wood. From that point onward, he knew that he wanted to be an artist; living in an economically depressed area such as Fayette, however, he had to prepare for another profession such as teaching. However, he ordered his own tools and instruction manual. Since that time, Hamberlin has been painting, sculpting and woodcarving in his spare time as a hobby. He has also displayed part of his artistic works at universities, schools, and civic art exhibits. His greatest pleasure is fulfillled when his wife, Mary and his two children express appreciation for his work.[3]

Joseph Overstreet
Painter

Joseph Overstreet, painter, was born in 1934 in Conehatte, Mississippi. He studied at the California School of Arts and Crafts and participated in "New Black Artist," an exhibit at the Brooklyn Museum in 1969. Recently, his canvasses have avoided racial themes to concentrate instead on vivid color and original configuration. Thus, many of his abstractions are based on a medley of African and Indian colors. However, Overstreet's memorable and artistic pieces are those that depict some aspect of racial subject matter. Of note are "Jazz in 4/4 Time" and "Keep on Keeping On," both oil on canvas.[1]

Beah Richards
Author and Actress

Vicksburg native, Beah Richards, author and Broadway actress, has compiled a long and impressive acting career. Beah starred in the Broadway production of *A Raisin in the Sun*. She also gave impressive performances in such film successes as *Miracle Worker, Purlie, Hurry Sundown, In the Heat of the Night, Guess Who's Coming to Dinner,* and *Mahogany.* Her TV productions include: "Room 222," "The Bill Cosby Show," "Ironside," "Hawaii Five-O," and "A Dream for Christmas." In addition, Beah Richards found time to author a book of poetry, *Black Woman Speaks,* and a play, *One is a Crowd.*[1]

William Fischer
Composer

Born in 1935 in the Mississippi Delta, William Fischer—a performer, composer-arranger, and musical director—was educated at Xavier

University (Louisiana), Colorado College, and the Academy of Music in Vienna, Austria. He was the recipient of numerous awards, such as a German State grant, Deutsches Atcademischer Austauschdienst, Rockefeller Foundation grant, and a Fullbright fellowship. His compositions include several works for solo piano, solo viola, solo saxophone, and chamber groups; five for symphony orchestra; two concertos for jazz quintet and symphony orchestra; three operas, several songs, a few with lyrics by black poets, and four electronic pieces. His electronic works are *Batucada Fantastica*, *Gift of Lesbos*, and *Time I*.[1]

Frederick Douglass Hall
Music Educator

An organist and music educator, Frederick Douglass Hall wrote compositions for voice and piano, chorus, and chorus with orchestra. Hall, a graduate of Morehouse College, received additional musical-training at Chicago Musical College, Columbia University, and Royal College of Music in London. He earned his Ph.D. in music education from Columbia Teacher's College in 1952. His musical career and teaching experiences include serving as director of music at Jackson State College, Clark College in Georgia, Alabama A & M College, and Dillard University. He is a member of the American Guild of Organists and continues a successful and distinguished music career.[1]

Raeschelle Potter
Opera Singer

Raeschelle Potter, who first sang in New Bethel Baptist Church in Biloxi, signed a two-year contract with the reputable Graz Opera Company in 1974 and left for Austria to start rehearsals for *Don Giovanni*. The Gulfport native, a graduate assistant at Southern Illinois University, sang leading roles in the university's operas and won grants from WGN-Chicago and the American Opera Guild. Afterwards she performed a number of supporting roles at the Metropolitan. She now chooses to perform in Europe until she is assured of leading roles in American opera.[1]

Lucia Hawkins
Opera Starlet

Lucia Hawkins, an off-Broadway soprano artist toured the circuit with the "Porgy and Bess" Trio; in collaboration with Avon Long, the original Sportin' Life, and Levern Hutcherson as Porgy, she sang in a presentation entitled "Highlights of Opera and Broadway." The trio received excellent reviews in national and international theatrical circles.

As a soloist, the Vicksburg native has appeared as a guest performer at Radio Center Music Hall, the Saskatoon Symphony in Canada, and on the Johnny Carson Tonight Show, and the Symphony of the Air. During the John F. Kennedy and Lyndon Johnson administrations, she sang at the White House.[1]

Albert King
Performer

Albert King, native of Indianola, grew up on a dirt farm in Arkansas after the separation of his parents. "When I was young," he unabashedly says, "We couldn't afford a Christmas tree. We were real, real poor." That may well be the reason why the 255-pound, six-foot-four hushed-voiced King, declared war in 1976 on the then rising disco mania and was doing his best to put the blues back into the main stream of American music.

Like other black musicians, Albert King produces emotional lyrics of rejected love and mental and economic depression. He carries a V-shaped guitar named "Lucy." After more than thirty years his albums ascended the musical charts, and now he usually performs before packed or overcrowded night club audiences. The sixty two year old Albert King electrified enthusiastic audiences who hooted and hollered after each song of sadness, sorrow, and suffering.

When Albert King performed, Sunday January 28, 1973, at Jackson's white First Baptist Church, several blacks, including the wife of white civil rights attorney Frank Parker, were denied admittance to regular Sunday morning worship.[1]

Little Milton
Blues Singer

"Little Milton," as he is professionally known, was born Milton Campbell in Inverness, where he, like most of his contemporaries, spent his childhood plowing, picking, and chopping cotton. Like most black singers he began singing in church. At fifteen he got his first job in a night club singing for $1.50 a night. Later he made "big money" at $3.00 a night. After recording his first songs "Somebody Told Me" and "Alone 'N Blue," he moved from one record label to another. In 1973 his Stax recordings were among America's best sellers.[1]

Levion Dillon
Pianist

Blind pianist, Levion Dillon, a Tylertown native, was attracted to the piano by a fellow classmate at the Piney Woods School. From Piney Woods, Dillon launched his professional career with his first performance at the Club Riviera in St. Louis, Missouri, with Dinah Washington in 1949.

Dillon played in every major city from New York to Los Angeles. He performed with such notables as Count Basie, Duke Ellington, Nat King Cole, and others. Currently, he enjoys a semi-retirement in Vicksburg, where he is featured regularly at the piano and organ in a popular restaurant.[1]

Ike Turner
Soul Singer

One of the most popular husband and wife teams in "hard rock and hot buttered soul" of the nineteen-sixties was Ike and Tina Turner. Ike, the son of a minister, was born in Clarksdale, where he played the piano "in a church lady's house." The lady allowed him to play in return for cutting wood. After selecting and playing a few notes of "Blues in the Night" and other tunes that were popular at the time, he begged his mother to buy him a piano. When school closed that year, he took home a better than average report card. Soon thereafter a new piano appeared in his house. A few years later, Ike and Tina performed at the small clubs of the "chitlin' circuit" throughout the South. Until their divorce, they were featured at the top-drawer places, where they received $15,000 or more for an evening's work. Presently Ike Turner performs with his band as a soloist on the nightclub circuit.[1]

Bukka White
Bluesman

In 1977 Booker T. Washington "Bukka" White, one of the last of the W. C. Handy-era bluesmen, died at the age of 89. The Houston, Mississippi, native known for his gravely voice and trainlike rhythms on his steel-bodied guitar, musically trained a number of blues musicians who graduated to the top. One contemporary star, Bob Dylan, recorded one of his tunes.[1]

Bobby Bryant
Trumpeter

Bobby Bryant, Hattiesburg trumpet specialist returned to his native city on May 11, 1971, and packed the University of Southern Mississippi Auditorium in a concert of contemporary music, featuring jazz mixed with blues, rock, and soul. He was assisted by the University Jazz Lab Band and the Greenbacks.

    Bryant had organized his own dance band by the time he entered high school. In 1957 he earned a bachelor of music degree with a major in trumpet. The top studio trumpet player in the Hollywood area and top trumpeter for the NBC Orchestra on the West Coast, Bryant also played a four-week engagement at the Los Angeles Playboy Club. His career includes teaching in Chicago and performing engagements across the continent from Broadway to the Monterey Jazz Festival.[1]

RELIGION

The cornerstone of Mississippi black communities has historically been and still is the black church. Political, social, cultural, and economic affairs emanated from this religious structure. The church provided the necessary training for preachers who espoused biblical truths, moral welfare, political action, civil rights, and economic nationalism. Orators and politicians received lessons in oral and written communication, acquired skills in forensic arts, and learned to appeal to the emotions—fear, hate, and love. Actors, musicians, and songsters were taught drama, prose, acting, musical compositions, lyrics, and rhythms. Through the church adults and children learned to read and write as well as to interpret the Bible. Religious auxiliaries and benevolent societies utilized the church for cultural and fund-raising activities, such as fairs, bazaars, dinners, and picnics, in order to build schools, lodges, and other charitable structures and to aid the poor, the elderly, and the unemployed. Lastly, it was the home of the saint, hypocrite, and sinner. The church has been the house of worship and repentance, the community center, the school, the political forum, the stage, and the business establishment.

From slavery to freedom, the church was the refuge from oppression and racism. Because of slaves' preoccupation with death, the church described the "invisible institution," heaven, as a place for the sufferer. The Christian religion also taught obedience and passivism as well as techniques necessary to isolate the slave from his master. In the north, black churches were centers for abolitionist activities and stations for the underground railroad.

With the advent of the Civil War and Reconstruction that followed, emancipation was paralleled with the coming of the Lord and religious segregation. During slavery times, the slave worshipped with his master; but after the Civil War, the free blacks separated from whites and established their own religious institution. With separation came a tremendous growth within the Baptist, Methodist, and Pentecostal churches. As a result, there emerged a black leadership that consisted of females as well as males who spread the gospel through an intelligent ministry that morally uplifted the black race. Some became politicians, entrepreneurs, and educators. A representative few of these leaders are mentioned within this section.

The Baptist movement spread rapidly among black Mississippians throughout the state. Thus, Baptist became the largest denomination. Emotionalism oozed from the campfire meetings and revivals as blacks, seeking salvation, became annoited with baptism and filled with the Holy Spirit.

When the Pentecostal movement, characterized by intense religious fervor, began in Mississippi, many Methodists and Baptists converted to this new religion, which swept through the black communities. In 1895, Charles H. Mason and Charles P. Jones met in Jackson, Mississippi, to establish a Holiness Pentecostal church similar to the one in Los Angeles, California.[2] In 1897, Mason and Jones journeyed to Lexington, Mississippi, where they converted an old cotton gin into the Church of God in Christ. Soon thereafter, with the aid of Dr. Arenia Mallory, they established a holiness school at the site, Saints Institute, that is still operating as a private high school.[3]

One of the early converts and founders was Jesse Eaton, who pastors a Church of God in Christ in Columbia, Mississippi. Dave Pitchford, another convert who received his Doctor of Divinty in January 1963 from Trinity Hall College and Seminary in Springfield, Illinois, has served as District Superintendent in northern Mississippi for approximately nineteen years.[4]

Black Mississippians have extended themselves into the ranks of the ecclesiastical leadership of our nation. The United Methodist Church elected five black natives to the bishopric. Lorenzo H. King, Alexander P. Shaw, Prince A. Taylor, Charles Golden, and Scott Allen. A few others rose to prominence as religious assistant or as a church official. Such was the case of George H. Jackson.

At St. Mark's Episcopal Church in Raymond on May 13, 1874, George H. Jackson, a former slave, "was the first Negro ordained as a deacon by the Episcopal Church in Mississippi and possibly the first in the South. At his side stood his friend and former master, Colonel Thomas Dabney."

Few blacks in Mississippi, except those living along the Gulf Coast, are Catholic. Others are sparsely scattered across the state. The first black bishop ordained in the state of Mississippi was Joseph Lawson Howze, a former parish priest in Asheville, North Carolina.

Religion

On January 28, 1973, at age 49, he was ordained bishop and became auxiliary-bishop to Catholic Bishop Joseph B. Brunini, Natchez-Jackson Diocese. Howze was the third black priest to be named a bishop in the history of the Catholic church. The historic ceremony brought together the largest group of bishops, priests, religious laity, and representatives of other faiths, ever to be gathered for a Catholic ceremony in Mississippi."[5]

Alexander Preston Shaw
Bishop

On April 18, 1879, in Abbeville, Lafayette County, in a log cabin that was the Methodist parsonage, a son was born to the Reverend Duncan Preston and Marie Petty Shaw. He was named Alexander Preston.

Young Preston received his early training in the public schools of Lafayette County. Later, he enrolled for his preparatory and college training at Rust College in Holly Springs, where in 1902 he received his bachelor's degree. In 1906 Shaw received his bachelor of divinity degree from Gammon Theological Seminary in Atlanta, Georgia, and he did graduate studies at Boston University.[1]

Shaw answered the call to the Christian ministry in 1908. On March 27, the elders affiliated with the Washington, D.C., Conference of the Methodist Church admitted Shaw to the ministry on a trial basis. In 1910, he was ordained as an elder and presided as parish minister in Winchester, Virginia; Harrisburg, Pennsylvania; and Westminister, Maryland.[2]

As a parish minister Shaw made his most exemplary contributions as a preacher. He enjoyed the opportunities it afforded, and he made a reputation as a powerful pulpiteer.

In 1915, Shaw transferred to Wesley Church, Little Rock, Arkansas, where he served for two years, before transferring to the predominantly white Southern California Conference, in 1917. Only two blacks were members of that conference, and it was one of the largest in the nation. The Board of Elders of the Southern California Conference selected Shaw as pastor of Los Angeles Wesley Methodist Church where he remained for fourteen years. Because of his outstanding work and pleasing personality, he attracted special attention from his white peers. By popular vote that conference elected Shaw as delegate to the General Conference in 1928. Prior to that time only one black man was so honored—W. H. Brooks, in 1920, by the New York Conference.

Since Shaw personified achievement and excellence, when Lorenzo H. King resigned his post as editor of the *Southwestern Christian Advocate* in 1931, Alexander P. Shaw was unanimously elected his successor. Shaw began to use his pen as he had used his voice to spread the message of evangelical Christianity. "His editorials soon became the first thing read in the *Southwestern Christian Advocate*. He remained in that position until his elevation to the episcopacy.

On May 14, 1936, Alexander Preston Shaw was chosen general superintendent of the Methodist Episcopal Church, the first Mississippi circuit rider to be so honored. He was elected on the fifth ballot with 462 votes. He was assigned to the New Orleans Area and supervised it for four years. In 1940 the Methodist Church created the Central Jurisdiction and Bishop Shaw was selected to serve the Baltimore region, where he remained until his retirement.

At his retirement dinner in 1952, Bishop Shaw was hailed as an outstanding evangelist who delivered electrifying sermons, such as the one delivered at the Central Jurisdiction Conference in 1944. He admonished the conference for its racist policy when he exhorted:

> We accept the setting apart of a Central Jurisdiction only as an administrative arrangement for the Negro membership in the Methodist Church. We are not all in harmony with any Methodists or others who think such a plan is necessary in a truly Christian brotherhood. We consider it expedient only on account of the Christian childhood of some American Methodist who need a little coddling until they can grow into full grown manhood and womanhood in Christ Jesus.
>
> We are hopeful that in the near future our Methodism may become sufficiently Christian in character and maturity to find a more excellent way.

On March 7, 1966, he closed his earthly biography. Bishop Shaw's funeral was held at the Holman Methodist Church in Los Angeles, on March 12, 1966. The eulogy was delivered by Bishop Willis J. King. Bishop Shaw had spent fifty-eight years in the Methodist ministry, having risen from humble surroundings to the highest office in Protestant Christianity.

Sherman Lawrence Greene, Sr.

Sublime Churchman

Natural forces destroyed the original site in Warren County, where on June 15, 1886, Delia Greene presented her husband Henry with their seventh child, Sherman Lawrence. Sherman grew to be a man of six feet, one inch in height, weighing 230 pounds. His father, a former slave and pioneer rural preacher, and his mother, a faithful and devout churchwoman, reared their seven sons and one daughter in a Christian environment.[1]

When Sherman reached age eleven he revealed his ambition to enter the ministry of the African Methodist Episcopal Church. After finishing the Warren County Schools, he enrolled at Alcorn A. & M. College. That same year he was licensed to preach at Bourbon, Mississippi. Afterwards, he studied theology at Shorter College in Little Rock, Arkansas. He was admitted to the South Arkansas Annual Conference at Wilmar, in November 1906, and was ordained a deacon in 1908. Desirous of more education, the Reverend Greene went to Wilberforce University in Ohio and studied at Payne Theological Seminary. In 1910 he was ordained an elder at Urbana, Ohio.[2]

Reverend Greene returned to Arkansas and began a fruitful pastorate. He was presiding elder of the Monroe District, the Greenville District, and the Little Rock District. After eighteen years as a traveling elder, Greene was elected and consecrated the fifty-first bishop of the A.M.E. Church at the general conference in Chicago, Illinois, in 1928. Bishop Greene presided over the Eighteenth Episcopal District, which consisted of countries in South America and the West Indies. Subsequent assignments included Arkansas, Mississippi, and Louisiana. Beginning in 1946, Bishop Greene supervised the religious activities of Philadelphia and Delaware's annual conferences; the Ninth Episcopal District (Georgia); the Twelfth District (Arkansas and Oklahoma); the Eleventh District (Florida); and the Second District (District of Columbia, Maryland, North Carolina and Virginia).

The law of the denomination stipulates that the presiding bishop shall become the chancellor of the educational institutions of the area. It was in this capacity that Bishop Greene made some singular contributions. He served as president of Lampton College, Alexandria, Louisiana; Shorter College, North Little Rock; and Campbell College, Jackson, Mississippi. He succeeded in renovating existing buildings or constructing new ones on every campus of the schools under his jurisdiction. One notable example is the former S. L. Greene Administration Building at Jackson's Campbell College, which is presently the New Education Building of Jackson State University.

Dr. G. H. J. Thibodeaux, President of Campbell College, recalled the return of Bishop Greene to Mississippi as presiding prelate of the area in 1932:

> We cannot forget those dark days: Campbell College's doors closed; and how we were dispossessed and evicted ... And when the sable curtains of despair covered us as the dew of heaven covers Dixie, we mourned and bade farewell to this precious heritage. Then came the mighty Giant, big in body, large in heart, and great in spirit, to lead this defeated, dejected, and despaired group into a New Era ... Campbell College at the beginning of this era, existed only in name—without funds, without buildings, without collaterals, without credit, without teachers, and without students. Our Bishop Greene sounded the death knell to defeat. And buoyed our sinking spirits until we caught a perspective of the future.[3]

In many instances when turmoil and strife surfaced, the African Methodist Episcopal Church relied upon the wisdom and legal talent of Bishop Greene. For example in Cleveland, Ohio, in 1932, a group of protestors tried to disrupt the proceedings of the General Conference. The police urged admittance of a small committee of the protesters, with the understanding the mass would then quietly disperse. Some of the leaders wanted to yield to the will of the mob, but Bishop Greene allied the forces of the delegates behind him, and with the following statement rescued the situation: "We have come to this city by invitation and the promise of protection ... under Almighty God and with His help, if you (authorities) cannot protect us, we will protect ourselves." With that the mob left.[4]

In another instance, the academic status of Morris Brown College was challenged. As usual Bishop Greene weathered the storm, saved the academic status of the school in the Atlanta university system, and led in a financial campaign that increased the school's endowment. Also, Bishop Greene advocated divorcing the episcopacy from the administration of the internal affairs of the church's colleges, thus paving the way for a higher respect from the regional accrediting agencies.[5]

As a youth, Sherman L. Greene represented the A.M.E. Church at the World Conference of Methodism in London. That experience inspired him to become involved in ecumenical affairs. In 1957 Bishop Greene became the first nonwhite elevated to the office of vice-president-at-large at the World Conference. In forty-five years of ecumenical involvement Bishop S. L. Greene made sixteen voyages abroad, including that to the much heralded World Conference on Faith and Order, at Edinburgh, Scotland. He played a prominent role at the World Council of Churches in 1954 at Evanston, Illinois. He was one of the leaders in the organization of that body and served on its executive board until his voluntary resignation.[6]

Bishop Greene helped organize the National Fraternal Council of Churches, a predominantly black group, serving as president and later as chairman of the board. His recommendation at the Annual Meeting in Washington, D.C., 1922, set in motion the steps that led to the March-on-Washington movement in 1941 and inspired the Civil Rights Act of 1964.[7]

Bishop Greene worked tirelessly with Negro Methodists in an attempt to bring them together. One of his last pronouncements to the General Conference of the (United) Methodist Church, as a fraternal delegate, was that the white Methodists must clear the atmosphere and create the climate necessary for a merger of all Methodist bodies.[8]

Bishop Greene continually sought to make the church a viable force in civil, social and fraternal affairs. Early in life he identified with the Republican party and in 1940 was a delegate to the national convention. As a pastor in New Orleans he was a member of the board of directors of the Keystone Life Insurance Company and of the New Orleans Urban League. Upon his return as bishop he served as president of the Gulfside Interdenominational Ministers Conference and the Mississippi State-Church Cooperative Council, and on the executive committee of the Mississippi Inter-racial Council.

Bishop Greene held membership in the Free and Accepted Masonic Order (Prince Hall), the Knights of Pythias, the Odd Fellows, Elks, and Kappa Alpha Psi Fraternity. Other memberships included the American Academy of Political and Social Sciences and the NAACP.

Bishop Greene was a forceful preacher, an astute administrator, a dynamic leader, and a builder of men. One of his many talents was the ability to find and inspire young men to enter the ministry. And once he found them he guided and encouraged them. Many of A.M.E. Church leaders were Bishop Greene's proteges.

Despite his attainments Bishop Greene never lost the common touch. He loved people. He never forgot those who helped him. Former neighbors near Yokena, Mississippi, delight in telling how even after he became a bishop he would stop by and visit with them. The Reverend Neal Cowans, a ninety-five year old resident, states that Bishop Greene came to Yokena soon after his election to the bishopric, went inside the little old church there and knelt in prayer.

His tenure as bishop spanned thirty-nine years, the second longest in the history of the denomination. He served as president and secretary of the Council of Bishops. In 1952 the general conference reorganized the financial structure of the A.M.E. Church, establishing the general board and Bishop Greene was elected chairman. According to a Methodist publication, "Bishop Greene's creed was Truth; his service-domain Man; his sphere of influence, the Globe. Like John Wesley, the world was his parish, and like Richard Allen, he lifted as he climbed."[9]

At the General Conference of 1964 Bishop Greene was given a special assignment to write the policy of the A.M.E. Church. That was his terminal appointment. The gallant soldier of Christ and leader of men died on Tuesday, July 25, 1967, at the Hugh Spalding Pavilion, Atlanta, Georgia.

His first wife, Pinkie B. Greene, whom he married in 1905, died in September 1961. To that union were born two children, a son, Dr. Sherman L. Greene, Jr., and a daughter, Lillian G. Powe. On May 28, 1962, he married Callie Colston Logan.

Lucy C. Jefferson

Business, Club, and Religious Leader

Lucy Crump Jefferson, a stalwart of the black community, was born in Jackson on November 3, 1866. During her youth, Lucy's parents moved to Vicksburg, where she completed her primary and secondary education. She achieved honor for her leadership skill and academic excellence.[1]

The Crumps were devout Christians who greatly influenced Lucy's commitment to religious endeavors. As a child, Lucy joined Bethel A.M.E. Church, where she held several distinguished positions and actively participated as a member of the Missionary Society, trustee board, secretary to the board of stewardesses, and president of the Women's Christian Union of Vicksburg. As president, she led that group in purchasing property on which they built an old folks' home and orphanages. Throughout her life, she dedicated herself to religious concerns. Because of her faithfulness, the missionary society was named in her honor. Lucy Jefferson has been described as "a great church and society worker" who has "those qualities which make up true womanhood."[2]

In spite of her dedication to religious matters, Lucy Jefferson stringently engaged in and supported the Women's Club movement. While a prominent member of the Colored Women's Federated Club of Mississippi, she assumed the responsibility as chairman of the committee on site and prices. Her duties involved raising funds and locating a suitable site for a state headquarters.[3]

Later, Lucy Jefferson sought means to improve the quality of life for black Mississippians; therefore, she readily accepted the position as grand treasurer of the National Knights and Ladies of Honor, a benevolent organization that stressed black education and economic nationalism. Within the black community, she symbolized progress and prosperity and "was pointed to with pride as one of the leaders of her race."[4] Consequently in 1966, the Vicksburg Board of Education named one of its junior high schools in her honor.

While active in religious, cultural, and social activities, Lucy Jefferson did not neglect her personal life. On June 20, 1889, Lucy Crump married William Henry Jefferson, Jr., whose father was a semi-wealthy Virginia freedman. When Jefferson's father died, he inherited his valuable property. On December 1, 1894, the Jeffersons used the inheritance to establish the W. H. Jefferson Funeral Home, which according to one historian was "the first (business) in the state for, and by Negroes."[5] At the death of her husband, Lucy Jefferson became owner and manager of the funeral home, positions she held until her death on April 24, 1953.

H. Hartford Brookins

Bishop, Civil Rights Activists, Humanitarian

As a small child, H. Hartford Brookins was up at five o'clock every morning working in the cotton fields, milking cows, and feeding chickens alongside his parents, seven brothers, and two sisters. He hated it and was determined to improve his lot in life.

From those humble beginnings, Brookins managed to work his way through school, obtaining degrees from Wilberforce University and Payne Theological Seminary in Ohio, an awesome accomplishment for the son of a black sharecropper from near Yazoo, Mississippi. He is presently a bishop of the African Methodist Episcopal Church, the largest black church in the world. He presides over the Fifth district, which covers seventeen western states. He has become a nationally recognized spokesman in the fight for equality and social justice.[1]

The religious dedication of his family and his parents' desire for an education greatly influenced Brookins's life. His mother insisted upon their attending services every Sunday. At an early age Brookins became interested in the ministry and enjoyed public speaking. As a child, he frequently conducted funerals for dead animals.

To fulfill his educational and career goals, Brookins attended high school at Jackson's Campbell College, where he did odd jobs to pay his expenses. Immediately after graduation, Brookins enrolled at Wilberforce University's Seminary where he was accepted on probation. When asked how he would pay his tuition, he replied that his parents would give him financial assistance, therefore talking his way in without money. He worked in the cafeteria, did other jobs and graduated with a high grade point average. "I was dead serious by then" Brookins asserted, "because I knew if I flunked, they would throw me out . . . Finally, graduation day came and I still owed the university money. They pulled me out of the graduation line, but I got right back in. I was determined to get across that stage."[2]

After graduation, he was sent to a little mission in Topeka, Kansas, called Mud Town, where he met his wife. Two years later he moved to Lawrence, site of the University of Kansas, where he enrolled for graduate courses. He defined his religious beliefs as, "very practical. I've always believed that you have to keep some sense of balance between the ultimate and the now, the metaphysical and the physical. What happens in the ministry is not just the Sunday morning occasion, it's really doing something about people's lives."[3]

In the midst of various political discourses, particularly the Civil Rights movement, the Reverend Brookins chose to be a "moderate" voice and subsequently received invitations for public speaking engagements. Later, he was elected president of Wichita's Interracial Ministerial Alliance, composed of approximately two hundred clergymen, of whom about ten percent were black.

Despite his community involvements Brookins did not neglect his parish or religious responsibilities. He assisted his Wichita congregation in a fund-raising venture that resulted in the construction of a half-million dollar edifice.

Following a fruitful pastorate at Wichita, Brookins assumed the pastorate of the prestigious First African Methodist Episcopal Church of Los Angeles, California. Soon after his arrival in Los Angeles, he interwove his religious duties with civil affairs. Because of the Watts riots, he relocated First A.M.E. Church, built its present multi-million dollar facility, and added hundreds to its membership, including that of Thomas Bradley, whose political elevation Brookins helped design. Bradley, currently campaigning for a third term as mayor of Los Angeles, chose his former pastor and present bishop as co-chairman of his campaign.

In 1972, the A.M.E. board of elders elected Brookins as the ninety-first Bishop of the A.M.E. Church at Dallas, Texas. Commenting on his appointment Brookins stated, "My election was difficult for many reasons. I had become very politically and socially active and some of the leaders' views were more orthodox regarding the church agenda. Many thought I was just seeking headlines and taking too much time away from the church. At the election meeting in Dallas, one powerful bishop said, 'Of all the people running, Brookins will only be elected over my dead body.' I was elected and he died of a heart attack three minutes later."[4]

Bishop Brookins was assigned to the seventeenth district which included five Central African countries and Zimbabwe (Rhodesia). When the 1974 uprising occurred in Rhodesia, Brookins could not identify with the black Freedom Fighters who were opposing the white minority regime. Politically, he could not become involved in the internal affairs of the country. However, as a result of the bishop's honesty, courage, and economic assistance to the Freedom Fighters, he earned the respect of exiles from Rhodesia. He and his wife Helene, a University of Kansas student, raised funds to aid the guerrilla movement and urged his congregation to provide asylum in their sanctuaries. Five years later, he received an invitation to attend the installation of the new president of Zimbabwe.

Now in his second quadrennium as the Presiding Prelate of the Fifth Episcopal District, Bishop Brookins successfully established the first economic development program within the A.M.E. Church. Under his inspiring leadership, the congregation invested over a half-million dollars in The People's Trust Fund. Designed by bankers, lawyers, and insurance executives to insure its credibility while generating revenue for church and community projects, the funds assisted black entrepreneurs who were denied bank loans, helped churches to obtain loans at reduced rates, provided scholarships for black theology students, and issued emergency funds to the elderly and the indigent.

Demonstrative of his zealous concern for viable social action, he chairs the board of directors of the South Los Angeles Development Corporation, a $6,000,000 program funded by the state of California. The purpose of the corporation is to equip unemployed black youth with necessary skills for successful competition in the job market. The corporation offers training courses in wood processing and electronics and operates a reciprocal referral service and placement for those individuals needing subsidized employment through work experience.[5]

Formerly chairman of the board of directors for Operation PUSH, Bishop Brookins now heads its division of International Religious and Civic Affairs. He served as co-chairman for The Gathering, a coalition of two hundred clergymen to construct a black agenda of issues affecting black people across denominational lines. And presently, he is a National Board Member of the recently formed TransAfrica Organization to review American Foreign Policy regarding Third World Countries.[6]

During the summer of 1980 the Reverend H. Hartford Brookins was selected as president of the Council of Bishops of the A.M.E. Church. Formerly, he held the chairmanship of the influential Budget and Finance Committee. Despite his preeminence, Bishop Brookins has not forgotten his roots. Each year he returns to the Mississippi Homecoming, often delivering the "Medgar Evers Eulogy," to a huge crowd of sympathizers. He is the recipient of several honorary degrees.

Homer C. McEwen, Sr.

Minister

In 1946 the Reverend Homer Clyde McEwen, Sr., came to Atlanta, Georgia, as the youthful minister of First Congregational Church—a church, according to McEwen, "that was feeling a little cocky, although the Ku Klux Klan still marched by it occasionally." He and his wife soothed their relatives' fears by saying they would probably stay no longer than three years. June 1979, after thirty-three years of service, Dr. McEwen became the first minister to retire from First Congregational Church.[1]

McEwen was born December 4, 1913, in Aberdeen, Mississippi, to Julia Clay and Reverend Beverly Tolbert McEwen. His father was an elder of the Methodist Episcopal Church and his mother was a teacher at Rust College. He graduated (B.S.) summa cum laude, from Straight College (now Dillard University) in 1934 and won varsity letters in football, basketball, tennis, and track. In 1940 he received the B.D. degree, cum laude, from Chicago Theological Seminary and did further study on a Ford Foundation Fellowship at the University of Chicago, 1940–1942. In 1942 he received the master of divinity degree from Chicago and was awarded the doctor of divinity in 1963.

One of the distinguishing features of Dr. McEwen's ministry has been his leadership role in the church and community. During the three-year interval between graduation from college and enrolling at seminary, he worked for the Federal Emergency Relief Administration, Work Progress Administration Labor Gang, Dryades Street Branch YMCA, and the Federal Writers Project. McEwen served on the boards of the Metropolitan Atlanta Association for the Blind, Carrie-Steele-Pitts Children Home, Dillard University, and the Southeast Conference, United Church of Christ.

In addition, to combat racism in the predominantly black city of Atlanta, Reverend McEwen and members of his First Congregational Church sponsored public forums that led to the integration of the Atlanta Police Department; developed and implemented programs that combatted the welfare freeze; co-sponsored with the National Association for the Advancement of Colored People seven youth who integrated Georgia Institute of Technology; and launched the Atlanta boycott which began the modern drive towards openness and humanity in race relations. Also, McEwen endeavored with other concerned citizens to eradicate school segregation. He created a multiple interracial ministerial staff which persuaded several predominantly white churches to employ interracial staffs.

McEwen is the author of several poems and essays published in *South Today* and "Conversation With A Grave Digger," *Preaching About Death*. McEwen, a former professor of homiletics and worship at the Interdenominational Theological Center, is presently employed as a regular columnist in the *Atlanta Daily World*.

Joseph Harrison Jackson
Preacher, Administrator

In 1953 at Miami, Florida, Joseph H. Jackson was elected president of the National Baptist Convention, U.S.A. Incorporated, the world's oldest and largest organization of black Baptists, headquartered in Chicago, Illinois. At that time the group boasted of a membership of over six million and about a dozen different national boards. The organization established a publishing house that reported 1974 sales totaling more than two million dollars, exceeded only by the giant Southern Baptist and the United Methodist Publishing Houses. Prior to 1974, the "stogy old Baptist Convention, which for many years, under beloved but aging and therefore less-than-vigorous leadership, had inched along much like a sluggish ore carrier with a damaged rudder."[1]

Immediately, Jackson brought the convention to life. Well educated, a world traveler, a respected writer-thinker, and one of the most effective preachers in all Protestantism, he began moving the convention beyond "its traditional once-a-year get-together" role to one of church involvement in both the national and international affairs. Some church officials claimed that "Jackson was too conservative and controversial, but the majority agreed that he steered the organization into new spheres of influence, notably into a more active role in the civil rights struggle."[2]

Jackson was born in Jonestown, a rural community in east Mississippi, on September 11, 1900, to Mr. and Mrs. Henry J. Jackson. As a youth he taught himself arithmetic, spelling, and reading while leading cows to pasture or doing other chores. Unable to accumulate sufficient funds, he acquiesced in attending college. One day when he lamented over his lack of funds to attend college his mother instructed him to look under a pile of quilts and to get the fifty dollars which represented her lifetime savings. "Take it," she said, "and go and make a man of yourself."[3]

Jackson took her advice. He received his A.B. degree from Jackson State College, a B.D. from Colgate Rochester Divinity School, and an M.A. from Creighton University. Since then he has had bestowed upon him honorary degrees from more than a dozen other institutions. He was ordained into the Baptist ministry in 1922 and pastored at First Baptist Church, McComb, Mississippi; Bethel Baptist Church, Omaha, Nebraska; and Monumental Baptist Church,

Philadelphia, Pennsylvania. He left Monumental Baptist Church in 1934 to accept his present pastorate at Chicago's Olivet Baptist Church.[4]

One of the most ambitious ventures initiated by Jackson under the auspices of the Negro Baptist Convention was the Liberian land investment program. The objective was to develop extensive farms on 100,000 acres of Liberian land and to raise funds for missionary activities in Africa. The convention also purchased four acres in Fayette County, near Jackson, Tennessee.

Prior to his election as president of the NBC, Dr. Jackson served as secretary of the foreign missions board of the NBC. He has also held membership on the central committee of the World Council of Churches and on the executive committee of the Baptist World Alliance.

Jackson was the first black vice-president of the World Baptist Alliance. In 1960 after attending the World Baptist Alliance in London, England, Jackson journeyed to Russia. During that visit he delivered twenty-one addresses and attracted the attention of swarms of curious Russians who converged on him, blocking streets and stopping traffic.[5]

Further demonstrating ecumenicity, Jackson was the only Baptist invited to the Second Vatican Council in Rome, Italy, in 1962, during which time he had a private audience with Pope John XXIII. His travels also took him to Asia, Europe, and the Middle East. On these tours, he taped a series of messages for the Voice of America.[6]

Among the books he has authored are *A Voyage to West Africa and Some Reflections on Modern Missions* (1936), *Stars in the Night* (1950), *The Eternal Flame* (1956), *Many But One: The Ecumenics of Charity* (1964).

On September 3, 1963, Jackson, a fluent public speaker and a very popular pulpiteer, delivered a historic address on civil rights at Cleveland, Ohio, before an audience of more than twenty thousand. Reaction to the speech was clearly positive:

> It was one of the greatest addresses delivered on civil rights since Frederick Douglass; It was a great plea for the freedom movement within the framework of the Federal Constitution and the American philosophy of freedom; This was more than an address, it was a directive and a charter for action in the present and future struggle for civil rights; and This is the voice of a Christian statesman who has faith in himself, in his race, his nation and his God.[7]

In early 1975, much controversy centered around the issue of whether blacks should participate in the American Revolution Bicentennial. *Ebony* magazine published a much heralded article, "Should Blacks Celebrate the Bicentennial?" Joseph H. Jackson responded with an essay in the affirmative, from which the following excerpt was taken:

> Further, Negro Americans are taking part in this historic celebration because they recognize that they are a part of American life. Their achievements and growth as a people are vital parts of the past 200 years of this nation's history. In the days of the pioneers, men of color helped to clear the forest, till the soil, cast in the seed, and harvest the ready grain. In the time of crisis and in practically every war, the blood of Negro soldiers has been mixed with the blood of other protectors of American life and democracy. It was Crispus Attucks who was the first to fall on Boston Common in the Boston Massacre, and from then until now the story of heroism and courage on the battlefield has included the daring deeds and sacrifices made by men and women of color.[8]

Dr. Jackson married Maude Thelma Alexander in 1926. They have one daughter, Kenny. After over forty years at Olivet and nearly a quarter-century as president of the NBC, his mother probably would agree that he took her advice and made a man of himself.

L. Venchael Booth

Founder and Past President, Progressive Baptist Convention, Inc.

Frederick and Mamie Powell Booth of Collins, Covington County, had four children, three boys and one girl, including Lavaughn Venchael Booth who was born on January 7, 1919. His father, a member of the deacon's board, made religion a meaningful part of their daily existence. And his children attended school regularly. When Lavaughn completed high school, he enrolled at Alcorn A. & M. College and received his B.S. degree in 1940.[1]

Prior to attending college, Lavaughn had experienced a call to the ministry. Determined to prepare himself spiritually, he attended Gammon Theological Seminary in Atlanta, Georgia; after his first year he transferred to Howard University Divinity School, where in 1943 he obtained the bachelor of divinity degree.

During his study at Howard, young Booth accepted invitations to preach in Maryland and Virginia and was ordained in 1941. Subsequently, he became pastor of First Baptist Church, Warrenton, Virginia. One year later Reverend Booth went to First Baptist Church, Gary, Indiana, and pastored there for eight years. While in Gary, he simultaneously fulfilled his ministerial obligations and the requirements for an M.A. degree at the University of Chicago. In 1952, he was called to Zion Baptist Church, Cincinnati, where he is today. Under his leadership Zion Baptist Church completed one of the most extensive building programs among black churches in Ohio. The congregration built a $500,000 sanctuary and a $400,000 fifty-bed nursing home.[2]

Reverend Booth intertwined his ministry with civic activities. In 1962, he organized a membership drive and $100,000 fund-raising venture to erect a new headquarters for the Cincinnati Community Chest. After blacks were disfranchised through gerrymandering, he founded the "Berry Backers," a political group that succeeded in getting vice-mayor and councilman, Theodore M. Berry, a liberal, reelected to the city council. In 1963, Booth spearheaded the membership campaign for the Cincinnati branch of the NAACP and successfully increased the membership by fifty percent. For two years, he served as president of the Negro Sightless Society of Ohio, Cincinnati branch. In 1965 he acted as campaign chairman for the committee to elect attorney William N. Lovelace as Cincinnati's first black municipal court judge.[3]

During the early sixties, many youthful Baptist disenchanted with the leadership and civil rights stance of the venerable National Baptist Convention called for change within the organizational structure. L. V. Booth, a leader in the movement, helped organize in 1961 the Progressive National Baptist Convention. Its membership included thirty-three representatives from fourteen states. Presently, the National Baptist Convention affiliates consist of 1,200 churches representing forty-five states. Dr. Booth is the immediate past president of the convention.

The energetic minister and civil rights activist L. V. Booth has written several religious songs, one of which, "Brothers Joined in Heart," was sung by an interracial couple at the Baptist World Alliance at Brazil in 1960; a book of radio sermons, *Showers of Blessings*, 1950; *Who's Who in Baptist America*, 1960; and is a contributor to *Outstanding Black Preaching*.[4]

Among his many honors are "Cincinnati's Man of the Year," 1961;

Distinguished Service Award—Baptist Churches of Detroit, 1963; Progressive National Baptist Convention's Founders Award, 1969; listed in Ebony's Success Library, 1978–1974—"100 Most Influential Black Americans;" and Governor's Outstanding Mississippian Award, 1974.

In 1942, Dr. Booth married Georgia Anna Morris, a graduate of Talladega College, Alabama. They have four children: Lavaughn V. Jr., William Douglas, Anna Marie, and Georgia Annita.[5]

Mae Frances Spencer
Church Worker

Mae Frances Spencer, a native Mississippian and former educator in the state, is a regional staff member for the United Methodist Church, serving as liaison between the New York office and her relating conferences.[1] Spencer, an employee within the women's division of the Board of Global Ministers of the United Methodist Church in Washington, D.C., is responsible for nine conferences covering six states on the East Coast.

SCIENCE, MEDICINE AND SOCIAL WORK

Unequal rights and opportunities in education and jobs have kept Negroes from gaining the knowledge and experience necessary for scientific achievement. This is especially true of the black experience in Mississippi. For too long, blacks were denied an education; many could not obtain knowledge in the natural sciences because of Jim Crowism. Only a very few, such as George Washington Carver, managed to achieve without formal training. Unjust laws prevented black inventors from receiving patents for their inventions or discoveries. Under the institution of slavery blacks were considered not citizens but chattel; therefore, the government could not enter into an agreement with someone other than a citizen. Unscrupulous whites therefore, often stole their inventions or occasionally paid meager fees for them.

Some white scientists used pseudo-scientific arguments in an unsuccessful attempt to prove that blacks were naturally inferior to whites and incapable of attainment in arts and sciences. The first director of the Red Cross blood bank actually separated blood given by black and white blood donors and labeled each carton either white or black. Dr. Daniel Hale Williams, who performed the world's first successful heart operation; Dr. A. M. Mackel of Natchez, president of National Dental Association; and Dr. Charles Drew, who discovered blood plasma, are striking examples that the hypothesis of black inferiority was false.

During the early 1900s the ratio of black to whites with doctorate degrees was one-to-1,277 (about .08%). In the 1960s it was 480 to 32,675 (about 1½%). According to census data, there were only 3,374 black engineers, 1,998 black dentists, and 4,706 black doctors. Very few of these resided in the South.

When blacks entered the scientific world, training was restricted to three black institutions with limited facilities and revenues. After the passage of civil rights bills and anti-discriminatory laws, white institutions implemented a quota system of admission, which determined the number of blacks in science and medicine.

Obviously, the situation has changed particularly in Mississippi where many black doctors have established private practices and cater to low-income families in predominantly black towns and counties. Previously, black doctors could not do their residency training or use local hospital facilities. Today, black doctors in Mississippi, such as Dr. Charles E. Smith and Frank Jones of Hattiesburg, have white patients. Dr. Jones is also the administrative head of family practice at Forrest General Hospital in Hattiesburg.

Discussed in this section are a few black doctors and others in the related field of social work who achieved success in spite of racial obstacles. These individuals gained respect and confidence, not because they were black, but because they were qualified.

Sidney D. Redmond
Physician-Surgeon, Lawyer-Politician

Charles and Esther Redmond, sharecroppers, lived on a remote farm in Holmes County near Ebenezer, Mississippi. Formerly slaves, they were poor but ambitious, black but possessing a profound sense of race pride. They had six children, two of whom became medical doctors; two others completed college. Their son, Sidney Dillion Redmond, was born in a two-room log cabin in the backwoods of Holmes County on October 11, 1871.[1]

Redmond's early educational opportunities were very meager, because of working and living so far from the nearest school, which opened only five or six weeks a year. As a result, he was thirteen years old before he learned to count and to write his name. Young Sidney often walked fourteen miles a day to and from school. He completed the second grade, and then his education was interrupted. When he returned to school, he promoted himself to the fifth grade. While in the fifth grade the teacher taught him reading, writing, arithmetic, and spelling.

His mother, though herself unlettered, was determined that her children should be educated. She insisted they study every night, the year around, whether in school or out, and on days when the weather did not permit working in the fields. Her constant cry as soon as they came home was, "Boys get those books." He credits his mother with having saved him from demotion and dropping out of school.

Sidney Redmond aspired to be a country school teacher, but as he grew older he became thoroughly disenchanted with farming and rural life. He associated poverty with rural existence. His father, a farmer and community blacksmith, allowed credit because his customers were poor farmers and could not pay cash; therefore, the Redmonds never had enough money to make ends meet. The longer they farmed, the poorer and more deeply in debt they became. At age fourteen, Sidney "concluded that farming was a myth, an unending dream of rainbow chasing."

Although Sidney resolved to leave the farm, the family's indebtedness after his father's death caused him to reconsider. He moved the family near Ebenezer and "entered into a new contract with his father's old creditors, two merchants of Ebenezer, agreeing to put two yokes of oxen and the mules on the road to do all those merchants' haulings." This meant hauling cotton to Yazoo City and bringing back supplies. His contract was for one year, and the proceeds applied to the old debt.

This new arrangement meant that Sidney had to spend three or four months a year camping on the roadside. "And as he would lie awake those nights alone, gazing at the stars as they darted and played across the heavens, and the scampering clouds as they meandered on their never ending journeys he prayed: 'God make me a man.'"

Since the money from the haulings went toward the old debt, Sidney spent his days off working the family crop or transporting produce to Yazoo City to obtain additional cash for the family. Fortunately, the farm yielded a good crop, farm prices increased, and Redmond paid off the old debts. Sidney convinced his mother to sell out and move to Holly Springs, where he and his siblings entered school.

Sidney was thirteen before he saw a train and was eager to ride it to Holly Springs, but farmers had painted such lurid pictures about the dangers of "train ridin'," that Sidney and his brother Augustus rode their favorite mules, Pete and Tobe, the two hundred mile distance. (They later used the mules to do local hauling at Holly Springs.) They arrived safely after the six-day journey and purchased a home.

Soon after Redmond's arrival in Holly Springs, he enrolled at Rust College in the fall of 1887. During the summers, Sidney worked in a hotel for ten dollars per month and board. At the end of four months he had earned forty dollars with which to reenter school. Throughout his college experience he labored—chopping wood, waiting tables, or serving as a pullman porter.

In 1893, Sidney graduated from Rust College and accepted a position as vice-principal and later principal of Mississippi State Normal School in Holly Springs. That same year he married Ida Revels, the daughter of ex-U.S. Senator Hiram Rhodes Revels.

When Governor James R. Vardaman abolished State Normal School to fulfill a campaign promise, Redmond lost his job. (Vardaman believed that blacks should use their hands and not their heads.) Redmond then accepted the principalship at Haven Institute in Meridian. Later, he taught mathematics at Rust until he resigned to enter Meharry Medical College. After a short stay at Meharry, Redmond became seriously ill and left school. After he had recuperated, he entered Illinois Medical College at Chicago where he remained until he graduated.

When Redmond began medical school, he had saved eight hundred dollars to apply toward his studies. As time passed he invested in the stock market and hoped to make enough money to finish school and open an office "in grandiose style." At first he made a little money and thought he had found the "easy road" to fame and fortune. Later, he began to lose. Finally, the Democrats nominated William Jennings Bryan who advocated for free, unlimited coinage of silver at the ratio of sixteen to one. A panic ensued. The New York Stock Exchange closed down for four months, and Redmond lost every dollar of his hard earned money.

To finance his education he taught in a country school by day and practiced medicine by night on a temporary medical license. After accumulating the necessary finances, he returned to Chicago, graduated at the head of the class, and passed the medical examinations of the Illinois State Board of Health.

He did post-graduate study at Harvard Medical College, Massachusetts General Hospital, and the Mount Sinai Hospital in Boston. Dr. Redmond then opened an office in Jackson, Mississippi.

He arrived in Jackson broke but "immaculately dressed in a Prince Albert coat, striped trousers, patent leather shoes, kid gloves, and a silk hat." Since black doctors had been unsuccessful in Jackson, it was almost impossible for Dr. Redmond to find suitable accommodations for a home and an office. Undaunted, Dr. Redmond did obtain living quarters with Professor P. A. Wardlaw. Unable to get an office, he arranged with a blacksmith to rent one corner of his shop as an office. When Redmond began refurnishing the shop, the owner of the property, Ned Farish, objected, and the doctor had to move.

When Ramsey Wharton, later mayor of Jackson, learned of Redmond's difficulties, he informed Redmond of two vacant rooms in the Burburvich Building. Redmond established his office and remained there for three years.

For the first three months business was slim. The first month he collected only thirty dollars, and the second month sixty dollars—not enough to pay his rent on his house, office, or horse.

During the third month, Sam Jackson, a former driver for Mississippi Insane Asylum-Whitfield, consulted Dr. Redmond about his paralysis. Upon examination Dr. Redmond discovered "Jackson had a depressed fracture of the skull, of several years standing and suggested an operation to remove the pressure from his brain." Jackson refused Redmond's offer to operate and then discussed the operation with Dr. Mitchell, his banker, adviser, confidant, and former employer. Dr. Mitchell advised against it, saying it might kill him. Later Jackson decided to have the operation, and Mitchell offered to perform the operation for Jackson without charge. But Jackson replied, "No, Sir; I thank you, Doctor, very much. You say it might kill me and Dr. Redmond says it won't." He chose Redmond instead.

Although there was no hospital, sanitorium, or trained nurse in Jackson, Dr. Redmond improvised the means and performed the operation. Within three or four weeks Sam Jackson was walking, and within six months he had regained full use of his limbs. Dr. Mitchell sent Dr. Redmond a check for a $250 professional fee, out of the deposit Jackson had with him.

Soon after Jackson's operation, two white doctors consulted with Dr. Redmond about George Hackett who had a strangulated inguinal hernia, and Dr. Redmond diagnosed gangrene of the intestine and advised an immediate operation. Since the white doctors were not surgeons, they asked Dr. Redmond to perform the operation.

Redmond performed the operation in the old Stamps House, "which had not a screen, nor a mosquito bar in it." The operation was successful. Because Hackett had no family, friends, or money, Dr. Redmond neglected his own bills and paid Hackett's room rent, board, and medical supplies for six weeks.

The success of Redmond's operations on Sam Jackson and George Hackett established Dr. S. D. Redmond's reputation as a well-qualified physician. He had proven himself as a skilled surgeon. Following those successes Redmond performed many operations. Within eight months after the date of his arrival, Redmond had paid his debts. When the city of Jackson experienced a yellow fever epidemic, Dr. Redmond contained the disease and his reputation as a skilled physician spread throughout the state.

Dr. Redmond saved E. Bealls, another black physician, from being lynched. Dr. Beall had treated a white male alcoholic who had taken several grains of morphine mixed with alcohol. He asked for a drink to sober up, without telling Dr. Beall that he had previously consumed several grains of morphine. When Beall administered a "hypodermic of ½ grain, [alcohol]," the patient collapsed. Dr. Redmond was summoned. Having declared that death was inevitable, Redmond then notified the patient's brother and explained matters before the patient died. Not knowing the relative's reaction, Redmond advised Beall to leave town until the problem was resolved. Rumors spread that Dr. Beall had killed the man, and a revengeful mob gathered to lynch him. But, Dr. Redmond explained Dr. Beall's position in the situation, assuring them that Beall was not responsible or guilty of any wrong doing. Redmond's explanation was accepted, the mob dispersed, and Beall returned.

In 1904 Mississippi Governor James K. Vardaman, a racist demagogue, invited all of Jackson's white doctors to attend his inauguration. On the day of inauguration a white man, Bell, chose to go hunting and shot himself in the foot, causing uncoagulated bleeding. Since the white doctors were attending the inauguration, Bell asked Dr. Redmond to treat him. As Vardaman delivered his bitterest invectives against black education, Redmond amputated Bell's foot, in which there was gangrene. When Bell's neighbors heard of the incident, they asked Redmond to be their attending physician. In light of the racial climate in Mississippi, Redmond politely declined.

Because of Dr. Redmond's reputation as a skilled surgeon and physician, McLelland, an established businessman who refused to assist Redmond upon his initial arrival in Jackson, guaranteed Redmond credit at his bank. Thereafter Redmond and McLelland became friends and business associates. Together as the largest stockholders, they purchased, with the financial assistance of a few others, the Capitol Light and Power Company.

After fourteen years of practicing medicine in Jackson, Dr. Redmond, organizer and first president of Mississippi Medical and Surgical Association, had increased his business investments and enterprises. He purchased a house on Church Street which he had earlier been unable to rent "because they said he would never be able to pay the rent." He also bought the old blacksmith shop and half of Farish Street block, on which he built three brick buildings, to be used primarily as offices for black professionals, in the hope they would be spared the difficulties he had once experienced. Dr. Redmond also pioneered in the operation of black owned drugstores in Jackson, all of which did a thriving business.

As one of the organizers of the American Trust and Savings Bank of Jackson, he served as its president for several years. When business declined, Dr. Redmond placed an advertisement in the paper advising all depositors to call at the bank and receive their money. This was a first for Mississippi.

By the 1920s, Dr. Redmond became active in Mississippi politics and was elected chairman of the Mississippi Republican state executive committee, which position he held for more than twenty-four years. He was a delegate to numerous Republican national conventions and personally helped nominate ten Republican candidates for president and vice-president of the United States.

On numerous occasions Dr. Redmond presented memorials to the Mississippi legislature and petitions to the U.S. Congress, all in behalf of the welfare of blacks. In 1924 he addressed a joint session of the Mississippi legislature requesting economic and political assistance to uplift the status of black Mississippians. For several years he led a movement to establish a school for derelict youth. The school finally materialized in 1944 when the legislature appropriated $100,000 for building such an institution. In 1919, twelve years before the federal government set up its WPA night schools, Dr. Redmond's first night school was established at Smith-Robertson school.

Dr. Redmond traveled extensively. In 1919 he went to Paris as a delegate of the Pan-African Congress, whose stated purpose was to improve race relations throughout the world. He was also a correspondent of the Paris Peace Conference which terminated World War I. Following the close of the peace conference, Dr. Redmond visited other countries in Europe. He also traveled to Canada, Mexico, and the West Indies.

In the early 1900s the overriding demands of his medical practice took its toll on Dr. Redmond. In 1913 his health began to fail, because of overwork and the constant strain of an ever-increasing practice. Believing that law was less exhaustive or taxing, he exchanged his Hypocratic Oath for Blackstone's law books. He passed the bar and replaced his medical shingle with that of a lawyer. He received a bachelor of law degree from the Illinois College of Law in Chicago. In 1915 Campbell College conferred upon him the degree of doctor of laws; Rust College, his alma mater, conferred upon him an honorary master of arts.

Dr. S. D. Redmond, the charismatic physician, politician, lawyer, and financier died on February 11, 1948. Left to mourn his death were his second wife, Johnnie Grace King Redmond and three children, Esther, Sidney II, and Ruth. His first wife, Ida Revels Redmond, had died in 1914.

L. T. Miller

Delta Doctor-Humanitarian

Prior to the Civil War, a slave named Wash Miller, married a mulatto, named Emily. Emily worked in the prestigious antebellum mansion, Melrose, of Natchez. That marriage produced several children, of whom three were girls. Thereafter, Wash's master moved to California and took his slave with him. However, Wash's wife and children remained with her master. Wash was allowed to save his earnings to purchase his freedom and that of his wife and children.[1] After emancipation, Wash was given the funds he had saved, and he returned to Natchez.

One day, as Rachel, Emily's and Wash's youngest daughter, was playing in the yard, a man appeared at the gate, introduced himself, and began to question the thirteen-year-old, who had been an infant when her father was taken away. Emily ran inside and said to her mother, "There's a black man out there, and he says he's my father."[2]

At Natchez, Wash bought a home for his family, and after their reunion Emily bore him three sons—J. H., William, and Lloyd. Later Wash sold his home to the Illinois Central Railroad and invested a portion of the funds in a livery stable. He used draft horses for drayage and beautiful carriage horses hitched to attractive surreys for travelers and sightseers.[3]

Lloyd Miller the seventh, and favorite child was born in Natchez, on December 6, 1874. His mother had wanted a girl and she referred to the unborn child as "Daisy." As a child Lloyd seemed somewhat frail and was still called Daisy. (After he grew up "Daisy" was shortened to "Dais.") Early in life he displayed a leaning toward a medical career by playing nursemaid to the sick animals in the neighborhood. Lloyd was sent to St. Louis, Missouri, to attend high school. Afterwards he returned to Natchez and attended Natchez College. Later he matriculated at Meharry Medical College and received his medical degree in 1893.[4]

Upon his return to Mississippi, Dr. L. T. Miller, for reasons unknown opened his medical office in Yazoo City. There the rich flat Delta country joins the foothills; and there the dense black population offered a large clientele. And for about sixty years, the doctor of the lower Delta, the Yazoo basin, was Dr. L. T. Miller. Dr. Miller, a short, balding man, performed more than 35,000 operations and rendered service to a vast majority throughout the Delta.[5]

Douglas Adams assisted Dr. Miller in getting his medical practice established in Yazoo City. Adams worked for Howard Coast, a white general merchandise store owner. Adams approached Coast and recommended Dr. Miller as a competent black doctor. Coast, impressed with Miller's credentials, publicly announced, "We have a good young colored doctor here and I want all of you to go to see him." Not only did that provide patients, but it also assured Dr. Miller that the white man would pay the bill. Dr. Miller never forgot that kindness.[6]

Another individual responsible for Dr. Miller's successful medical practice was his wife, Emma Burruss, a local belle whose father had once served as treasurer of Yazoo County. She used her inheritance, which included property and money, to aid her husband's medical career.[7]

Soon after Dr. Miller's arrival in Yazoo City a smallpox epidemic engulfed the area. This severely taxed the county's medical resources. Many of the victims were confined to quarantine barracks called "pest houses." Dr. Miller was summoned to treat stricken patients regardless of race or color.[8] Elderly blacks recalled that after the smallpox epidemic ended, many whites came to Dr. Miller's side door for office visits and treatment. Others waited until nightfall to come. He was the acknowledged "Doctor of the Delta." One woman remembered that a renowned white native credited and thanked Dr. Miller for saving his life.

Dr. Miller discovered that many of his patients needed surgery, but there were no hospital facilities. His ingenuity led him to secure rented beds in private homes for the post-operative healing of his patients, thus enabling Dr. Miller to save many lives. Previously, he was averaging some thirty operations per month, in addition to running his own drug store. His recovery rate was exceedingly high, despite the absence of the most favorable conditions.

Without trained nurses or proper facilities he transformed his office into a makeshift clinic, accomodating a dozen patients. In 1907 Dr. Miller opened "Miller Infirmary," Yazoo County's first and the only sanitarium in Mississippi for blacks. That eighteen-bed facility more than doubled the available hospital bed space for the blacks.[9]

Dr. Miller co-founded with Tom J. Huddleston, the first black-owned and operated hospital in Mississippi had conceived the idea. Huddleston, a school teacher, farmer, and businessman, believing it to be a worthy venture, Huddleston and Miller formulated their plan and co-founded the Afro-American Sons and Daughters, a fraternal and benefit association which financed the construction of a $50,000 hospital in 1928. As early as 1924, the organization had 1,000 chartered members.[10]

Dr. Miller became chief surgeon at the Afro-American Sons and Daughters Hospital, where he performed from three to seven operations daily. Dr. Miller saved the life of a patient whose intestines were punctured eighteen times, and another patient who had been shot so close to the heart that x-ray photos showed that only a miracle had saved her from immediate death.[11]

Two young physicians who interned with Dr. Miller—Dr. George A. Carmichael of Canton, Mississippi, and Dr. Robert E. Fullerlove of New Jersey—held him in high esteem. Whenever the opportunity afforded, Dr. Miller counseled young doctors and employed them on his staff. According to Dr. Carmichael, most black doctors in the state had profited from Dr. Miller's skills and wisdom. Some received from him financial aid to continue their professional training. Many observed his surgical skills in the operating room. Dr. Miller often reminded aspiring young surgeons, "You'll never get any further than you are now if you continue to watch somebody else. The only way you can learn is by doing it yourself."[12]

Dr. Carmichael described Dr. L. T. Miller as skillful, modest, unassuming, and generous. "If some of the almost incredible surgical operations that Dr. Miller performed had been reported and written up in medical journals," Carmichael asserted, "he would be in the Hall of Fame. Not only that, but he performed these on people who were not able to pay for them. Some paid the small fees, but many more brought vegetables, chickens, eggs, and fruit."[13]

He often did the unorthodox—or perhaps it was the best under the conditions that existed. Even in the "modern" facilities of the Afro-American Hospital with its two operating tables in one room, a northern visiting doctor was aghast when he observed Dr. Miller at one table and Dr. Fullerlove at the other: "I never saw anything that looked like a complication from that practice although textbooks would not approve it."[14]

Nevertheless, in the midst of house calls, private practice, and surgery, Dr. Miller found time for relaxation and recreation. With regards to his personal habits, he was a strict disciplinarian. He was an early riser. By eight o'clock, he was at the hospital, where he made daily visitations and performed surgery. Reading professional texts and journals and playing an occasional game of bridge occupied him until his ten o'clock bedtime.[15]

Dr. Miller suffered a stroke late in the afternoon on December 17, 1950, after an unusually busy day. He died on March 8, 1951, with final rites held at St. Stephen's United Methodist Church and attended by blacks and whites from throughout the area.[16]

In later years Dr. Miller's widow established a ten thousand dollar L. T. Miller Scholarship at Meharry Medical School. The annual interest on this amount was presented to a medical student who had attained the highest cumulative average at the end of his junior year. In the late 1960s the L. T. Miller Community Center was erected in his honor in Yazoo City. This modern public facility serves hundreds of Yazooans of both races.[17]

George H. Lane

Physician

George H. Lane, born July 2, 1902, in Jonestown, Mississippi, completed grammar and secondary school as well as undergraduate studies at Alcorn State University. After graduating with a bachelor's degree from Alcorn, he matriculated at and received his medical degree from Meharry Medical College in Nashville, Tennessee. Upon completion of his internship, Lane opened general practice at Greenwood in 1932.

Lane, did not remain in Mississippi but migrated to Milwaukee, where he combined his work in internal medicine with cardiovascular diseases. After a great deal of hard work, Lane succeeded in establishing a Sickle Cell Center at Milwaukee's Deaconess Hospital.[1]

Deborah Hyde-Rowan

Neurosurgeon

A thirty-four year old native of Laurel, Mississippi, Deborah Hyde-Rowan, is presently a neurosurgeon at the Guthrie clinic, a medical institution in Sayre, Pennsylvania. Her clientele includes individuals within the forty-county area of rural northeastern Pennsylvania and south central New York. According to Marilyn Marshall, an editor with *Ebony* magazine, there are only 3,300 neurosurgeons in America, and less than 60 are black and even fewer are women. Neurosurgery, a highly specialized field, encompasses the diagnosis and treatment of injuries and disorders affecting the nervous system, which includes the brain, spinal cord, and nerves.[1]

Dr. Rowan, the daughter of Ann McDonald and Sellus Hyde, is the first member of her family to attend college. Dr. Rowan's education for the medical profession began at Tougaloo College, where she earned a bachelor's degree in biology. While at Tougaloo, she was chosen Miss Tougaloo College and Miss Alpha Phi Alpha. Upon graduating, she matriculated at Cleveland State University where she obtained a master's degree in biology. Undecided about the doctoral program and influenced by fellow classmates at Cleveland State University, she applied, was accepted, and graduated from the medical college of Western Reserve Medical School. She completed her internship and residency at University Hospital in Cleveland. Afterwards, in July 1982, she joined the staff of physicians of Guthrie Medical Center. Dr. Rowan is married to Hugh Rowan.

Dr. Deborah Hyde-Rowan is proud of her accomplishment and believes that her success demonstrates that "black women have the determination, discipline, and dedication to succeed in an area such as neurosurgery."

Eliza J. Pillars

State Health Department Nurse

In an effort to reduce sickness and death among blacks, the Mississippi State Board of Health hired in 1923 Eliza J. Pillars, a graduate of the School of Nursing-Hubbard Hospital, Meharry College. For decades, Mississippi had a large black population, low economic status, and the highest infant and maternal morbidity among blacks in America. In the late 1930s, eighty percent of black babies born in the state were delivered by midwives who lived on plantations, remote sections in the backwoods, and small towns; therefore, Eliza J. Pillars's task was to make the midwives more efficient and safe. With the assistance of another black nurse, Pillars conducted classes for midwives throughout Mississippi. Utilizing a manual prepared by the State Department of Health, Pillars taught midwives the techniques of prenatal and postnatal care and actual baby delivery. Charts were used to supplement actual demonstrations. Also, each midwife had a nursing bag fully equipped for her work. Every month, these bags were inspected by Nurse Pillars.[1]

Distrustful of scientific trained health officials and medical techniques, many of these illiterate and superstitious midwives were unreceptive to the use of prophylactics for the eyes of the new-born immediately after birth. Since ninety percent of the blindness in the United States was caused by infection of the eyes at birth, medical authorities strictly enforced the prophylactics method. Since Nurse Pillars had profound understanding and tact as well as possessed the requisite professional background, she convinced the midwives to place several drops of the solution in each of the baby's eyes immediately following birth. In addition, Nurse Pillars checked their methods, and the freshness of the solutions.[2]

Because of dire poverty, ignorance, superstition, and the indifference of the authorities, funds were not provided for health care centers; consequently, Nurse Pillars converted rooms in rural shanties into delivery rooms. Each community had a delivery room where midwives learned the basics for a safe delivery.[3]

Because of practices of racial exclusion and few opportunities for preliminary medical or professional education in the South, midwives were readily accepted within the black communities. As a result of so many professionally trained persons engaged in medical practices, the State Board of Health required that all midwives must be licensed by the State Board. In order to obtain a license, the midwives had to pass a test after completing the course of instruction and a physical examination. Because of Eliza Pillars's work with midwives, documentation revealed that Mississippi's midwives were in good physical condition.[4]

By rendering this invaluable medical service, the Jackson, Mississippi, native, Eliza Pillars assisted in saving many lives and the preservation of health; thereby serving her race and the nation. In preparing for this life career, Pillar graduated from Meharry Medical College's School of Nursing, actively participated in Lambda Pi Alpha Sorority (Medical), and served as president and financial secretary of the Southern Region of the National Association of Colored Graduate Nurses.[5]

Rhetaugh G. Dumas
Psychiatric Nurse

Rhetaugh G. Dumas, a Natchez native, began her professional career as a nurse-teacher in the public schools of Mississippi. After that, she served as professor and chairman of Yale University's psychiatric nursing program, where she combined teaching, research, and nursing. Later, she accepted the directorship of Nursing Service at Connecticut Mental Health Center. The National Institute of Mental Health (NIMH) under the auspices of the Department of Health Education and Welfare appointed Dumas Chief of Psychiatric Nursing Training.[1]

Her duties as director entailed conducting extensive research in various areas related to mental health and supervising graduates in training for psychiatric nursing. Within the Institute's Division of Manpower and Training, Dumas supervised a program designed to expand and improve training in psychiatric and mental health nursing, to utilize trained nursing personnel in providing community service in critical areas, to implement special programs in gerontology, juvenile delinquency, alcoholism, and drug abuse in urban communities. Many of these programs were directed at increasing the number of nurses in psychiatric-mental health, and expanding the content of advanced training in nursing schools.

In addition to her administrative duties, Dumas found time to write extensively for professional journals, serve as consultant for group relations conferences, and present papers at scholarly conventions.

In preparation for a professional career, Dumas obtained her B.S.N. degree from Dillard University. She engaged in graduate studies in the Department of Education and Psychology at Alcorn State University and Dillard University. In 1961, she received the M.S.N. degree from Yale University in mental health and psychiatric nursing.

Jessie O. Thomas
Pioneer Social Worker

Jessie O. Thomas, a pioneer social worker born in Pike County, Mississippi, December 21, 1885, was the second child in a family of six children—four boys and two girls. Until the advent of the Civil War, his parents were labeled as slaves. When emancipation seemed inevitable, they exchanged their plantation existence for that of sharecropping and tenant farming. Since there was an abundance of food and livestock on their property, Jessie assumed that his family was economically secure.[1]

On one particular day Jessie was shocked to learn that his family did not own the land that they cultivated. His father, greatly distressed and disappointed, informed the family that their landlord had rented the property to another family willing to pay a higher rental fee. Jessie determined to avoid this type of arrangement and, therefore, struggled to get an education.

In spite of racial segregation and discrimination in Pike County, neither Jessie nor any member of his family ever worked for local whites. They were self-sufficient. Therefore, he was shielded from involvement with whites, a situation that historically often led to an inferiority complex within southern blacks. Generally, black and white tenant families and landowners co-existed amicably and peacefully. White and black children played baseball and other sports without consciousness of inferiority or superiority, although schools were segregated.

His school consisted of a one room shack where approximately one hundred pupils ranging from grade one to seven were taught by one teacher. As a pupil, his most unforgettable learning experiences were the spelling bees and oratorical contests. He traced his oratorical skills as a public speaker to that one-room schoolhouse in Pike County, Mississippi.[2]

Jessie's desire to learn was inspired by his father. His father, possessing only a fourth-grade education, had taught himself to read and write. He had a perpetual hunger for knowledge and information and read everything he could that was, in his language, "uplifting." What he lacked in education he made up for in honor and upright living.[3]

During most of Jessie's childhood, his mother was ill; she died when he was fourteen. On his way home from her funeral, Jessie decided to pack his belongings and disappear unannounced. He and a schoolmate, David Davis, traveled together to the mechanized culture of the sawmill community of Natalbany, where they were employed. Immediately he suffered from loneliness, homesickness, and physical illness caused by the intense heat and mosquitoes. He felt uncomfortable among his fellow employees who took advances on their wages, gambled, drank alcohol, and engaged in prostitution.

He did, however, enjoy the thrill of making money and being independent. Jessie sent his father as "a peace offering" for having left home, groceries and several pairs of shoes. He was greatly relieved when his father sent a letter of thanks, an admonition to stay out of bad company, and the assurance that he would always be welcomed home.

During a visit to McComb Jessie was informed by a friend, of Tuskegee Institute, a school where students worked while pursuing a trade or vocation. He applied for admission and was accepted.

Jessie O. Thomas arrived at Tuskegee on Sunday morning, September 6, 1906, dressed in a new suit and smoking a Cremo cigar, with sixty-five dollars to his name. When he entered Captain C. B. Hosmer's office to register, the captain took Thomas aside and lectured him on the rules and regulations, which forbade smoking. That afternoon he attended a meeting of the Mississippi State Club, where he met his "statemates." When the meeting adjourned, he met a fellow-classmate named Wysinger who pledged to assist Jessie in adjusting to the institute. Wysinger encouraged Jessie to apply for admission to the freshman class and join his section. However, Dr. David G. Houston, an administrator, assigned Jessie without an examination to the senior high school class.

Jessie identified with various campus organizations, such as the debating society, mid-week prayer meetings, Y.M.C.A., choir, and glee club. He developed into such a promising bass singer that the choir directress requested his release from drill duty for rehearsal. The next semester the commandant commissioned him second lieutenant, which drew protests from other officers who knew Jessie did not attend drill and other military activities. The commandant countered that Jessie exercised such a wholesome influence on the total student body that his presence honored the staff more than the appointment honored him.

During the summer of 1907, the end of his first school year, Jessie went to Birmingham to work at the blast furnace of the Tennessee Iron and Coal Company. At that time a laborer could work overtime, and Jessie worked ten hours a day with a half-hour for lunch in order to enroll his sister at Tuskegee. This decision affected his health. Although he saved $150, eating poorly cooked and selected food had given him a chronic case of indigestion. Within three weeks after returning to school he was hospitalized and the physician advised him to leave school until he had fully recovered.

Discouraged and depressed, Jessie left school and obtained employment in Montgomery without informing his family. His stomach ailment had developed so that a glass of water caused him as much discomfort as a piece of steak. Adhering to the advice of a black physician, he stopped drinking coffee and drank hot water before each meal. His condition improved.

In 1908, he returned to Tuskegee and was elected president of the Y.M.C.A. Jessie Thomas organized the first student council on Tuskegee's campus. The organization's effectiveness impressed the administration so that the student government was permitted to make recommendations to the executive council of the college.

During the 1909–1910 academic year the students complained to the administrative steward concerning the cafeteria food. The steward made minor modifications and then food conditions worsened. It was customary for President Booker T. Washington to assemble the students together and inquire as to conditions. On this occasion the students very loudly complained about the food. He queried as to why they had not appointed a committee and reported the matter. They informed him of their previous actions. He conferred with the steward and then transferred him to another area, replacing him with a person recommended by Jessie Thomas. At the dedication ceremony for a new cafeteria, Thomas represented the student body.

The composition and delivery of Thomas's presentation greatly impressed several trustees, one of whom sent Jessie a check for fifty dollars. President Washington recommended Thomas, as field secretary, to solicit aid for Tuskegee from northern philanthropists.

Jessie Thomas graduated from Tuskegee Institute in May 1911 and in June assumed responsibilities as Tuskegee's fund raising field secretary in Rochester, New York. En route to Rochester he was met in New York City by Frank Chrisholm, senior field director, who sent him to Albany on an assignment. While his area of specialization had been carpentry and architecture, his total training, experience and association had been with blacks. His new appointment entailed patronizing white philanthropists, who would donate large sums of money to Tuskegee. He recalled that on one occasion, he had to raise ninety thousand dollars within thirty days for the payment on a heating plant. "With this type of objective," he said, "there would be no point in wasting one's time with 'after collections' in Negro churches."

Thomas's assignment carried him to New York and Pennsylvania to solicit funds from the most affluent church groups and civic clubs, and persons of wealth. Unlike some field directors in other schools, Washington had worked out a system which gave dignity to the job. The field director of Tuskegee was not employed on a commission basis, but on a fixed salary plus living and traveling expenses. During the first year of his assignment, Thomas raised more money than any other field director, even though some had been out on the job twelve years.

In the spring of 1916, nine months after the death of Booker T. Washington, Jessie O. Thomas accepted the position of principal of Voorhees Industrial School near Denmark, South Carolina. That institution, founded by a graduate of Tuskegee, was often referred to as the "Tuskegee of South Carolina." Named in honor of its largest benefactor, it occupied some fifty acres of land and had an endowment of more than a hundred thousand dollars. The administrative turnover at Voorhees following the death of the founder "was unceremoniously rapid," in part because the treasurer and paymaster was, among other things, a dictatorial and a "Tom."

Thomas had been duly warned of the situation but believed that his contacts would enable him to succeed where others had failed. Between his inauguration on May 16, 1916, and September 15, he had raised enough money for the installation of the school's first steam heating plant. In addition, he increased the school's financial resources, enriched the curriculum, and added important persons to the board of control. It became possible, that year, for graduates of Voorhees to receive certification to teach in the public schools of the state without having to take an examination.

In 1917, Thomas took a sabbatical from Voorhees to accept a position as state supervisor of Negro economics for the state of New York and examiner-in-charge of the United States Employment Service in New York City under the auspices of the United States Department of Labor.

Thomas found it increasingly difficult to get many executives to train blacks as stenographers, bookkeepers, clerks, electrical engineers, steamfitters, or to employ them in their firms. Therefore, he created interracial advisory committees composed of the civic-minded, public-spirited, prominent citizens in each community to interpret the nature of his work and its relation to the World War I effort for total employment. Impressed with Thomas's organizational skills and leadership potential, a wealthy Jewish woman, who served on the committee and the board of directors of the National Urban League convinced the League's board and executive secretary to utilize Thomas's service within their organization. As a result, he became southern field director of the National Urban League and established the southern office of the National Urban League in Atlanta, Georgia.

In spite of several delicate controversial issues, Jessie O. Thomas became an indefatigable personality throughout the South and particularly in Atlanta. Every movement for racial advancement and goodwill had his support. When two of Atlanta's most prominent churches were destroyed by fire, Thomas appeared before the Atlanta city council and the county board of commissioners and requested financial assistance to rebuild those edifices. The council and board of commissioners responded with a contribution of $5,000 each. He helped organize forums, business and professional clubs, his most auspicious monument being the Atlanta University School of Social Work.

In 1936, Texas observed its centennial with a budget of ten million dollars. Negroes were given an opportunity to present a complete display of their contributions to American culture. This challenging enterprise was under the direction of Jessie O. Thomas, general manager, and A. Maceo Smith, assistant general manager, with a staff of more than a dozen specialists.

In October 1941, Jessie O. Thomas secured a leave of absence from his duties as southern field director of the National Urban League to accept the position of senior promotional specialist with the United States Treasury. As was customary with Thomas, he set out to have the state war Bond staffs integrated. Integration he insisted, would give blacks full participation in the bond drive. Subsequently, Ted Gamble, executive assistant to the secretary of the treasury, informed Thomas: "We are going to give you a blank check on the United States Treasury so that you can secure whatever talent you and your promotional committee may decide upon as participants for the rallies at each one of the four cities to be covered."

The impact of Thomas's efforts was shown in the appointment of fourteen blacks as deputy administrators and eighteen as associate state administrators and in the thousands of blacks who attended,

Walter Washington

Jacob L. Reddix

Ernest A. Boykins, Jr.

John A. Peoples, Jr.

George A. Owens

Laurence C. Jones

Jane Ellen McAllister

Cleopatra D. Thompson

William Arthur Butts

Willa B. Player

Romeo Benjamin Garrett

William Smith Demby

Charlemae Hill Rollins

Moorland-Spingarn Research Center, Howard University

Gladys Noel Bates

H. Hartford Brookins

L. Venchael Booth

George H. Lane

Jennifer O. Hicks

Walter Payton

Thomas J. Money, Jr.

Glennie M. Rowland

Jesse Leroy Brown

participated in, and financed the war bond rallies. And as Thomas said, "Few positions I have held afforded a greater opportunity for the exercise of creative imagination. . . ." After his resignation was submitted and accepted, he was retained on the staff of the treasury with the title of "expert consultant" for three years.

Another successful venture involved the inclusion of blacks within the administrative staff of the American Red Cross. According to J. O. Thomas, the American Red Cross consistently denied blacks the opportunity to apply their skills either on local, area, or national levels as bona fide professional or administrative employees. In 1942, as a result of positive actions by blacks, Jessie O. Thomas was appointed assistant to the vice chairman of the American Red Cross and several other blacks were hired by the organization. Thomas said, "Beginning at zero in 1942, by April 1945 Negroes employed on domestic and foreign soil by chapters and the national organization were drawing salaries alone of approximately $1,940,000."

Thomas returned to Atlanta after his retirement in 1953 and devoted his time to community activities and racial advancement. One such activity involved the Atlanta Chapter of Frontiers of America, which he served as president for five years. He declined reelection, but served as president emeritus until his death.

In his newspaper column "My View," Dr. Benjamin Mays eulogized Jessie O. Thomas: "Without Jessie O. Thomas, the Urban League would not be what it is today and Atlanta, the South, and the Nation are better because of the contribution that Jessie O. Thomas made." Left to mourn his death was his wife, Nellie Mitchell, and his foster children.

Lucille Price

Social Worker

Lucille Price, member of a distinguished Natchez family, was Mississippi's first black professional social worker. During the depths of the Great Depression she worked with the Works Project Administration (WPA) in Mississippi and was the only worker who remained throughout the 1930s.[1]

Price completed requirements for the baccalaureate degree at

Tougaloo College. Later, at Atlanta University, she took a "crash course" in social work which was administered by the Emergency Relief Administration (ERA), to prepare personnel to handle the mass of unemployed, aged, and destitute people. Governor Paul Johnson believed that Hinds, Warren, and Bolivar counties should have "colored" social workers, and she was the first to serve in that capacity. Lucille Price, however, assisted the poor, the proud, and the deceptive of both races when the WPA certified hundreds of workers for the construction of Hawkins Field, Jackson's first commercial airport.

As a black social worker Lucille Price experienced racism. For instance, all black federal employees rode the freight elevator to conferences in Mississippi public buildings. Whites and blacks who came to her for certification often displayed hostility and resentment that she should occupy such a position. Yet, it was common for them to say, "Lady, please take my application?" As an administrator, she was segregated from white administrators, but she persisted, and gradually blacks and whites accepted and respected her.

Price later enrolled at the University of Chicago and engaged in graduate studies within the division of social sciences. On returning to Jackson she was employed as a child welfare worker at Oakley Training School near Raymond, until she retired. She is married to Dr. G. A. Price, a dentist; they have one son, who is a dentist in a Chicago northside suburb. Dr. Robert W. Harrison a dentist from Yazoo City, and the only black member of the Board of Institutions of Higher Learning, is her nephew.

Cleo Walter Blackburn

Social Worker, Minister

Cleo Blackburn was born near Port Gibson, in Claiborne County, to David and Sarah (Sneed) Blackburn, on September 27, 1909. His grandfather, once a slave, was emancipated after he rescued his master's daughter from a runaway horse. The ex-slave then became an ordained minister of the Disciples of Christ. His grandson, Cleo, also affiliated with the same faith. He practiced and applied his faith to the betterment of mankind.[1]

Sarah Blackburn, a school teacher, made sure that Cleo received the best elementary education available. He attended Southern Christian Institute at Edwards and planned to enroll in college. However, disaster struck. His mother was hospitalized and a flood washed away most of the family farm. Nevertheless, his mother scraped together every penny she could. With the sum of $7.19, young Blackburn journeyed to Butler University in Indiana. He worked his way through college as a janitor, busboy, and dishwasher.[2]

After studying at Butler, Blackburn secured scholarships at Fisk and Pendle Hill, the latter a Quaker-operated school in Pennsylvania. He desired to complete doctoral studies in sociology, with concentration in the area of black migration. However, finances dictated that he seek employment. Subsequently, he went to Tuskegee and worked on the Negro Yearbook that Booker T. Washington had initiated. Pleased with his job, Blackburn contemplated accepting a position as a research assistant; however, he met Dr. Robert E. Park, a sociologist at the University of Chicago.

Park advised Blackburn to work at Flanner House in Indianapolis for seven years, before getting an advanced degree. Blackburn went to Flanner House, worked, studied and learned, but he never received his Ph.D., although he later was awarded several honorary doctorates.[3]

While at Flanner House, Blackburn directed a sociological study of the Negro community, in Indianapolis, which was financed by the Indianapolis Foundation.

Blackburn worked for several years as a social worker in settlement houses. Because of his effectiveness as director, his work attracted widespread attention in the academic world. When offered, the presidency at Jarvis Christian College in Hawkins, Texas in 1953, he graciously accepted. As president he persuaded several prominent Dallas businessmen to support the five-year economic program of the college, for which they raised three million dollars. He was president of Jarvis until 1964.

Three years later the U.S. Congress chartered one of its first welfare agencies, the Board for Fundamental Education. Blackburn was named director.[4] He served in this capacity until 1969 at which time he became chairman of the board.

Blackburn's work experience, illustrative of his administrative and academic achievement included: sociology research at Fisk University, Nashville, Tennessee, 1932; research director of study made by Tuberculosis Association in Chester, Pennsylvania, 1933.

Because of his commitment to improving mankind, Blackburn was the recipient of numerous awards and honors, which included: the 1940 Indianapolis Junior Chamber of Commerce Distinguished Service Award, 1955; Honorary Doctor of Divinity Degrees from Northwest Christian College, Eugene, Oregon and Drake University, Des Moines, Iowa; Honorary Doctor of Humanities degree, Indiana Central College, Indianapolis, Indiana; and Honorary Doctor of Humane Letters from Wabash College, Crawfordsville, Indiana, and Butler University, Indianapolis, Indiana.[5]

Articles regarding his work appeared in national publications such as: Survey Graphic, Time, Reader's Digest, Wall Street Journal, Newsweek, Coronet, Business Week, Fortune, Christian Herald, Journal of Housing, Today, and The Lilly Review. An eight-minute presentation of his work in housing was included in a nationwide NBC special telecast on Wednesday, November 29, 1961.

On May 9, 1934, Dr. Blackburn was married to Fannie Elizabeth Scott, who died on November 17, 1965. He later married Dora Atkins Powell. He has three children: Harriet Virginia (Mrs. C. J. Reynolds), Walter Scott, and Sara Ann (Mrs. Eldridge L. Morrison).[6]

Walter Massey
Physicist

The former dean of the college at Brown University, Walter Massey, a native of Hattiesburg, Mississippi, was appointed Director of the Argonne (Illinois) National Laboratory, a top United States Defense Department research facility. Dr. Massey, a Morehouse graduate, is also a faculty member within the physics department at the University of Chicago.

Argonne Laboratory, located twenty-five miles southwest of downtown Chicago, is one of the U.S. Department of Energy's major research centers. Dr. Massey is the primary supervisor of more than fifty employees and manages a million dollar-plus budget.[1]

Natalia Tanner Cain
Ephebiatricist

Natalia Tanner Cain, presently of Detroit, Michigan, is a pioneer in ephebiatrics—one of five hundred multi-disciplined professionals nationwide who are members of the Society of Adolescent Medicine, which concentrates on treating teen-agers and their illnesses. Dr. Cain was born in Jackson in 1923.[1]

Margaret Lawrence
Child Psychologist

Dr. Margaret Lawrence, is currently a practicing child psychiatrist and psychoanalyst at Harlem Hospital Center in New York and an associate clinical professor of psychiatry at Columbia University College of Physicians and Surgeons. She has received numerous awards and completed extensive research in her field. In 1975 she spoke at the annual meeting of the Hinds County Association for Mental Health. Originally from Mississippi, Dr. Lawrence now lives in Pomona, New York.[1]

Gwendolyn Nero Loper
Social Worker

Gwendolyn Nero Loper, Greenwood native, is a social worker at Jackson Veteran's Administration Hospital and a field instructor for Mississippi University for Women. She served as the first black president of the Jackson Young Women's Christian Association and the first black appointee to the State Board of Mental Health. In addition to her professional responsibilities, Gwendolyn Loper is a prominent civic and religious leader.[1]

Georgie Catchings Coleman
Nurse Anesthesiologist

Recognized as a woman with a mission, Georgie Catchings Coleman, a nurse anesthesiologist, commanded the respect of surgeons, physicians, nurses, and others with whom she worked. Formerly, an instructor of operating-room procedures in the New York City Hospital, she followed a suggestion to study anesthesiology and entered a program at Bellevue Hospital, where after graduation she remained as an instructor in that program.

In 1970, Coleman, a Jackson native returned to Mississippi and taught in the nurse-anesthesiology program at the University of Mississippi Medical Center. One year later, the university's trustee appointed her chairperson of that program. As chairperson, she converted, in 1974, the anesthesiology program from a certificate granting one into a baccalaureate curriculum, and in 1976 the first B.S. degree class in anesthesiology graduated. Currently, there are only ten such programs in the nation. Until June 1978, Coleman chaired the Medical Center's program. She resigned to become national educational consultant to the ten anesthesiology programs.[1]

Jennifer O. Hicks
Obstetrics and Gynecology Specialist

Jennifer O. Hicks, a native of Vicksburg and the daughter of Mr. and Mrs. Roosevelt Hicks, was appointed in July 1983 to the staff of the Claiborne County Community Health Center as obstetrics and gynecology specialist.

A graduate of Rosa A. Temple High School in Vicksburg, Dr. Hicks obtained the bachelor degree from Jackson State University and M.D. degree from Meharry Medical College in Nashville, Tennessee. While a student at Meharry Medical College, the student body elected her Miss Meharry in 1977. She also received the Robert Wood Johnson and Public Health Service scholarship.

Prior to joining the Claiborne County health staff, Dr. Hicks interned at the Homer G. Phillips Hospital in St. Louis, Missouri, and spent her first year of residency at the Max C. Starkloff Hospital of St. Louis University. Afterward she completed residency requirements at Baroness Erlanger Hospital at the University of Tennessee—Chattanooga.[1]

SPORTS

Among blacks, the realm of sports has provided the opportunity for success, escape from slums, and the avenue for fame and fortune. Yet, sports perpetuated the myth of blacks' brawn and whites' brains. Black athletes were generally viewed as nonintellectuals, symbolized as potent studs, and utilized as objects. In very few instances, did black athletes rise above these negative images. The media and the power brokers in recounting the lives of the black athletes never emphasized their academic achievements, service to the community, or capacity to engage in another profession.

For decades, blacks were excluded from professional sports beyond the collegiate level until 1947 when Jackie Robinson joined the Brooklyn Dodgers as a professional baseball player in a major league. Earlier James Owens had proven his ability to achieve at the 1936 Olympics in Munich, Germany, where he was the first American, black or white, to win three gold medals in track and field. His success astounded Adolf Hitler who believed in white supremacy. Jack Johnson's victory over Jack Dempsey crushed America's "Great White Hope" and blacks entered the boxing arena as champions. Blacks' success in these fields paved the way for black basketball and football collegiate players to compete professionally. And, black Mississippians entered the competition in record number. To name a few, there were such outstanding athletes as Marvin Woodson (football), Eugene Short (basketball), Willie McGee (track and field, football), Harold Jackson (football), Tommie Townsend (football), Reggie Collier (football), and the list is endless. Mentioned within this section are only a few of America's as well as Mississippi's greatest athletes.

Other black Mississippians have carved some enviable niches in athletics. Jack Spinks, of Toomsuba, was the first black Mississippian drafted into professional football. Spinks played professionally with the Pittsburgh Steelers, Green Bay Packers, and the New York Giants (NFC). He proudly wears the ring as a full-fledged member of the Giants championship team of 1956.

Bill Foster of Rodney was the first black from the state to play professional baseball. He was with the former Chicago American Giants for ten years.

A few other top competitors include, Willie McGee, Hattiesburg (Alcorn), coholder of the world's record 60-yard dash and the 100, who signed with the Los Angeles Rams. Also listed among professionals were: Willie Howard, Clarksdale (Alcorn); L. C. Greenwood, Canton (Arkansas); Roy Hilton, Hazlehurst (J.S.U.); Jerome Barkum, Gulfport (J.S.U.); Joe Owens, Columbia and Alex Price, Yazoo City (Alcorn); Donald Watts, Natchez (Xavier); John Outlaw, Clarksdale, Vernon Biggs, Gulfport (J.S.U.); Larry Estes, Louisville, (Alcorn); Floyd Rice and Larry Cameron, Natchez (Alcorn).

Walter Payton
Professional Football Record Breaker

Born under the sign of Leo, July 25, 1954, to Peter and Alyne Payton, Walter Jerry Payton grew up on the dusty streets of Columbia, Mississippi. There, evading the night watchman, he and playmate, Damon Earl, ran barefoot through the pickle factory located next to his home. Alone, Payton jumped aboard the flatbed freight cars as they eased through town or impersonated Sir Lancelot, Zorro, or Robin Hood. On one occasion he opted for solitude and fantasy football as Payton played to a cheering imaginary crowd in his backyard. "I'd throw up the ball, pretend it was a kickoff," reminisced Payton, "then run and fake and flip and fall down and get up again and call another play. Sometimes I'd pretend it was a pass. I'd run and catch it or dive for it."

Payton's fantasy transformed into reality, after graduating from Marion County Training School and enrolling at Jackson State University where he was awarded a baccalaureate degree in special education and matriculated as a graduate student in the master's degree program. As an undergraduate, Payton attracted the attention of pro scouts when he set an NCAA scoring record with 66 career touchdowns. Looking for a centerpiece for their rebuilding effort, the Chicago Bears selected the 5' 11", 204-pounder as their number one draft choice in 1975. This began the professional football career of Walter Payton.

The phantom crowds that cheered and applauded Walter as a boy showered him with accolades as a superstar for the Chicago Bears of the National Football League. He transformed the Windy City into "Payton Place," where adoring fans and the daily papers called him "Wonderful Walter." His fluid running style earned him the nickname "Sweetness," but his fearless approach to his job sometimes scared Chicago coach Jack Pardee and hometown fans. Still alive in the crowd's and coach's memory was the unforgettable running back, Gale Sayers who retired prematurely in 1971 after several knee operations. "There's a time when runners need to learn to give up, and Walter never gives up," says Pardee. "You don't keep twisting and turning when you know you're going to get killed." "He's always squirming," commented Sayers, "but he may pull something one of these days when somebody's got hold of him."[1]

In spite of the danger, Payton did not and does not disappoint his fans, team mates, or opponents. During his rookie year, former Cleveland Brown's fullback, Jim Brown watched and scrutinized Payton as he ran two plays and pegged him for the pinnacle. Thereafter, Brown remarked, "Walter had the quickness and the moves and the instincts of just a great runner. He was the most impressive back that I've seen come into the league in a long time." Fred O'Connor, Chicago's backfield coach asserted: "God must have taken a chisel and said, 'I'm gonna make me a halfback.' "[2] Payton, unaffected by fame and fortune constantly proved his concern for his fellow man, particularly his teammates; for instance, in the fourth quarter of a game between the Bears and the Lions, wide receiver James Scott of the Bears lay writhing on the ground, his ankle severely twisted. Suddenly, Walter Payton appeared, hefted the 191-pound Scott onto his shoulder, and carried him to the locker room. Provisions in his contract did not stipulate that Payton had to play medic. On the contrary, superstars stand in the huddle staring impassively at their own feet until the casualties have been removed. Walter Payton is not just a superstar, one of the highest-priced players in the National League, but he is a caring humanitarian who is sensitive to his teammates' emotional wounds as to their physical injuries. For example, Bob Avellini, newly deposed as the Bears' starting quarterback, was sent in to mop-up for starter Mike Phipps, with the Bears leading the Lions 35-7. As soon as Bob set foot on the field, the crowd greeted him with a barrage of boos. A cruel and insensitive moment, Bob endured and no one would have noticed if Payton had stayed on the sidelines and ignored the incident. Instead, he turned and confronted the Soldiers' Field mob with lusty cheers. The fans got the message, and turned an ugly situation into positive accolades. Had anyone else acted as Payton had, cynics would have suspected self-gratification and a narcissan would have waited to take his bows before the media. But Payton had dressed and left when the press arrived.[3]

Whenever possible, Payton shared the "limelights" with his teammates. At Jackson State where Payton scored 464 points, Payton habitually took a lineman with him whenever he was interviewed, a practice he maintains to this day. The blockers appreciated how he gave the football to them to spike everytime he scored. Usually the spiker was Guard Revie Sorey, because he usually got to the end zone first. "We don't get to be in the limelight very often," Sorey stated. Sorey, the most creative spiker on the squad, ordinarily delivered a smashing overhand. Once Sorey pretended the ball was a bomb. Revie placed the ball gently in the end zone, then he and Payton stared at it while slowly backing away and hissing. Then they ran off shouting, "Pow!" "Pow!" and waving their arms wildly. At the end of the 1976 season Payton was a bit more elaborate, he handed each offensive lineman more tangible evidence of his gratitude: an engraved gold watch. "Maybe it's all right to brag if you're Billie Jean King or Muhammad Ali," Payton declared. "But I'm in a team sport. It takes ten more guys, and I don't see why I should rip all the glory. But if my teammates didn't do their job well, mine would be a lot tougher and I wouldn't be the player I am."[4]

First impression would lead one to believe that Payton's vocation would have been working with children and basking in the glow of college-sweetheart-turned-wife Connie. Besides, it must be remembered that pro football is not exactly fun. "It's work," Payton says. "It's a job. It has never been fun for me." Actually, he never intended to play professional football. But the NFL paid big bucks—much more than special education teachers made—and Walter could not suppress his God-given ability.

Furthermore, Payton acknowledged God's role in his success as a football player. Walter's faith in God is something instilled in him by his mother and late father, Peter. According to Payton that strong religious faith has helped him to rise above the football mania of contract disputes, an over-bearing media, fickle fans, and losing seasons.

Religion with Walter is a personal matter and though he does not talk much, when he does people are impressed by his religious fervor and sincerity. "Whatever I accomplish I don't do by myself. The credit belongs to God—and the offensive line." "I've got peace of mind now," says the 26-year-old Payton. "When you've got peace of mind, you can deal with the adversity of not getting to the playoffs, not playing in the Superbowl because the Lord has something better for you. Life is like a maze. I choose which direction I'm going and then whatever happens after that is already planned. I don't have any control over it. The Lord always has something in store for you, so, I don't worry about it. I know that my relationship is with Christ. He shows me the way."[5]

Furthermore, Payton is duly humble in the presence of established greatness. "It's an honor or a challenge competing against O. J. Simpson," he says. "I always thought O. J., Jim Brown, and Gale Sayers were the premier running backs of all time. To be able to compete on the same level, that's really an honor. I just hope I can achieve as fast as O. J. When he went over 2,000 yards in 1973, I walked around campus jokingly saying that 2,000 yards in the NFL was my next goal. Now I wonder if I might ever be able to reach that. Records are made to be broken."

Walter Payton possesses self-confidence. When he was drafted in the first round by the Bears in 1975, without false modesty he proclaimed to the press: "I'm the best running back in the draft and everybody knows it." Then, he proceeded to prove his point when he voluntarily requested the rookie trials. He ranked first among the Bear rookies in pull-ups, bench presses and other tests, and further demonstrated his point by leap-frogging over the head of a six foot four inch Bear assistant coach. True, in his rookie year, he gained only a modest 679 yards. But, the very next season, he was off and running, rushing for 1,390; 1,852; 1,390; and 1,610 yards in the following four seasons. In 1979, if you add the 313 yards he contributed on pass receptions, Payton accounted for an unbelievable 41 percent of the Bear's total offense.

After the 1976 season in which he glided, collided, thumped, bumped, scratched, clawed, and ran 1,390 yards, Walter received a telegram from O. J. Simpson, the only running back that year to rush for more yardage. It read:

> Congratulations on an outstanding season. Having gained only 486 yards in my second season in the NFL, I marvel at your tremendous accomplishments for the Bears this fall. I know that before your career is finished, the records I own today will be gone and forgotten.[6]

Additional testimonies to his outstanding achievements came from sport writers and other athletes: Ron Harris of *Ebony* wrote, "Walter Payton is no doubt the best running back in football today." Alan Page, defensive tackle for the Bears, who played with the Minnesota Vikings in 1977 when Payton blew past them for 275 yards—the National Football League's single game rushing record, claimed Payton "can do it all. He can run around you, through you, over you, by you, and beside you." In addition, Tampa Bay Buccaneers defensive end Wally Chambers commented, "He's the best, no doubt about it. We held him to 42 yards rushing one game, and what does he do? He turns a screen pass into a 65-yard touchdown. The man is dangerous!" With only five years in the game, he is already over the 6,000 yard career mark. Except for his rookie year, Payton has rushed for over 1,000 yards each season, amassing a career high 1,853 yards (third to Simpson and Jim Brown) in 1977. Only a few players stand between Payton and Jim Brown's record of 12,312 yards. A perennial all-Pro, Payton also holds the records for most rushing attempts in one game (40) and one season (383).

When the 1980 season opened, Payton had amassed within five years an amazing 6,926 yards rushing record. Assuming that Payton remains healthy, it is predicted that he will surpass Simpson's total career yardage in three years, and Brown's in four. Already, he has practically erased Gale Sayer's name from the record books. However, by Payton's own admission, he is not a finesse runner. Rather, he's a big bruising back who runs over people. That's his style, and that is what some think may be his undoing. Bobby Bryant of the Minnesota Vikings, had this to say about defending against the pulverizing Bear runner: "The way I look at it, it's like trying to rope a calf. It's hard enough to get your hands on him and once you do, you wonder whether you should have."

Linebacker Jack (Hacksaw) Reynolds of the Anaheim Rams declared: "You can't tackle him below the waist, because his legs are going all over the place. The best place to zero in is right at his middle. You've got to get a firm hold on him there, like you would on your wife or your girl friend."

Jim Trimble, New York Giants' director of pro personnel compared Payton to Wilbert Montgomery of the Philadelphia Eagles, when he stated: "Walter is a blithe spirit. He's a bouncer, kicker, and hopper. Where Montgomery is more patient, Payton is like a pinball. He has unusual strength for a running back his size and, when he smashes into the line, you don't know where he's going to come out."[7]

Some sport critics however, castigated Payton for carrying his loyalties too far, and trying to shoulder too much of the Bear's burden alone. For example, in the 1979 playoff against the Eagles, Payton's 84-yard breakaway at the outset of the half was disallowed because of an illegal motion penalty. A disconsolate Payton, who carried the ball only five times for twenty-one yards in the second half, blamed himself for having let his teammates down. That day, the breaks were with the Eagles, who won 27-17.

Loyalty is a way of life for Payton, but coupled with that loyalty is a profound sense of dedication and perseverance. He surpassed Sayer's rushing record. During the best day of his two-year pro career, Payton ended the afternoon with 1,341 yeards on the ground—nine more than O. J.'s 1,332. Making and breaking records is not Payton's ultimate goal. "Records don't really matter to me," says the nonchalant hero who would be more comfortable labeled as Connie's husband, than the premier running back in football. With only six years behind him, Payton has over 8,000 yards rushing. Jim Brown, the Hall of Famer turned film idol, retired after nine seasons with 12,312 yards. Simpson quit in 1979 with 11,236 in 11 years. "I doubt that I'll play as many as eight years," predicted Payton. "I don't really care about catching Brown or anyone else. My only goal in this game is to quit football when I'm ready, and not when it forces me to quit."[8]

Payton, optimistically looks forward to his retirement day. "I realize that football is only a stage that I am going through. It will be over very soon," Payton lamented. "I've made plans to take care of my family and I'm glad that football gave me the opportunity to do it."

Payton is a man who comes from some place more important than a football huddle, however, and is headed for something bigger than a goal line or dusty record books. For three years he served as honorary chairman of the Illinois Mental Health Association. He makes appearances for the Boy Scouts, March of Dimes, Cancer Foundation, and the United Way. He has also been actively associated with the American Diabetes Association. His off-the-field interests include helping deaf and retarded children. After his rookie year, he began studying for a master's degree in education for the deaf.[9]

However he got his nickname "Sweetness," he has certainly sweetened the pot for his future. With the aid of his millionaire Mississippi attorney he is wisely investing his money. He is the sole stockholder of Walter Payton Enterprises, a project that would make Mother Goose jealous. Besides having a major interest in an antique Rolls-Royce business, Sweetness has a string of condominiums in San Diego, over nine hundred acres of timberland in north Mississippi, a seven-million-dollar, two-hundred-room Holiday Inn in Hattiesburg, a twenty-six acre shopping center nearby and owns a Lear jet."[10]

And there is a role-model for youth everywhere, irrespective of race, class or color.

Lusia Harris Stewart
Delta State's Lady Statesman

The athletic teams at Cleveland's predominantly white Delta State University (DSU) call themselves "Statesmen." In 1974 Lusia Harris, who prefers to be called "Lucy," was the first and only black basketball player to be recruited. Her statesmanship was never in question as she led the virtually unknown Delta State to three state championships, two regional titles, two national championships, and was a member of the Pan-American and U.S. Olympic Women's Teams.

Lucy the basketball phenomenon and the seventh of nine siblings, grew up on a vegetable farm in Minter City, population 200, located about 24 miles east of Cleveland. The dean's list student started playing basketball with her brothers and sisters in their backyard when she was about eleven or twelve years old. She played on the Tucker Young Junior High School and the Amanda Elzy High School teams in Greenwood. Lucy recalls that they had a very good team then. "We always got to the state (finals), but we never won."[1]

For approximately three years, Lady Statesman Harris set record after record for Delta State and the nation. "With a 31 point average per game, Lucy held 15 of 13 individual DSU records and in the summer of 1976 set an Olympic record which will never be broken when she scored the first basket ever recorded in women's Olympic basketball. Not only did she make the first score, but Lucy led the silver medal-winning U.S. team in total scoring for the entire games. The U.S. team had never placed better than eighth in international competition before."[2]

A survey of coaches in *Sports Illustrated* named Lucy "the best all around offensive player in women's basketball."[3] And she was among the thirteen women athletes nominated by Women Sports Athlete of the Year (1977).

Delta State Statesmen, the first Mississippi team to play in Madison Square Garden, defeated Queens College in 1976 and capped a 51 game winning streak. Lucy Harris scored a dazzling 47 points and broke the Garden's high score record that season for male or female, college or pro. At that time the all-time record for the Garden was 56 points. Lucy's high was 58.

Lucy Harris broke other records at Delta State. After the 1976 Olympics, Mississippi Governor Cliff Finch proclaimed "Lusia Harris Day" in the Magnolia State and led a state delegation to Cleveland to pay tribute to one of Mississippi's best known personalities. In 1975, Delta State University's student body selected Lucy as its first black homecoming queen. DSU's president, Kent Wyatt said, "She's just fantastic. She is the best thing we ever had. . . . She is more than just a superior basketball player. She is a B+ student, a campus leader, and a goodwill ambassador for our university, the state of Mississippi and the country."[4]

Reportedly, the 6' 3" black woman was very conscientious about her school work. Unlike many athletes she did not cut classes, nor did she accept special treatment. Even while on the road, she traveled with her textbooks. After a home game in which she scored 37 points to lead the team to a victory, Lucy was asked if she would go out and celebrate. "No," she replied, "I am going to my room. I have six classes tomorrow. I can't afford to celebrate tonight."[5]

Pete Brown

Professional Golfer

Of the few top black golfers, Pete Brown, born near Port Gibson, ranks high. In 1964 Pete Brown won the Waco Turner Open, the first PGA tournament ever won by a Negro. But to fully appreciate Pete Brown one has to remember that at age twenty-four he was cut down by polio, after his biggest success to that time, the 1956 Michigan Open. "Everything he strived for seemed lost. And he was lost, over 1,000 miles from home, penniless, virtually friendless. But Pete Brown dared to hope . . . dared to persevere . . . dared to envision rising to greater heights than any black man despite his affliction. His enthusiasm finally proved his salvation."[1]

In February 1970, Pete Brown won a dramatic sudden-death play-off victory over Britain's Tony Jacklin in the $150,000 Andy Williams-San Diego Open. "Faced by a battery of photographers and TV cameramen, Brown cheerfully accepted the $30,000 first-prize check from singer Williams."[2]

In June 1970 Mississippi honored Earlie "Pete" Brown for his outstanding achievement. Mayor Russell Davis presented Brown with a Jackson City Council resolution in the form of a plaque, citing his achievements as a professional golfer and his contributions to the rest of the nation on behalf of Mississippi. Mayor Davis called Pete

Brown the "best golfer Jackson ever produced." "It is rare that a Negro is honored in Mississippi for any sort of professional achievement," said David Davidson, sports writer, of the *Jackson Daily News*.[3]

Spencer Haywood
Basketball Superstar

Spencer Haywood, basketball superstar, native of Silver Springs, led the U.S. to the gold medal in basketball at the 1968 Olympics in Mexico City. He matriculated at the University of Detroit but signed with the ABA's Denver Rockets after his sophomore season. He quickly became the ABA's leading scorer and rebounder, its Most Valuable Player and Rookie of the Year (1970). Supposedly several ABA teams propositioned Haywood to leave Denver during that season. When Rocket-owner, Bill Ringsby, learned of those behind the scenes maneuvers, he "rewarded" his young star with a new six-year contract reportedly valued at $1.9 million. Over the summer, Haywood decided that his contract was not all it was alleged to be and refused to report for the new season.

So, after only one year as an ABA allstar, Haywood jumped leagues and joined the Seattle Super Sonics. Both moves, of signing a professional contract as an undergraduate and switching leagues, were pro-basketball firsts. In 1972, Haywood became the youngest team captain in the NBA and Seattle's first black captain.[1]

Eugene Short
Basketball Pro

Eugene Short of Hattiesburg, the six foot, five inch forward, led Jackson State University's basketball team to a number one ranking in the National Association of Intercollegiate Athletics, polls in 1975. After pleading financial hardship, he signed what is believed to be the richest pack contract ever inked by a Mississippian, when he joined the New York Knickerbockers of the National Basketball Association. The contract, negotiated for Short by Hattiesburg attorney Bud Holmes, was a long-term agreement worth just over one million dollars. Short spent only two years in the NBA, however, before he was traded to the Seattle Supersonics. He later went back to the Knickerbockers and was cut from the team. Eugene Short's brother, Purvis, made the NBA with the Golden State Warriors.[1]

George Scott
All-Star Baseball Player

George Scott, one of the best known Mississippi athletes, started his baseball career as a youngster, using old broom handles for bats and cheap balls with sawdust stuffings. He is now making in excess of $100,000 per year as a member of the Boston Red Sox and is a favorite in the traditional All-star game.

After graduating from Greenville's Coleman High, Scott stated that approximately sixty colleges offered him baseball scholarships. UCLA even wanted me to go out there and play baseball. But the lure of immediate cash as a pro-baseball player proved too great for Scott to refuse, and he signed with the Boston Red Sox in 1962. Scott still spends considerable time in Greenville during the off season, conducting baseball clinics and visiting his mother.[1]

Mildrette Netter
Track Gold Medalist

Mildrette "Midge" Netter, Rosedale native, has received many honors as Mississippi's most prominent female athlete, including a Gold Medal at the 1968 Olympics. Alcorn track coach, Dr. G. A. Dungee, declared Netter as one of the best women athletes he has ever coached, notwithstanding the fact that he has served twice as the U.S. Olympic female track coach. She obtained the B.S. and M.Ed. in physical education from Alcorn State University.[1]

MILITARY

Although black Mississippians have fought and died for America's freedom out of a sense of patriotism—voluntarily, in most instances—it took approximately eight wars and 300 years before they and other blacks gained any semblance of equality in the military. On July 26, 1948, President Harry S. Truman issued executive order number 9981 which declared that "there shall be equality of treatment and opportunity for all persons in the armed services without regard to race, color, religion or national origin. This policy shall be put into effect as rapidly as possible. . . ."[1]

From the French and Indian War to the war in Viet Nam, blacks have fought to preserve freedom and democracy, not only abroad but in the United States as well. Prior to Truman's proclamation, "the military was frought with prejudices; fears of insurrections by armed black men in the early days of the Republic; charges of cowardice by black men in the face of the enemy, and numerous other subterfuges designed to deny the Negro his rightful place as a citizen of this nation."[2]

Initially, fear of revolts and race wars prevented the recruiting and enlisting of blacks into the armed services. Lack of available manpower and total mobilization of white soldiers forced the government to enlist blacks in the military. In every war and battle, blacks were exemplary of loyalty and heroic action and deeds. They fought in the American Revolution for freedom, in the War of 1812 for commercial right and freedom of seas, in the Civil War for the preservation of the union, in the Spanish-American War for American expansionism and manifest destiny, in World War I and World War II to insure the balance of power in Europe, and to make America safe for democracy and, in Korea and Viet Nam for the containment of communism. In each of these wars, the black soldier experienced racism. In spite of Truman's executive order and desegregation of the military, subtle racism and discriminatory practices still exist.

Black Mississippians in the military, like Ensign Jesse Leroy Brown, have achieved military honors and displayed conspicuous bravery. Others like Colonel Thomas Money have commanded battalions, companies, and regions. But many, enlisted men and officers, have been poorly treated when stationed abroad, not by the citizens of foreign countries but by the rank and file within the military. Many were denied promotion and technical training because they were black. They were segregated into all-black units and placed on the front line of the battle zone. When they returned to Mississippi and other southern states, they were discriminated against and, in most instances, not employed.

Racism in the military has been legally banned, but one cannot legislate away racism ingrained in attitude. And one day, it is hoped, when a black and white soldier from Mississippi are fighting in the same foxhole, neither will wonder "Will he stand with me when the shooting starts? Will he try to help me if I am wounded—even though there is a good chance it might cost him his life?"

Thomas J. Money, Jr.
Military Officer-Community Leader

Thomas J. Money, Jr., United States Air Force, retired, was born in Vicksburg, Mississippi. After graduation from Magnolia Avenue High School in 1935, he enrolled in Morehouse College, Atlanta, Georgia, where he received a B.S. degree in June 1939. In September 1939, he attended Atlanta University where he remained one semester before accepting employment with the Welfare Administration, Chicago, Illinois.[1]

Colonel Money was drafted into the armed services on March 7, 1941. Upon completion of basic training at Camp Wolters, Texas, he was retained as an instructor and battalion clerk. In 1941 he was transferred to the Army Air Corps at Chanute Field, Illinois, and Tuskegee Air Field, Alabama. During his first seven months in the Army Air Corps, he held the grades of private, private first class, corporal, sergeant, staff sergeant, technical sergeant, and master sergeant. As an Aviation Cadet, he entered Officer Candidate School at Miami Beach, Florida, in June 1942 and was commissioned a Second Lieutenant, Army Air Corps, in September 1942.

During World War II, he served in Italy with an F-51 fighter group under the command of Benjamin O. Davis, Jr. He returned to the States in 1945 and was stationed at Godman Field, Kentucky, and Lockbourne Air Force Base, Ohio, with a B-25 group. Upon desegregation of the U.S. Air Force and the closure of the all-black Lockbourne Air Base in 1948, Colonel Money was assigned to the Pentagon, Washington, D.C., where he worked in the Officers' Assignment Division for four years. His next military assignment took him to Bitburg, Germany, where he was Wing Personnel Officer for an F-86 fighter day wing. From Bitburg, the Air Force transferred Money to 12th Air Force headquarters Ramstein, Germany, where he remained for two years as the Director of Military Personnel.

Returning to the States in 1957, Money was employed as Professor of Air Science, AFROTC, at Howard University in Washington, D.C., where he taught for three and one-half years. From Howard University he was sent to Headquarters command, USAF, Bolling Air Force Base, Washington, D.C., where he acted as assistant Deputy Chief of Staff for Personnel. Upon his promotion to Colonel in March 1963, he was reassigned as the Deputy Commander for Personnel, Bolling Air Force Base, until his departure for Japan in August 1965.

Colonel Money served as Director of Personnel at Tackikawa Air Base, Japan until September 1968 at which time he returned to the United States and assumed duties in the Office of the Assistant Secretary of Defense for Manpower and Reserve Affairs, the Pentagon. In August 1970, he became Director of Compensation Administration, in the Office of the Assistant Secretary of Defense and fulfilled his obligations in this capacity until his retirement on July 1, 1971. His decorations and awards as a member of the Armed Forces include: the Legion of Merit, Army Commendation medal, Air Force Commendation medal with two Oak Leaf Clusters, Certificates of Appreciation from Presidents John F. Kennedy and Richard M. Nixon, and key to Tokyo, Japan, from the Governor of Tokyo Metropolitan Government.

Upon his retirement from the Air Force, Colonel Money journeyed to Vicksburg where he became involved in volunteer work in the community. In April 1972, he was employed by the Mississippi Power and Light Company in Jackson as Administrative Assistant to the President. One year later the U.S. Army Engineer Waterways Experiment Station hired him as the Equal Employment Opportunity Officer in Vicksburg.

Colonel Money, in addition to working full-time at the Waterways Experiment Station, is active in the community. He has served as president of the Vicksburg-Warren Branch NAACP; treasurer, League of Women Voters of Vicksburg Area; board member of the League of Women Voters of Mississippi, the Warren County Alcohol and Drug Advisory Committee, the Children and Youth Clinic Advisory Committee, the Central Sub-Area Council of the Mississippi Health Systems Agency, and the Kuhn Hospital Ambulatory Care Governing Board. Colonel Money is a member of the Port City Kiwanis Club, Alcorn State University Industry Cluster, Tougaloo College Industry Cluster, and the Unity Breadfeast Club in Vicksburg.

In 1946, Colonel Money married Annie Lucy Dillard. They have a daughter, Rose, who resides with her husband in Washington, D.C.

Jesse Leroy Brown
First Black Naval Aviator

Born in Hattiesburg, Mississippi, on October 13, 1926, Jesse Leroy Brown, one of five children—four boys and a girl—of Alice Brown a school teacher, and John Brown, a farmer, became the first black naval aviator. Described as a serious, witty, unassuming, and very intelligent individual, Brown graduated from Eureka High School in Hattiesburg as salutatorian of his class. While in high school, Brown was a member of the basketball, football, and track team. After graduation, he matriculated at Ohio State University's college of engineering, where he maintained a straight "A" average for three years, prior to enlisting in the U.S. Naval Reserve, July 8, 1946. The following year on March 15, he reported for active duty.[1]

Less than a month later, April 15, Brown's enlistment ended, and he accepted the appointment as a naval midshipman. Afterwards, he enrolled at the Navy's "lily-white" pre-flight school in Ottumwa, Iowa, and completed his flight training at the naval air training centers in Pensacola and Jacksonville, Florida. While training in Pensacola, Jesse Brown was confronted with overt racism. In order to cope with "Nigger" taunts and ridicules by flight instructors and classmates, Brown, a self-disciplined and determined individual risked wings, commission, and future naval career to secretly marry his high school sweetheart, Daisy Pearl Nix, who later mothered his only child—Pamela, born December 23, 1948. (Naval regulations forbade marriage while in flight training.) His devoted wife and companion provided him with support and encouragement during trying periods of frustration. Despite acts of overt racism by naval personnel and colleagues, Brown was one of six graduates out of an initial enrollment of approximately one hundred. His perseverance earned him the distinction of becoming the first black aviator on October 21, 1948, eight days after his 22nd birthday. Seven months later, he received his commission as ensign and was attached to the Air Force, U.S. Atlantic Fleet.[2]

For Jesse Leroy Brown, his commission symbolized a dream realized. No longer would he pick cotton or gaze up at the sky when he heard an airplane and proclaim, "Someday I'm going to fly one of those".[3]

Although racial discrimination did not cease, being an officer brought relief. Subsequently, he earned the respect of fellow officers as he proved his capabilities as a naval pilot. In January 1949, Brown joined Fighter Squadron Thirty-two and as a pilot of that squadron, operating from the U.S.S. aircraft carrier, LEYTE (CVL-49), he flew twenty missions in the combat area off the northeast coast of Korea, from October to December, 1950. As a pilot of Fighter Squadron Thirty-two, Ensign Brown became a section leader and was posthumously awarded the Air Medal "for daring attacks against enemy lines of communication, transportation, facilities, military installations, and troop concentrations at Wonsan, Chongpu, Songjim and Senanju" during the Korean conflict. He skillfully led his section into hostile anti-aircraft fire, thereby "inflicting serious losses on the enemy and provided effective support for friendly ground forces".[4]

Brown's reputation as a skillful naval pilot was almost impeccable. As Lieutenant Thomas Hudner related, "I knew who he was when we new aviators joined the squadron. Jesse had been aboard for about a year and had one Mediterranean cruise under his belt, and with an experience like that he was recognized by those who knew him as being one of the squadron's more experienced pilots." Also, the operations officer of the Leyte, Commander E. Day asserted, that Brown "was a man and sold himself as a man."[5]

However, Brown made a few flight mistakes, such as landing his aircraft on deck of the ship. For example, according to Ensign Lee Nelson—one day "(Jesse) was high and slow at the 'cut' and dropped in hard on the landing, and bounced high—ten or twelve feet. The hook did not catch a wire, and we expected him to fall out of the sky for another hard landing and probably crash into the barrier." But, Jesse Brown's skill, intelligence, and experience allowed him to make a routine carrier landing after his airplane "Veered to the right, just missing the front end of the island structure".[6] Irregardless of the mishap, Jesse Brown proved his aviation skills and gave his life for freedom while on a naval mission in Korea.

Perhaps on the eve of December 3, 1950, Jesse Brown had a premonition that his assigned mission scheduled for December 4, might be his last. That night he wrote his wife Daisy concerning Christmas presents for their daughter; he also expressed his fears about the inclement weather and his squadron's efforts to support marines who were trapped by the Chinese. In closing his correspondence to his wife he expressed his love and loneliness when he remarked, "I honestly dread going to bed, but I usually dream of you so I'll manage to make it until we share our bed together again—darling, pray that it'll be soon. I have to fly tomorrow. But so far as that goes my heart hasn't been down to earth since the first time you kissed me, and when you love me you 'send' it clear out-of-this world. I'll write again as soon as I can. I'll love you forever."[7] This was the last correspondence Daisy Nix Brown received before her husband's death.

On December 4, 1950, Ensign Jesse Brown was one of four naval pilots scheduled to make an armed reconnaissance flight that afternoon. The other pilots were Lieutenant Commander Richard L. Cevoli, Lieutenant Thomas Hudner, Jr., and Lieutenant William Koenig.

An hour after launch, the four pilots had observed nothing of significance, then Brown's plane was struck by enemy fire and crashed. Prior to the crash, explained Lieutenant Hudner, "Brown called out that he had been hit, that he was losing oil pressure, and that he could not maintain altitude."[8] Brown, trapped in his burning airplane behind enemy lines, waved to his fellow commanderies for assistance. Hudner responded in subfreezing temperature. Hudner landed about 100 yards from Brown's wreckage where he discovered that Ensign Brown's leg was pinned down by a broken fuselage, and that Brown had discarded his helmet and gloves in a futile effort to free himself. As a result of this endeavor, Brown's hands were virtually frozen. Disregarding danger to himself, Hudner with bare hands packed the fuselage with snow to keep flames away from Ensign Brown, and unsuccessfully attempted to free him. Hudner radioed for help. A rescue helicopter manned by First Lieutenant Charles Ward, a marine arrived but Jesse was barely conscious as he plead with the men to rescue him. Working with an ax and fire extinguisher, Ward and Hudner worked for about forty-five minutes but could not remove Brown from the burning wreckage. Wavering between consciousness and unconsciousness, Brown spoke of his wife and daughter, but fate would not allow him to see either of them again. As dusk approached, Ward and Hudner returned to the base after assuming that Brown was dead. Brown's body was never retrieved; however, sometime later, "several pilots flew to the crash site, found the plane, and saw Jesse's body still in the cockpit, but now stripped of clothing. In a Valkgrian tribute to their fallen friend, they flew over him and dropped napalm, cremating the Navy's first black aviator," who thus became the first black American naval aviator to lose his life in combat.[9]

He was awarded posthumously the Air Medal, and the Distinguished Flying Cross. The Distinguished Flying Cross citation read in part as follows:

"For heroism and extraordinary achievement... in action... from October 12 to December 4, 1950, his exceptional courage, airmanship, and devotion to duty in the face of great danger reflect the highest credit upon Ensign Brown and the United States Naval Service. He gallantly gave his life for his country."[4] In addition, he received the Purple Heart Medal for wounds received in enemy action. To accept his awards were Daisy Brown, his widow, and Pamela Brown, his daughter.[10]

To further honor the heroic Ensign Jesse Leroy Brown, a U.S. naval ship was named the USS Jesse L. Brown (DE-1089), a knox class ocean escort which is capable of conducting search patrol, rescue, evacuation, blockade, and surveillance operations. This ship was constructed and then launched March 18, 1972, at the Avondale Shipyards in Westwego, Louisiana, under the sponsorship of his widow, Mrs. Daisy Brown Thorne. At the christening or commissioning of the ship, his daughter Pamela served as Matron of Honor. The principal address was given by Captain Thomas L. Hudner, USN.[11] At this date, 1983, Hattiesburg's city officials plan to memorialize Ensign Jesse Brown with a granite citation located in the town's square. A street and Elk club bear his name.[12]

John Mitchell Brown

Brigadier General, United States Army

A native of Vicksburg, Mississippi, John Mitchell Brown, who was born December 11, 1929, received his B.S. degree in engineering from the United States Military Academy and the M.B.A. degree in comptrollership from Syracuse University. Later he matriculated at the University of Houston, where he completed the advanced management program. Realizing the importance of superior military training, Brown successfully completed basic and advanced courses in military science at the army's infantry school. Soon afterward, he continued his military education at the United States Army Command and General Staff College and the Industrial College of the Armed Forces.[1]

Because of his excellent academic and military achievements, Brown was rapidly promoted from second lieutenant on June 3, 1955, to Brigadier General on June 3, 1979. During his twenty-six years in the Army, his military assignments included several important positions. He worked as operation research analyst and later as chief of the cost methodology branch and directorate of cost analysis for the office of Comptroller of the Army in Washington, D.C. From August 1970 to July, 1971, he served as assistant secretary of the general staff and then as commander of the first Battalion, 87th Infantry, 8th Infantry Division in Europe. He was a student at the Industrial College of the Armed Forces at Fort Lesley J. McNair in Washington, D.C. He also served as executive to the comptroller of the Army Washington Command, 3rd Brigade, 2nd Infantry Division in Korea, as assistant chief of staff comptroller of the United Nations Command in Korea, and as assistant division commander of the Second Infantry Division in Korea. In 1979 Brown was promoted as deputy director of Material Plans and Programs and Acquisition for the United States Army in Washington, D.C.

For his heroism, military astuteness, and educational training, Brigadier General John Mitchell Brown was decorated and awarded the following medals: Legion of Merit, Bronze Star, Meritorious Service, army commendation medal (with two oak leaf clusters), combat infantryman badge, parachutist badge, and the ranger tab.

Modis A. Smiley
National Guard

Specialist Four Modis A. Smiley of Philadelphia became the first black Mississippi National Guardsman to receive the state's Magnolia Cross award and a medal for an act of valor. The presentation was made by Governor Waller and Major General E. A. Beby, adjutant general of Mississippi. He joined the Mississippi National Guard in 1970. Awards are not new to Smiley, pastor of the Bakley Avenue Church of Christ in Philadelphia. A veteran of the Korean War, he holds the Korean Service Medal with three bronze stars, the United Nation's Service Medal, and a National Defense Service Medal. This most recent citation was for rescuing three people from a burning automobile, following a two-car collision in which without regard to his personal safety, he pulled Jesse Hardy, Jr., and his two daughters, from the flames just before the gasoline tank exploded engulfing both cars.[1]

Glennie M. Rowland
First Female Officer-ASU

Few females, black or white, have been allowed in the heirarchy of the military until recently. Today, they are few in number. Among that group is Major Glennie M. Rowland, a native of Lake, Mississippi. The Military Police Corps Branch Officer received a bachelor degree in business administration from Mississippi Valley State University and a masters degree in criminal justice from Troy State University in Alabama. Before becoming the first female officer assigned to the teaching staff at Alcorn State University, Major Rowland served as First battalion executive officer for the First battalion School Brigade at Fort Benning, Georgia. At Alcorn, Major Rowland serves as administration officer and instructor of the military science senior class.[1]

Daniel L. Jennings
Viet Nam Veteran

Claiborne county native, Daniel L. Jennings, retired as one of the most decorated men of the Viet Nam War. While serving in Viet Nam, Jenning's valor was exemplified in the number of medals awarded the United States Army such as the Silver Star, Bronze Star, the Army Commendation Medal for Valor, two Purple Hearts, and the Vietnam Cross of Gallantry.[1]

Notes

POLITICS

1. The 'grandfather clause' stipulated that a person was qualified to vote if his relatives voted prior to January 1, 1867. Blacks in the south received the right to vote March 1867.
2. The "understanding clause" required a prospective voter to be able to read and interpret a section of the state or federal Constitution.
3. The white primary law stipulated that in order for a voter to cast a vote in the general election, he must have voted in the primary. By law only white Democrats could vote in the primary.
4. Black individuals convicted of misdemeanors or felonies were denied the right to vote.
5. Jackson *Advocate*, 21–27 February 1980; New York *Times* 27 February 1980.
6. Ibid.
7. Ibid.
8. Ibid.

Hiram Rhodes Revels

1. A. C. McClure, *The South* (Philadelphia: Lippincott, 1886), 115–16; Hiram R. Revels, "Autobiography" (Unpublished ms., John D. Boyd Library, Alcorn State University, Lorman, Mississippi); Joseph G. de R. Hamilton, "Revels, Hiram Rhodes," *Dictionary of American Biography*.
2. Hiram R. Revels, "Memoirs" (Unpublished ms., John D. Boyd Library, Alcorn State University, Lorman, Mississippi); Benjamin Brawley, *A Social History of the American Negro* (New York: Collier-Macmillan Co., 1970), 269.
3. William J. Simmons, *Men of Mark* (New York: Arno Press and New York Times, 1968), 948–50.
4. Ibid.; George A. Sewell, "Hiram Rhodes Revels: Another Evaluation," *Negro History Bulletin* 38 (December 1974-January 1975): 336–38.
5. Revels, "Memoirs."
6. Melerson Guy Dunham, *A Centennial History of Alcorn A & M College* (Hattiesburg: University and College Press of Mississippi, 1971), 11; Maurine Christopher, *America's Black Congressmen* (New York: Thomas Y. Crowell, 1971), 2; John J. Morant, *Mississippi Preachers* (New York: Vantage Press, 1958), 47.

7. Revels, "Memoirs"; Lerone Bennett, "Black Power: Freedmen Seize Reins in the South Backed By Strong Vote Bill," *Ebony*, November 1965, 32.
8. John R. Lynch, *Facts of Reconstruction* (New York: The Neale Publishing Co., 1913), 38–44.
9. John Hope Franklin, *An Autobiography of John R. Lynch* (Chicago: The University of Chicago Press, 1970), 80; *Political Participation* (Washington, D. C.: U. S. Commission on Civil Rights, 1968), 3.
10. Simmons, *Men of Mark*, 949; Norman P. Andrews, "The Negro in Politics," *Journal of Negro History* 8 (October 1920): 423.
11. Samuel D. Smith, *The Negro in Congress* (Port Washington, New York: Kennikat Press, 1940), 15.
12. Smith, *The Negro in Congress*, 17; Monroe N. Works, *Negro Year Book: An Annual Encyclopedia of the Negro, 1914–1915* (Tuskegee Institute, Alabama: The Negro Year Book Publishing Company, 1915), 207.
13. Christopher, *America's Black Congressmen*, 5.
14. Ibid., 7.
15. Smith, *The Negro in Congress*, 17.
16. Ibid., 19.
17. Samuel D. Smith, "The Negro in the United States Senate," *Essays in Southern History*, ed. Fletcher M. Green (Chapel Hill: University of North Carolina Press, 1949), 52.
18. Smith, "The Negro in the United States Senate," 20.
19. Ibid.
20. Christopher, *America's Black Congressmen*, 9.
21. *The Congressional Globe*, February 8, 1871, 41st Congress, 3rd Session, 1059–60.
22. James A. Garner, *Reconstruction in Mississippi* (Baton Rouge: Louisiana State University Press, 1968), 368.
23. Ibid., 369–70; Revels, "Autobiography"; Dunham, *A Centennial History of Alcorn A & M College*,18.
24. Dunham, *A Centennial History of Alcorn A & M College*, 18.
25. Ibid.
26. Lerone Bennett, *Before the Mayflower* (Chicago: Johnson Publishing Co., 1962), 20.
27. Harry Gholson to R. B. Garrett, October 1958, collection of George Sewell.
28. Simmons, *Men of Mark*, 950.
29. Vernon L. Wharton, *The Negro in Mississippi, 1865–1890* (New York: Harper and Row, 1965), 160.

Blanche Kelso Bruce

1. Christopher, *America's Black Congressmen*, 15.
2. Frank Ellis Smith and Audrey Warren, *Mississippians All* (New Orleans: Pelican Publishing House, 1968), 46.
3. Ibid.
4. Lynch, *Facts of Reconstruction*, 80; Smith, *The Negro in Congress*, 26; John W. Cromwell, *The Negro in American History* (Washington: The American Negro Academy, 1914), 163.
5. Smith and Warren, *Mississippians All*, 47.
6. Ibid., 49.
7. Ibid.
8. Ibid.
9. Ibid., 50.
10. Cromwell, *The Negro in American History*, 167.

11. Christopher, *America's Black Congressmen*, 16; Smith and Warren, *Mississippians All*, 50–51.
12. Smith and Warren, *Mississippians All*, 51.
13. Christopher, *America's Black Congressmen*, 16; Smith and Warren, *Mississippians All*, 50–51.
14. Christopher, *America's Black Congressmen*, 16; Smith and Warren, *Mississippians All*, 50–51; Andrews, "The Negro in Politics," *Journal of Negro History*, 421–23, 431.
15. Smith and Warren, *Mississippians All*, 28; Christopher, *America's Black Congressmen*, 180.
16. *Biographical Sketch of Hon. Pinckney Benton Stewart Pinchback*, Moorland-Spingarn Collection, Manuscript Division, Howard University, Washington, D. C.; David Houston, "A Negro Senator," *Journal of Negro History* 8 (July 1922): 244; Christopher, *America's Black Congressmen*, 18–19; Blanche K. Bruce Papers, Moorland-Spingarn Collection, Manuscript Division, Howard University, Washington, D. C.; John Hope Franklin, *From Slavery to Freedom: A History of Negro Americans* (New York; Alfred A. Knopf, 1967), 320.
17. Corinne Hare Williams, "The Migration of the Negro to the West" (M.A. thesis, Howard University, 1944); Mark M. Krug, "On Rewriting of U. S. History Textbook," *Journal of Negro History* 66 (April 1961): 153; Christopher, *America's Black Congressmen*, 19.
18. Ibid.; Benjamin Brawley, *Negro Builders and Heroes* (Chapel Hill: The University of North Carolina Press, 1937), 129–31; C. C. Mosley, *The Negro in Mississippi History* (Jackson: Hederman Brothers Publishers, 1950), 51–52; Blanche K. Bruce, *The Mississippi Election: Speech of Blanche K. Bruce in the U. S. Senate March 31, 1876* (Washington, D. C. 1876), 9–13.
19. Letters addressed to Bruce regarding violence in Mississippi, Blanche K. Bruce Papers, Moorland-Spingarn Research Center, Manuscript Division, Howard University, Washington, D. C.
20. Christopher, *America's Black Congressmen*, 19–20; Patrick W. Riddleberger, "The Radical Abandonment of the Negro During Reconstruction," (April 1960): 88–102; J. J. Spellman to Bruce, 15 March 1896, Bruce Papers, Moorland-Spingarn Research Center.
21. *Cincinnati Commercial Appeal*, 8 February 1878; J. Multon Turner, Consul Minister to Liberia, to Bruce, Bruce Papers, 1877.
22. *Detroit Plaindealer*, 15 February 1878.
23. *New York Times*, 15 February 1878.
24. Smith and Warren, *Mississippians All*, 53–54.
25. Ibid.
26. Brawley, *Negro Builders and Heroes*, 129–31.
27. Ibid.; *New York Tribune*, 17 October 1883; J. W. Manigaulte.
28. Smith, *The Negro in Congress*, 40–41.
29. Cromwell, *The Negro in American History*, 170; Sadie Daniel St. Clair, "The National Career of Blanche K. Bruce" (Ph.D. dissertation, New York University, 1947); Mosley, *The Negro in Mississippi History*, 49. However, Smith (*The Negro in Congress*) says Bruce was buried in Woodlawn Cemetery where J. M. Langston was buried (p. 4).
30. Brawley, *Negro Builders and Heroes*, 127.
31. Smith and Warren, *Mississippians All*, 58.

John R. Lynch

1. *The Clarion Ledger–Jackson Daily News*, 15 March 1973.
2. John Hope Franklin, ed., *The Autobiography of John R. Lynch* (Chicago: University of Chicago Press, 1970), 10 (hereafter cited as *Autobiography*).

3. *Autobiography*, 14.
4. Ibid., 41.
5. Ibid., 42–43.
6. John R. Lynch, *Facts of Reconstruction* (New York: Neale Publishing Co., 1913), 27.
7. Ibid., 29.
8. Ibid.; *Autobiography*, p. xiii.
9. *Autobiography*, 84.
10. Ibid.
11. Lynch, *Facts of Reconstruction*, 64–65.
12. Ibid., 67–68.
13. *Autobiography*, p. xiv.
14. Ibid., 102–03; Andrews, "The Negro in Politics," *Journal of Negro History*, 426–36.
15. *Autobiography*, p. xv.
16. Ibid., p. xv–xvi.
17. Ibid., p. xvi.
18. John R. Lynch file, Mississippi Department of Archives and History.
19. Wharton, *The Negro in Mississippi, 1865–1890*, 162.
20. Ibid.; Samuel D. Smith, *The Negro in Congress* (Port Washington, New York: Kennikat Press, Inc.), 86.
21. *Congressional Record*, 43rd Congress, 2nd Session, 943.
22. Kenneth E. Mann, "John Roy Lynch, U. S. Congressman from Mississippi," *Negro History Bulletin* 37 (April/May 1974): 238.
23. Ibid.; *Autobiography*, p. xvii.
24. L. E. Murphy, "The Civil Rights Law of 1875," *Journal of Negro History* 12 (April 1927): 110–27.
25. Christopher, *America's Black Congressmen*, 59.
26. *Autobiography*, p. xix.
27. Ibid., 167.
28. Ibid.; Christopher, *America's Black Congressmen*, 60.
29. Christopher, *America's Black Congressmen*, 60.
30. *Autobiography*, 174–75; Smith, *The Negro in Congress*, 87.
31. *Autobiography*, 181–83.
32. Ibid., 186–87.
33. Lynch, *Facts of Reconstruction*, 191.
34. *Autobiography*, 186.
35. Christopher, *America's Black Congressmen*, 62.
36. *Autobiography*, 226.
37. Christopher, *America's Black Congressmen*, 63.
38. Ibid., 63–64.
39. Ibid., 64.
40. *Autobiography*, p. xxix.
41. Ibid.; Christopher, *America's Black Congressmen*, 63–64.
42. Mann, "John Roy Lynch, U. S. Congressman from Mississippi," 240.
43. Robert Stephen Newbery, "John Roy Lynch" (M.A. thesis, University of Wisconsin, 1970): 10.

James Lynch

1. Wharton, *The Negro in Mississippi, 1865–1890*, 154.
2. Ibid.
3. Ibid., 154–55.
4. William C. Harris, "James Lynch: Black Leader in Southern Reconstruction,"

Historian 34 (November 1961), 42.
  5. Ibid.
  6. Ibid., 43.
  7. Ibid.; Wharton, *The Negro in Mississippi, 1865–1890*, 146–49.
  8. Harris, "James Lynch: Black Leader in Southern Reconstruction," 44–45.
  9. Ibid., 44.
  10. Ibid., 45; Wharton, *The Negro in Mississippi, 1865–1890*, 261–62.
  11. W. E. B. DuBois, *Black Reconstruction in America 1860–1880* (New York: Atheneum, 1969), 436.
  12. Harris, "James Lynch: Black Leader in Southern Reconstruction," 45–46.
  13. Ibid., 44–46; Wharton, *The Negro in Mississippi, 1865–1890*, 151–52.
  14. Wharton, *The Negro in Mississippi, 1865–1890*, 151.
  15. Ibid., 152–53.
  16. Ibid., 153.
  17. Harris, "James Lynch: Black Leader in Southern Reconstruction," 47.
  18. Wharton, *The Negro in Mississippi, 1865–1890*, 153–54.
  19. Harris, "James Lynch: Black Leader in Southern Reconstruction," 49.
  20. Ibid., 49–50.
  21. Wharton, *The Negro in Mississippi, 1865–1890*, 154.
  22. Ibid., 154–55; Harris, "James Lynch: Black Leader in Southern Reconstruction," 51.
  23. Harris, "James Lynch: Black Leader in Southern Reconstruction," 51.
  24. Ibid., 52; Lynch, *The Facts of Reconstruction*, 46.
  25. Harris, "James Lynch: Black Leader in Southern Reconstruction," 57.
  26. Ibid., 54–55; Secretary of State's Report to Governor Alcorn, December 1870, Correspondence File E—88A, Mississippi Department of Archives and History, Jackson, Mississippi.
  27. Harris, "James Lynch: Black Leader in Southern Reconstruction," 57–59.
  28. Ibid.
  29. Ibid., 59–60.
  30. Ibid.
  31. Ibid., 60.
  32. W. H. Hardy, "Recollections of Reconstruction in East and Southeast Mississippi," *Publications of the Mississippi Historical Society*, 4 (1901): 126–27.
  33. *New Orleans Times Democrat*, 7 March 1900.
  34. Harris, "James Lynch: Black Leader in Southern Reconstruction," 61.

James Hill

  1. Ruth Watkins, "Reconstruction in Marshall County," Publications of the Mississippi Historical Society, 12 (1912): 172.
  2. Wharton, *The Negro in Mississippi, 1865–1890*, 163.
  3. Ibid.; Lerone Bennett, Jr., *Black Power U. S. A.* (Chicago: Johnson Publishing Co. Inc., 1967), 223; *Autobiography*, 44.
  4. *Hinds County Gazette*, 9 August 1882, Mississippi Department of Archives and History, Jackson, Mississippi; Vincent P. Desantis, "The Republican Party and the Southern Negro, 1877–1897," *Journal of Negro History* 65 (April 1960): 84; Petitions from Citizens of Lauderdale County to James Hill for appointment of a Mr. Smith, 8 March 1879; S. Hurst request for financial assistance, 31 May, Moorland-Spingarn Collection, Howard University, Washington, D. C.
  5. P. B. S. Pinchback to members of the National Executive Committee of the American Citizens' Equal Rights Association, 12 February 1890, P. B. S. Pinchback Papers, Manuscript Division, Moorland-Spingarn Collection, Howard University, Washington, D. C.

6. *Hinds County Gazette*, 9 August 1882.

Dr. Thomas W. Stringer

1. Wharton, *The Negro in Mississippi, 1865–1890*, 149.
2. Monument, City Cemetery, Vicksburg, Mississippi.
3. John J. Morant, *Mississippi Preachers* (New York: Vantage Press, 1958), 57, 71.
4. Revels A. Adams, *Cyclopedia of African Methodism in Mississippi* (Natchez, 1902), 190–91.
5. Ibid., 191.
6. Wharton, *The Negro in Mississippi, 1865–1890*, 149, 271; Monument, City Cemetery, Vicksburg, Mississippi.
7. Monument, City Cemetery, Vicksburg, Mississippi.
8. Wharton, *The Negro in Mississippi, 1865–1890*, 149.
9. Ibid., 151.
10. Mrs. Ruth Fleming, interview with author, 18 March 1974; Morant, *Mississippi Minister*, 192.

Josiah T. Settle

1. Material for this article came from Wilhemena S. Robinson, *Historical Afro-American Biographies* (Cornwell Heights, Pennsylvania: The Association for the Study of Afro-American Life and History, 1979), 123–134; "Black Legislators During Reconstruction," unpublished manuscript, Mississippi Department of Archives and History, Jackson, Mississippi.

Roscoe Conklin Simmons

1. Marcus Bouleware, "Roscoe Conklin Simmons: The Golden Voiced Politico," *Negro History Bulletin* 29 (March 1966): 132; David Tucker, *Lieutenant Lee of Beale Street* (Nashville: Vanderbilt University Press, 1971), 21.
2. *New York Times*, 29 April 1951, 88; Bouleware, "Roscoe Conklin Simmons," 131.
3. Tucker, *Lieutenant Lee of Beale Street*, 21.
4. Ibid.
5. Bouleware, "Roscoe Conklin Simmons," 132.
6. Ibid.
7. *New York Times*, 29 April 1951, 88; Bouleware, "Roscoe Conklin Simmons," 131.
8. *Ebony*, 18 August 1951, 102.
9. Ibid.
10. Roi Ottley, *The Lonely Warrior* (Chicago: Henry Regnery Co., 1955), 135.
11. *New York Times*, 29 April 1951, 88.

Robert H. Wood

1. Ruth Watkins, "Reconstruction in Marshall County," *Publications of the Mississippi Historical Society*, 12 (1912): 172; Wharton, *The Negro in Mississippi, 1865–1890*, 12–18; Franklin, *Autobiography*, p. xi, 21, 131–36; Garner, *Reconstruction in Mississippi*, 28.
2. Wharton, *The Negro in Mississippi, 1865–1890*, 170.

3. Franklin, *Autobiography*, 102.
4. Ibid.
5. Microfilm, Armstrong Library, Natchez, Mississippi; William C. Harris, *The Day of the Carpetbagger: Republican's Reconstruction in Mississippi* (Baton Rouge: Southern University Press, 1979).
6. "Minutes . . .," 4 January 1871, Armstrong Library, Natchez, Mississippi.
7. Ibid.
8. Franklin, *Autobiography*, 103–06.
9. *Journal of Negro History* 2 (1917): 357.

James Charles Evers

1. Charles Evers, *Evers*, ed. Grace Halsell (New York: World Publishing Company, 1971), 23–24; James J. Flynn, *Negroes of Achievement in Modern America* (New York: Dodd, Mead and Company, 1970), 220.
2. Evers, *Evers*, 27–30.
3. Ibid., 29.
4. Elton C. Fax, *Contemporary Black Leaders* (New York: Dodd, Mead and Co., 1970), 132.
5. Ibid., 196.
6. Evers, *Evers*, 41.
7. Ibid., 42.
8. Ibid., 53; Jason Berry, *Amazing Grace* (New York: Saturday Review Press, 1973), 151.
9. Walther Rugaber, "The Brothers Evers," *New York Times Magazine*, 4 August 1968, 14.
10. Evers, *Evers*, 80–86.
11. Fax, *Contemporary Black Leaders*, 135.
12. Evers, *Evers*, 88–89.
13. *True*, May 1970, 74.
14. Ibid.
15. George R. Metcalf, *Black Profiles* (New York: McGraw-Hill, 1970), 200.
16. Evers, *Evers*, 112; Charles Evers, interview with *Playboy*, October 1971; "The Dawn of a New Era in Mississippi," *Press Review* 1969, 397.
17. Ibid., 115; Arthur Schlesinger, Jr., *Robert Kennedy and His Times* (New York: Ballantine Books, 1978), 724.
18. *The Crisis* (June/July 1973): 188–89; Evers picture, "More Race Bars Fall in Mississippi, *The Crisis* 72 (March 1965): 178.
19. Roy Wilkins, "Full Speed Ahead," *The Crisis* 84 (June/July 1977): 295; "Fayette's Negro Mayor," *Dixie Magazine: New Orleans Times-Picayune*, 30 November 1969, 30; *New York times Magazine*, 26 December 1976, 55; Pittman, *Mississippi Official and Statistical Register, 1980–1984*, 290.
20. Ibid.
21. *Dixie Magazine: New Orleans Times-Picayune*, 30 November 1969.
22. William Simpson, "The Birth of the Mississippi Loyalist Democrats (1965–1968)," *The Journal of Mississippi History*, 44 (February 1982): 34–35; Lawrence Guyot and Mike Thelwell, "The Politics of Necessity and Survival in Mississippi," *Freedomways* 6 (Spring 1966): 120–32; William Strickland, "The Movement in Mississippi," *Freedomways* 5 (Spring 1965): 310–13.
23. *Time*, 15 November 1971, 16.
24. James Loewen and Charles Sallis, *Mississippi: Conflict and Change* (New York: Pantheon Books, 1974), 217; "Five Years of Progress in Fayette," A Pamphlet, 1975; *New York Times*, 24 April 1973; *The Clarion-Ledger–Jackson Daily News*, 11 February 1973.

25. *The Clarion-Ledger–Jackson Daily News*, 3 November 1982; *The Fayette Chronicle*, 13 May 1981.

Unita Blackwell Wright

1. "Lady Mayor of Mayersville: Rights Worker Becomes Mississippi's First Black Woman Mayor," *Ebony*, December 1977, 53; Pittman, *Mississippi Official and Statistical Register, 1980–1984*, 295.
2. *Vicksburg Sunday Post*, February 1978; "Lady Mayor of Mayersville," 53; Julie Chenault, "Her Honor the Mayor," *Essence*, 14 July 1983, 17; Sparkla Harmon, "Unita Blackwell: The 'Grassroots' Mayor," *Sunbelt*, May 1980, 6–7; Eric Brown, "We the Willing . . . Do the Impossible," *Sunbelt*, November 1979, 38.
3. "Lady Mayor of Mayersville," 55–56.
4. Ibid., 60–63.
5. Ibid., 56–63; Harmon, "Unita Blackwell: The 'Grassroots' Mayor," 7.

Eddie James Carthan

1. Shelia D. Collins, "The Trials of Mayor Eddie Carthan: The Revenge of the Good Ole Boys," *In These Times* 6 (January 20–26, 1982): 8; Eric Brown, "We the Willing . . . Do the Impossible," *Sunbelt*, November 1979, 38.
2. Collins, "The Trials of Mayor Eddie Carthan," 8.
3. Ibid., 8–9.
4. Ibid., 9.
5. Ibid.
6. Ibid.
7. "Carthan Still Victim of Mississippi Brand of Justice Despite Acquittal," *Black Press Review* 2 (December–January 1983): 10.
8. *Hattiesburg American*, 17 October 1982, 3a.
9. Ibid.
10. Ibid.
11. Ibid., 20 October 1982, 1.
12. Ibid., *The Clarion-Ledger–Jackson Daily News*, 4 November 1982.
13. *The Clarion-Ledger–Jackson Daily News*, 4 November 1982.
14. Ibid.
15. Ibid.
16. Ibid.

Marion Shepilov Barry

1. *Who's Who in America, 1980–1981*, 191.
2. Ibid.; *Time*, 6 August 1979.
3. *Time*, 6 August 1979.
4. *The Clarion-Ledger–Jackson Daily News*, 3 November 1982; "Marion Barry Reelection," *Jet* 63 (18 November 1982): 9.

Evan Doss

1. Evan Doss, interview with Margaret Dwight, 7 July 1983; Leadership Development Program," Southern Regional Council, 1974–1975.
2. Regina Devoual, "The People of Claiborne County," *Southern Exposure*, March/

April 1982, 35.
   3. James Devoual, *Claiborne County's Black Elected Officials* (n. p., n. d.): 9; Douglas St. Angelo and E. Lester Levine, "Black Candidates: Can They Be Aided By A New Populism?" *Journal of Black Studies* 3 (December 1972): 167–82; Leslie Burl McLemore, "Toward A Theory of Black Politics—The Black and Ethnic Models Revisited," *Journal of Black Studies* (March 1972): 323–32; Evan Doss, interview.
   4. Evan Doss, interview; Barbara Phillips and Joseph Hutties, Jr., *Mississippi Property Tax: Special Burden for the Poor*, Jackson, Mississippi: Black Economic Research Center, 1973, 50–57.
   5. Ibid.
   6. Phillips and Hutties, *Mississippi Property Tax*, 50–57.

W. E. Mollison

   1. Material for this article came from Irvin C. Mollison, "Negro Lawyers in Mississippi," *Journal of Negro History* (January 1930): 38–71.

Constance Slaughter-Harvey

   1. *The Clarion-Ledger–Jackson Daily News*, (n. d.).
   2. Ibid.
   3. Pittman, *Mississippi Official and Statistical Register, 1980–1984*, 442.
   4. Ibid.

Henry J. Kirksey

   1. Henry J. Kirksey, "A Chronology," unpublished autobiographical sketch.
   2. Ibid.
   3. Ibid.
   4. Ibid.
   5. Ibid.
   6. Ibid.
   7. *The Clarion-Ledger–Jackson Daily News*, 10 October 1978.
   8. Ibid.
   9. Ibid.
   10. Ibid., 4 June 1980.
   11. Ibid., 3 November 1980.
   12. Ibid., 4 June 1980.
   13. Ibid.
   14. Edwin Lloyd Pittman, ed., *Mississippi Official and Statistical Register, 1980–1984* (Jackson: Office of the Secretary of State, 198), 51.

Robert Clark

   1. Phyllis Garland, "A Taste of Triumph for Black Mississippians: Election of 22 Negroes to Office Stirs Hope for Future," *Ebony*, February 1968, 26.
   2. Ibid., 25–27; Pittman, *Mississippi Official and Statistical Register, 1980–1984*, 6.
   3. Garland, "A Taste of Triumph for Black Mississippians," 26.
   4. Ibid., 28; William Simpson, "The Birth of Mississippi Loyalist Democrats," *Journal of Mississippi History*, 35; *Political Participation* (Washington, D. C.: U. S. Commission on Civil Rights, 1968), 218.

5. Committee to Elect Robert Clark, "Robert Clark, Democrat, Second Congressional District," a Pamphlet, 1982; Roy Wilkins, "Full Speed Ahead," *The Crisis* 84 (June/July 1977): 295; Janet Wells, "Voting Rights in 1975: Why Minorities Still Need Federal Protection," *Civil Rights Digest* 8 (Summer 1975): 16.
6. *The Clarion Ledger Jackson Daily News*, 3 November 1982.
7. Ibid.; Ibid., 19 September 1982; Ibid., 25 September 1982.
8. *Hattiesburg American*, 17 October 1982.
9. *The Clarion-Ledger Jackson Daily News*, 4 November 1982.
10. Ibid.
11. Ibid.
12. *Hattiesburg American*, 17 October 1982.
13. Ibid.
14. Ibid.
15. Ibid.
16. Ibid.; Lawrence Guyot and Mike Thelwell, "The Politics of Necessity and Survival in Mississippi," *Freedomways* 6 (Spring 1966): 120–32; Guyot and Thelwell, "Toward Independent Political Power," *Freedomways* 6 (Summer 1966): 246–54.

Aaron Henry

1. "Mississippi Emergency Relief Fund," *The Crisis* 75 (February 1968): 63; "Christmas in Mississippi," *The Crisis* 72 (February 1965): 121; *The New Republic*, 10 October 1964; A. Theis and Edmund R. Henshaw, Jr., *Who's Who in American Politics* (New York: R. R. Bowker Company, 1969), 152.
2. Guyot and Thelwell, "The Politics of Necessity and Survival in Mississippi," *Freedomways* 6 (Summer 1966): 131; Jack Minnis, "The Mississippi Freedom Democratic Party: A New Declaration of Independence," *Freedomways* 5 (Spring 1965): 264–77; Staughton Lynd, "The Freedom School: Concept and Organization," *Freedomways* 4 (Spring 1964): 302–03; Council of Federated Organizations, *Mississippi Black Paper* (New York: Misseduc Foundation, Inc., 1965), 7; James C. Harvey, *Black Civil Rights During the Johnson Administration* (Jackson: University Press of Mississippi, 1973), 24; Pittman, *Mississippi Official and Statistical Register, 1980–84*, 71; Freedom Primer No. 2: The Freedom Vote and The Right to Vote and Freedom Primer No. 1: The Convention Challenge and The Freedom Vote, Special Collections, Mitchell Memorial Library, Mississippi State University; Eric Morton, "Tremor in the Iceberg," *Freedomways* 72 (Fall 1965): 318–23.
3. "They Know They're Niggers," *New South* 17 (October 1962): 6.
4. *Sunbelt*, April 1980.
5. Ibid.; Aaron Henry, "Economic and Political Power," Walter M. Matthews, ed., *Mississippi, 1990* (Jackson: University Press of Mississippi, 1977), 67–73; Gordon Henderson, "Mississippi: the Most Open Place," *New South* 20 (October 1965): 14.
6. "The Mississippi Freedom Vote," *Civil Rights Digest* (December 1968): 10.
7. Henry was referring to United State Senator Jacob Javits, liberal Republican from New York, and longtime conservative Mississippi Democrat, Senator James Eastland.
8. *Sunbelt*, April 1980; *Hattiesburg American*, 18 August 1983.
9. Ibid.
10. *Sunbelt*, April 1980.

Douglas Leavon Anderson

1. *Jackson Advocate*, 1–27 February 1980; Pittman, *Mississippi Official and Statistical Register, 1980–1984*, 47–85; Phyllis Qualls-Brooks, "Black Lawmakers Outstanding in State Legislature," *Sunbelt* 1 (May, 1980), 32–33.

Politics

Fred Lee Banks

1. Ibid.

Horace Lawson Buckley

1. Ibid.

Credell Calhoun

1. Ibid.

Tyrone Ellis

1. Ibid.

Hillman Jerome Frazier

1. Ibid.

Isiah Fredericks

1. Ibid.

David Leo Green

1. Ibid.

Clayton P. Henderson

1. Ibid.

Leslie Darnell King

1. Ibid.

Barney J. Schoby

1. Ibid.

Charles Bernard Sheppard

1. Ibid.

Percy Willis Watson

1. Ibid.

Charles Lemuel Young

1. Ibid.

Deborah Jones Gambrell

1. *Hattiesburg South Mississippi Weekly*, 9 September 1982; Pittman, *Mississippi Official and Statistical Register, 1980–1984*, 217.
2. *Hattiesburg South Mississippi Weekly*, 9 September 1982.

Melvin Redmond

1. Material for this article came from the *Vicksburg Sunday Post*, 19 June 1980, 6 July 1981.

James Winfield

1. Material for this article came from the *Vicksburg Post*, August 1977.

Eddie Lucas

1. Material for this article came from *The Clarion-Ledger–Jackson Daily News*, 10 June 1980, 3a.

Eddie L. McBride

1. Material for this article came from *The Clarion-Ledger–Jackson Daily News*, 9 September 1982, 2 October 1982, and 3 November 1982.

Clifford Jennings

1. *The Clarion Ledger-Jackson Daily News*, 30 July 1974.

James C. Cooper

1. *The Clarion Ledger-Jackson Daily News*, 30 July 1974.

Vernon C. Johnson

1. *The Vicksburg Sunday Post*, 29 June 1975.

Charles E. Pugh

1. *The Clarion-Ledger Jackson Daily News*, 7 December 1975.

William K. Dease, Sr.

1. *The Jackson Clarion Ledger*, 1 August 1973.

Betty Jones

1. *Atlanta Daily World*, February 1980.

CIVIL RIGHTS

1. The Louisville, New Orleans, and Texas Railroad Company v. State of Mississippi, 133 U. S. 784 (1889).
2. Chrisman v. Mayor of Town of Brookhaven, 70 Mississippi 477 (1893).
3. Green v. State of Mississippi, 72 Mississippi 522 (1885).
4. P. B. S. Pinchback to Members of National Executive Committee, Washington, D. C., 12 February 1890.
5. Rosalyn Terborg-Penn, "Discrimination Against Afro-American Women in the Women's Movement, 1830–1920," in *The Afro-American Woman: Struggles and Images*, ed. Sharon Harley and Rosalyn Terborg Penn (New York: Kennikat Press, 1978), 118.
6. Gerder Lerner, *Black Women in White America: A Documentary History* (New York: Columbia University Press, 1978), 613.

Ida Wells Barnett

1. Bert James Loewenberg and Ruth Bogin, ed., *Black Women in Nineteenth Century American Life: Their Words, Their Thoughts, Their Feelings* (University Park: The Pennsylvania State University Press, 1976), 253.
2. Edgar A. Toppins, *A Biographical History of Blacks in America* (New York: David McKay Co., Inc., 1971), 448.
3. Ida B. Wells, *Crusade for Justice: The Autobiography of Ida B. Wells*, Alfreda

Duster, ed. (Chicago: University of Chicago Press, 1970), 18.

4. Chesapeake and Ohio & Southwestern Railroad Company v. Wells, 85 Tennessee 613 (1887).

5. Ida B. Wells, *Crusade for Justice*, 20.

6. Ibid.; Gerda Lerner, ed., *Black Women in White America: A Documentary History* (New York: Vintage Books, 1972), 196.

7. David M. Tucker, "Miss Ida Wells," *Phylon* 32 (Summer 1971): 112.

8. Ida B. Wells, *Crusade for Justice*, p. xx.

9. Tucker, "Miss Ida Wells," 114.

10. Ibid.; Ida B. Wells, *U. S. Atrocities* (London: 1892), 1–3, 11–19; Ida B. Wells, *Southern Horrors: Lynch Law in All Its Phases* (New York: The New York Age Print, 1892), 1–24; Ida B. Wells, *A Red Record Lynchings in the United States* (Chicago: Donohue and Henneberry, 1894), 1–101; Ida B. Wells, "Lynch Law in America," *Arena* 23 (January 1900): 15–24; Ida B. Wells, "Lynching; The Excuses for It," *Independent*, 16 May 1901.

11. Monroe M. Majors, *Noted Negro Women: Their Triumphs and Activities* (Freeport, New York: Books for Libraries Press, 1971), 192.

12. Ibid.

13. Tucker, "Miss Ida Wells," 118; Lerner, *Black Women in White America*, 196–97.

14. Langston Hughes, *Famous Negro Heroes of America* (New York: Dodd, Mead and Co., 1958), 160.

15. Ida B. Wells, *Crusade for Justice*, p. xx.

16. Ibid., p. xxi–xxii; Langston Hughes, *Famous Negro Women in America* (New York: Dodd, Mead and Co., 1958), 24–26.

17. William Loren Katz, *Eyewitness: The Negro in American History* (New York: Putnam Publishing Company, 1967), 363; Ida B. Wells, *Crusade for Justice*, 250–51.

18. Ida B. Wells, *Crusade for Justice*, 251; Loewenberg and Bogin, *Black Women in Nineteenth Century American Life*, 253.

19. Ida B. Wells, *Crusade for Justice*, 250–51; Martha Leslie Allen, "Black Women Journalists and the Black Press in the South at the Turn of the Century, 1895–1904," Seminar Paper, Howard University, 1978, 8–12.

20. Allen, "Black Women Journalists and the Black Press," 8–12.

21. Rosalyn Terborg-Penn, "Discrimination Against Afro-American Women in the Women's Movement,"; Sharon Harley and Rosalyn Terborg-Penn, ed., *The Afro-American Woman: Struggles and Images* (Port Washington, New York: Kennikat Press, 1978), 22–23; Edward T. James, ed., *Notable American Women, 1607–1950*, 3 (Cambridge, Massachusetts: Harvard University Press, 1971): 566; Eleanor Flexner, *Century of Struggle: The Women's Rights Movement in the United States* (Cambridge, Massachusetts: Harvard University Press, 1959), 43–44; Mary Church Terrell Papers, Manuscript Division, Library of Congress, Washington, D. C.

22. Emma Lou Thornbrough, *T. Thomas Fortune* (Chicago: University of Chicago Press, 1972), 184.

23. Ibid.

24. Ibid.

25. James, *Notable American Women*, 566.

26. Thornbrough, *T. Thomas Fortune*, 355–57.

27. Hughes, *Famous Negro Women in America*, 26.

28. Loewenberg and Bogin, *Black Women in Nineteenth Century American Life*, 253; *Chicago Defender*, 26 March 1931.

29. L. A. Scruggs, ed., *Women of Distinction: Remarkable in Works and Invincible in Character* (Raleigh, North Carolina: L. A. Scruggs, 1893), 39.

Margaret Murray Washington

1. Geneva B. White and Eva Bishop, ed., *Mississippi Black Women* (Jackson: Mis-

sissippi Bicentennial Commission, 1976): 2; Elizabeth Ross Haynes, "Margaret Murray Washington," *Opportunity* 3 (July 25): 207–09.

2. Lerner, *Black Women in White America*, 444–59.

3. Ibid.; Benjamin Brawley, *Negro Builders and Heroes* (Chapel Hill: University of North Carolina Press, 1965), 157, 261.

4. Cynthia Neverdon-Morton, "The Black Woman's Struggle for Equality in the South, 1895–1925," in Harley and Terborg-Penn, ed., *The Afro-American Woman*, 51–52; Rosalyn M. Terborg-Penn, "Afro-Americans in the Struggle for Women Suffrage" (Ph. D. dissertation, Harvard University, 1978): 146, 168.

5. Harley and Terborg-Penn, *The Afro-American Woman*, 51–52; Lerner, *Black Women in White America*, 444.

6. Harley and Terborg-Penn, *The Afro-American Woman*, 54–56.

Jack Henry Young

1. Jack H. Young, Sr., interviews with George Alexander Sewell, 20 November 1975 and 30 December 1975.

2. "Jack Harvey Young, 1908–1976," *The Crisis* 83 (December 1976): 349.

3. *The Clarion-Ledger-Jackson Daily News*, 15 June 1961, 1.

4. W. Haywood Burns, *The Voices of Negro Protest in America* (London: Oxford University Press, 1963), 56.

Medgar Evers

1. Charles Evers, *Evers*, Grace Halsell, ed. (New York: World Publishing Company, 1971), 23–24; James Flynn, *Negroes of Achievement in Modern America* (New York: Dodd, Mead and Co., 1970), 220; Tom Dent, "Portrait of Three Heroes," *Freedomways* 5 (September 1965): 250–63.

2. Evers, *Evers*, 24.

3. Ibid., 26, 42, 53; *Current Biography* (April 1969): 18; Walter Rugaber, "The Brothers Evers," *New York Times Magazine*, 4 August 1968, 14; Elton C. Fax, *Contemporary Black Leaders* (New York: Dodd, Mead and Co., 1970), 132.

4. Flynn, *Negroes of Achievement in Modern America*, 221.

5. Ibid., 221–22; Evers, *Evers*, 88–89.

6. Fax, *Contemporary Black Leaders*, 199; "Mrs. Medgar Evers," *The Crisis* 75 (May 1968): 205; Myrlie Evers, *For Us the Living* (New York: Doubleday, 1967), 1–378.

7. Fax, *Contemporary Black Leaders*, 199.

8. Ibid.; "The Mississippi Freedom Democratic Vote," *New South* (December 1962): 10.

9. George R. Metcalf, *Black Profiles* (New York: McGraw-Hill, 1970), 200.

10. Evers, *Evers*, 88–89.

11. Metcalf, *Black Profiles*, 200.

12. *True*, May 1970, 76.

13. *Look*, 1 June 1965, 63.

14. Metcalf, *Black Profiles*, 204.

15. Ibid.

16. Ibid., 204–05.

17. Evers, *Evers*; Cleveland Donald, Jr., "Medgar Wylie Evers: The Civil Rights Leader As Utopianist," *Mississippi Heroes*, ed. Dean Faulkner Wells and Hunter Cole (Jackson: University Press of Mississippi, 1980), 223; Carl Brauer, *John F. Kennedy and the Second Reconstruction* (New York: Columbia University Press, 1978), 180; Arthur Schlesinger, Jr., *Robert Kennedy and His Times* (New York: Ballantine Books, 1978), 341, 370.

18. Flynn, *Negroes of Achievement in Modern America*, 221; "Victims of White Supremacy, 1951–1965," *The Crisis* 72 (April 1965): 245.
19. Metcalf, *Black Profiles*, 211–13; Alfred Baker Lewis, "Progress in the Equal Rights Struggle," *The Crisis* (April 1976): 138.
20. Ibid.; Brauer, *John F. Kennedy*, 240; "Medgar W. Evers: In Memoriam," *The Crisis* (June/July 1977): 270–72; James C. Harvey, *Black Civil Rights During the Johnson Administration* (Jackson: University Press of Mississippi, 1973), 5.
21. *The Crisis* (June/July 1973): 188–89.

Fannie Lou Hamer

1. Fax, *Contemporary Black Leaders*, 116.
2. John Egerton, *A Mind to Stay Here: Profiles from the South* (New York: Macmillan Co., 1970), 95–96.
3. Ibid., 96; John Egerton, "Fannie Lou Hamer," *The Progressive* 41 (May 1977): 7.
4. Egerton, *A Mind to Stay Here*, 96.
5. Fax, *Contemporary Black Leaders*, 116–17; J. H. Odell, "Life in Mississippi: An Interview with Fannie Lou Hamer," *Freedomways* 5 (Spring 1965): 232.
6. Odell, "Life in Mississippi," 233–34.
7. Ibid.
8. Ibid.
9. Ibid., 232–33.
10. Egerton, *A Mind to Stay Here*, 97.
11. Fax, *Contemporary Black Leaders*, 118.
12. Ibid., 122–23; Wiley A. Branton, "To Register to Vote in Mississippi," *New South* 20 (February 1965): 10–15.
13. Fax, *Contemporary Black Leaders*, 122–23.
14. Ibid., 123–24.
15. Egerton, *A Mind to Stay Here*, 98–99.
16. Fax, *Contemporary Black Leaders*, 123–24, "The Cotton Vote in Mississippi," *Council of Federated Organization News*, 11 December 1964, Special Collections, Mitchell Memorial Library, Mississippi State University; Sepia, 32.
17. Fax, *Contemporary Black Leaders*, 124.
18. Egerton, *A Mind to Stay Here*, 98; Gordon Henderson, "Mississippi, The Most Open Place," *New South* 20 (October 1965): 13.
19. Egerton, *A Mind to Stay Here*, 98–99.
20. Sepia, 32.
21. Ibid.
22. Egerton, *A Mind to Stay Here*, 101.
23. Ibid.
24. Ibid.; "The Birth of the Mississippi Loyalist Democrats (1965–1968)," *The Journal of Mississippi History* 44 (February 1982): 27.
25. Fax, *Contemporary Black Leaders*, 126–27; *Freedom Primer No. 1: The Convention Challenge and The Freedom Vote*, Special Collections, Mitchell Memorial Library, Mississippi State University.
26. *Freedom Primer No. 1*; Clarice T. Campbell and Oscar Allan Rogers, Jr., *Mississippi: The View from Tougaloo* (Jackson: University Press of Mississippi, 1979), 214.
27. Fax, *Contemporary Black Leaders*, 126–27; Leslie McLemore, "The Mississippi Freedom Party," *Journal of Black Studies* 2 (September 1971: 87.
28. Egerton, *A Mind to Stay Here*, 101; Council of Federated Organizations, *Mississippi Black Paper* (New York: Misseduc Foundation, Inc., 1965), 18; *Freedom Primer No. 2: The Freedom Vote and The Right to Vote*, Special Collections, Mitchell Memorial Library, Mississippi State University.
29. Egerton, *A Mind to Stay Here*, 100; Council of Federated Organization, 1–92.

Fax, *Contemporary Black Leaders*, 127.
30. *Sepia*, 30.
31. Ibid., 29; Harvey, *Black Civil Rights During the Johnson Administration*, 24; Leslie B. McLemore, "The Effect of Political Participation upon a Closed Changing Political Climate in Mississippi," *Negro Education Review* 23 (January 1972), 6–7.
32. Fax, *Contemporary Black Leaders*, 128.
33. Ibid., 114–15.
34. Lerner, *Black Women in White America*, 609, 612.
35. Egerton, *A Mind to Stay Here*, 106.
36. William Faulkner, *The Faulkner Reader* (New York: Modern Library, 1961), 325–26.

Clyde Kennard

1. Mrs. Sarah Webb (Clyde Kennard's sister), interview with Margaret Dwight, 23 August 1983.
2. Tom Dent, "Portrait of Three Heroes," 256–60; William L. Higgs, *Mississippi Political Handbook*, Segregation and Integration, Miscellaneous Collection, Mitchell Memorial Library, Mississippi State University.
3. Ibid.
4. Dent, "Portrait of Three Heroes," 256–60.
5. Ibid.
6. Ibid.; Mrs. Sarah Webb interview.

James Chaney

1. William Bradford Huie, *Three Lives for Mississippi* (New York: Signet Books, 1964), 58–66.
2. Ibid., 58–60.
3. Lawrence Guyot and Mike Thelwell, "The Politics of Necessity and Survival in Mississippi," *Freedomways* 6 (Summer 1966): 120; J. H. O'Dell, "The Threshold of a New Reconstruction," *Freedomways*, 5 (Fall 1965): 508; Document #4, "An Address by Mrs. Fannie Lee Chaney of Meridian, Mississippi at the Metropolitan A. M. E. Church in Harlem October 23, 1964," *Freedomways* 5 (Spring 1965): 290–91.
4. Alfred Baker Lewis, "Progress in the Equal Rights Struggle," *The Crisis* (April 1976): 138–139; "Victims of White Supremacy, 1951–1965," *The Crisis*, 72 (April 1965): 245.
5. David Llorens, "Mississippi Revisited: Five Years After Summer Project, Editors Find Little Change," *Ebony*, July 1969, 52.
6. Buie, *Three Lives for Mississippi*, 110–11, 160; Kenneth S. Tolliett, "Southern Justice for Blacks: Legal System Is Dominated by Racist Police, Court Officials," *Ebony*, October 1971, 58–73.
7. Buie, *Three Lives for Mississippi*, 160.
8. O'Dell, "The Threshold of a New Reconstruction," 499.

James H. Meredith

1. Metcalf, *Black Profiles*, 219–20.
2. Ibid., 220; James Meredith, *The Life and Story of James Meredith* (Jackson: privately published, 1974), 1.
3. Metcalf, *Black Profiles*, 220.
4. Ibid.
5. Ibid., 221.

6. Ibid.; Louis E. Lomax, *The Negro Revolt* (New York: New American Library, 1963), 124; Bryan Fulks, *Black Struggle, A History of the Negro in America* (New York: Dell Publishers, 1969), 266.
7. Metcalf, *Black Profiles*, 221; James H. Meredith, *Excerpts from Three Years in Mississippi* (Jackson: Privately published, 1975).
8. Flynn, *Negroes of Achievement in Modern America*, 162.
9. Meredith, *Excerpts from Three Years in Mississippi*, 52.
10. Metcalf, *Black Profiles*, 224–43.
11. "The Will to Die: Rights Activists Recall Torment and Danger of the Civil Rights Fight," *Ebony*, May 1973, 154–60.
12. Dent, "Portrait of Three Heroes," 256–60.
13. "The Will to Die," 154–60.
14. *The Clarion-Ledger–Jackson Daily News*, 19 September 1982, 26 September 1982.
15. *The Clarion-Ledger–Jackson Daily News*, 26 September 1982.
16. Ibid.
17. Ibid.; Brauer, *John F. Kennedy and the Second Reconstruction*, 181–98; Schlesinger, Jr., *Robert Kennedy and His Times*, 341–52; Governor Ross Barnett's speech to White Citizen Council, White Citizen Council's Paper, Special Collections, Mitchell Memorial Library, Mississippi State University; "Mississippi: The Mood of the Deep South," *New South* 17 (October 1962): 13–16; *The Washington Post*, 7 October 1962; David Lawrence, "Illegality Breeds Illegality," *U.S. News and World Report*, 8 October 1962; "They Know They're Niggers," *New South* 17 (October 1962): 3–4.
18. Ibid.
19. Ibid.; *Ebony*, May 1973, 154–60.
20. Ibid.
21. Ibid.
22. Ibid.; Harvey, *Black Civil Rights During the Kennedy Administration* (Hattiesburg: University and College Press of Mississippi, 1971), 67.
23. *The Clarion-Ledger–Jackson Daily News*, 26 September 1982.
24. *Ebony*, December 1962, 26.
25. Ibid., 32.
26. Metcalf, *Black Profiles*, 246.
27. Ibid., 247–48.
28. Duncan M. Gray, Jr., "Paranoia, Guilt and Atonement," *New South* 18 (March 1963): 10–13; "A Day of Repentance," *New South* 18 (March 1963): 3; "That All Men Are Brothers," *New South* 18 (March 1963): 14–15.
29. Metcalf, *Black Profiles*, 251; Lomax, *The Negro Revolt*, 176–77.
30. Metcalf, *Black Profiles*, 251–53.
31. Ibid., 253–54.
32. Ibid., 254.
33. Meredith, *The Life Story of James Meredith*, 24–25; Simpson, "The Birth of the Mississippi Loyalist Democrats," *Journal of Mississippi History* (1965–1968): 33; *Cincinnati Ohio Enquirer*, (n. d.), Special Collections, Mitchell Memorial Library, Mississippi State University.
34. *Memphis Commercial-Appeal: Mid-South Magazine*, 21 November 1971.
35. *The Clarion-Ledger Jackson Daily News*, 26 September 1982; "Ole Miss 20th Anniversary," *Time*, 9 October 1982, 8; "James Meredith," *Jet* 63 (18 October 1982): 9.
36. "James Meredith," *Jet* 63 (18 October 1982): 9.

Willie Tatum

1. *The Hattiesburg South Mississippi Weekly*, 9 September 1982.

BUSINESS

William T. Johnson

1. Unless otherwise indicated, material for this article was taken from Edwin A. Davis and William R. Hogan, *The Barber of Natchez* (Baton Rouge: Louisiana State University Press, 1954), 262–71; James T. Currier, "From Slavery to Freedom in Mississippi's Legal System," *Journal of Negro History* 65 (Spring 1980): 117; Mrs. Mary Louise Miller, Interview with Margaret Dwight, 10 September 1983; *Delta Democrat Times*, 10 September 1983.
2. "Home," William T. Johnson papers, Mississippi Department of Archives and History, Jackson, Mississippi.
3. *Delta Democrat Times*, vertical file, Mississippi Department of Archives and History, Jackson, Mississippi.

The Montgomerys: Father and Son

1. Lewis O. Swingler, ed., *Jewel of the Delta*, A Souvenir Bulletin, 1962, 9; Janet Sharp Hermann, *The Pursuit of a Dream* (New York: Oxford University Press, 1981), 16–18.
2. Hermann, *The Pursuit of a Dream*, 16–18; Hudson Strods, *Jefferson Davis: American Patriot* (New York: Harcourt, Brace & Co., 1955), 112.
3. Frank E. Everett, *Brierfield* (Hattiesburg: University and College Press of Mississippi, 1977), 86.
4. Ibid.; Maurice E. Jackson, "Mound Bayou-A Study in Social Development," (M. A. thesis, University of Alabama, 1957), 38.
5. Henry Baker, "The Negro in the Field of Invention," *Journal of Negro History*, 2 (1917): 24.
6. John Hope Franklin, *From Slavery to Freedom* (New York: Alfred Knopf, 1964), 196–97.
7. Swingler, *Jewel of the Delta*, 9; Strods, *Jefferson Davis*, 113.
8. Carter G. Woodson, *The Education of the Negro Prior to 1861* (New York: G. P. Putnam's Sons, 1915), ch. 11, cited by J. H. Harmon in "The Negro As a Local Businessman," *Journal of Negro History*, 14 (1929): 116–17; Saunders Redding, The Lonesome Road (Garden City: Doubleday & Co., 1958), 94.
9. Strods, *Jefferson Davis*, 113.
10. Everett, *Brierfield*, 72.
11. Ibid., 76–77.
12. Redding, The Lonesome Road, 96.
13. James W. Garner, *Reconstruction in Mississippi* (Baton Rouge: Louisiana State University Press, 1968), 252.
14. Redding, The Lonesome Road, 96–97; Everett, *Brieffield*, 82–88.
15. Warren County, Mississippi: Land Records, Chancery Clerk's Office, Deed Book, 14.
16. Vernon Lane Wharton, *The Negro in Mississippi, 1865–1890* (New York: Harper & Row, 1965), 42.
17. Redding, The Lonesome Road, 109.
18. Ibid.; Garner, *Reconstruction in Mississippi*, 164: Lerone Bennett, "6Black Power: Freedmen Seize Reins in the South Backed by Strong Vote Bill," Ebony, November 1965, 38.
19. Redding, The Lonesome Road, 109.
20. Ibid., 111.

21. Everett, *Brierfield*, 88–94.
22. Warren County, Mississippi: Land Records, Deed Book zz, 529.
23. Redding, *The Lonesome Road*, 112–18.
24. Ibid.
25. Ibid.; William F. Holmes, "The Demise of the Colored Farmer's Alliance," *The Journal of Southern History* 41 (May 1975): 192–97.
26. Holmes, "The Demise of the Colored Farmer's Alliance," 192–27.
26. Ibid.
27. Ibid.
28. Redding, *The Lonesome Road*, 119–20.
29. John J. Morant, *Mississippi Preachers* (New York: Vantage Press, 1958), 143.
30. J. W. Gibson and W. H. Crogman, *Progress of a Race* (Miami, Florida: Mnemosyne Publishing Co., 1969), 238.
31. Redding, *The Lonesome Road*, 119; Bryan Fulks, *Black Struggle: A History of the Negro in America* (New York: Dell Publishing Co., 1969), 195; Norman P. Andrews, "The Negro in Politics," *Journal of Negro History* 8 (October 1920): 431; Mignon Iris Miller, "The American Negro Academy in Intellectual Movement During the Era of Negro Disfranchisement, 1897–1924," (M. A. thesis, Howard University, 1966), Moorland-Spingarn Research Center, Howard University, Washington, D. C.; William Cohen, "Negro Involuntary Servitude in the South, 1865–1940: A Preliminary Analysis," *The Journal of Southern History*, 42 (February 1976): 36; John R. Skates, *Mississippi: A Bicentennial History* (New York: W. W. Norton and Co., 1979), 122–23.

George Washington Lee

1. David Tucker, *Lieutenant Lee of Beale Street* (Nashville: Vanderbilt University Press, 1971), ix.
2. Ibid., 4.
3. Ibid., 5–6.
4. *Greenwood Commonwealth*, 7 November 1902.
5. Tucker, *Lieutenant Lee of Beale Street*, 9.
6. Ibid., 10.
7. Ibid., 10–11.
8. Wendell Phillipps, *Speeches and Letters* (Boston: J. Redpath, 1863), 468–69.
9. Tucker, *Lieutenant Lee of Beale Street*, 12–13.
10. Ibid., 16.
11. G. P. Hamilton, *The Bright Side of Memphis* (Memphis, 1908), cited by Tucker in *Lieutenant Lee of Beale Street*, 24–25.
12. Ibid., 28.
13. Ibid., 30.
14. Ibid., 33–34.
15. Ibid., 42.
16. Ibid., 49.
17. Ibid., 52.
18. Ibid., 158–59.
19. Ibid., 112.
20. Ibid., 111.
21. Ibid., 119.
22. Ibid., 201.
23. David M. Tucker, "Black Pride and Negro Business in the 1920s: George Washington Lee of Memphis," *Business Historical Review* 43 (Winter 1969): 435–51.

Joseph Edison Walker

1. Unless otherwise indicated, material for this article was taken from T. J. Johnson, *From the Driftwood of Bayou Pierre* (Louisville: The Dune Press, 1949), 20–101.
2. Milan W. Davis, *Pushing Forward* (Okolona: Okolona Industrial School, 1938), 90–91.
3. Ibid.
4. Maceo Walker, letter to Joseph Edison Walker, 18 March 1975.

Clarie Collins Harvey

1. Clarie C. Harvey, interview with George Sewell, 24 April 1974.
2. Ibid.
3. Ruth Weber, "The New President: A Face to the Rising Sun," *The Church Woman*, 37 (June/July 1971): 20.
4. Ibid., 20–21.
5. Ibid., 21.
6. Clarie C. Harvey, interview; Alpha Kappa Alpha, *Women in Business*, Heritage Series # 3 (Chicago: Alpha Kappa Alpha Sorority, Inc., 1970), 10.
7. Ibid.
8. Weber, "The New President," 24.
9. Ibid., 22.
10. Clarie C. Harvey, interview.
11. *News Release*, Church Women United, 21 November 1971.
12. Clarie C. Harvey, interview.
13. Weber, "The New President," 22; *News Release*, Church Women United.
14. Weber, "The New President," 24.
15. *New Release*, Church Women United, February 1974; *The Clarion-Ledger Jackson Daily News*, 20 September 1974.
16. Weber, "The New President," 24; *News Release*, Church Women United, December 1973.
17. Weber, "The New President," 22–24; News Release, Church Women United.
18. *The Clarion-Ledger Jackson Daily News*, 11 May 1974.

George Johnson

1. Material for this article was taken from Gwendolyn Robinson, "George Johnson: Mississippi Experiences," *Sunbelt*, 1 February 1980, 6–8, 21; "Cooperation Pays Off," *Ebony*, November 1982, 130.

Robert Earl James

1. Unless otherwise indicated, material for this article was taken from Morris Brown College *Alumni Bulletin* (Spring 1972): 1; Linda Buford, "Making It: Dr. Robert James," *Sunbelt*, 1 July 1980, 29–30.
2. "Youngest Black Bank President," *Jet*, December 1971.

Jessie R. Chambliss

1. Material for this article came from an unpublished biographical sketch.

Sam Baker

1. Material for this article came from Rose Ragsdale, "Sam Baker: A New Man in the Small Business Administration," *Sunbelt*, 10 August 1980, 40–42.

Vernon Floyd

1. Material for this article came from the *Hattiesburg South Mississippi Weekly*, 9 September 1982.

Charlene Owens

1. Unless otherwise indicated, material for this article was taken from the *Hattiesburg South Mississippi Weekly*, 9 September 1982; Clipping File, National Association of Negro Business and Professional Women's Clubs, Inc., Washington, D. C.

Rose Morgan

1. Material for this article came from Alpha Kappa Alpha, *Women in Business*, 14.

Louise K. Quarles

1. Material for this article came from Alpha Kappa Alpha, *Women in Business*, 17.

E. W. Green

1. Material for this article came from William Anthony Avery, "The Negro in Business," *Republican* 15 September 1912, Newspaper Clipping File, Manuscript Division, Hampton Institiute, Hampton, Virginia.

Thelma Sanders

1. Material for this article came from Alpha Kappa Alpha, *Women in Business*, 18.

Randolph T. Myrick

1. Material for this article came from *Black Enterprise*, November 1973.

Emorrie Jenkins

1. Material for this article came from *Black Enterprise*, undated magazine clipping.

Naomi Sims

1. Material for this article came from "Have Black Models Really Made It?" *Ebony*, May 1970, 152–60.

EDUCATION

1. Van S. Allen, "Fulfilling the Role of Being a National Resource," *Sunbelt*, 1 August 1980, 10–11; Linda Buford, "Colleges: The Research Function," *Sunbelt*, 1 August 1980, 12–15; Lynette J. Shelton, "Benjamin E. Mays: A Man of Dignity," *Sunbelt*, 1 August 1980, 7–9.
2. Shelton, "Benjamin E. Mays," 7–9; Marvel Lany, "An Agenda for the Survival of Black Institutions of Higher Learning," *Sunbelt*, 1 May 1980, 26–29; Jay T. Smith, "The Land Grant College and Industrial Education," *Sunbelt*, 1 February 1980, 38–39.
3. Nulton Morris, "Black Institutions," *Black Collegian*.

John D. Boyd

1. *Who's Who in America, 1964–1965*, 223.
2. Melerson Guy Dunham, *Centennial History of Alcorn A. & M. College* (Jackson: University Press of Mississippi, 1971), 96.
3. Ibid.
4. Ibid., 76.
5. J. D. Boyd, letter to George A. Sewell, 20 November 1975.
6. Ibid.
7. Dunham, *Centennial History*, 76.
8. Ibid.
9. Ibid., 77–78.
10. J. D. Boyd letter.
11. Dunham, *Centennial History*, 78; *Port Gibson Reveille*, 7 April 1966.
12. J. D. Boyd letter.

Walter Washington

1. Billy M. Bishop, "Public Education in Mississippi, 1910–1954," (M. S. thesis, Starkville, Mississippi State College, 1963), 33.
2. *Alcorn State University General Catalog, 1982–1984* (Lorman: Alcorn State University, 1982), 39, 48–49; George A. Sewell, "Alcorn A. & M.: Pioneer in Black Pride," *The Crisis* 79 (April 1972): 126.
3. Sewell, "Alcorn A. & M.," 126.
4. Dunham, *Centennial History of Alcorn A. & M. College*, 80; *Leaders in Education* (New York: R. R. Bowker Co., 1974), 1142.
5. Biographical Materials, Alcorn State University, Office of Public Relations.
6. Ibid.
7. Ibid.; Clarice T. Campbell and Oscar Allan Rogers, Jr., *Mississippi: The View from Tougaloo* (Jackson: University Press of Mississippi, 1979), 265.

B. Baldwin Dansby

1. Material for this article came from *The Clarion-Ledger–Jackson Daily News*, 21 November 1975.

Jacob L. Reddix

1. Unless otherwise indicated, material for this article was taken from Jacob L.

Reddix, *A Voice Crying in the Wilderness* (Jackson: University Press of Mississippi, 1974), 52.
  2. *Jackson State College Catalogue, 1971*.

John A. Peoples

  1. Unless otherwise indicated, material for this article was taken from *Who's Who in American Education, 1967–1968*, 664; Dr. John A. Peoples's letter to George A. Sewell, 2 April 1974.
  2. *The Clarion-Ledger–Jackson Daily News*, 10 August 1983.

Ernest A. Boykins

  1. Material for this article was supplied by the public relations officers of Alcorn State University and Mississippi Valley State University.

Joe Louis Boyer

  1. Unless otherwise indicated, material for this article was taken from *The Clarion-Ledger–Jackson Daily News*, 19 September 1982.
  2. Curriculum Vitae submitted by Dr. Joe Boyer to Dr. Margaret L. Dwight, 5 November 1982.

George A. Owens

  1. *Time*, 27 December 1968, 48.
  2. Ibid.
  3. Ibid.; Campbell and Rogers, *Mississippi: The View from Tougaloo*, 219–21, 223–25, 231–37.
  4. *Time*, 49.
  5. Dr. George A. Owens's letter to George A. Sewell, 4 April 1974.

Laurence C. Jones

  1. Laurence C. Jones, *Piney Woods and Its Story* (New York: Fleming H. Revell Co., 1922), 48.
  2. Ibid.
  3. Ibid., 26–27.
  4. Ibid., 30–31.
  5. Ibid., 31–32.
  6. Ibid., 50–56.
  7. *Readers Digest*, December 1956, 168.
  8. Jones, *Piney Woods and Its Story*, 53.
  9. Ibid., 54–55.
  10. Ibid., 56–57.
  11. Ibid., 66–67.
  12. Ibid., 78–79.
  13. Ibid., 90–91.
  14. Ibid., 110.
  15. Ibid., 111.

16. Ibid., 112–113.
17. *The Pine Torch*, (July/September, 1975): 2.
18. Ibid.
19. Laurence C. Jones, Jr. to Arthur B. Spingarn, Spingarn Papers, Moorland-Spingarn Research Center, Manuscript Division, Howard University, Washington, D. C.
20. *The Pine Torch*, 2.

Jane Ellen McAllister

1. Cynthia Parsons, "Two Women with a Vision," *Southern Education Report* 4 (April 1969), 20; W. William Burns, "Jane Ellen McAllister: First Black Woman to Earn the Doctorate in Education in the World," *Sunbelt*, 1 August 1980, 18–19, 36–38.
2. Janie M. Gardner to George Sewell, June 1964.
3. Ibid.
4. Ibid.; Parsons, *"Two Women with a Vision,"* 22.
5. Mable Carney, "Doctoral Dissertation and Projects Relating to the Education of Negroes," *The Advanced School Digest* 8 (February 1942): 1.
6. Ibid.
7. Alleane M. Currie to George Sewell, 2 April 1974.
8. Cynthia Parsons and W. Bruce Welch, "Mississippi Beehive College," *American Education* 4 (December 1967/January 1968): 19.
9. Ibid., 20; Alleane M. Currie letter.
10. Parsons and Welch, "Mississippi Beehive College," 21–22.
11. Ibid.; Dr. Margaret Walker, interview with George Sewell, 7 October 1975.
12. *Project Enrichment Newsletter*, October 1962, Jackson State College; Parsons and Welch, "Mississippi Beehive College," 21.
13. Parsons and Welch, "Mississippi Beehive College," 21; Winona Williams-Burns, "Jane McAllister: Pioneer for Excellence in Teacher Education," *The Journal of Negro Education* 51 (Summer 1982): 355–57.
14. Williams-Burns, "Jane McAllister: Pioneer for Excellence," 355–57.
15. *Project Enrichment Newsletter*.
16. Ibid.
17. Parsons and Welch, "Mississippi Beehive College," 21.
18. Ibid., 22.
19. Parsons, "Two Women with a Vision," 23.
20. Unpublished biographical data on Jane Ellen McAllister.
21. Alleane M. Currie letter.
22. Ibid.; Parsons, "Two Women with a Vision," 29.
23. Parsons, "Two Women with a Vision," 29.
24. Ibid., 23.

Florence Octavia Alexander

1. Material for this article came from unpublished biographical notes given to George Sewell.

Cleopatra D. Thompson

1. Unless otherwise indicated, material for this article was taken from personal papers of Dr. Cleopatra D. Thompson, Jackson, Mississippi.
2. *Alcorn Herald*, 15 May 1982.
3. Ibid.; *Jackson Advocate*, 27 January 1983, 2 February 1983.

Hazael McFarland Thompson

1. Material for this article came from an unpublished biograpical sketch.

William H. Holtzclaw

1. Material for this article was taken from R. Fulton Holtzclaw, *William Henry Holtzclaw: Scholar in Ebony* (Cleveland: Dillion and Liederback, Inc., 1920); Edith M. Mc Millan, "In Darkest Mississippi," *Opportunity* 2 (October 1924): 294–97.

Willa B. Player

1. Unless otherwise indicated, material for this article was taken from Jacques C. Press, *Leaders in Education* (New York: R. R. Bowker Co., 1974), 869; Peter Murray Papers, Moorland-Spingarn Research Center, Howard University, Washington, D. C.

William Arthur Butts

1. Material for this article came from a letter from the Office of Public Relations, Kentucky State University, 20 January 1976.

Edward Allen Jones

1. Unless otherwise indicated, material for this article was taken from Dr. E. A. Jones, interview with George Sewell, April 1982.
2. Unpublished biographical notes, Jones Papers.

Romeo Benjamin Garrett

1. Unless otherwise indicated, material for this article was taken from Romeo Benjamin Garrett letter to George A. Sewell, 23 October 1975.
2. National Council for Black Studies, "Spotlight on Dr. Romeo Garrett, Professor Emeritus of Bradley University," *Voices in Black Studies: A Newsletter* 6 (March/April 1982), 3, Bloomington: Indiana.
3. Ibid.
4. Ibid.
5. Ibid.

Melerson Guy Dunham

1. Material for this article came from Melerson Guy Dunham letter to George Sewell, 14 February 1976.

Charlemae Hill Rollins

1. Unless otherwise indicated, material for this article was taken from Charlemae Hill Rollins, letter to George Sewell, 13 March 1974.
2. Rosey E. Pool Papers, Moorland-Spingarn Research Center, Manuscript Division, Howard University, Washington, D. C.

Ruby Stutts Lyell

1. Material for this article came from Ruby Stutts, interview with George A. Sewell, August 1980.

Joffrey T. Whisenton

1. Material for this article came from J. T. Whisenton letter to George Sewell, February 1976.

William Smith Demby

1. Material for this article was taken from "William Smith Demby," unpublished manuscript in the possession of George Sewell; William Smith Demby, interview with George Sewell.

The J. E. Johnsons

1. Unless otherwise indicated, material for this article was taken from Anselm J. Finch, "As I Knew J. E. Johnson," *Mississippi Educational Journal* 30 (January 1954), 63–76; Melerson G. Dunham letter, 12 August 1925.
2. C. C. Mosley, *The Negro in Mississippi History* (Jackson: Hederman Brothers, 1950), 69–70.
3. Ibid.
4. Mosley, *The Negro in Mississippi History*, 69–70.
5. Dunham, *Centennial History of Alcorn* A. & M. College (Jackson: University Press of Mississippi, 1971), 88.
6. Program Booklet of Southeastern Association of Women's Clubs, Miami.

Arenia C. Mallory

1. Unless otherwise indicated, material for this article was taken from Benjamin Brawley, *Negro Builders and Heroes*, (Chapel Hill: The University of North Carolina Press, 1937), 263.
2. *The Durant News*, 3 February 1966.

McKinley Charles Martin

1. *Jackson State University Newsletter*, Spring 1960, 6.

Joyce Ladner

1. Ann Allen Shockley and Sue P. Chandler, *Living Black American Authors* (New York: R. R. Bowker Co., 1939), 93.

Gladys Noel Bates

1. Material for this article came from biographical information furnished to George Sewell.

Lou Emma Holloway

1. *The Clarion-Ledger–Jackson Daily News*, 29 September 1974; Campbell and Rogers, *Mississippi: A View from Tougaloo*, 231.

Janice White Sikes

1. Material for this article came from Janice White Sikes, interview with George Sewell, June 1980.

Dorothy Gordon Gray

1. Material for this article came from Dorothy Gray, interview with George Sewell, 1980.

Julius Eric Thompson

1. Material for this article came from unpublished biographical information given to George Sewell.

LITERATURE AND JOURNALISM

Richard Wright

1. Michel Fabre, *The Unfinished Quest of Richard Wright*, trans. Isabel Barzun (New York: William Morrow & Co., Inc., 1973), p. xvii, headnote from "Introduction," p. xv.
2. Ibid., 1.
3. Ibid., 1–2.
4. Ibid., 2.
5. Constance Webb, *Richard Wright, A Biography* (New York: Putnam's Sons, 1968), 13.
6. Fabre, *The Unfinished Quest*, 3.
7. Ibid., 3–4.
8. Ibid., 6–7.
9. Ibid., 7.
10. Richard Wright, *Black Boy* (New York: Harper and Brothers, 1945), 15–16.
11. Ibid.,
12. Ibid., 31–32; Fabre, *The Unfinished Quest*, 15–16.
13. Wright, *Black Boy*, 37–39.
14. Ibid., 34.
15. Ibid., 40.
16. Ibid.
17. Ibid.
18. Ibid., 37–39.
19. Ibid., 75–78.
20. Ibid., 92–94.
21. Webb, *Richard Wright*, 42–43.
22. Wright, *Black Boy*, 95–97.

23. Fabre, *The Unfinished Quest*, 28–30.
24. Ibid., 36.
25. Wright, *Black Boy*, 60.
26. Fabre, *The Unfinished Quest*, 36.
27. Wright, *Black Boy*, 150–59.
28. Ibid., 182–85.
29. Ibid., 59.
30. Webb, *Richard Wright*, 169.
31. Wright, *Black Boy*, 228–40.
32. Ibid., 267.
33. Ibid., 271–73.
34. Ibid., 276–81.
35. Fabre, *The Unfinished Quest*, 77.
36. Quoted in Webb, *Richard Wright*, 92.
37. Ibid., 98.
38. Fabre, *The Unfinished Quest*, 88; see also Webb, *Richard Wright*, 99–100.
39. Quoted in Webb, *Richard Wright*, 103.
40. Ibid., 109.
41. Fabre, *The Unfinished Quest*, 117–18.
42. Ibid., 121–22.
43. Webb, *Richard Wright*, 122.
44. Ibid., 123–24.
45. Ibid., 125–26.
46. Ibid., 130–32.
47. Ibid., 135–36.
48. John M. Reilly, "Richard Wright: Apprenticeship," *Journal of Black Studies* 2 (June 1972): 439–60.
49. Ibid., 141–42.
50. Ibid.; David Bakish, *Richard Wright* (New York: Frederick Ungar Publishing Co., 1973) 18; John M. Reilly, "Richard Wright's Discovery of the Third World," *Minority Voices* 2 (Fall 1973): 47–53.
51. Bakish, *Richard Wright*, 19.
52. Ibid., 27–28.
53. Ibid., 29–30; Richard Wright, letter to Arthur Spingarn, 9 February 1941, Spingarn Center, Howard University, Washington D.C.
54. Bakish, *Richard Wright*, 41–42.
55. Webb, *Richard Wright*, 187–88.
56. Bakish, *Richard Wright*, 51.
57. Webb, *Richard Wright*, 208–09.
58. Bakish, *Richard Wright*, xii, 53–54.
59. Webb, *Richard Wright*, 400.
60. Ibid., 6.

Margaret Walker Alexander

1. Unless otherwise indicated, material for this article was taken from Margaret Walker Alexander, interview with George A. Sewell, 1980.
2. Rose Ragsdale, "At Home with Dr. Margaret Walker Alexander," *Sunbelt*, 1 May 1980, 9.
3. Ibid.
4. Margaret Walker Alexander interview.
5. Ibid.
6. Bonnie L. Jackson, "Margaret Walker Alexander Day," *Sunbelt*, 1 July 1980, 38.
7. Ragsdale, "At Home with Dr. Margaret Walker Alexander," 10; Clarice T. Camp-

bell and Oscar Allan Rogers, Jr., *The View from Tougaloo* (Jackson: University Press of Mississippi, 1979), 265.
  8. Margaret Walker Alexander interview; "Margaret Walker-Four Poems," *New Challenge: A Literary Quarterly* 2 (Fall 1937): 49.
  9. Ragsdale, "At Home with Dr. Margaret Walker Alexander," 10–11.
  10. Margaret Walker Alexander interview.

Anne Moody

  1. Ann Allen Shockley and Sue P. Chandler, *Living Black American Authors* (New York: R. R. Bowker Co., 1973), 111–12; Gerda Lerner, ed., *Black Women in White America: A Documentary History* (New York: Vintage Books, 1972), 425–31; Anne Moody, *Coming of Age in Mississippi* (New York: Dial Press, 1968), 235–39; Campbell and Rogers, *Mississippi: The View from Tougaloo*, 201; Carl Brauer, *John F. Kennedy and the Second Reconstruction* (New York: Columbia University Press, 1978), 313, 318.

Percy Greene

  1. Material for this article came from an interview with Percy Greene by George A. Sewell, 31 December 1975, and Mrs. C. C. Mosley, *The Negro in Mississippi History* (Jackson: Hederman Brothers Publishers, 1950), 59.

The William A. Scott Family

  1. Cornelius Aldolphus Scott, Interviewed by George A. Sewell.
  2. James S. Smoot, "The Negro Press: Voice for Civil Rights," *Freedomways* 3 (September 1963): 202–14.

Lerone Bennett, Jr.

  1. Harry A. Ploski and Ernest Kaiser, *The Negro Almanac* (New York: The Bellwether Company, 1971), 666; "Twenty Years of Ebony," *Ebony*, November 1965, 79.
  2. Ibid.
  3. Correspondence, Public Relations Office, Johnson Publishing Co.
  4. Ibid.; Lerone Bennett, "Unity in the Black Community," *The Black Position* 1 (1971): 6–7.
  5. John Henrick Clarke, "Lerone Bennett: Social Historian," *Freedomways* 5 (Fall 1965): 481–92.
  6. Ibid., 484–85.
  7. Ibid., 488.
  8. Ibid., 489.
  9. Ibid., 491–92.
  10. *Ebony*, August 1975, 40.
  11. Correspondence, Public Relations Office, Johnson Publishing Co.

William Dilday

  1. Lynette Shelton, "WLBT-TV 3—New Beginnings," *Sunbelt*, 1 January 1980, 5; "Coloring TV in Mississippi: William Dilday Is the Nation's First Black TV Station

Manager," *Ebony*, March 1973, 108–12.
  2. Shelton, "WLBT-TV 3—New Beginnings," 5.
  3. Ibid.; *Ebony*, "Coloring TV in Mississippi," 112.

Sarah Harvey Stevens

  1. Biographical notes, private collection of George A. Sewell.

Jessie Mosley

  1. Biographical notes, private collection of George A. Sewell.

William Gordon

  1. Material for this article came from Atlanta *Daily World*, (n. d.).

Elizabeth Taylor Greenfield

  1. Eileen Southern, *The Music of Black Americans: A History* (New York: W. W. Norton & Co., 1971), 245; Benjamin Brawley, *Negro Builders and Heroes* (Chapel Hill: University of North Carolina Press, 1965), 249; George C. Grant, "The Negro in the Dramatic Arts," *Journal of Negro History* 16 (January 1932): 32.
  2. Monroe N. Works, *Negro Year Book: An Annual Encyclopedia of the Negro, 1914–1915* (Tuskegee Institute, Alabama: The Negro Year Book Publishing Company, 1915), 268.

William Grant Still

  1. Verna Arvey, *William Grant Still* (New York: J. Fischer & Bros., 1939), 46; Edgar Toppin, *A Biographical History of Blacks in America* (New York: David McKay, 1971), 418; John E. Skates, *Mississippi: A Bicentennial History* (New York: W. W. Norton, 1979), 148.
  2. Toppin, *A Biographical History*, 415.
  3. Eileen Southern, *The Music of Black Americans: A History* (New York: W. W. Norton & Co., 1971), 454.
  4. Arvey, *William Grant Still*, 9; Toppin, *A Biographical History*, 416.
  5. Arvey, *William Grant Still*, 9–10.
  6. Ibid., 10.
  7. Toppin, *A Biographical History*, 416.
  8. Arvey, *William Grant Still*, 11.
  9. Ibid.; Alain Locke, "Toward A Critique of Negro Music," *Opportunity* 12 (November, 1934): 331.
  10. Arvey, *William Grant Still*, 11.
  11. Ibid.
  12. Ibid., 12; Edwin R. Embree, *13 Against the Odds* (Port Washington, New York: Kennikat Press, 1968), 209–10.
  13. Toppin, *A Biographical History*, 416.
  14. Ibid.; Arvey, *William Grant Still*, 12.
  15. Toppin, *A Biographical History*, 416; Embree, *13 Against the Odds*, 204.
  16. Arvey, *William Grant Still*, 12–13; Toppin, *A Biographical History*, 416–17.

17. Arvey, *William Grant Still*, 13.
18. Ibid.
19. Ibid., 13–14; Embree, *13 Against the Odds*, 205.
20. Arvey, *William Grant Still*, 14.
21. Ibid., 23.
22. Ibid.; Toppin, *A Biographical History*, 416.
23. Toppin, *A Biographical History*, 416.
24. Southern, *The Music of Black Americans*, 456–60.
25. Arvey, *William Grant Still*, 46; William Grant Still letter to Harriet Gibbs Marshall, 29 December 1938, Washington Conservatory of Music Papers, Moorland-Spingarn Research Center, Howard University, Washington, D. C.
26. Embree, *13 Against the Odds*, 208.
27. *The Clarion-Ledger–Jackson Daily News*, 15 November 1974, 4.
28. Langston Hughes, *Famous Negro Music Makers* (New York: Dodd, Mead & Co., 1955).
29. Embree, *13 Against the Odds*, 209.
30. Hughes, *Famous Negro Music Makers*, 89.

Leontyne Price

1. Time, 10 March 1961, 59; *Current Biography*, 1961, 374; Skates, *Mississippi: A Bicentennial History*, 148.
2. Time, 63.
3. *Ebony*, April 1961, 185.
4. Time, 59.
5. Hattie V. J. McInnis, "My Most Famous Student," *National Retired Teachers Association Journal* 25 (May/June 1974), 61.
6. *Ebony*, 185.
7. Ibid.
8. Time, 59–60; Southern, *The Music of Black Americans*, 501–03, 505, 508.
9. *Current Biography*, 374.
10. Time, 59–60.
11. Toppin, *A Biographical History of Blacks in America*, 390.
12. *Current Biography*, 374.
13. Charlemae Rollins, *Famous Negro Entertainers of Stage, Screen and TV* (New York: Dodd, Mead & Co., 1967), 88.
14. Time, 60.
15. Rollins, *Famous Negro Entertainers*, 88.
16. Time, 60.
17. Ibid.
18. Rollins, *Famous Negro Entertainers*, 88–89.
19. Ibid., 89; *Current Biography*, 374.
20. *Current Biography*, 375.
21. Time, 10; Frank Smith and Audrey Warren, *Mississippians All* (New Orleans: Pelican Publishing House, 1968), 38.
22. *Current Biography*, 375.
23. Ibid.
24. Time, 60.
25. *Current Biography*, 375.
26. Ibid., Rollins, *Famous Negro Entertainers*, 90.
27. Rollins, *Famous Negro Entertainers*, 90.
28. Ibid., 91; Smith and Warren, *Mississippians All*, 38.
29. *Ebony*, 12 December 1966, 188.
30. Time, 58.

31. Current Biography, 375.
32. Ebony, 185.
33. Time, 58.
34. Smith and Warren, *Mississippians All*, 39.
35. Time, 58.
36. Ibid., 59.
37. Ibid., 64; Smith and Warren, *Mississippians All*, 40; Time, 64.
38. Smith and Warren, *Mississippians All*, 40–41; Current Biography, 375.
39. Smith and Warren, *Mississippians All*, 390; Rollins, *Famous Negro Entertainers*, 92.
40. Ebony, 185; Smith and Warren, *Mississippians All*, 35.
41. Smith and Warren, *Mississippians All*, 35.
42. Ibid., 41–42.
43. Time, 24 March 1967, 80.
44. Ibid.
45. Saturday Review of Literature, 9 September 1972, 32.
46. Time, 62–63.
47. Current Biography, 375; Rollins, *Famous Negro Entertainers*, 91–92.
48. Rollins, *Famous Negro Entertainers*, 91–92; Current Biography, 375.
49. Time, 63; "Who Has Class and Style," Ebony, 5 March 1978, 44.

B. B. King

1. Henry Pleasants, *The Great American Popular Singers* (New York: Simon and Schuster, 1974), 315.
2. Ibid.; "Blues a la King," concert, Toronto, Canada. Jeanette Roach, librarian, Tougaloo College, and her staff made available photocopies of materials published by Tougaloo College and by King's public relations officer. In many instances these carried no author or date.
3. Pleasants, *The Great American Popular Singers*, 35; Boston Sunday Globe, 21 November 1971.
4. Pleasants, The Great American Popular Singers, 315–16; Current Biography, 1970, 227.
5. George Goodman, "B. B. King," Look, 29 June 1971, 55; James H. Cone, *The Spirituals and the Blues: An Interpretation* (New York: The Seabury Press, 1972), 108–42.
6. Pete Fox and Joseph Belsito, "B. B. King—King of the Blues" (New York: Indianola Productions, Inc.).
7. Pleasants, The Great American Popular Singers, 316.
8. Goodman, "B. B. King," 56.
9. Pleasants, *The Great American Popular Singers*, 316.
10. Ibid., 316–17.
11. Ibid.; Fox and Belsito, "B. B. King—King of the Blues."
12. Goodman, "B. B. King," 56.
13. Memphis Press-Scimitar, 21 August 1971.
14. Fox and Belsito, "B. B. King—King of the Blues."
15. Memphis Press-Scimitar (n. d.).
16. Ibid.
17. Pleasants, *The Great American Popular Singers*, 317.
18. Ibid.
19. B. B. King, "Every Day I Have the Blues," recording.
20. New York Post, 26 April 1974.
21. Pleasants, *The Great American Popular Singers*, 309.
22. Current Biography, 227.

23. *Savannah Morning News*, 17 December 1972.
24. *Esquire*, December 1970, 139.
25. Goodman, "B. B. King," 57.
26. *Club Calendar*, 1 (1973), 4.
27. McColloch, 31 January 1972. B.
28. *Savannah Morning News*, 17 December 1972.
29. *Los Angeles Times*, (n. d.).
30. *The New York Times*, 26 April 1974.
31. "B. B. King and Lucille."
32. Ibid.
33. *Blues & Soul*, 1973.
34. Ibid.; *New York Post*, 26 April 1974.
35. "Grapevine," 15 November 1971.
36. *Playgirl*, October 1973.
37. *Paris International Herald Tribune*, 2 November 1973.
38. *Music Week*, 4 November 1972.
39. Pleasants, *The Great Amereican Popular Singers*, 330.
40. Ibid., 18.
41. *New Zealand Herald*, 5 March 1974.
42. All the above-mentioned honors are from a sheet "B. B. King," published by Sidney A. Seidenberg, Inc., King's manager.
43. B. B. King Collection, Tougaloo College Library, Jackson, Mississippi.

Bo Diddley

1. Unpublished biographical sketch of Elias "Bo Diddley" Mc Daniel.
2. Ibid.
3. Ibid.
4. William Ferris, *Blues from the Delta: An Illustrated Documentary on the Music and Musicians of the Mississippi Delta* (New York: Doubleday, 1979): 9; Theodore Mc Daniel, "The Political Economy of Black Music," Paper presented at Fifth Annual Conference of CIC, Summer Institute, Ohio State University, Columbus, July 1983.
5. James R. Mitchell, "The Marketing of Black Music," *Contributions in Black Studies* 4 (1980/1981): 10; Unpublished biographical sketch.
6. Unpublished biographical sketch.
7. Ibid.

Charley Pride

1. Public relations materialsl furnished by Hortense C. Jones, 4 April 1974.
2. *The Clarion-Ledger–Jackson Daily News*, 8 December 1974.
3. *Forward Times*, 3 March 1973; *The Clarion-Ledger–Jackson Daily News*, 11 April 1974.
4. *Vicksburg Sunday Post*, 9 May 1971, 5.
5. Ibid.; *Ebony*, March 1967, 62.
6. *Vicksburg Sunday Post*, 5.
7. Ibid.
8. *St. Louis Dispatch*, 12 March 1973.
9. *Esquire*, March 1971, 60.
10. *St. Louis Dispatch*; *Ebony*, 64.
11. *Vicksburg Evening Post*, 9 May 1971.
12. *Vicksburg Sunday Post*, 9 May 1971.

13. Ibid.
14. *St. Louis Dispatch.*
15. Ibid.
16. Ibid.
17. Ibid.
18. *Time,* 6 May 1974, 52.
19. Public relations materials, Hortense C. Jones.

Arthur Crudup

1. Material for this article came from Charles W. Tisdale, "Big Boy Crudup: The Forgotten 'Blues' Hero," *Jackson Advocate,* February 1980.

Frederick O'Neal

1. "O'Neal Will Keynote Black Heritage Program," UFT Bulletin—New York Teacher (February 1982): 2; Charles Wesley, *The Quest for Equality: From Civil War to Civil Rights* (Cornwells Heights, Pennsylvania: The Association for the Study of Afro-American Life and History, 1969), 206.
2. Harry A. Ploski and Ernest Kaiser, *The Negro Almanac* (New York: The Bellwether Company, 1971), 780; Peter Bailey, "Black Theater Group Goes on Broadway: Negro Ensemble Company Scores with Taut Family Drama," Ebony, 8 June 1973, 84–94.
3. "O'Neal Will Keynote Black Heritage Program," 2.
4. Ibid.

James Earl Jones

1. *Current Biography,* 1969, 226.
2. Ibid.
3. Ibid.
4. Ibid.; *Newsweek,* 2 December 1963, 68.
5. *Newsweek,* 68.
6. *Current Biography,* 226.
7. Ibid.
8. Ibid., 227.
9. Ibid.
10. *Ebony,* 7 June 1969, 54.
11. Ibid., 60.
12. Ibid.
13. *Current Biography,* 227.
14. Sherry Johnson, "Video-Land: Our Image, Our Destiny," *Sunbelt,* 1 July 1980), 10, 13–14.
15. *Current Biography,* 228; *Newsweek,* 68.
16. Quoted in *Current Biography,* 227.

Richmond Barthé

1. Unless otherwise indicated, material for this article was taken from Ploski and Kaiser, *The Negro Almanac,* 706–07.
2. Benjamin Brawley, *Negro Builders and Heroes* (Chapel Hill: University of North Carolina Press, 1965), 249.

Sam Gilliam

1. Material for this article came from Ploski and Kaiser, *The Negro Almanac*, 712–13.

LaVern Hamberlin

1. Material for this article was taken from LaVern Hamberlin, interview with Dr. Margaret Dwight and Dr. Ray Davis, 25 January 1982; *Natchez Democrat*, 4 January 1981.

Joseph Overstreet

1. Ploski and Kaiser, *The Negro Almanac*, 718.

Beah Richards

1. *Vicksburg Sunday Post*, 6 February 1977; *Leading Afro-Americans of Vicksburg, Mississippi* (Vicksburg: Biographia Publishing Company, 1908), 15.

William Fischer

1. Southern, *The Music of Black Americans: A History*, 481.

Frederick Douglass Hall

1. Southern, *The Music of Black Americans: A History*, 453.

Raeschelle Potter

1. *The Clarion-Ledger–Jackson Daily Newes*, 30 July 1974.

Lucia Hawkins

1. Material for this article came from the *Vicksburg Sunday Post*, 6 February 1977.

Albert King

1. Material for this article came from *The Clarion-Ledger Jackson Daily News*, 29 January 1973.

Little Milton

1. *Memphis Commercial-Appeal*, 30 September 1973.

Levion Dillon

1. *The Clarion-Ledger–Jackson Daily News*, 30 June 1975.

Ike Turner

1. *Ebony*, undated clipping.

Bukka White

1. *Atlanta Journal-Constitution*, 1977.

Bobby Bryant

1. *The Clarion-Ledger–Jackson Daily News*, 9 May 1971.

RELIGION

1. *Vicksburg Sunday Post*, 24 September 1972; Henry Y. Warnock, "Southern Methodists, the Negro and Unification: The First Phase," *Journal of Negro History* 52 (October 1967): 287–304; Eugene Portlette Southall, "The Attitude of the Methodist Episcopal Church: South, Toward the Negro from 1844 to 1870," *Journal of Negro History* 15 (January 1930): 359–370; Gene Ramsey Miller, "A History of North Mississippi Methodism, 1820–1900" (Ph. D. dissertation, Starkville, Mississippi State College, August 1964).
2. German R. Ross, *The History and Formative Years of the Church of God in Christ* (Memphis: Church of God in Christ Publishing House, 1969), 1–50.
3. Ibid.; Lawrence W. Levine, *Black Culture and Black Consciousness: Afro-American Folk Thought from Slavery to Freedom* (New York: Oxford University Press, 1977), 170.
4. Elder Dave Pitchford, Theola McSwain, and Dora Connors, interviews with Margaret Dwight, 1 November 1982.
5. Ibid.; *Ebony*.
6. *The Clarion-Ledger–Jackson Daily News*, 29 January 1973; Joseph Butsch, "Catholics and the Negro," *Journal of Negro History* (October 1917): 393–410; John P. Alston, Letitia T. Alston and Emory Warrick, "Black Catholics: Social and Cultural Characteristics," *Journal of Black Studies* (December 1971): 245–55.

Alexander P. Shaw

1. Unless otherwise indicated, material for this article was taken from John H. Graham, *Mississippi Circuit Riders, 1865–1965* (Nashville: Partheon Press, 1967), 206–08.
2. Karl E. Downs, *Meet the Negro* (Pasadena: Login Press, 1943), 146.

Sherman L. Greene

1. *This Is Your Life*, a pamphlet (Six Episcopal District, African Methodist Episcopal Church, 1962), 1.

2. Ibid.
3. *Three Quadrenniums of Outstanding Service of a Great Leader*, a pamphlet (Jackson: Campbell College, n. d.), 13–14.
4. *This Is Your Life*, 2.
5. Ibid.
6. Reverend Joseph T. McMillian, Obituary.
7. Milton Mickens, *Bishop S. L. Greene: Twelve Years of Record Breaking Service*, A Pamphlet (Jackson: Campbell College, n. d.), 4.
8. McMillian, Obituary.
9. *Three Quadrenniums of Outstanding Service of a Great Leader*, 1.

Lucy Jefferson

1. W. H. Jefferson, III, interview with George A. Sewell, 17 January 1975.
2. *Leading Afro-Americans of Vicksburg* (Vicksburg: Biographia Publishing Co., 1908), 46.
3. Mrs. Charles C. Mosley, *The Negro in Mississippi History* (Jackson: Hederman Brothers, 1950), 121.
4. *Leading Afro-Americans of Vicksburg*, 46.
5. Mosley, *The Negro in Mississippi History*, 121.

H. Hartford Brookins

1. Stacey Peck, "Helene and H. Hartford Brookins," *Los Angeles Times Home Magazine*, 16 May 1980, 66; James B. Browning, "The Beginning of Insurance Enterprises Among Negroes," *Journal of Negro History* 22 (October 1937): 417.
2. Peck, "Helene and H. Hartford Brookins," 69.
3. Ibid.
4. Ibid.
5. Biographical notes: Morris Brown College Centennial Founder's Day program, 17 March 1981.
6. Ibid.

Homer C. McEwen, Sr.

1. Material for this article came from unpublished biographical notes.

Joseph H. Jackson

1. *Ebony*, December 1964, 77; Kenneth K. Bailey, "Protestantism and Afro-Americans in the Old South: Another Look, *Journal of Southern History* 41 (November 1975): 466–71.
2. Harry A. Ploski and Ernest Kaiser, eds., *Negro Almanac* (New York: Bellwether Company, 1971), 617.
3. Ethel L. Williams, *Biographical Directory of Negro Ministers* (New York: Scarecrow Press, Inc., 1965) 190; *Time*, 6 April 1970.
4. Williams, *Biographical Directory of Negro Ministers*, 190.
5. *Ebony*, December 1964, 79.
6. Ibid.
7. National Baptist convention public relations material.
8. Ibid., August 1975, 35–36.

I. Venchael Booth

1. Mrs. W. C. Boykins (Dr. Booth's sister), interview with George Sewell, 2 March 1976.
2. Unless otherwise indicated, material for this article was taken from L. V. Booth, letter, 12 January 1976.

Mae Frances Spencer

1. *The Clarion-Ledger–Jackson Daily News*, 30 November 1975.

MEDICINE

Sidney Redmond

1. Unless otherwise indicated, material for this article was taken from the unpublished papers of Dr. Sidney Dillion Redmond, which were made available through the kindness of attorney Jack Young, administrator of the S. D. Redmond estate.
2. Monroe N. Works, *Negro Year Book: An Annual Encyclopedia of the Negro, 1918–1919* (Tuskegee Institute, Alabama: The Negro Year Book Publishing Company, 1919), 202.

Dr. L. T. Miller

1. Daisy M. Greene, letter to George A. Sewell, 11 March 1974.
2. Ibid.
3. Ibid.
4. *Ebony*, March 1950, 29.
5. Ibid.
6. D. W. Wilburns, interview with George A. Sewell, Wilburns home, Yazoo City, April 1974.
7. Ibid.
8. Ibid.
9. *Ebony*, March 1950, 29.
10. Ibid.
11. Ibid.
12. Dr. George A. Carmichael, interview with George A. Sewell, 5 April 1975.
13. Ibid.
14. *Ebony*, March 1950, 28.
15. Ibid.
16. Mrs. J. B. Overton, telephone interview with George A. Sewell, 18 November 1975.
17. Robert C. Grant, Executive Secretary, Alumni Affairs, Meharry Medical College, letter to George A. Sewell, 24 April 1974; *The Clarion-Ledger–Jackson Daily News*, 18 April 1974.

George H. Lane

1. Material for this article came from *Excellence*, Fall 1980, 11.

Deborah Hyde-Rowan

1. Material for this article came from Marilyn Marshall, "Neurosurgery: Two Black Women Surgeons Are Pioneers in Highly Specialized Medical Field," *Ebony*, September 1983, 72–76.

Eliza J. Pillars

1. Willa M. Maddix, R. N., "A Pioneer in Mississippi," *Opportunity* 15 (November 1937): 332; Estelle Massey Riddle, R. N., "The Negro Nurse: The Supply and The Demand," *Journal of American Medical Association* 108 (March 1937): 1047; Dorothy Deming, R. N., "The Negro Nurse in Public Health," *Opportunity* 15 (November 1937): 333–35.
2. Maddix, "A Pioneer in Mississippi," 332; "Friends of Humanity: Bricks Without Straw," *Opportunity* 15 (November 1937): 324–25.
3. Maddix, "A Pioneer in Mississippi," 332; WPA, "Concerning Children and Childbirth," WPA Papers Manuscript Division, Mississippi Department of Archives and History.
4. WPA, "Concerning Children and Childbirth"; Mabel Keaton Staupers, R. N., "The Negro Nurse in America," *Opportunity* 15 (November 1937): 339–41; "What Are the Opportunities for Colored Girls to Acquire Nursing Training in the South?" *Opportunity* 15 (November 1937): 330–31.
5. Maddix, "A Pioneer in Mississippi," 332.

Rhetaugh G. Dumas

1. Material for this article came from a news release, National Institute of Mental Health, U. S. Department of Health, Education and Welfare, 8 June 1972.

Jessie O. Thomas

1. Unless otherwise indicated, material for this article was taken from Jesse O. Thomas, *My Story in Black and White* (New York: Exposition Press, 1967), 10.
2. Dr. Benjamin E. Mays, "My View," *Pittsburgh Courier* (undated clipping supplied by Mrs. Melerson Guy Dunham).
3. Jessie O. Thomas, "Economic Deadlines in the South," *Opportunity* 4 (February 1926): 48–49.

Lucille Price

1. Material for this article came from *The Clarion-Ledger–Jackson Daily News*, 19 October 1975.

Cleo W. Blackburn

1. Charles W. Ferguson, "Americans Not Everyone Knows," *Parents and Teachers Association Magazine*, October 1968, 21.
2. Ibid.
3. Ibid.
4. Ibid.; Cleo W. Blackburn, letter to George A. Sewell, 16 November 1975.

Walter Massey

1. Material for this article came from "1979 Highlights in Pictures," Ebony, January 1980, 51.

Natalia Tanner Cain

1. Ebony (n. d.), 47–58.

Margaret Lawrence

1. The Clarion-Ledger Jackson Daily News, 30 November 1975.

Gwendolyn Nero Loper

1. Paul E. Baker, "Mental Hygenics for Negroes in the South," Opportunity (June 1937): 211–13.

Georgie Catchings Coleman

1. Material for this article came from Sunbelt, December 1979, 11.

Jennifer O. Hicks

1. Port Gibson Reveille, 11 August 1983.

SPORTS

1. Lerone Bennett, Jr., "Jesse Owens; Olympic Triumph Over Time and Hitlerism," Ebony, December 1983, 140–146; Harry A. Ploski and James Williams, The Afro-American (New York: John Wiley & Sons, 1983), 23, 922, 928–29, 950.
2. Marino Casem, letter to George Sewell 13 February 1976.
3. Marino Casem interview with George Sewell, 11 February 1975.
4. Marino Casem, letter.

Walter Jerry Payton

1. Marino Casem, letter.
2. "Multi-millionaires Under 30," Ebony, March 1984, 134.
3. Newsweek, 5 December 1975, 63.
4. Sports, n.d., 27.
5. Sports Illustrated, December 1976, 70; Time, 19 December 1977, 16.
6. "Walter Payton," Ebony, December 1979, 106.

7. Ibid.
8. *Sports*, January 1980, 32.
9. *Black Stars*, November 1980, 23.
10. Ibid; *Newsweek*, 5 December 1977, 63.
11. *Ebony*, February 1977, 88.

Luisa Harris Stewart

1. Andrew Harris, "Luisa Harris Stewart: Lady Statesman," *Sunbelt* (August 1980), 20–21, 35.

Pete Brown

1. *Newsweek*, 16 February 1970; Harry A. Ploski and James Williams, *The Afro-American* (New York: John Wiley & Sons, 1983), p. 937.
2. Ibid.
3. *Jackson Daily News*, 30 June 1970.

Spencer Haywood

1. *Newsweek*, 15 February 1971.

Eugene Short

1. *Jackson Daily News*, 17 August 1975; Andrew Love, "Eugene Short: Short Changed? *Sunbelt*, January 1980, 30–31.

George Scott

1. *Jackson Daily News*, 15 July 1975.

Mildrette Netter

1. *Alcorn Herald*, Fall 1969.

MILITARY

Thomas J. Money, Jr.

1. Material for this article came from an unpublished biographical sketch, "Money Papers," Thomas J. Money, Jr., family collection.

Jesse Leroy Brown

1. Daisy Brown Thorne, interview with Margaret Dwight, 22 August 1983; "Ensign

Jesse L. Brown," Department of the Navy, Naval Historical Center, Washington Navy Yard, Washington, D. C.; Richard T. Speer, Navy Ship's Histories Branch, to Bravitt Manley 14 May 1980.

2. Daisy Brown Thorne, interview; John E. Weems, "Black Wings of Gold," *U. S. Naval Institute Proceedings* (July 1983): 36.

3. Weems, "Black Wings of Gold," 36; Rose Ragsdale-Bozeman, "If I Make It, I'll Be the First," *Sunbelt*, February 1980, 23.

4. "Yesterday, Today and Tomorrow: New DE Honors First Black Aviator," *Cruiser Destroyman*, Naval Historical Center.

5. Weems, "Black Wings of Gold," 36.

6. Ibid., 37.

7. Ibid., 38; *Ebony*, April 1951.

8. Weems, "Black Wings of Gold," 38–39.

9. "Exceptional Courage, Airmanship and Devotion," *Fly Navy: The Magazine of Naval Air Training* (21 September 1971): 6–7; *Washington Post*, 9 February 1971; Weems, "Black Wings of Gold," 38–39.

10. "Ensign Jesse L. Brown," *Washington Star*, 9 April 1971, Naval Historical Center.

11. "Navy Secretary Names Destroyer for First Black Naval Aviator," *News Release*, 8 February 1971, Office of Assistant Secretary of Defense—Public Affairs, Washington, D. C.; "Ship Honoring Black Navy Hero to Be Launched," *News Release*, 17 March 1972, Office of Information: Biographies Branch (01-0111), Washington, D. C., 4 December 1972; L. A. Olsson, "USS Jesse L. Brown," 15 November 1971, Department of Defense, Washington, D. C.; "USS Jesse L. Brown to Be Commissioned," *News Release*, Office of Assistant Secretary of Defense—Public Affairs, Washington, D. C.

12. "Responses: Family Tree," *Sunbelt*, June 1980, 4, 41; Daisy Brown Thorne interview.

John Mitchell Brown

1. Resumé provided by the late Lt.Colonel Norman S. Calhoun, PMS, Department of Military Science, Alcorn State University; Harry A. Ploski and James Williams, *The Negro Almanac: A Reference Work on the Afro-American* (New York: John Wiley & Sons, 1983), p. 888.

Modis A. Smiley

1. *The Clarion-Ledger–Jackson Daily News*, 18 September 1974.

Glennie M. Rowland

1. *Alcorn State University Weekly Bulletin*, 9 September 1983.

Daniel L. Jennings

1. *Port Gibson Reveille*, 21 October 1976; Phillip Drotton, *Black Heroes of Our Nation's History*.

Appendix

APPENDIX A
Black Members of the Mississippi Legislature in 1872

SENATE

Member	County
Hiram R. Revels	Adams
William Gray	Washington
Thomas W. Stringer	Warren
Peter Barrow	Warren
Charles Calwell	Hinds
Robert Gleed	Lowndes

HOUSE OF REPRESENTATIVES

Member	County
Henry Jacobs	Adams
John R. Lynch	Adams
Reuben Kendrick	Amite
Joseph Smothers	Claiborne
Thomas McCain	De Soto
J. H. Johnson	De Soto
Monroe Bell	Hinds
William Johnson	Hinds
Charles Reese	Hinds
F. Steward	Holmes
H. H. Trueharts	Holmes
Perry Howard	Holmes
Richard Griggs	Issaquena
R. W. Houston	Issaquena
William Landers	Jefferson
J. D. Cessar	Jefferson
A. Handy	Madison
J. J. Spellman	Madison
Arthur Brooks	Monroe

William Holmes	Monroe
A. K. Davis	Noxubee
Isham Stewart	Noxubee
Randle Nettles	Oktibbeha
John Cooke	Panola
J. H. Piles	Panola
H. C. Carter	Warren
I. D. Shadd	Warren
William H. Mallory	Warren
Charles W. Bush	Warren
J. E. Morgan	Washington
John D. Webster	Washington
H. M. Foley	Wilkinson
George White	Wilkinson
James M. Dixon	Yazoo
F. D. Wade	Yazoo
G. W. Gayles	Bolivar
James Hill	Marshall
Gilbert Smith	Tunica

Source: *Journal of Negro History*, Vol. 5, pp. 74, 75
New National Era, (March 28, 1872)

APPENDIX B
Mississippi Black Elected Officials—1982

STATE SENATORS

Douglas Anderson–District 27
Henry Kirksey–District 28

STATE REPRESENTATIVES:

Fred Banks–District 69
Horace Buckley–District 70
Credell Calhoun–District 68
Robert Clark–District 49
Tyrone Ellis–District 40
Hillman Frazier–District 67
Isiah Fredericks–District 119
David Green–District 98
Clayton Henderson–District 9
Aaron Henry–District 26
Leslie King–District 5
Barney Schoby–District 95
Charles Sheppard–District 87
Percy Watson–District 104
Charles Young–District 84

COUNTY SUPERVISORS:

Howard T. Bailey–Holmes
Willie Bunton–Issaquena
Eddie Burrell–Claiborne
George Curry–Oktibbeha
John Eggleston–Claiborne
Bilbo Ferguson–Wilkinson
John Ferguson–Warren
Noble Frisby–Jefferson
Sylvester Gaines–Jefferson
Louis Gaulden–Wilkinson
James Hamberlin–Jefferson
Neal Holliday–Clay

Sol Jackson–Jefferson
Charlie Johnson–Claiborne
James Johnson–Holmes
Herman Leach–Yazoo
Sylvester Reed–Quitman
William Matt Ross–Claiborne
Alix Sanders–Leflore
Ralph Sewill, Sr.–Humphreys
Eddie Smith–Coahoma
George Smith–Hinds
Kermit Stanton–Bolivar
Joseph Stevenson–Noxubee
Bennie Thompson–Hinds
Bernice Totten–Marshall
Phillip West–Adams

ELECTION COMMISSIONERS:

Ellis Braxton–Jefferson
Theodore Briggs–Marshall
Charles Clark–Claiborne
Georgia Clark–Holmes
Henry Clarke–Holmes
Roy Davis–Madison
Jennetter Dawson–Wilkinson
Katye Dukes–Adams
Johnnie Durham–Claiborne
Inez Franklin–Jefferson
James Gray–Claiborne
Bernard Handy–Quitman
George Hooper–Humphreys
Sam J. Horton–Holmes
George Huff–Amite
Betty Hunt–Hinds
Maggie Jackson–Jefferson
Kermit James–Humphreys
Ernestine Johnson–Leflore
Nellie Johnson–Tunica
Annie L. Keys–Jefferson
Bowen Lane–Clay
Aletha Lucas–Covington
Isabell Nash–Claiborne
Walter Pitchford–Holmes
Alice Scott–Madison
Ruth Shirley–Hinds
Louella Singletary–Coahoma
John Taylor–Marshall
Eddie Williams–Marshall
Marvin Williams–Humphreys

OTHER COUNTY OFFICIALS

Annie Brown–Tax Assessor & Collector–Holmes
Alvin Carter–Coroner–Ranger–Clay
William Crawford–Circuit Clerk–Tunica
Evan Doss, Jr.–Tax Assessor & Collector–Claiborne
Stella Jennings–Chancery Clerk–Claiborne
Julia Jones–Circuit Clerk–Claiborne
Leander Monroe–Coroner–Ranger–Claiborne
Everett Sanders–County Prosecutor–Claiborne
Horace Stringer–Coroner–Ranger–Jefferson
Bennie Turner–County Prosecutor–West Point

ALDERMEN

Shirley Allen–Metcalfe
Melvin Amos–Falcon
Ellis Atkins–Rosedale
Curtis Austin–Columbus
John Beamon–Renova
Silas Bell–Gloster
Edward Bishop Sr.–Corinth

STATE ALDERMEN

Floyd Boclair–Grenada
Lucille Bonney–Arcola
A. Z. Booker–Jonestown
George Booker–Oakland
Hollie Booth–Tylertown
Otis Boyd–Morton
Johnny F. Bradley–Pace
Hattie Braxton–Coahoma
Richard Brooks–Macon
Frank Brown–Beulah
Hezekiah Brown–Hollandale
Robert Brown–Crawford
A. J. Buckhalter–Crawford
Theodore Bullock–McComb
Angie Lee Butler–Coahoma
Clyde Cadney Jr.–Fayette

Appendix

John Calmese–Gunnison
William Percy Calvin–Yazoo City
Annyce Campbell–Mound Bayou
Lee Aaron Causey–Renova
Howard Chambliss–Fayette
Mamie Chase–Coahoma
Terry A. Chewe–Pontotoc
Laura Christian–Jonestown
James C. Clarke–Forest
Manuel Coleman–Renova
Robert Collins–Holly Springs
Roger Cooperman–Aberden
James B. Curry–Beulah
Dudley Davis–Bolton
Melvin Donaldson–Falcon
James H. Edmond–Grenada
Joe Edwards–Ruleville
Shirley Edwards–Ruleville
Fred Esco Jr.–Canton
Henry W. Epsy Jr.–Clarksdale
Harry J. Farve–Bay St. Louis
Mildred Fleming–Mayersville
Milton Webster Forte–Louin
Jason Gibson–Tchula
George P. Gillespie–Olive Branch
Roosevelt Granderson–Tchula
Boyce E. Grayson–Tupelo
Roosevelt Greenwood–Jonestown
Etta B. Greer–Pickens
Roosevelt Grenell–Cleveland
Edward L. Griffin–Shelby
Lonnie Gunns–Shaw
Will Hall Jr.–Gunnison
Melvin Harris–Magnolia
William B. Henley–Holly Springs
Walter D. Holland–Metcalfe
Jerry Howard–Goodman
Johnny Howard Jr.–Winstonville
Milton Hunt–Renova
James Ingram–Yazoo City
Sylvester Ingram–Moorhead
Levon Jackson–Gunnison
Louis Jackson–Moss Point
Monroe Jackson–Falcon
Eddie Jakes–Friars Point
Charles James–Woodville
Albert Zena Johnson–Fayette
Charles Johnson–Oakland
Clarence Johnson–Brookhaven
Herman Johnson–Mound Bayou
Sara H. Johnson–Greenville
Walter Lee Johnson–Coahoma
Joe Jones–Winstonville
Joni Jones–Ellisville
Luther Jones–Picayue
Joseph Jordan Jr.–Crawford
F. C. Kelson, Jr.–Crenshaw
Rogers W. King–Fayette
Henry Knox–Pace
Hobert Kornegay–Meridan
Sylvester Kyles Jr.–Shaw
John T. Lawson–Gunnison
Theodore Lawyer–Pass Christian
L. C. Leach–Bolton
Aaron Lee–Edwards
Solomon Leflore–Crenshaw
Carl Lewis–Beulah
Luther Malone–Roxie
Edgar Lee Marshall–Friars Point
Stuart Mason–Winstonville
Virginia McDavid–Metcalfe
John F. McGee–Goodman
Nan Ella McGee–Goodman
Billy McKenzie–Beulah
James McNeese–Falcon
Tom Meeks–Rosedale
J. W. Morgan–Brookhaven
John A. Morris, Sr.–Itta Bena
Shelly Newell–Arcola
George Nichols–Canton
Robert Norvell–Moss Point
Helen F. O'Neal–Crawford
Leroy Parker–Leland
Ben Patterson–Oakland
Robert Patton–Shelby
Henry Perkins–Winstonville
Willie Peterson–Mayersville
Judge Price, Sr.–Edwards
Matthew W. Prophet
Noah Rankin–Fayette
Percy Rawls–Brookhaven
Melvin E. Redmond–Vicksburg
Minnie Ripley–Mayersville
Arthur Roberts–Jonestown
Ernest Robinson, Jr.–Bolton
James E. Rodgers–Shaw
Thomas R. Sanders–Hollandale
Joe Sawyer–Friars Point
Jimmy Shannon–Philadelphia
Claude Smith–Renova

Henry R. Smith–Ruleville
Herman Smith–Shaw
Nerissa Gray Smith–Edwards
Robert Smith–Edwards
Thomas Smith–Falcon
Edward Snyder–Picayune
J. R. Spillers–Moss Point
Riley Swearengen–Oakland
Felix Tate, Sr.–Mound Bayou
Donald Thomas–Coahoma
Kenneth Thomas–Rosedale
Lawrence C. Thompson–Bolton
Ned Tolliber, Jr.–Cleveland
Dewey Townsend–Winona
Robert Vick–Summit
Ivory Walker–Metcalfe
Thomas N. Walker–Edwards
Jaurine Wallace–Mayersville
Harold Ward–Mound Bayou
David Washington–Pace
Willie Washington–Moorehead
Reuben Watson–Shaw
William T. Welch–Pass Christian
George F. West–Natchez
Richard West–West
Desota White–Arcola
Alberta Williams–Pace
Harold E. Williams
J. C. Williams–Friars Point
Jewel Williams–Friars Point
Larry Williams–Rosedale
Robert T. Williams–Mayersville
Thomas Williams–Glendora
Willie Wilson–Winstonville
Alton Witherspoon–Magnolia
Edmund Yung–Beulah

OTHER MUNICIPAL OFFICIALS:

Myltree Adams–Tax Collector–Coahoma
Annie Griffin–Clerk–Friars Point
Helen R. Harris–Clerk–Bolton

JUDICIAL AND LAW ENFORCEMENT:

Reuben Anderson–Judge, County Court–Jackson
Cleve McDowell–Judge, Tunica Co.–Tunica

MAGISTRATES, JUSTICES OF THE PEACE, CONSTABLES:

Lindsey D. Adams–Constable Dist. 3–Rolling Fork
James Allen–Constable Dist. 2–Benton Co.–Lamar
Larry S. Benson–Judge, Justice Court–Humphreys Co. Dist. 5–Louise
S. B. Bonds–Constable Dist. 3–Bolivar Co.–Shelby
Marjorie W. Brandon–Judge, Justice Court–Claiborne Co. Dist. 1–Port G.
Austin Brown–Constable–Warren Co. Dist.–Vicksburg
Mildred Coleman–Judge, Justice Court–Jefferson Co. Dist. 5–Lorman
Cleveland Collins–Constable Dist. 1–Marshall Co.–Holly Springs
Ernes Lee Cook–Constable Dist. 3–Quitman Co. Marks
Melvin Cummings–Constable Dist. 3–Humphreys Co.–Silver City
Earnest Cunningham–Judge, Justice Court–Marshall Co. Dist. 1–Holly Springs
Mack L. Davis–Constable Dist. 3–Claiborne Co.–Port Gibson
Roosevelt Dotson–Constable Dist. 3–Claiborne Co.–Port Gibson
Jimmy Ellis–Constable Dist. 2–Claiborne Co.–Port Gibson
Jerry Fisher–Judge, Justice Court–Holmes Co. Dist. 1–Lexington
John B. Foster–Constable Dist. 4–Adams Co.–Natchez
Bernice Frisby–Judge Justice Court–Jefferson Co. Dist. 4–Natchez
Debbie Gambrell–Judge, Justice Court–Hattiesburg
Edna H. Garner–Judge Justice Court Claiborne Co. Dist. 2–Port Gibson
Genova Garrett–Judge, Justice

Court, Madison Co. Dist. 4, Canton
Larry Giles–Judge, Justice Court, Yazoo City
Jimmy S. Harris–Judge, Justice Court, Wilkinson Co. Dist. 4, Woodville
Johnny Hartzog–Judge, Justice Court–Jefferson Davis Co. Beat 5–Prentiss
Walter Hawkins–Constable Dist. 4–Lowndes Co.–Glendora
Sam Hill–Constable Dist. 4–Lowndes Co.–Crawford
Gene Hudson–Constable Dist. 2–Coahoma Co.–Clardsdale
Robert E. Hughes–Constable–LeFlore Co. Dist. 4–Itta Bena
Erma Inge–Judge, Justice Court–Bolivar Co. Dist. 3–Mound Bayou
Clifton Jeffery–Constable Dist. 2–Warren Co.–Vicksburg
Paul S. Johnson–Judge, Justice Court–Coahoma Co. Dist. 4–Clarksdale
T. C. Johnson–Constable Dist. 4–Holmes Co.–Lexington
David Kemp–Constable Dist. 2–Sharkey Co.–Cary
Robert Lay–Judge, Justice Court–Marshall Co. Dist. 4–Waterford
Coy Lott–Constable Dist. 4–Jefferson Davis Co.–Prentiss
Samuel B. Minor–Judge, Justice Court–Wilkinson Co. Dist. 2–Woodville
Eddie Myles–Constable Dist. 4–Claiborne Co.–Hermanville
Tommie Nalls Jr.–Judge, Justice Court–Humphreys Co. Dist. 3–Silver City
Shirley Neal–Judge, Justice Court–Holmes Co. Beat 4–Lexington
Gussie Nichols–Constable Dist. 3–Jefferson Co.–Fayette
W. W. Owens–Justice of the Peace–Hinds Co. Dist. Pos. 1–Jackson
Otis Parker Jr.–Judge, Justice Court–Issaquena Co. Dist. 4–Mayersville
Shirley Perkins–Judge, Justice Court–LeFlore Co. Dist. 4–Itta Bena
Mabel Peterson–Justice of the Peace–Warren Co. Dist. 3–Vicksburg
Fred Robinson Jr.–Judge, Justice Court–Jackson Co. Dist. 2–Moss Point
Leroy Robinson Jr.–Constable Dist. 5–Jefferson Co.–Lorman
Randolph Robinson–Judge, Justice Court–Jefferson Co. Dist. 2–Lorman
Willie James Robinson–Constable Dist. 4–Coahoma Co. Clarksdale
Mary H. Russ–Judge, Justice Court–Wilkinson Co. Dist. 1–Centerville
Robert Lee Smart–Constable Beat 3–Holmes Co.–Pickens
Melvin L. Smith–Constable Dist. 3–Issaquena Co.–Mayersville
Norman Smith–Constable Dist. 2–LeFlore Co.–Greenwood
Jessie Stewart–Constable Dist. 2–Wilkinson Co.–Woodville
Charles G. Taylor–Constable Dist. 4–Jefferson Co.–Natchez
George C. Thomas–Constable Dist. 5–Hinds Co.–Raymond
Willie Thompson–Judge, Justice Court–Jefferson Co. Dist. 3–Fayette
Willie B. Thompson–Constable Dist. 1–Wilkinson Co.–Woodville
James Turner–Constable, Dist. 3–Washington Co.–Greenville
Charles Van Wells–Constable, Dist. 2–Hinds Co.–Clinton
George Walker–Judge, Justice Court–Hinds Co. Dist. 2–Jackson
McEwen Walker–Constable Dist. 4–Marshall Co.–Waterford
Peter Walker–Constable Dist. 2–Jefferson Co.–Lorman
Willis C. Wallace–Judge, Justice Court–Issaquena Co. Dist. 3–Mayersville
Marcus C. Ward–Judge, Justice Court–Jefferson Davis Co. Dist. 4–Prentiss

James A. Washington–Constable, Beat 5–Madison Co.–Pickens
Marvin Williams–Constable Dist. 5–Scott Co.–Lake
Mack Arthur Williamson–Constable–Madison Co. Dist. 4–Canton

OTHER JUDICIAL OFFICIALS:

Thomas C. Tolliver, Jr.–Chancery Clerk–Wilkinson County

POLICE CHIEFS, SHERIFFS, AND MARSHALS:

Willie Bass–Marshall–Friars Point
Osborne Bell–Sheriff–Marshall Co.–Holly Springs
Harry Cooper–Marshall–Coahoma
Frank Davis–Sheriff–Claiborne Co.–Port Gibson

EDUCATION–SCHOOL BOARD MEMBERS:

Ida Bedford–Bolivar Co. Dist. 6–Mound Bayou
Parker Bell–Holly Springs City Sch.–Holly Springs
Arthur Bingham–Jefferson Co., Dist. 3–Fayette
Charles Blakely–Sec., Sch. Bd., Panola Dist. 1–Sardis

EDUCATION–SCHOOL BOARD:

Orie S. Branson–Madison Co. Dist. 4–Canton
Claudine Brown–Leflore Co. Dist. 2–Greenwood
J. Mathilda Burns–Holmes Co. Dist. 4–Tchula
Henry Cannon–Rankin Co. Dist. 3–Braxton
Richard M. Coleman–Bolivar Co. Dist. 3–Shelby
Sarah Conwell–Boliver Co. Dist. 6–Mound Bayou
Dempsey Cox–Pres. Sch. Bd.–Panola–Sardis
Jimmy Curry–Chair, Sch. Bd. Claiborne Co. Dist. 4–Hermanville
Robert Dantzler–Jasper Co.–Heidelberg
Jihnnie L. Daughterty, Sr.–Benton Co. Dist. 2–Lamar
Bessie Earls–Oktibbeha Co.–Starksville
King Evans–Aquilla Line Sch. Dist.–Anguilla
James Figgs–Quitman Co. Dist. 2–Marks
Charlie Floyd–Wilkinson Co. Dist. 1–Centreville
James Gray–Humphrey Co. Dist 1–Belzoni
John W. Green–Wilkinson Co. Dist. 4–Woodville
Willie Gregory–Coahoma Co. Dist. 4–Clarksdale
Marvin Hayes–Panola Co. Dist 1–Sardis
John E. Hollins–Coahoma Co. Dist. 3–Jonestown
Cornelius Horton–Hinds Co. Dist 2–Edwards
Charles Howard–V. Pres. Sch. Bd. Hazelhurst–Hazelhurst
Bertyle Hughes–Wilkinson Co. Dist. 5–Crosby
Gussie Mae Hughes–Marshall Co. Dist. 2–Red Banks
Regina Hughes–Hazelhurst
David Hunter–Wilkinson Co. Dist. 2–Woodville
Lucious Ingram–Coffeyville–Coffeyville
James Jackson–Senatobia City Sch.–Senatobia
Helmon Johnson–Marion Co.–Columbia
James Jones–Canton City Sch.–Canton
Samuel Jones–Bolivar Co. Dist. 3–Shelby
Sharbor Jones–Jasper Dist.–Heidelberg
Willie H. Jones–Bolivar Co. Benoit
Bennie Knox–Claiborne Dist. 1–Lorman

Martha Lee–Jefferson Co. Dist. 2–Lorman
Freddie Love–Hollandale Dist.–Hollandale
O. P. Lowe–Leflore Co. Beat 4–Itta Bena
Amanda Malone–Marshall Co. Dist. 4–Waterford
Cornelia F. Montgomery–Holmes Co. Dist. 2–Durant
Thomas H. Moore–Bolivar Co. Dist. 6–Mound Bayou
Leonard Morris–Batesville City Sch.–Batesville
Essie Morrow–E. Jasper–Heidelberg
Burnell Newsome–Hazelhurst City Sch.–Hazelhurst
John S. Parker, Sr.–West Point Sch. Dist.–West Point
Earl Phillips–Bolivar Co. Dist. 1–Rosedale
Equilla Reynolds–Holmes Co.–Tchula
John Eddie Rogers–Watervalley Sch. Dist.–Water Valley
Leroy Russ–Wilkinson Co. Dist. 3–Centreville
Shirley Simmons–Madison Co. Dist. 5–Canton
Willie L. Simmons–Bolivar Co. Dist. 4–Cleveland
Roosevelt Sims–Clay Co. Dist. 3–Cedar Bluff
D. M. Smith–Bolivar Co. Dist. 4–Cleveland
Jimmy Smith–Claiborne Co. Dist 2–Port Gibson
John Calvin Smith–Leake Co.–Carthage
Robert Smith–Holmes Co.–Lexington
Willie Smith–Anguille Line Dist.–Anguille
George Spears–Bolivar Co. Dist. 6–Mound Bayou
Douglas Stewart–Amite Co. Dist. 2–Gloster
Richard L. Thomas–Bolivar Co.–Beulah
Leonard Thompson–Pres. Sch. Bd. Oxford–Oxford
James Madison Waters–Chair–E. Jasper Dist.–Heidelberg
Kurtcher Watson–Hollandale Sch. Dist.–Hollandale
Hattie White–Quitman Co.–Darling
Robert L. White–Jefferson Co. Dist. 4–Jefferson County
John T. Williams–Bolivar Co.–Shelby
Robert Lee Williams–Jefferson Co.–Lorman
Roosevelt Williams–W. Tallachatie Dist.–Glendora
Betty J. Wilson–Hollandale Sch. Dist.–Hollandale
Robert W. Wilson, Jr.–Amite Co. Dist. 3–Crosby
Willie Wilson–Bolivar Co. Dist. 6–Winstonville
James Woods–Trustee Bolivar Co. Dist. 5–Shaw
Roosevelt Yaroborough–Claiborne Co.–Port Gibson

OTHER EDUCATION OFFICIALS–SUPERINTENDENT OF SCHOOLS:

Lawrence Autry–Marshall Co.–Holly Springs
William Dean–Holmes County–Lexington
Reece Dixon–Noxubee Co.–Macon
Marion L. Hayes–Jefferson Co.–Fayette
Lonnie Haynes–Humphrey Co.–Belzoni
Charles Johnson–Wilkinson Co.–Woodville
Joseph Travillion–Claiborne Co.–Port Gibson

Source: National Roster of Black Elected Officials, Vol 12, 1982 (Washington, D.C.: Joint Center for Political Studies, 1982)

1983 Black Mayors

Bartley, Charles (Shaw)
Blackwell, Unita (Mayersville)
Butler, Lawrence (Bolton)
Gray, Robert (Shelby)
Jones, Franklin (Oakland)
Jones, William (Coahoma)
Leflore, Robert (Pace)
Leggette, Violet (Gunnison)
Lindsey, S. L. (Metcalf)
Lucas, Earl S. (Mound Bayou)
Lucas, Maurice (Renova)
Middleton, Kennie (Fayette)
Pritchard, Daron (Edward)
Smith, Fannie (Falcon)
Thomas, Richard (Beulah)
Thomas, Johnny (Glendora)
Todd, Johnny (Rosedale)
Tutwiler, Milton (Winston)
Washington, James (Friars Point)
Wilkins, Jimmy (Jonestown)

Source: Newton, Edmund, "Taking Over City Hall," *Black Enterprise* 13 (June, 1983): 163–164.

Index

Abbott, Robert, 57
Adams, Douglas, 362
Adams vs. Califano, 191
AFL-CIO, 83
Africa, 129–130, 179, 230, 246, 247; and the arts, 250, 283, 284, 326. See also individual countries
Africa (Still), 290
African Methodist Episcopal Church: ministers of, 7, 8, 15, 50, 338–341; members of, 109, 117, 178, 183, 231, 241, 341–342, 343–345; and Campbell College, 161
Afro-American Sons and Daughters, 363
Afro-American Symphony (Still), 290
Afro-American Women Suffrage Association, 101
Agnew, Spiro T., 275
Alcorn, James L.: and Revels, 10, 14; and Bruce, 17, 18, 20, 21; and Alcorn University, 28; and John Lynch, 29, 59; and gubernatorial candidate, 44
Alcorn Agricultural and Mechanical College: founding of, 14, 28, 45; presidents of, 15, 193–198; students at, 61, 118, 165, 170–171, 182, 223, 240, 367; honors from, 66, 167, 241; graduates of, 73, 91, 94, 186, 238, 242, 248, 286, 326, 338, 349, 364; teachers at, 206, 207, 224, 226, 236, 248, 400
Alexander, Mr. and Mrs. Columbus (parents of Florence), 222
Alexander, Ellis, 79
Alexander, Firnist James (husband of Margaret), 268
Alexander, Florence Octavia, 222–223
Alexander, Margaret Walker, 250, 267–269
Alexander, Dr. Will W., 202
Ali, Mohammed, 324, 383
All About Health and Beauty for the Black Woman (Sims), 188
Allain, Bill, 65

Allen (Maryland governor), 276
Allen, Richard, 341
Allen, R. J., 63
Allen, Scott, 334
American Citizen's Equal Rights Association, 49, 100
American Negro Short Stories, 278
American Negro Theater, 321
Ames, Adelbert: and Revels, 8, 11, 15; and Bruce, 18, 19, 21; and John Lynch, 27, 29, 59; as governor, 43, 46; and J. Hill, 48
Anderson, Douglas Leavon, 87
Anderson, Marian, 296
Anderson, Reuben, 5, 280
Andrews, George W., 288
Andrews, Jim, 68–69
And They Lynched Him on a Tree (Still), 291
Archer, Dr. Samuel H., 232
Arledge, Jimmy, 145
Arthur, Chester A., 36
Atkins, Chet, 318, 319
Atlanta Compromise, the, 163
Atlanta Daily World, 274, 275, 276, 277, 282, 346
Attaway, W. A., 171
Attucks, Crispus, 278, 349
Avellini, Bob, 382
Ayer, President and Mrs. Charles, 218

Baer, Max, 263
Bailey, F. Lee, 308
Baker, Barbara Willis, 184
Baker, Sam, 183–184
Ballou, C. C., 167
Banks, Fred Lee, 80, 87
Baptist Church, 334, 347–349, 349–351
Barber, Rims, 83
Barber, Sam, 296
Barbour, Japtha, 203
Barksdale, Ethelbert, 42, 43, 47, 48
Barkum, Jerome, 380

Index

Barnett, Ferdinand L., 107
Barnett, Horace Doyle, 145
Barnett, Ross, 133, 139, 141
Barnette, Travis, 145
Barry, Marion S. (Sr.), 72
Barry, Marion Shepilov, Jr., 72
Barry, Mattie B., 72
Barthé, Richmond, 284, 325
Basie, Count, 330
Bass, Mrs. Nellie, 217
Bates, Gladys Noel, 246
Bates, J. M., 246
Battles, Harriett, 151
Batucada Fantastica (Fischer), 328
A Bayou Legend (Still), 291, 292
Beale Street: Where the Blues Began (Lee), 169
Beale Street Sundown (Lee), 169
Beall, Dr. E., 358–359
Beby, Major General E. A., 399
Beck, Jeff, 310
Before the Mayflower (Bennett), 278
Bellafonte, Harry, 321
Bennett, Alma Reed (mother of Lerone, Jr.), 277
Bennett, Constance (daughter of Lerone, Jr.), 280
Bennett, Courtney (daughter of Lerone, Jr.), 280
Bennett, Gloria Sylvester (Mrs. Lerone, Jr.), 280
Bennett, Joy (daughter of Lerone, Jr.), 280
Bennett, Lerone, Jr., 268, 275, 277–280
Bennett, Lerone, Sr., 277
Bennett, Lerone III, 277
Berry, Theodore M., 350
Bevel, James, 125, 128
Bicentennial, The American, 279–280, 349
Biddle, Mrs. Francis, 291
Biggs, Vernon, 380
Bilbo, Theodore, 60, 266
Birdsong, T. B., 100
Bishop, Elvin, 310
Black, Hugo, 139
Black Boy (Wright), 256, 266, 267
Blackburn, Dr. Cleo Walter, 374–376
Blackburn, David (father of Cleo), 374
Blackburn, Dora Atkins Powell (Mrs. Cleo), 376
Blackburn, Fannie Elizabeth Scott (Mrs. Cleo), 376
Blackburn, Sarah Sneed (mother of Cleo), 374
Blackburn, Walter Scott (son of Cleo), 376
Black Code, The, 99, 156
Black Power, 163
Black Power (Wright), 267
Black Power, U.S.A., The Human Side of Reconstruction, 1867–1877 (Bennett), 278
The Black Woman (Ladner), 246
Black Woman Speaks (Richards), 327
Black World Publishing House, 278, 280
Blaine, James G., 36, 37
Blake, Eubie, 289
Blease, Cole, 56
Bloomfield, Mike, 306, 307, 310
"Blueprint for Negro Literature" (Wright), 264
Blue Steel (Still), 291
Bolden, Vincent Earl, 69, 71
Bomar, J. H. D., 157
Bonner, M. W., 173
A Book of Prefaces (Mencken), 259
Booth, Anna Marie (daughter of L. V.), 351
Booth, Georgia Anna Morris (Mrs. L. V.), 351
Booth, Georgia Annita (daughter of L. V.), 351
Booth, L. Venchael, 349–351
Booth, Lavaughn V., Jr., 351
Booth, William Douglas (son of L. V.), 351
Bost, W. M., 242
The Bottom Rail and Up Through Difficulties (Jones), 217
Boutwell Committee, the, 22
Bowers, Samuel, 145
Bowles, Preston Sewell, 244
Boyd, Cleopatra Carter (Mrs. John D.), 195
Boyd, Elizabeth Fry (mother of John D.), 193
Boyd, John (Sr.), 193
Boyd, John Dewey, 193–195
Boyd, Katye Carlotta (daughter of John D.), 195
Boyer, Joe Louis, 208–209
Boykins, Earnest A., Jr., 206–207
Boy Scouting, 183, 197, 227, 241
Bradley, Thomas, 344
Bradley University, 233, 234
Brawley, Benjamin, 26
"Breath of a Rose" (Still), 291
Bridges, Hallie Gail, 70
Brierfield (Everett), 155
"Bright and Morning Star" (Wright), 265
Brinkley, Sam, 115

Index

British Negro Theater, 322
Britton, Dr. Albert, 280
Brooke, Edward, 26
Brookins, H. Hartford, 342–345
Brooks, Gwendolyn, 237
Brooks, W. H., 336
"Brothers Joined in Heart" (Booth), 350
Brown, Alice (mother of Jesse), 395
Brown, Charles, 303
Brown, Daisy Pearl Nix (Mrs. Jesse), 395, 396–397, 398
Brown, Gallatin, 43
Brown, Jesse Leroy, 391–398
Brown, Jim, 382, 383, 384, 385, 386
Brown, John (father of Jesse), 395
Brown, John Mitchell, 398–399
Brown, Pamela (daughter of Jesse), 395, 396, 397, 398
Brown, Pete, 388–389
Brown, R. Jesse, 114, 116
Brown, Sterling N., 25
Brown vs. Board of Education, 190, 194
Bruce, Blanche Kelso, 3, 16–26, 33, 35, 37, 49, 160; on women's suffrage, 100, 101
Bruce, Josephine B. Wilson (Mrs. Blanche), 25
Bruce, Roscoe (son of Blanche), 25
Brunini, Joseph B., 335
Bryan, William Jennings, 55, 357
Bryant, Bobby (musician), 331
Bryant, Bobby (football player), 385
Buchanan, Noah, 9
Buckley, Horace Lawson, 87–88
Bunche, Ralph, 122, 219
Burden, Eric, 314
Burns (Meridian attorney), 116
Burr, Aaron, 166
Butts, Mr. and Mrs. Sylvester (parents of William), 230
Butts, William Arthur, 230–231

Cain, Natalia Tanner, 376–377
Calhoun, Credell, 88
Calhoun, John C., 11
Calhoun, John L., 276
Califano, Joseph, 146
Cameron, Larry, 380
Cameron, Simon, 12
Campbell, Milton. *See* Little Milton
Campbell College, 50, 161, 338, 343, 360
A Candle in the Dark: A History of Morehouse College (Jones), 233
Capers, Walter W., 271
Caribbean Melodies (Still), 291

Carlton, Frank, 70
Carmichael, Dr. George A., 363
Carmichael, Stokley, 66, 163
Carney, Mable, 218
Carrol, Earl, 289
Carson, Johnny, 307
Carter, Hodding, Jr., 149
Carter, Jimmy, 83, 268
Carthan, Eddie James, 67–71
Carver, George Washington, 353
Cassidy, Hiram, 30
Catholic Church, 334, 335
Cavett, Dick, 307
Cayton, Horace, Sr., 16
Cayton, Susie Revels, 16
CEEP (Continuing Education Enrichment Project), 221
Cevoli, Richard L., 397
Chadwick, George W., 289
Chalmers, James R., 34, 35, 36, 54
Chambers, Wally, 384
Chambliss, Captain Carroll R. (son of Jessie), 183
Chambliss, Chris (son of Jessie), 183
Chambliss, Jessie R., 182–183
Chambliss, Marcus (father of Jessie), 182
Chambliss, Norah Robinson (Mrs. Jessie), 183
Chambliss, Susan Claiborne (mother of Jessie), 182
Chaney, James, 143–145, 279
Chess, Leonard, 313
Chess, Phil, 313
China, 67
Chisholm, Mrs. Alexander, 294, 295
Chisholm, Jean, 294
Chisholm, Peggy, 294
Chrisholm, Frank, 370
Chrisman, Elizabeth, 99
Christian, Charlie, 304
Christmas Gift (Rollins), 238
Church, Robert R., Jr., 55, 56, 167, 168–169
Churches, 114, 333–351; World Council of, 179, 339, 348. *See also particular denominations*
Church of God in Christ (COGIC), 117, 245, 303, 334
Civil Rights, Commission on, 178
Civil Rights Acts, 4, 14, 32, 33, 104, 340
Civil Rights Movement, 99–146; individuals' involvement in, 66, 67, 72, 85, 343, 348; beginnings of, 100, 112, 114, 121; women in, 101, 102, 178, 179, 269;

and business, 145, 147; in the universities, 195, 210; reporting of, 280; and music, 284; and Baptist Church, 347, 350; and education, 353
Civil War, The: black soldiers in, 8, 17; slaves in, 26–27, 48, 156–157; freedmen in, 39–40; migration during, 52; and literature, 269; and religion, 333. *See also* Emancipation; Freedmen
Clapton, Eric, 310
Clark, Arthur B., 70
Clark, Essie Austin (Mrs. Robert G.), 84
Clark, Robert George, 5, 80–84
Clark, Robert III, 84
Clark, Wandrick (son of Robert G.), 84
Clarke, John Henry, 279
Clay, Henry, 11
Clayton, Powel, 36
Cleaver, Eldridge, 272
Clement, Jack, 317, 318
Clements, Dr. Rufus, 276
Cleveland, Grover, 37, 162
Coahoma Junior College, 245
Coast, Howard, 362
COFO (Council of Federated Organizations), 85, 100, 127
Cole, Nat King, 330
Coleman, Georgie Catchings, 377–378
Coleman, J. P., 119
Coleridge-Taylor, Samuel, 287
Colfax, Schuyler, 11
Collier, Reggie, 379
Collins, Isaac (grandfather of Clarie Harvey), 176
Collins, Malachi C. (father of Clarie Harvey), 176
Collins, Mary Augusta Rayford (mother of Clarie Harvey), 176
Collins, Shelia D., 69
Color Curtain (Wright), 267
Colored Fair Association, 49
The Colored Veteran, 272
Colored Women's Federated Club of Mississippi. *See* Federation of Colored Women's Clubs
Coming of Age in Mississippi (Moody), 270
Communist Party, 262, 263, 264, 265, 266
"Completely Well" (King), 311
Compromise of 1877, 3
Confrontation: Black and White (Bennett), 278
Congregational Church, 345–346
Conklin, Roscoe, 20, 21, 53

Connolly, John, 322
Connolly, Maggie, 322
"Conversation With A Grave Digger," *Preaching About Death* (McEwen), 346
Cooper, James C., 95–96
CORE (Congress on Racial Equality), 85, 113, 127, 144, 269
Costello (postmaster), 58–59
Costaso (Still), 291
Cotton Blossom Singers, 216
Cousins, Dr. Robert E., 220
Cowan, Rossie, 238
Cowan, T. F., 238
Cowans, Neal, 340
Cox, Minnie, 168, 171
Cox, Wayne, 165, 167, 171, 172
Cox, William Harold, 145
"Crackin' Up" (Bo Diddley), 313
Crawford, Eloise, 255
Crudup, Arthur, 320–321
Crump, E. H., 169
Cupit, Danny, 84

Dabney, Thomas, 334
Dale, Johnny, 68
Dana, N. J. T., 157
Danger Son (Rollins), 238
Danielewski, Tad, 323
Danks, Dale, 268
Dansby, B. Baldwin, 198
Darker America (Still), 290
Davenport, Alonza, 223
Davenport, Lizzie Blanchard, 223
Davidson, David, 389
Davis, A. K., 19, 23
Davis, Benjamin (Communist Party), 264
Davis, Benjamin O., Jr. (U.S. Air Force), 393
Davis, David, 369
Davis, Garrett, 11
Davis, Jefferson, 9, 10, 12, 15, 155, 159
Davis, Joseph E., 155, 156, 157–158
Davis, Ossie, 321
Davis, Russell, 388
Davy, Gloria, 296
Day, Beth, 217
Day, E., 396
The Day They Marched (Saunders), 278
Dease, William K., Sr., 96–97
The Death of White Sociology (Ladner), 246
Dee, Ruby, 321
de la Beckwith, Byron, 122
Delany, Paul, 275

Index

Dellums, Ronald V., 70
Delta Penny Savings Bank, 172
Demby, Allene Smith (mother of William S.), 240
Demby, Melissa Pope (Mrs. William S.), 241
Demby, William Clarence (father of William S.), 240
Demby, William S., Jr., 241
Demby, William Smith, 240–242
Democratic Convention (1968), 65, 67
Democratic Party: racism of, 3–4, 40–41, 42; relations of, with individual blacks, 15, 37, 47, 49, 83, 84, 162; and U.S. Congress, 24; election practices of, 21–22, 33, 34, 35; and 1868 election, 43; and Republicans, 54; and MFDP, 64–65, 85, 128; and Mississippi Negro Democrat Association, 272
Dempsey, Jack, 379
DePriest, Oscar S., 37, 56
Devine, Anne, 102
Diddley, Bo. See McDaniel, Ellas
Dilday, William, 280–281
Dillon, Levion, 330
Disciples of Christ, 374
Discrimination. See Civil Rights Movement; Integration; Segregation; Violence; Voting rights
Doar, John, 140
Dobbs, Mattiwilda, 296
Dockins, Johnetta, 195
Dominican Republic, 14
Doss, Evan, 73–75
Douglass, Frederick, 25, 106, 160, 348
Dow Chemical Company, 146
Dowdy, Wayne, 66, 94, 95
Downing, George T., 10
Drew, Dr. Charles, 353
DuBois, W. E. B., 148, 267, 279
Dumas, Rhetaugh G., 367
Dunbar, Paul Laurence, 291
Dungee, Dr. G. A., 390
Dunham, Melerson Guy, 236–237
Dwight, Lula, 102
Dylan, Bob, 331

Earl, Damon, 381
Eaton, Jesse, 334
Ebon Chronicle (Still), 291
Ebony magazine, 275, 277, 278, 279, 349
Economic Enterprises, Inc., 72
Education, 189–248; of slaves, 16, 33; of freedmen, 17; and James Lynch, 44, 45; compulsory, 51; separate but equal, 99, 105. See also Integration; Segregation; *particular institutions*
Edwards, Ralph, 216
EEOC (Equal Employment Opportunity Commission), 146
Eisenhower, Dwight D., 279
Elections, illegal practices in, 33, 34, 35, 36, 42, 252. See also Redistricting; Voting rights
Ellington, Duke, 330
Ellis, Robert B., 137, 139
Ellis, Tyrone, 88
Ellison, Ralph, 265
Emancipation: laws concerning, 26; of individual slaves, 151–152, 252, 361, 374; effects of, 283, 333, 368
Emancipation Proclamation, 278–279
Episcopal Church, 334. See also African Methodist Episcopal Church
Estes, Lary, 380
The Eternal Flame (Jackson), 348
"The Ethics of Living Jim Crow" (Wright), 265
Everett, Frank E., Jr., 155
Evers, James (father of Charles and Medgar), 59, 117
Evers, James Charles, 59–66
Evers, Jessie Wright (mother of Charles and Medgar), 59, 117
Evers, Medgar, 117–122; and Charles Evers, 59, 62; memorial to, 63–64; and H. Kirksey, 79; assassination of, 114, 128, 179; work of, 115, 132, 137, 279
Evers, Myrlie Beasley (Mrs. Medgar), 118, 120
Evers, Nannie Magee (Mrs. Charles), 62
"Everyday I Have the Blues" (King), 306

The Facts of Reconstruction (John Lynch), 37
Fadiman, Clifton, 169
Fairley, J. C., 132
FAIRR (Foundation for the Advancement of Inmate Rehabilitation and Recreation), 308
Famous American Negro Entertainers of Stage and Screen and TV (Rollins), 238
Farish, Ned, 357
Farmer's Alliance, the, 160
Farmer's Conference, the, 228
Farr, W. E., 162
Faulkner, William, 131
Faust, Dr., 219

Feather, Leonard, 307
Fabre, Michel, 266
Federal Negro Theatre, 262
Federation of Colored Women's Clubs, 223, 236, 239, 244, 342
Festive Overture (Still), 291
Fifteenth Amendment, 3, 13
Finch, Anselm J., 243
Finch, Cliff, 5, 66, 76, 387
"Fire and Cloud" (Wright), 265
Fischer, William, 327–328
Fish, Hamilton, 36
Fisk University, 72, 75, 104, 111, 218, 237, 375
Fitzgerald (congressional candidate), 35
Fitzhugh, Combash Charles, 51
Fitzhugh, Robert, 29
Flannes, Alvin, 280
Fleming, Karl, 141
Florey, H. T., 18
Floyd, Vernon C., 184–185
Foley, Red, 317
Ford, Gerald, 179, 275
Ford, James W., 264
Ford, Sharkey, 68
Forman, James, 125, 127
For My People (Alexander), 268, 269
Forney, John W., 10
Fortune, T. Thomas, 106, 110
Foster, Bill, 380
Foster, E. C., 6
Foster, Robert, 212
Fourteenth Amendment, 3
Franklin, Webb, 82, 83, 84
Frazier, Hillman Jerome, 89
Fredericks, Isiah, 89
Freedmen, 39, 52
Freedmen's Bureau, 8, 44, 157, 158, 189
Freedmen's Savings and Trust, 24, 36
Freedom Day (Canton, Miss.), 144
Freedom Farm plan, 130
Freedom Riders, 113–114
Freedom Schools, 269
From the Black Belt (Still), 290
From a Deserted Plantation (Still), 291
Frost, David, 307
Fuller, T. O., 168
Fullerlove, Dr. Robert E., 363

Galloway, Henry, 199
Gambrell, Deborah Jones, 92–93
Garfield, James, 24
Garrett, Charles Edward (father of Romeo), 234
Garrett, Naomi Sanders (Mrs. Romeo), 236
Garrett, Ponkie Duncan (mother of Romeo), 234
Garrett, Romeo Benjamin, 233–236
Garvey, Marcus, 109
Gatewood, Mary, 151
Gayles, Dr. Allene D., 241
Gentry, Ira, Sr., 231
George, J. Z., 49, 162
Gershwin, George, 295
Ghana, 267. *See also* Africa
Gibson, Jason, 68, 70
Gibson vs. Mississippi, 100
Gift of Lesbos (Fischer), 328
Gillem, Alvin C., 42, 43
Gilliam, Sam, 325–326
Giovanni, Nikki, 268, 269
Goin' Down Slow (Rollins), 238
Golden, Charles, 334
Goodman, Andrew, 144, 145
Goodwin, Lynn "Cato," 307
Gordon, William, 275, 281–282
Graham, Bill, 307
Granderson, Roosevelt, 68, 69, 70
Grand Gulf, Battle of, 157
Grant, Ulysses S., 11, 21, 33–34, 53
Graves, Howard, 277
Gray, Dorothy Gordon, 248
Gray, Victoria, 102
Green, Ben (19th c. planter), 157, 159, 160
Green, Ben (20th c. lawyer), 116
Green, E. W., 187
Green, David Leo, 89–90
Green, Jerome, 313
Greenberg, Jack, 141
Greene, Callie Colston Logan (Mrs. Sherman, Sr.), 341
Greene, Delia (mother of Sherman, Sr.), 337
Greene, Frances Reed (Mrs. Percy), 272
Greene, George Washington (father of Percy), 270
Greene, Henry (father of Sherman, Sr.), 337
Greene, Percy, 120, 270–273
Greene, Pinkie B. (Mrs. Sherman, Sr.), 341
Greene, Sherman L., Jr., 341
Greene, Sherman Lawrence, Sr., 337–341
Greene, Sylvia Stone (mother of Percy), 270
Greenfield, Elizabeth Taylor, 285
Green vs. State of Mississippi, 100
Greenwood, L. C., 380

Greer, Everline, 294
Greggory, Tom, 94
Gregory, Dick, 70, 121, 132, 133
Gresham, Walter, 37
Griffin, H. C., 9, 58
Griffin, Merv, 307
Griggs, Sutton E., 168

Hackett, George, 358
Hadas, Moses, 220
Hall, Carsie, 113, 114, 115, 116
Hall, Frederick Douglass, 328
Hall, Walter G., 280
Hamberlin, Lavern, 284, 326–327
Hamer, Fannie Lou, 66, 101, 122–131
Hamer, Perry (husband of Fannie), 125, 126, 128
Hancock, William, 10
Handy, W. C., 170, 288, 305
Hanna, Mark, 55
Hanson, Howard, 290, 292
Hardy, Jesse, Jr., 400
Hargett, Steve, 94
Harlem Renaissance, the, 267, 283
Harris, James, 69, 71
Harris, Ron, 384
Harris, William V., 82
Harrison, Alferdteen, 217
Harrison, Benjamin, 25
Harrison, Jay, 296
Harrison, Lou, 296
Harrison, Robert W., 374
Hartfield (Altanta mayor), 276
Harvey, Clarie Collins, 176–180
Harvey, Martin Luther, Jr. (husband of Clarie), 177–178
Hastie, William, 219
Haughton, G. R., 114
Haussler, A. G., 235
Hawkins, Lucia, 329
Hayes, John Edgar, 68, 70
Haywood, Spencer, 389
Heflin, Tom, 56
Henderson, Clayton P., 90
Hendrix, Jimi, 310
Henry, Aaron, 5, 63, 83, 84–87, 280
Henry, Edd (father of Aaron), 84
Henry, Mattie Logan (mother of Aaron), 84
Hester, David Earl, 69, 71
Hicks, Jennifer O., 378
Highway No. 1. U.S.A. (Still), 291
Hill, Abram, 321
Hill, Allen G. (father of C. Rollins), 237

Hill, Birdie Tucker (mother of C. Rollins), 237
Hill, James, 18, 19, 20, 29, 35, 48–49, 160; on women, 100
Hilton, Roy, 380
Hinds County Educational Federal Credit Union, 204
Hinds Junior College. *See* Utica Institute
Hitler, Adolf, 379
Holloway, Lou Emma, 246–247
Holmes, Bud, 390
Holtzclaw, William H., 228
Hooker, John Lee, 313
Hoover, Herbert, 56, 57
Hopkins, Lightning, 321
Horne, Lena, 121
Hoskins, Maggie, 255, 256, 257, 260
Hoskins, Silas, 255, 256
Hosmer, Captain C. B., 369
Houston, David G., 369
Howard, Maggie Revels (Mrs. Perry), 16
Howard, Oliver O., 44
Howard, Perry W., 16, 116
Howard, W. C., 172
Howard, Willie, 380
Howard University, 25, 53, 87, 288, 349, 393
How I Wrote Jubilee (Alexander), 269
Howze, Joseph Lawson, 334–335
Huddleston, Tom J., 362–363
Hudner, Thomas, 396, 397, 398
Hughes, Langston, 110, 249, 278, 291
Hume, Peter, 296
Hunt, Thomas W., 34, 35
Hutcherson, Levern, 329
Hyde, Ann McDonald, 365
Hyde, Sellus, 365
Hyde-Rowan, Deborah, 364–365
Hyman, Earle, 321

Idom, Guyton, 76
Illinois Eighth Colored Regiment, 108
"I'm a Man" (Bo Diddley), 313
Immigration bill, against Chinese, 23
"I'm Sorry" (Bo Diddley), 313
Integration: of schools, 13, 32, 63; of universities, 14, 132, 136–143; of housing, 40; of police, 95; of public facilities, 122, 269; of military, 166, 391, 393; and Church, 346; in government, 372. *See also* Segregation
Interracial Cooperation, Committee for, 112
Ireland, Samuel, 17

Island of Hallucinations (Wright), 267

Jacobs, Henry P., 9, 51
Jacklin, Tony, 388
Jackson, Andrew, 279
Jackson, George H., 334
Jackson, Harold, 379
Jackson, Mr. and Mrs. Henry J. (parents of Joseph), 347
Jackson, Joseph Harrison, 347–349
Jackson, Lonnie, 304
Jackson, Maude Thelma Alexander (Mrs. Joseph), 349
Jackson, Maynard, 276
Jackson, Sam, 357–358
Jackson Advocate, 270, 272
Jackson State University: students at, 81, 88, 115, 136, 222, 270–271, 381; teachers at, 87, 223, 224, 268, 328; graduates of, 96, 245, 347, 378; presidents of, 198, 203–204, 205, 206; influence of, 217–218; programs at, 219, 220, 221, 222; sports at, 389
James, Annie M., 181
James, Jimmie, Sr., 181
James, Robert Earl, 181–182
Japan, 135–136, 393–394
"Jazz in 4/4 Time" (Overstreet), 327
Jefferson, Blind Lemon, 304, 309
Jefferson, Lucy Crump, 341–342
Jefferson, William Henry, Jr., 342
Jeffords, Elza, 35
Jenkins, Emorrie, 187
Jenkins, Monroe, 64
Jennings, Clifford, 95
Jennings, Daniel L., 400
Jet magazine, 275, 277
Jim Crowism. *See* Segregation
John Reed Club, The, 262, 263
Johnson, Andrew, 20, 27, 157
Johnson, Ann Battles (Mrs. William), 151–152
Johnson, Bertha LaBranche (Mrs. J. E.), 242–245
Johnson, Charlie (father of J. E.), 242
Johnson, Ella Kaigler (mother of J. E.), 242
Johnson, George, 180–181
Johnson, Jack, 323, 324, 379
Johnson, Jack D., 317, 318, 319
Johnson, Jonas Edward, 194, 242–245
Johnson, Mrs. J. P., 174
Johnson, Leroy, 276
Johnson, Paul, 374
Johnson, Robert E., 275

Johnson, Vernon C., 96
Johnson, William T., 149–154
John XXIII, Pope, 179, 348
Jones, Betty, 97
Jones, Carrie Cox (mother of Edward), 231
Jones, Charles P., 334
Jones, Edward Allen, 231–233
Jones, Dr. Frank, 354
Jones, George H. (father of Edward), 231
Jones, Grace Allen (Mrs. Laurence), 217
Jones, James Earl, 322–324
Jones, Laurence Clifton, 211–217
Jones, Robert Earl (father of James), 322
Jones, Ruth Williams (mother of James), 322
Jordan, Louis, 303
Jubilee (Alexander), 269

Kaintuck (Still), 291
Katzenback, Nicholas, 140
"Keep on Keeping On" (Overstreet), 327
Kelley, Gwendolyn Greene, 272
Kennard, Albert (brother of Clyde), 131
Kennard, Clyde, 121, 131–133, 138
Kennard, Dorothy (sister of Clyde), 131
Kennard, Lawrence (brother of Clyde), 131
Kennard, Melvin (brother of Clyde), 131
Kennard, Will (father of Clyde), 131
Kennedy, Edward, 82
Kennedy, John F., 66, 121, 122, 133, 195, 394; and Meredith case, 136, 139, 140
Kennedy, Robert, 66, 133
Killen, Edgar Ray, 145
Killens, John O., 323–324
Kimball, Florence Page, 295, 299
King, Mr. and Mrs. Albert (parents of B. B.), 302
King, Albert (performer), 329
King, B. B., 302–311
King, Billie Jean, 383
King, Clennon, 138
King, Ed, 128
King, Leslie Darnell, 90
King, Lorenzo H., 334, 336
King, Martin Luther, Jr., 66, 71, 122, 139, 170, 272; and Bennett, 277, 278, 279
King, Riley B. *See* King, B. B.
King, Willis J., 337
Kirkland, Joe, 97
Kirksey, Audrie M. Neal (Mrs. Henry J.), 78
Kirksey, Charles (brother of Henry J.), 77
Kirksey, Charlie S. (father of Henry J.), 77

Index 461

Kirksey, Henry Jay, 77–80, 83, 93
Kirksey, Henry, Jr., 78
Kirksey, Kevin (son of Henry J.), 78
Kirksey, Nettie M. (mother of Henry J.), 77
Klingman, Charlie, 165
Koenig, William, 397
Korean War, 396, 399
Ku Klux Klan, 129, 144, 345

LaBranche, Jules Alcee, 242
LaBranche, Onie Smith, 242
La Guiablesse (Still), 290
Ladner, Joyce, 102, 246
Lamar, Lucius Q. C., 22, 24, 29
Lamb, Ella, 231
Lampton Institute, 193
Landon, Alf, 56
Lane, Dr. George H., 364
Langston, John M., 25
Latting, A. A., 116
Lawrence, Margaret, 377
Lee, Abner (brother of George W.), 164
Lee, Reverend George (father of George W.), 163
Lee, George Washington, 163–170
Lee, Hattie (mother of George W.), 163, 164
Lehmann, Professor, 288
Lenox Avenue (Still), 291
"A Letter to International Publishers" (Wright), 265
"Levee Land" (Still), 291
Lewis, Arthur B., 138
Lewis, Cudjoe Kozolla, 184
Lewis, John, 127
Liberia, 23, 204, 224, 227, 348. *See also* Africa
Lincoln, Abraham, 36, 252
Lincoln League of America, 56
Liston, Sonny, 323
Little Milton, 330
The Little Professor of Piney Woods (Day), 217
Locke, Alonzo, 166
Lockwood, Robert Junior, 303
Lodge, Henry Cabot, 36
Long, Avon, 329
Longino, Andrew H., 47
Loper, Gwendolyn Nero, 377
L'Ouverture, Toussaint, 165, 325
Louis, Joe, 263, 308
Louisville, New Orleans and Texas Railroad Company vs. State of Mississippi, 99

Love, J. P., 82
Lovelace, William N., 350
Lowery, Joseph, 70
Lowry, Robert, 49
Lucas, Eddie, 94
Luizzo, Viola, 67
Lyells, Ruby Stutts, 238
Lynch, Cora Williamson (Mrs. John), 37
Lynch, Ella W. Sommerville (Mrs. John), 37
Lynch, James D., 9, 15, 38–48, 50
Lynch, John Roy, 5, 26–38; and Revels, 8; and Hill, 18, 48; and James Lynch, 44, 46; and Wood, 58, 59; and Montgomery, 160, 162
Lynch, Patrick (father of John), 26

McAllister, Flora McClelland (mother of Jane), 217
McAllister, Jane Ellen, 217–222
McAllister, Richard (father of Jane), 217
McAlpin, Harry S., 276
McBride, Eddie L., 94–95
McBride, James, 65
MacBride, Thomas H., 211
McCary, Robert, 151
McCary, William, 29, 58, 59
McCormick, Medill, 55
McDaniel, Ellas "Bo Diddley," 312–315
McDaniel, Gussie, 312
McEvoy, J. P., 289
McEwen, Reverend Beverly Tolbert (father of Homer), 346
McEwen, Homer C., 345–346
McEwen, Julia Clay (mother of Homer), 346
McFerrin, Robert, 296
McGee, Willie, 379, 380
McInnis, Hattie, 293
McKay, Cliff, 275
Mackel, Dr. A. M., 353
McKinley, William, 25, 37, 76, 108
MacLaine, Shirley, 67
McLelland, Dr., 359
McLemore, Leslie, 83
McShane, James, 140
The Magic of Books (Rollins), 238
Mallory, Arenia C., 245, 334
Many But One: The Ecumenics of Charity (Jackson), 348
Marlow, W. D., III, 126
Marriage, legal, 51, 112
Marshall, Marilyn, 365
Marshall, Thurgood, 137

Martin, McKinley Charles, 245
Mason, Charles H., 334
Mason, Dr. Gilbert, 122
Masonry, 40, 50, 226
Massell, Sam, 276
Massey, Walter, 376
Matthews, Professor, 256
Mays, Dr. Benjamin, 373
Meharry Medical College, 240, 356, 361, 364, 365, 378
Melin, Henry, 151
Mencken, H. L., 259–260
Meredith, "Cap" (father of James), 133, 134, 142
Meredith, James, 114, 121, 133–143
Meredith, Mary Jane Wiggins (Mrs. James), 136
Methodist Episcopal Church, 39, 40, 336–337, 346. *See also* African Methodist Episcopal Church
Middleton, Kenneth, 65
Military, blacks in, 13, 61, 108, 118, 166, 201, 391–400; during Civil War, 8, 17. *See also* Veterans, black
Miller, Adelia (Mrs. James), 150, 151
Miller, Emma Burruss (Mrs. L. T.), 362
Miller, Emily (mother of L. T.), 361
Miller, James, 150
Miller, J. H. (brother of L. T.), 361
Miller, Lloyd T., 361–364
Miller, Wash (father of L. T.), 361
Miller, William (brother of L. T.), 361
Miller's Ferry Normal and Industrial Institute, 200
Mills, Florence, 289, 291
Millsaps College, 179
Miracle in Mississippi (Purcell), 217
Mississippi, University of, 14, 45, 90, 119, 121, 136–143, 378
Mississippi Association of Teachers in Colored Schools, 228
Mississippi Constitutional Conventions; of 1890, 4, 6; of 1867, 41, 49, 51
Mississippi Council on Interracial Cooperation, 198, 340
Mississippi Freedom Democratic Party, 64, 67, 85, 128, 129
Mississippi Inter-racial Council. *See* Mississippi Council on Interracial Cooperation
Mississippi Life Insurance Company, 168, 171, 172, 173
Mississippi Negro Democratic Association, 270, 272

Mississippi Negro Teachers' Association, 119
Mississippi River Commission, 24
Mississippi Southern College, 132
Mississippi Southern Rural Women's Network, 102
Mississippi State-Church Cooperative Council, 340
Mississippi State Normal School, 356
Mississippi Teachers' Association, 78, 193, 225; officers of, 197, 198, 223, 227, 244
Mississippi Valley State University, 87, 206–207, 208–209, 230
Miss Sally's Party (Still), 291
Mitchell, Dr., 358
Mize, Sidney, 100, 139
Mollison, W. E., 75–76
Mondale, Walter, 82
Money, Annie Lucy Dillard, 394
Money, Thomas J., Jr., 392, 393–394
Montgomery, Benjamin Thornton, 154–159
Montgomery, Isaiah T., 49, 154, 156–163, 171
Montgomery, Martha Rabb (Mrs. Isaiah), 163
Montgomery, Mary (Mrs. Benjamin), 156
Montgomery, Wilbert, 385
Moody, Anne, 102, 269–270
Moore, Mr. and Mrs. Caesar, 247
Moore, Carman, 307
Moore, Winston E., 308
Morehouse Academy, 231
Morehouse College, 96, 232, 233, 274, 277, 376, 393
Morgan, A. T., 13, 22
Morgan, Rose, 185, 186
Morris, Milton, 191
Morrison, Sara Ann Blackburn (Mrs. Eldridge), 376
Moses, Robert, 66, 127
Mosley, Jessie (Mrs. C. C.), 243, 281
Motley, Constance Baker, 137, 138
Mound Bayou, 154, 160, 161, 171
Mounger, William D., 280
Myrick, Randolph T., 187

NAACP (National Association for the Advancement of Colored People): and C. Evers, 63; and Henry, 85; origins of, 109; and Civil Rights Movement, 113, 114, 132, 137, 141, 145, 346; and M. Evers, 117, 118, 119, 122; members of,

127, 178, 233, 269, 281, 291, 340, 350; and integration of army, 166; honors from, 265, 299
National Afro-American Council, 109
National Association for the Study of Negro Life and History, 281
National Association of Colored Graduate Nurses, 366
National Association of Colored Women, 111
National Council of Negro Women, 67, 224, 229, 281
National Federation of Afro-American Women, 111
National Federation of Colored Women, 101
National Fraternal Council of Churches, 340
National Negro Business League, 161, 168, 175
National Negro Insurance Association, 168
National Urban League, 110, 372
Native Son (Wright), 115, 249, 259, 265, 267
Neal, Robert, 280
Negro American Baseball League, 316
Negro Baptist Convention, 348
Negro Fellowship League, 110
The Negro in Mississippi History (Mosley), 281
The Negro Mood and Other Essays (Bennett), 278, 279
Negro Newspaper Publishers' Association, 276
Negro Yearbook, 375
Nelson, Lee, 396
Netter, Mildrette, 195, 390
New Negro Poets: U.S.A. (Hughes), 278
New Symphony in G Minor (Still), 290
Niagara Movement, 109
Nineteenth Amendment, 101
Nixon, Richard, 136, 275, 394
Nkrumah, Kwame, 267
Norris, C. F., 46
Nye, James W., 11

Oakley Training School, 244, 374
Oak Park High School, 293, 299
Oak Park Vocational School, 242, 244. See also Oak Park High School
O'Connor, Fred, 382
October Journey (Alexander), 269

Office of Economic Opportunity, 86, 179, 221
O'Neal, Frederick, 321–322
One Hundred, the Committee of, 194, 243
One Is a Crowd (Richards), 327
Operation PUSH, 345
Ord, E. O. C., 158
Orff, Carl, 297
Otis, Jessie R., 61, 194
Otis, Joseph, 132
Outlaw, John, 380
The Outsider (Wright), 267
Overstreet, Joseph, 327
Owens, Charlene, 185
Owens, George A., 209–211, 311
Owens, James, 379
Owens, Joe, 380
Owens, Ruth Douglas (Mrs. George), 209

Pagan Spain (Wright), 267
Page, Alan, 384
Papp, Joseph, 323
Pardee, Jack, 381
Park, Dr. Robert E., 375
Parker, Frances Lorraine, 272
Parker, Mrs. Frank, 329
Parker, L. P., 166
Pastorela (Still), 291
Patterson, Joe, 139
Payton, Alyne (mother of Walter), 381, 383
Payton, Connie (Mrs. Walter), 383, 386
Payton, Peter (father of Walter), 381, 383
Payton, Walter, 381–386
Pearson, Drew, 273
Pease, Henry R., 44, 46
Pentecostal Church, 334
Peoples, John A., Jr., 204–206
Peoples, John A., Sr., 204
Peoples, Maggie Rose (mother of John, Jr.), 204
Perce, L. W., 29
Perkins, A. E., 165, 167
Perry, Herman, 168, 274, 275
Pershing, General John J., 279
Phillips, Wendell, 13, 165
Phipps, Mike, 382
Piles, J. H., 30
Pillars, Eliza J., 365–366
Pinchback, P. B. S., 21, 36, 37, 101
Piney Woods and Its Story (Jones), 217
Piney Woods Country Life School, 211, 213–217, 223, 330
Piney Woods School (Harrison), 217

Pioneers of Protest (Bennett), 278
Pitchford, Dave, 334
Plain-Chant for America (Still), 291
Player, Beatrice Day (mother of Willa), 229
Player, Clarence C. (father of Willa), 229
Player, Willa B., 229–230
Poem for Orchestra (Still), 291
Poetic Educations: Conversation Between Nikki Giovanni and Margaret (Alexander and Giovanni), 269
Poindexter, David, 263
Poitier, Sidney, 321
Porter, David D., 156–157
Port Gibson, Battle of, 157
Posey, Billy Wayne, 145
Potter, Raeschelle, 328
Poulenc, Francis, 296
Powe, Lillian G., 341
Powell, Adam Clayton, 143
Powers, R. C., 9, 44, 47
Prentiss Normal and Industrial Institute, 242, 243, 244
Presley, Elvis, 320, 321
Price, Cecil, 100, 144, 145
Price, Charles E., 276
Price, Dr. G. A. (husband of Lucille), 374
Price, George (brother of Leontyne), 293
Price, James Anthony (father of Leontyne), 292
Price, Katherine Baker (mother of Leontyne), 292, 293
Price, Leontyne, 292–301
Price, Lucille, 373–374
Pride, Charley, 315–320
Pride, Inc., 72
Pride, Rozene Cochran (Mrs. Charley), 316
Prophets For A New Day (Alexander), 269
Proscription policy, 41, 43
Pugh, Charles E., 96
Pulliam, Joe, 123–124
Purcell, Leslie Harper, 217
Purvis, Charles, 10

Quarles, Louise K., 186

Racism: in politics, 3, 42; incidents of, 59–60, 61; in Carthan case, 71; and elections, 83; in entertainment, 319; and Church, 346; in education, 246, 353, 366; in government, 374; in military, 391–392, 395. *See also* Integration; Segregation; Violence

Radical Republicans' Reconstruction plan of 1867, 3
Rainey, L. C., 100, 145
Ransom, Bishop R. C., 109
Reagan, Ronald, 65, 66, 82
The Reason Why the Colored American is Not in the World's Exposition (Wells), 106–107
Reconstruction, 3, 7, 99, 147, 189, 333; and James Lynch, 41, 43, 45
Redding, Saunders, 156
Reddix, Daisy Uvasine Shirley (Mrs. Jacob), 202, 204
Reddix, Frances Brown (mother of Jacob), 199
Reddix, Jacob L., 78, 198, 199–204, 219
Reddix, Joseph (brother of Jacob), 204
Reddix, Nathan (father of Jacob), 199
Redistricting, 4, 79, 83, 84, 92–93, 350; plan for, 29, 34, 36
Redmond, Augustus (brother of S. D.), 356
Redmond, Charles (father of S. D.), 355
Redmond, Esther (mother of S. D.), 355
Redmond, Esther (daughter of S. D.), 360
Redmond, Ida Revels (Mrs. S. D.), 16, 356, 360
Redmond, Johnnie Grace King (Mrs. S. D.), 360
Redmond, Melvin, 93
Redmond, Ruth (daughter of S. D.), 360
Redmond, Sidney D., 16, 116, 271, 355–360
Redmond, Sidney R., 115, 271, 360
A Red Record: Tabulated Statistics and Alleged Causes of Lynchings in the U.S., 1892–94 (Wells), 107
Reinhardt, Django, 310
Republican Party: and Revels, 9, 10, 12, 13, 15; and Bruce, 18, 21; in Mississippi, 19, 21, 22, 29, 35, 45; and John Lynch, 27, 32, 36, 37; and James Lynch, 38, 40–41, 46, 47; and Negro suffrage, 42; factions in, 43, 44; and Hill, 48, 49; and Settle, 53–54; and Simmons, 56; and Wood, 58; and Democrats, 54, 160; blacks in, 162, 163, 272; and Lee, 169, 170; and Scott, 275, 276; and Greene, 340; and S. D. Redmond, 359–360
Revels, Hiram Rhodes, 7–16; as Senator, 3, 30, 45; and Republicans, 37; and James Lynch, 40; as minister, 50; on women's suffrage, 100, 101; as president of Alcorn, 194

Index   465

Revels, Phoeba Bass (Mrs. Hiram), 16
Reynolds, Jack (Hacksaw), 385
Reynolds, Harriet Virginia Blackburn (Mrs. C. J.), 376
Rice, Floyd, 380
Richards, Beah, 327
Ringsby, Bill, 389
River George (Lee), 169
"Road Runner" (Bo Diddley), 313
Roberts, Alton Wayne, 145
Robeson, Paul, 295
Robinson, Jackie, 298, 379
Robinson, Willard, 289, 290
Rodgers, Jimmie, 315
Rolling Stones, The, 306, 314
Rollins, Charlemae Hill, 237–238
Rollins, Joseph Walter (husband of Charlemae), 237
Rollins, Joseph Walter, Jr. (son of Charlemae), 237
Roosevelt, Franklin Delano, 57, 276
Roosevelt, Theodore, 36, 55, 171
Rosenwald (Julius) Fund, 202, 203, 218, 268, 325
Rowan, Hugh, 365
Rowan, L. J., 167
Rowland, Glennie M., 400
Rust University: teachers at, 176, 223, 224, 346; honors from, 179, 360; graduates of, 236, 336, 356; benefit at, 300

Sahdji (Still), 291
Saints Junior College, 245, 334
Sanders, I. S., 188
Sanders, Thelma, 187–188
Sauguet, Henri, 296
Saunders, Doris, 278
Savage Holiday (Wright), 267
Savine, Red, 317
Saxton, Pauline, 268
"Say Man" (Bo Diddley), 313
Sayers, Gale, 381, 383, 385
Schoby, Barney J., 91
Schwerke, Irving, 290
Schwerner, Michael, 144, 145
Schwerner, Rita, 144
SCLC (Southern Christian Leadership Conference), 85, 127, 145
Scott, Cornelius Adolphus (son of William), 273–276
Scott, Emmeline Southall (Mrs. William), 273–275
Scott, George, 390

Scott, James, 382
Scott, Stanley Southall, 275
Scott, William Alexander, 273–274
Scott, William Alexander II, 273–275, 282
Seal, Roderick, 33
Segregation: of public facilities, 31–32, 63, 99, 104, 133, 135; of schools, 43, 51, 52, 60, 121, 164, 190, 199–200; in military, 61, 108, 118, 201, 391–392; effects of, 80, 255, 368; of universities, 119, 121, 132, 191. *See also* Civil Rights Movement; Integration; Violence; Voting rights
Seidenberg, Sidney A., 306
Self Help Elementary Program (SHEP), 221
Self Help Opportunity Project (SHOP), 221
Selma, March on (1965), 67
Senegal, 233. *See also* Africa
Senghor, Leopold Sedar, 233
Settle, Josiah (father of Josiah T.), 52
Settle, Josiah T., 52–54
Settle, Nancy (mother of Josiah T.), 52
Settle, T. T. Vogelsang (Mrs. Josiah T.), 53
Sharpe, Jerry, 145
Shaw, Alexander P., 334, 336–337
Shaw, Duncan Preston (father of Alexander), 336
Shaw, Marie Petty (mother of Alexander), 336
Shaw University, 45
Sheppard, Charles Bernard, 91
Shepperson, Charles B., 286
Sherman, General William, 39
Short, Eugene, 379, 389–390
Short, J. W., 35
Short, Purvis, 390
Showers of Blessings (Booth), 350
Sikes, Janice White, 247
Simmons, Roscoe Conklin, 55–57
Simmons, William J., 15
Simms, Hilda, 321
Simon, Miss (orphanage directress), 254
Simpson, O. J., 383, 384, 385, 386
Sims, Naomi, 188
Sinclair, Tom, 44
Slaughter-Harvey, Constance, 76–77
Slavery, 155, 199, 249, 353. *See also* Civil War, the; Emancipation; Freedmen
Smiley, Modis A., 399–400
Smith, A. Maceo, 372
Smith, Dr. Charles E., 354
Smith, Hazel Brannon, 86

Smith, Leona Kennard (Mrs. Silas), 131
Smith, Samuel, 16
Smith, Silas, 132
Smith-Hughes Act, 201
Smith vs. Allwright, 4
SNCC (Student Non-Violent Coordinating Committee), 67, 72, 85, 127, 269, 279
Snowden, James, 145
Sorey, Revie, 382–383
Southall, Amanda, 273
Southall, Daniel, 273
Southern Association of Colleges and Secondary Schools, 193, 194
Southern Education Foundation, 220
Southern Manifesto, the, 190
Southern Mississippi, University of, 132, 197
Southern Regional Council, 178
Spelman, J. J., 49
Spelman College, 176, 177, 179, 247
Spencer, Mae Frances, 351
Spense, Robert, 5
Spinks, Jack, 379
Stanton, Edwin M., 39
Stars in the Night (Jackson), 348
State Mutual (Federal) Savings and Loan Association, 178, 204, 228
Stengel, Casey, 317
Stennis, John, 83
Stevens, Sarah Harvey, 281
Stewart, George, 156
Stewart, Lusia Harris, 387–388
Still, Carrie Frambo (mother of William, Jr.), 285, 286–287
Still, Verna Arvey (Mrs. William, Jr.), 292
Still, William Grant, 283, 285–292
Still, William Grant (Sr.), 285, 286
Stockton, J. P., 11
Stokowski, Leopold, 290
Strasberg, Lee, 323
Straus, Mrs. Austin. *See* Moody, Anne
Stravinsky, Igor, 296
Stringer, Thomas W., 40, 44, 49–51, 226
Strong, Ariel Perry, 275
Stuart, M. S., 171, 172, 173
Suarez, Matt, 144
Suffrage. *See* Voting rights
Sullivan, Ed, 307
Summerville, Lucy, 271
Sumner, Charles, 11, 13
Superior and Talented Student Project (STS), 220
Sylvester, Mr. and Mrs. Elliott, 280

Taft, Robert A., 169
Tanner, Henry O., 325
Tatum, Willie, 145–146
Taxes: poll, 4, 62, 127, 162; property, 73–75
Taylor, B. T., 68
Taylor, Prince A., 334
Tchula Seven, the, 69–70
Terrell, Robert H., 37
They Showed the Way (Rollins), 238
Thibodeaux, G. H. J., 338
Thomas, Henry, 114
Thomas, Jessie O., 368–373
Thomas, Nellie Mitchell (Mrs. Jessie), 373
Thomas vs. The City of Jackson, 114
Thompson, Allen, 121, 180
Thompson, Dr. Cleopatra Davenport, 223–226, 227
Thompson, Hazael McFarland, 50, 226–228
Thompson, Julius Eric, 248
Thompson, Virgil, 295
Thompson, William Hale, 261
Thorne, Daisy Brown. *See* Brown, Daisy Pearl Nix
Those Who Wait (Still), 291
"Three O'Clock Blues" (King), 305
"The Thrill Is Gone" (King), 311
Tickenor, Gabriel, 152
Till, Emmett, 126
Time I (Fischer), 328
Tingle, Willie, 60
Tisdale, Charles W., 320
Tomorrow's Tomorrow (Ladner), 246
Tougaloo College: graduates of, 76, 184, 188, 196, 198, 226, 239, 246, 269, 365, 374; and Civil Rights Movement, 112; presidents of, 209–211; teachers at, 224, 227, 246, 248; honors from, 268, 311
Touré, Kwamé. *See* Carmichael, Stokley
Toure, Sekou, 130
Townsend, Tommie, 379
To You, America (Still), 291
Trimble, Jim, 385
Tri-State Bank, 174–175
Troubled Island (Still), 285, 291
Truman, Harry S., 391
Tubman, Harriet, 279
Tucker, David, 165
Tucker, Sophie, 289
Tucker, William, 126
Turner, Ike, 330–331
Turner, Nat, 7, 279

Turner, Tina, 330, 331
Tuskegee Institute: and Booker T. Washington, 55, 111, 375; graduates of, 88, 184, 228, 242; trustees of, 179; honors from, 245; and Jessie O. Thomas, 369–371
Tyrone, L., 243

Uncle Tom's Children (Wright), 265
Underground railroad, the, 333
United Methodist Church, 177, 334, 340, 351
United States Justice Department, 129, 140
United States Supreme Court, 4, 14, 99, 114, 119, 139, 190
United States vs. Guinn, 4
Universal Life Insurance Company, 173
Universal Negro Improvement Association, 109
Utica Institute, 193, 213, 228
Utica Junior College, 197

Vanderpool, Dawn Constance, 204
Vanderpool, Shirley Reddix, 204
Van Eaton, Henry S., 36
Vardaman, James K., 164, 356, 359
Varese, Edgar, 289
Veteran, black, 272, 392–400. See also Military, blacks in
Vicksburg, Battle of, 156
Vicksburg, Port City Cooperative of, 240
Vietnam, 179, 400
Violence: and civil liberties, 3, 4, 43, 126, 127–128, 140; white fear of, 19, 164, 391; in elections, 22, 34, 35, 162; against individuals, 60, 105, 123–124, 144, 215–216, 256, 259; responses to, 64, 100, 106–109, 119, 120, 147. See also Civil Rights Movement; Segregation
A Voice Crying in the Wilderness (Reddix), 204
Voices of Negritude (Jones), 233
Von Karajan, Herbert, 297, 298
"The Voodoo of Hell's Half-Acre" (Wright), 258
Voorhees, Don, 289
Voorhees Industrial School, 371
Voter registration drives, 62, 63, 73, 118, 144; women involved with, 66–67, 125–127, 178, 269. See also Civil Rights Movement; Voting rights
Voting rights: for blacks, 3–4, 40, 42, 67, 99, 101, 162; for women, 100, 101, 108; use of, 243–244. See also Civil Rights Movement; Violence; Voter registration drives
Voting Rights Act of 1965, 4
A Voyage to West Africa and Some Reflections on Modern Missions (Jackson), 348

Walker, A. Maceo (son of J. E.), 174, 175
Walker, Madame C. J., 109
Walker, Mrs. J. E., 174
Walker, Joseph Edison, 170–176
Walker, Marion Dozier, 267
Walker, "Aunty Patsy" (mother of J. E.), 170
Walker, Sigismund Constantine, 267
Walker, T-Bone, 304
Wallace, George, 121
Waller, William, 65, 74, 180, 282, 399
Walls, Johnny, 71
Walthall, E. C., 49
Ward, Charles, 397
Wardlaw, P. A., 357
Warfield, William, 301
Warren, H. W., 28
Washington, Booker T., 163, 228; and Tuskegee Institute, 55, 370, 371, 375; principles of, 109, 147, 200; and National Negro Business League, 161, 175; Institute (Liberia), 204
Washington, Carolyn Carter (Mrs. Walter), 197–198
Washington, Dinah, 330
Washington, George, 279
Washington, Josephine Fairley, 185
Washington, Reverend and Mrs. Kemp (parents of Walter), 196
Washington, March on: of 1963, 278; of 1941, 340
Washington, Margaret Murray, 55, 101, 111–112
Washington, Walter, 195–198
Waters, Muddy, 313
Watkins, John, 94
Watson, Percy Willis, 91–92
Watts, Donald, 380
Webb, Constance, 259
Webb, Sarah Kennard, 131, 133
Webster, Daniel, 11
We Build Together (Rollins), 238
Wells-Barnett, Ida, 101, 103–111
Wesley, Charles, 295
Wesley, Charlotte, 295

Wesley, John, 341
Wharton, Ramsey, 357
Wharton, Vernon L., 58
What Manner of Man (Bennett), 278
Wheeler, William A., 23
Whisenton, Joffre Conrad, 240
Whisenton, Joffre T., 239–240
Whisenton, Zadie Elizabeth Beford, 240
White, Bonnye Moore (Mrs. Willie J.), 247
White, Booker T. Washington "Bukka," 304, 331
White, Catherine, 26
White, Mr. and Mrs. James R., 247
White, Willie J., 247
White Citizens Council of Mississippi, 100, 190
White League, The, 22, 34
White Man, Listen! (Wright), 267
Whiteman, Paul, 289
The White Problem in America (Ebony), 278
Whitten, Jamie, 129
"Why I Sing the Blues" (King), 308
Wilkens, Roy, 122
Williams, Andy, 388
Williams, Dr. Daniel Hale, 353
Williams, Eddie, 275
Williams, Hank, 315
Williams, J. M. P., 9
Williams, Liles, 66, 94, 95
Williams, Nat, 305
Williamson, Sonny Boy, 305
Williamson, Q. V., 276
Willis, A. W., 173
Wilson, Flip, 307
Wilson, Henry, 11, 20, 37
Wilson, J. T., 172–173
Wilson, Margaret Bolden (Mrs. Richard), 252, 253, 254, 257, 258
Wilson, Richard, 252, 255, 258
Winfield, Gertrude (mother of James), 93
Winfield, James, 93–94
Winfield, Lawrence (father of James), 93
Winn, Baylor, 154
Winter, William, 76, 83, 94, 268
"Winter's Approach" (Still), 291
Womanpower Unlimited, 178

Women, 100, 101, 102, 108, 271
Women, Mississippi Commission on the Status of, 180
Wood, Martha, 64
Wood, Robert H., 29, 58–59
Wood, Walter, 271
Wood, W. R., 201, 202
Woodford, Stewart L., 54
Woodson, Marvin, 379
WPA (Work Projects Administration) Writer's Project, 262, 267, 360, 373
Wright, Ella Wilson (mother of Richard), 253–258, 260, 261
Wright, Ellen Popular (Mrs. Richard), 266
Wright, Julia (daughter of Richard), 266
Wright, Leon Alan (brother of Richard), 253, 254, 257, 260, 261
Wright, Nathan (father of Richard), 252, 253, 254
Wright, Nathaniel (grandfather of Richard), 252
Wright, Richard, 115, 249, 250, 252–267, 269
Wright, Rose Dhima Meadman (Mrs. Richard), 265
Wright, R. R. III, 175
Wright, Unita Blackwell, 66–67
Writh, Mary, 262
Wyatt, Kent, 388

X, Malcolm, 279, 324

"You Can't Judge a Book by the Cover" (Bo Diddley), 313
Young, Andrew, 128
Young, Aurelia Norris (Mrs. Jack H.), 113, 116
Young, Charles, 280
Young, Charles Lemuel, 92
Young, Henry H., Sr. (father of Jack), 115
Young, Jack Harvey, Sr., 112–117
Young, Jennie, 102
Young, Jennie V. (mother of Jack), 115
Young, Whitney, 122

Zander, Karin, 78
Zimbabwe, 344. *See also* Africa

www.ingramcontent.com/pod-product-compliance
Lightning Source LLC
Chambersburg PA
CBHW030330240426
43661CB00052B/1580